D1320183

Owen Hargreaves

Owen Hargreaves

The Biography of Manchester United's Midfield Maestro

Ian Macleay

JOHN BLAKE

Published by John Blake Publishing Ltd,
3 Bramber Court, 2 Bramber Road,
London W14 9PB, England

www.blake.co.uk

First published in hardback in 2008

ISBN: 978 1 84454 589 6

British Library Cataloguing-in-Publication Data:

A catalogue record for this book is available from the British Library.

Design by www.envydesign.co.uk

Printed in the UK by CPI William Clowes Beccles NR34 7TL

1 3 5 7 9 10 8 6 4 2

Papers used by John Blake Publishing are natural, recyclable products made from wood grown in sustainable forests. The manufacturing processes conform to the environmental regulations of the country of origin.

Contents

Acknowledgements

First and foremost for my family who supported me every step of the way. Heartfelt thanks to my wife Marie and my daughter Jacalyn and her husband Adrian.

An enormous thanks to my publisher John Blake for your encouragement and belief in the origination of the project. Special thanks to Chris Stone and Stuart Robertson for their hard work. Thanks also to Joanne in the office for her help.

For my own little back up team, Ravi Mistry my IT hotshot, Patrick Hagglund for his assistance with aspects of my research and my lawyer Peter Harris. Eirik Havdahl looks after the European scene for me and his contribution continues to be invaluable.

My twin brother Ken has been a great help throughout. One of the first football matches we ever saw together involved George Best and Denis Law scoring at Stamford Bridge. Terry Venables captained Chelsea that night and I never dreamt that one day he would be showing interest and support in my writing.

Lastly this book is dedicated to Gareth Hart who supported another team in red and in his lamentably short time with us touched the lives of everyone he came in contact with.

Ian Macleay

Spring 2008

'And I watched over one dear project of mine for five years, spent a fortune on it and failed to make a go and the history of which would make a very large book in which a million men would see themselves as in a mirror and they would testify and say... Verily this is not imagination, this fellow has been there'

Mark Twain, *A Connecticut Yankee in the Court of King Arthur* (1889)

Chapter One
The Calgary Kid

'He was young but it was obvious he was a different breed, with a different mentality. He had that great belief, determination and mental strength to want to improve. I have seen him grow and grow.'
Steve McLaren

'When I see this boy with the ball my heart leaps.'
Franz Beckenbauer

It was raining that bitter night. That is what he would remember most about it.

Like the rain back in Canada that later turned to sleet. He watched the match from the bench, Terry Venables was seated just a few rows in front of him, he had asked Steve McClaren to have put him on earlier. It was when Crouch had equalised to bring it to two each and England were going to the Euro 2008 Championships.

They could bottle up the midfield now; he could cover the area in front of Sol Campbell, block any attacks and just run down the clock. Then Croatia scored, he could see the move building, the neat pass followed by a sharp turn and then a strong shot that flew into the net. Carlson could only watch as it ripped past him. His hopes died then, he knew he would not get on now. McClaren would field an attacking player to try and salvage it.

Darren Bent went on and had one half chance, but the game was soon over and the booing started. Later on he was in a bar in Central London, too tired to sleep, the adrenaline pumping through him. Some fans came over to his table; approachable and respectful as always he grinned and nodded, nobody knew what to say. Soon he would be famous for the game that he did not play in.

He glanced into the mirror; somewhere a woman's voice was singing. Something about the closest thing to heaven. His thoughts went back an eternity. Thinking about a small boy with curly hair, out in the rain then the sleet, kicking a ball around in a yard halfway across the world.

Owen Lee Hargreaves, born 20 January 1981 to Colin, a former Bolton Wanderers and Wigan Athletic youth team player and Margaret in Calgary, Alberta, Canada. He has two older brothers Darren and Neil. Darren, the eldest, played for the Canadian youth team. Bolton offered him an apprenticeship but his career was terminated by a knee ligament injury.

Colin's mother died when he was just 15 and it hit him hard. He decided to emigrate from England and make a new start for his family. After leaving professional football he was working in the steel industry and this gave him scope to travel. He had the options of Australia, USA and Canada; he chose the latter as the best environment to bring up his young family.

They settled in Calgary, set in the rolling foothills of Alberta with the backdrop of the majestic Canadian Rockies to the west and the Canadian Prairies to the east. Calgary is the third largest city in Canada and was recently ranked the 'World's Cleanest City' in a survey published in 2007 by *Forbes* magazine. Owen grew up in a happy, loving family in one of the most beautiful, safest, healthiest countries in the world. He was lucky: his idyllic childhood gave him the bedrock that formed his affable personality and iron will. It was to prove invaluable in helping him overcome the many obstacles that were to litter his path to the stratosphere of the modern game.

The name Hargreaves was of Anglo-Saxon origin and the Doomsday book of 1086 traces it back to Cheshire. Broken down, the 'Har' means grey whilst Greaves means 'thicket'. The most famous Hargreaves apart from Owen was the author of the Mr Men books. Another famous Hargreaves was James who died in April 1778. Blackburn born James was credited with inventing the 'Spinning Jenny' which was a major factor in sparking the Industrial Revolution. Along with that of Arkwright, Hargreaves was the most famous name of the Revolution.

Strange that a player with such a cosmopolitan background, born 4,000 miles away had such strong Lancashire roots and an archetypal Northern name. What's in a name? I suppose United could have bought the Celtic star Jan Johannes Vennegoor of Hesselink or the Brazilian midfielder Creedence Clearwater Revival Couto, still pinging them around in Belgium for Lierse.

Research indicated that over the centuries the Hargreaves clan were not afraid of migrating abroad to what was known in those times as the New World. Some of the first immigrants to cross the Atlantic bore the name of Hargreaves. A majority of the million people who lived in Calgary declared themselves to be of European ancestry. Of the ethnic population almost a quarter of the émigrés were English. Other famous names who were Canadians of English descent include actors Dan Aykroyd, Keanu Reeves and tennis star Greg Rusedski.

In America, the 20th of January was traditionally the day that the US Presidents were sworn in. The date of 20/1 is an exceptionally lucky number for those who believe in alternative mythologies. Buzz Aldrin the astronaut was born on that day as was 'Dr Who' actor Tom Baker. The most famous footballer born on the same day, in 1874, was Steve Bloomer. The striker was a legend who played for Derby and Middlesbrough. Steve's England record was impeccable, scoring 28 goals in 23 appearances. After retiring as a player, Bloomer coached in Berlin and was interned at Ruhlben for the duration of the First World War.

1981 was the year when Israel destroyed Iraq's nuclear reactor. Clint Eastwood, acting with an ape, had the top movie with *Any Which Way You Can*. The *Dukes of Hazard*, with Daisy Duke and that red car was one of the most popular programmes on television. Race riots broke out in Thatcherite Britain. A group called the Specials (Nothing to do with Jose Mourinho) had a huge hit with a record called 'Ghost Town' which caught the mood of the time. Speaking of Ghost Towns, 11,569 had crammed into a crumbling Stamford Bridge to see Chelsea Football Club lose 0-1 to Cardiff City in a Division Two fixture.

At Old Trafford, a few weeks after the birth of Owen, a crowd of 46,685 saw Manchester United beat high flying Ipswich Town 2-1, a defeat that contributed to the Suffolk side being pipped to the title by Aston Villa. Scorer of the first United goal that day was Jimmy Nicholl, one of only three Canadian born players to represent United. Jimmy was born in Hamilton on 28 February 1956 and moved to Ireland with his family when he was a toddler. All in all he played 235 games (13 subs) and scored another five goals in the period 1974–1982. An accomplished defender, Jimmy won 73 caps for Northern Ireland and even found time to manage Millwall. Like Owen, Jimmy opted to play for the land where his father was born, rather than Canada.

The second player born in Canada was Roy Kilin who was born in Toronto but signed with United in 1947. Comprehensive research indicates that he did not make the first team. The remaining member of the trio was Owen Lee Hargreaves.

There is little record of Owen's early years in Calgary; he lived simply and happily in the 'Little House on the Prairie'. Superman was Owen's favourite superhero when he was growing up. It was around that time that the Superman films franchise was at its peak with the ill-fated Christopher Reeves taking the lead role. There was Kryptonite everywhere.

Although they lived in Canada Owen was brought up in an English household with traditional North Country values. Owen's grandfather Henry had also moved to Canada to live with his son and his family. Henry was a life long fan of Bolton, a love that his son Colin inherited. Colin was a very skilful player himself, his generation was brought up on the flair players like George Best and the bombastic Rodney Marsh. He continued to play well in his 50s in veteran tournaments and still displayed flashes of the talent that had almost taken him to the big time.

The Hargreaves clan were still mad about English football

and followed the matches very closely. There was no instant fix of the Internet available then but many English games were shown on TV that were broadcast about seven in the morning due to the time difference. Henry had strong opinions on the modern game. Owen told the *Daily Telegraph*, 'My grand dad would sit downstairs in his robe and watch the games. He was very opinionated.'

One game Owen vividly remembered was the 1990 Cup Final on 17 May involving Manchester United against Crystal Palace. Three generations of the Hargreaves family were around the breakfast table early that Saturday morning sipping coffee and savouring the wonderful Canadian bacon and avocado sandwiches. The first game between the sides was an exciting 3-3 draw with Mark Hughes scoring twice. Hughes had a season on loan at Bayern Munich in the late 80s, after his move to Barcelona had not worked out. That cup final was the first game where United really made an impression on the youngster. Bryan Robson was in his pomp and was a big favourite of Owen's. Little did he dream that one day Robson would tell the press that Hargreaves brought similar attributes of control and bite to the national side that he did.

Owen told the ShortList.com magazine about those times: 'We hardly had any live games televised in Canada. When a big United or Liverpool game came on, my dad would make a huge deal about it. We would all wake up early and watch it in our dressing gowns. I loved all sports but basketball was my main passion, so it took a big United game to get my mind off Michael Jordan.'

Growing up in Canada, Owen followed the Calgary Flames in the National Hockey League. His burning interest at the time though was basketball and he was a huge fan of the Chicago Bulls. This was when the goose-bump inducing Michael Jordan was in his prime. Michael was Owen's boyhood idol. When he grew up and played for Bayern Munich Owen wore the club shirt with the number 23 emblazoned on his back, out of respect. Basketball is still a passion of Owen's; Steve Nash the Canadian professional basketball player is a close friend of Owen's accompanying him to Euro 2004 and the 2006 World cup.

Owen is also a frequent contributor to the NBA.COM Blog garnering great reviews about his friend Steve and his exploits playing point guard for the Phoenix Suns of the National Basketball Association.

The young Owen never really supported any particular football team as a boy; he grew up watching a number of clubs, notably the long running grudge match between the two teams in red; Liverpool and Manchester United were the big two then with the Merseyside club dominating the 80s but the balance of power shifting back to the aristocracy of United in the 90s. Arsenal flew the flag for London by winning titles but a porcelain Chelsea, pre- Abramovich, were strictly lightweights, lacking glamour and any financial clout. One of Owen's favourite players was the legendary Steve McManaman who left Liverpool for a successful stint at Real Madrid. McManaman's career had some remarkable parallels to that of Hargreaves, the only other English player to win Champions League honours whilst playing for a foreign team. Both shared similar temperaments and personalities: laid back, quiet, intelligent, thoughtful, both committed to long term partners they had known since their teens. Both players were seriously undervalued and underrated by the fans. Owen's fan worship for the Beckham phenomena had not yet developed as the Chingford born youngster was still making his bones in junior football.

Owen first started playing football at the age of 5 for a team known as the 'Peanuts', wearing shirts with a big peanut logo on the front. His early school days were spent at Glenbrook Elementary, Andrew Sibbald elementary and then Nickle Junior High.

In 1988 Calgary staged the Winter Olympics, they were a huge success and helped transform the host city into the modern, vibrant place it is today. That was the Olympics when Eddie 'The Eagle' Edwards exploded onto the scene. One of the most famous sporting failures of all time, Eddie's glory (or the lack of it) was to live on as Steve Coogan (Alan Partridge) was making a film about the life of the Cheltenham born plasterer. It was not known if Owen witnessed any of the Eagle's exploits but he had a great passion for skiing from an early age. The Winter Olympics were to have a profound effect on Owen because he grew up literally in the middle of one of the World's most famous sporting events. The huge crowds of tourists that came to the Olympics and the blanket coverage on television seeped into his consciousness. To be caught up in all that excitement, just because they were a sportsman, doing something they believed in and excelled at. That passion was soon to grip Owen and propel him to stardom. Owen's father and grandfather were naturally anxious that he took up the round ball although as he recollected to the *Gauntlet* 'My parents were great in letting me make my own decisions at a young age. I think I always had a mind of my own and they said "do what you think is best"'.

Today soccer is the biggest participation sport in Canada. It really began to take off around the time Owen began to show he was born with great mobility, the ability to move fast. It was soon apparent that he possessed a God-given talent for football. In his early teens he was soon playing against older boys but his talent was making him stand out in any crowd.

The year Owen was born saw a downturn in the economy. Calgary had a booming economy in the 70s as it was linked heavily with the oil business. A sudden drop in oil prices triggered the collapse of the boom and the rise in unemployment. However Calgary quickly became far more economically diverse and by the end of the decade its economy was in recovery.

Colin Hargreaves played semi-professional football for Calgary Kickers who joined the CSL in 1987, its inaugural season. They ended up as champions but their success was short lived and the whole League imploded in 1989. Owen was desperate to follow in his father's footsteps, and quickly progressed through the junior levels to play for Calgary Foothills, the local amateur side. Foothills Soccer Club was one of the oldest youth organizations in Calgary with over 25 years of history and Foothills alumni. Today they have been ranked as one of the Canada's top ten sides based on the amount of medals earned at club nationals. Recently they have been implementing sophisticated high-tech systems to improve the coaching of young players proving what a go-ahead organisation they are.

Tony Taylor played left back for Crystal Palace in the 70s and had emigrated to Canada when his career finished. He was manager of Canada's under 17-side and upon hearing of the rapid progress of the young kid from Calgary gave him a trial with a view to making him a Canadian international. Owen failed to impress Taylor who ditched him from the squad. Thomas Niendorf who discovered

Owen as a 13- year-old told the FA.Com the reasons behind it. 'Owen was very technically gifted but not as physically strong as the other players. Just as importantly, Calgary is a long way away from Toronto and Montreal and they didn't like the idea of all the travel costs.'

Life is all coincidence: youngsters think that they are at the middle of the universe but they respond and go in a particular direction by the luck of the draw. Owen's whole life was changed by a random act of fate. Thomas Niendorf used to work in East Germany for the über-efficent Dynamo Berlin. When the Wall came down Thomas fled to Canada and started doing what he did best, working with footballers. Niendorf ended up at Calgary Storm. Thomas must have had a sharp intake of breath when he first saw the young Owen playing community soccer.

After the disappointment of the Canadian rejection Thomas arranged for the distraught Owen to have a short trial in Germany with Bayern Munich in October 1996. It was very brief but he must have done well because the following spring Bayern invited the Calgarian teenager and his parents over for an induction. Colin and Margaret Hargreaves visited the flat brick building that was home for the club's apprentices. They had been drawn from all over the world, as Bayern had the greatest infrastructure of a youth set up in the world.

Owen was just 15 and now faced the prospect of starting a completely new life in a foreign country and having to master a foreign language. It was a tremendous challenge. Owen had fond memories of a trip he had made with a Canadian youth side to Scotland. That was the sum total of his overseas excursions but his nomadic lifestyle was about to begin. Colin knew how hard it would be for his son to make it in the professional game. He had given it his best shot himself and almost made it to the big time with the twin advantages of playing in his own country with the support of his family and friends around him. Hargreaves Senior was a football man, and just like his father two things made him make up his mind.

The first was that he knew what an opportunity it was for the youngster. Bayern Munich were one of the top three sides in the world and for them to give his son a chance to play for them was beyond even his wildest dreams. Secondly, Colin had tremendous belief in Owen's ability; he seemed to have it all, pace, power, skill and an unflappable manner. Even then, such was his football knowledge and vision he correctly guessed that Owen also had the strength of character, profound football intelligence and temperament to make it in Munich.

So on the 1 July 1997 Owen left Canada to join the youth set up of Bayern Munich.

Field Marshall Erwin Romell, Germany's greatest soldier once said: 'The best form of welfare for the troops is first class training.'

No team in the world had a better training scheme than Bayern Munich. The records indicate that the Bavarian side were one of the most successful club sides of all time. They were formed in the first year of the twentieth century by members of a Munich gymnastics club. Their first major honour came in 1932 when they won the German Championship. Bayern were left as a regional league side following the formation of the national Bundesliga in 1963. In 1965 they won promotion to the Bundesliga and won the cup in the next two seasons – 1966 and 1967. The year of 1967 was a watershed for them because that was the year that they tasted their first European success scooping the European Cup Winners Cup (Now transformed into the UEFA Cup).

In 1969 they won the league and cup double. The dominant figure that emerged in this period was Franz Beckenbauer who was born in Munich in September 1945. They say in football that one man does not make a team but the pre-eminence of Bayern Munich is to some extent also the story of him. Beckenbauer invented the plum role of the 'libero' position, an attacking sweeper. This was a combination of the ultra defensive player who when occasion demanded would break quickly into attack.

The difference between that and the 21st century midfield anchorman role perfected by Owen was that the libero played behind the back four whereas Hargreaves protected the area in front of the back four. When United nuked Newcastle 6-0 in early January 2008 Rio Ferdinand scored the pick of the goals with a marvellous run from his own half, before then spearing home the fourth. A typical Beckenbauer finish and blindside run. Unless teams were prepared to put a man on the libero all the time it was almost impossible to counter.

The 70s were as Bowie crooned 'Golden Years' for Bayern and Beckenbauer as they embraced the concept of 'Total Football'. Bayern won the West German Cup in 1971 and then a hat trick of Bundesliga titles in '72, '73 and '74. 1974 also saw them lift the first of their three successive European Cup wins. Atletico Madrid were annihilated 4-0 after a replay in the first of them, thus Munich became the first German side to lift the trophy. In the following season Leeds United were beaten 2-0 and in 1976 St Etienne were defeated by a solitary goal to confirm their dominance of Europe. They became Champions of the World the same year when they beat Cruzeiro of Brazil 2-0 on aggregate in the World Club Championship.

At the heart of this was Franz Beckenbauer, nicknamed the 'Kaiser' by the fans for the authority he brought to everything. Franz was named European Footballer of the year twice and captained Germany to World Cup and European Championship wins. In all he played 424 games in the Bundesliga, scoring 44 times. His career in management was equally as spectacular, the high spot being when he managed West Germany to win the World Cup in 1990. When he returned to Bayern Munich he coached them to the Bundseliga title in 1994 and the UEFA Cup in 1996. After that he was promoted to president of the club.

Of course there were other fantastic players who wore the famous colours of Bayern. Their names read like a whose who of German football: Sepp Maier, Gerd Muller, Uli Hoeness, Karl-Heinze Rummenigge, Jurgen Klinsmann, Michael Ballack and Paul Breitner amongst them. Franz was president when Owen arrived at the club. They were managed at that time by Giovanni Trapattoni who had just guided them to the title.

Owen had travelled over to Germany with a great friend of his, Kevin McKenna, with whom he had grown up and played youth soccer. Both the lads were keen to make their football fortunes. Kevin was a lanky defender, his pal a smaller, tough midfielder. Owen took the high road to Munich whilst his compatriot ended up in Eastern Germany playing for Energie Cottbus, a small provincial club. Although McKenna's parents were both Scottish, like Owen, he was Canadian-born, and ended up opting to play for Canada. In an interview with the *Sunday Herald* he spoke about his friend: 'I have always considered him my idol as well as my best friend because soccer is something that comes so easily to him. He is the best player Canada has ever produced.'

It must have been tremendously hard for Owen to leave Calgary. He left everything behind to pursue the dream of making it abroad. In an interview with the *Guardian* he explained, 'I left my mum and dad, my girlfriend, my mates and my school in Canada for a completely new life in a strange country. I was alone when I came to Germany. I did not even have email then, so I wrote these long letters home every week. My mum and dad would also phone me. I was only 16 but I was proud and did not want to show them I was struggling in any way. So I came here with open arms ready to embrace everything and learn the language. It was exciting but incredibly difficult.'

Those words best summarise the character of Owen Hargreaves even at that tender age. He did not want to give up despite the difficulties and the upheaval in his life. Compare this to Ian Rush who famously described his move from Liverpool to Juventus as 'Like living in a different country'. Owen was highly intelligent, with the ability to learn a foreign language. He was given a thorough education not just in football but in his studies. As part of the system, the youngsters were given tuition and educated up to the standard German certificate.

Owen kept to his word of embracing the culture: one of his first trips on his tourist trek was to King Ludwig 11's Neuschwanstein Castle, built by a 19th century theatre designer in homage to Richard Wagner. This German castle was the inspiration for all of the Walt Disney castles which he had seen on the Canadian Cartoon channels. The castle was the setting for *Chitty Chitty Bang Bang*. Owen, who loved reading and history, was fascinated to learn Ludwig never lived in the castle and it was not even finished till after he had drowned his psychiatrist and himself in a nearby lake.

He adapted to the language and quickly picked it up. The main problem was eating and getting used to the classic Bavarian cuisine which used only regional produce. The daily menu included local specialities and large roasts. One speciality was Furstliche Braunbierbratwurste (princely brown beer sausages) washed down with large tankards of Marstall Dunkell – a highly powerful unfiltered lager beer. Owen was too young to indulge in such practices, even a few sips would have necessitated carrying him back to the Youth House. Next door to the building was the infamous 'Insider Bar' where the fans met up to celebrate their love for Bayern Munich, strong beer, sausages and heavy metal music.

Owen recalled that in his early days the place was pitch dark and the menu consisted of sausages and schnitzel. For anyone not familiar with it, schnitzel is a traditional Viennese dish which consists of thin strips of veal coated in bread crumbs and fried. Schnitzel formed the staple part of his diet and he claims to have lived off it for the first six months of his time in Germany.

Owen admits that at that time, one of the walls in his room was covered with pictures of David Beckham. The Manchester United star was the first of the 'Golden Generation' that promised to win the World Cup for England in the new millennium. In the summer of 1997 he was about to climb the stairway to global superstardom. Becks had just turned 22 and recently acquired his first Premiership medal and England Cap. In 'Scarface' there was the scalp prickling scene where Tony Montana, having just eliminated his rivals, takes over the crime empire of Miami.

He goes out onto the balcony and sees the airship with the slogan 'The World is Yours' emblazoned on its side. Beckham must have seen the airship too because he was about to dominate the world.

The schnitzel diet must have agreed with Owen because for the next two and a half years he played for the Bayern Under-19 side. This consisted of playing all over Bavaria on muddy village pitches. The tackling was hard and more often than not the kid from Calgary with the strange accent was a target for the local hard boys. This was nothing new though because back home in Calgary he had always been a target in junior football for the same reason. Whoever said that 'Whatever does not kill you makes you stronger' had it right. Owen grew in stature. He could look after himself without resorting to 'getting his retaliation in first'. Plus he was a highly gifted player, with the ball control to dribble out of tight situations, the acceleration to leave opponents standing and a complete lack of fear. The player Owen was most like at that age was a young Paul Gascoigne, but a Gazza who never gave in to drink. Bayern had a great find, and now their system would turn him into a star.

Owen was spurred on because nobody on either side of the pond gave him a candle for his chances of making it in Bavaria. In an interview with the *Independent* he told of the negativity that surrounded his sojourn to Germany. 'When I left Canada for Bayern people said. "You will never make it. You will be back in a year". I stopped going to school because I said, "I am going to do this". They said "You have got no chance". My teachers, friends and other people were very sceptical. It was the same at Bayern, they said, "He's got no chance"'.

The coaches watched his rapid progress with interest. At

the end of each season they had the heart-breaking task of rejecting those boys that did not quite make it, who lacked the little extra to make the jump to the next level. Colin Hargreaves had failed at the final hurdle, Kevin McKenna did also but the difference was finite, infinitesimal; the difference between success and failure. Neither player became disenchanted with football though. Owen we will learn went onto play for two of the biggest teams in world football and earned millions. Kevin McKenna is currently playing for FC Koln who are in the German Second Division.

In 1998 Owen almost tasted his first success for Bayern as the Under-19s reached the final of the German Championship. The final was played against Borussia Dortmund on their home ground at the Dortmund Rote-Erde Stadium. Owen's side lost after a penalty shoot-out. This was not to be the last time that a penalty shoot-out was to loom large in his life.

The next stage of his development was to spend six months with the amateur team.

In the spring of 1999 Owen travelled to the Nou Camp with his team-mates in the Under-19 side. They were about to play in a youth tournament in Rotterdam but as a reward for their recent endeavours they were amongst the 90,245 that packed Barcelona's ground that magical evening. They were about to witness the most astonishing climax to a final in the history of the competition. Bayern had got to the final of the European Champions League and were playing against the mighty Manchester United. The English side were just one win away from a historic treble, having already won their domestic league and cup competitions in style. Already the magic of Manchester United was starting to weave itself into the life of Owen Hargreaves.

Bayern had beaten Dynamo Kiev 4-3 on aggregate to reach the final, thus denying Kiev the honour of being the first Russian side to reach the European Cup Final. Andriy Shevchenko had scored 11 goals in their run. For Bayern it was their sixth final, the hat trick of wins in the Beckenbauer years had been followed by defeats in 1982 and 1987 to Aston Villa and Porto. By a quirk of fate it was played on the anniversary of Bayern's unlucky defeat to Villa in Rotterdam. Owen was swotting up on the history of his club and the more mature fans would still talk in awe of the save that the substitute goalkeeper Nigel Spink made from Rummenigge.

Both teams were forced by injuries to field weakened sides. Bayern were without long term casualties, French defender Bixente Lizarazu and the Brazilian Giovane Elber. Manchester United were without their midfield superstars, Roy Keane and Paul Scholes, both suspended as they rampaged around Europe. Owen had been looking forward to seeing them in action as he was particularly interested in analysing their style of play.

Bayern tasted first blood after five minutes when Mario Basler's free-kick deceived Peter Schmeichel, playing his last game for United. That was how it stayed, as Beckham's free-kick was United's best chance in a scrappy, niggly first half. Early in the second half Carsten Jancker burst into the penalty area and fired in a shot which Schmeichel saved brilliantly. Owen had mixed feelings about the whole evening. Of course, his loyalty was with his employers who had given him such a wonderful opportunity to progress his career. Deep down though a part of him was a United fan, having being forged in those early morning TV shows in Calgary and the love of Northern football instilled in him by Colin and Henry Hargreaves.

United had the majority of play but Bayern looked more dangerous on the break. Jesper Blomqvist shot over from close range but then Schmeichel made another fine save from Stefan Effenberg with just over a quarter of an hour to go. With ten minutes left Bayern's goal scorer Basler set up Mehmet Scholl for what should have been the killer blow. Instead his delicate chip beat Schmeichel but not the post. Bixente Lizarazu was sitting near Owen and he watched as the World Cup winner shook his head and muttered with a resigned acceptance, 'C'est la guerre'.

Five minutes later Bayern amazingly hit the woodwork again, as Jancker came over on his back to bicycle kick against the bar. Owen looked across at his coach Ottmar Hitzfeld and for the first time in the match he saw just a flicker of concern. Hitzfeld had won the Champions League with Borussia Dortmund in the 1997 final, beating a classy Juventus side. The game had been played in Munich a few months before Owen had turned up there. En route to the final Borussia had knocked out United in the semis, but Ottmar knew that they were never more dangerous than in the dying minutes of vital matches.

Owen could only watch. United had all their subs on including the experienced Teddy Sheringham and Ole Gunnar Solskjaer, the deadliest substitute of them all. Everyone has their own version of those crazy closing moments. Like when President Kennedy was assassinated it was said that people could remember exactly where they were and what they were doing. Bayern were about to be assassinated by the man with the 'Baby Face'. Owen could tell you where he was that night, he was right there watching it unfold.

The 45 minutes were up and the UEFA officials were

attaching Bayern's ribbons to the Cup. Owen was close enough to see them performing the task. The fourth official signalled that there was to be three minutes of extra time. In the first of those Beckham took a corner. Owen remembered thinking how beautifully he had struck it and wondered what Schmeichel was doing up there... There was a scramble before Sheringham steered it home.

Steve McClaren, another who was to figure significantly in this volume was United's number two that night. Above the din he turned to Sir Alex Ferguson and told him that United would go on now to win the game in extra time. Sir Alex shook his head and said it would not be necessary.

Perhaps that story best illustrates the difference between the two men. Sir Alex had already correctly judged that Bayern had gone and that the Cup was theirs. Owen Hargreaves, who was to later play for both men, knew it too. United came down the field like a hurricane. Another Beckham corner, Teddy flicked on and Solskjaer, with icy commitment, hit it into the net for the most famous goal in the modern game.

Owen told the *Guardian* about his experiences that night. 'In the end we threw it away in the last minutes. I remember watching David Beckham, who was playing in central midfield and trying to bring some of the things he did into my game. It was slightly different from me being a fan of Manchester United but I still lost my voice because we screamed so much. We just sat there shocked because it had been so comfortable. And then it was gone.'

Little did Owen realize that in just two years' time he would be playing in a Champions League Final himself. A few years after that he would be playing for Manchester United also. The dream was already coming true.

Chapter Two
A Small Town in Germany

'He played clear, simple balls was very committed and stuck to his job.'
Stefan Effenberg (Upon his replacement Owen Hargreaves' performance against Real Madrid)

Ray Liotta's opening line in the seminal Mafia film 'Goodfellas' was 'As far back as I can remember, I always wanted to be a gangster'. For Owen you could paraphrase it to 'As far as I can remember, I always wanted to be a footballer'.

Owen was living in Germany's third largest city, having graduated from the toughest finishing school in football at the Bayern Munich Youth Academy. If his birthplace Calgary was named the 'Cleanest City' in the world then Munich was considered to be the city with the fifth best quality of life. Bayern had been voted the top club in the world that summer by the International Federation for Football History and Statistics after studying Hargreaves employer's national and international results.

Owen played in his first ever Bundesliga game on 12 August 2000 against Hertha BSC Berlin. He came on in the 83rd minute of the home match played at the Munich Olympic stadium. This was the famous ground that had been built for the 1972 Olympic Games. The player he replaced was the bald-headed striker Carsten Jancker, the forward that had hit the Manchester United woodwork at the Nou Camp. Bayern won the match 4-1 and Owen looked very comfortable and confident as he gained his first experience in one of the world's toughest leagues. Owen's friend Kevin McKenna had already beaten him to the record of being the first Canadian to play in the German First Bundesliga. Kevin's team Energie Cottbus had already won promotion to the top flight.

After his introduction to the big-time Owen went back to the Bayern reserve team who had started the campaign successfully. Udo Bassemir was in charge of the reserve team at the time. The youngster had picked up a calf injury and was struggling for full fitness.

Owen made his first international debut for England at that time when he was called up to play for the Under-19 side against Georgia. The Canadian public were not best pleased that he had opted to play for England rather than the country he had been born in. The 'Canadian Slam' website ran a scathing attack on Owen accusing him of being a traitor because he turned his back on 'his' country which needed success and a star to sell the sport. They were completely wrong, as Owen was once quoted as saying 'When I was interested in Canada they were not interested in me.' The same year he had signed for Bayern he had in their parlance been 'cut' from the Canadian youth side. Even though he had been brought up in Canada, England was his country.

Bayern hit the top of the league with a 3-1 win over Wolfsburg in early September 2000. September was to be a very busy month for them with eight games in 24 days.

Owen played in his first Champions League game on 13 September 2000 in Bayern's 3-1 win in Helsingborg. The youngster replaced Hasan Salihamidzic six minutes from time and soaked up the atmosphere of the occasion. Owen was to grow to love the atmosphere of those big European nights, the roar of the crowd, the smell of the greasepaint. It was Owen's first international trip with the first team squad. The trip to Sweden for the Group F fixture was an adventure for him, the first of many guerrilla raids into other countries in the European continent. At the end of his time in Germany they could have opened a museum with all the booty he had accumulated and what he achieved during his Bayern career.

Three days later Owen made his first start in the Bundesliga against Sp Vgg Unterhaching at the Olympic Stadium in front of 48,000 on a Saturday evening. Owen put in a polished midfield performance as Bayern cantered to a 3-1 victory. Danny Schwarz put lowly Unterhaching ahead after 20 minutes with a deflected drive. Giovane Elber equalised for Bayern after 38 minutes with a terrific individual goal.

Hitzfeld replaced Elber shortly afterwards, sparing him for the European games, and Owen was pushed further forward. Skipper Scholl put Bayern ahead from the spot. Owen watched closely, mentally taking notes and studying techniques – he was anxious to perfect his penalty skills. Jancker, Elber's replacement, wrapped it all up with the third to make it a highly satisfactory 90 minutes for Owen.

A few days later Bayern overcame the Norwegian side

Rosenborg Trondheim 3-1 at home. Hitzfeld was bringing Owen on slowly and he did not participate in this particular game. Hargreaves was delighted at his progress though and told *Gauntlet Sports* his feelings about winning a spot in the Bayern squad: 'This has been my goal all along. And now I hope to continue to take steps forward and try to make myself a better player all around. I am still learning new things all the time and I want to continue to do that. I want to make myself better and work on my weaknesses.'

Bayern won Group F with 11 points gleaned from 3 wins and 2 draws, their only loss was to second placed Paris Saint-Germain. Vice President Karl-Heinz Rummenigge told the *Der Bild* that they had about 50-100 million Marks to invest in four or five players to establish themselves at the top of the European pile. Thomas Rosicky, then at the Czech Champions Sparta Prague, was a player he visualised linking up with the young Hargreaves. A mouthwatering prospect that unfortunately never materialised.

The next stage that Bayern found themselves in was in Group C, pitted against Arsenal, Lyon and Spartak Moscow. Bayern won the group comfortably, amassing 13 points from 6 matches (four wins, a draw at Arsenal and only one reverse 0-3 to Lyon).

This put them into the knockout stages of the quarter-finals. England had three teams in the last eight, the same number as Spain. For once there were no Italian sides in the mix. Owen's team were drawn against Manchester United, a repeat of the epic encounter that Owen had witnessed in the Nou Camp two years before. The City of Manchester again loomed large in his life. What was it about the club in red and white that seemed to cross his paths at certain stages of his career?

Owen Hargreaves

Sir Alex Ferguson's team had won the 1999 Champions League with four Englishmen in their team. The Bayern Munich side had a much higher proportion of Germans in theirs.

Manchester and Munich were inextricably linked because of the air disaster that occurred on Thursday 6 February 1958, twenty-three years before the birth of Owen Hargeaves. The Manchester United party were returning to London after a refuelling stop following a European Cup game in Belgrade. At 3.04pm the BEA Elizabethan airliner G-ALZU made its third attempt to take off from the main runway at Munich airport. This time the plane crashed, killing 23 people; eight of them were Manchester United players, members of the 'Busby Babes', arguably the greatest team that ever played at Old Trafford. Potentially they were the most brilliant club side in the history of the European game.

Their brightest star was Duncan Edwards, a man who could play anywhere and who seemed set for a place amongst the pantheon of the world's finest players. At 21 years of age he was at that time the youngest international in the history of England. Edwards was a giant in every sense of the word, weighing in at over 13 stone and standing over 6ft tall. Big Dunc would not have been out of place in the company of Pele, Cruyff, Maradona, Beckenbauer, etc. Even today Edwards is regarded as one of the finest players ever produced in this country. A player that earned £15 a week that was reduced to £12 in the summer. Whenever United fans of a certain age sit around and chew the fat over who was their 'greatest ever' player Edwards is the only name to consistently beat that of George Best. The United colossus was fatally injured in the crash but hung on for two weeks in the Rechts der Isar hospital. Duncan's injuries included damaged kidneys, broken ribs, a collapsed lung, broken pelvis and a fractured thigh. It was inconceivable to many that his wonderful body, so cruelly damaged in the accident could put up such a heart-breaking fight for so long.

Owen was steeped in the history of the crash of the 47-seater BEA high wing monoplane. Colin, his father, was only an infant at the time of the crash but his grandfather Henry, like everyone of that generation, knew exactly where they were and what they were doing when the scarcely credible news of the crash broke. We have discussed in the previous chapter the impact of the Ole Gunnar Solskjaer goal in the subtext of the assassination of President Kennedy. Those last three minutes in the Nou Camp were the most dramatic in the career of the referee that night, Pierluigi Collina. The death of Kennedy in 1963 happened 5 years after the Munich crash and led to the freeze-framing in time of a certain moment linked to a particular incident.

The story of the Munich crash was passed down through the Hargreaves family from grandfather to grandson, via father. Henry Hargreaves was particularly upset as for a long time it looked as if Duncan, probably the most valuable youngster ever, was going to sign for his beloved Bolton Wanderers. Duncan's cousin Dennis Stephens was already on their books.

Owen's grandfather spoke about a song called the 'Flowers of Manchester' that had been anonymously sent to a local paper a few days after the crash. A song reverently spoken of, yet narrowly sung. Owen, sitting in a kitchen in Canada listening earnestly to the tales, could hardly have guessed that one day he would be a thread in the tapestry of one of the most tragic yet inspiring stories in sport.

Inspiring? Yes, because of two of the survivors catapulted into the snow from the burning shell of the aircraft. Sir Matt Busby and Sir Bobby Charlton helped rebuild the club into the biggest and most famous in the world. The courage and basic, intrinsic values of those men created a template for modern players like Hargreaves. It would be wrong and unfair to mention Owen in the same context as those icons but at the time of writing Owen had never been sent off in his career and was a perfect role model to youngsters with his off field behaviour. The England international had shown remarkable courage in overcoming the setbacks, racism and painful injuries that had beset him throughout his career.

Perhaps it was down to the Munich connection. The modern player uses an airport like the average commuter uses his railway station. As his career blossomed Owen was always being whisked away by jet planes to some fixture whether it was for Bayern or on international duty for his country. The same country that Duncan Edwards represented 18 times, this was in an era when England caps were not dished out like free DVDs with the weekend papers. Sometimes when waiting in the Bavarian capital for his flight to be called Owen would gaze out through the windows, across the runways and think about the aircraft that tried to lift off that dark winter's afternoon.

The people of Munich had a bond with those of Manchester, they had stolen the Cup from them in the Nou Camp but always the date of 6 February 1958 kept them together. It was the same bond that made the soldiers of two warring armies get out of their trenches on a freezing Christmas morning in 1914 and kick a battered leather ball around. It was the love of football.

Stanley Matthews was born in 1915, second only to Best as the greatest winger in the history of the game. His tribute to Duncan was succinct. 'I cannot remember any other player that size who was quick like that.'

Bayern beat United in both of their matches to gain revenge for the Nou Camp defeat. In the first leg played on 3 April a late goal from substitute Paulo Sergio in the 86th minute gave Bayern victory at Old Trafford in front of 66,584. Stefan Effenberg set the goal up with a cleverly flighted free-kick. Before the match the Bayern skipper had told the media that the 'whole world is talking about this game'.

Owen travelled with the team but did not play in either tie. It was his first visit to the ground and it left a lasting impression on him, the gloomy and sepulchral Manchester was to be his future home. His family were continuing to monitor his career closely and this was seen as another milestone.

Franz Beckenbauer, the Bayern president, was delighted with the great result in Manchester. In an interview with the German tabloid *Bild am Sonntag* he described the victory at Old Trafford as a 'highly promising platform'. He went on to say, 'If we show the character that we did in Manchester, we will get through to the semis. We could win it although in our section Manchester United and Real Madrid are the best in Europe.'

Bayern tore into United in the return match, anxious to put the game out of their reach. Nobody knew better of their recuperative powers and how dangerous Ferguson's side could be when they were wounded. Hitzfeld's plan was to grab an early goal that would demoralise them. It worked perfectly, Elber turning in Michael Tarnat's cross in the fifth minute. The goal settled Bayern and just on half-time, Jens Jeremies quick-witted cross was cleverly laid off by

Giovane Elber for Mehmet Scholl to kill the game with the second of the night. United refused to give in though and fought hard throughout the second half. Ryan Giggs ran through to lob Oliver Khan and pull a goal back but there was to be no fairytale ending this night as Bayern smothered the Reds' midfield.

It was a bizarre night in many ways: before the game, United fan Karl Power, dressed in the full away strip, managed to get on the pitch and had his picture taken with the chaps. Roy Keane gave his team-mates a real shellacking at the end of the game – he must have wondered how many other impostors in United colours were out there on the pitch. Around that time Keane was expressing the view that the great treble winning side of 1999 was losing its hunger and focus.

Now the real glory was to come quickly to Owen as he was to get his chance against Real Madrid in the semi-final of the Champions League. Owen did not play in the first leg in Madrid. The score lines went the same as in the quarter-final against United. A 1-0 victory in Madrid followed by a 2-1 home victory in the Olympic Stadium. Their brilliant Brazilian striker Giovane Elber scored vital goals in both legs. At the Bernabeu on the 1 May 2001 his goal was the result of a mistake by the young Madrid goalkeeper, Iker Casillas. Elber's long range shot, not powerfully hit, crept past him in the 55th minute to give Bayern a priceless victory.

The legendary midfielder/left back Paul Breitner played for both clubs and covered the match in his capacity as a pundit. He wrote in the *Bild am Sonntag* about how he saw the tie. 'My verdict, advantage Bayern in every respect. If it had been 2-0, Real would have been forced to turn on the turbo boost immediately. 1-0 was an ideal result.'

Steve McManaman dominated the first game, outshining the superstars Figo, Raul, Effenberg et al. The Bayern defence tied the Madrid attack up in knots but could not subdue the ex-Liverpool man, lightning fast but unorthodox. Hip and cosmopolitan, the first English Euro-player twice carved out great chances for himself and thundered in searing shots that somehow the Bayern keeper Oliver Kahn kept out.

A week before the return game in Germany Owen called his pal Kevin McKenna who was now on loan at Hearts. He knew something that was being kept top secret from the media. This was the fact that he was replacing the suspended team captain Stefan Effenberg in the vital return game against Real Madrid. Effenberg was the heart of the team, a Roy Keane type of leader with great vision and a languid style. The Hamburg born player was a hard act to follow but his replacement was a product of the finest youth set up in the world and knew what was required. That was so typical of Owen, he still kept in touch with his pals from the early days in Canada. Fate had showered the young midfielder with more than his share of gifts and good fortune but he was still anxious to preserve his roots.

The Madrid game was the one that earned Owen the critical acclaim. The previous season Madrid had beaten Bayern 3-2 in the semi-final. This was after the Bundesliga champions had comprehensively beaten them 4-1 at home and 4-2 away in the second group stage. The clash between Madrid and Bayern had a history of being one of the tournament's tetchiest grudge fixtures. It dated back to the first leg of the 1976 European Cup semi-final played in Spain. At the end of a bad tempered 1-1 draw a Madrid fan attacked the legendary striker Gerd Muller and the Austrian referee Erich Linemayr. Muller had scored Bayern's goal that night and subsequently scored two more to knock out the Spanish side in the return match. A culture clash started then – the Spanish fans hated the defensive, Teutonic style of Bayern. Their German counterparts showed little respect for the perceived 'fancy Dan' foppery of Madrid.

In 1979 when Uli Hoeness took over at Bayern Munich his blueprint for success was to re-create a model of Real Madrid. In the opening years of the 21st century it could be said that the German giants were at least the equal of the Madrid maestros. A highly significant stat indicated that the two clubs with the highest amount of goals in European competitions were Real Madrid and Bayern Munich. The management of Bayern always believed in producing their own talent rather than paying out extortionate transfer fees. Madrid's purchase of Nicolas Anelka for £23m from Arsenal was a textbook example of their spending sprees. The 21-year-old prima donna was an exceptional talent but at that stage it was imprisoned by his moody, self-obsessed, materialistic image. The term mercenary could be safely applied to him. As Hoeness once remarked, 'He has scored one goal in ten months'.

Compare this to Owen, the product of the Bayern youth system. Apart from him it had created some of Germany's top stars such as Andreas Ottl, Thomas Hitzlsperger and Philipp Lahm. Despite coming from Canada, Owen had adapted to the new environment and integrated himself with his team-mates. Anelka had not bothered to communicate at the Bernabeu preferring the company of his PlayStation and brothers. One of the main differences between the teams was that the dressing room inhabited by Owen and his team seemed very harmonious compared to that of the ego riddled

Madrid team. The buzzword for Bayern which kept cropping up in interviews was 'Collectivism'.

Owen had a wonderful game, slipping seamlessly into the team and giving a faultless display against the star studded Madrid side. Bayern's tactics were simple, to protect their lead and stifle the opposition. Steve McManaman talked about the game in his autobiography *El Macca*. 'Bayern Munich always have the same game plan; defend, defend, defend and try to hit us on the break.'

Owen was deployed against Madrid as a defensive midfielder. Detecting danger from Figo and co before it reached his back four, cutting out passes, harassing his former idol Steve McManaman and preventing his diagonal runs. It must have been an amazing feeling for him to shadow-mark one of the players that he was such a fan of when he was growing up.

Bayern were given a great boost when Elber popped up to score a vital goal after seven minutes. The prodigious speed of Elber was always a problem to the Madrid defence. The Cup holders hit back and within eleven minutes had equalised. Referee Milton Nielsen awarded them a penalty and Figo smashed it home. Madrid had only to score once more to go through on away goals. The game could not have been more finely balanced than at that time. Owen must have had to pinch himself when he found himself on the same pitch as the player with the then world record transfer fee (£38m) Luis Figo, the record breaking striker Raul and Roberto Carlos, one of the greatest backs of any era.

Near half-time the Bayern midfield player Jens Jeremies scored from a free-kick to make it 3-1 on aggregate. Madrid now had to score two more and with their desperation rising by the minute poured forward. This was when Owen came into his own as his physical strength and tactical skills came to the fore. In the closing weeks of the season Ottmar Hitzfeld had concentrated on building up the player's physical strength which had been sapped by the demands of the long campaign waged on different fronts. This was despite the rotation system employed successfully and with surprisingly good effect by Hitzfeld.

This was the genius of the man, he would send the team on distance running on the Monday afternoon after a Bundesliga game. Owen had the dual advantages also of his youth and the fact that he only made 14 domestic appearances that season. Put simply Owen ran the Madrid forwards into the ground. Their manager, at the time Vicente Del Bosque, put the star striker Fernando Morientes on for the defender Aitor Karanka and then replaced McManaman with the speedy Sivio. Bayern held out though with Hargreaves outstanding, his exceptional stamina helped him cruise through the closing stages.

Hargreaves had obliterated his hero McManaman that night and hastened the end of his career in Madrid. It was a watershed moment in both of their careers. Although he was to remain at the Bernabeu for two more years his position was never to be the same. Steve's performance was unjustly criticised by Alfredo di Stefano.

Stung by their exit at the hands of Bayern Madrid purchased FIFA World Player of the Year Zinedine Zidane in the following summer for £50m from Juventus. With the addition of the most complete footballer in the world and the politics surrounding it McManaman found himself squeezed out of the Madrid midfield. That was the nature of the most ruthless business in the world where the difference between success and failure was literally the width of Oliver Kahn's fingertips.

If McManaman was criticised by one football god then Owen was eulogized by another one for his performance in the same match. Franz Beckenbauer told BBC Sport the next day how well he performed in the glorious Bayern victory over their old adversaries. 'It is hard to believe Hargreaves could turn in a performance like that. Perhaps he never had a chance to show what he could do, but last night he did.'

Coach Ottmar Hitzfeld told the media that Owen was a key player for Bayern. The General Manager Uli Hoeness said that this proved that all young Bayern players would get a chance if they were good enough.

The tributes came in thick and fast, but no one was prouder than Thomas Niendorf who had natured Owen's career since the early days in Calgary. Speaking from there, the man who introduced Owen to Bayern told the same BBC website: 'Owen is an example to all young players here. So much of being able to play at an elite level is courage and conviction. To see him play in one of the world's biggest soccer tournaments and hold his own is a tremendous thing. I cannot say enough about the way he performed. He had poise and played with intelligence. I do not think he put a foot wrong. Being allowed to take set pieces shows the type of respect his team-mates have for him already.'

By virtue of the fact that he had an upbringing in Canada Owen, had different qualities than if he had been brought up in England. For example, because of the climate the young players had two completely different seasons, the outdoor and the indoor. The latter was five-a-side soccer. The playing area was surrounded by boards which meant that the ball was always in play. This heightened the intensity of the game, improved players' reflexes and concentration because they were never able to relax.

Bayern were very astute and they slapped an interview ban on their newest star. They were desperate to protect their latest prospect and steadfastly shielded him from the demands of the press and the glare of unwanted celebrity. This worked perfectly, because he may well have been saddled with more expectation than he could have coped with. There are no post-match interviews or quotes in the archives from this period. Owen never courted the media and let publicity be his pimp like Beckham. What did Rilke write about Rodin? 'Fame is only the sum of those misunderstandings which gather around a new name?'

In a way it was a pity about the interview black-out because Owen could have articulated his answers in faultless German. Because of the education he had received at the Academy he had a strong grasp of the German language. Now he could speak fluent German without any trace of an accent.

The emergence of Hargreaves on the scene was like that of McManaman, largely ignored by the English press. A year before, Real had beaten Valencia 3-0 in the Stade de France Paris to win the UEFA Champions League. McManaman had a devastating game and scored the second goal, an event that was generally overlooked in this country.

The final this year was against Valencia in Milan on 23 May. With Stefan Effenberg back from suspension the papers speculated that Owen, the hero of the hour, might be relegated to the subs' bench. First though, there was the question of the Bundesliga to wrap up. This was done on the last day of the season in Hamburg and gave them a hat trick of Bundesliga titles. Up to the start of season 2007–08 they had won 17 titles. The victory gave them a huge psychological boost going into the UEFA Champions League final.

Owen won his first medal and had contributed to the title win by chalking up 14 domestic appearances. Just the start but he had got off the mark very impressively.

The 19-year-old Owen was chosen for the opening line-up in the final which was a battle between the beaten finalists of the two previous seasons. Jens Jeremies, who had scored the winning goal against Real Madrid, missed the final with inflamed muscles, so once again the youth team graduate stepped up to the plate. Jeremies was one of the most decorated players in the history of German football and a model of consistency.

Hitzfeld included half-a-dozen players who had taken part in the reckoning with Manchester United three days short of exactly two years before. They were Stefan Effenberg, Oliver Kahn, Sammy Kuffour, Mehmet Scholl, Thomas Linke and Hasan Salihamidzic. Two key players; the Brazilian Giovane Elber and French defender Bixente Lizarazu had both missed the Nou Camp match but started in Milan. Two other survivors from the 1999 defeat, lanky striker Carsten Jancker and Alexander Zickler were on the bench.

The new kid on the block was Owen, who told the *Daily Telegraph*: 'What happened in Barcelona made us more than determined when we found ourselves in the final two years later. I knew we were not going to lose. We had won the Bundesliga in Hamburg on the Saturday and then on Wednesday it was the Champions League Final. I was so focused, so determined and so excited to play and there was no doubt in my mind what was going to happen.'

The trip to Milan was planned with all the precision of a moon landing. Hitzfeld ordered that the party travel two days before the game which was a break from usual procedure. The ghosts of the Nou Camp still haunted the team, the pressure on them was mounting. The 52-year-old wanted to get away from Munich, which was in the grip of Cup fever, and obtain some well earned rest before the game. He correctly guessed that the German media would continue to harass the team for interviews. Owen was a particular favourite of theirs.

Before the final the news agency DPA asked famous sportsmen their take on things, here are some of the biggest names.

Boris Becker (former tennis ace and huge Bayern fan): 'I am a passionate Bayern Munich fan. I spend every waking moment thinking about this final. Of course I am nervous but we will win it.'

Michael Schumacher (Formula One World Champion): 'I am wishing Bayern Munich to win obviously. And I think they will win. The way Bayern are playing it could be tight. But it will not go wrong.'

Way to go Michael.

A quarter of a century had elapsed since Bayern had last tasted success in the European Cup. That was the night in Paris when Franz Roth's goal had beaten St. Etienne. Now they were up against Valencia who were a classy, attacking side managed by the Argentinean Hector Cuper. They had some fine players including Roberto Ayala and Gaizka Mendieta. It was him who gave Valencia the lead after just three minutes in this amazing final. Mendieta, who had been voted the 'European Midfielder of the Season' in consecutive years, easily scored from the spot. Within five minutes the Dutch referee Dick Jol awarded a penalty to Bayern. Mehmet Scholl missed the chance to level as the Valencia goalkeeper Santiago Canizares saved his kick. Owen helped drive Bayern forward but they made no real clear cut chances in the rest of the half.

Early in the second half Bayern were awarded their second penalty and this time the meticulous Stefan Effenberg made no mistake. That was about it for the rest of normal time. Owen had a more flexible role than in the Madrid game – his job was to ensure that Valencia midfield players did not enjoy time on the ball. The intelligence of Owen Hargreaves was such that, despite having only just a handful of games in the most important of European competitions, he could adapt in a disciplined manner to whatever situation occurred.

Valencia almost stole it in the dying moments of normal time when substitute Zlatko Zahovic brought a fantastic save out of Oliver Kahn. It was the equal of the saves he made from Steve McManaman in Madrid. Alex Stepney had made a great save in the closing stages of the European Cup Final in 1968 to deny Eusebio and help United win the trophy.

Another 30 minutes of extra time were ground out and Bayern finished the stronger as they went looking for the winner. Owen made sure that Valencia's attacks were limited to a few sporadic raids, that was his particular strength breaking up counter attacks. Then it was down to penalties, which was to be to some extent also the story of his England career. It started badly for Bayern with Paulo Sergio missing their first kick. Gaizka Mendieta opened the penalty sequence for Valencia and scored as crisply as he had in normal time. The Basque born winger had been a constant threat to the German team throughout the match. The next three penalties were rattled in, two of them emphatically scored by Bayern. Then as the pressure started to gnaw away the next three were missed. Two of them by Valencia. The score now was 2-2 with each side having taken four kicks.

Effenberg scored with his kick to edge Bayern ahead.

Earlier in the season sport director Karl-Heinze Rummenigge had criticised Stefan's commitment to perform and the midfielder responded in the best possible fashion. Valencia equalised through Ruben Baraja to peg it back to 3-3. With the pressure mounting, both sides scored their sixth penalty of the contest. Bixente Lizarazu was successful for Bayern and Kily Gonzalez kept Valencia in it to tie it at 4-4.

With the tension almost unbearable, Bayern's Thomas Linke scored their fifth penalty out of seven. Owen was gazing broodingly from the halfway line. He was about to go on. It was a nerve wracking moment as he told the *Independent*: 'The penalty shoot out went on for ages – there was just me and Carsten Jancker left to take one. He was 26 and I thought I should be respectful so I said you should go next. He looked at me and said "Forget it"'.

So Owen would have been on next and who knows what would have happened, but it was not required. Kahn saved Valencia's next effort and Bayern Munich had won the Champions League for 2000–01.

Hitzfeld was carried shoulder-high by his ecstatic players at the end of the evening. He was now officially a legend at Munich and had become only the second manager in history to win the Champions League with two different clubs. His other success came with Borussia Dortmund in 1997. Ernst Happel had become the first to do so, winning it with Feyenoord (who had beaten Celtic in the final also played in Milan) and Hamburg. Jose Mourinho had won the Champions League with Porto but was unable to repeat the trick in his turbulent spell at Chelsea.

Hitzfeld was a brilliant motivator and his skill with people was underrated. The selection of Owen for the return semi-final game was a stroke of genius. The introduction of fresh blood lifted the whole squad and focused their talents. Owen's early success seemed to be pre-ordained regardless. Critical superlatives were heaped on Owen by the German media.

How did Owen celebrate the most famous victory of his fledgling career? The standard joke was that he would don lederhosen and quaff beer from one of those massive glasses. Some years later he was asked the same question by *Sport* magazine and replied. 'Of course that is standard procedure. As Munich players, we get fitted with lederhosen for Oktoberfest. If we win the championship, we dress up and celebrate with the fans. It is funny to see the foreign players faces when they have them on – it is just so different from anything they are accustomed to.'

Owen later confirmed that they did not do the funny little leg slap dance. It would appear that when the boys from Bayern partied they did not dance. That image of Owen in lederhosen fascinated the media. When he moved to Manchester the *Guardian* would run a little feature every Monday entitled 'Kulturshock'. This consisted of a snap of Owen with Rooney and Ronaldo dressed in lederhosen and with a caption underneath. The caption was either a satire on recent events at Old Trafford or of the differences in the lifestyle. The cartoon ran well into January 2008 with the humour invoked by the subject of the caption being of a consistently high standard.

In a review of the singer Mika's live show one critic memorably described his outfit as looking 'like Owen Hargreaves dressed as a gay Bavarian goatherder'.

Owen was sitting on top of the world. He had made the desired progress to such an extent he now possessed the highest domestic honours achievable in football in his first season. The rollercoaster ride was just starting though.

Chapter Three

Kraftwerk

'There is no better place to learn your trade. You are not attuned mentally when you arrive at the club. It is something you acquire when you are there week in and week out.'

Oliver Kahn

A strong recommendation from the world famous custodian, voted the best goalkeeper in Europe for four years running. Kahn's memorable saving of three Valencia penalties in the shoot-out was a remarkable achievement even by his standards. In the aftermath of the famous victory the 31-year-old Kahn joked that he only saved important penalties.

Bayern returned to Munich at lunchtime the next day to a hero's welcome. Owen could scarcely believe how quickly things had happened for him.

In a few days they were flying out again this time to America. They played a long standing friendly against the New York/New Jersey Metro Stars and then spent some time unwinding after the exertions of their highly successful season.

The new season 2001–02 started in July with a shock 1-0 defeat to the newly promoted Borussia Monchengladbach. That was to be the story of the season in many ways. The next week they bounced back with a 3-0 victory over Schalke who had finished runners-up to them last season. This win gave them the motivation to defend their title and they went on an 11-match unbeaten run. This included thumping wins over Kaiserslauten (4-1), VFB Stuttgart (4-0) and 1860 Munich (5-1). After 12 games normal service appeared to have been resumed with Bayern at the head of the table having rattled in 30 goals.

It was an exciting time for Owen as he won his first cap for England against Holland. Sven-Goran Eriksson had instructed him to play on the left when he sent him on in the second half. Owen was somewhat bemused by this as he explained to the *Times*: 'I had never played on the left before, and he asked me to do it, explaining that he knew I was a central midfield player. At the time I had just won the Champions League with Bayern and the expectations were high.'

Then the Bayern starlet came on as sub against Germany on his home ground, the Olympic Stadium, after 78 minutes. That was the night of the historic 5-1 thrashing, the zenith of Sven's England tenure. Years later their paths crossed again in Manchester. Owen had just joined United and the Swede had just commenced his duties at Manchester City. Both men were staying in the plush Lowry Hotel and most mornings they would pass one another in the foyer on their way to their respective training grounds. That match was always in their minds when they briefly spoke of this and that.

Owen's appearance in the German debacle was to temporarily affect his place in Ottmar Hitzfeld's all-stars, as he confided to the *Independent*: 'That cost me my starting place with Bayern for a couple of weeks. They got over it.'

That period in Owen's career was a steep learning curve but his exposure to the inner workings of the German psyche was invaluable. In the space of a few months he had seen both sides of the coin: the ruthless manner in which Bayern had annexed both major trophies in the space of a couple of days and then the reaction of the German players to what must have been a demoralising defeat at the hands of their oldest rivals.

For the first time in his spell at Bayern Owen was linked with another club. Arsenal manager Arsene Wenger made a firm enquiry for him that was instantly rebuffed by Bayern. Wenger had been impressed with the marking job he had done on Luis Figo in the second leg of the semi-final against Madrid the previous spring. Their midfield ace Patrick Vieira was unsettled and close to leaving Arsenal. The Munich giants were a buying club, not a selling one, and a youngster with huge potential like Owen was regarded as a prime asset. Wenger had a wonderful network of scouts dotted around Europe which had unearthed the goldmine of talent that has rolled off the North London production line over the years. It was typical of him to try to lure Owen to London at that early stage of his career before his price in Euros sky rocketed.

Then it was back to UEFA Champions League action with the holders in Group H of the 2001–02 competition contesting with Feyenoord, Sparta Prague and Spartak Moscow.

Bayern beat Spartak Moscow 3-1 in the Russian capital at the end of September 2001. Ottmar Hitzfeld introduced Owen just before the end to give him another taste of the big time. Kahn was beaten for the first time in 445 minutes of Champions League football when Baranov's free-kick eluded him. The winners of the 2000–01 UEFA Champions League easily qualified from their group winning four and drawing two of their six games.

In the next qualifying group they were pitted against Manchester United for the third time in four years. On this occasion both games finished level, United drawing 1-1 in the first leg in Munich watched by 59,000 at the end of November. Ruud Van Nistelrooy scored United's goal, he had a fabulous competition that season, finishing top marksman with ten goals. Bayern played poorly in the match, particularly in the second half where they kept giving the ball away. Sir Alex Ferguson told the after match press conference that he was very disappointed at not winning.

On 18 October 1956 a United team including 'Busby Babes' Roger Byrne, Tommy Taylor and Duncan Edwards played the first leg of a first-round European Cup tie against the West German champions Borussia Dortmund. It was staged at the Moss Side ground of Manchester City because United still did not have floodlights. The match attracted a record crowd of 75,598, a huge crowd for a midweek game. David Pegg, the England winger scored the winner in a 3-2 victory, yet another great talent to perish on the runway at Munich in less than eighteen months time. The fixture was the first Anglo-German clash in European competition, since then there have been over a hundred.

After their exhausting Champions League tussle with United, Bayern flew to Tokyo to take on the Argentinean side Boca Juniors in the Toyota Cup. This was the annual clash between the winners of the UEFA Champions League and the winners of the South America Cup.

Owen had not been born when Bayern had last won the

World Club Championship, as it was known then, back in 1976. In this particular match they had beaten the Brazilian side Cruzeiro Belo Horizonte 2-0 on aggregate. They had won 2-0 in Germany and drew 0-0 in the return match in Brazil.

Bayern took the match very seriously and with the same attention to detail that they had demonstrated in the Champions League final. The party left Munich on the Sunday in a Lufthansa Jumbo and arrived the next day. Hitzfeld tried to acclimatise his players as quickly as possible. Bayern took around 1,000 fans across the globe to Tokyo but they were heavily outnumbered by a huge contingent of Argentinean fans. The German team won the match by a solitary goal scrambled in the 19th minute of extra time by the big Ghanaian defender Sammy Kuffour.

Owen had a fine match and was heavily involved in the action of a bad tempered, exhausting battle. He did a marvellous marking job on the star player for Bocca, the 23-year-old playmaker Riquelme. Like Owen, Juan Roman Riquelme divided opinions deeply. On his day Riquelme was a world beating playmaker and the heart of the current Argentina side. Doubts persist though about the fragility of his play and his lack of pace. In the Toyota Cup Final Owen pressured him throughout the game and denied him both time and space to use his sublime skills. The experience Owen was obtaining just being on the same field as a talent like Riquelme was priceless.

Earlier in the season Bayern had lost 2-3 to Liverpool in the European Super Cup which had been played in the Stade Louis 11 in Monaco. This was the curious fixture played in August between the reigning UEFA Champions League winners and the UEFA Cup Winners. Liverpool raced to a 3-0 interval lead with goals from John Arne Riise, Emile

Heskey and Michael Owen, (thc duo who were to inflict such punishment on Germany in a few weeks time). Bayern pulled back two second half goals in the match played on the pitch laid over an underground car park.

Domestically Bayern found the going harder. Owen was playing regularly but teams were raising their games against the double champions. Bremen became the second team to beat them in the Bundesliga. This came a few days before their home draw with United in November. Their title challenge came off the rails just before the mid-season interval with a run of two away defeats and three successive home draws. This put them down to fifth position in the league.

The year ended on a high note for Owen though when the news came through that he had won the 2001 European Under-21 player of the year award. A tremendous achievement by Owen considering the circumstances he had been confronted with. To make it a great double for the club, Hitzfeld was voted the best club coach of 2001. This award was made by the International Federation for Football History and Statistics.

Schalke thrashed Bayern 5-1 at the end of January to add to their woes. With the score at 1-4, Owen was put onto the field to replace Scholl but he could do nothing to stem the flow. The defeat left Bayern eight points behind the leaders Bayer Leverkusen. They met in the next fixture and Bayern put themselves back in the race for the title with a fine 2-0 win. Owen played well and helped subdue the Bayer star Michael Ballack. Ballack had agreed to join Bayern in the summer and was seen as the coming force in German football. There was an interesting duel between him and Stefan Effenberg which the veteran just shaded.

The rollercoaster dipped again a few nights later when FC

St Pauli beat Bayern 2-1 in another shock. The equivalent in English football would have been Millwall beating Manchester United. Hitzfeld admitted to the media that it was a season of transition for them and compared the team to one of Schumacher's Ferrari cars in that everything had to be working perfectly for it to function.

Bayern played the return against Manchester United on the 13 March at Old Trafford. The game ended in a 0-0 draw, it was the first time that Owen appeared on the pitch of the Theatre of Dreams. It was the first time that he clashed with Roy Keane at Old Trafford. Owen was surprised how relaxed it was in the United dressing room. He could hear the sound of music playing in the room before the match which was unheard of in Germany. The background staff contributed to the atmosphere, and some went out of their way to make him feel welcome because of his English roots.

The match was a case of familiarity bringing just a hint of contempt, both sides knew each other very well and stood off. Owen was operating on the right side of midfield and must have impressed the watching England coach Sven-Goran Eriksson with his huge appetite for work. Owen nearly opened the scoring when he let fly from long range and his shot whistled just wide with the Reds' keeper Fabien Barthez just an onlooker. The French keeper had recently succeeded Kahn in the rankings of the IFFHS world's best goalkeeper.

Hargreaves was prominent again shortly afterwards when he set up a chance that was missed by Pizarro. Near half-time a nasty lunge by Keane on Effenberg went unpunished. Solskjaer, Bayern's bête noir, put the ball in the Bayern net but it was disallowed for some inexplicable reason.

Owen's fine form continued into the second half. A free-kick, awarded for a foul on him, almost brought the first goal of the evening. Barthez made a superb save though from Claudio Pizzaro's header. Later Owen won a corner and Effenberg nearly scored from the ensuing scramble. The game petered out into a draw as news filtered through that the other two sides in Group A, Boavista and Nantes had drawn. This score line guaranteed both the teams at Old Trafford were through to the quarter-finals.

Bayern's opponents were Real Madrid again, and the Spanish aces were bitterly disappointed at the draw. They wanted to play their most difficult rivals in what would have been a classic final. Madrid were a much different proposition from the team that had been put out in the semis last year. They swaggered into the same visitor's dressing room that they had slunk away from the previous season. McManaman started the match on the bench. Madrid took the lead after 11 minutes when Geremi their wing back scored. Geremi later joined Chelsea where he struggled to re-capture some of the form he had displayed at Madrid. That was how it stayed for nearly all of the remainder of the match. Owen had a chance to level the scores but his shot flew narrowly wide.

Towards the end Bayern were awarded a penalty but the Madrid goalkeeper Cesar made a fantastic save to deny Stefan Effenberg. Bayern seemed to be heading for defeat but in the closing minutes put up a huge bombardment on the Spanish goal. Steve McManaman came on to renew his duel with Owen as Madrid looked like going home to Spain with a crucial lead and a priceless away goal. Bayern turned the tie on its head though with two late goals. Effenberg made amends for his penalty miss though when he drove in the equaliser with a great shot after clever work by the Brazilian Elber.

The closing minutes were pandemonium, mainly played out in the Madrid penalty area. Even Owen, after keeping things steady for so long in front of the back four, was pushed forward as Bayern went for the winner. They got it after a furious skirmish in the Spanish six yard box when Claudio Pizarro thumped home. Owen was on the outside of the penalty box, clearing up and waiting for any rebounds to fall his way. He was one of the first to congratulate Pizarro as the Olympic Stadium erupted in celebration of Bayern's sixth win over Madrid in the last three seasons. This was a fact that Ottmar Hitzfeld was great at pains to remind the media about.

Speaking about the game Owen told *Der Bild*. 'Today it was a strange game. Thank God we won in the end. At times Real tried to turn on the exhibition style. It all looked very pretty but did not achieve the advantage and hopefully we will go through.'

Oliver Kahn poured petroleum onto the bonfire of their vanities by informing the media that Madrid would not put two past him in the return at the Bernabeu. Oliver was incorrect though as this was precisely what Madrid did in the return match eight days later. In a tense battle Bayern defended splendidly for 70 minutes as Real Madrid poured down on them. Owen was given the task of marking Zinedine Zidane, the player he rated as his greatest midfield opponent. He did well against the undisputed greatest player on earth. Figo, who had missed the first leg through injury, also made an appearance that night and gave a masterclass display of wing play.

Owen's disciplined pressing helped keep Bayern afloat and his determination forced the Madrid midfield into a number of careless passes. Around half-time Bayern enjoyed their best period of the game as they forced Madrid back on their heels and created a half chance for Elber.

Stung by Bayern's impudence Real cranked up the machine as they sought to reap the harvest of their brilliance. Zidane hit what the American's call the Upper 90, when he smashed a shot against the angle of post and crossbar. Eventually though the immense pressure told and Ivan Helgura scored after Madrid's 14th corner of the night was turned on by Roberto. That was sufficient for Madrid to advance to the semi-finals as they had the away goal. Five minutes from time though the holders crashed out as their substitute Gutti scored a second from Raul's pass. It was Bayern's first defeat in 20 UEFA Champions League games. The Bayern management team admitted that there was only one team in it whilst the Madrid coach Vincete del Bosque stated that it was a 'Great advertisement for European football.'

Madrid went on to win the Champions League, beating their arch-rivals Barcelona in an epic semi-final and then winning 2-1 against Bayer Leverkusen in the final at Hampden. The talented Leverkusen side included Ballack and the young striker Dimitar Berbatov in their side. They had disposed of United in the semi-final edging through on the away goals rule.

Bayern were also knocked out of their domestic Cup competition by Schalke 2-0 after extra time. Owen had a busy game and was occupied even more when Kuffour was red-carded and he had to drop deeper to cover. The 10 men battled bravely but two goals in extra time put them out of the competition.

In the late winter Bayern went on another fine run in the Bundesliga winning 5 games and drawing 2. Owen's best performances in this spell came in a 2-1 victory over TSV

1860 and a goalless draw at Hamburg. In this match he almost broke the deadlock with a searing 20-metre drive that hit the right-hand post. Sandwiched between the titanic battles with Madrid was a 2-2 draw with Bremen. Owen missed the game as he had been suspended and the dropped points raised serious questions as to whether or not Hargreaves' team would even qualify for Champions League football the following season.

Following their loss of the Champions League trophy Bayern regrouped and made one last gallant attempt to retain their Bundseliga title. Three straight wins guaranteed Champions League football. It also meant that on the last day of the season they still had a chance of winning their fourth Bundesliga in a row. Owen was a dominant figure in all these matches. Whilst other members of the team were exhausted by the demands of the long season Owen was still fit and strong and full of running. After the defeat in Madrid, Franz Beckenbauer was telling the media about their need to inject 'fresh young blood' into the side. Owen was the living embodiment of this.

There was no fairytale ending to the season though. Bayern duly won their last fixture against Hansa Rostock 3-2 but Dortmund's victory made them champs for the sixth time. This condemned Owen's side to third place in the table, but just two points behind. So Hitzfeld's Heroes finished potless for the first time since 1995. Not counting the little matter of World Club championship they had acquired in Tokyo.

For Owen personally though, it had been a great season. He occupied the midfield holding role against Rostock, his favourite berth in the side. In a turbulent term he had broken through to establish himself as a cornerstone of the team, making 47 appearances (29 in the Bundesliga, 4 in the domestic cups, 13 in the Champions League and his appearance in the Toyota World Club Championship game).

Normal service was resumed the following season. The chips fell more kindly for Bayern in 2002–03. Owen had another highly successful season though it was beset by injury. It had been a hectic summer for him, and after World Cup duty with England he took a three week vacation to see his parents in Canada and then a trip to Mexico. In mid July he reported back to the Bayern training camp. There were some new faces there – Michael Ballack and Ze Roberto. There was also severe competition for who would play in the defensive midfield position alongside Ballack. Apart from Owen there was Jens Jeremies, Niko Kovac and Thorsten Fink in contention.

Jens Jeremies started the season in front of Owen as he was selected for the 0-0 draw against Borussia Monchengladbach. The problems with Owen's fitness started around then. Having been injured in the World Cup (see Chapter Five: England's Dreaming), Owen was not able to take full part in the punishing pre-season training. This was important because the work done at that time established the fitness levels for the coming months. It also provided a shield against the niggly injuries that disrupted training schedules and stopped players from attaining maximum fitness.

Owen was back for the next game an UEFA Champions League Third Qualifying Round tie against Yugoslav champions Partizan. The 2001 winners of the competition cantered to a 3-0 win, while in the return match Bayern again scored three goals with Partizan managing one. In this match Owen played at right back and displayed his versatility. That was the season that Bayern played their away games in all white with a new sponsor's logo. In the two previous Bundesliga matches Owen had played in both full back positions, deputising for injured defenders. Bayern had easily won the games but they gave him the opportunity to display his adaptability and skill.

Owen's next European game was an appearance against Deportivo La Coruna in the Group G home match. It turned out to be a disastrous evening as Bayern were beaten 3-2 and lost their 29 game unbeaten Champions League home record. The damage was caused by the Dutch striker Roy Makaay who scored a tremendous hat trick. Makaay was later to join Bayern and the performance that he put in that night meant that he passed the audition with flying colours. Trailing to two opportunistic goals from Makaay at the break, Ottmar Hitzfeld read the riot act and switched to 4-4-3. He also introduced Owen as a wing back. His surging runs unsettled the Spanish rearguard and Bayern clawed themselves back into the game. Hasan Salihamidzic pulled a goal back from a rebound and then Owen's perfect cross was thumped home by Elber. Owen was virtually unplayable at this stage, displaying tremendous power and pace. With the score at 2-2 Bayern should have kicked on and won the game from their opponents. However they seemed to run out of gas and let Deportivo back into the game. A quarter of an hour from time Makaay beat the feeble offside trap to grab the winner.

Bayern never gave up and in the dying minutes Owen sent over a wondrous cross that Ballack soared to head against the bar. When referee Graham Poll blew to end the game Bayern had just launched another huge frontal assault on the Deportivo goal, but the damage was done and three precious points were already lost.

Owen was in the starting line up for the next game, a 3-1 victory over Energie Cottbus which put them four points clear of the Bundesliga with 12 matches played. It was noticeable that Owen was taking command of most of the set pieces, taking the majority of corners and free-kicks.

The next European fixture was a trip to the Stade Felix Mollaert to play RC Lens. Owen was picked in midfield and started brightly. Ballack, rapidly establishing himself as a major force in the side, put Bayern ahead after 23 minutes heading in Ze Roberto's free-kick. Owen almost won a penalty shortly afterwards when he burst into the box and ex-Liverpool defender Rigobert Song appeared to bring him down. Owen claimed a penalty but the referee rather harshly booked him for diving. It was a pivotal moment in the game, if not the season, because a second goal then would have effectively killed the game. In the second half Lens grabbed a scarcely deserved equaliser when Utaka headed home Moreira's corner kick to deprive Bayern of more precious points.

It got worse, as the star-packed AC Milan came to Munich on 1 October 2002. Owen was picked at right back, but after a short time he was switched into midfield when it became apparent that Milan had not really come to attack. This liberated Ballack to a more attacking role. The Milanese game plan was to use their superb goal taker Filippo Inzaghi to hit Bayern on the break. Filippo struck early in the second half when Clarence Seedorf set him up for a simple tap in. The marking by the Bayern defence was very poor.

Bayern came back down the field and equalised quickly when Pizarro out-jumped the Red and Black's sweeper Alessandro Nesta to equalise. Like in the match against Deportivo that should have been the wake up call to take the game by the scruff of the neck. But Bayern seemed hesitant and Milan had time to re-organise. Owen, relishing the atmosphere and seemingly unaffected by the tension, tested the Milan keeper Dida with a long range effort. How he would have loved to have scored in a fixture of that prestige. Back home in Canada his family were still monitoring his progress and watching the Euro Sports stations to chart his progress in fixtures of this magnitude. The game looked to be running down to an inevitable draw. Milan had come for what they wanted – a point and the precious away goal. Then Inzaghi struck again four minutes from time. Climbing to meet the substitute Serginho's long range cross to glance it goalwards, Kahn, who won the FIFA World Cup Golden Ball award for 2002, could only push it into the net.

Three games and one solitary point. Bayern, pre-tournament favourites, were going out of Europe after barely a handful of matches. The year they had won the UEFA Champions League they were like a well oiled machine. It reminded Owen of those big Mercedes Benz cars he used to see in the black and white movies. Now injuries, loss of form, changes in personnel all contributed to the stuttering performance of the team culminating in a sudden and dramatic decline in the Bavarians Euro fortunes.

Injuries laid Owen low in the early autumn. In September he had torn a thigh muscle and in the following month in the away win at Rostock he tore another muscle, this time in the calf. This precluded him from playing in the return match at the San Siro which ended in another 2-1 victory to AC Milan. Inzaghi scored the winner after Kahn had been forced out of the match after tearing a muscle himself. Both players missed the trip to Spain to play against Deportivo La Coruna.

The nightmare continued there. Roy Makaay's last minute volley clinched a 2-1 victory and sent Bayern crashing out of Europe. It was the first time in their history that they had gone out of the competition in the first round. It would have been unthinkable a few weeks ago that Bayern would have been dumped out of Europe after just five games. To make matters even worse Lens' 2-1 victory over Milan condemned Bayern to finish bottom of Group 'G'. The 'group of death' is a football cliché, but in this instance it turned out to be the death of their hopes.

Their ignominious exit was the talk of Europe and the press reacted accordingly. Here are some samples of their hysterical reaction.

Austria

Kronenzeitung: 'Bye Bye Europe! Bayern's world in ruins'

Belgium

Het Laatste Nieuws: 'Deportivo sign Bayern's death sentence'

England

The Sun: 'Bayern bashed'

Switzerland

Blick: 'Bayern's 40 Million flops'

Spain

El Periodico: 'The huge favourites shuffle out of the rear entrance'

Marca:	'Bayern on the road to hell'

Holland

De Telegraaf:	'Bayern unable to play the role of the cat with nine lives this time around'

Italy

La Gazzetta dello Sport:	'Addio Europa'

It was a bad season for German clubs in the UEFA Champions League. With the subsequent elimination of Borussia Dortmund and Bayer Leverkusen, there were no German sides in the last eight for the first time since 1992–93.

The hangover carried over into the Bundesliga as Bremen beat them 2-0 in the Weser Stadium the following Sunday. Owen returned to first team action and almost scored his first senior goal in German football but was denied by a flying save in the opening minutes. The following week he played for the first half of the 2-1 victory over Dortmund in which their goalkeeper Jens Lehmann was dismissed. After not playing in a couple of matches Owen came on as substitute for Scholl to play the last 20 minutes of the Hertha Berlin game. Two Michael Ballack goals clinched the points for Bayern and maintained their bid to regain the title.

The result meant that Owen and his pals had won the 'Herbstmeisterschaft' or the 'Autumn Championship' which was bestowed on the team heading the table when the season entered its mid season break. Around that time he signed a new contract which extended his stay to 2006. Speculation always surrounded Owen that Arsenal had renewed their interest in him. The English tabloid press were running stories about how Sir Alex Ferguson had been charting his career following his performance against them at Old Trafford in the Champions League the previous season.

Owen flew to Marbella with the 42-strong Bayern party for their winter break. It was snowing in Germany when they left for the warmer temperatures of Spain. Ahead lay a lot of hard training and the chance of getting a winter tan. The trip was marred by the tragic death of Owen's team-mate Sammy Kuffour's daughter Godiva.

Upon his return Owen celebrated his 22nd birthday by treating his team-mates to a traditional Bavarian breakfast of Weisswurst and Brez'n – which featured white sausages. Later the chaps ate sauerkraut and drank whiskey from tumblers. There must have been a few hangovers in the team the next day.

The England international had something else to celebrate six days after his birthday when he scored his first Bundesliga goal in the game against Borussia Monchengladbach. It had been a long time coming – nearly 100 appearances in two and a half years. Owen told the Bayern Munich website how pleased he was with things, 'Naturally the win was more important. Sure, it was great, especially scoring the opener. I am happy in this position. My athleticism comes into play and there are plenty of one to one situations out on the flanks. I am very happy here.'

Having passed that personal milestone Owen doubled his goal tally 10 days later when he scored from a free-kick in the 8-0 cup win over FC Cologne. Bayern cruised to their 18th National title in the course of the next few months. One of the high spots for Owen was when he put in a sterling performance against Nuremburg in February. On this occasion he was playing in the right back position and it earned him very high ratings. The next month Owen was playing in his favoured midfield anchor role against Rostock – a game that Bayern won thanks to an own goal. His performance in that match earned him further kudos and emphasised his versatility. At this point Bayern led Dortmund, to whom they had leased their title the previous season, by 15 points.

Bayern actually clinched the title in the 30th Bundesliga match of the season with a 2-0 win over a Wolfsburg side including Stefan Effenberg. Also playing in the ambitious Wolves side was Martin Petrov who was in the Manchester City side that won at Old Trafford in February 2008. There was still four matches left to play, the last time Bayern had achieved such a feat had been 30 years before.

As the season concluded Owen ran into more hassle with injuries. This time it was adductor problems, which meant he missed the last weeks of the run-in. He did however return for the Cup Final and had an outstanding game. Bayern had a leisurely 3-1 victory over Kaiserslauten in the Berlin Olympic Stadium watched by a crowd of 70,490. They saw Owen set up the opening goal after just three minutes when his perfect cross was headed home by Ballack. Hitzfield had appointed Ballack as the captain of the team which turned out to be an inspired move. Owen was chopped down for the second goal and Ballack converted the penalty.

In all that season he made 25 Bundesliga appearances, four cup games and three in the ill-fated Champions League campaign.

Owen had a good month's vacation after the exertions of the double winning season and made the most of it. First of all he travelled to Calgary visiting his folks and hanging out with his brothers Neil and Darren. After that he rented a house in Barbados for a week where he played golf and worked on his fitness with runs on the beach and gym work. After returning to Calgary he visited California with his girlfriend Janelle. In LA he visited all the tourist attractions like Hollywood and the film studios.

Then it was time to return to Germany for pre-season training for what turned out to be a disappointing season. Roy Makaay, who had been instrumental in putting Bayern out of Europe the previous season was now a Bayern player having joined them from Deportivo. The Brazilian star Elber had left Bayern to play for Lyon.

It started brightly enough with the champions disposing of newly promoted Eintracht Frankfurt 3-1.

Eintracht will always be remembered in football history for the part they played in arguably the greatest European Cup Final of them all in 1960 when Real Madrid beat them 7-3 (Puskas 4, Di Stefano 3). Eintracht were no slouches having beaten Glasgow Rangers 12-4 on aggregate in the semi-final. Owen's grandfather watched the game on television never dreaming that one day his grandson Owen would be on the same field as one of the most famous teams in the world.

Without reaching the heights achieved by Puskas and Co Bayern played some neat football and raced to a 3-0 interval lead. The new boys in the Bundesliga became more used to life in the fast lane in the second half and pulled a goal back. Seven minutes from time Owen was replaced by Jeremies, he had grown philosophical about being subbed now. As long as he was happy he had done his job and it was for the good of the team he accepted it. He was annoyed about a harsh booking he had received from the referee for what seemed to be an innocuous challenge. Having gone through the combat of the previous season without such much as a caution this seemed a tad unfair.

Trouble was around the corner though when Bayern lost their first game of the season to Wolfsburg. It was a bizarre match in which the champions, 2-1 up at one stage, went down to two late goals. A sell out crowd of 30,000 shoe-horned into the V W Arena to watch what was always going to be a tricky match for Owen and his team. The home side got what they wanted – an early lead to fire the crowd. Bainano scored after an error in the Bayern defence. Owen surged forward as Bayern hit back, the England player cut in from the right and hit a fierce shot just over. Then his fine run and cross was headed down by his friend Roque Santa Cruz but Salihamidzic fired wide when he really should have equalised.

Bayern pressed but did not get back into it till early in the second half when midfielder Schweinster scored with a low drive. Owen set up Bayern's second on the hour. His incisive pass found Scholl whose perfect cross was volleyed first time by Roy Makaay into the roof of the net. Dancing with Wolves.

That should have been it. Owen should have dropped back to bottle up the midfield. Now where have we heard that before? Instead Bayern went looking for the third that would have made it safe. Out of the blue Baiano equalised for Wolfsburg with a thumping toe punt passed Kahn. As so often in these types of matches the team that looked down and out recovered to create a shock. In the last minute the Bayern back four again failed to clear their lines and Diego Klimowicz drilled the winner home from twelve yards.

The fall out from the defeat was not good. Some said that Kahn, the world's best goalkeeper, was at fault for at least two of the goals that flew into his net that day. At that time Kahn was coming under intense media pressure for events in his private life. The blond keeper had split from his wife Simone following an affair with a former barmaid. Injuries had also contributed to a decline in his game. Sometimes in life, as most goalkeepers will tell you, attack is the best form of defence. In an amazing outburst the combustible Kahn criticised Owen. The incident was later retold in the *Guardian* where Kahn's words were repeated: 'We are lacking discipline in our defensive midfield area' Kahn said haughtily 'because Hargreaves and some others are making too many mistakes. The way they ran around like hunted deer was unacceptable.'

Hargreaves replied by saying: 'You expect this at Bayern where there's so much politics and in-fighting. I am not German and I never will be, no matter how long I stay here. I am taking the spotlight away from German internationals when I play; and Kahn definitely enjoys the spotlight. But everyone knew I had nothing to do with those goals. I have learnt how to handle those situations; they are not easy at the time but they make you a stronger person.'

A composed reply from Owen, whereas Kahn's comments gave some insight into his psychological state. Particularly the reference to 'hunted deer' which may have been how Kahn viewed himself, caught in the glare of the spotlight of tabloid publicity. Like a deer in the headlights.

Owen had grown up fast, and in early interviews he talked of how unapproachable the older England players like David Seaman and Teddy Sheringham seemed to him when he first joined the England set up. This was because it was not 'the done thing' in German football. Now he could stand up to intimidating characters like Kahn and hold his own.

The games were coming thick and fast. Celtic were the

next team to visit Munich in the first match in the 2003–04 UEFA Champions League Group A series of games. Bayern, recalling the memory of last season's dismal performances, were determined to be more solid in defence. Celtic fielded a highly experienced and powerful strike force of Chris Sutton, John Hartson and Henrik Larsson. The stats indicated that Owen won 70 per cent of his tackles on the ground but he found it much harder to establish any superiority over them in the air. In fact Celtic stole the lead after 57 minutes with a headed goal from their tricky winger Alan Thompson.

Roy Makaay once again came to the rescue of Bayern with two goals. The first was a wonderful volley and the winner after 86 minutes was a shot-cum-centre that was a real 'slow roller'.

Another goal spree was a 3-3 home draw with Bayer Leverkusen which also had a missed penalty, six bookings and a red card. Owen's stats for the game were as encouraging as those for the Celtic game, and they were boosted by the part he played in creating Bayern's second goal. This was cleverly finished by his pal Roque Santa Cruz.

Owen's parents were staying with him having come over from Calgary on a short trip. On his day off after the Bayer Leverkusen game Owen played a round of golf on the Mangfalltal Course with his father. Owen was working on improving his golf game and had spent some considerable time in Marbella on the golf course. Owen did not play football for the next two weeks as he recovered from flu and a calf injury. His next start came in the away trip to RSC Anderlecht. The game ended in a 1-1 draw which was a highly credible performance considering striker Claudio Pizarro was sent off for two bookable performances after 35 minutes.

Owen played for 63 minutes before he was subbed,

exhausted after still suffering the after effects of the flu. This was very debilitating and Owen could feel his strength being sapped the longer he played. Before he had travelled to the game Owen had a workout with the rehab coach Bjorn Andersson, veteran of the European Cup Final with Leeds in 1975.

Owen played in the 5-0 German Cup drubbing of Borussia Neunkirchen from the Oberliga (fourth division). He played for 70 minutes before being replaced by Bastian Schweinsteiger and had hardly left the field before Roque Santa Cruz completed a fine hat trick.

Bayern qualified from their Champions League group by finishing second to Lyon. They won two matches and drew three including a 0-0 draw in the return match with Celtic. Their only reverse was a 2-1 home defeat to Lyon. UEFA had changed the structure of the competition again scrapping the second group stage and replacing it with an extra sudden death knock-out round. This reduced the clutter of the seemingly endless maze of group matches. By a strange quirk Bayern were drawn against the hardy annuals of Real Madrid in matches to be played in the early spring of 2004.

Owen missed some games with a groin injury but was back in training around the period just prior to the winter close down. A 6-0 pulverising of Freiburg put them in second place in the league with their Cup hopes very much alive. As 2004 loomed, the future once again looked full of possibilities.

Owen flew off to Canada for his Christmas break, full of confidence for the coming battles.

Chapter Four

All Roads Lead to the Allianz Arena

'He cannot only shut down the opposing playmaker but also take the initiative himself. Owen can become better than I was.'
Lothar Matthaus

'Determination is very important. I arrived at Bayern with a lot of other players from other countries who had great potential but could not go to the next level. Some went home after two weeks. It was not lack of ability but more to do with their mentality. You must have the desire to compete.'
Owen Hargreaves

The early weeks of 2004 found Owen in one of his favourite places on earth, Dubai. On a rest afternoon he must have been wondering if life could get any better with nothing more taxing to look forward to than a round of golf followed by a lazy evening relaxing and reading. The Bayern party had exchanged the cold climate of Munich for an eight day stint of training in the 26-30 degrees of the Arab state. This was the first time that the Bavarian team had ventured into that part of the world for their week of intensive winter training but it was soon to be a firm favourite with everyone. Even when the Lufthansa plane touched down early in the morning the temperature was touching 20 degrees, a bit different from Germany. Owen loved the weather and the modern city that was building skyscrapers and state of the art luxury hotels everywhere he looked. Despite being born in Canada and being used to the harsh winters he loved the sun and the warm sea.

Perhaps that was one of the reasons why he was such a successful player, being able to adapt to the very cold conditions that he sometimes experienced when playing for Bayern in the winter months yet also thriving in the heat. Particularly so when on England duty in the major tournaments, which were always played in the summer months.

The team stayed in the luxurious Jumeirah Beach Club Hotel but the training camp had been set up in the Dubai Police Officers Club sports centre. The facilities were excellent and the training pitch was ideal. The plan was simple: regenerate and concentrate on building up strength and stamina to meet the rigours that lay ahead. Owen was still concerned about his fitness levels. All season he had been slightly below par. The mid-season training ended with a low-key, friendly match against Southampton, then still in the Premiership. The game ended in a 1-1 draw with Owen, delighted to be back in England, playing the full game.

Owen celebrated his 23rd birthday by playing in a friendly against Mainz.

Even then thoughts of the upcoming clash with Real Madrid dominated everyone's thinking. Uli Hoeness said at the time of the draw, 'A fantastic draw, wonderful perfect. I am looking forward to two massive evenings.'

The Madrid fans, taking the moral high ground, had a nickname for Bayern – they called them 'The Dark Beast'; it showed a mixture of fear and respect for them and sounded like something out of a Dennis Wheatley novel about the occult. Bayern had been reviled in certain parts of Europe but had an excellent record against Madrid. Before their current clash they had beaten Madrid 9 times out of the 15 times they had met, drawing on two occasions.

The first leg between the gargantuan talents of European football was a personal tragedy for Oliver Kahn. It was his error that gifted Roberto Carlos with a late equaliser that the Galacticos scarcely deserved. To give some indication of the heritage behind the teams the fixture was Bayern's 187th at that elite level of competition whilst Madrid had played in UEFA tournaments for 47 years, 34 of them in either the European Cup or the Champions League.

Owen had a bright game and was responsible for creating Bayern's best goal scoring chance in the first half when Roy Makaay's brilliant flick put Owen in for a long range shot that he connected with perfectly. The shot would have beaten most goalkeepers in the world but Casillas made a breathtaking save. Iker Casillas was in the top three keepers in the world along with Petr Cech and the £34 million Juve keeper Gianluigi Buffon. A goal then and Bayern might well have gone onto win the tie.

It was Makaay who put Bayern in front 15 minutes from time when he thundered in a header, the freezing fans celebrated wildly but their celebrations were cut short when Madrid equalised. Roberto Carlos struck a 30-yard free-kick solidly but not savagely. Kahn should have gathered it but in an error reminiscent of the England keeper Scott Carson against Croatia he spilled it and watched along with the rest of the Olympic Stadium as it trickled into the net.

Bayern flew to Madrid knowing that they had a major task in front of them. A stricken Real Madrid were in a state of flux – Ronaldo was out with a torn muscle, and Roberto Carlos was suspended. Ugly rumours and racist remarks appeared in the Spanish press accusing Bayern of exerting undue pressure to get him banned. Steve McManaman had returned to England to play for Manchester City, muttering about the 'Disneyfication of Real Madrid', Claude Makelele had sniffily left Madrid to join Chelsea who had recently been taken over by Russian billionaire Roman Abramovich. The young oligarch was spending money like the French trader Jerome Kerviel. Madrid did not recover from the sale of him for several seasons and failed to win anything until the pragmatic Fabio Capello clinched the Spanish league playing with two defensive midfielders in the mould of Claude and Owen. Capello's back four played with the brutality of Aussie Rules football.

Here was the dilemma of players like Owen: in being defensive they were not seen as being glamorous. Makelele would always complain that amongst the 'Galacticos' he was treated as an inferior being. The Galacticos, Beckham, Zidane, and the alpha male Ronaldo had the image rights and inflated salaries based on shirt sales. The bean counters' argument was always who would want a Makelele shirt when you could buy Zidane's? At Manchester United today, Cristiano Ronaldo, Wayne Rooney and Carlos Tevez sell the shirts but the sweat equity is provided by Owen Hargreaves and Michael Carrick. The picture remains unaltered in February 2008; the 'Football Rich List' was published with the top two spots being occupied by Real Madrid and a rapidly closing Manchester United. Bayern Munich had climbed to seventh spot, leapfrogging Liverpool and Internazionale.

Owen described the build up to the match on the official home page of the English FA, fa.com. 'At around five o'clock we will have a pre-match meeting at the ground, in which a few specific instructions will be given but the emphasis on match-day is very much on relaxation and focus. Generally, I will have around 10-ish, maybe have a light training session to loosen the legs, relax by reading a book or something and then after our meeting, we will set off for the stadium at around 7pm. The idea is to keep your energy for the evening really. Our energy levels should be high tonight because, with the snow in Germany we did not get to train much.'

Owen got to renew his burgeoning friendship with Beckham, and they had even more in common now that David had gone to a different country to play for a massive club. They had recently been on England duty together and had been ribbing each other about the forthcoming showdown between their clubs. The honeymoon period between Beckham and the Spanish media was over. His lack of impact in Spain was bringing him under fire in the press and soon the *News of the World* was to break its story of his affair with a former personal assistant. After his own dizzying rush of fame, Owen just kept his head down and carried on doing what he did best: play football. As time goes by Beckham is remembered less for his football but more for his underwear ads and celebrity life.

Bayern had travelled to the Iberian Peninsula and stayed in the luxurious Hotel Villa Magna-Park Hyatt. Real won a hard fought match by a solitary goal ghosted in by the world's greatest player Zinedine Zidane. The Frenchman scored after 32 minutes and the 75, 000 crowd went mental. Owen looked up and saw just a blur of red and yellow flags. Some had that silhouette of the black bull on them, the whole event had a quasi-religious intensity quite unlike anywhere else.

Owen went off at half-time as Hitzfeld gambled. The stakes were high as he was playing for his job; Bayern were not going to win the league that year and Owen would finish without any honours for the first time in his professional career. He was replaced by the young prospect Bastian Schweinsteiger in an attempt to attack Madrid more. Schweinsteiger created two half chances towards the end of the game but was unable to convert them and Bayern were knocked out of the competition.

Franz Beckenbauer was annoyed at the manner of Bayern's exit and the length of time it took them to switch from defence to attack.

The chairman, Rummenigge, emphasised that the Estadio Bernabeu exit had no financial implications as they had only costed revenue streams to come from the Group A games. Real Madrid went out in the quarter-finals to Monaco, Fernando Morientes, on loan from Madrid scored the goals that eliminated them. Ironic also that Madrid were paying £30,000 a week of his wages.

Owen's form held up well in the games around the Madrid clashes, he was given a very high rating by the German soccer magazine *Kicker* for his performance against Dortmund. The problem was that Bayern lost 0-2. He also had a fine match against Vfl Bochum away where the 'imp Statistik' match stats indicated that his angular frame had touched the ball a hundred times. This was more than any other Bayern player. The stats also indicated that he was the second best tackler in the match and the best passer. Once again despite his excellence it was not enough to prevent his team from losing by a solitary goal. With those defeats evaporated any hope Bayern had of catching Bremen at the top of the league.

A far more damaging defeat to the image and morale of the side was a 1-2 exit at the hands of second division Alemannia Aachen in the quarter-final of the cup. It was a typical cup shock where Aachen, fired up for match and roared on by a fanatical home town crowd, scrambled home. There was no excuse for a shoddy performance from the Bayern team which included 10 internationals who had amassed over 300 caps between them.

After 26 minutes Aachen went in front when a 30-yard shot from Blanks whistled into the net with Kahn just an onlooker. Bayern equalised after the only bit of football they played in the match. A quick fire interchange of passes between Willy Sagnol and Owen ended with Ballack heading home in the dying seconds of the first half. Owen almost put Bayern in front at the start of the second half with a powerful free-kick but the home goalkeeper Straub denied him. The game was set up for a shock and a late goal from the former Liverpool player Meijer was enough to dispose of the record championship winning side.

Ballack's influence in the midfield had dwindled and he started to receive criticism in the press and was having a difficult relationship with his own fans.

Owen's pelvic problems started in March of that year. X-rays did not indicate any reason for it and around that time it was suggested that his legs were not the same length. The mystery ailment had plagued him for most of the season and only his innate ability to overcome obstacles gave him the motivation to keep going. The condition worsened when he had to spend anytime on the ball or hit long passes. The Bayern Doctor Hans-Wilhelm Muller-Wohlfahrt worked closely with Owen trying to cure the problem.

Hitzfeld had been keen all season to improve the physical aspect of Bayern's game and had worked on their tackling especially. In the end though Bayern could only finish second in the table which, following on from their disappointing showing in the cup competitions, brought the curtain down on the six-year Hitzfeld era. He had won them eight trophies in his time there and was the most successful club manager in the history of German football. Owen had enjoyed a good association with him and his career had blossomed; how he would work with the new manager Felix Magath was open to conjecture. Magath had signed a three-year contract as head coach. Word was he was a tough man who had graduated out of the same charm school as Fabio Capello. He had no time for fools and was known as a strict disciplinarian. 50-year- old Magath made it clear that he would not tolerate any player who gave less than 100 per cent effort in every game.

The honours rolled in though as in the next two seasons Bayern did the double double winning the Bundesliga and the German cups in back to back years. In the summer of 2004 after his exertions in the Euros, Owen holidayed in the South of France. Then he joined his team-mates on a trip to Japan where they played two friendlies. Owen was one of the most popular players in the Bayern squad amongst the oriental fans, particularly the ladies.

Magath spent the time on the trip assessing players before

his first selection. Owen had little time to absorb any of the Japanese culture as he went from receptions and functions to intensive training sessions. One of the stadiums that Owen played in was the same one in which they won the 2001 World Club Final and he contributed such a lot by his marking job on Riquelme.

Speculation grew in the press about whether or not Owen would be moving to a Premiership club following his excellent performances for his country. The list of his suitors now included Middlesbrough, Aston Villa, Liverpool and Spurs. A new and highly significant one to add to the list now though was Manchester United. The tabloid *Der Bild* ran headlines 'Sir Alex Ferguson lures Hargreaves' and 'Hargreaves For 20m. Euro to Manchester', whilst the German football magazine *Kicker* wrote: 'Manchester United have contacted FC Bayern'.

A knock ruled Owen out of the first game of the season away to Hamburg but he was soon back in the team and played against Bayer Leverkusen who hammered them 4-1. Owen could do nothing to stop Dimitar Berbatov, an early lead which opened the floodgates. Berbatov was following on the heels of the 'Baby Faced Assassin', Ole Gunnar Solskjaer, in being one of the deadliest marksmen in Europe. Owen was criticised heavily in the press for his performance that day. Felix Magath was quick to spring to the defence of his player though in an interview with the *Suddeutsche Zeitung*: 'In my opinion the criticism of Owen Hargreaves is not justified. He was restless and nervous at the beginning, but this is actually normal. I allow young players to be nervous in their first match of the season. What was important for me and what looked good was the fact that he found his rhythm in the course of the match.'

Bayern had a fascinating run in the UEFA Champions League that season. To start with they were drawn in Group C which comprised Juventus, Ajax and the underdogs Maccabi Tel-Aviv. That is where the odyssey started with a drab 1-0 win in Israel thanks to a penalty from Makaay. A crowd of 20,000 watched the first Champions League match involving the side from Munich and an Israeli team.

Ajax, coached by the legendary Ronald Koeman, were next on the chopping block and Makaay plundered a hat trick as Bayern romped to a 4-0 victory. Owen shone brightly in his favourite midfield defensive role and even found time to set up the first goal. A rambunctious tackle won the ball in his own half and he advanced before hitting a perfect long pass up to Maakay who went on to score with ease. It was a mouth watering pass and excited the watching coach Felix Magath, who heaped praise on Owen in the press conference after the match.

Owen was now a highly experienced player in the Champions League. This was the fifth season in a row he had played in something most players could only dream about. This was why he was only keen in joining one of the top four sides in England that, like Bayern, could virtually guarantee Champions League football at every opportunity.

The experience was paying dividends. In the thrashing of Ajax Owen went up against the highly rated Rafel van der Vaart and completely obliterated him. So much so that Rafel did not make any forward passes and avoided any one-to-one scenarios with the hard tackling Bayern player. The *Kicker* magazine rated players on a 1-6 scale of performance (i.e. 1 for high, 6 for low). The Ajax man only managed a score of 4.5. Hamburg later purchased him and subsequently attracted interest from Chelsea.

After a shaky start to the campaign Owen was now in top form and produced two vibrant performances in the Bundesliga. His contribution powered Bayern to vital wins over Werder Bremen, who had beaten them to last season's title, and the season's surprise package, Wolfsburg. Both of these opponents possessed classy midfield aces who were negated by the power play of Owen. Johan Micoud of Werder Bremen received the 6 low score in the *Kicker*. Some Bayern fans joked that he had asked Owen for his legs back after one dazzling piece of footwork by Hargreaves had completely bamboozled him.

The Wolfsburg Argentinean international Andres Alessandro was another player whose threat had been removed by Owen in the 2-0 victory. The *Suddeutsche Zeitung* commented on Owen's performance in this manner: 'Hargreaves' stubbornness was the key to success because it gave the Munich side the chance to occupy the midfield early on.'

Lothar Matthaus, who had set a world record number of international appearances for Germany was another of the game's absolute legends who was impressed by Owen. He told his website, 'He is a fantastic player not only in terms of fighting spirit but also game wise and tactically. And he is very dangerous in dead ball situations.'

A perceptive comment by Lothar, for to this day Owen has never received the praise he deserved for the accuracy and power of his shooting. The problem was the paltry return in the number of goals he had scored. In the spring of 2008 the total amount of goals he had amassed in his career stood at 12. He had yet to 'break his cherry' for England.

Another milestone for Owen was his 100th Bundesliga match against Schalke at home. The stats read that in 100 games he had won 59, drawn 21 and lost 20 which included the defeat at the hands of the Gelsenkirchen outfit that day. Owen had been booked in just 13 of those matches giving him an average of just three a season.

The 'ton-up' boy put in another measured performance and the match stats indicated that he was the home player with the best passing average and the most contact with the ball. Schalke's German international striker Gerald Asamoah scored the only goal of the game with a short range header 15 minutes from time. The next morning Magath showed the Bayern team the video of their performance. He could not have been impressed with Owen's role, although the stats vindicated it, as he was not included in the squad that flew out to Turin to play against Juventus.

Without him Bayern went down 1-0 to the 'Old Lady' in Turin. The goal was scored by Pavel Nedved the blond Czech Republic midfielder. Magath had blundered badly because without Owen to mark him Nedved had the run of the park and caused havoc all night. In the return match at the Olympic Stadium Owen kept a much tighter rein on the big Czech. Even he could not prevent the mighty Juventus from completing a double over Bayern. The only goal came late in the game courtesy of another error by Oliver Kahn when he spilt a shot by Zlatan Ibrahimovic. The huge striker had just beautifully spun past Owen. Now not many players can do that but the big man was their point of reference. Another Juve legend Alessandro Del Piero scored from a yard. Juventus were soon to be involved in a series of scandals which was to lose them their title and relegate them.

It should be noted though what a fine team they were in their pomp with marvellous players like Nedved, the brilliant goalkeeper Gianluigi Buffon and Del Piero.

Another team with heritage behind them, 27 Italian championships, nine Italian Cups and two European Cups. At that time they were managed by Fabio Capello who must have been impressed with the defensive qualities of the young curly haired fellow with the English background. Their paths were to cross again he felt sure.

Bayern eased through to the last 16 of the Champions League with a 5-1 beating of Tel Aviv. Owen only played for the first 30 minutes and was then subbed after a clash of heads with Maccabi's Erez Mesika. Owen needed six stitches in a cut over his left eye and was withdrawn from the fray. Despite his injury and a migraine inducing headache, Owen was delighted that his team were through to the last 16 where they were drawn against Arsenal.

In one match towards the end of 2004 Owen was playing against Mainz 05 and Bayern were cruising along with a 3-0 lead. Magath's assistant coach Seppo Eichorn ordered 'Move forward to the ball'.

Owen responded by asking what he should do with it. Within two minutes he was taken off and replaced by Sebastian Deisler. The point was that in the event of any argument the management always won and any disputes were ruthlessly dispatched.

Bayern were top of the Bundesliga when proceedings ground to a halt for the winter break. An exciting 2-2 draw with Stuttgart was enough to give them the unofficial 'winter title'. Owen's last minute free-kick against Stuggart was headed on by Michael Ballack, which forced the Stuttgart goalkeeper into a fine save, and Guerrero turned in the equaliser. Owen spent the match marking Alexander Hleb, one of his trickiest opponents in the Bundesliga and soon to join Arsenal.

That was one of the most stable periods of Owen's career in that he had been relatively clear of injury. He had played in 16 out of 17 Bundesliga games and five out of six Champions League games.

Christmas was on the agenda once again. After attending the Bayern Christmas party Owen and his girlfriend flew to New York for a spot of shopping and a basketball game involving the New York Knicks. From the 17-23 December Owen rented a house in the Caribbean for his entire family. Then it was off to Calgary to spend a traditional Christmas with a tree, presents, turkey etc.

In early January he flew back to Germany and then onto the training camp in Dubai. They spent nine days under the desert sun before returning to the snow of Germany. Magath had devised some new training methods and mercilessly pushed his players through them. At times surrounded by the sand Owen must have thought he was in one of those French Foreign Legion movies were the Legionnaires spirit was broken by the ruthless Sergeant-major.

That was the time of the Tsunami in the Indian Ocean and the Bayern players donated a five figure sum to the victims. After every home game Owen donated and signed the shirt he had worn in the match to be auctioned for the disaster fund.

A disaster on a smaller scale hit the Bayern dressing room when news filtered through that striker Roque Santa Cruz's brother Oscar was killed in a car smash. Roque was Owen's closest friend at the club, a friendship that was to endure when both men were playing in the Premiership.

Bayern started their offensive for the title with a 3-0 win over Hamburg. Owen played well enough to merit a 2 rating in the tabloid *Der Bild*. The big game though was the clash with the English champions Arsenal and the first leg was scheduled to be played at the Olympic Stadium. Owen had flown to London in early February with striker Claudio Pizarro on a scouting mission to watch Arsenal take on Manchester United, who won 4-2. Ronaldo scored twice as his incredible skill started to burst through. The player that impressed Owen most though was Thierry Henry. Bayern won comfortably 3-1. A late goal from Kolo Toure gave Wenger's side a faint chance of salvaging something but generally the Bayern camp were very pleased with the result. An extraordinary fact that emerged was that until Ashley Cole came on after 75 minutes Owen was the only Englishman on the pitch. The irony was that he was playing for a German team. A few weeks earlier Arsenal had become the first Premiership team to field a side composed entirely of overseas players.

Even Cole was shortly to quit Arsenal to take the Euros of a Russian businessman and link up with another ensemble of mercenaries. At that stage there was a case for making Cole the best left back in the world. Whilst on England duty Owen had formed a friendship with the player whose fine career was later to be dogged with controversy. The whole fabric of the game had changed in those years that Hargreaves had first emerged as a major talent. There were eight French players on the pitch, six of them playing for Arsenal. Previously, reports in newspapers always referred to the away side as being 'the Londoners'. Cole was the only Londoner on the pitch that evening having joined the club at nine from a Sunday League side called Puma.

Bayern played well after Claudio Pizarro had given them an early lead. Pizarro scored again on the hour and Hasan Salihamidzic scored the killer third after 65 minutes.

Owen was a great fan of Arsenal's style and a few weeks

later he spoke to the *Daily Telegraph* of the contrasts between theirs and Chelsea's, who he had just played against: 'Arsenal and Chelsea are two different clubs. They are exactly the opposite. When you look at Arsenal, they were two goals down but trying to pass it through the middle. Chelsea are the opposite. They could not hurt us passing the ball and I do not think they created a chance.'

Owen was on the bench for the return at Highbury, Martin Demichelis retaining his place in midfield. Despite Owen's consistent form and polished play there was no guarantee of a place in the starting line up. A solid defensive display saw Bayern through to the last eight, for the first time since 2002. They lost on the night to a Thierry Henry goal but stood firm and went through 3-2 on aggregate. The Bayern defence restricted Arsenal to only one chance in the first half but Kahn saved from Patrick Vieira. Owen came on for Salihamidzic in the closing stages. It was the first time that he had played at Highbury and relished the chance before the Gunners moved down the road to the Emirates stadium. He loved playing in front of London crowds and was an admirer of their humour. Bayern nearly equalised near the end but Ballack and Pizzarro both frittered away chances.

Bayern were buoyed by beating Arsenal – going to Highbury with a dodgy 3-1 score line and getting through encouraged them to believe it could be their year again for the Champions League trophy. The draw put them up against Chelsea with the first leg at Stamford Bridge. Owen was interviewed by the London Evening News and bullishly told them, 'We have great players in every position and now fancy our chances against anyone.'

The controversial Chelsea coach Jose Mourinho had been

banned by UEFA for his deplorable behaviour against Barcelona earlier in the competition. Under Article 70, paragraph two of UEFA's Disciplinary Regulations he was banned from the tunnel, dressing room and technical area for both of the Bayern matches. Already Mourinho was sowing the seeds that would eventually lead to his sacking from Chelsea despite the success he had brought them. Bayern were without ace strikers Makaay and Pizarro, as big a blow to them as Chelsea losing Frank Lampard and Didier Drogba.

Bayern lost the first game 4-2 in a result that flattered Mourinho's marauders. Owen played for the whole match and was the highest rated Bayern player in the *Kicker* magazine. Chelsea's good fortune started in the fourth minute when Joe Cole's shot, as innocuous as Carlos's in Madrid, was deflected past Kahn by the Brazilian centre back Lucio. Bayern easily contained the Chelsea attacks for the rest of the half and deservedly equalised through Bastian Schweinsteiger after 52 minutes. Ze Roberto's powerful drive spun off Cech and Schweinsteiger rolled the ball home.

Lampard scored twice in the next ten minutes as in Hoeness's words Bayern let the game slip out of control. As usual Lampard took the glory but the man who caused the problems was Drogba whose strength in the air and power on the ground terrorised the centre of the Bayern defence. Drogba netted the fourth from close range and that appeared to have put the tie beyond reach.

In the closing minutes an incident occurred in the game that was to have particular relevance to Michael Ballack. The Dutch referee Rene Temmink pointed to the spot when Michael Ballack fell after contact from Ricardo Carvalho. The captain of Germany duly converted the penalty by smashing it past Cech. However the captain of England

Terry accused Bayern players of diving and criticised Temmink for giving the penalty.

If you wanted a good reason for Ballack's failure to make anything of his career at Chelsea a picture of the thuggish Terry sticking his face into Michael's may go a long way into explaining why. A picture saves a thousand words, they say. For Terry to accuse Bayern players of diving when he captained a side containing Joe Cole and Arjen Robben may sound a little like the pot calling the kettle black.

Owen joined in the argument when he granted an interview to the *Daily Telegraph* and countered Terry's ravings by claiming that the referee had favoured Chelsea towards the end of the game: 'In the last twenty minutes I thought he blew the whistle for Chelsea. He gave them too many free-kicks when I do not think he needed to and obviously influenced the game.'

When asked about the penalty the England star went on to explain, 'If you are fouled or you get shoved in the box and the referee gives it, then it's a penalty. The referee has given it and it's his responsibility, his job to judge the situation.'

Owen received a tremendous amount of coverage in the press, articles on the game including his quotes appearing in the *Times* and *Daily Mirror*. For some reason he was not included in the return match at the Olympic Stadium. The party line was that Felix Magath saw no tactical role for him although he had recently told the *Kicker* magazine that 'Owen is defensively the best midfielder in our squad'.

Bayern threatened to overwhelm Chelsea in the opening moments when they threw everything at them in wave after wave of attacks. Lampard's whole career was built on a series of deflections but the one he scored that night abused even his good fortune. Cole fed Lampard, who did what he always did and shot. His low shot clipped the heel of Lucio exactly as it had done in the first leg. Kahn could only pick it out of the net. The odds on winning the weekly Euro millions draw was calculated as being somewhere in the region of 86 million. Felix Magath was comparing those odds to the possibility of Chelsea scoring such deflected goals at such vital stages. Now 2-5 down, Bayern looked down and out with just their pride to play for now and a damage limitation exercise in place.

Cech, who looked anything but a world class keeper in the Bayern games, could not hold Ballack's header and Pizzaro thrashed the ball home, so it was still a contest. Chelsea went 6-3 ahead in the dying minutes when Drogba scored with a header from another break away. The crowd started to stream away in their thousands, in a scene reminiscent of the night England had scored 5 there and Owen had come on as sub.

Owen had talked to the *Times*, after the first match about the tactics Chelsea employ with Drogba: 'Only once they started to bring it forward with Didier Drogba flicking it on, did they cause us a lot of problems. It reminded me of Celtic when they had John Hartson and Chris Sutton up front with Henrik Larsson running on to the second ball. It is tough to defend because the ball can go anywhere and Drogba is good at attacking balls in the air.'

The drama still had some twists to unfold. Bayern scored twice in the dying seconds to grab an improbable win as goals from Paolo Guerrero and Mehmet Scholl rocked Chelsea. It ended 5-6 but Owen saw enough that night to doubt Chelsea's ability to go all the way and win the Champions League. They had been extremely lucky in their victory over Bayern and in the final analysis Mourinho's side lacked the character and quality to win Europe's biggest prize.

The young star was correct. Liverpool, the eventual winners, coached by Rafael Benitez proved too shrewd for Chelsea and knocked them out in the semi-final. For Owen the Euro trail ended but he had the consolation of winning the domestic double.

With five games left Owen scored a tremendous last minute goal in Hanover to give Bayern three priceless points. On the same day their nearest rivals FC Schalke and VFB Stuttgart both slipped up and the title race shifted dramatically in favour of Felix Magath's side. The strike by Owen was a contender for goal of the month, savagely struck after Claudio Pizzaro had laid the ball back into his path.

The last ever match played at the Olympic Stadium was Bayern's last home game of the season against Nuremburg. It ended in a 6-3 victory to the new champions after they had raced to a 5-0 half-time lead. Owen returned to the side after serving a one match suspension. The team was presented with their 19th Championship trophy; for Owen it was his third win in just five seasons in the top flight. Owen's brother Neil had flown over from Canada to see him collect the honour – another proud moment for the Hargreaves family.

The last two seasons Owen spent in Munich were all but wrecked by injury. In 2004–05 he played in a total of 27 Bundesliga games, three cup games and eight in the Champions League. In 2005–06 his total games were 15 in the Bundesliga, four cup and three in the Champions League.

It started so brightly for Owen, who came back very refreshed after some more globetrotting in the summer with his girlfriend. His first port of call was Majorca for the wedding of a friend followed by a trip to see his family in Calgary. It was the time of the world famous Rodeo and was incredibly exciting. The fabulous Hargreaves Boys also found time for some golf in Vegas.

Bayern began the new season playing in their new stadium, the state of the art Allianz Arena. With a capacity of 66,000 it was based on a design from Shakespeare's time when the people were right up close to the action. The architects were responsible for the award winning Tate Modern building on the South bank in London. Owen had recently done some photo-shoots there for Bravo Sport and the Bayern Magazine.

Owen made an entry for himself in the history books when he scored the first goal in new stadium in the 28th minute of the match against Borussia Monchengladbach. Bayern finished up easy 3-0 winners despite having a man sent off. The historic goal came about when Roque Santa Cruz cut the ball back to Owen who curled a drive into the right hand corner of the goal from the edge of the box. Very visual and spectacular. Owen was absolutely delighted to have the honour of scoring such a goal. Bayern must have been pleased that it was scored by the first product of their youth system to make it all the way to the very top and a young man whose image and humility made him a credit to the club. It was also the first goal scored in the 43rd Bundesliga season. (Of the five goals Owen had scored in the Bundesliga three of them were against Borussia Monchengladbach).

Owen started the match on the left of defence, a position he had been tinkering with in the pre-season friendlies. In the 44th minute new boy Valetian Ismael was dismissed for a second bookable offence and Bayern were reduced to 10 men. As part of the re-organisation Owen slotted into his favoured midfield anchorman role. Roy Makaay scored two second half goals as Bayern cruised to a comfortable victory. Owen was voted 'Man of the Match' and topped the stats for his massive contribution. Felix Magath, not known for praising his players unduly was impressed with the strength of Owen.

Further good news was announced when Owen extended his contract with Bayern until 2010. Bayern went from strength to strength equalling the Bundesliga record of 13 consecutive victories. Owen was a regular in his favourite position – the midfield anchorman. His average rating in the *Kicker* rankings was 2.5 which made him the third best player in the Bundesliga (Miroslav Klose, later to join Bayern was top rated) and also Bayern's best player.

The season was disrupted when Owen had to be subbed at half-time against Hanover on 17 September with groin problems. The adductor muscles seemed to be the cause. Owen had felt twinges before the game and took some painkillers. Then he was hit by the flu virus which really laid him low. Around that time the papers were dubbing him the 'English Patient' after the character in the award-winning book.

Further investigation by the teams of medics who looked after Owen indicated that the problem may have started with his back. Owen worked very hard to get fit by having daily rehab sessions at Sabner Strasse. Slowly he increased the intensity of his exercises. After an absence of seven weeks Owen was back in first team action against SV Werder Bremen and made a successful comeback in the 3-1 victory over their rivals. He continued to be in the wars though when he sustained a black eye after clashing with Martin Demichelis and took an elbow from the Argentinean in the Bruges Championship league game. Owen was very lucky not to sustain a fractured cheekbone.

After the Christmas festivities Owen travelled to the Dubai training camp. Each time he went back he enjoyed it more, revelling in the climate and the culture. His fitness was giving cause for concern though. On 3 February 2006 Owen underwent surgery on his groin in a surgical clinic in Munich Bogenhause. He had been complaining of increased pain in the groin area for the last few days and after a thorough examination and consultation it was decided to operate. The delicate operation was performed by the eminent surgeon Dr Gunther Meyer.

After some examinations Owen increased the volume of rehab sessions. He was unable to play in either of the matches against AC Milan in the Champions League. The first game at the Allianz Arena ended all square but in the return Milan outplayed the German side and ran out easy 4-1 winners. Inzaghi scored twice, with superstars Shevchenko and Kaka grabbing the others.

Owen played his first game in the Bundesliga in 2006 on 19 March. It went well although Bayern went down 0-3 against Werder Bremen. The appearance boosted his confidence and he was able to play his part in the coming weeks as Bayern completed the first back to back double. First he won the cup then he helped clinch the 20th Bundseliga, his fourth in six years.

Throughout the summer, rumours persisted that Owen would be joining Manchester United. They had already had talks with his agent one report said. Oliver Kahn was extremely perturbed at the situation and stated in the press that Bayern could not cope with his departure following Ballack's move to Chelsea. Uli Hoeness blamed Owen for trying to orchestrate a move, Sky Sports reported. Bayern were very anxious to hang onto their star man and citied tax laws as a strong motivation not to let him go.

On the 16 September 2006 Owen was playing in an away game against Armina Bielfield, a fixture that they were eventually to lose 1-2. In the 24th minute after being fouled Owen felt a pain in his left leg and hobbled off the pitch. Owen was immediately dispatched to hospital for scans and it was confirmed that he had broken his left fibula. The injury effectively ended his career in Munich. He came back to play a handful of matches for them. That season Bayern won no honours and in an even more humiliating turn of events failed even to qualify for the UEFA Champions League.

Chapter Five

This Is England

'It was my first England game. I was the new "Saviour" on the left side of midfield, although I had never played there before.'

Owen Hargreaves, August 2001

Owen Hargreaves's first appearance in an England shirt was on 31 August 2000. This was when he was called up by Howard Wilkinson to play in an Under-21 game against Georgia at the Riverside Stadium, Middlesbrough. England won 6-1; Owen played in further games against Italy and Spain.

Howard Wilkinson told the Bayern website, 'We need the best players we can get. He could have played for Wales or Canada but we invited him to join us.'

Ex-Arsenal star David Platt replaced Wilkinson as boss of the Under-21 side and soon became a fan of Hargreaves. He told the Bayern Munich website. 'He is the complete midfielder, a ball winner; he's consistent and can influence the direction of a match. He operates over a wide area just like Roy Keane.'

Owen was in a unique position because he could have played international football for any of four countries: England, Wales, Canada or Germany (under residency rules). To play for England and wear the three lions on his chest, was always his ambition though.

Stan Adamson, the executive director of the Canadian Soccer League (CSL) always had a dream that Owen would have appeared in the red shirt of the country of his birth. He told *Inside United*, 'The hope was he would play for Canada, but everyone understands that if you chose between the two countries, you would choose England.'

The first time that Owen played in the full England team was against Holland in a friendly at White Hart Lane on the 15 August 2001, the curly haired midfielder was 20 years and 206 days old. He wanted it when he arrived in Germany as a 16-year-old and being called up for England made him want it even more. Sven-Goran Eriksson had been impressed with his classy performances for Bayern and rewarded him with promotion to the seniors. The Swede had phoned Owen personally in Germany to tell him the glad tidings. A crucial World Cup qualifier loomed on 1 September against Germany. The German season started earlier than England's and the Holland game had been scheduled as a much needed run-out.

England lost 0-2 against a lively Dutch side that put an abrupt end to Eriksson's 100 per cent start for England. The resurgent Dutch side was packed with talent and included Edwin Van der Sar, Jaap Stam and Ruud van Nistelrooy, all of whom were to have successful careers at Old Trafford, even if the last two were to clash with Sir Alex. Other experienced superstars in the orange showcase that night included Marc Overmars, Patrick Kluivert and Boudewijn

Zenden. Edgar Davids could only make the bench in the impressively stellar array of players. The England team was: Nigel Martyn, Gary Neville, Martin Keown, Wes Brown, Ashley Cole, David Beckham, Paul Scholes, Jamie Carragher, OWEN HARGREAVES, Andy Cole, Robbie Fowler.

The troublesome left hand side of midfield was a perennial problem at that time and Owen was handed the role. A succession of players had been tried in what was a football 'black hole' – none had been able really to make it their own position.

Owen started brightly amongst the senior ranks and was not fazed, more fascinated, by the occasion. Early on in the game he broke forward to feed Paul Scholes. The ginger-haired United star fired in a fierce long range shot that was gathered by Van der Sar. After half an hour the zestful Owen made a surging run down the left and crossed for Andy Cole. The striker trapped the ball before firing in a shot that was kicked out by Van der Sar. Gary Neville smashed the ball back but the future United keeper tipped the ball over the bar.

Holland stunned England with two goals in two minutes just before half-time. Van Pommel's 35-yard effort fairly whistled into the net. Then van Nistelrooy smashed in the second after Zenden's beautifully flighted long range effort was only parried by Martyn. Holland continued where they left off in the second half and completely dominated the game. Owen only played for the first half and was replaced at the break by Michael Carrick as Sven swamped the pitch with subs. He used 22 players but the Dutch used 19 also.

Owen did not have the happiest of debuts, despite his comfort on the ball and accurate passing. As the half wore on he found it hard to penetrate the Dutch rearguard yet was unable to give adequate protection to his full back Ashley Cole, then still at Highbury. Cole was given a chasing that night by the former Barcelona winger Zenden who had recently joined Chelsea.

Jamie Carragher played in the midfield anchor role and struggled against the pace and guile of the Dutch midfield. Owen was at times perplexed by it. Perhaps Sven realized that night that Hargreaves' talents would be better employed in a more defensive position that would suit his style more. It was a landmark night for Owen though as he was the first English player in history who had neither lived nor played professional football in England. Eriksson seemed pleased with Owen's performance after taking into account the fact that he was playing out of position.

What should have been a historic day for the Hargreaves family turned out to be one of great sorrow. So often in life things are bittersweet. Owen's grandfather Henry died of cancer the day before he won his first cap for England. Henry was a fanatical Bolton fan. Amongst his favourite players was Frank Worthington the maverick England centre-forward.

In April 1979 at Bolton's old ground Burnden Park in a match against Ipswich Worthington had scored one of the greatest goals of all time. A moment forever enshrined in football folklore. The move started with a long throw in by a young Sam Allardyce. Heading down big Sam's throw the alert Bolton striker juggled with it before, with marvellous skill, he looped it over his head and, turning quickly, lost England defenders Terry Butcher and Mick Mills. Super Frank completed the magic by confidently volleying home past the Ipswich keeper. Worthington had caressed the ball five times without it touching the ground. It was one of the most breathtaking pieces of skilled improvisation ever displayed in this country. Henry Hargreaves was one of the lucky Trotters fans to witness it and it left an indelible mark on him. Owen's dad was a skilful player with a passion for the game inherited from Henry.

Henry had strong opinions on how football should be played and would shake his head at the lack of skill displayed in the modern game. Thus from an early age Owen had the importance of the skill factor of the game drummed into him.

The death of Henry hit Owen hard. Getting emotional when he talked of him, Owen told the *Daily Telegraph*, 'Cancer can touch anyone, kids, anyone, that's the scary thing. There was so much hype at the time on television around me because Bayern Munich had just won the Champions League and it was my first England game. So I turned off the television. It was a good thing I did because somehow the news had got out and television was saying my grandfather had passed away. He was massively into football. He would have enjoyed seeing my first England game.'

Owen's next game, the World Cup Group 9 qualifier was to prove to be one of the most significant matches in the modern history of England. By a strange coincidence it was against the country that been his home in recent years and on the home ground of the team that had nurtured his talents. The game turned out to be a 5-1 victory for Sven's men, easily the best result in the Swede's reign.

England v Germany was the highest profile fixture of them all. Steeped in history it could be traced back to the First World War when during the famous Christmas truce of 1914 it was said that troops from both sides played football together. In the official history of the Lancashire Fusiliers it is recorded that they had beaten a German unit 3-2.

The most famous match between the nations was England's 4-2 World Cup Final win in 1966 when West Ham striker Geoff Hurst scored the most famous hat trick in England's history. Hurst was a spectator in the 63,000 crowd at Owen's home ground. The match was also the high spot of Michael Owen's career as he blasted a hat trick.

The goal ace's Liverpool colleagues Emile Heskey and Steven Gerrard scored the others. Germany took the lead after six minutes when Jancker prodded past Seaman. Hargraves's Bayern team-mate Michael Ballack set the goal up with a neatly chipped cross that beat Rio Ferdinand and Ashley Cole. England's hopes of automatic qualification to the 2002 World Cup Finals looked in jeopardy. The Germans were group leaders with only one team gaining automatic qualification.

Michael Owen had other ideas though and within five minutes had equalised from Nick Barmby's flick header. Sebastian Deisler, the Hertha Berlin striker should have put Germany back in front when he blazed over from close range. The England midfield of Beckham, Gerrard and Scholes started to exert their authority. Just on half-time they went ahead with a text-book goal. Beckham floated over a cross for Rio Ferdinand to head down to Gerrard. 'Stevie G' immediately trapped the ball and exploded a 30-yard shot that swerved past Oliver Kahn. Gerrard was to miss the World Cup with a groin injury.

England tore into Germany early in the second half and Owen scored again on 47 minutes, volleying past Kahn from close range after Heskey's pass had released him. A fine piece of opportunism. The ruthless little striker completed his hat trick on 66 minutes when Gerrard put him in. The significance of the treble did not escape Owen as he became the first Englishman since Geoff Hurst to notch three goals against Germany. Owen celebrated with handsprings.

The rout was completed on 73 minutes when Beckham and Scholes shredded the German defence and Heskey ran through to beat Kahn.

Ballack had been withdrawn a few minutes before and been replaced by Klose, one of the players acquired by Bayern after Hargreaves had joined United. Hargreaves came on for Gerrard after 78 minutes and helped England wind down the clock. By this time thousands of German fans were streaming for the exits. At the end of the match only the hardcore remained whilst the large England contingent continued to shout and sing themselves hoarse scarcely believing what they had witnessed. Sven was telling everyone it was the 'stuff that dreams are made of'.

The Munich scoreboard reflecting the 1-5 scoreline became an iconic image shown on thousands of greeting cards. It was only Germany's second World Cup qualifier home defeat in their history and England's first win in Germany for three decades, Terry Paine's goal giving England a narrow victory in Nuremberg in May 1965. Despite the fact that he had only been on the field for a short time it was one of the high spots of Owen's career. Owen confirmed to Sky Sports his allegiance to the Union Jack. 'I am not German; I practise my trade here that is all. Everybody talks about England v Germany. I don't represent Germany. I am English. That's it.'

After the match German and England fans clashed on the Munich streets and 75 arrests were made. Estimates suggested more than 10,000 fans had made the trip to

Munich. They were met by an army of German police and border troops. There was a contingent of crack English police who were a specialist anti-hooligan force.

In the next match against Albania goals from super strikers Michael Owen and Robbie Fowler, in the closing minutes of each half, put England on top of the group by goal difference. Sven chose an unchanged team from the one that had started in Munich. There was an air of euphoria in the country following the famous victory. One tabloid had tried to present Sven with 'The Ashes of German Football'. Owen did not figure in the Albania match.

England went on to qualify for the 2002 World Cup thanks to Beckham's last minute goal against Greece in the theatre of dreams the following April. The apotheosis of the United midfielder was complete. Germany had failed to qualify automatically for a major tournament for the first time in their history. They eventually booked their tickets for Japan and Korea with a 5-2 aggregate play off win over Ukraine.

Owen admitted to Sky Sport that he would love to play in the Premiership in the future: 'I would love to play in the Premiership. It would be an honour for me. There are so many fantastic teams and the fans are great. It is not like that anywhere else in Europe. I am hoping my future will end up there.'

Being in the England squad meant that Owen was conversing with players in his mother tongue. Also he was learning of the excitement generated by the clashes of the big Premiership teams and the intense rivalry between their supporters.

Elland Road, Leeds, was the scene of Owen's next game for England in a friendly against Italy on the 27 March 2002. Sven had been impressed with Owen's performance in the 0-0 draw with Manchester United in the Champions League match on 13 March. The versatility of the youngster was of particular interest to him. There is no doubt that the assimilation of the Bayern midfielder into the England set up was aided by the shrewd management skills of the Swede. Sven had informed Owen that he had a chance of making the World Cup squad.

Owen told Sky Sports, 'Mr Eriksson called me a couple of weeks ago and told me that he was coming out to Munich to watch me and that I was still part of his plans. It's good to get that personal touch from a coach. He asked me how things were going and how I was feeling mentally and physically. I told him I was good.'

The tabloids were now exposing Sven's liaison with TV star Ulrika Jonsson. One of the snaps of the couple the *Sun* had published was taken at a charity breakfast in Manchester the morning after the United/Bayern game. The phenomenon of Sven as a playboy now started to obscure the fan's perception of him as a coach.

For the Italy match England started with a 4-4-2 formation with the Heskey/Owen combo up front and a midfield comprising Beckham, Nicky Butt, Lampard and Trevor Sinclair. Gerrard had withdrawn from the squad with groin trouble along with Scholes and Kieron Dyer. In a quiet, tedious first half the only real incident of note was when Juventus keeper Buffon made a fine block from Sol Campbell.

At half-time Sven made 11 substitutions. Bobby Robson, who had managed England so successfully, criticised Sven for his excessive use of subs. His argument was that it rendered the fixture meaningless. The game had moved on since Bobby's tenure. The difference now was that the demands of the Champions League meant that clubs were reluctant to let their stars play the full 90 minutes so a compromise was arrived at.

The injection of Owen, Joe Cole, Danny Murphy and Teddy Sheringham into the midfield transformed the game. Owen was in the centre of midfield alongside Murphy with Joe Cole on the left and Sinclair on the right. Cole set up England's goal for Robbie Fowler who had taken over as captain.

Joe Cole showed both sides of his game that night, his tenacious tackle on Alessandro Nesta enabling Robbie Fowler to open the scoring. Four minutes later Joe was caught in possession outside the England penalty area and lost the ball to Demetrio Albertini. The Italian then slipped the ball to Vincenzo Montella who instantly beat David James with a curling drive from 25 yards. Owen could only look on in horror, Joe just wanted the ground to open up and swallow him. David Lacey in *The Guardian* was of the opinion that 'Hargreaves was already ahead of Cole and has further enhanced his cause.'

Montella terrorised the England defence all game and James defied him with two great saves. Not to be denied though, he won the game with the last kick of the match from the penalty spot after James had brought down the on-rushing sub Maccarone. The Italians were coached by former Bayern coach Giovanni Trapattoni.

Owen had come out of the game with credit against a strong Italian side. He kept his place in the 25-man squad that was chosen for the game at Anfield against Paraguay on 17 April. It was not an easy game for England because Paraguay had beaten Brazil and drawn home and away with Argentina on their way to the World Cup Finals. The jet heeled Michael Owen – who else? – gave England an early lead heading in a cross from Gerrard. The fresh faced Owen was one of the six second half substitutes. Joe Cole, another of them, set up Danny Murphy for the second after 47 minutes. Further goals from Darius Vassell and an own goal off the back of Ayala completed the rout. Owen did a lot to enhance his rising reputation that night, his intuitive covering, important tackling and careful distribution caught the eye of Eriksson. What appealed most to the Swede though was his versatility as the Bayern star took stints on both flanks and finally at right back. The squad was riddled with injuries and Sven was assessing Owen as cover in various positions. Despite a tricky domestic season Owen had grafted tirelessly and done enough to make the squad for the 2002 World Cup in Japan and South Korea.

At the press conference held at the Café Royal to announce the squad, Steve Curry of the *Daily Mail* questioned Sven on the inclusion of Hargreaves: 'In the case of Owen Hargreaves were you attracted by his technical ability as much as his youth and potential?'

Sven: 'The technique was most important. A footballer these days needs many qualities, and technical ability is obviously among them. You must be clever out there, whether you are attacking or defending, and you have to be able to run and run. I have not picked anyone just because he's young or new. I have picked them because they are good.'

So the football equivalent of Greg Rusedski was on his way to Japan, it was a watershed moment for him. First off Owen met the squad at the Sopwell House Hotel, near St Albans, to attend a party held by the Beckhams. Owen kept a low profile that night avoiding the predatory gaze and the non-stories of the global media. After the party the squad flew from Luton Airport to Dubai for a five day break with their families and partners. Owen knew swanky Dubai well from the time he had spent there in training camps with Bayern in the mid-season break. The idea was to acclimatise to the heat they would face in the Far East. The party stayed at the billionaires hang-out called 'The Jumeirah Beach Club' located on the famous white sand beach strip. Owen tried to relax in the outdoor jacuzzis, sauna and steam rooms. Training was in the early mornings and the cool of the evening. He was in the best shape of his life and desperate to play a part in proceedings.

They then moved onto the beautiful JeJu Island off the coast of South Korea. There they played a friendly against South Korea and drew 1-1 in searing heat. Owen played on the left in a three man midfield alongside Paul Scholes and Danny Murphy. Owen set up England's first chance when he cleverly put Michael Owen through on goal. They young striker tried a lob but the chance was scrambled clear. He did score his obligatory goal on 25 minutes after Heskey's shot had been parried by the Korean goalkeeper. At the break Sven made eight changes which disrupted the flow of the game. South Korea equalised in the second half from a corner after some idiosyncratic marking. The game fizzled out but it was useful in terms of acclimatisation. Owen did exceptionally well, industrious and highly skillfull, he gave his best performance so far in an England shirt. He had picked up a slight knee strain in the game, which was iced after the game to reduce the swelling. Sven told the media, 'Owen Hargeaves has a slight knock, but I don't think it is serious. I think Owen played very well. He's hard working.'

The England team flew by BA charter flight to Japan and touched down at Osaka-Kansai airport. Beckham mania was at its height around that time and the party had to pick their way through a thronging crowd of chanting and screaming fans. It was like something out of the Beatles' first film *A Hard Day's Night* when the Fab Four were mobbed by hysterical fans. For Owen, who used to have posters on his wall of the England captain, it was a chance to witness the very high price of fame. The Bayern youngster was too down-to-earth to be blinded by his own growing fame.

The final warm-up game before the competition started was against Cameroon. Injuries had shorn the side of Seaman, Ashley Cole, Beckham, Dyer and Butt. Cameroon were the champions of Africa, drilled like a platoon and including in the side the fearsome Samuel Eto'o. The African players would soon become a significant force in the Premiership as their abilities matched their expectations. Eto'o blasted Cameroon into an early lead after a mistake by Martyn. Darius Vassell, playing alongside Michael Owen, nimbly equalised for England. Vassell was in a rich vein of form at the time – that goal was his third in five games. He failed to maintain his clinical opportunism though and his career stalled after a transfer to Manchester City and exposure to the fame that cripples so many.

Geremi put Cameroon back in front with one of his specialist free-kicks which comprehensively beat Martyn from 25 yards. Geremi was playing for Middlesbrough after joining them on loan from Real Madrid.

England looked like they would be losing the last of their warm-up games but Robbie Fowler, on for Vassell, saved the day for England with a late, late goal.

Joe Lovejoy's book *Sven-Goran Eriksson* recounts his tick-all-the-boxes praise for Owen in the post match press conference: 'Only Owen Hargreaves advanced his cause in the last two matches. It was understandable that half a dozen of them, who knew they were going to be in the team anyway, just did as much as they had to do. The opposite was true of Hargreaves. He improved a lot, really matured going into the contest.'

Owen featured in England's opening Group F match of the 2002 World Cup against Sweden. He was preferred to Nicky Butt in the midfield anchor role alongside the United pair Beckham and Scholes. The lumbering Heskey was deployed on the left, which raised a few eyebrows.

The Nordic team included Freddie Ljungberg and Henrik Larsson, two of the deadliest forwards in Europe who had melded into a lethal strike force. United fans will always have a soft spot for Henrik as his successful loan spell from Helsingborgs made an important contribution towards their 2006–07 Premiership win. The match kicked off at 6.30pm in a sweltering 84 degrees F. England started brightly and Owen featured in some crisp passing movements. Sol Campbell headed England ahead after 25 minutes from Beckham's impeccable in-swinging corner.

Owen seemed to run out of steam towards the end of the first half as Sweden edged back into it. In the second half Sven's side lost their grip on the game and the Everton winger Niclas Alexanderson cut inside to thump a great shot past Seaman. Shortly afterwards Beckham, clearly not fit following his broken foot, was replaced by Dyer. Only some smart saves by Seaman from Teddy Lucic and an appalling miss by Larsson kept England in the game.

The press had a field day with England's lacklustre performance and the tabloids were quick to criticize. The midfield had barely functioned in the untidy second half, failing to maintain possession and putting additional pressure on the defence. There were too many long balls for

Michael Owen to chase and for long periods Hargreaves watched the ball sail over his curly head.

The next group match was against Argentina in Sapporo. After Germany the South Americans were probably England's bitterest rivals of modern times. Nearly two decades had elapsed since Maradona's two goals had knocked England out the World Cup in Mexico, but the manner of the defeat would never be forgotten by many. Beckham was also keen to obtain revenge for his sending off against Argentina in France in the 1998 World Cup after his clash with Diego Simeone. The game needed a strong ref and they got one in Collina whose path had last crossed Owen's that night in the Olympic Stadium when England had scored five. The bald-headed one had also been in charge when Owen's future employers, Manchester United, had snatched the 1999 Champions League title from his current masters Bayern Munich. The Castrol ambassador for Euro 2008 described the heart-stopping finish as the most dramatic in his illustrious career.

Owen's World Cup campaign only lasted a further 19 minutes, as he collided with his team-mate Michael Owen and sustained a shin injury. That was enough to put him out for the duration. The injury was a freak accident. Owen did not see the challenge from the Liverpool predator and sustained a nasty injury from the clash. Trevor Sinclair replaced Owen, he went to the left with Paul Scholes partnering club mate Nicky Butt.

Near half-time, Michael Owen was tripped by Mauricio Pochettino and Collina pointed to the spot. Replays of the incident suggested that the Mersey Marauder had dived. A nervous Beckham scored the only goal of the game when he lashed home the penalty. Juan-Sebastian Veron, who had an unhappy spell in English football with United and Chelsea, was replaced at half-time. England held on to win another famous victory. Reportedly Argentina did not want to swap their blue and white shirts for the ones with the three lions.

After the game Owen told Sky Sports News, 'I put my foot out to block Zanetti and Michael Owen came up as well and accidentally ran through my leg. I thought I would be able to run it off just like you normally can but I had to come off. I think it is the bone or muscle at the back of my left leg which has been affected; it went numb right away. To have to come off in such a game and so early was so disappointing for me. It would have taken a lot to get me off the pitch.'

Without Owen England drew 0-0 in a drab match with Nigeria which was enough to take them out of the 'Group of Death' and put the favourites Argentina out. The temperature in the Niigata stadium touched 100 degrees F. A 3-0 stroll against Denmark meant England had a quarter-final tie against Brazil to contend with.

An X-ray showed no fracture to Owen's leg but the Bayern player was not fit to feature any more in the competition. The England medical team were hoping that Owen would have been fit to play in the Brazil match but the injury failed to respond to treatment. England press spokesman Paul Newman told the agencies, 'Owen is completely banned from doing any kind of training. We do not know for certain when he will be able to play again.'

Owen watched the match amongst the 47,436 crowd in the new state of the art Shizuoka stadium. Michael Owen gave England a dream start but Rivaldo equalised after Ronaldinho's step over had bemused Ashley Cole. Ronaldinho knocked England out of the World Cup when his bizarre long-range free-kick sailed over Seaman's head. It was a moment that was to haunt David for a long time along with a comparable error when conceding Nayim's goal in the 1995 Cup-Winners Cup Final. Seaman was vilified by the press and fans. Brazil went on lift the trophy beating Germany, of all teams.

The manner of England's exit from the tournament attracted vitriolic flak from the press. Eriksson seemed incapable of inspiring England to victory at the crucial time in the game when the scores were locked at 1-1. The match-winner Ronaldinho had been dismissed for a foul on Danny Mills and Brazil played for over 30 minutes with ten men. Despite the fact that the reverse was his first defeat in a competitive fixture, the choice of subs was severely criticised. Kieron Dyer for Owen's replacement Sinclair and Darius Vassell for Michael Owen. Joe Cole, potentially the most gifted player of his generation, had seen just 17 minutes of action in the whole tournament. This was seen by many as nothing short of dereliction by Sven. The only forward with the ability to leave defenders on their haunches was introduced against Sweden for Vassell. Darius, then at Villa, had formed a firm friendship with Owen during the trip when the pair roomed together.

Owen had a reasonable tournament, motivated and with a talent that distinguished him from others. The injury had curtailed his chance of showing the nation the full extent of his skills. What was notable about his performances was that Owen was the fittest player in the squad. The main factor in this was that he was the only member to have had a winter break. Sven had been petitioning the FA for the Premier League to take a winter break in early January. He was at pains to point out his plan to start the season earlier, finish it in late May and have a maximum break of three weeks after Christmas. He cited the fact that Bayern Munich's mid winter sabbatical had enabled Hargreaves to have a good rest. At the time of writing nothing had developed about the winter break or an even more radical plan to scale down the Premier League.

At the time Eriksson was hired in 2001, a five-year plan was envisaged with England winning the World Cup trophy in 2006. Hopes were high for the 2004 European Championship to be staged in Portugal.

Owen talked to Sky Sports of his experiences in the Far East, which had given him the desire to be part of England set up again in a big tournament: 'It is a shame that I got injured when I did, particularly as it was the first injury of my career. You get your ups and downs and maybe it was not meant for me this time.'

England were the youngest team at the World Cup and the term 'golden generation' was already being bandied around. The constituent parts Joe Cole, Beckham, Ferdinand and Owen were seen as the brightest stars in the firmament together with the young man from Canada, Owen Hargreaves. The future beckoned, his star was in the ascendant.

Chapter Six
England's Dreaming

'Frank Lampard and Steven Gerrard are world class but the balance is much better with Hargreaves in there. I suppose people would say those attributes are similar to the ones I bought to the team.'
Bryan Robson

Owen spoke of his World Cup experiences on the Bavarian giant's website: 'Things were going well and I am playing and then unfortunately I get knocked out ... But I am taking it in my stride and this has been the greatest time of my career, to be involved in a World Cup and with so many fantastic players.'

Bayern players had a good World Cup. Oliver Kahn won the player of the tournament award, very rare for a goalkeeper to win it. Michael Ballack, who had just joined the club, featured in the top 10 players of the World Cup compiled by the Technical Study Group.

Owen returned to the England set-up in September of that year champing at the bit, his appetite for England whetted by the World Cup trip to the Far East. Villa Park was the venue when he played in the 1-1 draw with Portugal in a friendly match. Owen was introduced after 45 minutes, replacing Steven Gerrard.

Owen was a huge fan of the Liverpool captain. He was included on Owen's six best midfielders in the world that he selected in the *Inside United* magazine. 'He's got an awesome all-round game. He is an extremely powerful player. He scores goals, he has a great range of passing, good presence and physique.'

Once again Sven used the fixture as a chance to blood new talent and try out a multitude of players and tactics. Flaubert tells us 'God is in the details'; Sven's painstaking attention to detail largely went un-noticed.

The home side were already a goal ahead following a headed goal after 40 minutes from 21-year-old Alan Smith, then plying his trade at Leeds. Another of his Elland Road colleagues Lee Bowyer created the chance. Smith had a spell at Manchester United but suffered a horrific broken leg and a dislocated ankle at Liverpool which restricted his chances.

Smith's versatility worked against him at Old Trafford. He joined the Reds as a striker but his ability to operate in midfield meant he was a squad player who was uncertain of a place in Sir Alex's starting line up. Owen had similar problems in his fledgling England career, his willingness to fill in at right back detracted from his qualities as a holding midfield player.

Portugal made wholesale changes at the interval, bringing on nine players and by full time the starting line-up had been completely replaced. They deservedly equalised in the second half when an unmarked Rodriguez Costinha headed home a simple goal from eight yards. Once again

England had been caught napping at a set piece. Owen had been stationed on the left hand post to cover such eventualities but such was the power and accuracy of the header he was powerless to stop it flying into the net.

The game petered out but Owen finished strongly, passing with speed and purpose. He had publicly acknowledged that he had learnt a few tricks in training from David Beckham whilst being around him for six weeks. The media were still transfixed by the angle of his cheekbones and fashion sense but Beckham was a huge influence in the dressing room. Naturally Beckham was included in Hargreaves' top six midfielders nominated in *Inside United.* Owen had this to say about the Los Angeles midfielder player whose poster adorned his walls in his teens: 'He has an incredible ability to pick a moment and decide a game, that is what the top players get paid for – to be the best against the best.'

Middlesbrough became the latest of the Premiership clubs to be linked with a transfer bid for Owen. Steve McLaren, Sven's chief honcho and the Boro coach, was weighing up a £8 million move for a player he had the utmost regard for. The Premiership champions Arsenal were also casting envious glances at the Bayern youngster. Arsene Wenger was a great fan of Owen and thought he would have bolstered Arsenal's squad. Julian Rigby, freelance journalist and Arsenal fan thought so also: 'Hargreaves would have been a brilliant buy for Arsenal. Wenger had been tracking him for ages. He had the English work ethic but what appealed most to him was his continental background. Imagine a midfield pairing of him with Cesc Fabregas. The problem was in those days the club had haemorrhaged cash in building the Emirates.'

Hargreaves's image was rising all the time. In interviews

his voice was well-modulated, speaking in the curious hybrid of mid-Atlantic and German. For all the puppy eyes and Pre-Raphaelite curls, Owen had incomparable backbone. What came across was a certain steeliness with a clear sight of his future global targets. Owen knew he had to play regularly in the side if he was to stand any chance of breaking through onto the world stage.

The man who discovered him, German coach Thomas Niendorf, was of the opinion that Premiership stars had an advantage over overseas-based players. The Canadian domiciled coach whose tutelage ignited Owen's career, reasoned that this was because they were under scrutiny from Eriksson all the time plus the intense attention they received from the media circus. Thomas told Sky Sports, 'I think Owen is realising that having had that initial recognition, he is having to work his way up again. He feels confident he's making the right decision going with England and is confident in his own ability, but he is now seeing that there are politics involved'.

On 12 October England travelled to Bratislava to play Slovakia in a Euro 2004 Qualifier. The draw had given England an easy run to Portugal. Compared to the 'Group of Death' in the World Cup, Slovakia, Macedonia and Turkey did not look too problematic.

Torrential rain for the three days leading up to the fixture turned the pitch into a quagmire and added to that the England players had to face a hostile crowd. Two England fans were gunned down in the street within earshot of the luxury hotel Owen and his chums were staying.

Beckham was back in the side after missing the Portugal game, Owen was one of the subs, the United trio of Beckham, Butt and Scholes made up the engine room of the midfield alongside Gerrard. Up front 'Bruno' Heskey got the nod over Alan Smith.

At the break England trailed to a Szilard Nemeth goal, they had played disappointingly and failed to create any clear-cut chances. The left hand side of the midfield continued to be a problem. Paul Scholes played there in the first half and was peerless in the central midfield berth but even he found it hard to dominate the left channel. Gerrard was switched there in the second half and England improved. They pushed up and after a concerted bout of pressure Michael Owen equalised when he touched in Beckham's trademark curling free-kick.

A United midfielder set up the winner, Paul Scholes crossing for ace marksman Michael Owen to score with a near post header eight minutes from time. This stung the Slovakians into action and in the closing minutes they threw everything forward in search of an equaliser.

An Owen replaced an Owen three minutes from the end, Hargreaves coming on for the two-goal hero. Sven wanted to shore up the defence against the frenetic Slovakia attacks. They almost snatched an equaliser when Butt hacked a shot from Zeman away but England grabbed three vital points. Owen got to wear an England shirt again even if it was only for a few minutes and it did end up sodden with rain.

Owen had to wait until the following February (2003) for his next run out with England. The match was against Australia at Upton Park two nights before St Valentine's day. It was no massacre but a poor result for England as they crashed 1-3 in their first defeat against Australia with the round ball. It was one of the most sensational matches in Sven's controversial tenure as England coach. Sven seemed more concerned with the machine than the mechanics in the lingo of the Aussies.

Wayne Rooney became the youngest ever player to represent England as the Swede substituted his entire 'first XI' at half-time. In the second half he sent on his 'youth side' including two of Manchester United's extraordinary future signings Rooney and Hargreaves.

Australia were determined to make a name for themselves on the international stage and fielded a side including experienced, talented players like Harry Kewell, Mark Viduka, Lucas Neill and Stan Lazaridis. In goal was Mark Schwarzer of Middlesbrough who had replaced ex-Manchester United goalkeeper Mark Bosnich, whose career ended so abruptly.

The East End ground was packed with a crowd of 34,590 which contained a large percentage of Australians now living in the capital and anxious to give their side the sort of vocal support reserved for their cricket and rugby sides.

They were given a rousing start when Crystal Palace defender Tony Popovic scored from Lazaridis's clever free-kick. They doubled their lead when Rio Ferdinand had one of his attacks of sleeping sickness and was caught in possession by Harry Kewell. The Australian was in peak form and free of the injuries that were to stymie his career at Liverpool. Running on through a decimated defence, he calmly slipped the ball past the onrushing David James.

That was how it stayed at the break when Sven introduced the young generation or the 'Under-26s' as they were dubbed. It might be interesting to compare the two sets of players.

Owen Hargreaves

FIRST HALF	SECOND HALF
David James	Paul Robinson
Gary Neville	Ledley King
Sol Campbell	Owen Hargreaves
Rio Ferdinand	Darius Vassell
Kieron Dyer	Paul Konchesky
David Beckham	Francis Jeffers
Michael Owen	Danny Mills
Paul Scholes	Danny Murphy
Frank Lampard	Jermaine Jenas
Wes Brown	Wayne Rooney
Ashley Cole	James Beattie

Interesting to note that for a variety of reasons only the future United duo Owen and Rooney and keeper Robinson really graduated to the higher echelon from the second half squad. Owen hit the big time when he hitched his star to the Old Trafford road show, Rooney still has the potential to be a world class player but Robinson's confidence and form deserted him in 2007.

Rooney, at 17 years and 111 days, became the youngest player ever to play for England at that level. Wayne was an Everton player at that time. The legend that was Duncan Edwards won his first cap for England against Scotland at the ripe old age of 18 years 183 days. Arsenal attacker Theo Walcott holds the record now, beating Rooney by 36 days. Other Reds who crashed the England party at tender years were Rio Ferdinand at 19 years 6 days, Phil Neville at 19 years 124 days and Michael Carrick at 19 years 302 days. Lee Sharpe made his England debut against the Republic of Ireland when he was three days older than the former West Ham and Tottenham midfielder.

The Toxteth terror sparked England and his terrific pass found Jermaine Jenas who delivered a fine cross for Francis Jeffers to nod home. For the remainder of the match England pressed for an equaliser and Owen featured in some neat moves down the left. It was Australia who clinched the game though with Brett Emerson scoring from a breakaway. Paul Robinson played well in goal in his spell between the sticks and moved ahead of David James in the pecking order. Owen tried hard but could do little to lift a lethargic side.

Sven received a lot of flak for the defeat but inside he must have been pleased with how things were progressing. Youngsters like Owen were just starting to find their feet at that level and gained valuable experience in the hot house atmosphere of Upton Park. Owen played there for United at Christmas 2007 and found it very hostile. As they trudged off the field the England players were booed by a section of the 34,590 crowd. Probably Aussies, enjoying the result over the whingeing Poms, joined in a good natured manner but it was also a sign of the discontent that was growing amongst the fans. The 15 players from Australia had soundly beaten the 22 from England. The *Sun* described their performance as 'One of the most lamentable in our football history.'

Despite the good showing he had put in, an element of the crowd was failing to appreciate the finer points of Owen's contribution to the cause. Seemingly impervious to criticism, the Bayern player was determined to make an impression in the Euro 2004 qualifying campaign.

Owen played for 45 minutes against Serbia-Montenegro at Leicester's new Walkers stadium on the 3 June. Nicky Butt was injured and Owen was handed the holding role.

Delighted to be playing in the position that he most favoured, Owen told Sky Sports, 'This is a great chance for me and one that I want to take. I have always said that my best position is as the anchor in midfield. It is where I spend most of my time playing and where I played for England in the World Cup. The best games I have played for Bayern or England have been in the anchor role.'

England won 2-1 in a friendly match used as a warm-up before the qualifying match against Slovakia the following week. Steven Gerrard put England ahead in the first half after an exchange of passes with Michael Owen. Near half-time the visitors equalised when Jestrovic headed home after slack marking by the England back four.

Sven rang the changes in the second half and Owen came on for Paul Scholes. Other changes included Wayne Bridge for Ashley Cole and Joe Cole for Lampard. Owen played efficiently as the tempo of the match dropped. This was as a result of the changes to the balance of the team. Joe Cole blossomed with the presence of Hargreaves alongside him, it was a partnership made in heaven. It was fitting that he scored the winner with a fierce free-kick eight minutes from time, Joe's first goal for England. That was about the only high spot in a tepid display by England against the 22nd best international team. The crucial point that came out during the match was that England were highly vulnerable to surrender any lead they had built up.

Sven talked to Sky about Owen: 'He has been playing for Bayern for most of the season, much of the time on the right of midfield or at the back. He is a very versatile player. As far as I am concerned, for the future, Hargreaves's best position will be in the centre of midfield. Can he play that anchor role? Yes.'

Eight days later Owen played for 46 minutes in the 2-1 defeat of Slovakia in a 2004 Euro qualifier. The game was played at the Riverside stadium in Middlesbrough where Owen had first made his debut for an England side when he featured in the Under-21 match. The combustible Danny Mills was the player that made way for Owen. The Bayern star immediately slotted seamlessly into the midfield combo of Lampard, Gerrard and Scholes. On paper it looked a dream combination. At that time Lampard was, fleetingly, playing some of the best football of his career; Gerrard was just starting to dominate the Liverpool midfield as his startling talent shone through, and Scholes was, well Scholes. It never quiet gelled though. Lampard was the dominant figure and took nearly all of the shots and free-kicks, Gerrard never seemed comfortable with Lampard partnering him. There was little adrenalin between them, it seemed flawed with little invention.

Owen pepped the team immediately as he turned in another fine performance with some crunchy tackles, strong runs and canny crosses. He was most effective at the back though, winning possession with some strong tackles or quick interceptions. Sometimes he would play safe with a percentage ball, on other occasions he would try to be more expansive. Another plus for the side was that he was prepared to run with the ball from deep. His yeoman heart though was his biggest asset, as he seemed unperturbed if the going became difficult. Owen had an unquenchable desire to succeed.

Football is a game of sequences and therefore a game of accumulation. Being successful is the result of an accumulation of many little things. A player improves by 10 per cent, he organizes on that then works on something else. Slowly it comes together, George Graham preached that when he was winning titles for Arsenal.

Janocko put Slovakia ahead after 31 minutes and England trailed at the break. Michael Owen equalised on the hour from the penalty spot after he had been brought down. The Liverpool striker was winning his 50th cap and was captaining England in the absence of the suspended David Beckham. Twelve minutes later he scored what proved to be the winner when he headed in Gerrard's cross.

Owen Hargreaves was delighted for the other Owen and wrote on his own website, 'It was the perfect evening for Michael – skipper in his fiftieth international and he goes and scores twice. I, too, am very satisfied. It is a good feeling to come on with the team a goal down and help it to turn things around.'

After the game Owen travelled back to Munich before packing his bags and heading off on holiday. His first stop was Paraguay where his chum Roque Santa Cruz was getting married. Neither would have dreamed that in a few years they would both be playing for famous teams in the Premiership.

In September 2003 Owen featured in the two qualifying matches in Group 7 against Macedonia and Liechtenstein which both resulted in victories for Sven's side. The away tie at Skopje Macedonia was a potential banana skin and England had to fight all the way for victory. Owen played the whole 90 minutes and was voted by the *Sun* as England's best player. This was the first time he earned any kudos from the English press, particularly the tabloids.

England started very slowly, they found it hard to get any rhythm going and failed to threaten the Macedonia goal. They found themselves a goal down after 27 minutes when a mistake by Ashley Cole led to Georgi Hristov scoring.

Errors by Sol Campbell and David James all contributed to the conceding of the goal. Sol mis-headed the weak left wing cross and ex-Barnsley striker Hristov's equally soft, half- hit shot still eluded keeper James.

Sven substituted the ineffective Lampard (this was before the fans were putting in a clammer for his removal from the team) at half-time. A careless pass from the Chelsea man almost set up Artim Sakiri for what would have been a killer second goal. Emile Heskey was introduced to play in a three pronged attack alongside Michael Owen and Rooney. The jury is still out on who is the best strike partner for Owen. Between 28 March 2001 and 23 August 2003 Owen scored 13 of his total of 14 goals playing alongside Heskey.

The electrifying Rooney equalised early in the second half with his first goal for England. It was a record breaker as he was just 17 years and 317 days old and beat the previous record set by Michael Owen. Pound for pound, Jimmy Greaves was probably the greatest goal thief in the history of English football (though you may get an argument from Gary Lineker/Michael Owen fans). The ex-Chelsea striker only made his scoring debut against Peru when he was a precocious 19 years and 86 days.

The goal was a cracker. Heskey had been racially abused by a section of the crowd throughout the game. Undaunted, the blunderbuss of a striker powered through to nod on Beckham's orthodox long ball. Wayne scampered onto it before bulleting a low drive into the bottom left hand corner of the goal.

The much-fcted Rooney's strike overshadowed Owen Hargreaves' contribution to the game. The England man operated on the left of midfield. With Sven's defence looking as shaky as a Nigerian bank draft it desperately needed Owen to shield it. Time and time again he broke up attacks and set them up with shrewd passes and accurate crosses. There was heavy traffic in the England midfield but Owen was the dominant player. It was a great moment for him because his parents watched his performance. On holiday from Canada they had first stopped off in London and rounded off the trip with a visit to Munich.

David Beckham, yellow carded, won the game for England with a smooth side-foot conversion from the penalty spot. It was awarded when John Terry was sent sprawling by Aguinaldo as he controlled Beckham's free-kick.

Owen made a statement about the game on his website: 'It was not easy to play there. The pitch was hard and uneven. The Macedonians were aggressive and consequently destroyed our game. We are really happy that we still managed to win the game. But with our committed and courageous performance, particularly after the break, we really deserved to win.'

Sven told the press that he had been particularly impressed with Owen's performance in the first half. A 'Sven-ism' which had now become a football cliché was his famous, 'First half good, second half, not so good.'

Now it was on to the Theatre Of Dreams to play Liechtenstein in front of 67,000 plus. A future United superstar replaced a current one when Owen came on for David Beckham after 58 minutes. England were already two goals up and cruising to a comfortable victory. Tiny Liechtenstein, a principality of 62 square miles, had put up a tremendous performance.

The first half was a dismal affair with both sides cancelling each other out. The no-nonsense Manchester fans made their feelings known when they booed England off the field at the break. Lampard was getting severe abuse from a section of the crowd.

Michael Owen broke the deadlock when he put England ahead early into the second half heading home Gerrard's swirling cross. It was his 24th goal for England and put him level with Geoff Hurst in 11th place in the all time England goal scorers, one below Bryan Robson.

Owen made a good impression in the closing stages and nearly scored with a long range drive that whistled inches over the bar. The Sky commentator purred in admiration at the power of the shot. Then he whipped over a perfect cross which Michael Owen just failed to convert.

Rooney scored the second after Beckham and Gerrard had combined. The win put England on top of the group and requiring just a point to qualify. They obtained that with a 0-0 draw in Turkey. Owen did not feature in a match remembered only for Beckham's missed penalty.

With England going to Euro 2004 in the summer, Owen was waiting for his call up to the squad. By the early spring of that year he had racked up 95 Bundesliga appearances and 25 in the Champions League. The battle-hardened midfielder made a statement on his website: 'I expect to play a role in Euro 2004, but I am not sure how big that role will be. We have a few warm-up games to try things out but I'm prepared to play anywhere. I can play anywhere, whether it's on the right or in the centre.'

The first of those warm-up matches was against the hosts of the competition and one of the favourites, Portugal. A four-minute cameo performance earned Owen his 16th cap for England when he came on in the Algarve Stadium in Faro in front of an excitable capacity crowd.

It was a special match for Luis Figo who was winning his

100th cap for Portugal. The ex-Barca winger almost gave the home side a dream start but David James robbed him of a goal with a marvellous save. It was England's David Beckham who set up the first goal when Ledley King deflected in his free-kick early in the second half. The classy Paulette equalised for Portugal on 70 minutes with a virtuoso free-kick straight out of the Beckham bumper book of set pieces.

As Portugal surged forward in the closing minutes Sven threw Owen into the blender to superimpose his presence on the back four. In such a short space of time he still managed one pass and took a corner. By the end of the game 39 players had added another cap to their collection. Owen told his website that a draw against the hosts was an 'Outstanding result'.

He went onto say, 'There was not enough time to shine. Nicky Butt had a good game in my position, that's why there was no reason to substitute him. I always enjoy being with the National team, even though I only had a brief appearance this time around. The next couple of months will show whether I will earn a place in the starting line up.'

Owen was next named in the 26-man squad for the trip to Gothenburg for the friendly with Sweden. This was to prove another step in the steep learning curve that was to take him to the pinnacle of the game.

The vital year for England was de-stabilised by Chelsea's efforts to tempt Sven to be their manager. A whirlwind had hit English football with the arrival of Roman Abramovich in the summer of 2003. The former plastic-duck salesman had made his money in the get-rich-quick supermarket trolley dash that had happened with the collapse of communism. Russia's youngest oligarch had purchased

Chelsea Football Club after seeing his first football match at Old Trafford in March 2003. The game was a Champions League match between The Reds and Real Madrid and ended in a 4-3 victory to the home side. The Spanish aces went through on aggregate though despite two great goals from David Beckham. Abramovich instantly fell in love with the beautiful game and since then has been flexing his financial muscles to re-create the magic he felt that special night.

In July 2003 a sheepish Sven was photographed leaving Abramovich's palatial Knightsbridge mansion with the super agent Pini Zahavi. The tabloids linked him with taking over the coaching duties at Stamford Bridge from the then manager Claudio Ranieri. Afraid of losing the Swede to the West London side the FA played hardball with the multi-billionaire and gave Sven a two year extension on his contract. In addition he almost doubled his pay to a net figure of £3m a year. The episode did nothing for team morale or Sven's rapidly declining popularity with the fans. It was an early warning of the effect that Abramovich's mammoth wealth was to have on the domestic and the international game. Things were never the same in the game after he came on the scene.

There was little doubt that the early purchases made by Chelsea and funded by Abramovich's wealth, Veron, Crespo, Joe Cole and Bridge were all players that had been recommended by Eriksson. They had either been managed by him in Italy or were bright youngsters that Sven was blooding in the England set up. If history had been different and he had taken over the reins at Chelsea then a move for Owen would have been in the offing. Bayern announced that Chelsea had shown interest in purchasing him around the time they were being knocked out of Europe by the West London team.

England lost their friendly with Sweden 0-1 but Owen had a tremendous match. The high spot of his performance was when he lashed a booming long range free-kick which smashed against the angle of the bar and post. The match was played in the Nya Ullevi stadium and on the hour Owen was replaced by the swashbuckling Joe Cole. Sweden scored the only goal of the game on 53 minutes.

Owen won the '*Sun* Man of the Match' award with a rating of 8/10. The youngster was exceptionally busy on the night, his style and work-rate giving inspiration to others in the team. He made a comment on his performance in the match to the press. 'It's a shame we did not convert our good chances in the first half. Personally I am of course pleased that I played well.'

Sven named Owen in his squad for the upcoming Euro tournament. It was a great moment for him and vindication for Sven. Two weeks before the commencement of Euro 2004 England played their penultimate warm-up match against Japan in the City of Manchester Stadium. Owen came on for Steven Gerrard after 82 minutes which won him his 18th cap for England.

Michael Owen had given England the lead after 25 minutes after his club mate Gerrard had fired in a low drive from outside the box. It was his first international goal for nine months, injuries were starting to hinder his progress. England did not get out of first gear though and Japan deservedly equalised through Feyenoord's Shinji Ono early into the second half. It was now five matches since Eriksson's side had registered a win. Not the best form to be in before a major tournament.

Owen displayed some impressive touches in his cameo and troubled the Japanese goalkeeper Narazaki with another of his specials from long range.

Owen made a statement on his website about the match: 'Japan have a good side, they have already proved it at the 2002 World Cup. They ran a lot and kept us busy. It was really a good test. We have a good atmosphere inside the team and so are in the best possible mood for the Euro.'

It was hard for Owen to progress any further at this stage. He had proved his versatility by playing across the midfield or slotting in at either full back position. The Bayern player was no jack of all trades though. Since the 2002 World Cup his opportunities had been limited. His profile was diminishing with the England fans at that time. Hargreaves was a very hard working, pragmatic midfielder not a flying winger like Ronaldo. The critical England fans singled him out for lacking dynamism and any real purpose in his game.

Owen's character and off field behaviour was exemplary. The England team had received a lot of bad publicity in recent years. Rio Ferdinand was banned for half a season for missing a drugs test. Nicky Butt had been permitted to play for England while on bail following his arrest for an alleged assault. (The case was subsequently dropped). Frank Lampard had been dropped after an incident in a hotel at Heathrow. Details of John Terry's £5k a week gambling habit had emerged. Owen was scandal free though and a great role model for youngsters.

England's first match of the 2004 Euro Finals was on 13 June against the mighty French side. Owen had high hopes for the competition and told the *Metro* 'It is about time, after so many years, that we bring back a title back to England. We have the potential. Of course you need a bit of luck to win a big tournament.'

Prophetic words for what lay ahead.

Chapter Seven

The First Exit to Portugal

'Sometimes nothin' can be a real cool hand'
LUKE (Paul Newman) COOL HAND LUKE

Owen appeared for 14 minutes in the first of England's 2004 Euro matches against France. The game was played in Benfica's ground, the rebuilt Stadium of Light (Estadio da Luz) on 13 June in front of 64,000. France, favourites for the competition, snatched an incredible late victory in a manner not seen since United had stolen the European Cup from Bayern Munich in 1999.

It was only Sven's second defeat in a competitive match and was a massive dent to their confidence. England started impressively, roared on by a huge army of fanatical fans. Both sides fielded strong line ups in the Group B match, which were as follows.

ENGLAND	FRANCE
David James	Fabien Barthez
Gary Neville	Lilian Thuram
Sol Campbell	William Gallas
Ledley King	Mikael Silvestre
Ashley Cole	Bixente Lizarazu
David Beckham	Robert Pires
Paul Scholes	Patrick Vieira
Frank Lampard	Claude Makelele
Steven Gerrard	Zinedine Zidane
Michael Owen	David Trezeguet
Wayne Rooney	Thierry Henry

The French subs bench was graced with such talent as Sylvain Wiltord, Marcel Desailly and Louis Saha. They looked the better side in the first half but did not create any chances. It was England who took the lead after 38 minutes when Bixente Lizarazu, Owen's Bayern team-mate, fouled David Beckham out on the right. The ex-United superstar lofted over the free-kick which Frank Lampard headed home.

Owen was watching from the bench and was highly encouraged by the first half showing.

France stepped up a gear in the second half but could make no impression on the tough England rearguard with Sol Campbell outstanding. With 20 minutes left Eriksson's side should have sealed victory. Strangely enough the incident involved players who at one stage of their fine careers had all played for Manchester United. In a high speed counterattack Rooney was chopped down by Mikael Silvestre and the German referee Markus Merk had no hesitation in awarding a penalty. Up stepped David Beckham but Fabien Barthez, who had replaced Mark

Bosnich as United's custodian, outguessed his former skipper and beat out the kick. Beckham had opted for power rather than precision.

Five minutes after the penalty had been missed Owen made his debut in the Euros. Another milestone in his star-studded, event-packed career. Hargreaves replaced another Old Trafford legend Paul Scholes. It looked game over for the French but events transpired which had echoes of that balmy night at the Nou Camp in May 99. England were defending stoutly and merely running down the clock. Owen, his usual tidy self, took up a slot in front of the back four to the left of Ledley King, who had played magnificently.

That identical position was Claude Makelele's speciality and he had made it his own playing for France, Real Madrid and Chelsea. At that time he was perhaps the finest exponent of that holding midfield role in the world. In the dying minutes though he was pushed forward in a desperate attempt by Les Bleus to salvage something. It smacked of desperation because little Makelele was not known for his attacking prowess.

Owen's appearance as a sub had been part of a double as Emile Heskey had replaced Rooney at the same time. Hindsight is a great thing because on such decisions games are won and lost. The frisky Rooney still looked a handful and was full of running, to replace him at that juncture did not look like one of Sven's better decisions. Put it down as an Ulrika moment.

Sure enough Heskey fouled Makelele on the edge of the box and Zidane blurred the ball past David James. It was a sublime piece of skill and opportunism, a real roof smasher. Malcolm Allison, another famous son of Manchester used to talk of 'deception and disguise' at free-kicks. The Madrid man must have had undoubted satisfaction at this goal. Zinedine Zidane was the best midfield player that Owen ever played against. He told the *Inside United* magazine. 'I played against him for Bayern Munich against Real Madrid and everything about him was top class. His ability, presence and physique were amazing. He seemed to be two steps ahead of everyone else.'

Karl Heinze Rummenigge had praised Owen's performance against Zinedine for Bayern Munich. That night playing for his country he could only watch the best player in the world win the game with his matchless skills.

England tried to re-group. Owen was now marking another Bayern Munich player Willy Sagnol who had also come on as a sub. France, driven on by Patrick Vieira, poured forward sensing blood. Steven Gerrard made a hash of a reckless back pass to James but a French forward intercepted. The forward was the worst player in the world that he could have given the ball to – Thierry Henry. The then Arsenal striker took the ball past James but was brought down by the keeper as he shaped to pull the trigger. Merk duly awarded the penalty kick for this incident. Zidane dispatched it clinically.

It was the third minute of injury time and the England players slunk off, shell shocked. James, then at Manchester City, was heavily criticised for the two goals, being beaten by the free-kick and for clattering Henry. James protested that he had never been shown any video footage of Zidane's free-kicks.

Owen was philosophical about events, he loved soaking up the atmosphere and knew that England had controlled most of the match. The important thing was to focus on the remaining group games.

The Switzerland game turned out to be a stroll for England as they cantered to a 3-0 victory in the Ciade de Coimmbra. Owen came on for Scholes again, Paul had not scored for England for three years and slowly his England career was winding down.

Scholes's departure was after 70 minutes with England leading by Wayne Rooney's headed goal. The match was played in the intense afternoon heat that sometimes touched 100 degrees F. The introduction of Owen pepped the England midfield who were still wresting control from the functional Swiss diamond formation.

Morale was still high within the squad despite the defeat to France. The match was effectively over after an hour when the Swiss full back Haas was dismissed for two bookable offences.

Owen helped set up the second goal which made the game safe for England. A strong tackle by the midfield sentry enabled him to win the ball in the penalty box. Pushing forward, a long clearance from him near the halfway line was picked up by his pal Darius Vassell. The striker cleverly beat a defender before setting up Rooney to score with a deflected drive that ricocheted off the back of the keeper's head.

Steven Gerrard pounced to make it three. Owen in the closing minutes was stronger than anyone, chivvying the back four for allowing Switzerland a chance and driving his side on. In the last minute he received a knock on his ankle from a Swiss player in his own penalty area. It was a deliberate foul and the ball was nowhere near him. Owen went over on it and received treatment.

His statement to the press was about how hot the match had been, but how confident he was of winning something.

Owen summed up the bullish mood in the England camp, the players were very confident that they could go all the way in the competition. Unfortunately he missed playing in the Croatia game as he was suffering from gastroenteritis. The midfielder claimed that he had eaten something bad after the Switzerland game. His stomach was badly upset and his sleep pattern was disrupted. It was bad luck because he had escaped serious injury to ligaments and bones when he was fouled late in the Switzerland game.

The medical team monitored Owen's health in the days leading up to the Croatia game. The midfield that started the game was Beckham, Gerrard, Lampard, Scholes but Sven considered Owen to be a key member of the squad and would have included him at some point in the game. Most of all Sven recognised his ability to do things capably in any situation. It was a tribute to the progress that he made in the Swede's reign that he was considered such an integral part of his plans.

England won a hard fought battle 4-2 against Croatia. The Bayern player Niko Kovac put Croatia ahead after five minutes. Paul Scholes ended his drought by scoring after 40 minutes and in first half injury time Rooney put them ahead. Rooney scored again after 67 minutes to raise his profile even higher. (Around this time Sven was comparing him to Pele). Croatia refused to lie down though and Tudor pulled it back to 3-2 after 72 minutes.

That was the stage of the game where Sven would have missed Owen the most. The game was set up for him to add solidity to the defence and shore up the midfield. By a quirk of fate Hargreaves was to be missed even more against Croatia when they met up again in November 2007. Lampard made it safe for England though when he made it

4-2 and set it up for a quarter-final showdown with the hosts Portugal on the following Thursday night.

Owen was delighted with the result over Croatia and put a very positive gloss on things. The fact that there were 40,000 England fans in the stadium particularly pleased him. He was sorry that he had not played in the match but hoped that he would get a chance against Portugal.

The Portugal game was one of the most exciting matches that England have been involved in recent times. It was back to the Stadium of Light in the Portuguese capital for a place in the semi-finals. This was easily the most important match Owen had played in since the World Cup clash with Argentina at the Sapporo Dome two summers before. Sven started with the same opening line-up for the third game in a row. England wore white that night with blue shorts and white socks.

They got the dream start that they craved when Michael Owen fired them ahead after just three minutes. James punted downfield, Costinha fluffed his header and Michael pirouetted to score.

The then Liverpool based striker had taken a back seat to Rooney in the tournament so far. Many in the media were doubting his ability to make any lasting impact with Wayne. The fact was that Michael held a very high attacking line which stretched the distance between the opponent's midfield and defence. This had the effect of creating more space for Wayne to create his own brand of havoc. If Hargreaves was in the side then Owen could float even more which in turn gave Rooney space to get onto the ball without the attentions of a man marker.

Michael had now become the first Englishman to score in four consecutive tournaments. It should have settled their jangling nerves and enabled England to dominate. Hargreaves was on record saying that the England game plan was to pressure from the beginning and try to control the match. Portugal had never beaten England in Lisbon. In 1947 when the sides first met the scoreline read Portugal 0 England 10. Times had changed though.

Their jangling nerves took over though and the England midfield faded badly, Beckham in particular looked tired with Gerrard and Scholes decidedly jaded. They had played so well against Croatia but Portugal had an extra day's break since their last group match. Fitness levels were starting to tell. The addition of Hargreaves with his young legs could have only been complementary to the older heads.

Things got worse when Wayne Rooney crashed out of the tournament with a broken metatarsal. The Everton man had a tendency to dive in recklessly like Gazza. The Geordie boy was the last player to make such an impact for his country, but the clash with Jorge Andrade's boot seemed innocuous at first. The loss of the talismanic youngster after 27 minutes seemed to signal the demise of England's hopes of winning the competition.

The balance shifted dramatically as Portugal poured down on the England back four. In hindsight Sven should have brought the defensive midfielder Owen on to stiffen the defence. They were in danger of being over-run at times but held firm somehow. Brilliantly marshalled by Sol Campbell and with the dominant Ashley Cole showing why he was then the best left back in the world England clung on. Portugal had two brilliant wingers in the Galactico Luis Figo and the heir apparent Cristiano Ronaldo, a future team-mate of Owen's.

Nine minutes from the end of normal time with England

still ahead Sven sent Owen on for the disappointing Gerrard. Stifled by the presence of Lampard and physically exhausted, Stevie G should have been replaced considerably earlier. Phil Scolari, the shrewd Portugal coach who was to be offered Sven's job, was shuffling the pack too. Figo, totally shackled by Gary Neville, was hauled off to be replaced by the ex-Spurs striker Helder Postiga. Rui Costa replaced defender Miguel and Simao came on for Costinha.

Hardly had Owen been on the field than Portugal scored the equaliser their non-stop pressure had warranted. It was created by a substitute and executed by one. Simao's cut back cross was headed home by Postiga from point blank range. The home crowd went wild as the English hearts sank. Terry was conspicuous by his absence, Owen could only watch as his dream slipped away, the sceptics in the press box nodded.

England could still have won it in the dying minute though. Owen made an impact on the left and won a free-kick. Beckham took the kick and Michael Owen soared to crash a header against the bar. Sol Campbell met the rebound and bundled it over the line. The goal was disallowed though for Terry's push on Ricardo. Terry was rapidly becoming the new Jack Charlton of football, a dinosaur of a player in the modern game. He had been lucky to reclaim his place from Ledley King but was determined to progress his career. Like Charlton had done for Leeds, an important feature of Terry's game was his treatment of the opposition goalkeeper at set pieces. The Swiss referee Urs Meier correctly blew for a foul and replays substantiated this. The tabloids wrote it up like the biggest robbery since Alfie Biggs and his accomplices had stopped the mail train. Owen had a bad case of the 'Wenger's' as he told the Press that he had not witnessed anything.

That foul cost England dear because after 110 minutes the ruby shirted Rui Costa fired home an unstoppable drive from well outside the box. The ball went in off the underside of the bar, England looked down and out. The only chance they created came early in extra time when Owen's perfect cross was nodded wide by Beckham. It was a bad miss by David who only seemed to come alive in the last 30 minutes.

Frank Lampard saved England, and prolonged the nation's agony, when he equalised in the 115th minute. The never-say-die attitude of England was well to the fore when Lampard swivelled to drive home Beckham's cross past the Portugal keeper Ricardo. So it went to penalties.

It was the first time that Portugal had been involved in a shoot-out but for England it was to follow an all too familiar pattern. The portents were not good. It was their fifth penalty shoot out in 14 years and they had lost three out of the first four. David Beckham strolled up to take the first kick, but he really should have been subbed long before Owen had come on for Gerrard. At the crucial moment, just as he made contact the ball appeared to bobble and ended up high in the night sky. It gave him an unwelcome hat trick of penalty misses after his failure in the French match and another miss against Turkey. There was a lasting image of Beckham staring down at the penalty spot like Tiger Woods checking out a divot after a poor putt. Beckham has become mythic in just a few short years but this was not one of his golden moments.

Michael Owen scored England's second penalty despite scuffing it badly. Owen watched silently from the halfway line, hands clamped to his hips. Midfield ace Deco and Simao successfully completed their kicks. The Chelsea duo

Lampard and Terry both scored from their attempts whilst Cristiano Ronaldo neatly scored for Portugal. An abysmal Rui Costa effort whistled over the bar to make it all square.

Then it was Owen's turn to take a kick. He described how he felt at that moment on his website: 'It does not matter if you converted your penalty or not since there is nothing you can do. In open play, it is easy to point to mistakes or to praise individual skill that lead to a decisive moment of a game but with penalties you cannot really speak of a team effort. I was pretty confident walking up to the spot taking my penalty but no matter how cool or decisive you are penalties just feel like Russian roulette. All that work and effort you have put in over 120 minutes will forever be forgotten and it is down to that Wild West inspired duel.'

It was a good analogy to the Wild West, High Noon all that gunslinger imagery. Owen was very confident and side-footed to the right side of the goal to make it four out of five kicks. It was a moment he will recall all his life and a testimony to his courage and coolness under fire. Once again Owen's gift for seizing opportunity was displayed. So it went on, the tension was now almost unbearable, down on the pitch, on the terraces and in millions of living rooms throughout the nation.

Portugal scored their next kick when Maniche, who had a spell with Chelsea, rolled home. That levelled it at 4-4. The rollercoaster rumbled on, later reports would reduce the story to cliché, if not fiction.

It was now sudden death with whoever missed going out. Ashley Cole floated home the Three Lions' next penalty and Postiga levelled for the hosts with an almost arrogant conversion.

Darius Vassell, Rooney's replacement, was next up to take

the seventh kick. Owen's chum hit it straight and true but the Portugal keeper Ricardo, sans gloves, threw himself sideways to keep out the shot. The keeper completed the execution of England when he beat his opposite number James rather fortuitously from the spot and scored the decisive penalty.

So that was it. England went out of a competition they should have won and Portugal lost in the final to a superbly organised but dull Greek side. Football was changing. The Portugal squad that knocked out England included the Porto players Carvalho, Maniche, Ferreira and Tiago who had just won the Champions League under their brilliant young coach Jose Mourinho. All these players were later to play for him at Chelsea as he took a flamethrower to the Premiership. The Portugal side also included the world class talents of Deco, Figo and the budding legend Ronaldo. For England to lose out to them so narrowly on their home ground was no disgrace.

Portugal's failure to go on and win the competition was even more ironic. They lost to a team representing all the virtues of a Mourinho side, hard work, good team spirit, organisation and a stubborn defence. This was coupled with a dour, win-at-all-costs attitude. Ever the narcissist, Mourinho would watch the teams most reflecting his image.

Fitness was now everything. Owen looked in superb shape – at the peak of his powers in terms of physical conditioning. Even when struck down by the stomach flu he had shrugged it off in a couple of days. Compare this to the listless Steven Gerrard who at times in the Portugal game looked completely shattered. The England midfield of Beckham, Scholes, Lampard and Gerrard appeared at times to be flat and one paced. It was only when Hargreaves was added to the mix any variation occurred. Three years on the problem was magnified.

Apart from his splendid performance against England, Zinedine Zidane had a poor competition. He was in good company, as fellow Galacticos Figo, Beckham and Raul badly underperformed. Totti, Vieri and Henry failed to live up to their megastar reputations as their countries crashed out.

The world order was changing. The hard running Hargreaves type of player was coming to the fore, equipped with lacerating pace and excellent control, superbly fit and technically aware, prepared to run all day in his tireless pursuit of the ball. Ostensibly required for defensive duties. What was considered anachronistic was the old fashioned ball playing luxury 'maverick' player.

So England limped home after the titanic battle which had raged for almost three hours. The *Daily Telegraph* praised Owen,'Worked himself down the left. Never gave up.'

Owen rented a house and stayed in Portugal for a few days to lick his wounds and try to get his head around England's exit. In interviews he talked of feeling empty after losing in a penalty shoot out. It was hard to leave the beautiful country. He had been convinced that England were good enough to have gone on and lifted the trophy there.

Hargreaves particularly felt sorry for Sven who had lost in the World Cup to Ronaldinho's fluked goal and now was out of the Euros by penalties. Dieter Hamann, who won Bundeliga titles with Bayern, had recently made the point to *The Guardian*. 'What can Eriksson do? Should he take the penalties himself?'

Later Owen nipped off to spend a week in France at the Cote d'Azur then back to Bavaria. Meanwhile Sven retreated to his huge villa in Sunne, in the heart of Sweden. There amongst the lustrous parquet floors and beautiful objets d'art he recharged his batteries and planned his assault on Germany in 2006.

The draw for the 2006 World Cup was kind to him. Cosy teams from Austria, Poland, Wales, Northern Ireland and Azerbaijan. Like a cherry picked list of opponents for a rising boxer it included no real problems or so it would seem.

It was August of that year when Owen next linked up with his England pals. With Wembley still being rebuilt, Newcastle was chosen as a venue for a friendly against Ukraine. It was an early Monday start for the Munich-based player. He had to be at the airport to check in at 5:15 to make the 6:00 flight to Amsterdam, and then onto Newcastle. The game was scheduled for Wednesday night and the team assembled on Monday afternoon for a spot of lunch. Sven was on hand to meet and greet his players wearing an immaculate Hugo Boss suit and warm smile.

It was a chance to meet up with some old pals, particularly Darius Vassell. Owen had felt gutted for him at his penalty miss but Sven's players had already consigned the Euros to the dustbin of history, particularly that fateful night in Lisbon.

It was a bit of a wasted journey for Owen as he had to sit out the match on the bench. Sven picked his strongest side in the first half and in the second opted to throw on some new faces like Glenn Johnson and Shaun Wright-Phillips. It was a new era after all.

At that stage Owen was in limbo, he had not aspired to Sven's 'First XI' or to use the Mourinho-ism the 'Untouchables'. Despite his callow youth he was hardly a new boy having been on the international scene for three seasons. The days of Sven throwing on complete new teams in the second half of matches were gone. FIFA had limited the number of subs in friendlies to a paltry six.

England cantered to an easy 3-0 victory on a cool, cloudy autumn evening. Michael Owen had joined Real Madrid in the summer to link up with his England captain Beckham. Both of the Galacticos scored that night with new boy Wright-Phillips adding the third.

Owen was sorry that he did not get on to play for his country. The next day he flew back to Munich via Amsterdam, the flight was late and Owen was almost missed training the next day. The trials and tribulations of an international footballer!

Travel hassles were to feature when Owen travelled to London en route for England's two World Cup qualifying away games against Austria and Poland. Once again he had an early Monday morning start but Owen was stuck in traffic on his way to the airport and missed his flight to Heathrow. (The airport traffic was always a problem. In an amusing incident at Christmas 2007 it was reported that motor racing legend Michael Schumacher took control of the cab he was riding in to beat the jams and make his flight.)

Michael was not around that day and this meant Owen had to catch a connecting plane in Berlin. The delay meant that he did not get to the England training camp till late in the afternoon. The players were already changed and participating in a training session. The laid back Eriksson told Owen to relax and go jogging instead. The patience and mildness of his temperament often surprised players more used to the self-glorification and detonations of different egos. Capello would not have been so benign; reports also mentioned that Sir Alex Ferguson was also to disagree with Owen over such matters.

Owen made the sessions at Arsenal's training complex at London Colney for the next two days before flying out on the Thursday afternoon. The match was on Saturday and was of vital importance to Owen. He relished the challenge of playing for England in the World Cup again, especially as it was in the country where had been living for the past seven years.

Austria held England to a 2-2 draw in Vienna. It was a laboured performance by Sven's side. Owen took no part in the match which saw England lose a 2-0 lead. Ranked 73 places behind England in the World Ratings it was a poor show, the amateurishness of the defending particularly worrying. Sven experimented with Wayne Bridge in midfield but Owen was missed in the line-up.

The Three Lions were back to winning ways in Poland though when they won 2-1. The match was played the following Wednesday night in Charzow and Owen saw some action when he came on near the end for David Beckham. There were to be no slip ups that night and Owen was sent on to stiffen defence and shield the back four. Sven had made the players watch a video of the Austria match, he was still angry at the slipshod manner in which they had conceded the lead.

Tottenham striker Jermaine Defoe had given England the lead after 37 minutes with a neat turn onto Beckham's pass and a cool finish. Early in the second half Maciej Zurawski equalised for Poland. England kept their nerve though and regained the lead with a scrappy goal. Ashley Cole crossed from the left and the Polish defender Glowacki, under pressure from Michael Owen, turned the ball into his own net.

The players boycotted the media after the game. It was a protest against criticism that they had experienced after the poor showing in Austria. The main bone of contention concerned the midfield. The lumpen, orthodox Gerrard/Lampard combination showed less spark than a dying novelty lighter. Owen was unable at this stage to make the transition from a bit part cameo player to a starting role in his favourite holding role.

Speaking after the game Owen told his fans that England were again on track to qualify for the World Cup.

Then it was off to Old Trafford in early October to play Wales in another qualifier. High profile games at Old Trafford were becoming a regular fixture for him and went a long way to explaining how he settled in so quickly at United. A 2-0 win put them on top of Group 6 with two wins and a draw.

Frank Lampard put England ahead after just three minutes, the goal actually went in off Michael Owen's heel and the new Galactico claimed it as his at first. Then the ubiquitous Beckham scored perhaps the best goal of his illustrious England career. This was a perfect chip into the top right-hand corner of the net from the corner of the penalty box. Five minutes from time Beckham went off to be replaced by Owen.

Once again Owen had replaced his former idol in midfield. His appearance came too late to have any effect on the game. In his lavish praise of Sven, Owen would always mention how despite his seemingly detached manner the Swede made an effort to follow his career in Germany very closely. Smoothing the way for the youngster, Sven would also tell the press how well Owen had been performing for Bayern in Germany. This was a great stepladder boost to his confidence even if the small cameos were frustrating to him. It also set him up as a scapegoat for England's shortcomings.

In November England played Spain in a gruelling friendly played at the Bernabeu Stadium. Owen's Champions League experience would have proved vital as he had already played there three times for Bayern Munich. Sven had called him into the squad but the injury jinx struck again when Owen took a knock on the hip in the Bundesliga match against Bochum. He flew to Madrid but after consultation with the Swede and conferring with the medical team it was decided not to risk him.

Owen watched the game from the sidelines and was impressed by a classy Spanish side. Their brawny defender Asier Del Horno, soon to be another Chelsea purchase, headed the only goal of the game after nine minutes. Robinson, the England keeper who had made his debut against Poland, saved Raul's penalty soon afterwards.

The game descended into chaos when Rooney lost it after being substituted just on half-time. Owen was shocked to see him tear off his black armband and discard it when he stormed off. The armband had been worn as a mark of respect to former England greats Keith Weller and Emlyn 'Crazy Horse' Hughes. When his captain Beckham tried to calm him down he received a torrent of abuse as Rooney flew into an incandescent rage. This was in marked contrast to Owen's banana grin, impeccable manners and avoidance of any reputation-tarnishing incidents.

Time moved on and it was not until February 2005 that Owen played for England again. This time it was against Holland at Villa Park, the team that the young greenhorn had made his debut against, 25 matches before. The game finished scoreless, uneventful save for the five changes that Sven made in the game. Owen came on for the second half for Lampard, amongst the other subs were the introduction of new caps Andy Johnson and Stuart Downing. There was not much to cheer the 40,705 crowd on a cold, late winter's evening. Roy Makaay, the Bayern team-mate of Owen missed a good chance for Holland and Dirk Kuyt smashed a shot against the post. Sven's flaring eyes were watching Owen closely and noticing the rapid progress he was making.

The following month Owen was called into the England squad for the two World Cup qualifying games against Northern Ireland and Azerbaijan. This was coming off the back of the news that in the Champions League his side had been drawn against multi-billionaire Abramovich's Chelsea, ensuring that he would be crossing swords against his England pals and the nucleus of both sides: Terry, Lampard and Joe Cole. As he took the early morning flight to London he looked forward to the banter with the Chelsea boys.

So it was back to Old Trafford on Easter Saturday to play against Northern Ireland, he knew how important it was for the national side not to show any weakness and keep the run going. There was no chance of it that day as England ran out easy 4-0 winners. Owen came on after 72 minutes replacing Steven Gerrard. He immediately took up residence in his favourite position in front of the back four and was highly impressive for the rest of the game. England were already 4-0 up with all the goals coming after half-time. Joe Cole had opened the scoring and put on a dazzling display of his great talent.

The following Wednesday, 49,046 partisan fans at St James's Park roared England onto another easy victory over Azerbaijan. The score was 2-0 with goals from Gerrard after 51 minutes and David Beckham eleven minutes later. Owen sat this one out. He held forth on his award winning website about the game.

'The coach told me that he was very happy with my performance against Northern Ireland. I also think that I played a decent game. It's always a shame when you don't get a chance to play. But the second match took place in Newcastle and with Jermaine Jenas and Kieron Dyer we have two players from Newcastle United in our squad. I can understand the coach opting for those two, but it is of course beyond all question that I always want to play and that I was disappointed.'

This quote encapsulated all the qualities that drove Owen onto superstardom, his ferocious determination and unquenchable hunger for success. Pensive and combative he was hardening into a complex character. At the time of writing, Owen, despite the grinding pain of his knee condition, was an integral part of both the England and Manchester United squads. Messrs Jenas and Dyer were both playing for London sides and had become minor celebrities tailored to the tabloid fantasy of the age. An allegory for the 'progress' of the Premiership but tellingly neither had established themselves as regulars in the England set up.

Those two victories kept England on top of Group 6 with 16 points, a point ahead of Poland. Owen's dream of a quixotic World Cup mission in Germany was inching nearer.

Chapter Eight

Atonement

'He's a very good player and a really great bloke'
David Beckham 'Sport Bild'

'It is my position – playing in the holding role – getting stuck in, winning tackles and laying it off. I feel very confident in that role.'
Owen Hargreaves (in the 2006 World Cup)

Owen missed England's summer tour of the US because of his duty to Bayern Munich. David Beckham went on to tell the German sports magazine *Sport Bild*, 'It's important that he does his duty for the club. Bayern opened their new stadium. That is why Owen missed our game against Columbia in New York.'

Owen missed out on a 3-2 win with the other Owen nabbing his second hat trick for England. Beckham was to later decamp to America to hitch his star to LA Galaxy. Owen was on American soil that summer, after visiting his family in Calgary he spent a few days in Las Vegas. The only contact Owen had with the England squad was when he phoned his close pal Darius Vassell to congratulate him on his transfer to Manchester City from Villa.

Owen received a text from Sven on his hi-tech mobile that looked like something out of a futuristic film. It was good news informing him that he had been included in the squad for the friendly against Denmark in Copenhagen on 17 August.

Eriksson was interviewed in the German newspaper *Welt Am Sonntag* about his midfielder: 'I had a scout at Bayern's match against Gladbach. (The first match in the new stadium that would be used in the World Cup). He told me that Owen, playing out of position, was the game's best player, that he is in terrific form and that he scored a wonderful goal. Owen is so incredibly talented and full of ambition.'

The Denmark match was played on a Wednesday night in the Parken Stadium; it turned out to be the heaviest defeat of Eriksson's reign. The first half was uneventful, the game played out in a ground with a *Blade Runner* eeriness to it. Owen replaced Lampard after 64 minutes with England two down and in danger of being pulverized. Three second half goals in seven minutes did for them.

The introduction of David James for Paul Robinson at the start of the second half was named as the main reason for the debacle, the Manchester City keeper being at fault for three of the goals. The first was a pantomime of errors, as Tomasson raced through the defence to set up a gift goal for Dennis Rommedahl to tap-in after James had failed to come out in time. A calamitous mistake that was to shatter England's fragile confidence. The Charlton winger Rommedahl created the second for Tomasson to turn home from close range.

England were three down shortly afterwards when James

missed Jensen's corner and Michael Gravgaard headed home from point blank range. Rooney shot a late consolation from Beckham's cross four minutes from time. The humiliation was complete though in the final minute when Soren Larsen ran through unchallenged to shoot past the forlorn James. Owen tried valiantly to plug the huge holes at the back but could make little impact in front of the misshapen back four.

The whole team was disorientated by Morten Olsen's classy side, who were recording their first home win over England. Owen and Beckham were the last Englishmen to leave the field, heads down, fists clenched.

The success of the England cricket team, winning the Ashes that summer, mirrored the publics concerns about their football team.

Henry Winter of the *Daily Telegraph* wrote of the 'nightmarish performances' of David James and Chelsea defender Glenn Johnson, a second half replacement for Gary Neville. James, it was claimed, upset the England camp again by complaining that he had been given no time to warm-up for his appearance.

The *Telegraph* went to town on the England defence in similar fashion to that of the Danish wingers. Jamie Carragher and Rio Ferdinand were also heavily criticised for their poor performances. Only Owen was exempted from any criticism. It was England's heaviest defeat since Wales had thrashed them at Wrexham a quarter of a century before.

Maybe the seeds of the Owen backlash were sown then. The fans and press were looking for scapegoats. Hargreaves playing for Bayer Munich was an obvious target; he was always at pains to tell them he was not German but playing for a German side. The least quintessentially English member of the side, who had never kicked a ball in the Premiership. To many in the game he was seen as Sven's protégé, a favourite chosen automatically. Another problem was that Owen was not a crowd pleaser like Joe Cole, equipped with his dazzling arsenal of tricks and flicks. Nor was Hargreaves a flying winger like Wright-Phillips or Ashley Young. The England crowd always loved wingers foraging deep into enemy territory.

Tord Grip, Eriksson's vastly experienced number two, told the press that his boss was very upset at England's 'awful' performance in the second half in Copenhagen. Grip was a huge fan of Claude Makelele and thought that the answer to England's midfield problems would be to play with a sitting midfield player. Tord told *The Guardian* of his high hopes for Owen: 'Hargreaves is playing there for Bayern Munich and is doing it very well at the moment. He is playing there regularly; Bayern have used him almost everywhere, left back, right back, left midfield, right midfield, but now he has that sitting role. Bayern Munich have some other very good players in that position but Felix Magath is saying that this is Hargreaves place.'

Both Grip's and Magath's clarity of vision about Hargreaves's best role for club and country tells us exactly how tactically astute and what shrewd judges of a player they were. Over recent seasons England's best performances had been when the midfield formation accommodated Hargreaves in a defensive holding role.

Football is a labyrinth of connections and coincidence which goes even beyond the exquisite talent of a Joe Cole or the omnipotence of a man like Abramovich. A fellow Swede Bjorn Andersson played for Bayern Munich in the

1975 European Cup Final against Leeds United. (Bayern won the second of their hat trick of 70s European Cups, the Leeds fans rioted and UEFA banned their team from Europe for a year.)

Gripp told *The Guardian* 'He was badly injured by Terry Yorath and is working for them as a scout. He had Hargreaves in the youth team. He started as a defensive central midfielder. He said that he is going to be a very good holding midfielder.'

Connections everywhere, Yorath's daughter Gabby, when not strutting her stuff on 'Strictly Come Dancing', presented Champions League coverage involving matches in which Owen featured. She was to interview him for the BBC TV *Inside Sport* programme in Munich. Bjorn was an old friend of Sven and Grip.

At the Millennium Stadium in early October England scrambled a 1-0 win over Wales, courtesy of a deflected Joe Cole low drive.

Owen replaced the Camden-born Chelsea star with 15 minutes to go. The midfield was subjected to a reconfiguration with Steven Gerrard pushed farther forward and Beckham shifted sideways. Owen's arrival bolstered the midfield, set the tone and secured their slender lead. England had 59 per cent of possession and played very cautiously. Some papers expressed surprised that Owen had edged in front of Michael Carrick, another classy holding player, in the England pecking order but his commitment and calm authority were impressing Sven more and more.

The Welsh fans did not give Owen a very good reception. Like the Canadians there was an element that thought Hargreaves should have opted to play for them (by virtue of his Welsh mother) rather than opt to play for their oldest rivals.

Prior to Owen coming on Beckham had been tried in the holding role in a 4-5-1 formation. After the battering they had received in Copenhagen Sven was reluctant to go with his normal 4-4-2 line-up. Beckham had a mixed reaction to his performance – his tackling, a pre-requisite for the role, was not nearly as sharp as that of Owen's. David's favoured pass was always the long ball but the short pass was always the most telling when made in such situations. This was particularly true when Lampard and Gerrard were selected.

The brief was simple: stay behind the ball, break up counter attacks and screen the back four. Lampard's career blossomed immediately that Makelele joined Chelsea. It was noticeable in recent seasons his effectiveness and incision had dropped as Makelele made fewer appearances for Chelsea as time caught up with him. By the winter of 2007 the press revealed that Makelele had an arrangement with new Chelsea coach Avram Grant to only play in the very important matches.

In an interview with *Shoot* magazine Owen spoke of his hopes for the 2006 World Cup. 'We are one of the best teams in the world now. There is strength in depth and there are very few weaknesses, if any. The expectation is always high, but I think this group of players can go all the way.'

Four days after their narrow win in Wales England played at Windsor Park against Northern Ireland. The last time Ireland had beaten England at home Charles Lindbergh had flown across the Atlantic and Newcastle had won the title. Northern Ireland were now ranked lower than Rwanda and Gabon. Like Wales they were a side comprised of players from the lower leagues and wannabes. Fired by local rivalry

Owen Hargreaves is one of the finest exponents of dead-ball kicking in Europe. Here he arrows over a corner for Bayern Munich.

© Clevamedia

The world is yours! Owen lifts the Champions League trophy as Bayern Munich beat Valencia on penalties in 2001.

© Clevamedia

'Fashion fades, style is eternal' – Yves Saint Laurent.
Owen at the BBC Sports Personality of the Year Awards, 2006.

For Queen and country…

Above: Owen stands alongside Sol Campbell and Sven-Göran Eriksson to meet Queen Elizabeth II. *© Stewart Turkington/REX Features*

Below: England play France, April 2008. Owen (fifth from left) is one of the two guarding midfield players chosen by new coach, Fabio Capello. *© Clevamedia*

Owen, on the ball for England (*right*), and celebrating after scoring his penalty against Portugal during the 2006 World Cup Quarter Final (*below*).

© Clevamedia

Above: New kids on the block. New signings Owen and Nani Almeida appear at a press conference in China held during the club's far-east tour.

© Sipa Press/REX Features

Below: Owen, making his Euro debut for United against SportingLisbon in November 2007. Despite the close attention of a Lisbon player he sets up another attack.

© Clevamedia

Owen leads the dash to the Champions League final showdown against Chelsea.

© Clevamedia

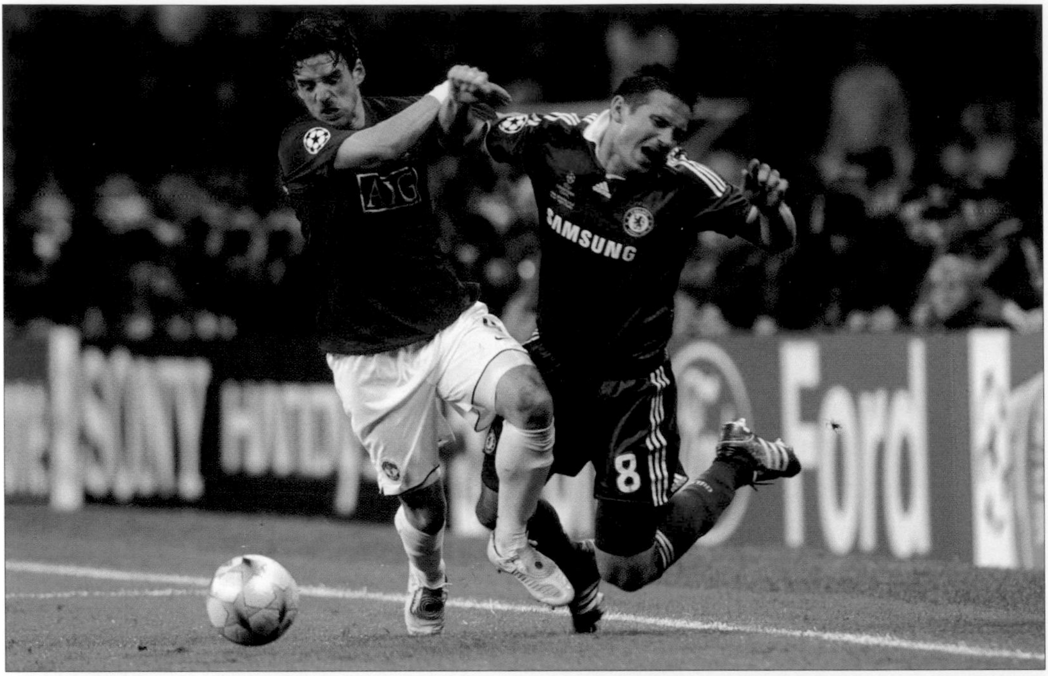

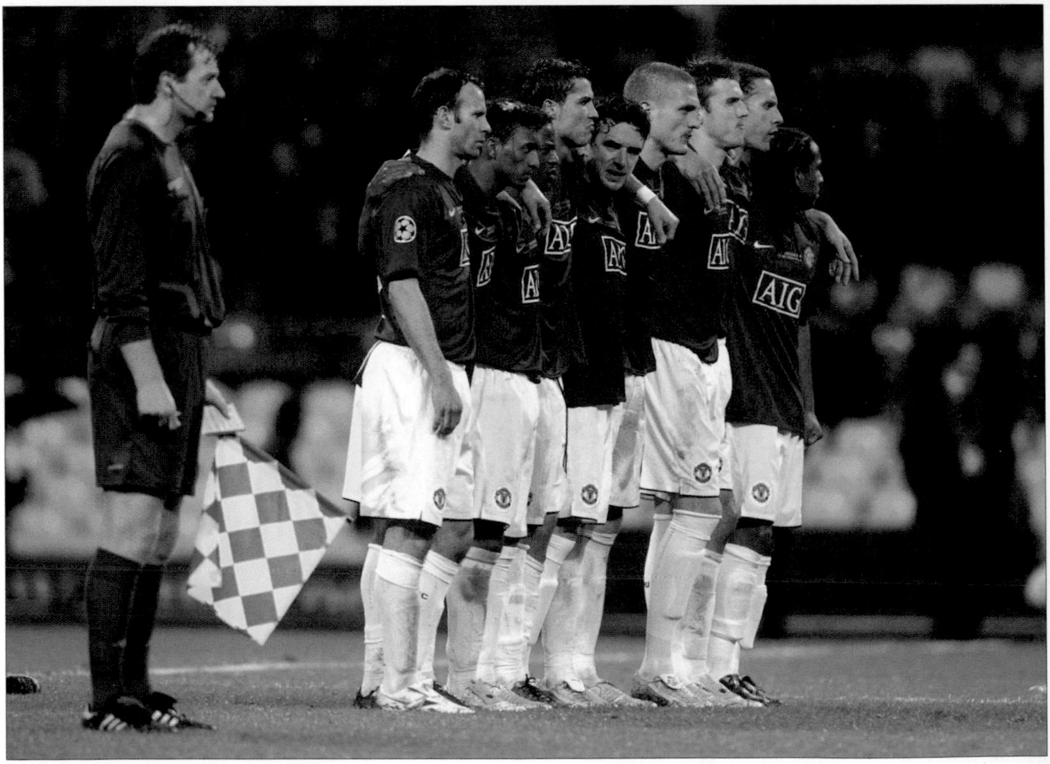

Owen played an important part in helping Manchester United to the most prestigious trophy in European football, the Champions League. He battled hard in midfield with Chelsea star Frank Lampard, before lining up to face the dreaded penalties before coolly slotting home his own spot-kick in front of a global audience of millions. His performance epitomized what it is to be a modern footballing professional.

and a passionate crowd they were an entirely different proposition from the side that had fallen apart in the second half the previous spring.

The only goal of the game was scored by David Healy after 73 minutes. This was enough to severely dent England's qualification hopes. The goal was another unfortunate blunder by keeper Robinson who was badly caught out of position at the near post. The man dubbed the 'King of Killyleagh' was once on Manchester United's books though his first team experience was restricted to just 30 minutes. Healy replaced Ryan Giggs in a 2-0 home win over Ipswich two days before Christmas 2000. Ole Gunnar Solskjaer bagged both goals for United.

United scouts spotted David's goalscoring potential when he played for Downpatrick Academy High School. Sir Alex was unconvinced as he considered him to be too lightweight. Plus he had a fit Ole Gunnar Solskjaer on the bench, the greatest United finisher of recent times.

Healy had a journeyman career in league football at Preston, Leeds and more recently Fulham. This was in marked contrast to his international career where as at the autumn of 2007 he had scored 33 goals. In addition he shattered the record for goals in a European Championship campaign. Healy's average was an amazing 0.55 goals per game in a mediocre side often playing against far superior opposition.

Owen came into the fray, on for Lampard after 80 minutes, but was unable to salvage any pride for his country. Sven had promised that things would improve but they were as bad as ever. The midfield had flopped once again with Gerrard and Lampard unable to create anything in tandem. The conundrum of Steven and Frank was to haunt Sven throughout his tenure with England. Their failure to mesh flummoxed the cream of the game's football brains and Mark Lawrenson. The more Sven tinkered with the DNA of the England midfield the worse it played.

Sven had perserved with the experiment of playing Beckham deep but this failed too. The first signs of the once-golden powers fading were starting to emerge. The jury was still out on him. Some were of the view that even at the height of his powers, the 1999–2000 treble winning season, Becks was only 66 per cent of a great footballer. Now age and injury were slowing him still further as his personal life was replacing his football.

Rooney was an accident waiting to happen, booked for a challenge on ex-United winger Keith Gillespie and continuing his running feud with his captain Beckham. What had gone wrong with the young colossus who looked like he could have won the Euros for England in 2004? Was it the relentless pressure of fame or the fact that he was playing in the wrong formation with the wrong players?

Only Owen played with any true authority. The problem was the limited time he was allowed to display his talents. Also there was the increasing pressure that was building on the Eriksson organisation. Owen left the field again for the second time in three weeks with the bitter taste of defeat in his mouth. The muscles in his face were tensed like a Gladiator returning from the arena. The Irish Kop end taunted the English with cries of 'Easy, easy, easy', whilst at the other end a section of the England support chanted 'Sack the Swede'.

Owen had played all over the world for club and country. He had appeared in hostile stadiums in Spain and Italy but that night for the first time he sensed unrest in the fans. An animosity was emerging from his own supporters against him. This confounded the young Bavarian based midfielder.

Shortly afterwards the *Sun* sent an imitation P45 around to Soho Square to present to Sven. England did qualify for Germany easily enough, but Owen, plagued by injury that season, missed the two victories over Austria and Poland at Old Trafford that secured a pass to the finals.

The BBC had asked Owen to join their commentary team for the Austria game. It would have been interesting to see how he would have made out with the flinty eyed Hansen and Co but once again his fans were denied the chance of seeing him in action. Even if it was to be in a different environment than they were used to seeing him. A heavy cold meant he had to cancel the trip to London and prevented him from appearing on TV.

Much has been made of Owen's accent. One football blog even went as far as creating a pie chart setting out the various influences on it. It merely listed his parents from Bolton and Wales, his Canadian upbringing, his lengthy career in Germany and in recent times his move to Manchester.

Plus there was the exposure to the various dialects, for example the Glaswegian of Fergie and the Swedish of Sven. Plus the Cockney and effected Estuary English vowels of Joe Cole, Frankie Lamps, Rio and the chaps. How this cocktail of accents and argot would have gone down with the 8 million plus viewers would be hard to say. It would have been a decided improvement on the incoherent Beckham and the inane mumblings of John Terry though.

A Lampard penalty after 25 minutes won the Austria match. On the hour Beckham received his marching orders. This was for two bookable offences inside a minute on Andreas Ibertsberger. An historic moment as he became the first English international to be sent off twice. Eriksson quickly threw on Ledley King in the holding role once Beckham had walked. It was obvious that the holding role was here to stay; finding the right player to fill it was the challenge.

Owen could only watch the turgid match from his sofa, in between he was sipping a hot beverage and trying to reduce his temperature. Later that evening the news filtered through that Holland had beaten the Czech Republic in Prague, thus ensuring a place for England in Germany.

Without Owen England beat a shot-shy Poland 2-1 at Old Trafford to win their qualification group. Michael Owen and Lampard with a searing volley scored the goals. Owen only played once more for England before the World Cup. The injuries that disrupted his season for Bayern curtailed his England appearances as Sven tried to regroup and organise his forces for the summer assault on Germany.

One particular game he was sorry to miss out on was the friendly against Argentina which for some reason was played in Geneva. He was just starting to get his fitness back but in view of his long lay-off he opted not to make the trip. It was an exciting game which England won. With only five minutes left England trailed 2-1 but two late goals from Michael Owen won the game and lifted their spirits for the forthcoming World Cup battles.

Owen watched the game from Vienna where he spent the weekend visiting his friend, the Rapid Vienna skipper Steffen Hoffman, who he had known since they had played together in the Bayern youth side. It was a very pleasant interlude for Owen, he had been invited over to the christening of his daughter Sophie-Marie to whom he was godfather.

Sven was playing down England's chances saying that they were just one of a number of countries who had the ability to lift the World Cup. However Owen was bullish on England's chances when he spoke to Sky Sports. 'Definitely, when you look at the squad we have. I have been in the squad ever since 2000–01 and this is definitely the best we have had, in my opinion since that time. The potential is extremely high and the expectation is also extremely high. The players are very confident because we have a great team.'

Owen's versatility was still seen as his greatest asset and there was speculation that he would be Gary Neville's understudy at right back.

Owen's last appearance for England before the World Cup was again at Old Trafford in the sedate 3-1 home victory overt Hungary. Owen was introduced for Jamie Carragher in the second half as the holding player. The score was 0-0 at the time and his arrival prompted a three goal burst. Crouch scored the third and celebrated by showing his weird robotic dance to the world. No gimmicks from Owen though, just solid, thoughtful football.

When he came off the bench he was greeted by some jeers. The backlash that he sensed in the defeat in Ireland started there. He made a rare error when he failed to close down Pal Dardai who went on to score the Hungarian goal.

Ian Wright lambasted Owen on BBC for his error. In an attack Wright went on unfairly to say that Hargreaves was in the squad because 'he knew something about Sven that others did not'. On that basis perhaps the ex-Arsenal striker must have known something about the hierarchy at the BBC because of his frequent appearances as a pundit. The ex-Arsenal striker was later to quit the show in a dispute over policy

Wright's step-son Shaun Wright-Phillips became a

regular in the England squad shortly afterwards and how much of this was down to the relentless promotion of his father cannot be gauged. The breadth of Shaun's odyssey is interesting to review. Suffice to say that the over-priced winger failed to fully establish himself at Chelsea after a staggering £22m move there from Manchester City. The diminutive player was one of the most heavily criticised members of the England squad whose dismal attempt to qualify for Euro 2008 ended in a rocky-horror show. As Oscar Wilde put it 'You would have needed a heart of stone not to have laughed.'

George Cohen, right back in the boys of '66 side, pontificated in the *Sun* that Owen should be dropped from the squad. The debate raged, Tony Woodcock ex-Arsenal and England star sprang to his defence on the BBC Sport website. Tony was a kindred spirit having played in Germany for Cologne. They both shared the same hair style, a tight curly perm.

Despite the jeering Owen was pleased with the Hungary game as he told Sky Sports. 'When Sven put me in central midfield it was great. It is the position I am most accustomed to and I had not played it for England in ages. For the first 15-20 minutes, it took time to get used to it. It is the same position, but it is just a bit different playing with England than it is with Bayern.'

Things hotted up, Sven was caught out by the bizarre fake Sheikh sting set up by a Sunday newspaper. The fallout from this escapade added to the pressure piling up on him. Speculation was rife as to who would be his successor. The name of Steve McClaren was being bandied around. A 7-0 thrashing of his Middlesbrough team by Arsenal did nothing to help his case.

Owen was the player most identified with the Sven era and consequently maligned the most. The Swede's multiple substitutions irritated the hell out of both the fans and media. The Hungary match was Owen's 30th cap but he had started in only seven of those. The last had been back in March 2004 when England had lost their friendly against Sweden in Gothenburg.

Things improved for Owen, Bayern won the double of the DFB Cup and the Bundesliga title. Then came the icing on the cake when it was announced that he had won a place in the 23-man squad to go to the World Cup. He was absolutely delighted at being selected and regarded it as high spot of his career. Sven had thought long and hard about including him, he had flown out to Germany to see Owen play against Stuggart. Owen played also for England 'B' against Belarus in the right back position.

Owen told Sky.sports.com 'Whenever I have been healthy, I have always been picked. So obviously it is something I am looking forward to in the summer. But I have been out, and missed so many games this year. This has probably been one of the most difficult seasons for me, missing so many games. I am starting to feel strong again, and am now looking forward to the coming games and whatever the gaffer decides, he decides.'

Owen attended the Beckham's send-off party on the Sunday night before the squad flew off to Germany. The event was hosted by the couple in a marquee the size of United's pitch, on the lawn of their Hertfordshire mansion. Amongst the elite guests were David Cameron, Sean Combs, Will Young, Elle Mcpherson, Ozzy Osbourne and Ray Winstone. Outside, teams of paparazzi fed like sharks off the whole culture.

Owen sat down to dinner in black tie at a table surmounted by birch trees decorated with silk butterflies which was planted in a bed of white tulips and roses. He nibbled at a grilled-tomato consommé with basil and mozzarella followed by carpaccio and seared tuna with a soy vinaigrette Label Anglaise chicken. For afters there was peanut butter parfait with cherry compote. As he supped coffee and tried to resist the Turkish delight there was the sideshow of Graham Norton hosting the Charity Auction. £50 clicks for Thierry Henry's boots; he wondered idly if they were ones that he wore when he went round David James' in the last World Cup. What about £150 clicks for a weekend at Combs's Hamptons' house?

Robbie Williams put on a 45 minute show. As the diaphanously clad Wags (that word was just being coined) drifted by, Robbie nodded across to Owen. The last time he had seen him was on the training ground in Munich when the Port Vale fan had asked to work out with the Bundesliga giants.

Williams was besotted by a footballer when he grew up in the Potteries, his name was Alan Hudson. The blueprint for the buccaneering 'Mavericks' was exiled in Stoke when his audaciously talented, squandered career at Chelsea came off the rails. Perhaps something in Hargreaves's game reminded him of the doomed Hudson.

That endless summer evening was concluded by James Brown, the Godfather of Soul, performing one of his last shows before he checked out to the great dance floor in the sky.

But Owen had left by then, his mind full of the coming weeks, he was on the cusp of life-changing success. The trick was to avoid the hideous spiral of fame that came with it.

Sven praised Owen when certain sections of the press expressed surprise at his inclusion in the World Cup squad. The Swede told the *Independent*, 'I can understand the reaction in England because the fans never see him play and because of that they do not really have a reason to think about him. He is a better player than he was two years ago in the European Championships or four years ago in the World Cup.'

England's first game of the 2006 World Cup campaign was against Paraguay in Group B on Saturday 10 June. The game was played in the Commerzbank Arena in Frankfurt aka the Waldstadion (stadium in the forest), a ground Owen had played on many times before. They had the perfect start when after just three minutes Carlos Gamarra headed Beckham's perfect free-kick into his own net.

The game kicked off at three in the afternoon and the temperatures touched 95 degrees. As had been the case in Japan England found it hard to acclimatise to the conditions and failed to kick on. The longer the game went on the more England wilted. The age old problem of England football teams was the failure to kill opponents off. Owen's great friend Roque Santa Cruz, the star striker for Paraguay and the new hero at Blackburn, expressed the view that the only way England would win the tournament was if it rained!

Eight minutes from time, Owen, wearing the number 16 squad shirt, came on to a storm of booing to replace Joe Cole. The reasons for this were twofold. The England fans sweltering in the baking heat were frustrated by their side's inability to finish off their functional South American opponents. Joe Cole was one of the most popular England players of recent years. His undoubted ability, hard work and likeable personality endeared him to the fans. Plus he was one of the few players with the bravado capable of winning a match on his own. To replace him with a defensive midfielder seemed a soft option to them. It smacked to them of ultra-defensiveness and desperation. (Strange to observe that Jose Mourinho had built his glittering career and formidable reputation on this very principal of hanging on to a lead, however slender. Yet he was the most popular choice of the fans in recent years to manage England.)

Owen was now the focal target of the boo boys. Public enemy number one. Crouch had received similar treatment in the Poland match. In his autobiography Crouch recounted his feelings at the time. 'I felt terrible. I knew up in the stands it would be killing my mum and dad. I was coming on the pitch to play for England, at home, for my third cap, in front of friends and family, and I was being booed by our own fans. So this was what it was like to be playing for England, in England?'

Sir Alex Ferguson had complained that in the 21st century we were living in a 'mocking culture'. Owen's future boss put part of the blame on reality television shows like *Strictly Come Dancing*. In the week of England's disastrous exit from Euro 2008 virtually every member of the squad was booed on Premiership grounds by disdainful fans, irate at their performance.

Former England legend John Barnes was voted off *Strictly Come Dancing* the same day. Barnes was one of the most skilful players ever produced by this country with the quickest feet and best balance of his generation. Yet for Saturday night prime-time entertainment this fine man was judged by so called 'experts' for his attempts to master complex dance steps.

Barnes himself received terrible abuse during his England career. This was motivated by racism – the National Front even paid for some members to travel the globe and abuse him. John had the last laugh though, scoring one of the greatest goals in England's history in the Maracana stadium against Brazil. The National Front members even tried to discredit it by saying it had been scored by a coloured player and did not count.

Owen was also on the receiving end of this Neanderthal bile from some of the travelling England fans because to many of them he was perceived as being German. He told Sky Sports, 'What did I think of the jeers when I came on? I think it is inevitable. I knew that was inevitable in the sense of myself playing in Munich. Obviously, my background is very different from all the other players. I knew that the jeering was eventually going to happen. I think for six, seven or eight months I had not played a game for England at all and had gone from the mind of the fans. In all honesty, it's the same in Germany; they want to see people who play in Germany and not abroad. From my angle I was not really surprised. Can I win the fans over at the world Cup? I hope so.'

So Owen's international career was in the balance at that moment. There was a lot of activity on the message boards about him, morons comparing him to Osama Bin Laden or the new Chris Waddle; others saw a chance to deplore the standards of the Bundesliga.

The comics Baddiel and Skinner (the description is used in the same context as the application of the word 'fans' is to the people who booed Owen in an England shirt) found Hargreaves an easy target for their sulphurous barbs. An advert for their humour free pod-cast asked what the reason was for Owen Hargreaves being in the squad?

Once again Sven spoke up for him, his natural football instincts told him that there was staying power in Owen Hargreaves. The England coach told *The Guardian* after the match, 'You could see today why Owen is so important to us. He wins the ball, plays it simple and gives more freedom to Lampard and Gerrard. The few minutes he was on the pitch Owen showed his usefulness to the England team. We will need him again.'

The Guardian's match report rated his performance highly, talking up his snappy challenges when Paraguay threatened and describing him as 'Quite simply England's best defensive midfielder. Not exactly an unimportant position in modern football, and the only man in the squad capable of playing the role in its broadest sense.'

The *Sun* had a different view of Owen at that stage and made a comment about him 'scurrying back and forth trying to look useful'. Usual tabloid attacks. In a guide to 'Watching England play in the World Cup in the pub' Hargreaves was named as the only English player it was 'ok to boo'.

Owen did not feature in England's next game, a 2-0 victory over Trinidad and Tobago, on a horribly muggy evening in Nuremberg. Late goals from Crouch and Gerrard helped England to their second successive victory in the group. It was a facile victory over the smallest nation ever to qualify for the World Cup finals but enough to earn them a place in the last sixteen.

Then it was onto the final group game against Sweden in Cologne. The match was played at the Rhein Energie Stadion reconstructed on the site of the old Mungersdorfer stadium where Woodcock had played. England had not beaten Sweden for 38 years. Owen was given a rare start.

Both Lampard and Gerrard had picked up bookings and Sven was anxious to avoid any suspensions.

The day before the game Owen spoke to Sky Sports at the press conference. Very relaxed, quiet and deferential, he was wearing that stripey Umbro polo shirt with the England badge. 'I did not know it was two years since I last started. It has been a while. I am told it was in Sweden and I think I got man of the match in that one. Maybe it's a good omen. Anytime you get an opportunity – especially in a tournament like this – to present yourself and help your team to win is brilliant and something you dream of as a footballer. It is important to take your chances and that is what I want to do. I feel I am now a much better player than I was four years ago so I feel confident going into the Sweden game.'

This turned out to be prophetic because Owen turned in a stunning performance in a highly exciting 2-2 draw. The match started with a blow for England when Michael Owen twisted his knee and sustained a cruciate ligament injury which nearly wrecked his career. Sven was royally gob-smacked.

Owen Hargreaves played heroically as Sweden probed the English defence. His pace and athleticism, coupled with some robust challenges broke up numerous attacks from the Scandinavians clad in yellow and blue. Joe Cole put England ahead after 34 minutes with the best goal of his England career and some would argue the best of the tournament. Niclas Alexandersson's headed clearance fell just right for him and Cole chested the ball down before exploding home a tremendous shot from over 30 yards. It soared and dipped past goalkeeper Andreas Isaksson. The spectacular goal was reminiscent of Sir Bobby Charlton in his heyday and is now a staple of all compilations of clips of England matches. It was an irresistible finish, the undisputed highlight of England's campaign, and should have set them up for a famous victory.

Sweden had other ideas and equalised six minutes into the second half. Tobias Linderoth floated over a corner and ex-Villa defender Marcus Allback soared to beat centre backs Terry and Ferdinand to the ball. The giant Swede's header floated over the flat-footed Robinson for the equaliser. Owen was on the 18 yard line and could do nothing to stop the goal.

Panic set in, as the Swedes pressurized the England back four in a state of paranoia about set pieces. Jamie Carragher appeared to handle the next corner earned by Sweden but the referee did not spot it. An incident that incensed Freddie Ljungberg who protested bitterly to the referee. Paul Robinson kept England in it when he turned Henrik Larsson's deflected header against the bar and Owen helped clear England's lines.

Rio Ferdinand limped off to be replaced by the old warrior Sol Campbell, Sweden pushed up as England conceded the midfield. This meant Owen came into his own as the rest of the defence looked decidedly vulnerable against the high ball. An increasingly jittery Terry, without the safety net of Rio to cover his lack of pace, was relying even more on Owen to shield him as Sweden began a massive frontal assault. Both Campbell and Jamie Carragher lacked mobility, the whole patchwork quilt was about to fall apart.

England's failure to defend set pieces was blatantly apparent. Another corner by the blue and golds was flicked on by Lukic and the Swedish skipper Olof Mellborg hooked against the bar. Owen dropped back even deeper.

Rooney so palpably unfit was replaced by Gerrard; Wayne showed his displeasure by trashing the England dug-out. With Michael Owen out of the tournament England were shorn of their first choice strike partnership.

With Owen Hargreaves in such commanding form Steven Gerrard was given a licence to roam and put England back in front five minutes from time. The hyper-active Joe Cole carved out the chance with another piece of sorcery. Another platform for victory but as Owen observed in his post match analysis Sweden moved up a gear.

Facing possible elimination, they threw everything forward and were rewarded with a late, late equaliser. It was created by the oldest trick of all, a long throw into the England box. The ball bounced over Sol Campbell's head, Terry stood transfixed as did Robinson. The old fox, ex-Celtic legend, Henrik Larsson reacted quickest and jabbed it home with his right foot. Lethal finisher Larsson had a remarkable late autumn to his career. After terrorising Arsenal in the Champions League final for Barcelona he went home to Helsingborgs to wind down his goal-drenched career. Sir Alex called him back to the big time though for his cold-blooded guile and experience. Henrik enjoyed a highly successful short loan spell at Old Trafford which contributed to their reclamation of the Premiership title.

Only Cole and Owen shone for England, both received star ratings of 8 in the *Sun*. The Hargreaves rating was as follows. 'Magnificent show in his first start in two years. Followed his job description, he won tackles, moved the ball on and added security to the team. Hard to leave him out now'.

For the first time in the press Owen was compared to Nobby Stiles. Another United legend and only the second Englishman from Old Trafford to win a World Cup winners medal. Stiles was one of the most ferocious tacklers in the history of the game who specialized in short passes to his team-mates. Stiles wore contact lenses when he played and was nortiously short sighted. The most famous game Stiles played was in the 1966 World Cup semi-final when his mind-boggling tackling completely obliterated the star of the competition, up to then, Eusebio. Nobby was the pro-type holding midfielder. In those days it was seen primarily as a stopper and a lot of the role involved very close man marking.

Stiles was a great exponent of this type of play. Chelsea captain Ron Harris was another player who was an intimidating man-marker. The tackling was much harder in those days, purists and fans of a certain age would argue. There was a famous story about George Best when he was at the height of his fame playing for Manchester United. A famous fashion chain had signed George up and as part of their advertising campaign they wanted some action shots of George in a red shirt. A photographer was detailed to take some pictures of George in action against Chelsea at Old Trafford. The picture editor was displeased as his photo-spread contained the bullet headed Harris in every one! So tight was Harris's marking of the Belfast Boy.

Owen preferred a different approach, his tactics relying more on reading the game and making timely interceptions. Not that he shirked tackles in the torrid second half as Larsson and his chums threatened to overwhelm England. They gleaned a point though which was enough to secure top spot in Group B and pitch them against Ecuador. Owen's dreams of World Cup glory were about to come true.

Chapter Nine
Lambs for Lions

'Owen Hargreaves has changed a lot in a very positive direction. His game is much more effective now and he has become a vital member of the team'
Karl-Heinz Rummenigge

'For somebody like Owen Hargreaves to get the criticism he has had has been amazingly unjust. To play a holding role like he did, I thought he was superb. I think he put a lot of fingers up to people to say "here I am".'
Mark Wright

After the Sweden game the praise was heaped on Owen about giving 100 per cent in every game and every position. The cracks about him being included in the party because he was a fluent German speaker and could help his team-mates order drinks in the Baden-Baden cafes had now stopped.

Hargeaves had done enough to suggest to Sven that he was the player for the important holding midfield role.

Owen was telling the media that there was a great sense of camaraderie and a tremendous atmosphere in the England squad following their qualification from the group. The longer they were in the competition the more the players got to know each other.

So Owen headed down the autobahn to Stuttgart to play Ecuador. The tabloids cranked up the hype. Rooney appeared in the *Sun* with his body painted in a St George's flag dripping with blood. His England buddies preferred the one the *News of the World* ran with Sophie Anderton in a similar pose.

Owen told Sky Sports in the build up to the game, 'I think it was a great opportunity especially in the World Cup to play and I am very happy to get the opportunity. I think every team that's made it this far can win it. It is going to be very difficult obviously. So far we have had three steps from seven to be in the final. Ecuador will be the fourth step and hopefully we can be very positive and win that game as well.'

England successfully negotiated the fourth step with an uninspiring solitary goal victory over Ecuador in the Gottlieb Daimler Stadion. Owen started at right back in place of Jamie Carragher with Michael Carrick slotting into the midfield holding role. Once again England struggled in the heat. The game kicked off at 5pm but at times the temperature reached 42 degrees C. The crowd was 52,000, two thirds of which were hardcore England fans.

World Cup minnows Ecuador had been battered 3-0 by Germany in the last of their group matches but nearly took a shock early lead. Terry, mediocre at best throughout the competition, made a hash of a back header which put in Carlos Tenorio for a gilt-edged chance. Strikers at that level usually convert those chances with impudence but he dithered and Ashley Cole deflected the chance onto the bar.

That was about it for the first half. Owen had an uncertain opening and was caught out of position on a couple of occasions. Near half-time he clashed with Augustin Delgado and came off second best. They both went for the same ball; Delgado missed it and accidentally clattered Owen, studding his shin and knee. The Bayern man went down as if clipped by Ricky Hatton and was taken to the sidelines for treatment. Sven was one of the first on the scene and ordered ice packs as immediate treatment. This went on throughout the interval but at least he missed the boos and whistles of the England fans annoyed at their team's failure to break down Ecuador.

Owen was luckily able to play the entire second half of the game. At first it was feared that he would be ruled out of the World Cup as he had been against Argentina in Japan. Beckham had scored the winner that day from a penalty and he came up with the winner again that day. This time it was one of his specialist free-kicks that bent over the wall and low into the far corner of the net.

It was enough to beat the team ranked 39th in the world and put England through to the last eight. This was the third consecutive major tournament that they had reached that far under Eriksson's command.

Beckham became the first England player to score in three World Cups; he was feeling the strain though. The England captain was physically sick a few moments before he struck with his free-kick.

The ploy of using Carrick behind the feeble pair Lampard and Gerrard failed, leaving Rooney marooned up front with just his excessive volatility for company. Owen had been missed in his holding role, but he was just glad to start for his country in any position. Carrick fed few passes through from the back as Robinson went route one with huge punts up the field.

Owen spoke to Sky Sports.com about the game: 'Becks's set pieces are his strengths. It was a great free-kick against Ecuador and it won us the game. He did his job. It takes time to find your gauge, especially when it is so humid, but David got his sights right when it really mattered. It is just about winning. So far we have won our games. The football will come in time.'

Owen was delighted to have played 90 minutes again for his country and progressed so far. The feeling amongst the media circus was that England had not yet hit form and the jury was still out on Sven. This was his last tournament for England. No one was quite sure how he had done it or what his game plan was.

Now it was a trip to Gelsenkirchen and a game against Portugal in the Veltins Arena, home of Schalke 04. A new state of the art stadium had been built for £131m with a huge cubic video, retractable roof and sliding pitch. When Mourinho's Porto had won the Champions League there it produced the memorable quote from a laconic Spanish journalist about the Special One's 'Anti-football being as cold and flat as Gelsenkirchen'.

It was not cold the night Sven took on 'Big Phil' Scolari's team, the third successive time he had crossed swords with him at that stage. Owen was desperate to turn the tables on them and book a place in the World Cup semi-final. The week had passed quickly and on the Monday night the team had a tasty barbecue with their families. Owen spent a fair amount of time in the gym using the exercise bike and working out on the weights.

All that hard work paid off, as he put in a wonderful

performance to be named as the England man of the match. Owen even scored a penalty in the mandatory shoot out when the game ended scoreless after extra time. The problem was, none of his colleagues managed to score from theirs and once again England crashed out on penalties in a major competition.

The 2004 Euro battle between the sides had been easily the best match of the tournament. It ended in a nailbiting 2-2 after extra time followed by the heart-stopping marathon penalty shoot out. The 2006 version hinged on the expulsion of Rooney. This came after an hour following a flare up involving the Chelsea defender Ricardo Carvalho and Wayne's United team-mate Ronaldo. The Portuguese players had set up an ambush which the England striker had naively walked into. Referee Horacio Elizondo showed him a straight red card and he walked.

England played for another hour with 10 men and held out till the shoot out. Owen was the dominant England player throughout the match. A hard man is good to find! Henry Winter of the *Daily Telegraph*, probably second only to Brian Glanville as the finest football writer this country has produced, wrote of Hargreaves's performance as follows: 'Comfortably the most impressive individual on the pitch. A rapid-response unit to Portuguese threats, Hargreaves unleashed tackle after tackle. Here was a two hour shift that embedded Hargreaves in the hearts of England supporters.'

Imagine how Owen must have felt when he realized that the England fans were chanting in the game, 'There's only one Owen Hargreaves.' Owen claimed that he had not heard his name being chanted as he was focusing on the game.

England's near hero coolly tucked his penalty away but

Lampard, Gerrard and Carragher all missed from the spot. The Portuguese goalkeeper Ricardo was the hero again, saving all the kicks except Owen's textbook conversion. Helder Postiga, Simao Sabrossa and Cristiano Ronaldo beat Robinson with their attempts to wrap it up at 3-1. It was the conclusion of England's hopes.

So that was it, no World Cup for another four years.

The FIFA Technical Study Group panel awarded Owen the man of the match. Their press release covering the award read as follows: 'Hargreaves served the team superbly throughout, with great positioning and covering tackles. Many times he also threatened the opponent's goal breaking from midfield. His play was at a constant high level.'

The *Daily Telegraph* and a host of newspapers gave him similar awards. Dan Freedman in his book *Kick off* was delighted with Owen's display. 'I was so happy for Owen when everything turned around for him at the World Cup in Germany. In the quarter-final against Portugal, when we went down to ten men, he was fantastic. He took responsibility and did the running of three people. He scored the only goal and was FIFA man of the match. Suddenly he was a wanted man by the press, and people around the world could see what a player he was.'

Dan was right about Hargreaves' fame spreading. Previously the only political reference to Owen was when the *Sun* compared him to John Prescott. This was at the time of the height of the abuse they were heaping at him. The punch line was that like Prescott he managed to stay in an elite group without anyone knowing what it was he actually did.

You know you have really made it when the Prime Minister talks about you. Tony Blair named David Miliband as the 'Cabinet's Wayne Rooney' and then compared Tessa

Jowell to Owen Hargreaves. The analogy was that they both received an inordinate share of undeserved flak. Way to go Tony!

The papers fell over themselves appeasing Owen; they had a lot to make up for. The *Telegraph* said that one of the pluses in Sven's five-year reign was that he was vindicated over his backing of Owen Hargreaves. The *Sun* who had compared him to a 'mass murderer' led the apologists.

For Owen it had been the most amazing year of his career. England's scandalous exit was an anti-climax but he had left Portugal as arguably the future of English football and with all his supposed competitors reeling in their tracks. After all he was the only Englishman to turn up and play.

In a poll on the official website of the English Football Association Owen was voted the best English player of the 2006 World Cup. In excess of 35,000 fans, approximately the number of England fans present in Gelsenkirchen, voted in the poll. Owen scooped a quarter of the votes romping home well in front of ex-Hammers Rio and Joe Cole.

Owen was delighted to receive the award although his main ethic in football, drummed into him at the Bayern finishing school, was that football was a team game. If one made it they all made it. He spoke of his feelings to the FA website. 'Anytime you can have the public's support is great. Obviously before the World Cup I got a taste of the other side but it is far better to be on the positive side of it.'

Now it was time to relax and the combative midfielder headed off with Janelle to Dubai. He had been captivated by the place when he had stayed there with the England squad prior to the 2002 World Cup and on subsequent visits when Bayern pitched their training camp in the desert state. Relaxing on Jumeriah Beach he would stare out into the

Gulf reflecting on how his fortunes had taken an upswing and what a cruel game football was.

Whilst on holiday some England fans approached Owen in his hotel and he told the FA website what happened next: 'They came up to me and thanked me for working so hard. It was an incredible thing. They just said "thank you", which is the best thing you can really say to someone.'

Then it was back to Munich before flying onto Canada to visit family and a spot of golf.

Steve McClaren, Sven's back-up man, was appointed as his successor. To many fans he was not the solution but part of the disease. Critics hinted that he was the fifth choice for the job. The term 'poisoned chalice' has become a cliché synomous with anyone taking the England job. With each fresh appointment though the job got harder as the pressure built. A crucial error was made in the selection process; the FA should have gone for a strong personality who had managed internationally before. Scolari, the scourge of Sven, was a firm favourite but the timing of the approach was bungled. Guus Hiddink, the manager of Russia, would have been an ideal choice as England were to find out to their cost. Hiddink was too clever to ever take the job; he valued the protection of his private life and the privacy of his loved ones too much to risk it.

Owen refused to accept that England lacked passion in the World Cup and scornfully explained to the *Times*, 'There would be something wrong if we needed Sven to instil passion in us before a World Cup quarter-final. The passion was there, and the ability, so that's why it was frustrating that we never hit our stride. Beyond the fact that it is such a fine line between success and failure I cannot put my finger on the reason.'

The technocrat McClaren's reign started impressively but the tide of hope and expectancy was soon to crash onto the beach. Terry Venables was appointed as McClaren's number two, a bulwark against the press was his main task. One of the few shrewd moves the ex-United number two made. Venables was immensely popular with the public and had accumulated a lot of goodwill through his highly successful stint as England coach from 1993–96. In addition to this his high profile roller coaster career as a player and manager gave him vast experience and huge knowledge of the game. For whatever reason, the McClaren regime failed to harness Venables's talents to improve England's dull image or their form on the playing field.

Owen won the Man of the Match for the second game in succession when he starred in the 4-0 dismantling of Greece on the 18 August. It seemed inconceivable that a team as poor as Greece had been European champions two years previously. Owen played in the number seven shirt vacated by the former captain Beckham. McClaren announced to the press that he wanted to take the team in a different direction when he dropped the then Real Madrid star from the squad.

What direction the bizarre appointment of John Terry as captain led England into is open to conjecture. McClaren tried to show the world who was boss by dropping Becks, just as Bobby Robson had ditched Kevin Keegan back in 1982. Both McClaren and Jose Mourinho had great faith in Terry and Lampard as their key players. However as time went by neither player was able to take England or Chelsea to the higher level the huge expectations demanded of them and both managers paid the ultimate price.

To feed the illusion Terry and Lampard both scored in the defeat of Greece, Crouch rattling in the other two. It was to be a false dawn. New manager, new captain but the same old pattern of play and ego-besotted selections.

The Abramovich factor cannot be dismissed at this stage. Abramovich's billions had meant Terry and Lampard had been surrounded at Stamford Bridge by world class players who had made them both appear to be better talents than they were. The fawning media bandwagon fuelled by Mourinho's hogwash and hyperbole, vigorously promoted by writers like Winter and pundits like Hansen, were instrumental in landing Terry the most prestigious post in the playing game. A task he was not up to mentally or even physically.

Steven Gerrard was Terry's nearest challenger but throughout McClaren's rocky tenure the Liverpool star's England form stuttered. Compared to players like Kaka or even the young Arsenal hot-shot Fabregas, Stevie G's style looked antiquated and lacking vision. The last really impressive international performance by him had been on Owen's home ground against Germany in the 5-1 mauling.

Owen missed the ostracised Beckham around the dressing room. Ever since the young waif had first played for England at White Hart Lane his boyhood idol had been around. Now it was different.

If McClaren had really wanted to take England in another direction he would have made Owen captain. He had the European experience and was a fitter, better player than the present incumbent without a blemish on his character.

Owen emphatically admitted to Sky Sports that he was determined to be a regular under McClaren: 'With the new manager we all know very well things will be different. There are new faces in the camp too, not only players, and the coaching staff will all have their own philosophy on how they want to train us. Everyone controls their own situation. Steve McClaren said that to us today, that every player in the squad today has the opportunity to prove himself and keep his England shirt.'

Next on the agenda were two Euro 2008 qualifying games in early September. The first was against the part-timers of Andorra, the weakest side in the group. They were put to the sword 5-0 at Old Trafford in a game watched by 56,000. Owen had another sterling game breaking up the Andorrans' infrequent attacks and driving England forward.

Another strength that would have made Owen an ideal captain is his linguistic skills. Frustrated at their inability to retain possession for any length of time they started to put some foul tackles in. Owen was quick to remonstrate with the Austrian referee in fluent German.

Crouch scored two more goals, giving him a total of 10 goals in his last nine games, Gerrard and Defoe (2) shared the others. Owen could have scored his first England goal but his 30th minute free-kick crashed against the centre of the crossbar. McClaren had got off to a flying start with nine goals scored and none conceded. Terry was comparing Owen to his Blues team-mate Makelele and telling the press how well Hargreaves had slotted into the set-up.

Owen faced a sterner test four days later when England travelled to Skopje to play the more resilient Macedonia. Owen was telling the media that he wanted to win Euro 2008 in Austria and Switzerland. Crouch scored the only goal of the game a minute after the break when he gleefully whipped in a fine overhead kick that went in off the bar.

That was the last game that Owen played for England for six months. Things had never looked brighter for him in the England set up. The top Premiership clubs had been jostling for his services but the link with Manchester United was now apparent. His former England boss Sven was still singing his praises to the media and told Sky Sports. 'I always thought that he would become a great player. I am happy for him now that all the biggest clubs in Europe want him. People used to criticise him but I always believed in him.'

McClaren had him in his plans for the midfield holding role, his favourite position. Then a few days later he shattered his left leg in the Bundesliga match against Arminia Bielefeld.

England effectively blew their chances of qualifying for the Euros in the two games played in October 2006 against Macedonia and Croatia. The Macedonia game was played at Old Trafford and ended scoreless. In Thucydides' *History of the Peloponnesian War* the Macedonian army featured strongly. The rearguard of the 2006 expeditionary force put up a similarly heroic performance.

It was a disgraceful performance by McClaren's men against a side ranked 51st in the world. For long periods England were outplayed.The clearest chance came after 85 minutes when the anaemic Gerrard's shot crashed back off the bar with the Macedonian goalkeeper Nikoloski beaten. The Crouch and Rooney partnership had little chemistry and could only fire blanks. Much pressure was heaped on Crouch's gangly shoulders as Rooney's post-adolescent angst got the better of him yet again. It was the midfield that was the most disappointing area of the team though with Lampard, who appeared to be coasting to say the least.

The Chelsea player was sucking up the play and unbalancing the already cumbersome strike partnership of Crouch and Rooney. Not only that but Gerrard's talent was again being negated. The problem was that other players had to adapt to play with him, never Lampard. The beauty of a player like Hargreaves was that he could dovetail around the defence and adjust his style for the midfield accordingly. Carrick played in his berth against Macedonia. The threat of their attack was negligible so his defensive duties were reduced to a minimum but little was created going forward. Futile short passing and wayward rectangular crosses.

If the loss of two points to Macedonia was a jarring setback then the defeat in Croatia was a full blown disaster. Croatia were the dark horses of the group, they had not lost a competitive home match for twelve years and were desperate to beat England.

The game ended in a bitter 2-0 defeat. Eduardo, later to join Arsenal, put them ahead on the hour with a neat header which left Terry flatfooted. It was the second goal though, 20 minutes from time, that was the killer. Gary Neville, who had missed a simple chance against Macedonia, tried a back pass to Paul Robinson which bobbled badly on the pitch. Robinson 'air-kicked' the ball and it rolled gently into the net. It was the joke goal to end all goals, sure to feature on every compilation DVD of bloomers for years to come. The odds of two extreme goalkeeping errors both being made in the two Croatia ties must have been extremely high.

The press wrote up Robinson's howler as the main reason for England's failure. The *Sun* had the most amusing headline of them all. 'It's down to you misses Robinson.' A subtle play on the old Simon and Garfunkel 60s hit 'Mrs Robinson'.

The point was McClaren's side suffered their first defeat at the hands of a far superior side, technically and tactically. They were managed by the ex-West Ham and Everton defender Slaven Billic, an intelligent character with a keen sense of humour. Croatia were a team of craftsman, all of them comfortable on the ball. The problem was that the media was so parochial that to a large extent great football nations like Croatia were ignored. As well as that, myths like only 'Iron Curtain' countries took the Euros seriously were pumped out.

Apart from Owen two others from the midfield were missing, the suspended Gerrard and Joe Cole who had picked up a bad injury on Chelsea's American tour. McClaren's 3-5-2 formation misfired badly, the three central midfielders Lampard, Carrick and Scott Parker, (making his first start), were obliterated. Parker, another of the nouveau riche Chelsea impulse buys was hailed in certain parts of the media as a doppelganger for Owen but failed to live up to expectations and was subsequently transferred to Newcastle and then West Ham. Lampard's reputation continued to curdle.

Hargreaves was missed the most; there was no defensive ballast as the tricky Croatia forwards at times dazzled the frail England back four. Ashley Cole and Neville were unable to push forward to supply Rooney and Crouch who again disappointed.

Predrag Zukina of the Zagreb daily paper *Jutarnji List* summed up things. 'We analysed your match against Macedonia and sometimes it seems as though your players are almost afraid. It looked as though, even against a team like that, you were concentrating on your defence and not attacking like you should.'

That was the last of the qualifying games until the spring of 2007. The performance of the England midfield in those two matches was very poor.

England without Owen played one more game in 2006, a 1-1 draw with Holland in Amsterdam. It was an improvement on the performances in October but the jury was still very much out on McClaren. It was going to be a hard winter in 2007 with no prospect of a sunny summer in 2008.

Meanwhile Owen fought hard to get fit. In January 2007 he received another marvellous accolade, being named as the official Nationwide England Player of the year for 2006. Thirty-three players had pulled on the shirt with the three lions badge in 2006 but it was the 1111th player that had been selected for his country that won it.

It was a landslide victory for Owen as he swept the poll. The continental style midfielder received nearly 30 per cent of the votes with Steven Gerrard second and Crouch a poor third. Lampard, who had won it the two previous years, was not even on the radar, neither was the man chosen as captain. You could not fool the punters, the guys that stood in the rain, spending their last Euro, risking batons and abuse; they would always choose Kelly Brook over Ugly Betty.

Owen was thrilled to bits to win this award because it was done by the real England fans that travelled the world to support their country. To win the hearts of them, many whom for whatever reason had a somewhat distorted vision of him to begin with, was a fantastic achievement. Owen has already won the highest honour a European player can achieve by attaining a Champions League medal. This is the jewel in the crown to go alongside the booty he plundered as Bayern blitzkrieged the Bundesliga. After winning more medals in Germany than Field Marshall Rommel Owen looks set to add to this haul with United. Even if he were to, perish the thought, scoop a World Cup medal in South Africa in 2010 nothing could really top this honour. Owen had done what the firebird had done, re-ascend in flames. The achievement was simply magnificent, whilst Lampard buckled and whined under the pressure Owen, so thoroughly professional in everything he did, just got on with it.

(Who can forget the self-pitying Lampard publicly airing his grievances and complaints to the *Evening Standard*: 'People have been on my back. I'm upset because I worked my socks off. I think I deserve a little bit of respect'. That's funny Frank because Owen earned his. That was the one thing that Abramovich could not buy, respect.) In the words of George Best's legendary fan letter to fellow maverick Alan Hudson 'He stuffed their words down their throats where it mattered – on the pitch'

Owen told the Football Association's official website of his delight at winning the award: 'Any time you can receive the support of the fans is very special. I am very nearly ready to start playing again and hopefully I will be back playing for England again soon. I have got my eyes on the big qualifiers in March.'

England had one more game before the visit to Tel-Aviv and that was a friendly against Spain which they lost 0-1. Ben Foster and Joey Barton won their first caps.

Steve McClaren talked to Sky Sports about what the absence of Hargreaves meant to the England team who had now gone four games without a win since his broken leg. 'The majority of big teams have someone in the middle who gets it all together. Roy Keane did it when I was at Manchester United. They are the ones who do all the unseen work and provide the glue that allows other players to go out and express themselves in a more effective way. We have seen Gerrard, Lampard and Hargreaves all play together so few times. In the games he did play Owen gave Frank and Steven more freedom to play.'

Owen was flattered by McClaren's comparison of him to the legendary Red Devils midfielder Keane. Sir Alex Ferguson concurred with the England coach's assessment. The United boss was bestowing his blessing on Owen as he intensified efforts to bring him to Old Trafford as the heir apparent to Keane. The Bayern Munich man told the *Sun*, 'It is important to win the ball in the middle of the park and try and get it forward in any game you play. I think I have shown I can do that. But although I play the same position as Roy Keane did we are very different. He had his qualities and I have mine.'

England only drew 0-0 against a particularly obstinate Israel in the Ran Gan Stadium, to make it five games without a win. That was the problem, McClaren failed to win the ones that mattered. The result was cordially detested by media and public. England played with the finesse of a cement mixer. Owen who had been telling the media all week how anxious he was to play for England did well enough. Even he though could not help England obtain the win they so desperately required. Points were being frittered away and that was making the task of qualifying increasingly harder.

Owen talked to Sky Sports about the draw: 'It was disappointing that we did not get the result we expected. The first 10 minutes Israel looked quite strong and came at us, but after that we controlled the game and could not put away the chances we had and it is disappointing and frustrating we could not score a goal.'

The frustration in his voice was very discernable; they had trained and prepared well for the game but at the end of the day it was not enough. Group E was turning into the group of death. The tabloids were turning the knife already dubbing McClaren 'McDonut' and making reference to the fans' chants of 'You don't know what you are doing'.

Andorra away was the next chapter in the unfolding horror story. The game was played on a stormy night in Espanyol's Olympic Stadium near Barcelona. At half-time the score was 0-0 and the travelling army of 15,000 sheltering under their saturated union jacks unleashed a torrent of abuse as fierce as the unrelenting downpour. There was an old Tommy Docherty quip about the game being so bad 'even the subs booed'. None of the England subs went that far to vent their frustration at their colleagues but it was noticeable that a couple of them actually ran towards the tunnel not just to get out of the blinding rain.

The second half was nearly as bad but England scored three times as Andorra, the football equivalent of a park team, tired. Gerrard knocked in a couple and in the dying seconds substitute David Nugent, fresh out of the Championship league, walked in the third. Unconvincing was not quite strong enough for it.

Owen only received a 4/10 rating in the *Sun* which brought his sequence of 'Man of the Matches' to a grinding halt. The beef was that his short passing game did not look like opening up the packed Andorran defence. His stats belied the rating though with a 91 per cent pass completion score and six tackles won. Elsewhere Rooney amassed a grand score of 3, the same as Aaron Lennon.

Booked in the match, Owen told the *Sun* that the Portuguese referee Bruno Paixao had failed to give the England side adequate protection. 'We kept our cool despite some of the tackles they put in and did the job we needed. Some of the challenges were shocking and I do not think the referee protected the players enough, and I told him so numerous times. They did not really come to play. People could have got injured. It is good that we got the job done and kept a clean sheet.'

The coach of Andorra, David Rodrigo believed England were by no means certain to qualify from Group E, maintaining that they would have to win in Russia to be certain.

That was the last game Owen played for England in 2007. He was now 26 years and 65 days old. It was 5 years and 225 days since he had made his debut against Holland. In that time he had played for England 39 times, starting 15 times and being substitute on 24 occasions. The number of full games he had played in was a dozen. Owen had been replaced only three times. Injuries and the recurrence of tendonitis in his knees curtailed his appearances under the short-lived reign of McClaren.

In June England won 3-0 against Estonia in Tallinn to revive hopes of a place in the Euros. Michael Owen scored his first international goal for a year. Beckham had been recalled to the squad.

The pressure hotted up in September as England had two qualifying home games against Israel and Russia in the newly revamped Wembley Stadium. Both fixtures finished in 3-0 wins to England. A thigh injury ruled Owen out of the games. To add to McClaren's dilemmas Hargreaves had been suffering from tendonitis which had restricted his training and delayed his much feted debut for his new team Manchester United. On the Tuesday, his first day's training at Arsenal's London Colney training complex, Hargreaves was restricted to just gym work. On the Wednesday he looked to be really struggling in training. McClaren told the *Evening Standard* after a team meeting at their Hertfordshire hotel, 'Owen's thigh felt tight after we started training so he sat out most of the session. As a precaution, he was sent for a scan. Thankfully, that only revealed a small problem and we are hoping it will clear. He is a determined character and we know he really wants to play. Naturally though we will not take any unnecessary risks with him.'

Strangely, while Owen was yet to play at Wembley, Bon Jovi had notched up more appearances. Owen's new accomplice at Old Trafford Michael Carrick looked the obvious choice to replace him but instead coach Steve brought Aston Villa's Gareth Barry back from the international wilderness. Barry had been in the form of his life as the claret and blues inspired by Martin O' Neill started impressively. The zealots that inhabited the Holte End would argue that their captain Gareth was a more inventive player than Owen. He lacked the pace, mobility and the biting tackle of the new United signing though.

Also Owen was battle-hardened in the trench warfare of the Champions League and had played against the likes of Pavel Nedved and Zinedine Zidane. A framed shirt of Zidane had pride of place in Joe Cole's Surrey mansion. It had been given to him by Claude Makelele and Cole, once touted as England's answer to the double Z, joked, 'it's up on my wall, so I have to pretend I played against him.'

Owen had been there and worn the tee-shirt or should it be the shirt of Zizou?

Israel tried to launch a war of words against England before the game. The Israeli midfielder Idan Tal claimed that England's style of football was 'ugly' and 'not smart', Owen bit back at the jibes and told the *Metro*, 'I do not know who he is or what he meant by it, it's obviously a poor comment. When you are at the top, people say things to try to bring you down by making headlines or provoking a reaction. It does not bother me, if you look at their team, I know which one I would prefer to have.'

Tal was currently playing for Beitar Jerusalem after unspectacular spells with Everton and Owen's father's old team Bolton. Owen was still protecting England even when he was not playing.

Owen failed a fitness test before the match and was ruled out. McClaren, treading on the eggshells of qualification, was upset. Luckily enough Israel were very unambitious and started with just one striker up front. Over-run in midfield and in defence they were ruthlessly dismantled by England. Gareth Barry in the Hargreaves role had an impressive game and grabbed his chance to show what he could do at that level. Barry had a hand in two goals by supplying the fine threaded pass for Michael Owen's second goal and the corner for Micah Richards to head the third. Gareth, a natural left footer, linked up well with the two Cole boys and his friend Stevie G.

The brouhaha surrounding the game was the usual guff. The papers wrote the victory up like the 1966 World Cup Final but in context Israel were even more lamentable than they had been in the goalless draw in Tel Aviv.

Bitterly disappointed at missing the game Owen could only watch as Barry staked a claim to his place and received the plaudits. It was starting to dawn on McClaren that Gerrard needed a natural foil in the middle of the park. Russia would be a tougher nut to crack though and the England coach wanted the insurance of Owen's solidity in the holding role. The stealth of the Russian captain Andrei Arshavin was seen to be a major threat and McClaren wanted Owen to counter it. Arshavin was a highly skilful player particularly adept at exploiting any space between the midfield and the back four. McClaren knew that Owen was astute enough to break up play before the back four became vulnerable.

It was not to be though, as he had a further scan on the injury. On the Sunday England's physio Gary Lewin took him for a special training session. Afterwards it was decided to send him back to Manchester for more treatment. All to no avail. The tabloids headlines on the morning of the game read, 'Hargo out'.

Russia were crushed by the now familiar 3-0 scoreline at Wembley to put the qualification of England in their own hands. It was the best performance by England in the McClaren era. Russia were awful at Wembley, their defending was the worst by a major nation for many years, the marking non-existent. A rejuvenated Michael Owen with space and time scored two first half goals and even Rio Ferdinand, (gearing up for the Christmas Party season) got into the act with a late goal.

Barry had another excellent game and set up Rio's goal. The papers sympathised with Owen who had established his niche in the team and now through the injustice of injury found his place in jeopardy.

England moved into second place. With Croatia crushing Andorra 6-0 to virtually clinch Group E, it was now a straight fight between the Three Lions and the Red Soviet Army for a ticket to Euro 2008. Venables accused Guus Hiddink of 'kidology' when he claimed England would not qualify.

Despite the good 180 minutes at Wembley the media was still wary of McClaren, Barry was the flavour of the month but the Russian Army had retreated back to Moscow where they would make their last stand. A plastic pitch awaited and there were misgivings about the England goalkeeper and back line. Owen's fitness level was still giving cause of concern. How important he was to the cause was to become very apparent in the coming weeks.

Chapter Ten

End of the Road

'Steve McClaren ignored a plea from Terry Venables to bring on Owen Hargreaves during England's defeat by Croatia. Venables believed with the score at 2-2, England were through to the European finals and the presence of Hargreaves in a holding role in front of a defence might protect the single point that would have ensured qualification.'

Michael Hart, Chief Football correspondent, *Evening Standard*

'I am afraid of what has happened to football. We need to come back to the game'

Michel Platini

Owen's favourite group were the Motown act 'Boyz to Men', best known in this country for their achingly beautiful cover version of the Gladys Knight song 'End of the Road'. Steve McClaren came to the end of his road in October 2007 when England failed to qualify for Euro 2008. The final nail in his coffin was the 2-3 home defeat to Croatia, but before then the road took a few twists and bends.

In early October it was reported in the press that Owen Hargreaves required a further month on the sidelines. His career at Manchester United had been limited to just three Premiership appearances. Owen was tipped to return to the side in UEFA Champions League action but on the Monday morning before the game he felt his knee go in training. It was decided to give him an injection in his knee to get rid of the tendonitis. Sir Alex Ferguson was of the view that he would be out for three to four weeks which ruled him out of the vital games against Estonia and Russia.

Estonia came to Wembley and were easily beaten 3-0 making it a triptych of those scorelines. For the record the goals were by Wright-Phillips, Rooney and an own goal. Lampard appeared after 70 minutes for Michael Owen to a storm of booing. Ashley Cole damaged his ankle.

The Estonia game gave another false impression of England's improvement. Not only was Owen ruled out of the tough trip to Russia but so was the papier-mache Terry. He had been complaining of a floating bone in his knee and in training it locked. Terry's physical condition had deteriorated in the last few seasons as the punishment his body had taken took its toll.

The plastic pitch in the Luzhniki stadium was a real worry to England. Terry Venables had pioneered plastic pitches when he managed QPR in the 80s. It had never caught on though and none of the current squad had played on that type of pitch. McClaren had organized two training sessions on an artificial surface at Arsenal's London Colney centre. There were fears that the Russians would flood the pitch before the game and when the temperature plummeted the ball would skid off at any angle from the freezing surface.

With Owen ruled out, Barry started again in Moscow,

Lampard was on the bench. Sol Campbell took Terry's place and Everton youngster Joleon Lescott came in for Ashley Cole. It was a tea time kick-off and the game started well enough with England going ahead after 29 minutes. Micah Richards' long ball was flicked on by Michael Owen and Wayne Rooney controlled brilliantly before volleying over the Russian keeper Vladimir Gabulov.

A great start; it should have been enough to give England at least a draw and a place in the Euros. Some fans were already daring to dream of the tournament. Russia were playing little better than they had at Wembley and looked uncomfortable on their own plastic pitch.

Then it all changed as the home side, clad in their Nike shirts, pushed up sensing an unease in England's play. Nervousness started to creep in as the tension continued to gnaw away at England. Steven Gerrard should have clinched the match after 50 minutes when he had a golden chance to double England's lead. Barry floated in a free-kick which found him unmarked at the far post. All he had to do was take the ball down, kill it and pick his spot. Instead he squeezed the trigger before he took proper aim. Stevie G snatched at the shot as soon as it came to him. The millions of TV fans back home could only watch it fly wide of the post. Close but no cigar, close but no Euros 2008. In that moment the game was won and lost, it could be said Steve McClaren watched his whole future just melt away.

Guus Hiddink gambled then, big time. Abramovich was present in the stadium, obligatory open neck shirt and Russian scarf. Mourinho was amongst the top three managers in the world but even he was expendable when things went wrong. Hiddink turned to another Roman in his hour of need. Roman Pavlyuchenko of Spartak Moscow.

The hero Rooney turned villain after 59 minutes when, with Lescott badly out of position, he tried some Pasodoble of a tackle and bundled Konstantin Zyrianov over. A penalty kick was awarded; England protested bitterly that the offence occurred outside the box. Up stepped Roman Pavlyuchenko to bury the penalty.

That is when it all started to go so terribly wrong for England; another massive crack in the McClaren Empire appeared. Perhaps the first one occurred when Macedonia took a point at Old Trafford and the second one around the time Robinson air-kicked in Croatia. Things were sliding now though and there could only be one outcome of this down-bound curve.

Owen Hargreaves was never missed more than at that moment. That is when his experience would have counted as well as his speed and strength. Russia were pouring forward into the gaps. Owen could have plugged them with his intuitive covering, if he had played like he had that night in Germany against Portugal in the World Cup it might have been enough. Barry was caught too far up field on numerous occasions. The pairing with Gerrard gave scant protection to the back four. About as much as when Lampard and Gerrard played together. The England midfield was simply over-run and out-gunned.

This let the Russians flood the midfield and wrest superiority from England. To quote from *Henry V*, Act III, Scene VII – 'Foolish Curs, that run winking into the mouth of a Russian bear and have their heads crushed like rotten apples!'

Four minutes after the penalty Russia went 2-1 up and effectively ended England's interest in the Euros. The story was to take a few more twists but the damage was done. The goal was the result of another error by Robinson, the hard running Zyrianov fired in a shot, Robinson could not hold it and Pavlyuchenko reacted first to turn the ball home. Robinson had been an accident waiting to happen for a long time but the dishevelled Lescott was also implicated as he reacted slowly to the situation.

England never looked like salvaging anything. Barry, winning his 14th cap, was criticised in the press for his stodgy performance. The *Sun* was of the view that he 'lacks the range of play to really succeed in a crunch match like this one.' Amongst the many headlines about Iron Curtains, sickles and labour camps, the *Times* said of the Villa man, 'Gareth Barry's pretensions to be an international holding midfield player have also been shattered.'

The rest of the England midfield was equally disappointing. Joe Cole looked a shadow of the player that had scored that wonder goal against Sweden in the World Cup. Wright-Phillips was abysmal – to call him one dimensional was being kind to him.

England limped home from Moscow like the remnants of Napoleon's army had done centuries before. England's last game of the group was against Croatia at Wembley. To have any chance of qualifying England had to beat them and hope that Russia would slip up somewhere in their remaining games away to Israel and Andorra.

Against all expectations Israel beat Russia 2-1 in Tel Aviv, everyone expected Russia to virtually clinch their qualification there. Owen watched the match on television in Manchester and was delighted that the result gave England a fighting chance.

The limitations of the Russian side were highlighted in the defeat by a makeshift Israel team. Hiddink's three-man back line struggled against the pace of the home side. Omer Golan became a celebrity for a short time after scoring the injury time winner. Manchester bookie and famous United fan Fred Done, of the BetFred betting shop empire, had promised a £50k top of the range Mercedes to any Israeli player scoring the winner. Fred was looking forward to a lucrative summer with England playing so the Merc would have been good business, but the Israeli FA banned Omer from accepting it.

Whilst on the subject of incentives, Roman Abramovich watched the match stony faced from the stands. The wealthy Russians who flooded into Tel Aviv to see their team qualify and soak up the winter sun had a nasty setback. Hiddink was still confident of qualifying though as he predicted Croatia would see off England at Wembley. The verbal knife-fights between the managers continued.

The evening before the benefit match in Israel England played a friendly against Austria in Vienna. Considering that McLaren's side had their face-off with Croatia on the following Wednesday it seemed a risky undertaking. Owen was ruled out of the game as he could not play two matches in quick succession because of his ongoing knee problems. It was a low key affair with Crouch scoring the only goal of the game. On the downside Michael Owen picked up a knock which ruled him out of the Croatia game. England were already without Rooney, also out following an accident in training. England looked very lightweight up front, McClaren had no luck with injuries that was for sure. His whole Euro 2008 campaign was jinxed from start to finish.

Franz Beckenbauer had been critical of England and told *The Guardian*, 'there is no life in this team. The first time I played against England during the World Cup in 1966 there was always a certain spirit. A European Championship without England would not be the same.'

Owen was declared fit for the Croatia game but was not selected for the opening line-up which included Barry. McClaren also chose Scott Carson in goal who had played in Austria. To play a rookie keeper in such a vital game was a foolish move by McClaren, particularly in view of the fact that England's loyal servant Steve James was top of the Premier League stats for keepers. Torrential rain hit London a few hours before kick-off which gave out a bad portent of what was to come.

Owen sat on the bench wearing the orange bib with the Nationwide logo, next to him was his friend David Beckham. Both men should have started the game. Three weeks before Wembley had hosted a NFL football game involving the Miami Dolphins and the New York Giants. It was another wet day and the pitch had churned up like a World War I battlefield.

'Kid' Carson, wearing a curious all yellow costume, made a disastrous start to the game and in doing so condemned England to the international wilderness. After just eight minutes Croatia scored when Srna tore past Wayne Bridge and slipped the ball to winger Niko Kranncjar. The Portsmouth player took a punt and his optimistic right-footed shot bounced in front of Carson. The Villa keeper bent down to save but he must have taken his eye off the ball and it flicked off his glove and into the net. It was a dagger blow to the heart of England. Owen felt his stomach churning.

If Carson goes on to win more medals than General Georgi Zhukov that moment will still haunt his career. In some respects though Carson was lucky, if he had committed an error like that playing for Colombia he would have probably been assassinated.

Six minutes later Croatia scored their second and left England facing an almost impossible task. Eduardo, who had opened the scoring in Zagreb and was later horrifically injured at Birmingham, waltzed through the England defence to put Olic in for a simple goal. Wright-Phillips stood with his arm in the air frantically and vainly claiming offside. This was not the case as his Chelsea cohort Wayne Bridge, too deep and too left, had played him onside. The England back was having a horror story of a game that Stephen King could not have written. Owen sank deeper into his seat as the rain lashed down, rubbing his eyes at the surrealism of it all.

The crowd were stunned, even before the two goal burst they were strangely quiet, even morose. The atmosphere was more suited to a Michael Buble concert than a make or break qualifying game. The Croat fans gave their side great support throughout the match chanting a marathon mantra.

It was like one of those Las Vegas magic shows, a total illusion. McLaren should have reacted then, Mourinho would have. In his time at Chelsea they had conceded an early goal to Fulham at Craven Cottage. With less than 20 minutes gone Jose had no hesitation in replacing both Joe Cole and Wright-Phillips. A similar course of action then would have been appropriate. As it was McClaren, always his own worst enemy, waited until half-time before bringing Beckham on for the hapless Wright-Phillips and Defoe for Barry. Gareth had another poor game, he had left too much space between midfield and the back line. Space that Croatia had thrived in. To single Gareth out though was unfair as the whole midfield was appalling. Gerrard was captain that night but had his worst game in an England shirt. Lampard was totally anonymous, as ineffective and lost as the other waxworks in white shirts.

Owen should have come on at the same time because without Barry they had no holding player to counter-act the tricky Croatian forwards. Instead the Manchester United star warmed up on the touchline as the England team came back out for the second half. Millions of viewers saw Owen shake his pal Beckham's hand and wish him luck as the new Armani model entered the fray.

A soft penalty decision awarded by Peter Frojdfeld put England back in the game eleven minutes into the second half. Siminic stupidly tugged back Defoe in the penalty area as he went for a Joe Cole cross that he had little chance of getting. Up strode Lampard to send the goalkeeper the wrong way and coolly convert the penalty, the only thing he did of note all night.

Beckham looked like he might have been England's saviour yet again when he set up the equaliser after 65 minutes. The LA Galaxy player hit a first time, succulent pass for Crouch to chest down and volley in a thrilling equaliser. Scarcely believing their luck the players celebrated, dizzyingly believing that they were going to the Euros at that moment in time. Russia were winning in Andorra but if the England score remained level then they were through to Austria and Switzerland. Owen was out of his seat celebrating like the fans in the bars. All they had to do was hang on.

Millions of fans were celebrating too, mentally arranging their holidays and days off. The Euros 2008, another endless summer of promise and hope. What was that banner on the Football Italiano show? Facci Sognare! Make us dream. You could smell the barbies and taste the cold Bud.

On that damp November night, it was reported that the England No.2, strategy consultant Terry Venables, had tried to get Hargreaves on. Owen was a specialist in the holding role, perhaps the best in Europe. Venables was too over-qualified to be McClaren's No.2. The ex-Chelsea star had a zoom-lens ability to home in with perfect clarity on a particular problem. Michael Hart of the *Evening Standard* wrote as follows. 'Steve McLaren ignored a plea from Terry Venables to bring in Owen Hargreaves during England's defeat by Croatia. Within seconds of Peter Crouch's equalising goal Mclaren's No.2 suggested introducing the Manchester United midfielder from the substitute's bench.'

Terry was convinced that the presence of Owen as the holding midfield player would preserve England the point they so desperately needed. It never happened. McClaren was swanning around on the touchline under a huge twirling umbrella, swigging tea. Sir Alf Ramsey had sat in the rain in October 1973 when Poland had knocked England out of the World Cup. It was the result which terminated his career as England manager. Sir Alf, the 'Daddy' of them all, the only manager to win a World Cup for England. Capello may work a miracle if he crystallizes his impact, but it looks a pretty safe bet that Sir Alf will be the only English manager to get his mitts on the trophy for a very long time.

Steve did not bring on Owen, instead he instructed the Tottenham striker Defoe to drop deeper. Defoe, not even a regular in the struggling Spurs side, was not noted for his defensive qualities.

Thirteen minutes from time the Croatian substitute Miaden Petric, on for Kranjcar, wandered unmarked into acres of space. Suddenly he unloaded an angled drive across Carson and into the far corner of the net. England were out.

The blood-curdling goal was scored in the precise area that Owen would have been patrolling. His main defensive brief was to stop precisely what had just happened. There was not a player in the game with better concentration around the penalty area. The goal could have been avoided, that was the real killer. After Barry's poor showing in Russia the England coach could have really gambled and played two holding midfield players in Owen and Carrick.

McClaren claimed he was about to bring on Owen when Petric pierced the England rearguard. Instead he brought on another Tottenham striker Darren Bent for the sporadic Joe Cole. Bent dropped a shot onto the roof of the net but the flat-line was showing on the screen. The camera lingered on the England bench, Owen, deep in his thoughts, was sat two rows behind McLaren, now slumped back on the bench, head down, his nerves frazzled. Joe Cole was in front, without a tracksuit top, shivering and soaked stewing glumly over the situation.

The England side that night had one record, the only English side not to feature a solitary player from Old Trafford in 115 games. The last instance was a friendly against Morocco in May 1998.

Billic's side had already qualified yet they went looking for the winner. The media thought that they might have just come to London for the shops and the clubs but nothing was further from the truth. Rumours abounded that Croatia had been offered gigantic bonuses by football-mad Russian oligarchs keen to see their country go through at the expense of England. One thing that did emerge was that Billic's team were excellent players, a throwback to the golden age of 'maverick' talents like Peter Osgood, Alan Hudson, Stan Bowles, Charlie George et al.

The whistle blew, the pipe dream of a European Championship was no more. Beckham was again last off, still dignified, saluting what was left of the crowd. The flummoxed McClaren, seeking sanctuary, headed down the tunnel and out of the big time.

The boos rang around the ground. The biggest was reserved for the jaw-dropping decision to award Lampard the man of the match award. Frank had not felt so bad since his finance Elen Rives had emptied out her wardrobe in a Red Cross shop after a domestic dispute. Everything that was wrong with the England football team was encapsulated in that award and McClaren's failure to bring on Hargreaves.

Owen left the stadium, his strong features looking mournful. The fashionable Light Bar in the St Martins Lane Hotel was his destination. Accompanied by some chums he ordered a couple of bottles of Louis Roederer Cristal champagne at £265 a pop. They spent some time chatting and drinking but the mood was sombre. The redtops tried to sniff round and write it up as some David Duchovny 'Californication' spree. In essence it was just some wealthy young professional men having a drink after a bad day at work. The London News wrote a piece on it and quoted some onlookers who described the group as 'well dressed' and 'charming'.

Across town John Terry and Wright-Phillips' 'celebration' party in the Mayfair hotspot Chinawhite was cancelled. A few weeks earlier at a birthday celebration for Wright-Phillips the captain of England's party piece had been to show off by urinating in a very public place.

The fall out from McClaren's horrendous 18-game reign was ugly. The damage to the economy was calculated at being nearly £2 billion. At 8.30am the following morning the FA board met and both McLaren and Venables were sacked. The headlines were hysterical, predicting to a nation awash with emotion the end of civilisation. The most amusing was one of those freebies, *City AM*, announcing that due to last night's result 'Summer 2008 is cancelled'.

MP Roger Godsiff tabled a motion to the House congratulating Croatia and Russia on qualifying. He went on to say, 'the House acknowledges that the Croatian team were far superior in technical ability, skill and commitment than the insipid and incpt England team'. The motion went on to criticise the £747 million Wembley Stadium for its playing service and talked of the disgrace brought to the England shirt by 'the over-hyped English prima donnas'.

England's failure to qualify for the European Championship meant that they have plummeted to 12th in the FIFA ratings. They were now seen as a banana republic of Europe by many. Roy Keane had some harsh words to say about the England set up, he mused briskly in the *Metro*, 'I do believe there are too many egos about in the England set-up and that has cost them dear. From the outside looking in, I tend to think there are too many egos in there, too many big heads. If you get carried away with a little bit of success then you are in trouble. You look at the England set-up and they do not appear to be a happy bunch I have to say.'

A fitting epitaph for the McClaren era, a good overview of the entire cyclorama of mis-management and disaster.

A mere 26 days after McClaren had been ousted, Fabio Capello was named as England manager after agreeing a four and a half year contract worth £6.5m a year with the Soho Square chiefs. Fabio, 61 years old, was a character straight out of the *Sopranos*, a tough guy that chewed diamonds and stood no nonsense. His record was impeccable with a total of seven domestic championships. They had been won in the world's toughest leagues Italy and Spain with Milan, Real Madrid, Roma and Juventus. As ruthless as a Robespierre and as austere as a Pentecostal Minister he had survived the complexities of football at the highest level. Possessed of a deep-water intellect, he worked without an agent and never read the press.

If he did he would have found some glowing tributes. *La Repubblica* said, 'the right man to put a stop to England players getting drunk and organising promiscuous parties between matches. Capello is going to put a stop to this circus of WAGs with players thinking about the glitzy impression their wives and girlfriends are making rather than what they have to do on the field.'

Corriere della Sera wrote about him in even better terms: 'A tough, extremely ambitious, extremely correct and very confident man who is a great connoisseur of football and of great footballers. He only speaks once and what he says is what he means. If you don't understand it then that's tough – no matter how big a salary you are on.'

Capello was an amazing step ahead for England, one of the few coaches capable of getting the Three Lions roaring again. Fabio was credited with perfecting the 'pressing game' used by AC Milan in the early 90s to lay waste to Europe. The style was based on midfield destroyers Marcel Desailly and Demetrio Albertini winning the ball in the 'killing zone' of midfield and feeding superstar striker Marco Van Basten.

Clarence Seedorf, who played for Capello at Real Madrid, was interviewed on Radio 5 about his boss and asked if he would tolerate the WAGs culture. Claude said that he would 'rather have less quality but committed players rather than quality players who are not committed.'

Owen appeared to tick all the boxes for Capello, he was an identi-kit footballer with all the credentials that the Italian looked for in a player. A huge sea change was about to rock the England international set-up. Capello was going to be the biggest thing to hit England since the bubonic plague. Already the jokes were doing the rounds. How would Capello solve the conundrum of Gerard and Lampard? Answer; he would drop them both.

Platini's comment at the start of the chapter seemed particularly apt at that time. We needed heroes like Owen Hargreaves to glorify the game. Capello was regarded as one of the most inventive players of his generation and the problematic midfield looked to be the area most in need of his attention. One thing was certain, Owen Hargreaves was about to enter another exciting and challenging phase of his career.

Chapter Eleven

Stranger in a Strange Land

'Owen is a great addition for us and will do a terrific job for us, particularly in Europe. I am positive about it.'
Sir Alex Ferguson

'We are the biggest club in the world, we want the best players and Owen is a top player. He will strengthen the team.'
Michael Carrick, July 2007

'I am delighted Owen has arrived.'
Rio Ferdinand, August 2007

Near the end of extra time in the 2007 Cup Final, the worst so far played in the 21st century (and arguably the worst final played in the previous century) Chelsea's Didier Drogba scrambled home the winner against an exhausted Manchester United side. It denied Sir Alex Ferguson his fourth League and Cup double in his honour drenched twin decades. United had landed the biggie though – the Premiership pennant – and snapped the stranglehold that Chelsea, collateralized by the Russian tycoon Abramovich, had exerted over the modern game.

With the balance of power slowly slipping back to Old Trafford, Sir Alex wanted to cement United's place at the summit. He was building teams with the impatience and imperiousness of a pharaoh constructing a pyramid. The Scot was of the view that they could have won another treble but missed out because they did not have enough players. In an interview with the *Sun* in the summer of 2007 he explained, 'Our downfall last season is that we came to the final part of the season without enough players for all the different competitions we were in. We had a great opportunity in all three competitions but just did not have enough bodies to stretch our squad and save some legs.'

On the Sunday night after the Cup Final it was announced by Bayern Munich president Franz Beckenbauer that Manchester United had purchased Owen Lee Hargreaves for a fee in excess of Euros 25m (£17.5m). Sir Alex had driven a hard bargain as reports in the tabloids earlier in the week had suggested that the protracted deal was in danger of crashing and burning as the total fee was spiralling to over £20m. The top Premiership sides, cash rich with the enormity of the increased TV money, embarked on a fresh orgy of buying. United were the highest rollers, scooping up more Latin talent in Nani from Sporting and Anderson from Porto for a combined fee of £32m. Fabulous potential, but players bought for the future, season 2008–09 or so it seemed. Eleven years earlier Ole Gunnar Solksjaer had been bought for his future potential but he had exploded onto the scene immediately because of his sharpness and meticulous finishing.

The first player signed by United that was not born or

resident in the United Kingdom was Nikola Jovanic. Dave Sexton, the United boss at the time, purchased him for £350,000 in January 1980. Nikola was a stylish defender but found it hard to adjust to the pace of the English game, he played 26 times for the Reds and scored four times (two against Leicester City) before returning home.

Michael Essien with his expressionless ferocity had browbeaten the United midfield in the Cup Final but it was hoped that the addition of Hargreaves would give a more combative edge to the Reds' languid midfield. Owen's purchase gave more variations and there was much speculation as to what permutations Sir Alex would opt for. Some critics suggested that Owen would slot into a defensive role alongside Michael Carrick with Paul Scholes pushed farther forward in a 4-2-3-1 formation. Louis Saha was pencilled in for the advanced role. There was increased speculation that Carlos Tevez would be joining from West Ham but the intrigue surrounding his actual ownership had muddied an already complicated situation.

Hargreaves was expected to patrol the no-mans-land between the back four and midfield with a brief to ruthlessly break up the opponent's attacks and set attacks rolling. The strength of his tackle and quickness to the ball was seen as a great asset. Some United fans were expressing doubts though that the inclusion of another defensive player would disrupt the attacking flow. Sir Alex was concerned at the havoc that Milan's Kaka had wreaked in the Champions League semi-final. Particularly when he had been in matador mode in the first leg at Old Trafford. If Owen had played that night the result might have been a lot different. Owen would have given more bite and confidence and there was no better man marker in Europe. Sir Alex envisioned, as so often in his career, what no other coach yet saw.

Owen told *The Guardian*, 'There are so many fantastic players in the United squad and I just think I'm another piece in that puzzle. Every player brings his qualities and I think mine are in the defensive midfield area. Hopefully I can win some tackles and protect the back four to ensure we keep a clean sheet and get the ball to the fantastic offensive players that we have.'

Owen injured a knee in pre-season training which slowed the start of his career in Manchester and delayed his first appearance in United colours. The condition was diagnosed as tendinitis. The injury precluded him from playing in any of the four matches on the Far East tour to Japan, China and Korea. The trip gave Owen the chance to catch up with the acquaintances he had made whilst on England duty – Wayne Rooney, Rio Ferdinand, Gary Neville, Michael Carrick and Wes Brown. Paul Scholes' England career had come to a premature end but Owen had played with him previously.

Sir Alex told the *Toronto Sun*, 'It's good to get Owen Hargreaves on board at last. His broken leg delayed the transfer but some players are worth waiting for – he is one.'

Owen landed around lunchtime at Tokyo's Narita Airport on 16 July with his new chums. The team was engulfed by hundreds of their fanatical fans in a wave of affection usually reserved for boy bands. The name of Owen Hargreaves was already well known in the Far East and because of his exploits with Bayern Munich and England they saw his mettle as heroic. Shortly afterwards Owen and Alan Smith, wearing their red United Polo shirts, went out on a community visit on behalf of the Manchester United

Foundation to the St Luke's paediatric cancer ward. The sight of the stricken youngsters, many desperately ill, soon made the United duo forget the fatigue of their long flight. It was one of Alan's last official acts for United as he joined Newcastle United for a fee in the region of £5m.

Before retiring to their luxury hotel the United players trained in front of hordes of fans, who appeared to spontaneously locate, at the Nishigaoka Stadium. Photos of Owen playing keepy-uppy with Rio and Rooney at the session appeared in the British tabloids confirming his arrival at the highest level. The next day United drew 2-2 with Urawa Red Diamonds. The high spot of the tour was the 6-0 crushing of Shenzen in Macau in China. The fans were treated to a magical goal from the skunk-haired Nani followed by his first back-flip celebration in a red shirt.

An amusing incident happened on the tour when Sir Alex told the players that the wining golf team would be awarded the prize of a bottle of wine from his cellar. Fergie's cellar was known throughout the club as being one of the best in the country, crammed with the finest wines known to man. Owen paired up with Rooney and they laid waste to their fellow team-mate's hopes. No bottle had arrived at the time of writing from the Ferguson camp though. Owen urged Rooney to challenge the United supremo on the subject but he seemed somewhat reluctant.

Owen gave an interview to the *Shortlist* magazine and talked of his first meeting with Sir Alex. 'I admit I was nervous the first time I met him. We had a strange encounter. He invited my girlfriend and I for breakfast. We went to meet him and I just sat there looking at him. I could not believe it was Sir Alex in front of us with his toast.'

Still the injury persisted and Owen did not play in the

2-3 defeat to Internazionale at Old Trafford. It was a poor display by United, much to the consternation of Sir Alex who warned his squad that they would 'not beat anyone' playing in that manner. Paul Ince, another competitor in the Hargreaves mould, once said that Sir Alex was a gent Monday to Friday then on Saturday 'out came the beast'.

Owen finally made his first appearance in a friendly against Peterborough United on Friday 3 August. The Posh (no relation to their former midfielder's wife) were managed by Darren Ferguson, the son of the great man. They had clashed swords when Darren was a player but this was the first occasion that they had met as opposing managers. Owen came on for 45 minutes in the second half.

The game ended up as a 3-1 victory to United who fielded a team of youngsters with Owen being the only marquee name in the line-up. In the opening minutes Peterborough were all over them like a cheap suit. Adam Eckersley gave United a first half lead but Peterborough equalised through Rene Howe. Owen started slowly but started cavorting as the game wore on; United wrapped it with goals in the last 20 minutes from Richie Jones and Fangzhuo Dong.

Owen told *Shortlist* magazine, 'At Peterborough they did not give me the warmest of welcomes to England. In fact they slaughtered me.'

Seventy-seven days after they had met in the Cup Final United played Chelsea again in the FA Community Shield. It seemed to many fans, still mentally shattered by the events of the previous season, that there had been hardly any break at all. Owen took no part in the latest clash between the two factions. The match was only marginally better than the anaemic Cup Final. After the wettest summer on record the game was played out in Dubai-like heat with the temperature on the pitch reaching 37. United won 3-0 on penalties after the game had finished 1-1 after 90 minutes. Ryan Giggs had put United ahead on 35 minutes. It was the Welsh wizard's first goal in a Wembley Final. Chelsea equalised on the break with about their only worthwhile attack in the game.

The first silverware of the season was regarded as just scrap to many fans. Its value, like that of the FA Cup Final, had diminished each year. The victors would always claim bragging rights whilst the losers would always denounce it as a mere training exercise pointing to the pitch choked with substitutes. Perhaps it was a case of familiarity breeding contempt. Only four Charity/Community Shields had been played since 1981 that did not involve the teams in red Liverpool or Manchester United.

Owen's England colleague Frank Lampard's lean spell continued, he was anonymous for most of the game and fluffed the crucial second penalty. The United fans abused Lampard throughout the game about his weight. Reworking a famous Chelsea chant to sound like, '10 men went to lift, went to lift Frank Lampard.'

Some were of the view that he missed the penalty because there was no one in front of him to get a deflection off. One United message board described him as the Ricky Gervais of football, a tiresome embarrassment, floundering at the vital moment. Gervais had recently put in a disappointing performance at the same venue when his act died on its feet at the 'Concert for Diana'.

It was interesting to compare Michael Ballack's goalscoring performances at Chelsea to those in Germany. When he played with Owen at Bayern Munich the German captain scored 43 times in the four seasons the England midfielder was shielding the back four. While Lampard dominated the Chelsea midfield in Ballack's first season in the Premiership Michael only managed four goals.

Owen was a great fan of Ballack and backed him, telling AOL Sport, 'Michael Ballack was extremely successful in Munich. He was Player of the Year every season he was there. People have not seen the best of him by any means, but given an opportunity, I am sure they will. For someone of his size, he has fantastic technical ability and his finishing, with both his head and feet, is among the best in the world.'

Owen's words were highly prophetic as in the closing stages of the season Ballack emerged as Chelsea's main driving force as they pushed United hard for the title

Owen watched the game from the bench, sipping water and wearing the white training sweat top with the AIG logo. He was given a tremendous reception by the United fans at the end of the match when he went to congratulate his new team-mates on their victory.

Dunfermline at East End Park was the venue of Owen's next outing. In a testimonial match for Scott Thompson, the midfielder played for 65 minutes. In a 4-0 steamroller of a victory he looked highly impressive. Linking up well with Paul Scholes, the pair gave hints that they may well form an effective partnership. Sometimes they switched roles. Owen beavered away, always tidy and neat with his distribution. The only worrying thing was he left the field with an ice pack applied to his knee.

Sir Alex missed all the fun. The boss's missus Cathy had him under house arrest as they moved home.

Mike Phelan was the gaffer that night and told the *Manchester Evening News*, 'We decided that Owen needed more than the 45 minutes he got last week, but he is fit and healthy and ready to play.'

Owen had not at that stage found anywhere to live and was enjoying the luxury lifestyle of the glass-fronted Lowry Hotel, Manchester's only five star hotel. Happily ensconced in his £325 per night billet on the banks of the River Irwell the early days in Munich seemed a long way off. He told *Shortlist*, 'Settling in at Manchester after my success in Munich has been surprisingly easy. I do miss the food in Munich and the lack of speed limits. There are lots of speed cameras in Manchester. I keep getting zapped.'

There was no record of Owen having to undergo any initiation ceremony upon joining the Reds. In earlier times players had to drink a yard of ale or had their Hugo Boss suits cut to pieces. Ryan Giggs had swerved the major ceremony because he had joined the club as a schoolboy and had worked his way up. The Cardiff-born winger would recount stories of being thrown fully clothed into a cold bath if he was late for training when he first broke into the first team.

A week later with the phoney war over the real thing started. United were at home to Reading, managed by the former United legend Steve Coppell. Owen watched the game from the director's box alongside Tevez whose transfer had finally been ratified after months of wrangling. The box must have been full because Sven-Goran Eriksson, City's new manager, was spying on United a week ahead of the derby. His suited credibility was still intact and with a billionaire to back him, that wolfish grin was in evidence once more.

United were poor on a muggy overcast afternoon and could not break down the stubborn Reading defence. Rooney went off with a hairline fracture of his left foot in a disappointing afternoon; rivals Chelsea, Liverpool and Arsenal all won their games and the Reds already trailed by two points. Sir Alex had emphasised the importance of a winning start.

Covering the match for Radio 5 Live, Mark Lawrenson said that he thought Hargreaves would figure in place of Carrick in the Champions League matches.

Three nights later United travelled to Portsmouth for a tricky looking fixture. In their run-in to the title the previous season United had lost at Fratton Park and their record had been poor there with three reverses out of the last four. Owen still did not figure in the line-up. Carlos Tevez made his debut in place of the crocked Rooney. Paul Scholes opened his and United's account for the season with a fine first half goal.

Portsmouth equalised early in the second half and United's misery was compounded when Cristiano Ronaldo was sent off for an alleged head butt as the game petered out into a draw. It was a match United had dominated, having 69 per cent of the possession. Chelsea had won their opening fixtures to open up a four point lead. In their opening 13 matches in their previous campaign the Reds had racked up 11 wins. The coyotes were already sniffing.

On the Sunday, United were involved in the Manchester derby against an unbeaten City side, rejuvenated under the management of Owen's mentor Sven-Goran Eriksson. It was as if the media had wiped Sven's CV from the records. It would have indicated 15 notable trophies won in Sweden, Portugal and his jaunt to Italy. Owen lavishly praised the Swede in the press conference convened to announce his arrival at Old Trafford. He told *The Guardian*, 'I think Sven is a fantastic manager. He had lots of success and I appreciate that he supported me along the way when other people possibly at times did not agree. He showed faith in me as a player and I tried to repay that at the World Cup.'

Owen made his debut in the match which kicked off at lunchtime on a cool, cloudy late August day. He had a fine game considering the fact that he had not played for so long. Energetic and industrious in the number 4 shirt, he soon caught the eye and won praise from the Radio 5 commentary team covering the match. They made the point that Scholes would particularly benefit from his presence in the team. It was a good seamless debut from Owen, calm in possession and authoritative when not. The downside was that United lost 0-1 to their arch-rivals and slipped even further behind in the title race. Deiberson Geovanni scored the goal with a long range shot that deflected off Nemanja Vidic's instep. Some sceptics harshly suggested that the goal had been scored in an area of the pitch that Owen should have been defending.

Kaspar Schmeichel the Danish son of arguably United's greatest ever custodian Peter kept a clean sheet for Eriksson's side. As had been the case in their previous two games United dominated the match (65 per cent possession) but could not translate it into goals. The midfield was chock-a-block all game. It was United's worst start to the season for 15 years as they languished in 16th place. In the period between 2 May to the date of Owen's debut in the City match on 19 August United had only scored three goals in all competitions. This was the first time since 1992 that they had scored less than eight goals in a nine match sequence. Football was all about sequences.

Alan Hansen on BBC's *Match of the Day 2* in the evening named Owen as United's best player. The England midfielder, interviewed on the programme, his curly hair still dripping wet, said that he was 'disappointed with the result but am sure there will be more wins in the future.'

It was so important that Owen's career at United got off to a good start. Bobby Charlton would always speak of players embracing the meaning of the club. He cited examples of Cantona and Schmeichel as players who gave early indications of their commitment to the cause.

Steve Mclaren watched Hargreaves's Premiership debut and was pencilling him in for the friendly clash against Germany three days later. Unfortunately the Calgary-born midfielder had slightly aggravated the tendinitis problem which kept him out of the 1-2 defeat by the Germans.

Owen made his home debut for United against Tottenham Hotspur on the Sunday that comprised part of the August Bank Holiday. No stranger to the Theatre of Dreams, Owen had played there for England and got to know the ground in numerous training sessions. The weather improved and a crowd of 75,696 watched one of the most vital games played in the reign of Sir Alex. Chelsea had gone back to the head of the table and anything other than a win would anchor United in the bottom three and leave them at least seven points behind the leaders. Spurs were tough adversaries, their likeable manager Martin Jol was under unbearable pressure following a similar poor start to the season. He did not last much longer, being replaced by the highly regarded Sevilla coach Juande Ramos.

In a tense battle, 20-year-old Nani won it for United with a marvellous goal volleyed in from 30 yards after 68 minutes. The shot clipped the head of Carlos Tevez and flew in past Spurs keeper Robinson. The Cape Verde born Nani was known to Hargreaves as he was one of the players that

Bayern Munich had targeted the previous season. Owen played a part in the goal as his run had been blocked, the loose ball was collected by Nani who swivelled and fired home the drive.

Owen put in another efficient performance which earned him a 7 out of 10 rating in the *Times*. Carrick lined up alongside him as United started with two holding midfielders, Owen was the deeper-lying of the two England internationals who alternated at collecting the passes from the central defenders Rio and Vidic. Spurs meekly surrender the midfield terrority not wishing to mix it up with the interchangeable components Owen and Carrick. Only Robbie Keane with his exceptional movement posed the slightest threat to Owen and Carrick. The inclusion of two defensive midfielders provided too much protection against a Tottenham attack lacking any real firepower. The ex-West Ham and Tottenham star gave way to Chris Eagles early in the second half as Owen started to push up and probe the Tottenham defence, his bustle and aggression growing by the minute.

Near the end the super-charged Hargreaves could be seen giving Rio Ferdinand a Keanesque type rollicking for a lapse in concentration that almost set up a Tottenham raid. The United rearguard, the bedrock of the previous season's triumph, had started the new campaign nervously with Rio looking especially jumpy. Owen's reprimand already started the fans thinking that he had all the hallmarks of a future Reds captain.

Sir Matt Busby spoke glowingly of the spiky Nobby Stiles giving a fearful rollicking to any team-mate who lapsed even for a few moments from giving less than 100 per cent. If the Reds were winning he would exhort them not to give up, Busby used the expression 'compelling' to describe

Stiles' immense value to the team. Hargreaves would have brought a smile to Busby's face. Already his big yeoman heart and enthusiasm were marking him out as a warrior in the best traditions of Nobby.

Ole Gunnar Solskjaer, the legendary United striker announced his retirement from the game a few days after. The 34-year-old Norwegian finally lost his long battle against the knee injury that he sustained against Wolves in 2003.

On the Tuesday after the Spurs game a new team picture was taken to include Owen, Tevez and the other summer signings. In a touching gesture Sir Alex insisted that Ole was included in the picture taken on the pitch at the Theatre of Dreams. Another poignant moment followed as Ole was held back and a guard of honour hastily formed by Owen and his new team-mates. The Baby Faced Assassin was then clapped onto the pitch by the players. Owen sadly never got the chance to play alongside the legend who wore the number 20 shirt.

On the following Saturday Roy Keane's Sunderland visited Old Trafford in a game that kicked off at 5.15pm. The class of 1999 was well represented that day because Roy had signed both Andy Cole and Dwight Yorke on free transfers. Three-quarters of the United treble winning strike force were re-united. Ole Gunnar Solskjaer was there, saying goodbye . Andy Cole and Dwight Yorke were in the Sunderland squad. Teddy was still playing in the Championship for Colchester United.

Sunderland, superbly marshalled by Keane, blocked United at every turn. For a long time it looked like they were going to escape with a point. Louis Saha, a second half substitute, headed the only goal of the game after 76 minutes. Owen had another fine game driving United on. He put in two fierce shots, one was parried by the Sunderland keeper, and the other even more powerfully hit flew over the top. The win lifted them into the top six.

Owen told the *Daily Star*, 'Anytime you do not have players like Wayne and Cristiano it is going to be difficult. They are two of the best players, so it will be great to have them back. Once we get everybody back, it will be very exciting.'

Then a thigh injury ruled out Owen who did not play in the 1-0 frantic lunchtime win at Everton. Goodison Park stewed as the temperature soared, it was a crucial win for United as Liverpool and Chelsea were both held to draws and dropped vital points. Vidic scored the only goal after 83 minutes, a towering header by the six-foot-four Serb. Every one of the five goals he had scored for United up to then had been with his head.

United won by the same score in Lisbon in the Champions League thanks to a diving header by Cristiano Ronaldo from six yards. Owen was struggling to regain fitness. He told the *Manchester Evening News* of his injury frustration: 'I have never really had this injury before so it is new territory. It is frustrating. I missed pre-season, then I had a run of games and I was enjoying it. I have to take it day by day. It is just disappointing to suffer something so niggly. But I think injuries come from last season when I broke my leg.'

The message boards were even this early referring to Owen as another 'sick note' and sarcastically pointing to his record of 37 games in the last two seasons. Another stat was that since 2000 he had totted up 145 appearances at the average rate of under-21 games per season. Anoraks were claiming that the stats pointed to him playing in 52 per cent of Bayern's games in his seven year stint in Munich.

The problem with Owen was that because of the style of his play he would always be amongst the casualties of war. A chronic knee injury that took months of treatment and where no surgery was involved was a worry to all at the club.

The broken leg Owen sustained the previous season meant that complications were a serious consideration. Owen was especially prone to muscular and hamstring injuries after months of inactivity. Plus regaining match fitness was always a problem. The bionic Solskjaer battled for three years against his knee problem and to regain match fitness was the most remarkable comeback story since that of Judy Garland. The assassin's comeback was all too brief, like Owen Ole relied on his speed off the mark. There was also the issue of trying too hard, which meant players who had been out for any period of time were always susceptible to knocks and setbacks.

In his absence though United started their ascent. Jose Mourinho left Chelsea in a storm of controversy in mid September. The exact story will never come out but Chelsea's party line was that it was because of an irretrievable breakdown in relations with Abramovich. There were three types of manager: the inspirational leader like Sir Alex who drew on emotional factors; secondly there was the seductive leader, the best example being the populist Arsene Wenger whose ideas transcend class and race distinctions. Mourinho was the third type, the charismatic manager. The problem with that type of leader was that when the charisma faded there was not much left. As time passed Mourinho's relationships with Abramovich and his captain Terry deteriorated. The fragility of it became apparent as questions were raised regarding the quality of the football played by Chelsea and Mourinho's lack of respect for other managers.

Everything and everybody has a weakness. Mourinho's weakness was that he was a winner. Whatever it took to win he did, his head had been in the fast lane for too long, United fans were delighted to see Jose go because of his spiteful manner and attempts to intimidate referees and fourth officials in the clashes between the two sides.

United could not have entertained Chelsea at a better time than when they came to Old Trafford for their first match sans Mourinho. Avram Grant had been promoted from director of football to take charge of the West London team although he had no UEFA Pro licence. By coincidence Claudio Ranieri's first game in charge of Chelsea was at Old Trafford in a 3-3 thriller at the start of the treble winning season. Owen took his seat in the stands and listened as the United fans baited the travelling Chelsea contingent with their chants of 'You've lost your Special One' and 'Sign on Mourinho'.

A diving header from Carlos Tevez, thumped home after stealing ahead of Terry, put United ahead in first half injury time. Tevez had missed the pre-season endurance work because, like Anderson, he was involved in the Copa America. Both were striking form now though. A Louis Saha penalty coolly scored at the end of the second half was enough to beat a still shell-shocked Chelsea side.

United won the midfield battle, particularly after John Obi Mikel was sent off for a perceived two-footed lunge on Patrice Evra. Mikel had been courted by United for a long time before he signed for Chelsea for upwards of £12 million. If things had worked out differently the belligerent Nigerian might well have been occupying Owen's role at Old Trafford. Obi was a hard player and like Owen could lay the ball off accurately first time but lacked Hargreaves's unselfishness and ball-keeping prowess.

It was sweet revenge for United for their unlucky defeat in the Cup Final and karma for Terry's ill judged early season taunts about catching Chelsea 'If you can'. The media was always trying to juxtapose Chelsea against United and claim that the Reds were a lesser club.

As Owen's injury continued to keep him out of contention, United racked up easy wins over Birmingham, Wigan and Villa. Owen told AOL Sports news 'I thought I would be fit but I have not trained.'

The press continued to question Sir Alex's summer purchases, asking why he spent more than £50 million on a winger and two midfielders when he needed a top class striker to replace Ruud van Nistelrooy. Did he really need Owen Hargreaves?

Sir Alex spoke in the *Manchester Evening News* about him, saying that 'Owen is a different player to anyone else we have got. He has fantastic speed and sees danger very well. He is a fantastic addition to our squad. Of course he has been frustrated. He came for a big fee and has only played three games, which is not what he is here for.'

Around that time Busby Babe John Doherty died of lung cancer at the age of 72. John was tipped to be a United great when he burst on the scene in the early 50s after a brilliant career in the youth team. Like Owen a half century later John had a marvellous football brain and a wonderful touch. When he won a League Championship medal in 1956 the future looked golden but John was plagued by knee problems and his huge potential was never reached.

United legend Liam 'Billy' Whelan was brought over from Ireland as a replacement for John. The quiet ball-playing Dubliner scored an amazing 52 goals in a tragically short 98 appearances. Ironically on the day that Doherty had the knee operation that ended his career Liam was killed in the Munich crash.

Medicine has improved immeasurably since those times but knee problems are still the main cause of the termination of careers. Owen had hoped to be back for the Champions League clash with Roma but faced another month on the sidelines after breaking down in training. Sir Alex told the media that Owen had to have an injection in his knee.

The burgeoning relationship up front between Rooney and Tevez continued to set the pulses racing. United travelled to the Ukraine and beat Dinamo Kiev 4-2, Rooney scored the second and dominated the match. This important win put them top of Group F and was their 10th win out of their last 11games. Their only reverse was when the second string lost to Coventry in the Carling Cup.

Anderson and Fletcher played in the centre of midfield in the absence of Owen in United's most comprehensive away win in the Champions League since they beat Brondby 6-2 in their treble winning season.

Eventually Owen made his comeback against Middlesbrough at Old Trafford. Sir Alex Ferguson announced his comeback to AOL Sport: 'Owen is fit to start. It has been frustrating for him, missing games is not why he came here for a big fee and he must be a bit disappointed with the way things have gone. But it is a long season and he is back which is terrific.'

Nani put United ahead after just three minutes and then Rooney put United back in front after Jeremie Aliadiere had scored a shock equaliser. It was the first away goal in the Premier League that a team had scored at Old Trafford that season. Strangely enough, the last one had been scored by

Carlos Tevez, then playing for West Ham. It was highly significant because it preserved the East Enders' status in the top flight. Now settled at United, Tevez struck two second half goals which gave the score some reflection of United's superiority. The stocky Tevez was always available for Hargreaves' short passes and was also adept at closing down defenders.

After an impressive comeback the *Manchester Evening News* gave Owen a mark of seven out of ten for 'a busy and efficient performance'.

Owen felt a bit sore and stiff after being out for so long but suffered no reaction to his comeback. More work was required on his fitness levels but he was enjoying himself in the Premiership and told the *Daily Telegraph*, 'There were sell-outs for every game in Munich but football is more exciting here. The referees contribute to making the game more exciting here. In Germany the referees blow for any contact. Here the football is more physical and played at an incredibly fast pace. You always have to be on your toes. Alert.'

Owen's return was timely because Paul Scholes was ruled out for three months after damaging knee ligaments. The ex-England man had been playing in a deeper-lying role at the base of midfield as Fergie toyed with the idea of the 4-2-3-1 system. Owen was seen as the pivotal holding midfielder in the line-up.

The biggest game in his fledgling United career was looming – 'The game that stopped the World' as it was billed by Sky TV. Arsenal away at the Emirates.

Chapter Twelve
Northern Rock

'Everything I have done in the past does not count. It is how I am performing now. I want to get into a position where people enjoy watching me play. But the most important thing to me is that my manager trusts me, team-mates trust me. Everything else is gravy.'

Owen Hargreaves, early autumn 2007

A random survey of football shown on television in October 2007 indicated that 93 hours of live football were televised on Sky digital. In addition there were 297.5 hours of separate recorded football including highlights and chat. This was some indication of the stranglehold football exerted over modern life towards the end of the first decade of the 21st century.

One match dominated the first half of the 2007–08 season, the match played on Saturday 3 November with a lunchtime kick off of 12.45. It was the crunch match between unbeaten league leaders Arsenal and Owen Hargreaves' new side Manchester United. Both teams had accumulated 27 points; Arsenal had played a game less and headed the table by virtue of the additional three goals they had scored. The Gunners boss Arsene Wenger spoke to the *Times* about the forthcoming clash of the titans: 'This game will stop the world, the whole football world will be watching. It is two teams who play flowing football at a high pace and that is always worth watching. The game can become an art when that happens.'

Owen had thought that United had become a bit complacent recently but was looking forward to the forthcoming trip to London and told the *Metro*, 'We have a lot to work on because at times against Middlesbrough we got a bit complacent. Arsenal have played extremely well and are playing some lovely football but I still think we are the top team in the country.'

Since Henry was sold to Barcelona Arsenal had changed dramatically. The team had become more compact with the back four pushing up. It was a fascinating encounter with little to choose between the sides. Arsenal's attacking full-backs Bacary Sagna and Gael Clichy may have slightly held the edge over their United counterparts because of their incredible speed. Up front United held the aces with their explosive pace and thunderous shooting. The greyhound Ronaldo was now the most exciting player in the Premiership, blurring feet, allied with great courage and skill. Cristiano could score from any range with either foot and, at six-feet-two, was deadly in the air.

It was in midfield that the contest was most evenly balanced. The rhythmic possession of the conductor Cesc Fabregas against the special qualities of technique and style summed up as the class of Owen Hargreaves. It was Owen's job to nullify the threat of the Spanish youngster with the uncanny ability to see killer passes. In the huge build up to the game the *Times* showed some graphics of the two players considered by many to be the new aristocracy. This consisted of a drawing of the pitch with a marker indicating every time the player had touched the ball in a particular area. Cesc's graphic, compiled in a recent match against Bolton, highlighted the fact that he operated generally in the centre of an area halfway inside the Wanderers half. As the Arsenal fans would tell you, he was just a boy but he was the man. Fabregas was spending more time around the box in the old fashioned inside forward position.

Owen's chart indicated that he operated inside his own half, terminating attacks, seldom approaching the opposition's penalty area. The graphic on the United player was compiled from a dossier of facts generated from his debut performance against Manchester City.

Sir Alex had learnt a lot from Arsenal over the years, the fusion of stamina and power (a staple of the midfield of the George Graham era) was an idea that Ferguson had assisimilated well. Owen could be said to be a throwback to Graham's player Michael Thomas. The Arsenal midfield anchorman was famous for his last minute title winner at Anfield.

In the romanticised promotion of the match Sky TV ran an advert in the press with the slogan 'When it really matters'. On one side of the ad there was a picture of a squinting Sir Alex wearing his black zipped up jumper next to Owen Hargreaves. Tevez and Rooney were the other United players in the picture. Opposite them was Wenger, Fabregas, Gallas and Hleb. Interesting that the images of Owen and Fabregas were seen as the dominant figures of the match. In previous years images of the snarling figures of the alpha male gladiators Roy Keane and Patrick Vieira grabbed the fans by their lapels.

Keane always said that Arsenal was always the game he looked forward to as so much depended on it. The Irish enforcer had a great willingness to go toe-to-toe with Vieira which set the tone for the skirmishes that ended in the notorious 'Battle of the Buffet' in 2004. That was when Arsenal's 49-game unbeaten run ended and Sir Alex had pizza chucked at him. Now it was more about the football although the rivalry was still there under the surface. The public spats between Wenger and Sir Alex had mellowed over the years.

The game started with United deploying two holding players in midfield, Owen and Anderson. The blueprint for their game plan was based on the roles of Silva and Dunga that Brazil had used in the 1994 World Cup. The pair were precursors of the modern midfield enforcers whose mantra was seek and destroy, disrupt and dismantle.

Owen was wearing the all black strip with the white and red trimming. The all black kit was first introduced back in the first season of the Premiership in 1993–94 when the referees no longer wore black. They were the first team to wear black though some purist fans disliked the blue and gold trimmings. To others it was always associated with the Kung Fu kick employed by Cantona at Selhurst Park. Owen felt at home in it because it was not too distant from the colours in which Bayern Munich had dominated Europe.

On a lovely autumn afternoon United just shaded the first half. Owen had a terrific tussle with Fabregas as he tried to break up the rhythm of the Arsenal midfield. Fabregas was too good a player to be snuffed out completely but Owen's constant harrying disrupted him enough to force him deeper. Owen's tackling was always fair as he made some crucial challenges.

United took the lead in injury time of an ugly, niggly first half. Ronaldo fired in a low cross that Rooney touched on. Unluckily for Arsenal the ball spun off their captain William Gallas and fell into the net. Gallas was an interesting player, Mourinho had blundered badly when he had allowed him to leave Chelsea as part of the Ashley Cole deal. The under-rated Gallas had been their best defender and had papered over many of the cracks in their seemingly impregnable back four.

In a masterstoke of management skills Wenger had appointed William captain of Arsenal. Gallas was already showing every sign of being a better leader than Henry, though as Arsenal's challenge for the title eventually faded, questions were raised.

Owen, who had been booked after 26 minutes spoke to the *Daily Telegraph* about the threat, posed by Arsenal in the first half: 'They had plenty of possession but were never threatening and football's about winning games and scoring goals.'

Fabregas equalised for Arsenal three minutes into the second half. They tore into United from the re-start with a gusto that surprised Owen. Deep in his own penalty area Cesc exchanged passes with Hleb who worked the ball forward to Emmanuel Eboue. Emmanuel Adebayor raced onto a chip from Eboue and crashed a shot against Edwin van der Sar. The ball broke at a radical angle to the Rasta-locked Sagna who rolled the ball to Fabregas to hammer into the net. Owen could do nothing to stop the goal.

Rooney should have put United back in front after 65 minutes after neat work by Giggs but headed wide from a good position. Owen continued to chase and harry as United pushed Arsenal back on their heels. A recent development in the Arsenal style had been the high speed relay passing. Chelsea would use Frank Lampard to open up games with long crossfield passes. Beckham in his pomp at United was perhaps the finest exponent of this type of pass. It dated back even further to the time of Glenn Hoddle; in Major League soccer they called it 'on the diagonal service'.

Wenger considered such passes as high risk on the basis that they can be intercepted or go astray. Instead he preferred the less risky, quick fire, short range, relay man to man passing movement. The only way to break this up was to get between the passers and disrupt the sequence. A player like Owen was essential therefore to counter this mode of play. Hargreaves' speed and ability to read where the next pass was going were great assets to his team.

On 73 minutes Owen pushed upfield and tried a speculative shot which whistled narrowly over the bar. Eight minutes from time United went ahead again with the goal that appeared to clinch it. Patrice Evra charged past the Arsenal substitute, Theo Walcott, and exchanged defence-splitting passes with Saha. Then he squared for the scintillating Cristiano Ronaldo to shoot home.

Arsenal looked beaten but in stoppage time Clichy put in a great cross that Walcott sliced horribly. The ball bounced just right for Gallas, his cheeks blown out like Miles Davis, who drove goalwards. Van der Sar, standing on the line clawed the ball away. England won the World Cup in similar circumstances. Darren Cann, the linesman, spotted that the ball had gone over and waved for a goal. This was duly awarded and Arsenal grabbed a vital point to stay ahead of their bitterest rivals.

Last season Henry's 93rd minute header had beaten United at the Emirates and given them a unique double over the new Champions. Despite this achievement they finished 21 points behind United. On the pre-season tour of Asia Sir Alex made a point of telling anyone that would listen that there was no way in the coming season that Wenger's team would be that far behind again.

The Govan born Scot, who wore a giant poppy on his dark overcoat, complained that a foul should have been awarded before Gallas equalised. After the match he was furious that twice United had thrown away their chance of winning. Owen trudged off the field, angry that two precious points had slipped away despite sweating blood all day. The England star had not felt so bad at the end of a match since the defeat on penalties to Portugal in the World Cup 17 months and a lifetime ago. Coral's paid 14-1 for a 2-2 draw, Owen had been 28-1 to open the scoring.

Continuing his dialogue in *The Guardian* Owen said, 'Both of our goals were beautiful pieces of play, while theirs were a bit scrappy and probably not typical of the way Arsenal play. It's great to keep the ball, like they did, but when you've got a team that are as good defensively as us, you can keep them at bay. The most important thing is that when you win the ball back you attack.'

Owen's display in the game 'that stopped the world' earned him 6/10 in the *Daily Mirror*. They wrote up his comments about Arsenal's lack of creativity in a manner that would antagonize Gooners and add fuel to the always simmering bonfire of tensions between the two clubs. The antipathy had mellowed slightly when both sets of fans had focused on Chelsea as the new enemy of football. It was the first time in the season that Arsenal had conceded two goals in a Premier League match. The Premiership stats of their meetings indicated that United had won 12 times. Arsenal had notched up 9 wins with 11 draws.

Sir Alex was encouraged that he had the strongest bench so far that season which enabled him to alternate the side when needs be. The game had been described as the 'Textbook Match' by Portsmouth coach Harry Redknapp. The ex-West Ham boss meant that the tactics employed by Wenger and Sir Alex would be commemorated for years to come by soccer boffins, aspiring coaches and anoraks. In fact anyone interested in studying the evolution of the modern game would have found it fascinating.

Owen Hargreaves' proficient play in the match would be for the subject of analysis and dissertations on the state of football in the 21st century. The principles of his game would be copied by purists and students alike, a palette of influences and inspirations.

The return match with Dinamo Kiev was next on the agenda on the Wednesday following the Emirates battle. Owen was again not risked by Sir Alex who was using him sparingly. His condition was still not strong enough to let him play in two encounters in four days.

Talking to the *Manchester Evening News* about the fixture Owen made the point, 'Dinamo seemed a bit afraid of us in Kiev. It is rare in the Champions League that you see someone pulled apart so easily and concede four goals at home. Normally, those types of game are difficult but Dinamo were really quite poor.'

Owen would have enjoyed playing in the 4-0 dismantling of the docile Ukraine side. Gerard Pique, another potential star in the making, put them ahead with his first goal for the club. Then the golden triumvirate of Tevez, Ronaldo and

Rooney took over and scored a goal apiece. Did any club in the world hold such firepower up front? Every defence in Europe was petrified of them.

Hargreaves conducted an interview with the *Sun* and quoted from Roy Keane's autobiography about the Champions League being the priority over domestic honours. He went onto say 'there are perhaps 10 teams who can win the Champions League and our current squad is strong enough to win the whole thing. But it is how we play in March, April and May that matters.'

On the following Saturday United were at home to Blackburn Rovers and beat them 2-0 to maintain their defence of the Premiership title. Owen played for 77 minutes of the match before being replaced by Michael Carrick. As always he was busy and efficient playing his part in a workman-like performance. He had two shots in the match, a free-kick that flew just wide in the first half and a more wayward one in the second. Owen's overall performance earned him 8/10 in the *Daily Express* match ratings.

United were without Rooney who had twisted his right ankle in a game of head tennis. England, about to go into battle against Croatia in the game that sealed their fate, missed him more than his club. The game was another exercise in showing exactly why Ronaldo was voted one of the top three players in the world. Two goals by him in a minute near the end of the first half killed the game as a contest. The first was a free header he leapt into the night sky to thunder in from a swirling Giggs corner. It skimmed in off the scalp of David Bentley; there was some in the media that said Bentley would be the new Beckham. David was still an infinitely better player than most though. Bentley's name had been spelt incorrectly and looked incongruous on the back of his shirt. With its luxury car connotations it would have been harder to find a more English name than Bentley amongst the Samba's, Pedersen's and Mokena's that were on the field.

Sixty seconds later Ronaldo, who some said was now the new Best, galloped through the middle to fire Tevez's low centre across Brad Friedel and into the far corner. The speed of counter attack, Vidic's headed clearance, Saha's superb flick on, Tevez's run and cross was over in seconds. It left Mark Hughes reeling and his old manager purring at the exhilaration of it all.

United went into cruise control for the second half. Owen stood guard over Ferdinand and Vidic. David Dunn, the Blackburn midfielder, received his marching orders for a clash with Saha. Earlier he had been booked by referee Chris Foy for tugging back Tevez. A man short in midfield, Blackburn stubbornly fought on but Owen locked and bolted the back four.

Radio 5 covered the match and commentator Alan Green praised Owen's 'controlled performance' in the game. Once again Owen was quick to the ball and strong in the tackle. Green talked about the ballyhoo around Sir Alex's comments earlier in the week about the quota of foreign players in the game. Many thought that this was a barb aimed at Arsenal and Wenger. The BBC man pointed out there were seven foreign imports in the Reds line up that day and then jokingly enquired about the nationality of Hargreaves!

Roque Santa Cruz, Owen's best chum from the Munich days, had the thankless task of playing up front for Blackburn that day. It was the first time that Owen had played against his friend since they had both acquired gainful employment in the north of England. Roque had made a good start at Blackburn and had scored with only his second touch in English football against Middlesbrough. The parallel careers between Owen and the player voted by *Die Welt* as the sexiest in the World Cup 2006 were uncanny. Both came as precocious youths from continents on the other side of the world to make their names with Bayern Munich. They found fame early and tasted instant success in the Champions League. In addition both players amassed numerous honours in the Bundesliga in the form of League titles and domestic cups.

Roque always remembered that the first player to welcome him in Munich was the young man with dark tousled hair, unearthly eyes and the curious accent. It was the start of a beautiful friendship. Owen was present at Roque's marriage to his stunning model wife Giselle and comforted him when his brother Oscar was tragically killed in a car smash. Both young men had their careers blighted by injury; Cruz never managed more than five goals a season for Bayern due to injury.

Happily settled at Blackburn, who had bought him for £3.8m, it turned out to be the bargain of the season. Roque had already scored six times prior to the United game. Owen saw to it that he was given no scope for a goal at claustrophobic Old Trafford. However in the following weeks he went goal crazy, scoring a hat trick at Wigan and two against Arsenal. Strangely enough he finished on the losing side on both occasions, but there was a strong feeling in the game that, like Owen, the best was yet to come. A further double against Manchester City two days after Christmas confirmed this.

The friends left the field arm in arm having a confab; it

must have been a very sweet moment for both of them. One in red, the other in blue and white halves playing in the Theatre of Dreams in front of 75,510 people in the English Premier League. Football was truly an international game now; Owen had been born in Calgary, Canada whilst Roque came from Asuncion in Paraguay. The friends had been tutored in Germany and had just competed against the cream of the best players in the world from such places as Portugal, Serbia, Argentina, Holland and Brazil.

Yet both had chosen to decamp to Manchester, Roque and Giselle had purchased a home in Bowden, Manchester's answer to Beverly Hills. The exceptionally handsome Roque bought his clothes at Prada and his accoutrements at Gucci. Roque was one of the few players in Munich who was sympathetic to Owen's credo of stylishness. In terms of mystique, poise and image he could almost rival Owen. Blackburn's new striker had even had a hit record in Germany, a top 40 song called 'Ich'.

Owen was still getting little icicles of pain in his knee after games. He was philosophical about injuries and accepted it as an occupational hazard.

Sir Alex told the *Times* that the bunch of players he had was the most talented he ever had at his disposal: 'I believe that this is the strongest squad I have ever had. So much so that I would be pushed to name my overall best team. We have got young players led by Wayne Rooney and Cristiano Ronaldo and more in the likes of Carlos Tevez, Nani and Anderson. In fact it is difficult to know when to stop talking about our important players'.

At first the press put this down to pure psychology and another mind game of Fergie. They saw it as the hyping of the potential of his players in an attempt to psyche out

Wenger and co. With Mourinho out of the picture there were less fractious relationships amongst the top managers. Both Benitez and Grant, decent men, had great respect for their opponents and their achievements. However after exhaustive comparisons with the great treble winning side of 1999 and the double winners of the 1993–94 season, it was true that the class of 2007 could hold their own with anybody.

Great players dripped off the tongue like honey, giants like Cantona, Keane, Kanchelskis and Hughes in the Fergie Mark 1 side. The celestial quartet of Beckham, Schmeichel, Scholes, and Giggs in Mark 2. That is just a sample, every Red has their own favourites. The 21st century United has more options possibly plus the blend of highly experienced maestros like Giggs and Scholes with youngsters like Ronaldo. The flexibility of a player like Hargreaves meant that when he dropped anchor in midfield United could attack with a variety of formations with three or sometimes four players.

Maybe Sir Alex and before him Sir Matt had sent out sides containing greater fabulous individuals but the overall strength in depth and the tactical acumen had never been higher. No player was indispensable anymore in the way that Cantona and Roy Keane had been in Sir Alex's earlier working models of the country's finest football team. The 2007 United squad probably had more 'bench' players of quality than its previous incarnations.

There was a short intermission in proceedings because of the international break. England were booted out of the Euros as Owen sat and watched in horror when he should have been playing. Then it was back to the cut and thrust of the Premiership.

On Saturday 24 November United travelled to the Reebok

Stadium to take on Bolton. They lost 1-0 in what was one of the biggest shocks of an event filled season. It was Bolton manager Gary Megson's first victory since he had replaced the hapless Sammy Lee, the short term replacement for Sam Allardyce. Bolton lay third from bottom of the Premier League at the time whilst United had gone 10 games undefeated since Owen's debut defeat against Man City. With Rooney still ruled out, injuries to Ronaldo and Vidic further weakened the line up. The weather that afternoon was appalling.

Owen played though and was voted the Man of the Match by *The Guardian*. The *Manchester Evening News* were harsher and only awarded him 5/10 in their match ratings making the point that it was his least effective game so far. Hargreaves did hit two thunderous free-kicks which just shaved the bar though.

United were poor throughout, their passing was inept and Tevez missed some great chances. The only goal was scored by Anelka after 10 minutes following a slip by Pique. Anelka was later to join Chelsea as they tried to bolster their squad in their unsuccessful bid to wrest the title from United.

Sir Alex was incensed by Bolton's intimidatory tactics and blasted referee Mark Clattenburg for not giving his side adequate protection. The treatment of Patrice Evra at the hands of Kevin Davies seemed to echo this. After 19 minutes the United defender retaliated after a late tackle by Davies. Four minutes later Davies was booked for another late tackle by the Bolton striker. On the half-hour Davies headed Evra in an aerial challenge and five minutes later Davies was given a final warning by the referee following another clash.

Evra told *The Guardian* about events. 'It was a big fight. I received more tackles in one game than I have had in my entire life. It was the same last year too. (United won 4-0 with Rooney scoring a hat trick). Davies kicked me then as well and I said to him. "Why did you do that?" He said, "Because I do not like you".

Sir Alex was so incensed he accused Clattenburg of allowing the first half to become a 'shambles' and was banished to the stands for the second half. In September 2003 Sir Alex had a huge bust up with referee Jeff Winter at Newcastle which earned him a £10k fine and a two game touchline ban.

Owen defended his manager to the *Manchester Evening News*. 'There were definitely a few challenges that were borderline, especially the one from Kevin Davies. I don't mind physical. That is why there is a ref out there but he struggled to keep the game under control.'

The last time Bolton had beaten United at home was nearly three decades ago when Owen's father's hero Frank Worthington had scored twice in a 3-0 drubbing.

Sir Alex pushed Owen further forward late in the second half in an attempt to salvage something. Carrick tucked in behind him in the holding role as United went for broke. Bolton's attacks were almost non-existent but they held on under tremendous pressure. In the dying minutes Owen almost saved it when he smashed a free-kick over the Bolton wall but the ball dropped onto the roof of the net. Just for a moment it looked as if he had scored. The fervent Bolton fans celebrated wildly.

The defeat was a blow to Owen but he was looking forward to making his UEFA Champions League debut for United against Sporting Lisbon the following Tuesday. Another milestone was achieved when he came on as sub for Saha with 11 minutes of the match remaining.

The score at that moment was poised at 1-1. The first 45 minutes were dire, as United, having already qualified, struggled to find any motivation for the task ahead. The Sporting Lisbon right back put them ahead after 21 minutes with a low drive from an acute angle that deceived the stand in keeper Tomasz Kuszczak. At the break Sir Alex, furious at his team's lacklustre performance, brought on Giggs and Tevez for Darren Fletcher and Nani. It was Tevez who equalised for United on the hour. Patrice Evra, recovered from the battering he took at Bolton, raced down the left and Saha turned his cross onto Tevez whose scuffed shot went in via a Sporting defender. A messy equaliser but it set up an exciting finish as United pushed up looking for the winner.

Owen came on after 79 minutes replacing Saha who had missed an easy chance and was struggling with the pace of the game. No such problems with Owen who lifted the team with his arrival. Saha had angered the Old Trafford aficionados with his profligacy and listless performance. It was evident that Hargreaves was already starting to be a favourite with the crowd as his integrity shone through.

In the amusingly named 'Man Untied pies' website a poll was conducted to nominate the next United captain. Owen scooped 46 per cent of the vote and had a landslide victory. The aggregate score of the next two in the contest – Rio (22 per cent) and Rooney (21 per cent) – did not beat Hargreaves' total. These polls were representative of the real fans' views and to earn their wholehearted respect after a handful of games was a very encouraging pointer to the coming new year. It was a good bet that in the not too distant future Owen would be pulling on the captain's armband.

Near the end Owen looked like he had won it when he

pushed forward and fired in a shot that just cleared the bar. That appeared to be it as thousands made their way out of the ground to beat the traffic. Millions more at home watching the match on ITV 1 prepared to switch over. Ronaldo had other ideas though. The Danish referee Claus Bo Larsen awarded a free-kick outside the box with two minutes of injury time already played. Owen had watched Ronaldo on the training ground recently practising an even more incredible variation of his free-kick. This involved hitting the ball at a certain spot, at a certain angle so it swerved and dipped in such an eccentric fashion it would be impossible for any goalkeeper to follow its line of flight.

That is precisely what he did, uncorking a wonderful shot past Patricio and high into the net. It was a wonderful goal not only because of the sheer artistry involved but also for what it meant to United's hopes of winning the UEFA Champions League. Ronaldo's last gasp winner meant that they were winners of Group F with five straight wins and avoided all other group winners. The draw a few days before Christmas put them up against French side Lyon with the advantage of the second leg being played at the Theatre of Dreams. The stats revealed that they had only lost one of their last 33 Champions League ties at home when they had gone down to a Herman Crespo goal against AC Milan in February 2005. Ironically both Arsenal and Liverpool, who had struggled in their groups, had been drawn against the Milanese clubs in the next round.

Another bonus was that Sir Alex could send out a team including youngsters and fringe players against Roma in the last game of the group at the Stadio Olimpico. This was played a few days before the epic 'Grand Slam Sunday' clash with Liverpool and Sir Alex wanted his key players rested before. Owen did not make the trip to Rome for that reason. Michael Carrick, wearing what appeared to be ruby slippers, played in his role. This was the true strength in depth which Sir Alex had alluded to in his recent statement. Carrick was an England international, a product of the wonderful West Ham academy that had invented the 'golden generation' by churning out players like Rio, Joe Cole, Lampard and Defoe. Now he was fourth choice in the pecking order of defensive midfielders.

The game suffered from a Sven-like excess of subs and by the end Roma were fielding very nearly their full strength side with World Cup winner Francesco Totti their star man. United included Dong Fangzhuo, Danny Simpson, Tom Heaton and Chris Eagles in their squad. Gerard Picque had put United in front after 17 minutes when he headed in Nani's corner but on 71 minutes the Brazilian striker Alessandro Mancini fired home a fine equaliser.

Owen told the *Manchester Evening News* that his manager was nursing him along: 'I feel great. The manager is keeping an eye on me and picking the times that I play. I really appreciate that. It is not that I might be tempted to push things too much, more that the manager is a great judge of how players are and how they feel. I trust him completely in that respect. He sees everything and makes the right decision.'

Before the Roma game Owen had played in the home victory over Fulham. It was the Monday night match played on a freezing December evening. A huge crowd of 75,055 defied the cold to watch another efficient win by United. The score was 2-0 with you-know-who Ronaldo scoring them both. Fulham were struggling at the foot of the table and manager Lawrie Sanchez was about to be sacked following a run of poor results. Owen had a storming game, making his mark early and dominating throughout. He played the whole 90 minutes and earned a 7/10 rating in the *Manchester Evening News*.

The match was covered on Radio 5 Live and the summariser Jimmy Armfield had some complimentary things to say about Hargreaves's performance. Extolling his virtues as a strong determined player, Jimmy said his best performances were in the central attacking midfield role. During the match Owen had spent a spell at right back, a position that Bayern and England had used him in. Nobody was better qualified to speak of his performance there than Armfield who was one of the finest right backs that England had ever produced, winning 43 caps and playing over 500 times for Blackpool.

Owen was down to play in United's next fixture, a home game against Derby County who were rooted to the bottom of the Premiership and without an away goal to their credit. Fans expecting to see Owen were surprised when Michael Carrick took his place, particularly when he had been spotted warming up. Actually that was where his problem started because it was during the warm-up a slight strain occurred to his calf. Sir Alex took no chances with the Liverpool game and a hectic Christmas period looming and withdrew him from the contest. Perhaps contest was the wrong word because Derby never threatened a shock of any kind as United yawned to a 4-1 victory.

Ryan Giggs opened the scoring on 40 minutes with his 100th League goal, a truly amazing record. The Welsh wizard had scored a goal in the Premiership every season since its inception. Gary Speed, the only player who could equal that, was leaving the Premiership around that time so it looked like Ryan would have another record to himself. Carlos Tevez hit two goals in the second half as United went for the jugular. Ronaldo wrapped it up in the last minute with a penalty. The little Argentinean was denied a hat trick but Ronaldo, with his own agenda, was anxious to score as many goals as possible.

There was a brief moment of glory for Derby though when the 25-1 outsiders scored through substitute Steve Howard to record their first goal, away from home, since the Championship play-off final in May. Owen could not help smiling when he watched the 3,000 travelling Derby fans celebrate as if they had won the Champions League. Extraordinary creatures, football fans. It gave him some insight into the power of United and the myths that hung over Old Trafford.

Jimmy Armfield again did the summarising of the game for Radio 5 Live and told the listeners that it was a great shame that Owen did not play that day. The ex-Leeds boss went on to say that it looked like Owen was really hitting some form after his fine display in the Fulham match.

The win over Derby helped United cut the gap behind Arsenal to one point but what was looming was a trip to Anfield to meet Liverpool. This was being billed as 'Grand Slam Sunday'.

Chapter Thirteen

Grand Slam Sunday

'I look at the places I have lived like chapters in a book. There is no point reminiscing. I am here now and enjoying it. At Munich, you were expected to know your place. There's a hierarchy. Here if you are good, you're good. There are no young and old players, they say only good and bad.'
Owen Hargreaves, March 2008

Grand Slam Sunday followed hard on the heels of the hype for the Liverpool v Manchester United clash. The Sky advert used to promote it was a copy of a medieval battle featuring Ronaldo going head to head with Liverpool captain Stevie Gerrard; Rooney, shaking his fist (what else?), was in the background. The other clash on that day was Arsenal v Chelsea and the usual suspects completed the ad – the obligatory Terry and Lampard with Fabregas cavorting.

The Liverpool game was scheduled for a 12.45 kick off with the Emirates pot boiler commencing at 4.05. For any football loving couch potato the highlights were on BBC 2 at 10.30, always worth watching because of the dry wit of

Adrian Chiles. If you got bored waiting you could always listen to the phone-in's 606 or Talk Sport.

Liverpool had not won the championship for 18 years, back when Lee Martin won the Cup for United and Owen was snowboarding in Calgary. Fellow clubs in the big time included Luton, Millwall, Crystal Palace, QPR, Norwich and Wimbledon. The modern day rivalry between the two clubs was still intense though. John O'Shea's injury time winner in the corresponding fixture last season had catapulted United to the title and still rankled with the denizens of the Kop.

Owen was in the starting line up at Anfield, wearing the same black ensemble that they had sported at the Emirates Stadium. Mark Lawrenson on Radio 5 told his listeners that in his view the season did not start until January. Obviously no one had bothered to tell the 44,459 fans that were shoehorned into the famous old ground or the millions of TV viewers worldwide.

Ray Wilkins spent five seasons at Old Trafford between 1979–84 and in many ways could be compared to Owen Hargreaves. Speaking to the *Metro*, the former England captain predicted that United would dent Liverpool's title aspirations in the Merseyside cauldron: 'United will have to defend for long periods on Sunday. If Liverpool come flying out and leave gaps they will pick them off left, right and centre with their pace and their ability. I think that's what United have, they have players all over the pitch who can win games for them.'

That proved to be the case when Carlos Tevez scored the winning goal two minutes from the break. Ryan Giggs hit a low corner to Wayne Rooney and his shot was imperiously flicked into the roof of the net by the little Argentinean. The

Liverpool defence were caught napping by the slick United move. Alvaro Arbeloa remained static on the goal line as the rest of his defence vainly pushed out trying to catch Rooney offside. For the second year running the match winner was scored from close range in front of the Kop end. It was Tevez's first goal for United away from home and against their fiercest rivals in the north-west. Owen was one of the first players to rush to congratulate him, Liverpool were furious at being caught out by the sucker punch move.

Owen had a brilliant game and earned a rating of 8/10 in *The Guardian.* The only other United player to rate so highly was Rio Ferdinand. The reason that the former Leeds player earned such a rating was the protection that Owen gave him throughout the game. Similar to the sterling work that Makelele had done for Chelsea in shielding Terry a few seasons before.

Alan Hansen focussed on Rio's performance in that evening's *Match of the Day* show. Owen did not get a mention in all of this. It would have needed a more insightful pundit than Hansen to appreciate the contribution of Hargreaves. To most United fans Hansen lost any credibility over a dozen years before when he made his crass statement about 'Never winning anything with kids'. The 'Kids' in question being Beckham, Scholes, Butt and the Neville boys the finest crop of youngsters Manchester United or the country had seen since the Busby Babes.

To overlook Hargreaves was a crime, in every clip of Rio's performance Owen could be seen hovering, covering, checking. Owen was still fitting in at Old Trafford, it took time and some brilliant players had never coped with the pressure. If you wanted to be hypercritical of his performance against Fulham earlier in the month then Owen was culpable of two errors. Allowing Clint Dempsey to dribble past him on the wing and into the box for a Fulham chance that was missed was the first. The second was when he was caught out of position and Kuqi missed a good headed chance. That day there was no lapses as Liverpool were deprived of any chances.

Fernando Torres had been seen as the main threat to United. Signed for a club-record £26m from Atletico Madrid, the fair haired Spaniard had already scored 12 goals in 19 games. The form striker was so quick and powerful that his strong running denied Ferdinand time to marshal his forces. Rio always had the option of Owen available to help. Torres missed an easy chance early on but apart from that he was dominated by Rio and his new pal.

The United number four's contribution to the victory could not be underestimated. His natural instinct was to break up the play and run forward a few yards before looking for a short pass. Having made the pass his style of play was to remain back and protect the immediate vicinity. The United style of play, as opposed to the continental way of Bayern Munich, was for the player to move into space to provide an option for another quick pass to be played. Some critics were of the view that when Hargreaves played the tempo of United's game dropped. The United coaches were faced with the dilemma of letting Hargreaves go forward and increasing the tempo but at the same time losing the effect of his defensive stability.

In the second half Owen handled the ball outside the box and a free-kick was given against him. The big Norwegian John Arne Riise crashed in a fierce shot but it was deflected wide by Owen who had stood his ground in the wall. Owen seemed to be everywhere as Liverpool grew increasingly desperate. Breaking up attacks, blocking a shot from the substitute Ryan Babel, cajoling more effort from his strikers. Brian Clough used to say the sign of a class player was the ability to pass under pressure. By comparison, his England team-mate Steven Gerrard struggled to impose himself on the game.

Rooney missed a great chance near the end when Ronaldo set him up. This was just before a Liverpool fan had chucked a golf ball at him but that went astray also. Owen shook his head, he had played in some tense battles for Bayern Munich and his country but nothing was quite like the atmosphere he encountered that day. His father had told him stories about the old Kop when it was a terrace and the most formidable end in the history of the English game. It must have been really something to play in front of that heaving mass of singing humanity.

Seven minutes from time Michael Carrick came on for an exhausted Tevez and immediately slotted in alongside Owen. That effectively signalled the end of the game for Liverpool as the two defensive England men sealed the midfield. Marcel Desailly also commented for *Match of the Day* and talked of the 'defensive block' that United had used to win the game. Capello had honed his defensive block at Milan to perfection and the game at Liverpool gave fans an early glimpse of what England would be serving up in the future under their new coach.

The game ended with United looking the stronger of the sides, they became the first opposing team since Everton in 1910 to keep four consecutive clean sheets at Anfield.

Owen, nearly breathless with exertion, talked to the BBC on Radio 5 Live after the match and was very happy with the way that things had gone. 'Very fast, very physical. I did enjoy it. A big game for the fans, when a chance occurred we needed to take it.'

The interview was concluded when he told the nation how tired he was and how much he was looking forward to a bath and a nice meal. He certainly earned it.

Grand Slam Sunday was a transitional point for Owen in his first season at Old Trafford. It was transitional because his previous games still reflected his Bayern Munich roots and habits he had picked up in his 39 England games. The game he played at Anfield looked forward to other possibilities and confirmed the partnerships he was already forging with Ferdinand and his midfield partners Anderson and Carrick.

There was a moment of clarity then, almost Zen, as Ferguson was aware. Something was being achieved with Hargreaves an increasing important figure to the team. Grand Slam Sunday continued with Arsenal beating Chelsea 1-0 thanks to a goal from Mr Gallas. A pernicious challenge by Eboue damaged Terry's foot; Petr Cech was starting to show his fallibility, his error leading to the goal. Arsenal, fast and fluent were emerging as the main threat to annexe United's title, Chelsea looked too political and injury prone to regain it.

United looked very healthy going into Christmas, always a crucial time in the race for the Premiership. Last Christmas Chelsea had stumbled and United picked up nine points out of nine with handsome wins over Villa, Wigan and Reading. Owen was looking forward to the games but a few days before, an incident occurred that was to damage both the image and the morale of the world famous club.

The Manchester United Christmas Party was held in the

£395 a night Great John Street Hotel. Allegations of rape were made against the promising young defender Jonny Evans who had recently played against Roma. Those allegations were later dropped and it must be stressed at this point that there was not the suggestion that Owen was involved in any of the shenanigans reported. Numerous pictures appeared in the press of the players attending the party but Owen was not seen in any of them, nor was he mentioned in any reports.

The public were disappointed to read of a 15-hour drinking spree involving the players and reports of their alleged £4k contribution each towards the cost of it. The reports made great play of the fact that 100 attractive girls were invited to the party whilst the WAGs were ordered to stay away. Of course none of this was new, United were always known as a drinking club in the old days. The exploits of such characters as Paul McGrath and Bryan Robson were urban myths. The alcoholism that destroyed George Best's career and eventually his life was triggered by the binges conducted in the Brown Bull public house near Salford Central station.

The WAGs' factor was a fairly new phenomenon, but even before that phrase was coined there were some amusing incidents. Going back a decade Line Berg, who was married to the Norwegian defender Henning, told an amusing story of her first trip to Old Trafford to see her husband play. It was a February day, not as cold as Norway, but she opted to wear old jeans, trainers and a woollen jacket. She wore no make up as she was only going to a football match. She was dismayed to find herself amongst a bevy of beautiful women wearing skimpy, gorgeous clothes and clutching expensive bags.

Even in those days a hierarchy existed, Posh ruled the roost with the Nevilles' womenfolk's important powers. The whole thing depended on whose husband was doing well in the team at the time. Ole Gunnar Solskjaer was always popular with the fans, especially after he scored the goal that clinched the treble, and consequently his girlfriend held an important position. Dwight Yorke had a dalliance with the world famous model Katie Price (aka Jordan) who clashed with Mrs Beckham over supremacy.

In December 1999 the United players held their private Christmas party at a club called Reform in downtown Manchester. It had been organised by Gary Neville, Roy Keane and Dwight Yorke. They laid on food, enough champagne to float *HMS Belfast*, music and a battalion of security guards to keep out the riff-raff. As was the case for the 2007 Christmas party no wives or girlfriends were invited. Instead Dwight Yorke had arranged for dozens of attractive girls to attend the party by phoning around modelling agencies, lap-dancing clubs, escort agencies etc. Manchester has always been a city packed with attractive young girls waiting for the opportunity to go to social events like that. The cost of the whip round for the evening was not recorded.

The party did not work out as planned. In protest the wives/girlfriends held their own Christmas party at the Sugar Lounge, one of Beckham's haunts before he went to Madrid. Later in the evening, fuelled by drink and curiosity the WAGs crashed the Reform club and broke up the players' fun.

The point was that nothing really had changed, boys would still be boys and have their boys' night out. Boys keep swinging. The personnel had changed, hell raisers like

Yorke and the under-rated Mark Bosnich had moved on. Critics said that they never reached their potential because of their lifestyles. Bosnich in particular paid a very high price for his. As the boxer John Conteh famously said when questioned if women and drink had undermined his once fabulous career, 'If it was not for women and drink I would not have done anything.'

Owen was the complete opposite of this, his partner had not yet moved to Manchester, preferring to stay anonymous. Since he had been in Manchester he had kept a deliberately low profile. To some extent he had been overwhelmed by the initial exposure to Manchester in an interview with *The Guardian*. 'I remember looking at Manchester United from a distance. I knew it was a massive club but it is even bigger than I anticipated. The biggest thing about the club is the history and the success. Look at the players who have been here, not only the players I know like Roy Keane but Bryan Robson, Bobby Charlton, George Best. To be part of that is a dream for any player.'

Despite his reluctance to take the centre of the stage Owen's profile had risen sharply in the short time he had been in Manchester. Rooney had the highest profile of the English players but somehow the public had never embraced him with the warmth that they had Beckham. Wayne could not compete with Becks in the looks stakes, the same as his girlfriend Colleen could never establish herself as the number one WAG. She had recently been spotted at Las Vegas attending the fight of another Manchester bruiser, Ricky Hatton, but looked distinctly out of place in the glamour of the occasion. On the New Year Graham Norton show Rooney was portrayed as a chimp when the Irish comedian was talking about his wedding plans.

Owen and Janelle could have been the number one celebrity couple in Manchester and probably England, they had the looks and the style. They chose not to. Roy Keane had an outburst in the press to the effect that the WAGs were running the players' lives and what a bad sign that was.

Don Revie, manager of the fearsome Leeds side of the 70s, always maintained that the role of the wife was integral to the success of the team. The former England manager always encouraged his players to marry young. The current English manager Fabio Capello must have studied the picture of four of his stars, Rio Ferdinand, Gary Neville, Michael Carrick and Wes Brown swaggering to the party. It looked like a revival of the *Reservoir Dogs* film with Rio wearing a velvet jacket and a black scarf, tied Mourinho-style at his throat, and Carrick in an expensive leather jacket.

Nowhere was Owen to be seen in any of the pictures. Perhaps in the words of one of the Sunday's that broke the story 'he made his excuses and left'.

This incident could not have happened at a worse time because the stock of the England team was at an all time low with their failure to qualify for Euro 2008. The perception of the average English footballer was of someone with limited ability, a fat wallet and a brain the size of a Malteser.

The public perception of a WAG was of a silicone-enhanced, grinning popsy little better than a prostitute who cared more about money than their own self respect. Peter Crouch made a quote almost as amusing as that as John Conteh's when he was asked what he would have been if he was not a footballer. 'A virgin' was his answer.

Another reason for the worrying antipathy of the working classes against their own sport of football was the sight of footballers with faces only their mothers could have loved in the company of beautiful women. Abigail Clancy, the partner of the beanpole Crouch, was particularly glamorous and could often be found gracing the front pages of the tabloids.

Rio Ferdinand is a superb player, possibly the best footballing defender since Bobby Moore, but he's not blessed in the looks department. Press reports indicated that the prime mover in the party was Rio. Fabio Capello was a huge admirer of Ferdinand, he had monitored his career since his West Ham days and when Rio was at Leeds he had expressed interest in signing him. Speculation was rife that Capello had pencilled in Ferdinand to be the new England captain. Terry was going down with the SS McLaren and all hands. Rio was now behaving in the same mode of behaviour that had raised doubts about Terry being a fit person to captain his country.

Sir Alex was furious that United's name was besmirched by the antics of some of his players at the Christmas Party. There was no one better equipped in the game to handle the situation than Sir Alex Ferguson.

On the Saturday United entertained Everton at Old Trafford. Rio watched the game from the stand. The official line was that he was injured but the United fans were saying that he had been dropped after receiving the mother of all rollickings from Sir Alex. The camera focused on him during the match hunched against the cold, soberly dressed in a dark overcoat, looking suitably chastened.

Owen missed the game also, he was not dropped but reports suggested that he had a back problem. The champions had four games over the Christmas period beginning with the visit of David Moyes' team, they went to Sunderland on Boxing Day and then a tricky visit to Upton Park. The last of the four games in 10 days was a home game with Birmingham. Knowing Hargreaves's fitness problems, Sir Alex would have used him sparingly in any event, with the Hammers game looking the most likely for selection. This was the first time for four years that Owen had not gone to Calgary for Christmas. Bayern Munich always had a winter break and he had taken advantage of the holiday to visit his family. There had been talk about a winter break for years in England but nothing had ever transpired. The Christmas fixtures were good earners for the clubs and the TV companies welcomed the games as a respite in their schedules from the traditional Christmas films.

The back problem was not a new issue. Doctors were puzzled that they could never diagnose the problem from the many x-rays that they took of him. It was eventually put to him that his legs were not the same length. This put stress on his back and numerous other areas. In Germany he had been fitted with special insoles to compensate and balance out his legs.

Sir Alex must have been aware of the problem before he splashed out a fortune for Owen. The pitch at Anfield had not been particularly hard, it had been a wet autumn rather than a freezing one but with the onset of winter the surfaces would change appreciably. In horseracing parlance the going would change from 'soft' to 'firm'.

Everton proved a tough nut to crack, unbeaten in 14 matches they were the form team of the Premiership. Michael Carrick played in Owen's role with Anderson alongside. A hangover from the party seemed to affect United and the crowd were even more subdued than of late. Ronaldo struck one of his specials after 22 minutes to put United ahead. The Portuguese superstar had missed the party because he had been in Zurich collecting his third place World Player of the Year Award. Tim Cahill equalised for the away side within five minutes and this is how it stayed till three minutes from time. Then Everton defender Steven Pienaar had a rush of blood to the head and needlessly brought down Giggs in the box. Cristiano Ronaldo slotted home the penalty to win three crucial points for United. It was stroked home and easily beat ex-United keeper Tim Howard for his 33rd goal in his last 50 appearances. Owen left the match with a smile on his face, United were still second in the league just a point behind Arsenal.

They were to hit the top on Boxing Day after thrashing Sunderland 4-0 at the Stadium of Light. Owen had made his home debut against them in September but once again was missing from the United line up. Roy Keane's problems increased as his Sunderland team were completely outclassed by United. They raced to a 3-0 first half lead and then cruised for the remainder of the match. Saha, criticised in the press and tipped to move on, notched two of the goals.

Owen was back for the West Ham fixture, always a problematic game. Last Christmas, in Alan Curblishley's first game in charge, the Hammers had scrambled a vital win with a late goal. Twice Sir Alex had seen his title hopes perish at Upton Park as the home side, spurred on by a fanatical crowd, had denied his team victory. This year was no different, they went down 1-2 in their poorest showing of the season so far and their third defeat away from home.

Cristiano Ronaldo scored again after 17 minutes when he headed home a simple chance. Owen had a poor game by his high standards, earning a 6/10 rating in the *Daily Mail.* West Ham had a makeshift side out but Scott Parker and Hayden Mullins aided by the veteran Freddie Ljungberg made it hard for him to stamp his authority on the game. Sunderland had been a breeze but the same hesitancy and lethargy that had affected their performance against Bolton started to appear in their play.

The West Ham crowd disliked United more than any of the other London crowds did. The great battles over the seasons with Arsenal meant that both sets of fans had a grudging respect for one another. Since Chelsea had been taken over by the Russian money the soul of the club had been eroded. The original hard core fans had drifted away, disillusioned by the prices and the sterile football. They had been replaced by glory hunters and new fans who had no heritage or concept of the scope of the fixture. Consequently the atmosphere at Stamford Bridge was usually stilted. West Ham were very different in that they still retained the roots of their original support. When old enemies such as United were in town they did not hold back, in fact fixtures like that were what they lived for. Tevez had almost single handedly kept West Ham in the Premiership the previous season and their fans showed their appreciation by giving him a wonderful reception upon his return. It was a marvellous tribute to a great player. Certainly no United player could have ever received such an ovation from an East End crowd. Tevez was an emotional player and the occasion seemed to get to him. When he acknowledged the cheers with a cross armed salute, a homage to the two hammers on the club badge, a massive chorus of 'There's only one Carlos Tevez' rang out. He was on record as saying that were he to score he would not celebrate. Ronaldo had done the same thing in the Champions League against his old club Sporting when he notched the winner.

Anderson replaced the muted Tevez on 64 minutes. The game should have been clinched but Ronaldo smashed a penalty kick wide. When Cristiano had scored the winner against Everton a week before he had clipped the penalty home. Throughout the game at Upton Park he had been subject to a stream of abuse from the crowd. Determined to win the game and at the same time make a point he raced forward in a Rooney-like frenzy and smashed the ball. It flew wide of the post and thudded against the hoardings. Cristiano was furious as he realized not only had he allowed his feelings to get the better of him but he had missed a golden chance to seal the match. Owen stood behind Ronaldo when he took aim, arms on hips, head slightly bowed. Once again Owen wore the black away kit which he had worn with such distinction at Anfield and in the Emirates Stadium. His heart sank as he watched the kick being squandered, it would be hard now, he thought, as he watched the Hammers fans celebrate.

Early in the second half Rio's brother Anton had come on for Parker. Scott had jarred his knee, something Owen was highly conscious of in the tricky conditions. Seven years younger than his sibling, the West Ham defender had been injured for most of the season. Like his brother, Anton had been involved in some colourful incidents off the field and the jury was still out on whether he would make anywhere near the impression in top class football Rio had. Thirteen minutes from time though he was the hero of the hour as he drifted behind Darren Fletcher to nod Mark Noble's corner kick past Tomasz Kuszczak. Owen was in the box but was stranded as Ferdinand Jnr outwitted Ferdinand senior and co.

Sir Alex was furious – he was watching the game from the stands as he was still banned from the touchline following his antics at the Reebok. Owen was subbed for the first time since he had joined the club. It was more tactical than anything as Nani was flung forward in an attempt to grab the winner. The gamble backfired as West Ham stole the game from under their very noses. Evra gave away a foul on the right and Noble curled over another high centre. The West Ham centre back Matthew Upson rose above Vidic to head in the winner. It was a terrible brace of goals to concede, old fashioned ploys and predictable plays.

United's recent weaknesses in the air were becoming a concern. At Anfield the only time United had been remotely troubled was when Peter Crouch had outjumped Evra at the far post. Owen had patrolled so well that day that very few crosses and chips ever reached that area but an Achilles heel had appeared. The other Mersey side had scored their equaliser at Old Trafford when Everton's Cahill had outjumped Evra to score. The Upton Park game was a shambles. Sir Alex told the press that United did not deserve to win the game, a fact substantiated by the West Ham fans who jammed the switchboards of the phone-ins crowing at their third straight win over his team. Anoraks poured over record books attempting to find when/if such a thing had ever happened before.

Ferguson was 66 on New Year's Eve, he was obviously still upset by the business of the Christmas party and the behaviour of some of his players. He spoke to AOL Sports on his birthday and his words must have chilled some of his party goers. 'Football has changed but you cannot lose your contract. That is why we make changes here at Manchester United when we see anyone interfering with this sense of contract. When we see this, then it's time to go because this club is based on everyone being together'.

When Sky bought the heart and soul of English football in 1992 the players got £300 for losing and £600 for a win. The incentives were clear but now it was blurred, and this is what concerned Sir Alex and his disciple Roy Keane. The top players in the Premiership were now in the comfort zone: why pull out all the stops every week when you were pulling down £80k a week and drove a Bentley? At Christmas the problems were worse with the temptations and distractions increasing.

One of the reasons he had purchased Owen Hargreaves was that he wanted him as an influence in the dressing room. Sir Alex bought into Hargreaves as a player and also his lifestyle.

The next day, the first day of 2008, United played Birmingham at Old Trafford. Owen was named on the bench. Sir Alex was still not exposing him to the rigours of two games in four days, he needed him to re-charge his batteries for the rigours of the new year. A first half goal from Tevez was enough to clinch the points. Birmingham had not won at Old Trafford for three decades and the first half was played out mainly in their half. Carrick played in Owen's position alongside Park Ji Sung returning from a long lay off.

As the game progressed Birmingham improved and the malaise that had affected United's play over recent weeks crept back into their game. The home team's midfield supremacy ebbed away in the second half and Birmingham shared more possession without ever creating any clear cut chances. Towards the end Sir Alex brought on Owen to protect their narrow lead. If Steve McClaren had taken similar action a few weeks earlier perhaps English football would have been looking a lot healthier at the start of a New Year.

Chapter Fourteen
The Flowers of Manchester

'No wonder any player who comes to Manchester United never wants to leave. The attention to detail here is fantastic. It's bigger than Bayern, better organised. I was ready for a change. I got stuck in a routine in Munich.'

Owen Hargreaves

Owen came on 11 minutes from the end of the third round FA Cup tie against Aston Villa on the first Saturday night in January. Fabio Capello had ventured out on a freezing winter's night to watch his first match in England and assess the form of some of his players. Villa had a strong contingent of young English players in their side but two of Capello's brightest hopes Rooney and Owen started on the bench. Rooney had come on ten minutes before Owen and looked very lively. United wore their white and black away strip.

Within a minute of Owen coming on for a listless Saha, United took the lead when Ronaldo scored from close range. Giggs had crossed to the far post and with the Villa defence caught square Ronaldo stole in to score his 19th goal of the season. Rooney brightened the evening and almost brought a smile to the watching Capello's face when he bulleted in the second. Sven used to leave matches with unseemly haste when he was coach but not the big Italian, who always looked as if he was wearing a shirt a collar size too small for him. Owen had little time to show what he could do in opposition to Gareth Barry who was one of Villa's better players. Sixty-two year old Capello must have pencilled Barry in for the forthcoming game against Switzerland. Looking through his trademark designer glasses Capello must have grimaced when he saw Owen lose possession shortly after coming on.

The 33,630 who watched the game together with the new England coach was Villa's lowest of the season. Also in the crowd was an elderly man in a beige overcoat and tartan scarf. Few people would recognise him as being former Villa winger Peter McParland who once scored two goals against Manchester United in the 1957 FA Cup Final. The defeat cost the Busby Babes the double. Some said that they would have won it if McParland's challenge had not shattered goalkeeper Ray Wood's cheekbone.

After the match Sir Alex Ferguson joked that after Rooney's goal scoring introduction from the bench he had found the new Ole Gunnar Solskjaer. It was no longer the Baby Faced Assassin but the Assassin Faced baby.

United announced a club record turnover of £245m and figures that indicated that they had a worldwide support of 139 million fans who claimed to follow the Reds. In the same week it was announced that Ottmar Hitzfeld was to quit Bayern Munich at the end of the season. Ottmar had returned to Bayern when Magath left. Owen saw a lot of similarities between his new boss and the man who had won two European Cups with different clubs. Both men were great observers and could tell a player's fitness and form by looking at them.

United moved into overdive by crushing the decaying Newcastle 6-0 at Old Trafford. The Geordies were in the Twilight Zone after the exit of the ill-fated Sam Allardyce (a decision that would have met with disapproval from Owen's father whose roots were firmly linked with Big Sam's old club Bolton). Cristiano Ronaldo was in inspired form, scoring his first ever hat trick for the club, the fans were beginning to wonder if he had sold his soul to the devil. Owen was rested. Carrick was playing well doing Owen's defensive duties. The product of the Wallsend Boys Club also found time to set up attacks with some well weighted passes. Like Veron, Carrick was a wonderful passer but lacked the energy and two footedness of the ball-keeper Hargreaves.

The Madejski Stadium was the scene of Owen's comeback against Reading. United won a hard-fought match 2-0 with the deadly duo of Rooney and Ronaldo again claiming the goals. Owen, watched again by Capello, had an astute game intercepting the attacks sparked by Dave Kitson and Leroy Lita. Owen, in his retriever role, brought a more physical aspect to the midfield as Reading, who had given United a hard game in the season's opener, pressed hard. Owen almost broke the deadlock with his first goal for United with a long range free-kick which whistled over the bar. United weathered the storm and waited patiently for their chance to come.

Owen went off after 70 minutes to be replaced by Nani, as he started to tire and his energy level dropped. Thirteen minutes from time, with Reading tiring, Rooney cushioned home Carlos Tevez's cross. This stung Reading who threw everything into a last ditch attack on the United goal. With Owen off the field, gaps appeared in front of the United back four and in one of them Kitson inexplicably shot narrowly wide. Ronaldo made it safe in the dying seconds when he burst through to fire in the second.

Owen did not return to Manchester after the game. Instead, with the rest of the United party, he took the coach down the M4 to Heathrow where they caught a plane to Saudi Arabia. Their destination was Riyadh where they were taking part in a testimonial match against Al Hilal for the former Saudi Arabia and Wolves forward Sami Al-Jaber. They travelled all night and did not arrive at King Khaled International Airport until 5.45 the following morning. The sun was rising when eventually the players crashed out in their hotel. Questions were raised about the wisdom of undertaking a daunting 6,000-mile round trip at that critical stage of an arduous season. The answer was moolah, United received a £1m fee plus all their expenses were paid. It was United's first visit to Saudi Arabia and they were besieged by fans who garlanded them with flowers.

The game was played in front of an all male 70,000 crowd. United lost 2-3 and Danny Welbeck missed a penalty. Sami Al-Jaber scored one of the goals for the home side. The papers were full of pictures next day of Sir Alex with the belly dancers and Park Ji-Sung on a camel carrying fine sherbets. The media circus was in full flow, banks of flashbulbs. As a United player, Owen had a large official wardrobe, suit, track suit, casual trousers and any number of club polo shirts and shorts. In the *Daily Mirror* there appeared an interesting picture of Owen walking near

Park's camel wearing a United polo shirt, cargo pants and the Arabian head gear.

United stayed in Riyadh until Thursday, warm weather training. The training started at 10am for a couple of hours. At 2pm they played golf and later sight seeing. It reminded Owen of the times he spent in Dubai training with Bayern. The journey home was fraught as the plane had to refuel at Cairo and they spent three long hours on the runway. Even when the exhausted party arrived in Manchester they had a further delay waiting for their luggage.

On the Sunday, showing no side effects from their jaunt United beat Tottenham 3-1 in the fourth round of the FA Cup. Owen played well again, averaging 7/10 in the ratings shown by the *Daily Mail*, *Daily Express* and the *Manchester Evening News*. Owen showed the fans what a tremendous engine he had in what turned out to be a crucial win over a rapidly improving side.

Tottenham came to Old Trafford on a crest of a wave. Whilst United had been catching the rays in Saudi, Tottenham had been hammering Arsenal in the semi-finals of the Carling Cup. A cup that they were to snatch from the clammy grasp of Chelsea in a few weeks time. Juande Ramos had replaced Martin Jol and had set about transforming the North London side. Robbie Keane had put Spurs in front after 24 minutes when his intelligent run put him on the end of Lennon's cross. Tevez equalised before half-time when Dawson's mis-header allowed Giggs the chance to set up Carlos.

Jermaine Jenas was giving Owen a difficult afternoon. Put on a new diet by his new boss Jenas had started showing the form and aeroplane pace that had made him such a prospect around the time Owen had broken onto the

England scene. Jenas shanked a chance wide when he skipped past his England colleague early in the second half.

United started attacking Spurs down the middle, they went in front after 69 minutes when Dawson handled from Rooney and the long limbed Ronaldo rolled in the penalty. The same player clinched it for United two minutes from the end when his low drive went under the Tottenham keeper Radek Cerny.

The match was being commented on by Radio 5 by Ian Dowie, soon to be sacked from his day job by Coventry. Dowie noted that Capello was again watching United and stated that Owen must be a certainty to play in Capello's first England game. Dowie was a fan of Hargreaves and eulogised his career in Germany, listing his honours. As always, there was plenty to interest Capello when United were playing.

Sir Alex Ferguson must have been pleased with Owen's performance. It was unsung. Ronaldo, Rooney, Giggs and Tevez could bring the crowd to their feet in a way that Owen never would but to Sir Alex his performance was just as important. The vital season-changing games were coming thick and fast and he was going to be a key member of the team.

The counter-attack was the basis of most of United play but it was not all about Ronaldo's pace or Rooney's power. It was also about where on the field the move started and more importantly how it started. That was where Owen came in, whether he won it by a tackle, an interception or block. Ferguson had it down to that one moment when the ball was conceded by one player and possession taken by another. The first pass was the most important, it had to be quick and accurate. It was his dictum that the start of the move decided how deadly the completion was.

Owen's Premier League stats at that point made interesting reading:

Minutes on Pitch 980
Shots on target 6
Shots off target 10
Assists 1
Fouls Conceded 11
Fouls awarded 7
Crosses 0
Yellow Cards 1

Owen was 27 the day after the Spurs game. He celebrated quietly; Gary Barlow shared his birthday, another son of Manchester who had a lot to prove in his career. A man who enjoyed enormous early success and then suffered a critical backlash that almost obliterated his career and that of what to all intent and purposes was his backing band. A man who swept back to the very top of his profession by a mixture of grit and fury.

On the Wednesday after the Cup match Portsmouth came to Old Trafford for a Premiership game. Owen did not start; Sir Alex still doubted his ability to play two games in four days. In that type of fixture Owen's particular skills were not required against a Portsmouth side whose game was based on damage limitation. Owen did come on for Ronaldo after 73 minutes, the Portuguese superstar having already won the game with two goals. The second of them was a candidate for goal of the season or possibly even goal of the decade. A free-kick struck with such accuracy and power it drew comparison with the all time greats. Beckham's against Colombia in the 1998 World Cup or Gazza's against Arsenal in the 1991 FA Cup semi-final at Wembley. Around that time Paul Gascoigne was sectioned as he travelled further down the road to nihilistic destruction.

Owen was the complete opposite of the troubled soul who lay in a hospital bed on suicide watch. Both men were famous for pulling on the England shirt but there the similarity ended. Owen spoke to the *Sun* about his first six months at Old Trafford.

'I have just completed my first full week's training since I joined United and this is the best I have felt for a long time. I arrived with a knee problem so was not training all week and just playing games. Maybe the injuries I have had this season have been a legacy of that broken leg. Perhaps it is the physical intensity of the English game even though I enjoy that side of things.'

Then it was Tottenham again at White Hart Lane in a Premiership clash. This was a very tough match for United because it was always that much harder to play a side directly after beating them in a cup competition. Owen played for the first 45 torrid minutes. Sir Alex had started with him and Scholes. Their combination in midfield did not release Ronaldo and Rooney quickly enough. Spurs were out for revenge and set about United from early on. Jenas was at the heart of everything and his duel with Owen continued where it had left off at Old Trafford. Ramos now had Jenas driving forward in a supercharged Lampard-at-his-best role rather than the holding/midfield general role which had inhibited him in recent seasons.

Spurs scored after 20 minutes. Owen caught Jenas's heel in the box. He went to ground appealing for a penalty. At the same time he appeared to handle the ball and push it out to Aaron Lennon. Jenas was clever, he looked away from the ball and blocked Owen from getting it. Instead

Lennon snapped the ball up and crossed low and hard. Van der Sar pushed it out but the intuitive Berbatov was on hand to slot the ball home. Like all great goal scorers he made it look so simple.

Owen became very heated at the situation – he was furious at the referee Mark Clattenburg for allowing the goal to stand. It should have been disallowed on two counts. The first being that Jenas had handled it and the second that he had impeded Owen when he tried to recover the ball. At the break Owen was replaced by Sir Alex who sent on Carrick against his old side. Later on in the half Anderson replaced Scholes and later Nani came on for Giggs. Spurs' pressing game, modelled on Ramos' successful Seville side, rattled United.

Anderson looked a real prospect, a cross between Vieira and Esslen with great pace and power. Spurs held firm and it looked like United would fall behind Arsenal even further. In the last minute though United scrambled an undeserved equaliser. Nani floated a corner to the near post, Tevez challenged Dawson for the ball, and it flew into the net. Tevez claimed it but it was Dawson who got the final touch and the goal was eventually put down as an own goal. United were lucky to escape with a point.

Then it was back to international duty for England and a return to Wembley were Owen had last spent a frustrating evening against Croatia on the bench. Most of the press had included him in their starting line up for the match against Switzerland. Rather surprisingly Owen did not make the opening line-up, Gareth Barry was given the holding role in midfield in preference.

It was always said about Capello that he picked the players in form who suited his system best. An obvious stipulation was that the player had to be fit. Possibly the fitness problems that had dogged Hargeaves' first few months at Old Trafford influenced Capello's selection.

England took the lead after 40 minutes when their best player Joe Cole set up an easy goal for Jenas. Switzerland equalised through their young debutant Derdiyok and England looked shaky but Wright-Phillips restored England's lead. It was that sort of night. Owen replaced Barry with 15 minutes to go to make his first contribution in the near era.

The papers gave him a few lines saying that he did well enough. There was still work to be done.

Then it was back to Old Trafford for the derby game with Manchester City but this was no ordinary derby. Not that there could ever be such a thing between the two sides. United were worried that the minute silence that would be held for the 50th anniversary of the Munich disaster would not be respected by a small element of the City fans. They need not have worried, their behaviour was exemplary as they maintained a total silence. A full minute's silence had been mooted to have been held before the England v Switzerland match at Wembley. Unfortunately some of the southern fans could not be trusted to show the quality of respect displayed by the City fans and only a brief silence was maintained before Capello's new side went into action. But it was an occasion for Manchester United, they had seen Duncan Edwards first, they had loved him first, anything else was surely an intrusion on private grief.

More than 300 United fans had travelled to the site of the crash in Munich. Local residents joined the throng as the wreaths were laid and bagpipes played. Owen's old governor Karl-Heinze Rummenigge represented Bayern Munich and described the disaster as 'A black day for Football'.

Back in Manchester, United had been given special permission by the Premier League to wear a retro 1950s kit. It was a one off sans logo or sponsors' names. No names on the back either. City got into the spirit of things with a similar strip without a sponsor. They were not available to buy. Owen was named as one of the subs. The number 12 was on his back as was the same for his fellow subs Carrick and Park.

Sir Alex and Sven laid wreaths in the centre circle. Sir Alex patted Sven's arm as they walked back from the spot. Sir Alex acknowledged the part City fans had played in the occasion and clapped them.

City spoilt the party though by winning 2-1. It must have felt strange for Owen that day, somewhere deep down he must have felt resentful that he did not start in a game that would go down in history. He was growing to accept the fact that with the rotation policy and his injuries he would not start every game. His time at Munich had stood him in good stead; at their peak Bayern had six great footballers challenging for three, sometimes four, midfield slots.

United just never got going, the occasion overwhelmed them, intoxicated by grief and nostalgia. It was understandable, no other team in the Premier League had been through the emotional mangle in such a manner. United just froze. City had something to prove as they had just gone out of the FA Cup to Sheffield United (too late to save the job of Bryan Robson though), and did not quite look ready to be a top four side yet. Sven must have done his homework because he stifled United and dominated midfield. Martin Petrov, whom Owen had played against in Germany had a fine match and set up his friend Darius Vassell for the first on 25 minutes. Vassell had been reduced to just a fringe player at City for a long time and the goal was a reminder of better days to him.

Benjani, who had played for Portsmouth at Old Trafford just a few weeks before, had joined City in controversial circumstances. Just on half-time he doubled City's lead after more good work by Petrov. The second goal proved insurmountable as United struggled again in the second half. Rooney, suspended for the game, was badly missed. Seventeen minutes from time Owen was sent on along with Carrick to try to salvage something. Carrick ran through to side-foot a goal in the dying seconds but it was too little to late.

A strange, morbid day. Perhaps it was fitting that they lost, a thumping win would not have fitted the occasion.

United proved it was just a glitch, the following week they destroyed league leaders Arsenal 4-0 in a fifth round Cup game. Arsenal were hit by injuries and did not look interested in the competition but the manner of the victory must have damaged their confidence.

Owen played in the Champions league match at Lyon. It looked as if Sir Alex was saving him for the tough Euro games. The highly rated Benzema gave Lyon the lead. Owen was slightly at fault for the goal as he chased the ball when Anderson had it covered and left a gap outside the box, Benzema ran in and scored. Tevez levelled in the dying minutes to increase United's hope of fresh Euro glory. Owen was determined to play his part in achieving it.

Newcastle were next on the agenda and were butchered 5-1 at St James Park. United had scored six against them a few weeks earlier and carried on the destruction of King Kev's team in another early Saturday evening match. Keegan had marched back to take over the Toon Army a few days after the thrashing at Old Trafford. Owen took no part in the match and watched as Ronaldo notched two more goals to turn the thermostat up on the ex-England coach. Keegan, grey haired and dark coated, must have wondered what he had let himself in for as his players plumbed new lows.

United's next match was of special significance to Owen as he scored his first goal for the club. It came in the fifteenth minute of the match against Fulham on a cold but sunny afternoon on the first day of March. Once again Ferguson shuffled the pack and put out a midfield of Owen, Nani, Scholes and Park. Carrick, Giggs and Vidic were not even in the squad. Tevez was fouled on the edge of the box by the gigantic defender Brede Hangeland and a free kick was awarded in the 'D'. With Ronaldo resting on the bench the situation was made for Owen. Up he stepped to scoop the ball over the Fulham wall and arc the ball low into the bottom left-hand corner of the net. The Fulham goal keeper Annti Niemi could do nothing about it.

Before the match odds were given of 22-1 of Hargreaves opening the scoring. Owen had accumulated just a handful of goals in Bavaria but there were few cleaner strikers of the ball in Europe. Nonetheless, his opportunities were restricted in Manchester, with two of the greatest exponents of dead-ball kicking in Ronaldo and Rooney. The goal was an important first for Owen – every player likes to break his duck and his long overdue goal reminded the fans of his all-round importance to the team and the Herculean effort he put in. His skill with free-kicks was to prove even more vital in the coming weeks. This was all the more remarkable considering the ball of pain that lived in his knee, 24 hours a day.

Ji-Sung Park scored the second just on half time when he headed home Scholes cross to give the red war machine an insurmountable lead. Rooney and his chief collaborator Ronaldo came on to stretch their legs for the last 20 minutes and shortly after their introduction, the champions went three up, with Fulham's Simon Davies punting home an own goal after the defence had got into a tangle. Owen briefly appeared on Match of the Day after the game to tell the nation how pleased he was to score his first goal in United colours. He looked super-smart in a tailored club blazer, spectre-white high collar shirt, his hair shining with vitality. The Daily Telegraph gave him 8 out of 10 for his performance.

In the return match against Lyon a 41st minute goal from Ronaldo was enough to put United into the quarter finals where they were drawn against Roma. The performance against the French side was muted. Despite his classy free kick at Fulham the rotation policy meant that he did not start the game. He told the Metro, 'We are all part of the jigsaw puzzle. Nobody is going to play in all the games at United. You trust the boss, don't you, with all the experience he has. So far as I am concerned he has picked the right team pretty much every time'

However some critics were surprised at the sight of Owen sitting on the bench. Surely in the past Sir Alex had told the media that Hargreaves had been bought expressly for European nights at Old Trafford such as this. Owen eventually got on the pitch in the last minute to replace the match winner Ronaldo. United seemed nervy in that match and their poor form carried on into their next match the following Saturday. This was a lunchtime kick off against Portsmouth in the sixth round of the FA Cup which saw the end of their aspirations of achieving a double 'treble'. Owen played for the first 68 minutes of the tie which ended in a 0-1 defeat. Portsmouth went on to win the cup

Michael Carrick replaced Owen and in the increasingly delirious closing minutes he missed the easiest chance of the season. A yard out he hit an air shot when all he had to do was roll the ball over an empty line. As the rain sluiced down a penalty had been awarded when Tomas Kuszcak pulled down Milan Baros in the box which ended in the United keeper being dismissed. Rio Ferdinand went in goal and Pompey's Sulley Muntari beat him from the spot. Owen struggled to get to grips with the game and was involved in some crunching exchanges with the ex-Arsenal and Chelsea midfielder Lassana Diarra, tipped by many to be the new Makele.

It was Portsmouth's first win at Old Trafford since 1957, when they had beaten a United team that included "Busby Babes" Whelan, Coleman, Foulkes and Pegg. Derby, the poorest team not to grace the Premier, were supposed to catch the backlash from the fall-out of the Portsmouth exit. Instead it just turned out to be a narrow 1-0 victory over a demoralised team that had accumulated just 10 points. Once again a team down and out on their feet raised their game to extraordinary levels against the champions. It was unfathomable to most United fans. Ronaldo volleyed home an awkwardly bouncing cross to win the match near the end. Owen sat it out again as Ferguson rotated the midfield interchanging Scholes with Carrick and Anderson with Fletcher.

Owen's father would have been pleased to see his son playing in the next match against Bolton at Old Trafford. With an important match against Liverpool looming,

Ferguson rested Wes Brown and played Owen at right back, a position he had sometimes occupied for Bayern Munich. He played an excellent match, easily slotting into the back four and easily containing the aggressive Kevin Davies. Davies had bullied Evra in the shock defeat at the Reebok but Owen was very aware of the striker even when he was back-pedalling. A lot of Owen's game was based on the distances in respect of his opponents.

Two heart-pounding Ronaldo goals in the first twenty minutes did for Bolton and enabled the star winger to smash George Best's record of the most goals scored by a winger in a season. Owen meanwhile was coming to terms with the demands that a club of the stature of Manchester United was placing on its players. His performance against Bolton typified the way he applied himself to a change in circumstances and the enthusiasm he had for the game.

Liverpool were easily dispatched 3-0 in the next match where Owen was a non-playing substitute, the camera panned on him at one stage – hunched up in a padded jacket, bobbling his head back and forth like a prize-fighter in the corner awaiting the first round bell. It was a fine performance by United who took a massive step towards retaining the title. Wes Brown restored to the side put them in front with only the third goal of his career. Liverpool's Javier Mascherano, nearly bursting with nervous energy, was sent off in a bizarre incident and the game ended as a contest. His absence left a gaping hole in the Liverpool midfield and Owen's particular talents were not required.

Owen would have liked to have played against Liverpool again. When he was a youngster he came over from Canada to play in an under-14 tournament that was staged in Wales. Liverpool had heard the rave reports about him and sent Steve Heighway, then in charge of their youth academy to assess him. Owen received the thumbs down from the former winger who told his father he was 'too greedy'. Fabio Capello did not share Heighway's view and called him up for the friendly match against France. Alongside him was Gareth Barry as the Italian went back to the formation of two guarding players in midfield that had served him so well at AC Milan. France played with two holding midfielders in direct opposition to the England double pivots. They were the underdisputed master, Claude Makele, and his apprentice, Jeremy Toulalan. Owen had a fine match and was voted England's best player in the Sun earning 7/10. The best of a mediocre bunch.

England went down 1-0 and lost to a penalty scored by Ribery, the new sensation of Bayern Munich. Ribery was an interesting player, his face scarred badly by a car crash he showed searing pace, a shot like a howitzer and exquisite skill. Once again Bayern had a player whose talent was undeniable. The penalty was awarded when Anelka burned his team mate Terry for pace and was clattered by David James, last seen performing heroics in goal for Portsmouth at Old Trafford. Even he could not stop Ribery from blasting home the penalty. Terry had lost the captaincy and Rio wore the armband that night. Terry was replaced at half time. Lampard never even made the team that night, complaining of stomach pains. It would appear that the Chelsea axis had run its course in terms of the England set-up and both figures were redundant in Capello's vision of England.

Michael Carrick, who had made the United team against Liverpool in front of Owen, was one of the players excluded from the Paris trip. In the rarefied atmosphere of the top sides in Europe the superstars were judged by how good your understudy was. Such was the strength of the United midfield, Hargreaves was the number one choice for England whilst Carrick at that time was keeping him out of the Reds team.

Owen appeared to have a future for England under Capello, as he had played the whole 90 minutes and his personal duel with Ribery was the focal point of the game. With the imminent departure of Beckham from the International scene perhaps more scope could be given to his dead ball prowess. Richard Williams in the Guardian was full of praise for Owen, singling him out 'as the one player in a red shirt to have distinguished himself over the full 90 minutes... He rose above a threadbare setting with a performance of verve and imitative'.

Owen and Barry met up again the following weekend when Aston Villa were the visitors to Old Trafford. Owen came on after 62 minutes for his Captain at the Stad de Paris, Rio Ferdinand. In one of their most sparkling performances of the season United blitzed the Midlanders 4-0. Owen came on with two other internationals, O`Shea and Anderson, as United replaced three internationals with three more. The gulf between them and wanabbes like Villa was becoming even more pronounced. The fact that they could introduce a player who had been acknowledged as being England's best player against France was just staggering.

United flew off to the eternal city for their first leg clash with Roma, currently lying second in Serie A. They were an elegant side but possibly too lightweight for United. Around that time a strange story was run by the Times about Owen. Oliver Kay and Matt Dickinson wrote that Sir Alex had been angered by Owen's poor time keeping and that he had restricted his appearances as a disciplinary measure.

It was alleged that Owen had arrived late at Manchester Airport on the Monday morning for the flight to Rome. The article quoted a source that made the point that even if Owen had only been the matter of a few seconds late it would have still been a misdemeanour to his boss. The article also made reference to Hargreaves being late for some team meetings. Doubts about his future at Old Trafford were raised for the first time. The story was quickly rubbished, however, by United and Sir Alex told the 'People', 'Carrick has been sensational and that has had a lot to do with Owen not starting games. He has had his injury problems early on and that stopped him from getting bedded in. But Owen played a vital role in Rome and brought the energy and pace to our midfield which turned it for us. He signed a five year contract last year, so of course he's got a future.'

Ferguson was right when he praised Owen's performance in Rome. He had even gone so far as to say that he should have brought him on much earlier in the game than the 62nd minute. At that time United were clinging to a one-goal lead thanks to a powerful Ronaldo header but Roma were causing problems down the flanks. Owen contained the problem and towards the end even found time to push forward as United eventually won 2-0.

On the following Sunday Middlesbrough held United to a 2-2 draw at the Riverside Stadium. Two goals from the Brazilian striker Alves and a second half snowstorm made it an uncomfortable afternoon for Owen and his team mates. Owen came on after 67 minutes with United trailing 2-1 but Rooney equalised soon after Owen's appearance.

Owen had his best game for United so far in the 1-0 victory over Roma in the return. He played in a more attacking role and was voted man of the match for his outstanding contribution. Twice he broke through to bring fine saves out of the Roma keeper Doni and twice he powered down the right to send in perfect crosses. Ryan Giggs failed to convert the first but Tevez scored the winner from the second. If this performance was inspiring it was topped the following Sunday when Owen scored the winning goal against Arsenal in a thrilling 2-1 home victory. Arsene Wenger later admitted that the defeat had cost them the title. He was convinced that the title was headed back to London when Emmanuel Adebayor put them ahead early in the second half. Ronaldo equalised with a twice taken penalty and then Owen won the game when he curled a free kick over the opposition wall and past goalkeeper Jens Lehman after 72 minutes. It was identical to the goal he had scored against Fulham a few weeks earlier and went a long way towards United retaining their title. In a few days Owen had shown exactly why Sir Alex had been so anxious to bring him to the club.

United dropped vital points in their next two Premier away games drawing at Blackburn and losing in dubious circumstances at Chelsea. Two of Owens ex-Bayern buddies did the damage – Roque Cruz scored Blackburn's goal, in a match that Owen missed through injury, and a Michael Ballack double upset them at Stamford Bridge. Owen came on for the injured Vidic after 14 minutes and played another storming game. Dubious refereeing decisions cost them dear in a hate-filled atmosphere as a desperate Chelsea clawed themselves back into contention for the title.

Owen had a happier experience playing in the semi finals of the Champions League against Barcelona. He played both matches at right back and did not put a foot wrong in either fixture. The first game ended scoreless at the Nou Camp and was best remembered for Ronaldo's missed penalty in the first minute. Paul Scholes rolled back the years to score the only goal of the tie in the return at Old Trafford. The green-eyed Owen was the unsung hero of the matches though as his coolness and class ensured that the star-spangled Barca attack was denied any chances. The Calgary Kid had returned home to England to fulfil his huge potential.

United retained their premiership title by winning their last two games. West Ham were over-run 4-1 at Old Trafford in a match that Owen played at right back. His strong run and perfect cross set up the second goal which helped to ease the Reds' nerves. His experience was a vital factor in winning those crucial points. This was again the case at Wigan where he was introduced to the action at a vital stage with United clinging to a solitary goal lead. Rivals Chelsea still had a chance of snatching the title but Owen sealed up the back and United went on to win 2-0 and take the biggest domestic honour. It was a great moment for Owen as he collected his medal in his first season in England.

What the future holds for this midfield maestro can only be guessed at. He has come such a long way, crossing oceans and continents to reach his current, unrivalled place for both club and country. However, one thing is for certain – his yeoman spirit and indomitable will to win will see that whatever challenges lie ahead, he will be at the very centre of the fight, battling with heart and soul.

Owen Hargreaves stepped up to take his penalty in the European Champions League final shoot-out on 21 May 2008. United were trailing 2-3 on penalties. Once again a shoot-out was to loom large on what was the most important game so far of his star-spangled career.

It had started so well for Hargreaves and United. Sir Alex Ferguson had picked him to play on the right side of midfield, the first time he had started for the Reds in that position, but the same berth he had occupied for Bayern Munich the night they had lifted the same trophy by beating Valencia on penalties. Owen was in direct opposition against his England colleague and friend Ashley Cole. Cole stood off Owen early in the game which allowed Owen to get forward and show the fans yet another side of his game.

On 26 minutes United went ahead, with Ronaldo heading his 42nd goal of the season, from a cross supplied by Wes Brown. They should have made it safe there and then but two world-class saves from Petr Cech denied first Tevez and then Carrick. Cech proved to the watching world why he was the best goalkeeper in it.

Just on half time Lampard equalised for Chelsea with the aid of not one but two lucky deflections.

That goal upset United and Chelsea looked the stronger side in the second half as they pushed forward with renewed vigour. Owen dropped back and played a vital role in containing the powerful Chelsea midfield. The game went to extra time; Chelsea looked exhausted while the United boys stayed on their feet as the game moved into a crucial phase.

Four minutes into extra time Lampard was unlucky to hit the bar and perhaps Owen's thoughts turned momentarily to the Nou Camp and Bayern's near misses. Giggs, on for Scholes, missed a golden chance to clinch it. In the closing stages Drogba was sent off in an incident with Vidic.

So to penalties. Tevez, Ballack, Carrick and Belletti

scored the first four. Then Ronaldo tried to beat Cech with his version of the Ali shuffle but the orange-clad keeper bluffed him and the kick was missed. Lampard rolled in his attempt and United trailed. Owen was under tremendous pressure now; if he fluffed his spot-kick United would be out. No chance. Completely unfazed, he smashed a powerful shot into the top left hand corner of the net. Cech never got near it.

John Terry, with the chance to win it for Chelsea, slid on the wet ground and missed his kick; Giggs converted his chance and then Van der Sar triumphantly saved from Anelka to take the trophy to Old Trafford for the third time.

Owen proudly collected his winner's medal and became only the second English player in history to win two Championship League medals, for two different clubs. (The other was Manchester United player Jimmy Rimmer, who came on as a sub in the 1968 win over Benfica, and then won a medal with Aston Villa). Somewhere in the stadium Terry and ex-United executive Peter Kenyon were crying; Owen stood proudly next to Sir Alex Ferguson – the man whose faith in Owen had been repaid.

Appendix

Statistics

(collated by Marie Macleay)

BAYERN MUNICH

SEASON	BUNDESLIGA	CUP	CHAMPIONS LGE	GOALS	TOTAL APP'S
2000–01	14	1	4	0	19
2001–02	29	5	13	0	45
2002–03	25	5	5	2	35
2003–04	25	3	6	2	34
2004–05	27	3	8	3	38
2005–06	15	4	3	3	22
2006–07	9	1	5	0	15
TOTAL	**144**	**22**	**44**	**10**	**210**

Honours won with Bayern Munich: Bundesliga **Title winners:** 2001, 2003, 2005 and 2006 **UEFA Champions League:** 2001 **Inter-Continental Cup (Toyota, World Club Cup):** 2001 **Domestic Cup (DFB Pokal):** 2003, 2005, 2006 **Premiere Ligapokal:** 2004

Individual Awards won while with Bayern: The European U-21 player of the year award in 2001

Ian Macleay

ENGLAND

DATE	OPPONENT	COMP	SCORE
26/03/08	France	F	0-1
06/02/08	Switzerland	F	2-1 (Sub)
28/03/07	Andorra	Euros Q	3-0
24/03/07	Israel	Euros Q	0-0
06/09/06	Macedonia	Euros Q	1-0
02/09/06	Andorra	Euros Q	5-0
16/08/06	Greece	F	4-0
01/07/06	Portugal	WC	0-0 (Lost on pens)
25/06/06	Ecuador	WC	1-0
20/06/06	Sweden	WC	2-2
10/06/06	Paraguay	WC	1-0 (Sub)
30/05/06	Hungary	F	3-1 (Sub)
07/09/05	Northern Ireland	WC Q	0-1 (Sub)
03/09/05	Wales	WC Q	1-0 (Sub)
17/08/05	Denmark	F	1-4 (Sub)
26/03/05	Northern Ireland	WC Q	4-0 (Sub)
09/02/05	Holland	F	0-0 (Sub)
09/10/04	Wales	WC Q	2-0 (Sub)
08/09/04	Poland	WC Q	2-1 (Sub)
24/06/04	Portugal	Euros	2-2 (Lost on pens; Sub)
17/06/04	Switzerland	Euros	3-0 (Sub)
13/06/04	France	Euros	1-2 (Sub)
05/06/04	Iceland	F	6-1 (Sub)
01/06/04	Japan	F	1-1 (Sub)
31/03/04	Sweden	F	0-1 (Sub)
18/02/04	Portugal	F	1-1 (Sub)
10/09/03	Liechtenstein	Euros Q	2-0 (Sub)
06/09/03	Macedonia	Euros Q	2-1
11/06/03	Slovakia	Euros Q	2-1 (Sub)

Owen Hargreaves

03/06/03	Serbia & Mont.	F	2–1 (Sub)
12/02/03	Australia	F	1–3 (Sub)
12/10/02	Slovakia	Euros Q	2–1 (Sub)
07/09/02	Portugal	F	1–1 (Sub)
07/06/02	Argentina	WC	1–0 (Sub)
02/06/02	Sweden	WC	1–1
26/05/02	Cameroon	F	2–2
21/05/02	South Korea	F	1–1
17/04/02	Paraguay	F	4–0 (Sub)
27/03/02	Italy	F	1–2 (Sub)
01/09/01	Germany	WC Q	5–1 (Sub)
15/08/01	Holland	F	0–2 (Sub)

As at April 2008 Owen had gained 41 caps for England with 22 wins and 11 draws.

Owen was voted England player of the year in 2006 as well as collecting the award for the England player of the 2006 World Cup.

MANCHESTER UNITED (as at 11/05/08)

Premiership	16 games	7 subs	2 goals
FA Cup	2 games	1 sub	
Champions League	4 games	3 subs	

YALE STUDIES IN ECONOMICS: 8

RICARDIAN

ECONOMICS

A Historical Study

BY MARK BLAUG

New Haven: YALE UNIVERSITY PRESS

1958

Printed in the United States of America by Vail-Ballou Press, Inc., Binghamton, N.Y.

Library of Congress catalog card number: 58-7187

Could it be that an Englishman, and he not in academic bowers, but oppressed by mercantile and senatorial cares, had accomplished what all the universities of Europe, and a century of thought, had failed even to advance by one hair's breadth? All other writers had been crushed and overlaid by the enormous weight of facts and documents; Mr. Ricardo alone had deduced, *a priori,* from the understanding itself, laws which first gave a ray of light into the unwieldy chaos of materials, and had constructed what had been but a collection of tentative discussions into a science of regular proportions now first standing on an eternal basis.

THOMAS DE QUINCEY, *Confessions of an English Opium Eater* (1821)

PREFACE

IN BROAD OUTLINE, if not in detail, the Ricardian phase of classical political economy represents familiar terrain to the historian of economic thought. Since the title of this book suggests another chronological survey, I take this opportunity of saying that its theme is the rise and decline of the school of Ricardo in England: the reasons for its survival, but also the causes of its decay. "Study problems, not periods," Lord Acton used to say, and I have tried to hold to this precept throughout the book. The reader should not be surprised, therefore, if such standard topics as the theory of international values and the quantity theory of money are neglected except insofar as they bear directly upon the central theme of this study.

Oswald St. Clair's *Key to Ricardo* (London, 1957) appeared after this book was written. Much as I would have benefited from Mr. Clair's study in the writing of the first chapter, on the whole my argument would not have been much affected. *A Key to Ricardo* is an immensely useful guide but on some analytical questions, such as the invariable measure of value and the controversy over Say's Law, it does not altogether succeed in dispelling the air of paradox which hangs over Ricardo's words.

The present work grew out of a doctoral dissertation submitted to Columbia University in 1955. I am indebted to G. J. Stigler and T. W. Hutchison, who jointly supervised my thesis, for valuable criticisms on matters of detail and general emphasis. R. K. Webb's constructive advice cleared up many additional loose ends. William Fellner read the last draft and offered many helpful suggestions, particularly with reference to the Malthus-Ricardo debate on gluts. My greatest obligation is to C. S. Shoup: my conception of Ricardo's system owes so much to the many illuminating discussions I had with him that I hardly know where my ideas leave off and his begin.

My thanks are due to Mrs. Anne Granger, the most patient of typists, and to the helpful attendants of the Goldsmith Library of the University of London and that haven for scholars, the British Museum Reading Room. Some of the material in Chapter 9 has been taken from my article on "The Empirical Content of Ricardian Economics" which appeared in the *Journal of Political Economy* in 1956. I wish to thank the editors of that journal for permission to republish.

My wife went over the whole manuscript many times, doing her best to translate it into English. It is to her that this book is dedicated. Needless to say, the responsibility for any lapses, and for all opinions expressed in this book, is entirely my own.

M. B.

New Haven, Conn.
September 1957

CONTENTS

CHAPTER 1

Introduction

THE RAPID ASCENDANCE and almost total supremacy of Ricardian economics in the half-century after Ricardo's death has long been regarded as "something of a curiosity and a mystery." [1] Keynes believed that the key to the puzzle was to be found in "a complex of suitabilities in the doctrine to the environment into which it was projected"; certainly, this defines the nature of the problem. As to the completeness of the Ricardian victory, Keynes had no doubt: "Ricardo conquered England as completely as the Holy Inquisition conquered Spain."

Ricardo was fortunate in winning aggressive disciples. And disciples must soon acquire a vested interest in the ideas they seek to popularize; this is at once the simplest and most obvious explanation of the hegemony of Ricardian economics. "Favorable as may have been the time, and peculiarly endowed the man and his manner, economic science would never have felt the Ricardian influence to the extent that it did, but for the intellectual tenacity, the irrepressible enthusiasm and the propagandist activity of the group of friends, disciples and expositors—James Mill, McCulloch, Torrens, John Stuart Mill, Mrs. Marcet, De Quincey—who promptly espoused the new dispensation and gave it widespread currency." [2] And yet, skillfully as Ricardian economics was disseminated, the Ricardianism which conquered England would probably not have received Ricardo's personal endorsement. A series of amendments and defenses thrown up against criticism soon covered and in the end almost buried the original doctrine. The dogmatism of Ricardo's followers and the weight of tradition did not in fact prevent the gradual surrender of most of the basic elements of Ricardo's system. That "complex of suitabilities" which made for doctrinal success included many strands of thought which were alien to the spirit, if not to the letter, of Ricardo's *Principles*.

The works of disciples, zealous or otherwise, often makes dull reading. Hence recent interest in the period has shifted to the dissenting and neglected economists whose writings contain the seeds of so much

1. J. M. Keynes, *The General Theory of Employment, Interest, and Money* (London, 1936), p. 32.

2. J. H. Hollander, *David Ricardo. A Centenary Estimate* (Baltimore, 1910), p. 121.

later doctrine. The works of such authors as Scrope, Senior, Lloyd, and Longfield followed each other so closely, each pursuing essentially similar arguments in opposition to Ricardo, that we can hardly avoid speaking of "two different and more or less contemporary schools . . . in England, the classical or Ricardian and the utility schools." [3]

Since the utility theory of value made its appearance in England around 1830 or thereabouts, some historians have seized upon that date as marking the end of the Richardian school.[4] Thereafter, the influence of Ricardo, it is maintained, showed itself only in isolated areas of the science, such as the theory of rent or the doctrine of international trade. Schumpeter has gone so far as to assert that the Ricardian school was never dominant in British economics, thereby completing the full circle from Keynes. If we count heads, Schumpeter insists, we shall find that "the Ricardians were always in the minority, even in England, and it is only Ricardo's personal force which, as we look back, creates the impression that his teaching . . . dominated the thought of the time and that the other economists were just opponents of what was then called the New School . . . The opposite is nearer the truth." [5]

Numerical minority or majority, however, is hardly an adequate basis for assessing the weight of doctrinal influence. Moreover, Schumpeter fails to spell out the views which are supposed to characterize Ricardian economics; consequently his bold generalization stands unsupported.[6] At one point, much later in his *History*, Schumpeter does refer briefly to what he calls "the specifically Ricardian elements in the 'classic' structure, such as, e.g., the labor-quantity theory of value" (p. 921 n.). If we insist on the labor theory of value as the essence of Ricardo's teachings, then of course it follows that Ricardian economics was stillborn and died, literally, with Ricardo in 1823. For Ricardo's theory of value was never adequately expounded or defended by any of his followers. But this is another matter. They were not less Ricardians for all that. Similarly, if we assume with Keynes that Say's Law of Markets was the keystone of Ricardian economics, nothing more needs to be said; since Malthus' attack on Say's Law attracted no attention the Ricardian victory was "complete." But the doctrine that supply creates

3. M. Bowley, *Nassau Senior and Classical Economics* (New York, 1949), p. 17. See also E. R. A. Seligman, *Essays in Economics* (New York, 1925), p. 120.

4. R. L. Meek, "The Decline of Ricardian Economics in England," *Economica*, February 1950.

5. J. A. Schumpeter, *The History of Economic Analysis* (New York, 1954), p. 598; also p. 480.

6. Schumpeter argues, for instance, that J. S. Mill's *Principles* (1848) was "no longer Ricardian"; but on problems of interest theory, Schumpeter agrees, Mill saw fit "to uphold Ricardian doctrine," and on other questions too he showed signs of "lingering Ricardianism" (pp. 529, 561, 654, 662).

its own demand was never a vital feature of the Ricardian outlook, much less its keystone. Most of Ricardo's critics accepted Say's Law and every one of Ricardo's followers entertained different versions of it.

The heart of the Ricardian system consists of the proposition that the yield of wheat per acre of land governs the general rate of return on invested capital as well as the secular changes in the distributive shares. This theorem was the basis of Ricardo's macro-economic model and on it depend all the practical Ricardian deductions with respect to economic policy. It is the presence of this element, rather than the Law of Markets or the special theory of value which Ricardo employed to obtain his results, which identifies a "Ricardian economist." By the test of avowed obeisance to the master, there was never more than a handful of Ricardians; by the test of doctrinal assent, almost every economist in the period came under the sway of the Ricardian tradition. In this sense, the theories of Ricardo did exert an overwhelming influence on British economic thought throughout the period from Waterloo to the Franco-Prussian War. In the 1830's, it is true, there were definite signs of the impending dissolution of the Ricardian school. But a strong revival in the forties and fifties postponed the final breakdown. Jevons had good reasons, as we shall see, to fulminate against "the noxious influence of authority" emanating from "the unity and influence of the Ricardo-Mill school."

A Note on Ricardo Criticism

The critical literature on Ricardo is vast; unfortunately its quality is inversely related to its bulk.[7] The manias of the historical school have put a blight on most of the German material (which accounts for some 50 per cent of the total). A good deal of the remainder is outdated and practically worthless for anyone interested in the analytical core of Ricardo's system. All in all, apart from the classic commentaries of Wicksteed, Wicksell, and Marshall, there are probably no more than a dozen articles and books on Ricardo in the major European languages that can be read with profit today.

Despite the fact that few economists have been so frequently interpreted as Ricardo, there is no unanimity regarding his essential message. Considering the common misconceptions that prevailed in his own lifetime and the rather prosaic treatment still accorded him in

7. No adequate checklist or annotated bibliography is available. A recent effort which was to have repaired this deficiency (B. Franklin and G. Legman, eds., *David Ricardo and Ricardian Theory. A Bibliographical Checklist* [New York, 1949]), cannot be recommended. It suffers from serious omissions, irrelevant entries, and frequent misprints, and the annotating comments, when supplied at all, are almost always misleading.

many modern histories of economic thought, it becomes necessary to ask, once again, what Ricardo really meant.

Nothing could justify another forced march over such well-worn terrain were it not that the recent edition of the complete *Works and Correspondence of David Ricardo* [8] has thrown new light on almost every aspect of Ricardo's writings.

Ever since Cannan's famous onslaught [9] it has been unnecessary to dwell on the obvious errors in formal reasoning committed by the classical authors. Few today subscribe to what he called "the faith that mistake was impossible to the more prominent English economists of the period 1776 to 1848." However, Cannan's destructive critique is open to the charge of rendering classical economics void of sense and logic. "Has anyone ever risen from reading it," Professor Ogilvie once observed, "without feeling that all economists from 1776 to 1848 must have been not silly merely, but almost imbecile." [10] Cannan himself must have realized this, for in the last chapter of his book he suddenly appeals to historical relativism in an effort to rationalize the gaps in classical analysis.

Whether we ought to give the "ancients" the benefit of historical insight or look down from present heights at their mistakes, in the belief that truth is concentrated in the last increment of economic knowledge, is largely a matter of taste and purpose. Nevertheless, I cannot suppress the conviction that an appraisal of a historical body of doctrine without reference to the conditions under which it was formulated or the contemporary state of analysis out of which it arose soon becomes an uninteresting display of omniscience. Seen exclusively through the lenses of the "marginal revolution," classical political economy takes on the character of a graveyard of elementary blunders; nothing survives, not even the questions which were raised.[11] But as the history of ideas is a matter not so much of what was said, but of why it was said, my purpose here is to place the evolution of Ricardian economics

8. Ed. P. Sraffa and M. Dobb (Cambridge, Eng., 1951–55). Vol. *1* contains the *Principles,* Vol. *2* the unpublished "Notes on Malthus," Vols. *3* and *4* pamphlets and papers both published and unpublished, Vol. *5* parliamentary speeches and evidence, Vols. *6–9* private correspondence, and Vol. *10* biographical miscellany.

9. E. Cannan, *Theories of Production and Distribution in English Political Economy* (London, 1893; reprinted 1953).

10. *Economic Journal,* March 1930, p. 22 n.

11. The following statement of this position by Professor Knight is, to be sure, a little extreme: "It cannot be maintained that Senior, or any member of the older classical school, used or grasped the elementary principles of analysis as applied to economic phenomena. They simply did not see that the fundamental economic concepts are magnitudes interrelated as function-and-variable, that the nature of the economic problem is to maximize something, and that this is done when 'final increments' (partial derivatives) are equalized through an appropriate

in a framework which can display its logical development, be it the logic of history or the logic of intellectual growth.

Of course, the substantive theoretical achievements of the Ricardian system go far beyond the range of problems to which it was initially addressed. Indeed, some of Ricardo's ideas have proved to be of lasting significance. The theory of comparative costs in international trade is, perhaps, the most obvious example. Quite apart from such specific analytical propositions, the Ricardian approach to economic development, broadly conceived in terms of a conflict between tendencies toward increasing or diminishing returns, may be said to survive down to the present. Judged by the experiences of the age in which it was evolved, the Ricardian system fell somewhat short of providing a useful tool for the analysis of economic growth: on a large number of questions it offered wrong predictions. Still, it might be argued that much of Ricardian economics has stood up well in the sense that successive generations have continued to weigh the same "tendencies," albeit with different conclusions. But as Ricardo and his followers actually employed it, the Ricardian approach was marked by an excessive emphasis upon population growth and natural resource scarcities. So interpreted, Ricardian economics is no longer an important influence upon our thinking about economic progress. However, the central problem which Ricardo posed, namely, the changes in the relative shares of land, labor, and capital and their connection with the rate of capital accumulation, remains our abiding concern. And his interest in the effects of technological change, even if it expressed itself as an afterthought in the famous chapter on machinery, was the starting point of a line of analysis which only now seems to be bearing fruition.

---

allocation of means made among modes of use subject to a principle of diminishing efficiency. This, it is true, virtually amounts to saying that as economic theorists they did not know what they were talking about. It is a harsh statement, but in our opinion the study of the history of theory should largely center around such negative, and harsh, judgements" (*Journal of Political Economy*, February 1939, p. 133).

CHAPTER 2

Ricardo's System

> And thence we plunged into the recesses of political economy. I know not why this study has been termed uninteresting. No sooner had I entered upon its consideration, than I could scarcely tear myself from it . . . but at that time my uncle's object was not to make a profound political economist. "I wish," said he, "merely to give you an acquaintance with the principles of the science . . . of all sciences, political economy is contained in the fewest books, and yet is the most difficult to master; because all its higher branches require earnestness of reflection, proportioned to the scantiness of reading. Ricardo's work, together with some conversational enlargement of the several topics he treats of, will be enough for our present purpose."
>
> SIR EDWARD BULWER-LYTTON, *Pelham, or Adventures of A Gentleman* (1828)

1. Corn Laws and Food Prices

RICARDO's theoretical system emerged directly and spontaneously out of the great corn laws debate of 1814–16. Even before the Napoleonic Wars were over the issue of protection for agriculture began to attract that steady stream of pamphlets which was to become a permanent feature of British life in the first half of the nineteenth century. Ricardo's first contribution to the dispute over commercial policy, revealingly entitled *An Essay on the Influence of a Low Price of Corn on the Profits of Stock,* appeared on the same day as Robert Torren's *Essay on the External Corn Trade,* and both came close upon West's *Essay on the Application of Capital to Land* and Malthus' *Inquiry into the Nature of Rent.* With a greater or lesser degree of clarity, all four pamphlets develop the familiar major theme of Ricardian economics: the growth of capital and population leads to extension of cultivation to less fertile and less accessible land and to decreasing returns on cultivated land upon the application of successive increments of labor and capital.[1] Likewise, these tracts share the notion that restrictions on the

1. On the emergence of the law of diminishing returns, see Cannan, *op. cit.,* pp. 116–23; J. H. Hollander, "The Concept of Marginal Rent," *Quarterly Journal of Economics,* January 1895; F. Oppenheimer, *David Ricardos Grundrententheorie* (Jena, 1927), pp. 84–106; G. J. Stigler, "The Ricardian Theory of Value and Distribution," *Journal of Political Economy,* June 1952, pp. 195–200.

importation of grain cause the price of wheaten bread to rise and that the price of this food article regulates the money wages of labor and the general rate of profit. Whatever the doctrinal precedence for such a view, this was nothing more than the common belief of the commercial classes of the day. As Richard Cobden observed years later: "In reading the debates upon the passing of the first stringent Corn-law of 1814 I am much struck to find that all parties who took part in that discussion were agreed upon one point,—it was that the price of food regulates the rate of wages. That principle was laid down, not by one side of the House, but by men of no mean eminence on each side, and of course of opposite opinions in other respects." [2]

Commonplace also was the tendency on the part of all four authors to confine the discussion to the effects of the corn laws on the distribution of national income between the so-called "main classes of society"—landlords, capitalists (including tenant farmers), and laborers. This simple conception of social stratification, implied in Adam Smith's tripartite division of revenues, served to link the theoretical argument to the standard parlance of journalists and politicians; it also provided a sense of practical realism which proved to be the decisive factor in the propagation of Ricardo's terse abstractions.

By 1815 Britain had long since ceased to be a grain-exporting country. In years of dearth the home-grown supply was hardly adequate to meet domestic needs. The scheme of importation adopted in the closing decades of the eighteenth century broke down in the face of bad harvests all over Europe and the restrictive effects of the continental blockade. Consequently the price of grain rose sharply during the war years despite improvements in agricultural methods and the rapid extension of tillage in the form of reclamation and enclosure of waste land. The landed classes, depending on the continuance of high prices, invested heavily in the improvement of inferior land and leased farms at proportionately higher rents. The high price of corn rendered the existing corn laws inoperative since the English price was almost consistently above the figure at which the duty would have come into effect. Real wartime difficulties in importation, however, afforded

2. *Speeches on Questions of Public Policy*, ed. J. Bright and J. E. T. Rogers (London, 1870), *1*, 16–17. Adam Smith had taught that "the money price of labour, and of everything that is the produce either of land or labour, must necessarily rise or fall in proportion to the money price of corn" (*Wealth of Nations* [New York, Modern Library, 1937], p. 477). However, Smith also asserted that "the wages of labour do not in Great Britain fluctuate with the price of provisions . . . in many places the money price of labour remains uniformly the same sometimes for half a century together" (p. 74). Elsewhere he both affirmed and denied the doctrine (pp. 36, 85, 187, 242, 476, 482). The significance of these hesitations will emerge subsequently.

effective protection to agriculture. But the bumper crop of 1813 produced a temporary fall in prices and the landed gentry now sought more rigorous protection.

As the war drew to a close it was predicted that "corn" (i.e., small grains such as wheat, oats, rye, and barley) would pour into England at ruinous prices. Furthermore, the danger of reliance on foreign food supplies seemed self-evident after a generation of warfare, and the agricultural classes clamored for protective legislation in the name of the general welfare. At the same time, the collapse of the agricultural boom coincided with a severe depression in industry and trade, giving rise to the demand for wider access to foreign markets which was thought to be conditional, reasonably enough, on Britain's willingness to import European corn.

Although Britain was still a nation dominated economically and politically by landed proprietors it became increasingly clear throughout the war period that the days of the assured ascendancy of agriculture were over. Large-scale production and mechanization were already fairly widespread in the iron, coal, and textile industries even before the turn of the century. Government outlays on the war gave further stimulus to these industries and others providing military supplies, while heavy capital exports, in the form of public loans and expenditures abroad, promoted a steady expansion of foreign trade. But inflationary forces also tended to divert resources from normal channels to investments in agriculture and unproductive war equipment. In the balance, government absorption of savings may well have inhibited domestic investment in producers' goods. Whereas the scale had begun to tip increasingly in favor of industry, agriculture had enjoyed a privileged position in the war-induced boom. Then as now, there was a good deal of disagreement about the relative gains of agriculture and manufacturing in the war prosperity.[3] Certainly there were grounds for the opinion expressed by Malthus: "Of the great additional quantity of capital employed upon the land in the country during the twenty years, from 1793 to 1813, by far the greater part is supposed to have been generated on the soil, and not to have been brought from commerce or manufactures."[4] But Ricardo took a different view, and echoes of this controversy appear as late as 1848 in John Stuart Mill's *Principles*.

Of course, contemporary impressions were based upon the most casual observation and on a small body of highly ambiguous data. The

3. For the view that the war had adverse effects on the development of industry, see W. W. Rostow, "Adjustments and Maladjustments after the Napoleonic Wars," *American Economic Review*, March 1942, pp. 21–2; A. D. Gayer *et al.*, *The Growth and Fluctuations of the British Economy, 1750–1850* (Oxford, 1953), 2, 647–9.

4. *Principles of Political Economy* (2d ed. London, 1836), p. 196.

census returns of 1801, 1811, and 1821 were not comparable to each other with respect to information supplied and were so inadequately framed as to shed little light on the question. The universal statistical source before the 1820's was Patrick Colquhoun's *Treatise on the Wealth of the British Empire.* It supplied detailed and exact figures on the distribution of income and occupations as of 1812 but gave no reliable sources for the data.[5] Colquhoun concluded that the gross value of agricultural output still somewhat exceeded the value created in manufacturing and foreign trade.[6] The inclusion of Ireland, however, may account for that result. In 1823 one of the best statisticians of the period estimated, on the basis of census data, that agriculture accounted for 30 per cent of the national income and 33 per cent of the labor force in Great Britain and ventured to say that its importance in the economy was rapidly declining.[7]

The latent conflict of interest between the landed and industrial classes, held in check by war, came sharply to the fore with the parliamentary debates on the corn laws in 1814 and 1815. The act of 1814, which abolished the outdated bounty on exportation, was a prelude to the act of 1815 which dispensed with the sliding scale of duties on imports, substituting absolute prohibition up to a fixed price and free importation above that level. Since the ceiling established by the bill was geared to the abnormal scale of prices prevailing in 1815, farmers were given a virtual monopoly of the home market.

The new law met with the combined hostility of manufacturers and factory workers, united in the belief that the price of bread might have been lower but for the import prohibition of cheap corn. By making food dearer the corn laws tended to reduce real wages even while raising money wage costs. In a sense, this argument was broadly consonant with experience. Throughout the years of the Napoleonic Wars changes in the price of wheat seem to have dominated the cost of living, while the upward drift of both money wages and wheat prices from 1730 to 1820, with the price of meat and dairy products keeping pace with the price of bread, gave support to the belief in a causal connection between money wages and the price of corn.[8]

5. For a summary of Colquhoun's findings, see G. D. H. Cole and R. Postgate, *The Common People, 1746–1946* (4th ed. London, 1949), pp. 144–6. See also P. Deane, "Contemporary Estimates of National Income in the First Half of the Nineteenth Century," *Economic History Review,* April 1956.

6. *Treatise on the Wealth, Power, and Resources of the British Empire* (2d ed. London, 1815), p. 65.

7. J. Lowe, *The Present State of England* (2d ed. London, 1823), p. 142.

8. See Gayer *et al., op. cit., 2,* 949–57. The evidence with respect to the correlation between wheat prices and money wages in the period 1790–1815 has been called into question (see W. D. Grampp, "Malthus on Money Wages and Welfare," *American Economic Review,* December 1956, p. 930). Of course, money wage data for the period represent too limited a sampling to support any flat

Nor is there any doubt as to the importance of wheaten bread in the workers' budget. Oatmeal was no longer the staple diet of the poor, and rye bread and inferior types of mixed cereals were rapidly being replaced by the white loaf. Despite the growing consumption of meat and vegetables there is considerable evidence at hand, in particular in Eden's famous survey of 1797, to indicate that bread accounted for some 40 to 60 per cent of the weekly expenditures of agricultural laborers and factory operatives.[9] The remainder went for house rent, other typical agricultural products such as peas, beans, butter, and cheese, a variety of beverages and condiments, and such manufactured wage goods as coal and articles of clothing. All this is perfectly reflected in Ricardo's observation that "corn, though an important part, is only a part of the consumption of the labourer," the rest being "soap, candles, fuel, tea, sugar, clothing, & c." [10] In all his numerical examples, Ricardo adheres to the working hypothesis that workers normally spend as much as half of their wages on wheaten bread regardless of relative prices.[11] But for analytical purposes Ricardo always employs "corn" as an omnibus term for all wage goods. In so doing, he concentrated his entire theoretical apparatus on the economic repercussions of the corn laws.

2. The Rentless Margin

Writing to Trower in 1814, even before the *Essay on Profits* was published, Ricardo declared that nothing but "a cheaper mode of obtaining food" can prevent a decline in the general rate of profit; this followed from the basic principle that "it is the profits of the farmer which regulate the profits of all other trades." [12] Despite subsequent refine-

---

generalization about total wage rates. Professor Grampp bases himself on Tucker's money wage index for London artisans, a particularly unsatisfactory series for his purpose since it displays almost no short-period variations. All that needs to be emphasized here is that money wage movements, particularly in agriculture, were more closely controlled by changes in wheat prices during the Napoleonic Wars than in the postwar era. In this connection it is interesting to note that the marriage rate conforms perfectly to cycles in the price of wheat up to 1822; thereafter it follows the state of industrial activity (Gayer *et al.*, *op. cit.*, 2, 963–70). And as Professor Grampp himself points out, the prevailing poor law system of tying agricultural wage supplements to the price of corn provides "some small justification in fact for believing that money wages were affected by the price of corn."

9. See J. C. Drummond and A. Wilbraham, *The Englishman's Food* (London, 1939), pp. 244–50, 388–97; R. W. Salaman, *The History and Social Influence of the Potato* (Cambridge, Eng., 1949), pp. 479–81, 496–7.

10. Ricardo, *1*, 306; also p. 20.

11. *Ibid.*, pp. 19–20, 103, 306; *2*, 98.

12. *Ibid.*, *6*, 104; also pp. 114, 194, 205.

ment this concept remained the controlling assumption of Ricardo's theoretical model.

In the *Essay* the matter was stated without recourse to a theory of value. Capital, wages, and the net product are estimated in the common denominator of "quarters of wheat," and the rate of profit is expressed as a ratio of corn output to corn input. The logical foundation of this procedure, as Mr. Sraffa points out, is the notion that in agriculture both the capital stock, as a fund of subsistence goods advanced to workers, and the final product are one and the same commodity, namely, corn. Moreover, manufacturers employ corn as circulating capital since wages are assumed to consist entirely of bread. A uniform rate of profit in all trades being postulated, the profit margins of non-agricultural industries comes to be adjusted to the rate of profit established in the production of corn. Under the influence of diminishing returns, profits in agriculture decline and eventually profits in industry and commerce must follow.[13]

This preliminary theory of profit is abandoned in the *Principles* but reappears in the proposition that the marginal productivity of the "last" dose of capital-and-labor applied to land determines the general rate of return on investment. Moreover, Ricardo continued to assume that the demand for grain products is highly inelastic with respect to price.[14] With some hesitation and considerable qualification, as we shall see, he conceived of the demand for corn as a unique function of the size of population (*1*, 79). Hence, in the absence of changes in population, investment and returns in agriculture remain unchanged and set the pace for investment in industry.[15]

Furthermore, the new version of the theory of profits treats the problem of factor pricing through the microcosm of the single farm, distributing its produce between landlord, tenant farmer, and hired laborers.[16] Indeed, the opening statement of the preface to the *Principles*, which defines class-income distribution as "the principal problem in Political Economy," neglects manufacturing entirely and speaks only of capital employed in agriculture. Since farmers are explicitly

13. This kind of reasoning probably owes a good deal to the 18th-century view (found in Petty, Turgot, and others) that the yield of capital in industry must, in equilibrium, equal the rent which the capitalist can secure by buying land.

14. *Ibid.*, *1*, 191–2, 193, 385; also *4*, 220, 259.

15. Citing Adam Smith's observation that "the desire of food is limited in every man by the narrow capacity of the human stomach," Ricardo went on to say: "Nature then has necessarily limited the amount of capital which can at any one time be profitably engaged in agriculture" (*1*, 293).

16. *Ibid.*, p. 49. Cannan has observed that Ricardo "always appears to treat a farm as a kind of type of the industry of the whole country, and to suppose that the division of the whole product can be easily inferred from the distribution on a farm" (*op. cit.*, p. 268).

subsumed under the label of "manufacturers,"[17] the chapter on "Profits" deals quite naturally with the net earnings of the farmer and only mentions industry in passing.

Having characterized the farm as the "representative firm" Ricardo was forced to draw a sharp distinction between rent and profit. In so doing he merely accentuated the existing separation between owners' rent and farming profits under the prevailing tenancy system. In England farms were let on long-term contract for money rents, the landlord being responsible for financing improvements of the soil, buildings, and roads, while the tenant farmer provided implements and other working capital. In principle, therefore, there was some institutional warrant for Ricardo's definition of rent as a payment for an inexhaustible and nonreproducible input, "the original and indestructible powers of the soil" (*1*, 67). The wording is clearly calculated to distinguish rent from payments for man-made improvements on the land which, insofar as they require replacement upon depreciation, form a part of "gross rent." Likewise, "pure rent" is meant to exclude most royalties for the extraction of minerals.

A rigorous definition of economic rent is fundamental to Ricardo's scheme inasmuch as he wanted to demonstrate that "the laws which regulate the progress of rent, are widely different from those which regulate the progress of profits, and seldom operate in the same direction" (*1*, 68). Nevertheless he admitted that, in practice, some improvements become permanently vested in the soil; the yield of such sunk capital is "strictly of the nature of rent, and is subject to all the laws of rent" (*1*, 262). But the admission that some profits on capital invested in agriculture take the form of quasi-rents was never allowed to affect Ricardo's fundamental conclusions.[18]

As is well known, Ricardo's theory of rent is based on the twofold assumption of an extensive and an intensive margin of cultivation. The former arises out of the alleged fact that land is essentially fixed in supply and widely variable in quality. To attract additional units of land into production the price of produce must rise sufficiently to recoup the cost of less productive tillage. The resulting increments in revenue on superior grades of soil accrue to the landlord; if they stayed with the tenant farmer his profit would exceed the yield of capital elsewhere and bring about a transfer of investment.

17. Ricardo, *1*, 34, 35, 111, 115, 122; *6*, 294.

18. It was Marshall's contention that "The more fully the distinctively English features of land tenure are developed, the more nearly is it true that the line of division between the tenant's and the landlord's share coincides with the deepest and most important line of cleavage in economic theory," i.e., between profits and quasi-rents or, more loosely, between earned and unearned income (*Principles of Economics* [8th ed. London, 1930], p. 636).

Ricardo's emphasis is always on rents arising from the extensive utilization of land, possibly because the idea of a "difference between the produce obtained by the employment of two equal quantities of capital and labour" is not so readily confirmed by casual observation.[19] With the onset of diminishing average and marginal returns per unit of variable input, the price of the marginal unit rises and, again, intramarginal differentials accrue to the landlord. But now the argument depends exclusively on the static principle of variable proportions, and diminishing returns are the result, not of fixity in supply or differences in quality, but of the indivisibility of land as a factor of production. On a formal level, competition must equalize the marginal productivity of the composite capital-and-labor dose on all units of land.[20] In this sense, Ricardo's rent theory is simply a marginal productivity theory applied to land which equates intramarginal receipts in excess of costs with the income of the landowning classes of contemporary England. However, while the law of diminishing returns is formally correct in its static version, the Ricardian formulation blends this approach with a questionable dynamic interpretation in which economic growth is viewed as having an inherent land using bias.[21]

In the Ricardian system resources are viewed as shifting between land and industry, never between different uses of land. Since land has no alternative uses, rental payments do not affect the supply price of agricultural produce. "Pure rents" are transfer costs and involve no using up of resources. And so we arrive at the famous Ricardian slogan: "Corn is not high because a rent is paid, but rent is paid because corn is high" (*1*, 74). The gist of Ricardo's argument was to eliminate rent as a factor in the pricing process: the exchange value of agricultural products is determined at the margins of cultivation where the product is exhausted by the shares going to capital and labor. Ricardo was well satisfied to conclude that "by getting rid of rent, which we may do on the corn produced with the capital last employed and on all commodities produced by labour in manufactures, the distribution between capitalist and labourer becomes a much more simple consideration" (*8*, 194).

19. Ricardo's approach may well have been conditioned by an inaccurate impression of war-time experience. At any rate, Joseph Lowe attributed only 15% of the increase in agricultural output during that period to an extension of cultivation (*op. cit.*, app., pp. 36–7).

20. Strictly speaking, of course, Ricardo recognized average, not marginal, productivity such that additional quantities of labor and capital employed, *ceteris paribus*, yield a less than proportionate increase in total product. On this matter Wicksteed's critique is definitive; for a summary of Wicksteed's argument, see G. J. Stigler, *Production and Distribution Theories* (New York, 1948), pp. 326–30.

21. See H. Sidgwick, *Principles of Political Economy* (London, 1883), Bk. II,

It appears that Ricardo was in full possession of the general theorem that marginal costs determine prices, not only in agriculture but in industry as well. This is to be doubted, however. It is true that Ricardo asserts that the value of all commodities, "whether they be manufactured, or the produce of the mines, or the produce of the land," is regulated by the quantity of labor required "under the most unfavorable circumstances."[22] But elsewhere he denies the existence of a cost ladder between firms in a manufacturing industry (*1*, 75), and specifically postulates conditions of constant returns: "One portion of the capital employed in agriculture regulates the price of corn, namely, that portion which pays no rent; whereas, in the production of manufactured commodities, every portion of capital is employed with the same results; and as no portion pays rent, every portion is equally a regulator of price."[23]

Ricardo seems to hold that manufacturing firms operate at the optimum scale along a horizontal long run supply curve, where average costs and marginal costs are always equal; therefore, changes in the output of manufacturing as a whole result solely from variations in the number of firms each producing a constant output. At any rate, this much is to be inferred from the fact that he paid no attention to differences in the size of firms; his analysis rests on a simple two-industry model consisting of agriculture and an undifferentiated bundle of manufacturing enterprises.

Moreover, Ricardo's theory of value requires the condition of constant returns to scale because individual prices are presumed to be unaffected by the pattern of demand.[24] The supply price of agricultural output, however, must affect the cost curves of manufacturing firms to the extent that raw materials and wage goods derive largely from the soil. The price of corn becomes, in Professor Viner's language, a "pecuniary external diseconomy" of production as the expansion of output absorbs increasing quantities of agricultural goods at higher prices. These may be offset by "technological internal economies," but Ricardo discounted this possibility. "There are few commodities which are not more or less affected in their price by the rise of raw produce, because some raw materials from the land enters into the composition of most commodities. Cotton goods, linen, and cloth, will all rise in

ch. 7, which is still one of the best discussions of the mixed character of Ricardo's rent theory.

22. Ricardo, *1*, 73; also pp. 363, 364.

23. *Ibid.*, p. 250. When Malthus drew a distinction in his *Principles* between the differential fertility of the soil and the uniform productivity of machinery employed in manufactures, Ricardo's only comment was: "This and the observations in the next two pages are excellent" (*2*, 169).

24. The assumption of producer's sovereignty is always implicit throughout the *Principles;* a clear expression of it is given in a letter to Malthus (*8*, 276–7).

price with the rise of wheat; . . . they rise on account of the greater quantity of labour expended on the raw material from which they are made." [25]

It must be emphasized that Ricardo did understand the distinction between such short period variations along the cost curves and downward movements in costs resulting from irreversible dynamic forces. "The natural price of all commodities, excepting raw produce and labour, has a tendency to fall, in the progress of wealth and population; for though, on one hand, they are enhanced in real value, from the rise in the natural price of the raw material of which they are made, this is more than counterbalanced by the improvements in machinery, by the better division and distribution of labour, and by the increasing skill, both in science and art, of the producers" (*1*, 93–4).

Marshall hardly does justice to Ricardo when he observes that since "a commodity chosen at random was just as likely to obey one as the other of the two laws of diminishing and of increasing return," Ricardo "thought himself justified in assuming provisionally that they all obeyed the law of constant return." [26] Though Ricardo ended up by treating the supply structure of industry as fixed within the relevant time horizon, he did not arrive at that conclusion without misgivings. Indeed, his preoccupation with the invariable measure of value is largely explained by his intuitive grasp of some of the issues raised by the laws of returns.

3. The Invariable Measure of Value

While at work on the opening chapter of the *Principles* Ricardo confided to Malthus that he had altered his views on the effects of a rise of wages on prices (*7*, 71–2). Earlier Ricardo had held with everyone else that a rise in corn prices is always closely followed by a proportionate increase in money wages and vice versa, the change in wages necessarily affecting the price of every other commodity. This dictum was firmly entrenched in received doctrine and Ricardo had no difficulty in citing authorities to that effect.[27] However, the monetary metal being a commodity like any other, a truly general rise of wages cannot affect the level of prices. By definition, an equi-proportionate change in the cost of producing commodities *and* specie leaves the quantity of commodities and the quantity of money unchanged and hence does not alter the real purchasing power of money over commodities.[28] "All

25. *Ibid.*, *1*, 117; also pp. 104, 121–2.
26. Marshall, *op. cit.*, p. 814.
27. Ricardo, *1*, 46, 302–3, 307–8, 315.
28. So long as the country in question is on the gold standard and notes are convertible, the argument holds even if gold is not domestically mined.

commodities cannot rise at the same time without an addition to the quantity of money," Ricardo declares.[29] However, the essential problem with which he was concerned called for abstraction from changes in the purchasing power of money. Constancy in the value of money became the sheet anchor of his theory; repeatedly he called this assumption to the attention of his readers.[30]

If the level of prices is given, the money price of a commodity becomes a perfect index of its relative price. But what of the effects of a change in wages on relative prices? "The principles of political Economy cannot be explained by the changes which take place in nominal price. Every one who attempts to explain those principles should adopt the best measure of real value that he can obtain, for that purpose" (*2*, 67). The "principles" in question refer to "the laws which determine the division of the produce of industry among the classes which concur in its formation." Having exhibited the effects of the "high price of corn" on factor returns for the individual farm Ricardo employs a "measure of real value" to translate these conclusions to the economy as a whole.

The idea of an invariant standard of measurement had arisen previously in the bullion controversy with respect to a criterion for estimating the magnitude of the depreciation of bank notes (*3*, 65 n.). In the corn laws debate the question of a standard arose once again. This time it had no reference to absolute prices but rather to the terms of trade between corn and manufactured goods. Adam Smith had shown that the commodity serving as the measure of value must itself be invariable, and this became the standard supposition of the economists of Ricardo's generation.[31] Ricardo himself was convinced at the outset that a commodity produced under conditions of constant labor costs, irrespective of time or circumstance, would furnish the requisite medium of measurement, while gold, silver, corn, and money wage units were all rejected as subject to perpetual fluctuations (*1*, 14–15). Ricardo realized that no such commodity could in fact be found. But a statement of the conditions which "the invariable standard" would have to satisfy could, he believed, serve to isolate the relevant factors governing the value of different commodities.[32]

A perfectly accurate measure of value is inconceivable for three reasons: a rise in the price of any input affects commodity values unequally owing to differences in (1) the proportions of fixed to circulating capital employed; (2) the durability of fixed capital; and

29. *Ibid.*, p. 105; also p. 169.

30. *Ibid.*, pp. 46, 48, 110 n.

31. See S. Bailey, *A Critical Dissertation on the Nature of Value* (London Reprints No. 7, 1931), pp. 242–6, for a list of citations.

32. Among numerous references see Ricardo, *1*, 17, 29, 43–4, 275.

(3) the rate of turnover of working capital. These three exceptions to the strict labor cost theory of value reduce to the single difficulty, as Ricardo pointed out, that production cycles differ widely in the time required for their completion (*8*, 193). Thus any commodity selected as the standard unit must itself undergo arbitrary variations in value with every rise or fall in factor costs. Ricardo's solution was to choose gold as the yardstick of value on the grounds that its production might be conceived to require fixed capital and working capital in proportions that approach the average for all commodities.[33]

The choice of money itself as the invariable measure was a pure hypothesis, Ricardo conceded (*2*, 82–3). But he drew comfort from the fact that the stock of gold and silver, being highly durable, was only remotely influenced by the labor cost of mining or the rate or current output of gold and silver mines (*1*, 86–7). Be that as it may, in terms of Ricardo's invariable measure a rise in wages raises the relative prices of goods produced largely with manual labor or with capital of less than average durability; at the same time it lowers the relative prices of goods produced with fixed capital of more than average durability.

A simple example may illustrate the argument. Consider a two-input, three-industry economy; fixed and circulating capital turn over once per unit-period so that only differences in "proportions" remain; and the ruling rate of profit is 10 per cent.

	Fixed Capital	*Circulating Capital*	*Profit at 10 %*	*Price*
A	10	30	4	44
B	20	20	4	44
C	30	10	4	44

Suppose now there is an all-round rise of money wage rates of 10 per cent (for reasons made clear later); if the price of machines rises in the same proportion, output is unaffected, prices rise by 10 per cent, and real wages and real profits are unchanged. But let us assume that the price of machines remains the same and that factor substitution, which should occur as a result, can be ignored. The impact of the rise in wages is then as follows:

	Fixed Capital	*Circulating Capital*	*Profit at 10 %*	*Price*
A	10	33	4.3	47.3
B	20	22	4.2	46.2
C	30	11	4.1	45.1

33. *Ibid.*, p. 45. See Mr. Sraffa's remarks on the changes in Ricardo's choice of a standard in the successive editions of the *Principles* (*1*, xl–xlv).

Due to the increase in wages the level of prices has risen from 44 to 46.2, or 5 per cent. Since the value of money is to remain constant, money prices must be deflated accordingly.[34] In consequence, the price of the commodity produced with a labor-intensive technique (A) rises, the price of the commodity produced with a capital-intensive technique (C) falls, while the rate of profit is reduced from 10 per cent to 4.76 per cent.[35]

	Fixed Capital	*Circulating Capital*	*Profit*	*Price*
A	10	33	2.1	45.1
B	20	22	2.0	44.0
C	30	11	1.9	42.9

To reiterate: A general rise of wages (including the gold industry) leaves the level of prices unaltered because it is impossible to raise both the money price of commodities and the money price of gold. A rise of wages (excluding the gold industry) lowers the value of money, which is ruled out by definition. When the level of prices is held constant, a rise in wages alters relative prices expressed in terms of commodity B. Industry B is, by definition, a scale model of the economy as a whole. Therefore, its wage-output ratio uniquely determines the general rate of profit. If industry B is now identified with the wage goods industry (as Ricardo assumed subsequently), it follows that every increase in the labor required to produce wage goods must alter the structure of prices; indeed, this is how the rate of profit is equalized. The argument is complete: the effect of a change in wages on prices does not constitute a violation of the labor-cost theory of value. For the present, Ricardo is satisfied with a weaker conclusion:

> In estimating, then, the causes of the variations in the value of commodities, although it would be wrong wholly to omit the considerations of the effect produced by a rise or fall of labour, it would be equally incorrect to attach much importance to it; and

34. We assume that the output of the three industries is the same, to avoid the problem of weighting.

35. The result is, of course, a consequence of choosing as the measuring rod a commodity produced with an average ratio of capital to labor. In the first edition of the *Principles,* Ricardo's yardstick was a commodity produced without any fixed capital; in terms of it *all* prices fell when wages rose (*1,* 59–60). It should also be noticed that if commodity B were gold itself there would be no need to deflate prices; the example above assumes that B is any commodity whatsoever in order to show that Ricardo's conclusions do not depend upon choosing the circulating medium as the measuring rod.

> consequently, in the subsequent part of this work . . . I shall consider all the great variations which take place in the relative value of commodities to be produced by the greater or less quantity of labour which may be required from time to time to produce them [*1*, 36–7].

Ricardo's "ideal money" is produced with a period of production that is a mean for the economy as a whole. The time period in question is that which elapses between the input of direct labor for the replacement of the most durable capital good and the sale of the final product to the ultimate consumer, and as such the concept is closely related to Böhm-Bawerk's "average period of production." Indeed, as Böhm-Bawerk defined it, the average period of production is the reciprocal of Ricardo's annual rate of turnover of capital.[36] However, Ricardo's representative production period is an unweighted arithmetic average, dependent upon technical conditions of production and not upon the rate of interest. In the end, Ricardo spoke of the annual production cycle of agriculture as typical of the general degree of roundaboutness of the economy (*4*, 405), thus implicitly substituting corn for gold as the invariable measure of value.

The purpose of Ricardo's numéraire was well expressed by Cournot, who spoke of the need for a "fictitious and invariable modulus" in order to "distinguish the relative changes of value . . . from the absolute changes of value of one or another of the commodities between which commerce has established relations." [37] If value is to be interpreted in a purely relative sense, as a matter of ratios of exchange, the source of a change in the structure of prices becomes a meaningless question: when some goods become cheaper, the rest necessarily become dearer. But the cause of a shift in relative prices is the very problem which interests Ricardo. If wheat buys more cloth now than before, is it that wheat has become more costly to produce or that the productivity of labor in the textile industry has risen? In an unfinished paper, written in the last few weeks of his life, Ricardo returns again and again to the necessity of going behind the observable ratios of exchange to the underlying changes in "absolute value" or "real value,"

36. Charitably interpreted, Ricardo's writings can be made to yield a theory of capital on Böhm-Bawerkian lines. (See K. Wicksell, *Value, Capital, and Rent*, trans. S. H. Frowein [New York, 1954], pp. 37–8; V. Edelberg, "The Ricardian Theory of Profits," *Economica*, February 1933.) Böhm-Bawerk paid tribute to Ricardo's prescient hints but dismissed his theory of interest, quite rightly I think, as "colorless" (*Capital and Interest*, trans. W. Smart [New York, 1932], pp. 87–96, 355).

37. *Researches into the Mathematical Principles of the Theory of Wealth*, trans. N. T. Bacon (New York, 1929), p. 21.

the latter denoting value expressed in terms of a yardstick that is produced with an average ratio of capital to labor.[38]

Ricardo's quest for "the chimera of an invariable measure of value" is often represented as a simple logical error involving the notion that "the rate of exchange between two commodities is to be treated like the ratio between the height of two men." [39] However, it is hard to believe that Ricardo was not cognizant of this type of objection, later advanced by Bailey. The peculiar feature of Ricardo's approach, which sets it apart from the common run of value theories, is its concern with value measurement of commodities located at different points in time instead of in different points of space at the same time; in short, intertemporal rather than intratemporal comparisons of value.[40] It never occurred to Ricardo to stress this fact, yet it is implied by the logic of his analysis and by many scattered remarks throughout the *Principles*. Consider the following statement:

> Two commodities vary in relative value, and we wish to know in which the variation has really taken place. If we compare the *present* value of one, with . . . other commodities, we find that it will exchange for precisely the same quantity of all these things as *before*. If we compare the other with the same commodities, we find it has varied with respect to them all: we may then with great probability infer that the variation has been in this commodity, and not in the commodities with which we have compared it (*1*, 17–18; my italics).

Similarly, the assumption of homogeneous units of labor is justified by the fact that the scale of relative wages does not change significantly through time: "In comparing therefore the value of the same commodity, *at different periods of time*, the consideration of the comparative skill and intensity of labour, required for that particular commodity, needs scarcely to be attended to, as it operates equally *at both periods*." Differentials in skill continue "nearly the same *from one generation to another;* or at least . . . the variation is very inconsiderable *from year to year*, and therefore, can have little effect, *for short periods*, on the relative value of commodities." [41] The same

38. Ricardo, *4*, 374–5; also 9, 3, 38, 297–300.

39. E. H. P. Brown, *The Framework of the Pricing Process* (London, 1936), p. 161.

40. This is frequently ignored by critics. But see J. M. Cassels, "A Re-interpretation of Ricardo on Value," *Quarterly Journal of Economics*, May 1935, p. 520; F. H. Knight, "The Ricardian Theory of Production and Distribution," *Canadian Journal of Economics and Political Science*, June 1935, p. 177 n.

41. Ricardo, *1*, 21–2 (my italics). Ricardo commentators have accused him of circular reasoning in making the scale of relative wages dependent upon a standard

preoccupation with variations in exchange ratios between two periods of time and, incidentally, the same carelessness with respect to the permissible length of the time span, is much more strongly in evidence in the unpublished paper on "Absolute and Exchangeable Value" (*4*, 374–83, 396). And in a letter to Malthus in 1820 Ricardo touches on this topic when he remarks that the labor cost theory of value "is less liable to objections when employed not to measure the whole absolute value of commodities compared, but the variations which from time to time take place in relative value" (*8*, 279).

To permit intertemporal comparisons of value the medium of measurement must remain invariant between the two periods under consideration. Consequently, Ricardo's measure of value seems to involve the familiar index number problem. Now it is true that the difficulties which Ricardo's yardstick seeks to resolve would disappear if aggregate output were perfectly homogeneous; nevertheless Ricardo is not concerned with the usual problem of deflating by a price series. His interest was focused on the effect of a change in the productivity of labor on the terms of trade between agricultural wage goods and manufactures. By measuring relative prices with a numéraire requiring constant labor inputs Ricardo hoped to locate the source of the factors making for diminishing or increasing returns and to connect these to the changing trends in the distributive shares.[42]

The import of Ricardo's reasoning is clearly conveyed by supposing that the labor inputs of the invariable measure shift in the same proportion as the average level of all labor inputs in the economy. In that case, diminishing returns in agriculture, while raising money wages, no longer entail any necessary consequences for profits and rents: relative prices would alter in an unpredictable manner, depending upon the capital structures of different industries and the weight of their output in the total product. In practice, this would make it impossible to pinpoint the source of changes in productivity. Hence, for Ricardo's purposes, the production cycle of the invariable yardstick must remain of equal length over the time period of the analysis. This

---

level of skills established through price formation in the market, while explaining the latter by relative wage costs. However, the postulate that "all men are equal" is legitimate enough if the question of relative wages and the structure of the labor force are not the subject of analysis. Furthermore, if it be true that Ricardo is fundamentally concerned with intertemporal variations of value the charge of circularity falls completely to the ground.

42. Since the value of inputs as well as output is estimated in terms of the invariable measure, profit per cent on capital invested (or rent per acre of land) is expressed as a net product embodying a certain number of labor hours; it is therefore perfectly comparable to wages per hour. (See Schumpeter, *op. cit.*, pp. 646–7 n.)

seems more reasonable if we remember that "in spite of his references to the gradual advances of society, he really had in mind the effects which would be brought about in a relatively short time by the imposition of a high tariff on corn." [43]

And again, suppose that agriculture is in fact an industry like A or C, instead of B. In that case, the rising price of wage goods may induce factor-substitution, leaving the rate of profit unaffected. By identifying agriculture with industry B, Ricardo postulated a rigid average capital intensity for the economy as a whole. Thus, no amount of factor-substitution elsewhere in the system can prevent diminishing returns in agriculture from depressing average profits.[44] In other words, the "ideal standard" is an essential element in Ricardo's system. Its effect is to abstract from changes in technology, while tying the income shares to the cost of obtaining corn.[45] Indeed, the whole purpose of the turgid discussion on value in the first chapter of the *Principles* is to clear the ground for a proof of the basic tenet of the Ricardian system: namely, that the quantity of resources devoted to the production of wage goods uniquely governs the rate of capital formation.[46]

4. The Fundamental Theorem of Distribution

Ricardo was wont to speak of wages in six quite separate senses: (1) labor's relative share of total income minus rent; (2) per capita money wages; (3) per capita real wages; (4) the long-run equilibrium wage rate dubbed "natural wages"; (5) short-period "market wages"; and (6) the value of goods which serve to remunerate labor. Moreover, terms such as "real wages," "the price of labour," or just "wages" are indiscriminately employed in a variety of contexts and sometimes carry two or three possible meanings. Natural wages are clearly defined, however, as that rate of wages which will maintain a given population, population being of course identified with labor force (*1*, 93). Obviously it is governed by the price and quantity of "food, necessaries, and conveniencies" that become essential to the laborer "from habit and custom" (*1*, 93, 96–7). Under the Malthusian principle, labor is produced as it were at a constant supply price. Thus the de-

43. Cassels, *op. cit.*, p. 531.

44. We return to this question below (see sec. 5).

45. See Professor Stigler's illuminating numerical example: "The Ricardian Theory of Value and Distribution," *Journal of Political Economy*, June 1952, p. 203.

46. See Mr. Sraffa's comments: Ricardo *1*, xlix.

mand for labor (rate of capital accumulation) determines the amount of population but not the equilibrium rate of wages in the long run; this is governed by the cost of producing wage goods. Market wages, on the other hand, are simply food baskets valued at the going price. They fluctuate about the natural rate depending upon the short-run demand and supply of labor. Since population adjusts but slowly to changes in the reward of labor, an accelerated rate of capital accumulation pulls market wages above the natural rate, permitting an improvement in the laborer's standard of living. Ricardo even commits himself to the view that this situation can continue "for an indefinite period" (*1*, 94–5), although this belies the logic of the Malthusian theory of population.

In value terms natural wages cannot remain constant with "the progress of society," but tend to rise as the labor content of wage goods rises. So understood, a rise in "wages" is quite compatible with a fall in hourly money and real wage rates or even a reduction in labor's absolute share of income.[47] This unusual definition of "wages" is geared to the paradoxical dictum that profits depend upon wages and nothing else: "Profits, it cannot be too often repeated, depend on wages; not on nominal, but real wages."[48]

The antithesis of wages and profits follows rigorously from the fact that prices are measured by the invariable standard of value.[49] Profits as a share of output are equal to the physical product at the margins or cultivation minus the subsistence wage fund. Hence average profits are high or low depending upon whether the "real value" of wages per hour is small or large relative to the "real value" of output per man-hour after rent has been deducted. Owing to the growth of population and the resort to ever poorer grades of soil, a greater quantity of labor comes to be embodied in each additional unit of agricultural produce; if we assume with Ricardo that wage goods are predominantly

47. See the revealing example in the closing pages of the first chapter on value. Here the matter is turned upside down: an improvement in "machinery and agriculture" is seen to double per capita output while prices fall 50%. Hence workers are better off. But since the labor inputs of wage goods as well as labor's relative share have declined, Ricardo concludes that wages may be said to have fallen (*1*, 50).

48. *Ibid.*, p. 143. The sentence quoted is a perfect illustration or ambiguous usage. One might be led to think that profits depend on the purchasing power of wages rather than on money wages. But this is not Ricardo's meaning. For similar passages see *1*, 102, 112, 119, 289, 411.

49. Even if absolute prices rose, as a result of an increase in wages, "the value of the medium only in which prices and profits are estimated would be lowered"; the employer gains nothing in money profits but as a consumer he suffers a reduction in real income (see *1*, 127).

the products of agriculture then the value of labor's reward must rise independently of its purchasing power and the value of returns to capital must fall.

In the end, the use of the invariable measure of value brings the argument back to the conclusions of the *Essay on Profits:* "The profits of the farmer regulate the profits of all other trades." By assuming that the turnover period of capital is one year, Ricardo identifies the annual wages bill with the amount of capital employed. The rate of profit on capital is now simply the ratio of profits to wages. Wages are fixed in terms of corn and corn is both input and output in agriculture. Clearly, the corn rate of profit in agriculture cannot differ from its money rate of profit. Corn is also the sole variable input of industry, and the money rate of profit is equal between industry and agriculture. Thus when corn becomes more costly to produce the money rate of profit in agriculture falls (the price of the invariable measure is unaffected by a rise in wages). The price of industrial goods, produced with capital-intensive methods, must fall and with it the money rate of profit in industry.[50]

The whole argument depends on the choice of the yardstick of measurement: the corn output of agriculture is assumed to be produced with an average ratio of labor to capital (of average durability) and from that everything follows. The same results could have been more succinctly expressed by stating at the outset that the relative price of the numéraire is by definition equal to unity (and, given constancy in the purchasing power of money, its money price is also equal to unity). Any change in wages alters only the ratios of the prices of other goods to the price of the numéraire. If the numéraire has the particular property of being produced with an average proportion of labor to capital, a change in the man-hours required to produce it will be accurately reflected in the relative prices of all other goods. If, in addition, the numéraire is the unique product of the wage goods industry, the labor inputs required per unit of output of wage goods rigidly determines the general rate of profit in the system. The assumptions may be far-fetched but the logic is impeccable. One can see why Ricardo did not put it this way: it would have called for a careful distinction between accounting prices and relative prices, a strange and unfamiliar distinction at the time.

Owing to Ricardo's muddled terminology the fundamental theorem that profits depend upon wages—changes in wages being regarded from the standpoint of resources devoted to producing wage goods—was largely misunderstood and led to interminable confusion. Marshall saw it as drawing a distinction between amounts of wages paid and average

50. The price of a third class of goods, presumably luxury articles, will rise.

wage costs per unit of output to the entrepreneur.[51] But Ricardo explicitly rejects this interpretation (*2*, 61–2). It would amount to saying that the profits of an enterprise depend upon wage cost when everything else is equal, which is true but not very helpful. Some of Ricardo's disciples, and many a modern critic, attempted to rescue the theorem by converting it into a truism about relative shares.[52] But this simple version will not do even though Ricardo himself suggested it by slipping into shorthand expressions such as "profits would be high or low in proportion as wages were low or high." [53] But surely Ricardo could not have meant anything so trivial as the proposition that two quantities vary inversely when their sum is given? Would this have required the involved analysis of the invariable measure, or the tortured discussion of the effects of "improvements" on "the value of the things on which wages are expended?"

In consequence of measuring both entrepreneurial outlays on wages and the real wages of the labor force in terms of corn whose own value always remains constant, a falling rate of profit per cent on capital goes hand in hand with a fall in average profits and in the profit share of the total product less rent. But this is a deduction from the theory, not an assumption. If Ricardo's theory of profit were only a matter of relative shares, it would be a self-evident proposition. But without Ricardo's measuring rod, a decline in capital's relative share does not necessarily entail a declining rate of profit. Besides, Ricardo's entire argument clearly depends upon the fact that entrepreneurs maximize a rate of profit per cent on capital employed.

Ricardo's mind was almost fatally attracted by the clear-cut result, yet his writings are filled with qualifications of his basic theorem. Ricardo's system is based on the notion that the price of corn is kept up by the irrepressible forces of diminishing returns. But what of the importance of corn in the diet of the working class? Is it not probable that the growth of industry would gradually shift consumption patterns away from land-using products? In fact, high corn prices might en-

51. See Marshall, *op. cit.*, p. 550.

52. Gide and Rist assure the reader that Ricardo's theorem is a tautology: "A cake is being shared between two persons. If one gets more than his due share is it not evident that the other must get less? . . . Ricardo's implication is just that. His law deals with proportions and not with quantities" (*History of Economic Doctrines*, trans. R. Richards [2d ed. London, 1948], p. 175; see also W. S. Jevons, *Theory of Political Economy* [3d ed. London, 1888], p. 265; L. Robbins, *The Theory of Economic Policy in English Classical Political Economy* [London, 1952], p. 84; Schumpeter, *op. cit.*, p. 473). Presumably what is meant in all these references is relative shares of output less rent, for in Ricardo's system the forces which lower the rate of profit increase aggregate rents without necessarily increasing the rental share.

53. Ricardo, *1*, 27; also pp. 35, 143; *2*, 266–7.

courage the development of cheaper food substitutes. If so, every change in the price of these substitutes would alter real wages. Hence the money rate of profit in industry would no longer be governed exclusively by the corn rate of profit in agriculture. As the composition of the wage goods basket changes, the compelling influence of diminishing returns on profits and rents must gradually peter out.

On this crucial question Ricardo's analysis is full of contradictions. The price of corn and money wages, he emphasized, vary together in the same direction but not proportionately.[54] This follows from the fact that approximately half of corn wages are normally exchanged for other goods; if the laborer consumes a bushel of wheat, the price of other goods remaining the same, "he would be quite as well paid with a bushel and a half of wheat, when it was 16 s. a bushel, as he was with two bushels, when the price was 8 s. a bushel; or with 24 s. in money, as he was before with 16 s. His wages would rise only 50 per cent, though corn rose 100 per cent" (*1*, 306).

It is not assumed that the laborer receives a constant corn wage whether the price is high or low but, rather, a money wage which will always allow him to buy the same quantity of corn and other commodities. In order to preserve his theory of profit Ricardo refused to admit the possibility of commodity substitution with a change in relative prices. An increase in the price of corn, everything else remaining the same, raises money wages and leaves the composition of the market basket unchanged. Corn wages are reduced simply because the relative price of the fixed amount of manufactures has fallen. Hence the laborer's "enjoyments," on the above supposition, would be precisely the same." [55] But immediately Ricardo adds: "As other commodities would be raised in price in proportion as raw produce entered into their composition, he would have to pay more for some of them

54. Ricardo, *1*, 305–15. Ricardo overlooks Smith's contention that money wages are not significantly correlated with the price of corn (see above, sec. 1) and advances what German critics have called the *Paralleltheorie*. See K. Diehl, *Sozialwissenschaftliche Erläuterungen zu David Ricardos Grundgesetzen* (Leipzig, 1922), *2*, 86–145.

55. Ricardo, *1*, 103–4. As Professor Grampp has shown, if commodity substitution is introduced, so that indifference curves can be constructed, the effect of tying money wages to a given basket of consumer goods is that the worker's welfare is improved when the price of corn rises relative to the price of substitutes (*op. cit.*, pp. 925–8). Ricardo's formulation avoided one of Malthus' arguments: If the laborer is paid in constant amounts of corn every increase in corn prices relative to other substitutes leaves the worker better off; he can consume as much corn as before and more of other goods. Professor Grampp considers one or two contemporary replies to Malthus which run along the same lines as Ricardo's answer. The whole discussion affords an excellent example of the sense in which classical economics is analytically deficient.

. . . and therefore, even with the above increase of wages, his situation would be comparatively worse." Since the initial rise in corn prices is due to long-run forces we ought to couple historically diminishing returns in agriculture with increasing returns in manufacturing. As we have seen, Ricardo himself admitted that "the natural price of all commodities, excepting raw produce and labour, has a tendency to fall in the progress of wealth and population." Ricardo never resolved this question and we are left with two diametrically opposite arguments.

> My object has been to simplify the subject, and I have therefore made no allowance for the increasing price of the other necessaries, besides food, of the labourer; an increase which would be the consequence of the increased value of raw materials from which they are made, and which would of course further increase [money] wages, and lower profits.
>
> . . . . .
>
> From manufactured commodities falling, and raw produce always rising, with the progress of society, such a disproportion in their relative value is at length created, that in rich countries a labourer, by the sacrifice of a small quantity only of food, is able to provide liberally for all his other wants [*1*, 97, 121–2].

The chain of causation is unhinged in a different sense by the recognition that the supply of labor is not perfectly elastic with respect to wages. That is why money wages cannot increase to the same extent as the price of corn: "If they did—population would never come to a stop." [56] Ricardo specifically considers a population lag behind a rise in money wages, promoting an upward shift in the standard of living (*1*, 165, 406). By the third edition of the *Principles* Ricardo had met with Malthus' argument that "a sudden increase of capital cannot affect a proportionate supply of labour in less than sixteen or eighteen years" (*2*, 263). Nevertheless, Ricardo never stipulated the duration of the lag as he conceived it. Phrases such as "a considerable interval," "in no long time," "at the end of a very few years" serve to remind us of the ambiguous meaning of the wages-population mechanism but do little to display its function in Ricardo's system.[57]

What are we to make of the concession that workers may accumulate private savings because "more is generally allotted to the labourer in the name of wages, than the absolutely necessary expense of production" (*1*, 348 n.)? Not that Ricardo rejected the "iron law of wages," whatever that may mean; despite his appeal to a type of sequence

56. Ricardo, *3*, 243; also *8*, 235–6.
57. *Ibid.*, *1*, 16, 165, 220, 332.

analysis of population spurts, he employs the empty concept of a subsistence level of wages whenever it suits his purpose.[58] By supposing that laborers always procreate up to the limit of the food supply he was able to assert that, whereas the landlord's real income grows with his money income, the laborer's lot fails to improve with economic growth.[59]

The same ambiguous resort to different clock periods vitiates Ricardo's dismissal of the possibility of serious influences arising from improvements in agricultural technique. These are "of two kinds": those which affect economies in the use of land itself and those which save capital per unit of cultivated land. Since their tendency in either case is to bring about a "temporary" fall in rents, landlords are characterized as having little incentive to introduce such improvements.[60]

Ricardo closes another possible loophole by setting aside the impact of an expansion of foreign trade. Though it adds to "the sum of enjoyments," an increase in imports and exports cannot of itself raise profits unless it lowers "wages" by reducing the price of "the necessaries on which wages are expended" (*1,* 129–32). Laborers suddenly do not consume "conveniences"! In his anxiety to emphasize the point Ricardo restates his theory of profit in the strongest possible language: "The rate of profit is never increased by a better distribution of labour, by the invention of machinery, by the establishment of roads and canals, or by any means of abridging labour either in the manufacture or in the conveyance of goods" (*1,* 133).

The upshot of Ricardo's argument is that landlords are the only beneficiaries of the corn laws: "The interest of the landlord is always opposed to that of the consumer and manufacturer." If the corn laws are not abolished to permit the transfer of resources to industry, the course of events must undermine the possibilities of further capital

58. *Ibid.,* pp. 15, 159, 407, and throughout the chapter "Taxes on Wages." No wonder Ricardo's "iron law" has been the subject of much fruitless debate. Marshall denied that Ricardo held a subsistence theory (*op. cit.,* pp. 508–9) and so did Cannan (*op. cit.,* p. 195). For the contrary view see W. J. Ashley, "The Rehabilitation of Ricardo," *Economic Journal,* September 1891; M. T. Wermel, *The Evolution of Classical Wage Theories* (New York, 1939), p. 158.

59. Ricardo, *1,* 102–3, 112, 125; also pp. 334–5, where Ricardo considers the effects of a shift to a potato diet and concludes that the resources released thereby will go to swell profits, not wages.

60. *Ibid.,* pp. 79–83; *2,* 112–19. See the excellent discussion of this issue by J. H. Hollander in his *Introduction to Notes On Malthus' Principles by David Ricardo* (Baltimore, 1928), pp. liv–lix. See also Marshall, *op. cit.,* pp. 833–7; Stigler, *Production and Distribution Theories,* pp. 90–1 n.; H. G. Johnson, "An Error in Ricardo's Exposition of His Theory of Rent," *Quarterly Journal of Economics,* November 1948.

accumulation and retard industrial progress. In view of vested interests in "the restrictive system" Ricardo called for a *gradual* reduction in grain duties over the next decade and a corresponding "drawback" on exportation to countervail the special taxes with which landowners were burdened.[61] But even gradual repeal, he admitted, would reduce rents and bring about disinvestment in agriculture. However, insofar as free trade would raise real income to the country as a whole, the loss of landlords from repeal would be offset by the gains of other classes. On the basis of what we would now call the "compensation principle," free trade increases "the general happiness." [62] In Ricardo's words: "If corn could by importation be procured cheaper, the loss in consequence of not importing is far greater on one side, than the gain is on the other." [63]

5. Pessimism versus Optimism

To sum up: In the "progressive state," characterized by a rising level of investment and growing population, every equal increase in labor inputs results in smaller increments of output (read: corn). As the real price of corn rises, corn rents per unit of output swell accordingly. Graphically, therefore, the curve of total physical product less rent is concave downward.[64] Assuming that the wage rate is given at a conventionally determined subsistence level and that the size of the labor force is a constant proportion of the total population, the wage bill in real terms is rendered by a straight line through the origin so that per capita real wages are always constant (tan WOA). In value terms, however, the same physical quantity of wage goods is depicted by a curve of increasing slope representing the increased labor inputs of addi-

61. Ricardo, *1*, 266–7; *4*, 33, 243–4, 263–4; *2*, 81–91.

62. *Ibid.*, *1*, 271. Ricardo seems to have had in mind also a subjective welfare benefit arising from the spread of industry and the increased variety of products consequent upon the repeal of protection (*1*, 264 n.).

63. *Ibid.*, p. 336; also *4*, 41. On this aspect of Ricardo's defense of free trade, see H. Myint, *Theories of Welfare Economics* (Cambridge, Mass., 1948), pp. 65–8.

64. So long as the total product curve is of normal shape (i.e., convex downward before a point of inflection and thereafter concave), this will be true regardless of the behavior of the rental share of income which is not determined in Ricardo's system. The left-hand diagram is from Professor Baumol's *Economic Dynamics* (New York, 1951), p. 18. His presentation of classical dynamics has been adapted here so as to express Ricardo's argument. For another graphic presentation of Ricardo's model, based on Wicksteed's rent diagram, see A. Paquet, *Le conflit historique entre la lois des debouchés et le principe de la demande effective* (Paris, 1953), pp. 22–5; N. Kaldor, "Alternative Theories of Distribution," *Review of Economic Studies, 23,* second series, No. 61 (1955–56).

tional wage goods (read: corn). At the same time, the value of money rents similarly expressed rise faster than corn rents, leaving a smaller money residual for profits and wages.

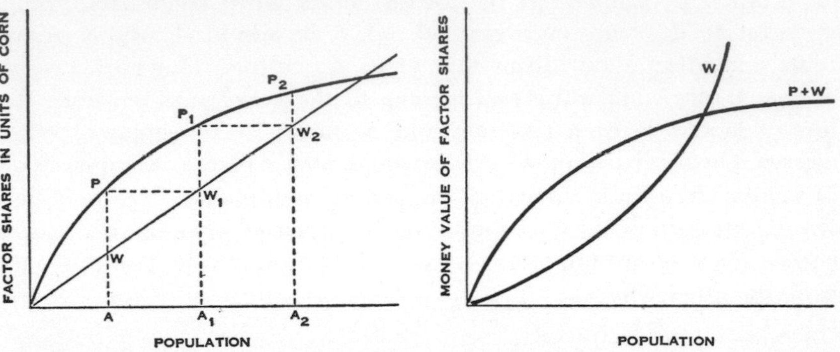

If we start with a population at A, the "natural" wage rate is given by AW divided by OA and the rate of profit by PW divided by AW (the amount of "capital" invested). Since Ricardo usually regards the supply of capital simply as a function of the power to invest, this situation leads to further investment which tends to raise "market wages" up to AP. In turn, population increases to A_1, whereupon wages fall back to the subsistence level (A_1W_1). Investment is stimulated once again and the same process shifts the wage bill to A_2W_2 and reduces profit margins. The expansionary process comes to a halt when wages have eaten up the total product minus rent. The intersection of the two curves defines "the stationary state" in which capital and population cease to grow as the motive for additional accumulation disappears.[65] The profits of farmers and manufacturers would then be "so low as not to afford them an adequate compensation for their trouble, and the risk which they must necessarily encounter in employing their capital productively."[66] Expressed in value units, the stationary state must be reached much sooner than when profits are considered in terms of units of product.

65. The stationary state is assumed to be a position of stable equilibrium, which is only true if an increase of population leads to a fall in the average product per worker but to an increase of total output less rent (as in our diagram). See A. T. Peacock, "Theory of Population and Modern Economic Analysis," *Population Studies*, November 1952, for a discussion of the Malthusian "cobweb."

66. Ricardo, *1*, 122; see also p. 335. A solitary quantitative hint indicates the belief that profits cannot fall to more than 3% or 4% (*1*, 36). Similar remarks elsewhere to the effect that profits are "only a just compensation" for waiting (*1*, 37) show that Ricardo admitted a "real cost" of capital, distinct from wages of management and a premium for risk, but on the whole the notion was not prominently in his mind.

It is clear that stagnation may be postponed by factor-saving innovations in agriculture which would lower "natural wages," but this possibility is not to be looked for. Given a constant state of technique, the only effective remedy is abolition of the corn laws. In permitting Britain to reap the benefits of her comparative advantage in manufacturing, repeal of the corn laws would act, so to speak, simultaneously on both curves so as to widen the distance between them.

We are now in a position to see just how much is "explained" by Ricardo's system. The behavior of the relative factor shares through time is the subject of the analysis, but we are not told of the actual division of the social product between wages and profits on the one hand, and rents on the other. The slope, but not the angle of inclination, of the subsistence wage line is accounted for. The level itself must be supposed to shift with the passage of time because increases in per capita income and density of population cannot fail to raise the customary standard of comfort. That is to say, the standard itself is simply posited as a datum. Even the movements of the relative shares are not strictly determined in the successive progressive periods; only the direction of change is indicated. For one thing, profits need not fall to zero before investment ceases; for another, labor is only slowly responsive to changes in the rate of reward. And the introduction of labor-saving devices, impelled by a rise in market wages, may cause considerable divergences between an increase in investment and a rise in the demand for labor. Therefore, capital may increase without putting any pressure on the available food supply. Furthermore, the sixteen- to eighteen-years population lag is surely too long a short run to permit abstraction from the influence of inventions in reducing the prices of manufactured "necessaries." We come back to the composition of wage goods as the keystone of the Ricardian arch.[67]

Much of Ricardo's reasoning is defensible if it can be supposed to refer to the secular movements of normal prices, caused by changes in technique, capital, and population. As Marshall suggested, this long period of stationary equilibrium, in which the adjustments of both variables and data are fully exhausted, is "unconsciously implied in many of the popular renderings of Ricardo's theory of value, if not in his own versions of it." [68] No doubt the Ricardian system makes implicit use of a stationary state as a methodological fiction. It combines this,

67. It is curious that the difficulty of defining the character of typical wage goods also wreaks havoc with Pigou's *Theory of Unemployment*. Pigou, like Ricardo, employs the distinction between wage and nonwage goods industries as a fundamental analytical concept.

68. Marshall, *op. cit.*, p. 379 n. See also Bowley, *op. cit.*, pp. 85–6.

however, with the notion of an actual stationary state toward which the economic system is tending, and superimposes on both a host of quasi-dynamical pieces of analysis. But Ricardo's concrete method is to compare an "ideal static state" with another position of stationary equilibrium which has been disturbed by import restrictions on corn.[69] Since the time lapse intervening between the two periods is considered to be short, or, strictly speaking, nonexistent, he ignores the likelihood of increasing returns in industry. At the same time the prominence of the law of diminishing returns is explained by the concentration on short-run changes as well as by the definition of agriculture as a single industry, a definition so wide in scope as to include all enterprises which employ land as a fixed factor of production.[70] Were Ricardo's analysis really concerned with long run economic growth, historical cost reductions in industry and agriculture would necessarily have come to the foreground.

It is not surprising then that Ricardo rarely addressed himself directly to the secular changes in the internal structure of the economy. Barring the maintenance of the corn laws, Ricardo believed that England was capable of becoming "the workshop of the world" and that its future was bound up with the growth of industry.[71] For all practical purposes, the limits to economic progress were political and not economic in character. Indeed, the alleged "pessimism" of Ricardo was entirely contingent upon the maintenance of the tariff on raw produce: "I contend for free trade in corn, on the ground that while trade is free, and corn cheap, profits will not fall however great be the accumulation of capital." [72] Even the notion of an impending stationary state was at most a useful device for frightening the friends of protection. In point of fact, Ricardo did not regard it as imminent. "Man from youth grows to manhood, then decays, and dies; but this is not the progress of nations. When arrived to a state of the greatest vigour,

69. The only sustained departure from the method of comparative statics comes in the chapter on machinery (see below, Ch. 4).

70. See P. Sraffa, "The Laws of Returns Under Competitive Conditions," *Readings in Price Theory* (London, 1953), pp. 183–4.

71. See Ricardo's comments in Parliament in reply to a member who expressed the view that "the country was more manufacturing than was good for it" (*5*, 180). See also the observation that Britain's comparative advantage in manufacturing already outweighed that of her neighbors (*8*, 358).

72. *Ibid.*, p. 208. The theoretical context of *das Richardosche Pessimismus,* the favorite subject of German criticism, is almost always overlooked. (But see L. Rogin, *The Meaning and Validity of Economic Theory* [New York, 1956], p. 116.) On the other hand, Elie Halévy's treatment of Ricardian pessimism in terms of a diametrical opposition in Ricardo between the principles of economic statics and dynamics (*The Growth of Philosophical Radicalism,* trans. M. Morris [New York, 1949], pp. 318–42) seems to me both forced and misleading.

their further advance may indeed be arrested, but their natural tendency is to continue for ages, to sustain undiminished their wealth, and their population."[73]

Writing for the *Encyclopaedia Britannica* in 1820 Ricardo remarked that economic growth knows no boundaries but those that arise from "the scarcity, and consequent high value, of food and other raw produce." But "let these be supplied from abroad in exchange for manufactured goods, and it is difficult to say where the limit is at which you would cease to accumulate wealth" (*4*, 179).

Misunderstanding on this score proved to be the decisive weakness of the Ricardian school. When free trade was not soon forthcoming, the disciples of Ricardo were faced with the problem of accounting for the rapid economic growth of the 1830's and 1840's. For without what Ricardo called "a substantially free trade in corn," the Ricardian "engine of analysis" predicted a rising price of corn and a rise in rents; although real wages would remain constant, investment incentives would necessarily disappear. Needless to say, Ricardo's legislative proposals were not enacted. The return in 1828 to the pre-1815 device of a sliding scale and other minor alterations in the law did little to lessen the protection of agriculture, which survived down to 1846. Yet the Ricardian prognosis failed to materialize. The necessity of amending the system in the light of these developments inspired the next half-century of economic debate in England.

6. A Labor Theory of Value?

Almost a generation after Ricardo's death his leading disciple, John Ramsey McCulloch, summed up the essence of his master's teachings: "Mr. Ricardo maintains, in this work, the fundamental principle, that the exchangeable value of commodities or their relative worth, as compared with each other, depends exclusively on *the quantities of labour* necessarily required to produce them, and bring them to market." Since this is the clue which unravels "the intricate labyrinth" of income distribution, McCulloch elaborated on his remark: "It follows that the cost or value of all freely produced commodities . . . (abstracting from temporary variations of supply and demand), depends wholly on the quantity of labour required for their production . . . so that, supposing the labour required to produce any number of commodities to remain constant, their cost and value will also remain constant."[74] What is so extraordinary in these assertions is the absence

73. Ricardo, *1*, 265; also p. 109.

74. "Notice of the Life and Writings of Mr. Ricardo," *The Development of Economic Thought*, ed. H. W. Spiegel (New York, 1952), pp. 165–6.

of any mention of an "invariable measure of value" as well as the stubborn insistence that the "relative worth" of goods depends "exclusively" and "wholly" on embodied labor time. This in the face of Ricardo's constant reminder that relative prices cannot be strictly proportional to relative labor costs owing to the varying productivity of different production periods.

The date of McCulloch's interpretation is not, in this instance, of any significance. His misunderstanding of Ricardo's argument goes back to their correspondence: McCulloch could see no point in seeking for a measure "which can never be found." "The real inquiry," he argued, "is to ascertain what are the circumstances which determine the exchangeable value of commodities at any given period." [75] Certainly this is the more familiar version of the so-called labor theory of value. But is it Ricardo's meaning?

In the first half of the nineteenth century critics and disciples alike concurred in regarding Ricardo as an exponent of the labor theory of value, but the bewildering variety of interpretations suggest no consensus on the meaning of that theory.[76] For some writers it implied no more than the belief that a given structure of prices is more strategically influenced by relative labor costs per unit of output than by, say, natural scarcities. In a still more anemic version, movements through time of relative prices are held to be conveniently measured, as a first and rough approximation, by standard units of labor time. From either point of view, the labor theory of value carries no ethical or meta-economic implications.[77]

However, an emphasis on the significance of labor costs goes back to seventeenth-century natural law doctrine which derived a judicial theory of the rights of property from the personal labor bestowed on appropriable objects. The classic presentation of this argument is found in the second of Locke's *Two Treatises of Government*, a work whose influence made itself felt on the economists of Ricardo's generation. Thus, McCulloch was of the opinion that Locke's essay "contains a far more distinct and comprehensive statement of the fundamental doctrine,

75. Ricardo, 9, 344.

76. See the comments by Professor Viner in a critical review of Schumpeter's *History* (*American Economic Review*, December 1954, p. 906) and the discussion of Mrs. Robinson's essay on "The Labor Theory of Value," *Science & Society*, spring 1954, which suggest that the confusion continues down to our own day.

77. So when Keynes expressed sympathy with the concept that "everything is *produced* by *labour*" and declared that "it is preferable to regard labour, including, of course, the personal services of the entrepreneur and his assistants, as the sole factor of production" (*op. cit.*, pp. 213–14), he was merely supporting his choice of wage units as the numéraire and not repudiating the utility theory of value.

that labour is the constituent principle of value . . . than is to be found even in the *Wealth of Nations*."[78] Though it was rarely made so explicit, the "philosophical" aspects of the labor theory of value, to use Wieser's terminology, were probably at the back of most of the "empirical" versions encountered in the literature of the period.[79] It turns up in the frequent assertions that labor is the only scarce original factor of production and that capital is "merely" hoarded labor. It underlies the controversy on the nature of profit which was never more than a hairsbreadth removed from the theory that returns to capital constitute expropriated labor time. In fact, not only the so-called Ricardian socialists but also John Stuart Mill said as much.

In all this Ricardo offered no clear guidance. Judged by the *Principles* alone one might easily have gained the impression that labor is merely the measure, not the source, of value, and that value means nothing more than exchange ratios between commodities. Ricardo was sometimes quite explicit in this regard:

> Before I quit this subject . . . it is necessary for me also to remark, that I have not said, because one commodity has so much labour bestowed upon it as will cost 1000 *L.* and another so much as will cost 2000 *L.* that therefore one would be the value of 1000 *L.* and the other of the value of 2000 *L.* but I have said that their value will be to each other as two to one, and that in these proportions they will be exchanged. It is of no importance to the truth of this doctrine, whether one of these commodities sell for 1,100 *L.* and the other for 2,200 *L.* or one for 1,500 *L.* and the other for 3000 *L.*; into that question I do not at present enquire; I affirm only, that their relative values will be governed by the relative quantities of labour bestowed on their production.[80]

And, as if to drive home the repudiation of any metaphysical concept of value, he added the famous footnote: "Mr. Malthus appears to think that it is a part of my doctrine, that the cost and value of a thing should be the same;—it is, if he means by cost, 'cost of production' including profits."

So the point of the chapter on value seems to be that, under conditions of perfect competition, relative prices of reproducible commodities tend to be proportioned to relative quantities of embodied labor; in addition, a hypothetical invariable measure may be employed to ascertain the source of changes in exchange ratios. Similarly, a careful

78. *Principles of Political Economy* (London, 1825), p. 69 n.

79. See F. V. Wieser, *Natural Value,* trans. W. Smart (London, 1893), pp. xxviii–xxix.

80. Ricardo, *1,* 46–7; also *2,* 101–2.

reading of the pages in the *Principles* in which capital is reduced to labor expended in the past reveals nothing more than the perfectly legitimate device of expressing the value of capital goods in man-hours: Ricardo goes so far as to make the point that capital goods are never produced by labor alone, not even in "that early state to which Adam Smith refers" (*1*, 21–2).

However, Ricardo's frequent contrasts between "relative value" and "absolute value" could be taken to mean that the latter is not just a subclass under exchange value but a coordinate cost value separate and distinct from ratios of exchange.[81] But there is nothing metaphysical in this: absolute value is simply a unit of social accounting. Ricardo employs the labor theory of value both to determine relative prices and to measure the components of total output. Thus, in the chapter on "Value and Riches," the problem of relative prices has disappeared. The wealth of a nation, or "riches," is said to vary with the physical magnitude of total output, whereas "value" is made to depend upon the productivity of labor. Consequently all goods can rise or fall together in "value." In fact, while augmenting riches, economic progress necessarily diminishes the direct and indirect labor inputs per unit of output and thereby reduces the cost value of "the general mass of commodities."[82]

Nevertheless, Ricardo does ultimately seem to adhere to the view that the expenditure of physical energy constitutes a unique real cost of production and a fundamental cause of value.[83] Even in the first edition of his *Principles* Ricardo spoke carelessly about labor as "the foundation of exchangeable value," and in his last paper there are unmistakable expressions of this idea (*4*, 397). But Ricardo's system does not rest, as Marx's system does, upon the philosophical significance of labor costs. If we drop the conception that labor alone imparts cost value to commodities, Ricardo's system remains unimpaired but Marx's theory loses its mainspring.[84]

An overriding interest in the effects of the corn laws led Ricardo to seek an intertemporal measure of value. Here too he drew on dubious analogies to the problem of measurement in the natural sciences[85] and, who knows, he may have been influenced by the Newtonian quest for

81. See C. M. Walsh, *The Fundamental Problem in Monetary Science* (New York, 1903), pt. II, chs. 2–6; L. M. Fraser, *Economic Thought and Language* (London, 1937), pp. 117–21.

82. Ricardo, *1*, 273–4.

83. See H. Biaujeaud, *Essai sur la théorie ricardienne de la valeur* (Paris, 1933), pp. 171–2; C. Turgeon and C. H. Turgeon, *La Valeur, d'après les économistes anglais et français* (2d ed. Paris, 1921), pp. 91–2; Schumpeter, *op. cit.*, pp. 594–6.

84. See App. A for comparison of Marx and Ricardo.

85. Ricardo, *1*, 284; *4*, 380.

an absolute yardstick of motion and velocity. But the invariable measure of value stands without such speculative support. The assumption of a single input coefficient was a drastic and dangerous oversimplification but it was not wrong. Preconceptions as to the "essence" of value Ricardo may have had, but when irritated by the difficulties in "this subject of value" he had no hesitation in declaring: "After all, the great questions of Rent, Wages, and Profits must be explained by the proportions in which the whole produce is divided between landlords, capitalists, and labourers, and which are not essentially connected with the doctrine of value" (8, 194).

CHAPTER 3

The Heyday of Ricardian Economics

As you and I are his two and only two genuine disciples, his memory must be a bond of connection between us.

JAMES MILL TO MCCULLOCH, SEPTEMBER 1823

1. The Triumph of the New Political Economy

IT WAS 1816 when Mrs. Marcet, already well known for a popular work on chemistry for juveniles, published her *Conversations on Political Economy,* a book that was to make her name a household word in England. In the preface she paid homage to "the great masters" of the science, namely, Smith, Malthus, Say, and Sismondi. "Political-economy is not yet become a popular science," Mrs. Marcet complained, "and is not generally considered as a study essential to early education." The dialogues between the omniscient "Mrs. B." and the credulous "Caroline" were calculated to remedy this situation. "It has now become high fashion with blue ladies to talk political economy," wrote Maria Edgeworth some years later,[1] and this was in no small way due to the popularity of the *Conversations.* Mrs. Marcet left no doubt about the character of her audience, for she disapproved of teaching political economy to the working classes[2] and sprinkled her discussion with voluble palaver about the fable of the belly and the limbs and the beneficent ordinations of Providence which had "so closely interwoven the interests of all classes of men." No wonder that the book was an instantaneous success and a second edition was soon called for. The publisher advertised its appearance in July of 1817. Some two months earlier Ricardo had published his *Principles of Political Economy.* Succumbing instantly to its arguments, Mrs. Marcet added Ricardo's name to the list of "great masters"[3] and led her pupils on a lengthy excursion through the "new" doctrine which concluded with Caroline's neat précis:

1. Quoted in Ricardo, *10,* 172.
2. *Conversations,* p. 158.
3. In March 1817 Ricardo wrote (*7,* 140) to Malthus that he had given Mrs. Marcet his opinions on some passages in her book and he may have shown her a MS copy of the *Principles.* Subsequently, he noted that the second edition of the *Conversations* was "very improved" (*9,* 122).

> In proportion as capital accumulates, the demand for labour increases, which raises wages, improves the condition of the poor, and enables them to rear a greater number of children—this increases the demand for subsistence, raises the price of corn, and induces the farmer to take more land into cultivation—if the new land be of inferior quality, the crops are produced at an increased expense, which raises the price of raw produce generally, and creates rent on superior soils. Corn, now become permanently dearer, causes a permanent rise of wages, and a corresponding fall of profits.[4]

This book went through seven editions in the next two decades without serious alterations and its popularity never waned. Ricardian economics had secured its first publicist.

A year later the *Edinburgh Review,* then the leading journal of Great Britain, carried a masterful and laudatory digest of Ricardo's *Principles,* written by John Ramsay McCulloch (1789–1864).[5] Like Mrs. Marcet, McCulloch did not spoil the effect by mentioning such conundrums as the invariable measure of value. Free trade is the desiderata for profits varied with labor's share of the produce and, while the corn laws were in force, dear food meant high wages and low profits. Ricardo's theory showed why profits were so high in America; it was because access to free land kept wages down.[6] Ricardo himself was well pleased with "the flattering critique," for as he told McCulloch: "I have already heard . . . that those who could not understand *me*, most clearly comprehend *you*" (7, 286).

McCulloch was as yet little known, but having gained a foothold on the *Edinburgh Review* he held fast to it. In the next two decades he wrote almost every economic article in the *Review,* ranging from strictly theoretical expositions to a variety of essays on concrete problems of economic policy.[7] In addition, he contributed economic re-

4. *Conversations* (2d ed. 1817), p. 231. Ricardo's *Principles* is frequently quoted verbatim, particularly in the chapters on foreign trade. However, Mrs. Marcet never adopted Ricardo's theory of value; throughout the seven editions of the *Conversations,* the treatment of value remained reminiscent of Adam Smith.

5. Other reviews were of a mixed character; most of the minor journals were hostile. A favorable notice appeared in the *Edinburgh Monthly Magazine* (May 1817, pp. 175–8); subsequently the magazine changed hands and under the name of *Blackwood's Edinburgh Magazine* became a rabid Tory organ which never ceased to attack the "new" political economy. The second edition of the *Principles* met with adverse comments from *The Monthly Review* (December 1820, pp. 416–30), and particularly from *Farmer's Magazine* (May 1820, pp. 129–46, 152–5). For Ricardo's reaction to another review see *1,* 219–20.

6. *Edinburgh Review,* June 1818, pp. 80–1.

7. For a list of McCulloch's articles (78 in all over a period of 19 years, and in a quarterly at that!) and an account of the enormous influence of the *Edinburgh*

views to *The Scotsman,* an important liberal weekly, and for a few years he was actually its editor. By the number of his readers, if by nothing else, McCulloch's voice gave leadership to public opinion on the great controversies of his day. Until his "retirement" into public service in 1837 he was undoubtedly the most prominent of all the contemporary economists and in fact "the veritable keeper of the economic conscience of England." [8] Were proof needed of his preeminence, it is found in the satirical references of literary opponents of economic science. Thomas Love Peacock derided "MacFungus" and his "ecoonoomical science" in *Paper Money Lyrics* (1831), and in *Crochet Castle* (1831) lampooned a "Mr. MacQuedy," advocate of "that curious fabric of postulates and dogmas . . . the science of political economy." McCulloch's magisterial position was, perhaps, the major factor in the rapid propagation of Ricardian economics in these early years.

The promotion of Ricardian economics to the status of "authoritative opinion" was virtually secured when McCulloch was asked to supply a definitive outline of the basic principles of political economy for the new edition of the *Encyclopaedia Britannica.*[9] Informed of the arrangement, Thomas Malthus (1766–1834) wrote to Napier, the editor, to question the wisdom of sanctioning "the theories of my excellent friend Mr. Ricardo" while these were as yet "*sub judice.*" [10] Napier sent Malthus' letter to McCulloch, who penned an angry reply:

> I think the *Supplement* will gain credit by being among the first publications which has embodied and given circulation to the new, and, notwithstanding Mr. Malthus's opinion, I will add correct, theories of political economy. Your publication was not intended merely to give a view of the science as it stood forty-five years ago, but to improve it, and to extend its boundaries. It

---

Review, see F. W. Fetter, "The Authorship of Economic Articles in the *Edinburgh Review,* 1802–47," *Journal of Political Economy,* June 1953.

8. Hollander, *David Ricardo. A Centenary Estimate,* p. 123.

9. Under the title "Political Economy" it appeared in the Supplement to the sixth edition of the *Encyclopaedia* in 1824 (reprinted with notes by J. M. Vickars [New York, 1825]), and formed the basis of McCulloch's *Principles* (1825). The Supplement also carried an article by Ricardo on the "Funding System" and several other essays by McCulloch and James Mill, but these dealt exclusively with practical issues.

10. *Selection from the Correspondence of the Late Macvey Napier* (London, 1879), p. 29. Malthus had written to Sismondi a few months earlier (March 1821): "I should say that though Mr. Ricardo's doctrines have certainly captivated some very able men, they are not spread very much among the great body of political Economists, and I am inclined to think that many of them will not stand the tests of examination and experience" (quoted in Ricardo, *8,* 376–7).

is, besides, a very odd error in Mr. Malthus to say that the new theories are all *sub judice.* He has himself given his complete and cordial assent to the theory of Rent, which is the most important of the whole; and the rest are assented to by Colonel Torrens, Mr. Mill, Mr. Tooke, and all the best economists in the country.[11]

In a sense McCulloch was quite correct. With the exception of Malthus, the spokesmen of economic science had already succumbed to the Ricardian system, in whole or in part. Let us survey the scene briefly.

Colonel Robert Torrens (1780–1864) openly adopted Ricardo's theory of differential rent in the second edition of the *Essay on the External Corn Trade* (1820); earlier he made use of Ricardo's theory of distribution in a vigorous article assailing the doctrines of Robert Owen.[12] In private discussions with Ricardo he proved himself a "convert" and his writings won Ricardo's personal endorsement.[13] In a new treatise, entitled *An Essay on the Production of Wealth* (1821), Torrens dissented from the labor theory of value; with that exception, however, the work bears an unmistakable Ricardian stamp. In later years Torrens was to change his mind twice over, but in the early 1820's he was clearly a follower of Ricardo.

James Mill (1773–1836) had established his reputation as an economist with *Commerce Defended* (1808), which led to a warm friendship with Ricardo. A footnote in the influential *History of British India* (1817) gave notice of his high opinion of Ricardo's work,[14] and with the publication of the *Elements of Political Economy* (1821) Mill furnished a readable exposition of Ricardian doctrine under the guise of "a school-book of Political Economy."

Thomas Tooke (1774–1858) was just beginning to be recognized as an important writer on economic questions. But a small-scale version of the later *History of Prices*, published in 1823, reveals no startling departures from the prevailing stream of thought. While no disciple he did not at least oppose Ricardo in print.

Among the older generation of economic writers, David Buchanan (1779–1848) took a skeptical view of the new dispensation. And as editor of the *Caledonian Mercury* he crossed swords with McCulloch over Ricardo's interpretation of agricultural distress. McCulloch advised Ricardo to limit the references in the *Principles* to Buchanan's *Notes on the Wealth of Nations* (1814) but Ricardo demurred.[15] Bu-

11. *Correspondence of the Late Macvey Napier*, p. 31.
12. *Edinburgh Review*, October 1819, pp. 453–77.
13. Ricardo, *7*, 180; *8*, 159–60, 163–4.
14. See *ibid.*, *7*, 228.
15. See p. 316 n., 353; *8*, 4; *9*, 206 n.

chanan published nothing more on economics until 1844 [16] and had no further influence on economic discussion. The Earl of Lauderdale (1759–1830) produced a second edition of his *Inquiry into the Nature of Public Wealth* in 1819; although the preface to the new edition stated confidently that "labour is no longer regarded as a measure of value . . . The distinction between productive and unproductive labour . . . is exploded. The origin and nature of the profit of capital is now universally understood . . . Parsimony has ceased to be the most active means of increasing public wealth," Lauderdale declined to notice Ricardo's views or the criticism bestowed upon his own work in Ricardo's *Principles.* Though an active member of the House of Lords, Lauderdale's efforts thereafter were entirely occupied with his favorite hobbyhorse, the public debt, and he too left the field of theory to the younger men.[17]

The appearance of an English translation of Jean Baptiste Say's *Treatise* (1821) might have provided a rallying point for opposition to Ricardo. Charles Prinsep (1789–1864), the translator, joined Say in expressing dissatisfaction with Ricardo's doctrine but sought to minimize the area of disagreement in the interest of the science as a whole:

> *In most important particulars,* there is no longer any difference of opinion; the sources and means of production; the nature of commerce; the benefits of freedom, of industry, and of the division of labour; the nature and uses of money; the operation of credit; the injurious effects of prohibition, monopoly, taxation, and, generally, of the interference of authority, on the business of production; the constant pressure of population upon the means of subsistence—all these are placed beyond doubt or controversy. The origin and nature of value; the effects of its oscillation upon productive power and activity; the limits of demand and supply; the power and benefit of national credit; the effect of national bankruptcy upon the productive classes; the peculiar pressure of each class of taxation—these . . . will probably for some time longer furnish matter of contention and argument.[18]

A small stream of pamphlets by lesser-known writers rejected the new orthodoxy, but these received little attention.[19] One of these

16. *Inquiry into the Taxation and Commercial Policy of Great Britain.* This work contains scattered comments on Ricardo, always hostile in character. See *Dictionary of Political Economy,* ed. R. H. I. Palgrave (London, 1894), *1,* 184.

17. See F. W. Fetter, "Lauderdale's Oversaving Theory," *American Economic Review,* June 1945, and a reply by M. Paglin, *ibid.,* June 1946.

18. J. B. Say, *Treatise* (London, 1821), pp. x–xi.

19. Most of these tracts were rediscovered by Karl Marx, and a number of them are discussed in Seligman's classic article "On Some Neglected British Economists," *Essays in Economics.* One or two came to Ricardo's attention (see 9, 27).

tracts was written by John Craig, an author of some standing, and constitutes in fact one of the first comprehensive critiques of the Ricardian system.[20] Yet McCulloch brushed it aside as "a very stupid book" which ought to be allowed to make "the quiet transit . . . to the pastry and the snuff shop." [21]

Standing almost alone, Malthus was unable to mobilize any general sentiment against Ricardo's theories. What told against him from the outset was his defense of the corn laws. In his belief that general gluts were possible he had few supporters and throughout the period he attracted only one or two genuine disciples.[22] When confronted with Malthus' double heresy on free trade and on gluts all the leading writers closed ranks and presented a united front. Say led the field with *Letters to Malthus* (1820). Torrens expounded the Law of Markets in the *Essay on the Production of Wealth* and dismissed Malthus' objections as "vague, fallacious, and inconsistent." [23] McCulloch classed Malthus with Sismondi and attacked both in a major article on "Effects of Machinery and Accumulation," which he later incorporated in his *Principles.*[24] James Mill devoted a long chapter in his *Elements* to a tenacious defense of the principle that consumption is necessarily coextensive with production. In the second edition of the book, which appeared in 1824, he added a new section which dealt specifically with Malthus' general argument. Despite continued dissension on the question of value, Malthus seems to have realized that Ricardo had won the day: in 1824 the *Quarterly Review* published an acrid attack on the "new school of political economy" which betrayed the hand of Malthus by its assertion that general overproduction is possible.[25]

The crosscurrents of discussion were still further complicated by the growing popularity of free trade doctrine under the impetus of practical, rather than theoretical, considerations. The presentation to the

20. Craig attacks the labor theory of value, the wages-population mechanism, the differential rent theory, and the inverse relation of wages and profits: *Remarks on Fundamental Doctrines in Political Economy* (Edinburgh, 1821), pp. 22–31, 53–60, 88–98, 128–37. See T. W. Bruce, "The Economic Theories of John Craig, a Forgotten English Economist," *Quarterly Journal of Economics,* August 1938.

21. Ricardo, 8, 378.

22. See the works of John Cazenove: *Considerations on The Accumulation of Capital* (London, 1822); *An Elementary Treatise on Political Economy* (London, 1840), pp. 143–7; supplement to a new edition of Malthus' *Definitions in Political Economy* (London, 1853). Of Malthus' other disciple, Thomas Chalmers, we shall have more to say below (see Ch. 5).

23. *Essay on the Production of Wealth* (London, 1821), p. 385.

24. *Edinburgh Review,* March 1821, pp. 102–23; *Principles,* pp. 175–86.

25. *Quarterly Review,* January 1824, pp. 297–334. John Stuart Mill replied in the *Westminster Review* (January 1825); he chided Malthus for identifying himself with old-fashioned views. For evidence of John Stuart Mill's authorship of this and other articles mentioned subsequently, see *Bibliography of the Published Writing of John Stuart Mill,* ed. N. MacMinn *et al.* (Evanston, Ill., 1945).

House of Commons in 1820 of the famous Merchants' Petition, drawn up by Thomas Tooke, inaugurated a general movement in favor of a more liberal commercial policy which cut across party lines. While "free trade" was on everyone's lips, political economy, Ricardian or otherwise, enjoyed increasing respect. Economists themselves grew conscious of the new status of the science: witness the formation of the Political Economy Club in 1821. The founding members included James Mill, Ricardo, Tooke, and Torrens among others. The club was to be more than a debating society, for the constitution enjoined the members to proselytize on behalf of "sound views in Political Economy." [26] Nor were Ricardo and his followers allowed to dominate proceedings. Malthus, Prinsep, and Nassau William Senior (1790–1864) were soon elected as members and at the second meeting of the club the question put up for debate was, "Can there be a general glut of commodities?" Observers testified that it was difficult "to find two members that agree on any point." John Lewis Mallet, whose diary affords occasional glimpses of the controversies that took place, noted that "on most occasions Ricardo and Mill led on one side, and Malthus and Cazenove on the other, Torrens and Tooke occasionally differing with both, and Prinsep being a sort of disturbing force." [27]

In the ebullient atmosphere of the boom of 1823–25 there was widespread sentiment in both parties in favor of Huskisson's efforts to scale down the tariff wall. When McCulloch came to London in 1824 to deliver the Ricardo Memorial Lectures he found himself addressing an audience which included prominent Whigs as well as several members of the Tory cabinet.[28] Despite Malthus and Lauderdale, "political economy" was tied up in the public mind with the doctrine of free trade; the growing prestige of free trade promoted the diffusion of Ricardian economics which succeeded, as it were, by quickening the trend which it had predicted.[29] In the corn laws debates of 1821–22 members of the House still quoted Malthus quite as frequently as Ricardo; by the mid-twenties, however, parliamentary discussions reveal the frequent use of Ricardian terminology and the adoption of Ricardo's theories by a number of speakers.[30] Henry Parnell, for in-

26. *Centenary Volume of the Political Economy Club* (London, 1921), *6*, 3–4.

27. *Ibid.*, p. 212; also pp. 217, 218, 248, 254.

28. Napier, *op. cit.*, pp. 39–42.

29. Such considerations are totally neglected by S. G. Checkland in his discussion of "The Propagation of Ricardian Economics in England" (*Economica*, February 1949). Moreover, Mr. Checkland conveys the erroneous impression that the unscrupulous tactics of Ricardo's disciples deprived the public of any knowledge of the rift between Malthus and Ricardo on gluts.

30. See W. Smart, *Economic Annals of the Nineteenth Century, 1821–30* (London, 1917), p. 414 n.

stance, who had been an outstanding exponent of protection in the debates of 1813–15, now professed his faith in free trade. Addressing the House in 1826, he pleaded ignorance of economics in the earlier years: "Since 1813, the subject of rent has been fully explained for the first time; whatever were the differences of political economists on other points, nearly all were unanimous in adopting the new views promulgated about rent. Since 1813, too, Mr. Ricardo published his new doctrines regarding wages and profits and upon the tendency of too low profits to promote the transfer of capital from this country to foreign countries." [31]

As the opposition between "corn and cotton" became more pronounced a number of landowners defaulted to the cause of free trade.[32] The protectionist camp went on the defensive and with increasing bitterness attacked the science of "political economy" as the ideology of the manufacturing classes, inspired by a hatred of the landed interests. Theoretical differences among economists were ridiculed as "quibbles"; gradually but perceptibly the "new" school of political economy lost its qualifying adjective. "There is a party amongst us," Lord John Russell told his electors, "distinguished in what is called the *Science* of Political Economy, who wish to substitute the corn of Poland and Russia for our own . . . Political Economy is now the fashion; and the Farmers of England, are likely, if they do not keep a good look out, to be the victims." [33] *Farmer's Magazine* pursued the same thought in a leading article: "Our cultivators, both landowners and farmers, are, in general, disposed to treat what is called, in the cant of the day, *political economy,* with a mixture of hatred and contempt. They perceive that their solid prosperity and comforts are to be sacrificed to the wild, fantastical fancies of a false science so called." [34] On a more serious level the very same arguments were being employed against Ricardo himself. As one contemporary critic put it: "The intended check it is meant to give to domestic agriculture, by confining it only to the very best lands, and supplying the nation with a great portion of corn from abroad, under the presumption that the culture of our second-rate

31. *Ibid.*, pp. 414–15.

32. The most able and celebrated convert to the cause of free trade was Viscount Milton (Earl Fitzwilliam), heir to one of the largest estates in England, and a vigorous critic of the corn laws in the House of Commons (1825–33) and thereafter in the House of Lords. His *Address to the Landowners of England* (1832), urging them to join the movement for repeal, was widely read. On the basis of unpublished correspondence it is evident that he had read Ricardo in the early 1820's. See D. Spring, "Earl Fitzwilliam and the Corn Laws," *American Historical Review,* June 1954.

33. Quoted in Ricardo, 9, 155.

34. Smart, *op. cit.*, p. 391 n.; also p. 463 n.

soils occasions the difference of price, but actually with a view of encouraging commerce at the expense of the landed interests, is, throughout the whole of Mr. Ricardo's work, very apparent." [35] The character of these attacks is as good an indication as any of the fact that political economy, free trade, and Ricardian economics had become so closely interwoven that they were no longer distinguishable.

2. The Only Two Disciples

The writings of James Mill and McCulloch are often said to have little theoretical interest. They were "faithful disciples" and as such it is supposed that they stood ready to sacrifice originality of thought for the sake of mere popular exposition and defense of Ricardo's doctrines. "In them the contradictions and confusions of Ricardo are either repeated, glossed over, or left out." [36] But the charge is unjustified; neither Mill's *Elements* nor McCulloch's *Principles* shows any tendency to repeat Ricardo by rote. Firstly, both authors go back to Adam Smith for certain concepts which Ricardo had simply accepted without comment: for example, the distinction between productive and unproductive consumption. McCulloch's *Notes,* attached to a new edition of *The Wealth of Nations* (1828), exemplify this effort to harmonize Ricardo's views with the enduring contributions of Adam Smith. Secondly, a number of ideas implicitly embodied in Ricardo's writings are drawn out and given a new emphasis by Mill and McCulloch; nowhere is this more evident than in their treatment of the wages fund.[37] Thirdly, Mill's proposal to tax the "unearned increment" of rental values goes far beyond Ricardo's own policy recommendations; indeed, Ricardo disapproved (9, 132–3) of Mill's suggestion, though it was only a logical deduction from the theory of differential rent. McCulloch, on the other hand, took strong exception to Ricardo's position on the machinery question and entered a protest to that effect in his *Principles.*[38] Lastly, both Mill and McCulloch recognized the fact that Ricardo had neglected to analyze the nature of profit in the light of the labor cost theory. In attempting to fill this gap in the Ricardian system they may have distorted Ricardo's meaning (Ricardo himself prepared a rebuttal of their interpretation), but nevertheless the intention was to generalize the doctrine so as to answer the objections that had arisen in the course of "the interminable controversy about the 'measure of

35. H. Jemmet, "Observations on Mr. Ricardo's Principles," *The Pamphleteer,* 27 (1826), 146. For Ricardo's reply to this charge in parliamentary controversies, see Ricardo, 5, 81–2; also 8, 182, 207–8.

36. E. Roll, *History of Economic Thought* (New York, 1956), p. 300.

37. See below, Ch. 6.

38. See below, Ch. 4.

value.'"[39] We may not rate their performance very highly but it cannot be denied that it represents an independent elaboration of Ricardo's theories.

The opening shot in the debate on the measure of value was fired by Robert Torrens in an article published soon after the appearance of Ricardo's *Principles*.[40] Torrens' position was simplicity itself: "If the rate of profit be equal, and if the market price of commodities exceed the wages of the labour by which they were produced, then it inevitably follows . . . that the products obtained by the employment of equal capital will be equal in value . . . when capitalists and labourers become distinct, it is always the amount of capital, and never the quantity of labour, expended on production, which determines the exchangeable value of commodities."[41] McCulloch took it upon himself to reply that capital was "accumulated labour" and that Torrens' measure of the value of commodities was only "an extremely cumbrous, roundabout and incorrect way of telling us, that their value depends on the *total quantity of labour* required to bring them to market."[42]

This answer satisfied neither Ricardo nor James Mill (*4*, 305–18), although they failed to clarify the nature of the disagreement. Torrens' theory is true by definition but explains nothing. McCulloch, however, failed to point out that value is never strictly equal to the "total quantity of labour required" when the rate of profit on capital is everywhere the same but capital-labor ratios differ from industry to industry. Two commodities produced with equal amounts of capital (having equal rates of turnover) will sell at the same supply price. With the same rate of profit on capital, their cost price must also be equal. Suppose one commodity is produced with more capital per worker. If the man-hours required to process the product and to replace machines worn out and raw materials used up accounted for the whole of the cost price, the labor theory of value would be correct. The ratios of living to stored-up labor would differ but their sum would be equal.

39. The phrase is Mrs. Grote's (see Ricardo, 9, 301).

40. Malthus joined the controversy with a work on *The Measure of Value* (London, 1823). John Stuart Mill (being 16 years old!) had made his debut in print the year before in an argument with Torrens on the same question (see *John Stuart Mill on the Measure of Value*, ed. J. H. Hollander [Baltimore, 1936]); this was followed by a critical review of Malthus' pamphlet in *The Morning Chronicle* (Sept. 5, 1823, p. 2). De Quincey wrote an equally unfavorable review in the *London Magazine* (reprinted in the *Collected Writings of Thomas de Quincey*, ed. D. Mason [Edinburgh, 1890], 9, 32–6). In 1824, and in the same journal, de Quincey defended Ricardo's measure of value with scholastic ingenuity: "Dialogue of Three Templars" (*ibid.*, pp. 37–112).

41. *The Edinburgh Magazine*, October 1818, pp. 335, 337.

42. *Ibid.*, November 1818, p. 431.

Value would be determined by the direct and indirect labor embodied in commodities. But this is never true. Machines are products and their supply price includes a going rate of profit. The more machines per worker, the greater the weight of nonlabor income in the cost price and the lower the ratio of wage costs to the sales price.

In Torrens' *Essay on the Production of Wealth,* the break with Ricardo is conceived along wholly different lines: "Market price, . . . instead of equalizing itself with natural price, will exceed it by the customary rate of profit . . . we cannot assert that profit . . . is included in the cost of production, without affirming the gross absurdity, that the excess of value above the expenditure, constitutes a part of expenditure . . . The profit of stock . . . is essentially a surplus—a new creation —over and above all that is necessary to replace the cost of production, or, in other words, the capital advanced" (pp. 51–4). This mark-up theory of profit is no better than Torrens' earlier effort: the level of the mark-up is unexplained.

Torrens' argument, however, suggested the need for a consistent explanation of the net returns arising from the ownership of capital.[43] In terms of the labor theory of value, a difficulty immediately suggests itself. When capitalists hire labor they exchange a quantity of past labor embodied in finished wage goods for a quantity of present labor that is to produce future output. But the general rule that products exchange in proportion to the amount of direct and indirect labor embodied in their production appears to be inoperative in the case of the exchange of capital for labor. Wage goods will never buy, or command, the same quantity of labor that was required to produce it; as McCulloch put it: "It will always exchange for more; and it *is this excess that constitutes profits.* No capitalist could have any motive to exchange the produce of a given quantity of labour *already* performed for the produce of the same quantity of labour *to be* performed. This would be to lend without receiving any interest on the loan." [44] From this it would follow that profit cannot be explained on the basis of the labor theory of value; profit is the reward of "waiting." As Adam Smith observed, capitalists earn profit because workmen "stand in need of a master to advance them the materials of their work, and their wages and maintenance till it be compleated." Since laborers cannot wait for the completion of the productive process they are made to part with a portion of output in return for advances of wage goods.[45] How-

43. Before the 1830's interest paid for the loan of capital was never clearly distinguished from the other components of profit, such as the premium for risk and the wages of managerial services. Nevertheless, the discussion was clearly concerned with "pure interest" in the modern sense.

44. *Principles,* pp. 221–2.

45. In modern language, workers are forced to pay a premium on present goods; the present value of future output (discounted at the rate of profit) is equal to

ever, if we add to this Adam Smith's doctrine of labor's receipt of the whole product "in the earliest stages of society," something like an exploitation theory of profit may still emerge: it is only because laborers have been dispossessed of capital and land that they cannot "wait."

But whereas McCulloch is quite insistent that "in the earliest stages of society . . . all the produce of labour must obviously belong to them," he avoids the conclusion that might be implied thereby. On the contrary, his mind ran in all directions but this one. In a letter to Ricardo in 1823 he visualized reward for abstinence and productivity of capital as alternative explanations of the phenomenon of interest:

> In so far as you differ with me on the vexata question of value, I think the difference principally hinges on the interpretation we are to give to the word profit— Whether [it] is the additional value we get back in exchange for a capital we have employed in production, a compensation for time, or for our forbearance in not having consumed the capital immediately, or is it a positive additional value resulting from the employment of the capital and not dependent on time? If we agree in our answers to this question I think we shall agree in our opinions on value.[46]

McCulloch's final solution to the problem was first advanced in the *Encyclopaedia Britannica* (1823) and then incorporated, in a slightly altered form, in his *Principles:*

> Mr. Ricardo was inclined to modify his grand principle . . . so far as to allow that the additional exchangeable value that is sometimes given to commodities by keeping them after they have been purchased or produced, until they become fit to be used, was not to be considered as the effect of labour, but as an equivalent for the profits the capital laid out on the commodities would have yielded had it been actually employed. I confess, however, notwithstanding the hesitation I cannot but feel in differing from so great an authority, that I see no good reason for making this exception [p. 313].

If we select wine and timber as typical cases in which time seems to be the only variable dimension of capital, their increased value after storage is not, he argued, "a compensation for the *time* that capital has been locked up," but rather the result of "the value of additional labour actually laid out on the wine." "Additional labour" is a figure of speech, for McCulloch really means the value of the initial outlay on labor compounded annually at the current rate of profit: the value of time-

---

the present value of wages. The inequality in the exchange between capital and labor is due to the fact that wages now are offered for output later.

46. Ricardo, 9, 366–7.

consuming articles must be estimated by the goods produced by a like amount of capital actively employed in engaging labor over the same period of time (pp. 314–18). In this sense, he spoke of profits as "only another name for the wages of accumulated labour" (p. 291). Therefore, he asserted, Torrens' theory that value is determined by the relative quantities of capital employed is "precisely the same as that just explained" (p. 319).

McCulloch had caught a glimpse of the fact that differences in the length of production cycles presuppose a rate of interest to equalize the returns per unit of time on capital invested. But this insight was unexplored and the whole analysis was given up in a subsequent amendment which generalized the term "labor" to cover the sum of all objects, animate and inanimate, that influence value: insofar as political economy is concerned "labour is any sort of action or operation, whether performed by man, the lower animals, machinery, or natural agents, that tend to bring about any desirable result . . . The labour of man and machinery . . . are in all respects the same."[47]

James Mill immediately adopted McCulloch's theory in the second edition of the *Elements* (1824). The illustration he chose was that of a producer of durable capital goods who decides to employ his own machinery in the manufacture of consumer goods. May we not suppose, for the sake of argument, that he has leased the machine to himself and so obtains his profit in terms of annuity payments over a certain number of years? After all, Mill declares, the quantity of embodied labor would have been the practical measure of value if the machinery had actually been sold; being "stored up," the machine merely releases its value over a period of time, but always in proportion to the original labor cost of production.

> It has been most pertinently and conclusively remarked by Mr. McCulloch, that time does nothing. How then can it create value? Time is a mere abstract term. It is a word, a sound. And it is the very same logical absurdity to talk of an abstract unit measuring value, and of time creating it.
>
> . . . . .
>
> It is no solution to say that profits must be paid; because this only brings us to the question, why must profits be paid? To this question there is no answer but one, that they are the remuneration for labour . . . They may, indeed, without doing any violence to language, hardly even by a metaphor, be denominated wages: the wages of that labour which is applied, not immediately by hand,

47. J. R. McCulloch, *Supplemental Notes to the Wealth of Nations* (Edinburgh, 1828), *4*, 75–7.

> but mediately, by the instruments which the hand has produced. And if you measure the amount of immediate labour by the amount of wages, you may measure the amount of secondary labour by that of the return to the capitalist.[48]

It should be obvious that both McCulloch and Mill are explaining the value of a given investment of capital, not profit or interest on capital. In so doing they already assume the existence of a discount factor, independently determined, at which to capitalize the expected stream of future earnings. Since this amounts to no theory of interest at all it does not matter whether we call it a "labor theory" or a "productivity theory." [49]

Ricardo denied that his disciples had resolved the dilemma of the time element. To McCulloch he wrote: "I question the propriety of calling these accumulated profits by the name of labour" (9, 358). In a letter to another friend he clarified the nature of the disagreement:

> MCulloch says he is not in search of a measure of value, his only object is to know what it is which regulates the relative value of commodities one to another, and that, he insists, is the quantity of labour necessary to produce them. But MCulloch uses the word labour in a sense somewhat different to Political Economists in general, and does not appear to me to see that if we were in possession of the knowledge of the law which regulates the exchangeable value of commodities, we should be only one step from the discovery of a measure of absolute value [9, 377].

Ricardo's unfinished dissertation on *Absolute Value and Exchangeable Value* reviews the whole controversy over the invariable measure of value, refuting in turn the interpretations of Torrens, Malthus, Mill, and McCulloch. After Ricardo's death the paper came into the hands of James Mill. Nevertheless, the second edition of Mill's *Elements* develops the very thesis which Ricardo had criticized. Similarly, McCulloch never altered his argument. In fact, in his biographical essay on Ricardo he intentionally omitted any reference to the existence of an unpublished essay by Ricardo on value.[50] Whatever one may think of the ethics involved it is probable that both Mill and McCulloch feared that political economy could not command a respectful hearing if its exponents differed point-blank on first principles. The time for controversy was over and tactical considerations called for consolida-

48. J. Mill, *Elements of Political Economy* (2d ed. London, 1824), pp. 99–100; (3d ed. 1826), pp. 102–3.

49. See Böhm-Bawerk, *op. cit.*, pp. 97–102, 297–300; Schumpeter, *op. cit.*, pp. 657–8.

50. See Ricardo, *4*, 358.

tion and a suppression of differences. At any rate motives such as these had led Mill to advise Ricardo not to publish the *Notes on Malthus* and McCulloch to condemn Ricardo's formal apostasy on the machinery question.[51] Torrens spoke not only for himself when he expressed the hope that "with respect to Political Economy, the period of controversy is passing away, and that of unanimity rapidly approaching. Twenty years hence there will scarcely exist a doubt respecting any of its fundamental principles."[52]

3. Bailey's Attack

The possibility of an early conciliation of existing differences respecting the foundations of political economy were rudely shattered by the publication in 1825 of a *Critical Dissertation on the Nature, Measure, and Causes of Value; Chiefly in Reference to the Writings of Mr. Ricardo and His Followers,* the most incisive and devastating of all the contemporary attacks on Ricardian economics. Samuel Bailey (1791–1870), the anonymous author of the work, had already displayed a wide knowledge of economic literature in an earlier study guide of *Questions in Political-Economy, Morals, Metaphysics, and Other Branches of Knowledge* (1823). The new work, however, combined a scathing critique of Ricardian value theory with hints of an alternative approach to the whole range of questions opened up by Ricardo's writings.

In the preface to the *Critical Dissertation* Ricardo is singled out as the writer "generally regarded as the ablest economist of his day," whose works have inspired "the political measures of the age" and "those sentiments of admiration and deference . . . so warmly manifested by men, themselves of no common talents" (pp. xii–xiii). But in the realm of value theory Ricardo's analysis is said to be shot through with loose and inconsistent employment of terms and with "an unperceived transition from one meaning to another . . . in the first steps of his argument."[53] The focus of Bailey's exposé is the concept of absolute value and the associated quest for an invariable standard of value. He distinguished two distinct senses in which economists had spoken of measuring value: "One of these senses, and the only proper sense, is, ascertaining the mutual value of two commodities by their separate relations to a third; the other is, ascertaining, when two commodities have varied in value, in which of them the variation has originated"

51. See Ricardo, *8*, 382.

52. *The Production of Wealth,* p. xiii.

53. P. xxiii. See the acute discussion of Ricardo's linguistic style (pp. xviii–xxii) and the illuminating catalogue of Ricardo's value terminology (pp. 233–9).

(p. 249). And of course it is the latter version, espoused by Ricardo, Mill, and de Quincey, which had given rise to the notion of intrinsic or absolute value in which value is not regarded as a relation between two objects in exchange but as "a positive result obtained by a definite quantity of labour."

The concept of "real value," as measured by an alleged invariant standard, is metaphysical, Bailey declared. First of all, the ultimate cause of value is not labor but rather the esteem in which a commodity is held. "Value . . . denotes, strictly speaking, an effect produced on the mind" (p. 1). However, even when we regard value, according to customary usage, as "a quality of external objects," the measurement of value always involves the determination of ratios of exchange since value means nothing else but "the power to command in exchange" (p. 26).

The effort to confine the term "value" to exchange value does not originate with Bailey. In fact, Torrens is quoted (pp. 32–3) as denying the concept of "cost value." Joseph Lowe in his *Present State of England* (1822) had been particularly insistent in asserting that value is "purely relative." Moreover, Lowe had gone on to speak of "general exchange value" and had advocated the construction of a "tabular standard" to measure the purchasing power of money over commodities. But the notion that changes in the level of prices may be measured by an appropriate index number is precisely what Bailey refused to accept. The whole of his key chapter on "Measures of Value" is taken up with a denial of any and all efforts at intertemporal comparisons of value, income, or prices.[54]

Having shown that neither money nor any commodity is a satisfactory measure of "contemporary commodities at any period" or of "commodities at different periods," Bailey goes on to criticize Ricardo for the failure to discern that his invariable measure would not "serve to indicate the variations in the value of commodities, but [only] the variations in the circumstances of their production" (p. 121). Bailey goes further: he grants that the search for an invariable measure is perfectly legitimate if only economists could be made to realize the futility of measuring value in the sense of the purchasing power of money. The whole passage in which this is admitted is worth quoting as an ironic commentary on the total misunderstanding of Ricardo's purpose; Ricardo is rebuked for not seeking what he in fact sought to do:

> Although Mr. Ricardo is professedly speaking of a commodity produced by invariable labour, in the character of a measure of

54. See in particular pp. 71, 72, 113, 117, 120, 136. In 1837, however, Bailey published a work on *Money and Its Vicissitudes in Value* in which he accepted the concept of index numbers. See Walsh, *op. cit.*, pp. 154–5.

> value, he is in reality, without being conscious of the difference, altogether occupied with the consideration of that commodity as capable of indicating variations in the producing labour of other commodities. The same remark will apply to economists in general . . . It is not . . . a measure of value which they are in pursuit of, but *a commodity which would indicate the sources of variation.* Whether there is any one object which would do this better than another, would at all events be a rational, and might prove a useful inquiry.[55]

Bailey's fundamental criticism of the labor theory of value, made many times since, is that the very idea of cost value leads to a vicious-circle argument. Value is conceived as being governed by the expenditure of labor and the value of labor itself is in turn made dependent upon the quantity of labor required to produce wage goods, and so forth.[56] Ricardo erred in "speaking sometimes of a commodity produced by an invariable quantity of labour as a measure and sometimes of the labour itself in that character." But since the invariable yardstick is intended to indicate "the variations in the cost of production, or producing labour of other commodities," Ricardo should have made it clear that when "he affirms labour itself to be a common measure of value, he . . . means, that when the quantities of labour respectively required to produce commodities are known, their values in relation to each other are thereby determined" (pp. 254–5). In other words, Bailey appears to have no quarrel with what I have called the "anemic version" of the labor theory of value; his fire is aimed solely at the idea of intertemporal accounting.

55. P. 127 (my italics). Once Bailey's distinction is understood it will be seen why it is incorrect to describe Ricardo's quest for an invariable measure of value as simply another milestone in the development of the concept of index numbers. See, for instance, T. S. Adams, "Index Numbers and the Standard of Value," *Journal of Political Economy,* December 1901, an otherwise excellent sketch of the history of index number theory from the invention of the tool in 1798 down to Jevons. See also L. Robbins, *The Nature and Significance of Economic Science* (2d ed. London, 1946), p. 60 n. Of course, Ricardo himself did not believe that changes in price levels could be measured by means of statistical averages. See J. Viner, *Studies in the Theory of International Trade* (New York, 1937), pp. 312–15.

56. Bailey, *Critical Dissertation,* p. 51. The criticism can be expressed in more general terms as asserting that the value of output can never be resolved into the sum of input values because the values of inputs are themselves explained by viewing them as the output of another process. But since "the value of labor" is determined outside the framework of the theory (i.e., by "habit and custom"), it is evident that no circularity is involved other than the familiar circularity of simultaneous equations. (See K. May, "The Structure of Classical Value Theory," *Review of Economic Studies, 17,* first series, No. 42 [1949–50].)

It is only in the closing chapter of his book that Bailey branches out from an exegesis of Ricardo to something like a critique of the whole superstructure of Ricardian economics. His method was to advance a threefold classification of commodities according to the "degree of competition." Firstly, there are so-called "monopolised commodities," which category is in turn divided into pure monopoly and imperfect competition; the latter is hopelessly confused, however, with inelasticities of supply that prevail during a market period. Skilled labor is included in this class because of the low elasticity of substitution between labor of different skills. Even labor as a whole comes under this heading because the supply is not immediately responsive to changes in wages (pp. 187–93). Secondly, there are commodities which can only be produced at rising costs, such as corn, raw produce in general, metal, and coal. The owners of the specialized factor in limited supply "enjoy a monopoly" and "it is simply out of this monopoly value that rent arises." It has nothing to do with differences in the fertility of land and is perfectly analogous to "the extraordinary remuneration which an artisan of more than common dexterity obtains beyond the wages given to workmen of ordinary skill" (p. 197). The third and last category comprises those commodities produced under conditions of perfect competition which Ricardo's theory of value is designed to explain. But even here labor alone does not determine prices. Not only is labor nonhomogeneous in quality, but "the discredit, the danger, the disagreeableness of any method of employing capital," and the necessary premium for time preference which must be paid, all tend to enhance the value of the product.[57] Moreover, the raw materials which go to produce this third range of articles frequently fall into the first two divisions. Therefore, instead of "protection from competition" affecting a very small part of the mass of commodities daily exchanged in the market, as Ricardo had claimed, "we have seen that it is a most extensive source of value, and that the value of many of the most important articles of interchange must be referred to this as its origin" (p. 229). Besides, while embodied labor may be "the principal cause" of value it is vain to resolve all the determining elements into one: "All that in reality can be accomplished on this subject is to ascertain the various causes of value" (p. 231).

The impact of Bailey's attack upon contemporary thinking was profound, judging by the number of references to it in an age not given

57. Pp. 206–22. Mill's theory of interest is refuted by the assertion that "we generally prefer a present pleasure or enjoyment to a distant one, not superior to it in other respects," and thus the wine producer must be compensated to overcome his inclination to undervalue the future (p. 218). This marks the first mention of Böhm–Bawerk's *agio* in the literature of the period.

to crediting sources. Malthus replied at once to Bailey's animadversions because of "the impression which it is understood to have made among some considerable political economists,"[58] at the same time condemning the value theorizing of Ricardo, Say, Mill, and McCulloch so as to leave no doubt about his differences with the Ricardians.

But the votaries weathered Bailey's criticism with admirable equanimity. James Mill's traditional exposition of the intertemporal measure of value in the third edition of the *Elements* (1826) does not mention Bailey's book.[59] McCulloch's *Principles* (1825), however, draws a clear distinction between relative value and cost value, shows that exchange values cannot rise or fall together, and cites Bailey as the author who first clearly pointed out "the condition essential to the production of an invariable measure of exchangeable value."[60] Having delivered himself of that, McCulloch sails on into a discussion of cost value; taking a leaf from *The Wealth of Nations* he assumes that the disutility per unit of common labor is constant and identical for everyone; now the standard of "real values" becomes a commodity produced with the same sacrifice of psychological pain, "by the products of equal quantities of labour, or of toil and trouble."[61] With a passing jibe at Bailey (for not perceiving the difference between "real value" and "exchange value"!) McCulloch concludes that "the proportion which the exchangeable value of a commodity bears to its real value, *at any given period,* may be easily determined."[62]

The Westminster Review, stronghold of the utilitarians, waved Bailey's strictures aside as entirely otiose,[63] while de Quincey, many years later, paid tribute to Bailey's analysis but nevertheless asserted that "with all his ability, that writer failed to shake any of my opinions."[64]

58. T. R. Malthus, *Definitions in Political-Economy* (London, 1827), p. 125. The second edition of Malthus' *Principles* (1836) shows Bailey's influence in the cautious discussion of the problem of value measurement (pp. 57–8, 111–22).

59. J. Mill, *op. cit.,* pp. 113–17.

60. McCulloch, *Principles,* pp. 211–14.

61. *Ibid.,* p. 217. Ricardo quoted the relevent passage from Adam Smith approvingly in the first chapter of his *Principles;* nevertheless, Ricardo typically treats labor as a physical expenditure of human energy.

62. *Ibid.,* pp. 220, 227. Later in the book Bailey is again condemned for denying that rent depends on differences in the quality of land (p. 285). None of these remarks were removed in later editions of the *Principles.* See also J. R. McCulloch, *The Literature of Political-Economy* (London, 1846; London Reprints No. 5, 1938), p. 33.

63. *Westminster Review,* January 1826, pp. 157–72. The article has sometimes been attributed, erroneously, to John Stuart Mill. Bailey wrote an unexciting reply: *A Letter to A Political Economist* (London, 1826).

64. T. de Quincey, *Logic of Political-Economy* (Edinburgh, 1844), published in *Collected Writings,* 9, 119.

The dominant note in many references to the *Critical Dissertation on Value* is a complaint of the nihilistic implications of the book. Charles Cotterill, himself a critic of the labor theory of value, could not help remarking that Bailey's treatment "leads to nothing less than absolute scepticism."[65] Another keen critic of Ricardian economics notes that Bailey "pulls down, but does not build up."[66] On the other hand, Bailey's failure to examine the concept of cost value with any care led one opponent of the Ricardian school to remark that Bailey treated value "as if it were a *mere relation of commodities between themselves;* whereas it appears to me that the idea of value in commodities *cannot even be conceived* without being mingled with the idea of their relation to mankind and to human labour."[67]

More typical, perhaps, of the average reaction is Torrens' notice of Bailey's *Dissertations* as "a masterly specimen of perspicuous and accurate logic; which furnishes an unerring test for the detection of that vague and ambiguous language in which some of our most eminent economists have indulged."[68] Thomas Tooke was also won over by Bailey's analysis, although he did not choose to make his views public. In a letter to Say in 1826, he expressed his disapproval of Ricardian economics with arguments drawn from Bailey.

> The error of the new school has a double origin; first, the assertion that . . . exchangeable value is solely determined by the price of production, and then in the idea that the costs of production always resolve themselves in labor. But, on the contrary, a mass of circumstances could maintain the supply of goods below demand and prevent prices from falling to the competitive level. The effect is that of a series of small monopolies, which are not so exceptional as Ricardo supposes. This may become the general rule and those cases, where unlimited competition can act at all, are possibly exceptional. The facts, therefore, deny the assertion that labor is the only determining element in cost-of-production.[69]

Tooke went on to assert, however, that Ricardo's treatment of international trade and taxation is sound and "capable of happy application"; although "the school of Ricardo . . . has not always been successful in proving its own assertions, it has often supplied the means

65. *An Examination of the Doctrines of Value* (London, 1831), p. 40.

66. J. Broadhurst, *Political Economy* (London, 1842), p. 9.

67. S. Read, *Political Economy* (Edinburgh, 1829), p. viii.

68. *An Essay on the External Corn Trade* (3d ed. London, 1836), p. xii. Torrens also recommended Tooke's *High or Low Prices* as a "corrective contrast to the premature generalizations, and pure abstractions, of the Ricardo school" (p. xiii).

69. Published by J. B. Say in his *Oeuvres diverses* (Paris, 1848), p. 530 (my translation).

to discover the sophisms in others." Here, once again, the advocacy of free trade colored the attitude to Ricardo's work and impeded the development of an active opposition.[70]

Nassau Senior seems to have been the only writer to have realized that Bailey's criticism contained the germs of a far-reaching reconstruction of basic economic concepts. In an appendix to Whately's *Elements of Logic* (1826) he adopted Bailey's generalization of the concept of rent as only a "species of an extensive genus," while avoiding Bailey's abuse of the term "monopoly."[71] Furthermore, Senior pointed out, what is spoken of as "profits" includes the "wages of the labour of the Capitalist," whereas much of what is included under "wages," such as the income of professionals, ought to be classed under "profits" in that the acquisition of professional skills is analogous to the investment of capital.[72] One need only glance at Senior's earlier economic writings to realize how much he had learned from Bailey.[73]

4. The Status of Ricardian Economics by 1830

Although Senior's attempt to overhaul the nomenclature of the science went unnoticed there was general agreement that the meaning which Ricardo had imparted to terms such as "wages" and "profits" could not be sustained. Ricardo's dictum that every increase of wages comes out of profits lent itself easily to crude protectionist arguments. If wage rates were lower on the Continent than in England, which no one denied, then it could be inferred that profits were higher there. Therefore, the removal of import duties on manufactured goods or the exportation of machinery would prove disastrous to Britain's ability to engage in "warfare for the markets of the world." McCulloch, called to testify before the Select Committee on Export of Tools and Machinery (1825), had the greatest difficulty in meeting this kind of reasoning. At the start, he admitted that the rate of profit in French industry exceeded that earned in British industry by virtue of low wages

70. The references above, if nothing else, should show how difficult it would be to test Schumpeter's assertion that "a poll of writers on value from 1826 to 1845 would produce a considerable majority for Bailey" (*op. cit.*, p. 487). The belief that economic opinion may be accurately canvassed like electoral preferences is one of the stranger prejudices pervading Schumpeter's *History*.

71. Bailey himself had precursors in Craig and Hopkins. See Bowley, *op. cit.*, pp. 131–2.

72. The appendix is reprinted with *Senior's Outline of the Science of Political Economy* (New York, 1951).

73. "Report on the State of Agriculture," *Quarterly Review*, July 1821, pp. 466–504. This essay contains a characteristic element of Senior's later work, the stress on historical increasing returns in manufacturing.

in France. This is false because Ricardo's theorem does not hold between countries.[74] Having implied a comparative disadvantage for Britain in the production of machinery, he should have concluded that its exportation might be unprofitable. But no, McCulloch declared that it would be impolitic to restrict the exportation of machinery. "Will you explain to the Committee why you are of the opinion that the French manufacturer would not undersell the English, seeing that his profits are larger than the English manufacturer?—Because if he were to offer to undersell the English, he can only do it by consenting to accept a less rate of profit on his capital than the other French capitalists are making on theirs, and I cannot suppose a man of common sense would act upon such principle." [75]

In his *Principles* McCulloch presented a watered-down version of Ricardo's theory of profit. Defining wages as "a certain proportion of the produce of industry," he noted that wages so defined may vary independently of real wages.[76] The notion that a rise or fall of money wages does not affect relative prices is defended in Ricardo's terms by assuming an average proportion of labor to capital as the measure of value. Therefore, "though fluctuations in the rate of wages occasion some variation in the exchangeable value of particular commodities, they neither add to nor take away from the *total value* of the entire mass of commodities." [77] But the inverse relation of wages and profits holds only if profits are taken to mean "the *real* value of the entire portion of the produce of industry, falling in the first instance, to the share of the capitalist." Thus understood, "Mr. Ricardo's theory holds universally." However, when profits are considered as net returns on capital invested then "there are very many exceptions to Mr. Ricardo's theory." [78] In fact, it is true only if "the productiveness of industry remains constant." [79] Since the latter interpretation robs Ricardo's formula of all its significant implications, McCulloch proceeds almost immediately to retract the qualification. Profits tend to decline because diminishing returns lessen "the quantity of produce to be divided be-

74. The question of international discrepancies in wage and price levels as determined by comparative cost ratios was first analyzed by Senior in his lecture "On the Cost of Obtaining Money" (1830). Senior drew upon broad hints in Ricardo's works.

75. McCulloch's testimony is quoted in full by Senior, *Political Economy,* pp. 144–5. McCulloch seems never to have fully accepted Ricardo's emphasis on comparative, as against absolute, cost advantage. See Viner, *Studies in the Theory of International Trade,* p. 488 n.

76. McCulloch, *Principles,* pp. 296, 363, 365.

77. *Ibid.,* p. 312.

78. *Ibid.,* pp. 367–8. For the fallacy of this argument, see above, Ch. 1, sec. 4.

79. *Ibid.,* p. 373. This interpretation seems to have been borrowed from Bailey (*Critical Dissertation,* pp. 65–6).

tween the capitalist and the labourer" and increase "the proportion falling to the share of the latter."[80] Loosely connecting the profit share with the rate of profit on capital, he concluded: "If equal quantities of capital and labour would always raise *equal quantities of raw produce,* the utmost additions to the capital of the nation could never . . . sink the rate of profits."[81]

Never far behind, James Mill followed McCulloch with similar revisions in the third edition of the *Elements:*

> The terms alteration of wages, alteration of profits, are susceptible of various meanings . . . When we say that the labourer receives a greater quantity of commodities, and when we say that he receives a greater exchangeable value, we denote by the two expressions, one and the same thing. In this sense, nobody has ever maintained that profits necessarily rise when wages fall, and fall when wages rise: because it was always easy to see, that, by an alteration in productive power, both may rise or fall together, and also that one may rise or fall, and the other remain stationary.[82]

But as Ricardo employed the word "value," wages and profits stand for proportionate shares of the product; and in that language "it is strictly and undeniably true, that profits depend upon wages."[83] Unfortunately, "in the common mode of expressing profits" reference is made to a percentage rate on capital and not to a quotient of output. "There is a great convenience in adapting our language to the rate upon the capital, rather than the shares of the produce," Mill concludes banefully. "This, however, it is evident, makes no difference in the truth of the doctrine."[84]

Two years later McCulloch came even closer to scuttling the antithesis of wages and profits: "In a theoretical point of view . . . Mr. Ricardo's doctrine with respect to profit is quite unexceptionable. But practically, it is of less importance; and may lead, unless the sense in which Mr. Ricardo understood profits be always kept in view, to the most erroneous conclusions."[85] Torrens, with a keen eye to doctrinal emendation, immediately observed that Mill and McCulloch had, in fact, admitted that "Mr. Ricardo's principles are tenable, only,

80. *Principles,* p. 376.

81. *Ibid.,* pp. 378–9.

82. Pp. 72–4. Both Mill and McCulloch overlook the fact that Ricardo's theorem is designed to analyze cases where "an alteration in productive power" has taken place.

83. *Ibid.,* p. 75.

84. *Ibid.,* pp. 75–6.

85. *Notes on the Wealth of Nations, 4,* 192–3. In the 3d ed. (1849) the phrase "of less importance" becomes "of little or no value" (p. 477).

when we pervert from their established acceptation the terms in which these principles are expressed. This is the same thing as admitting that the Ricardo doctrine of profit is erroneous."[86]

By 1827 every leading writer denied the Ricardian maxim that "profits depend on wages" except of course as a truism about relative shares. Tooke scoffed at the "proportional" conception of wages of which the Ricardians were so fond and wrote to Say: "I do not find that this School has up to now given a clear definition of the point which really separates wages from profits."[87] Sir Edward West, writing from India,[88] attempted to clear up the difficulty by introducing the distinction between wages as cost and wages as income. "The rate of wages may be increased without affecting the price of labour, or cost of production; and the rate of wages may remain the same, whilst from the increased exertions of the labourer, the price of labour and cost of production may be diminished. By Mr. Ricardo, however, all these distinctions have been confounded."[89] West's argument was promptly adopted by Nassau Senior, first incumbent of the newly created Drummond Chair of Political Economy at Oxford.[90] When prices, technique, and the productivity of labor are given, the profits of an individual enterprise depend upon wage costs per unit of output.[91] Who could object to that?

The extent of the reaction to Ricardo must not be exaggerated, however. Ricardo's theory, it is true, had been whittled down but it had not been repudiated. Ricardo's fundamental theorem provided the link that tied the rate of profit to the price of wheat and by way of the latter to the productivity of labor in agriculture. In abandoning Ricardo's dictum that "profits depend on wages," what was really abandoned was Ricardo's way of talking, not the idea behind the words. The rate of capital formation was still held to be governed by returns in agriculture, and the core of the Ricardian system, the law of diminishing returns, continued to dominate the body of economic thought.

So when Thomas Perronet Thompson (1793–1869), author of the *Catechism on the Corn Laws* (1826)—the most famous and certainly the most pungent of all the tracts evoked by the free trade movement

86. *Essay on the External Corn Trade* (3d ed. London, 1826), p. xiii.

87. Say, *Oeuvres diverses*, pp. 529–30.

88. See A. Plummer, "Sir Edward West (1782–1828)," *Journal of Political Economy*, October 1929.

89. E. West, *Price of Corn and Wages of Labour, with Observations upon Dr. Smith's, Mr. Ricardo's and Mr. Malthus's Doctrines* (London, 1826), p. 70.

90. When appointed to the Drummond chair in 1825 Senior had no reputation as an economist. The statutory requirements of the endowment, however, prevented the appointment of more likely candidates. See S. L. Levy, *Nassau W. Senior* (Boston, 1943), p. 111.

91. Senior, *Three Lectures on the Transmission of the Precious Metals from Country to Country* (London, 1828; London Reprint No. 3, 1931), pp. 75–6.

—attempted to show that the case for free trade did not rest on the Ricardian theory of differential rent,[92] he was effectively answered by a refurbished statement of the rent doctrine in McCulloch's *Notes on the Wealth of Nations.*[93] And while Torrens broke explicitly with Ricardo's rent theory in the fifth edition (1829) of the *Essay on the External Corn Trade* (pp. 136–44), he continued to look at the factors determining the rate of profit in exactly the same way as Mill and McCulloch.

At the close of the decade, however, the avowed partisans of Ricardo had all but disappeared. McCulloch remained his only active spokesman[94] and even he no longer commanded the same authority.[95] Among what Mallet called "the great guns of science" there was now no doubt that Ricardo's theory, as he expounded it, was rife with errors. A representative meeting of the Political Economy Club in 1831 will serve to illustrate the ambivalent, though largely critical, attitude to Ricardo. Torrens posed the question: "What improvements have been affected in the Science of Political Economy since the publication of Ricardo's great work, and are any of its principles first advanced in that work now acknowledged to be correct?" Mallet summed up the debate:

> Torrens held that all the great principles of Ricardo's work had been successively abandoned, and that his theories of Value, Rent and Profits were now generally acknowledged to have been erroneous. As to value the dissertation on the measure of value published in 1825 by Mr. Baillie [*sic*] of Leeds has settled that question. As Thompson had shown that Rent was not the effect of differences in the relative productiveness of soils, but the effect of demand and price; and as to profits, it is clear that the part that goes to replacing the capital employed, which Mr. Ricardo had omitted to take into account, was decisive of the unsoundness of his views. Tooke and McCulloch admitted the truth of the last observation, and Tooke also thought that Ricardo was wrong in

92. T. P. Thompson, *The True Theory of Rent, in Opposition to Mr. Ricardo and Others* (2d ed. London, 1827).

93. This note on "The Nature, Origin, and Progress of Rent" was written by John Stuart Mill expressly for McCulloch's book (see Ricardo, *4*, 7 n.).

94. James Mill had retired from the field to devote himself to other tasks. He ceased even to attend the Political Economy Club; the minutes record him as present on only three occasions after 1826.

95. A long struggle to establish a chair of political economy at the University of Edinburgh with McCulloch as its first incumbent resulted in total failure (see Ricardo, *8*, 205 n.; E. Swann, *Christopher North* [Edinburgh, 1934] pp. 133 ff.). In 1828 James Mill and Lord Brougham managed to secure McCulloch's appointment to a new but unendowed chair at University College, London; four years later the chair was still without an income and McCulloch resigned his position.

his Theory of Value, but they both considered that Rent was in point of fact the effect of differences in the productiveness of soils . . . McCulloch stood up vigorously for Value as well as Rent, and paid very high compliments to Ricardo; whom he still considered as right in most points, and at all events as having done the greatest service to the science . . . It was generally admitted that Ricardo is a bad and obscure writer, using the same terms in different senses; but that his principles are in the main right. Neither his Theories of Value, nor his Theories of Rent and profits are correct, according to the very terms of his propositions; but they are right in principle.[96]

Allowance must be made for Mallet's inaccurate reporting, such as citing Torrens in believing that Ricardo omitted to take into account depreciation of capital.[97] But the waning influence of Ricardo's theories is epitomized in Mallet's own amazement, shortly thereafter, at "McCulloch's speaking of Ricardo's theory with regard to the effect of tythes on the price of produce as one of the most rash speculations of that writer. I remember a time when McCulloch was the devoted and ardent disciple of Ricardo, his most able commentator, and the champion of all his opinions. So much for the progress of science!"[98] McCulloch had already expressed similar thoughts in print: "Though we highly prize the talent of Mr. Ricardo . . . we are not insensible to his defects; and to suppose, as some appear to do, that his work has fixed and ascertained every principle of the science, and that economists have nothing left but to comment upon and explain it, is altogether absurd."[99]

96. *Political Economy Club*, pp. 223–5.

97. It may be that Torrens did misunderstand Ricardo's manner of dealing with depreciation. In all his numerical examples Ricardo does not mention depreciation as a separate business expense. He supposes that part of the labor force is employed to maintain capital intact ("in its original state of efficiency"). Total outlays on depreciation are then shared among manufacturers in the form of direct wage costs proportionate to the durable equipment possessed: "Labor so bestowed may be considered as really expended on the commodity manufactured" (Ricardo, *1*, 39; also p. 388).

98. *Political Economy Club*, p. 254.

99. *Edinburgh Review*, September 1831, p. 97.

CHAPTER 4

Ricardo on Full Employment

> That machines do not, even at their first introduction, *invariably* throw human labour out of employment, must be admitted; and it has been maintained by persons very competent to form an opinion on the subject, that they never produce that effect. The solution of this question depends on facts, which unfortunately have not yet been collected.
>
> CHARLES BABBAGE, *On the Economy of Machinery and Manufacturers* (1832)

1. Ricardo's New Views on the Machinery Question

THE EARLY classical thinkers rarely conceived of technological unemployment as a problem requiring special analysis. Insofar as the demand for labor depended directly on the existence of profitable investment outlets, the cost-reducing features of machinery were thought to assure the reabsorption of displaced labor. What was "saved" instead of "spent," Adam Smith would say, went to purchase productive services rather than consumers' goods; the result was practically the same; purchasing power was simply transferred to the laborers employed "and nearly in the same time too."[1] In other words, "saving" was tantamount to "investment" since both took the form of an increased fund of provisions advanced to workers during the period of production.

The doctrine that the process of capital accumulation as such produced no surfeit of production was crystallized by Jean Baptiste Say in the slogan "supply creates its own demand." As stated in his *Traité* (1803), the Law of Markets was little more than an account of exchange in a barter economy which emphasized the identity of sales and purchases. But the idea was taken over by James Mill in *Commerce Defended* (1808) and reformulated with reference to a monetary economy. Ricardo succumbed immediately to "Mr. Mill's theory" (3, 108) and Say gave it further support in the second edition of the *Traité* (1814).

1. *The Wealth of Nations*, p. 321. On the predecessor of Adam Smith, and the entire stream of discussion therafter, see the excellent monograph by A. Gourvitch, *Survey of Economic Theory on Technological Change and Employment* (Mimeograph, Works Projects Administration, 1940), chs. 2, 3.

Whatever the many interpretations which later came to be attached to Say's Law the essential meaning of the doctrine stands out clearly in Mill's *Commerce Defended:* unlimited industrial expansion is possible without breakdown through barriers set on the side of demand. That the concept took hold so quickly is not surprising. The physiocrats had established the notion that production automatically creates the income with which goods and services are bought, the disbursement of income in turn generating additional production. But in ignoring changes in the demands of firms and households for cash balances Mill went beyond the useful idea that total income and total output are necessarily interdependent to the claim that the total output valued at current prices, whatever they are, is necessarily and always equal to the sum of all income payments.[2] Neglecting for the moment the relationship of the latter proposition ("Say's Identity") [3] to the looser versions of Say's Law, the practical implications of "Mr. Mill's theory" is that instances of overproduction and unemployment are always isolated phenomena; excess supply of some goods necessarily entails excess demand for others; but so long as all income received is *promptly* spent, the flow of capital from the overexpanded to the depressed branches of industry quickly restores any disrupted equilibrium within total output.

Ricardo's early views on the machinery question followed the conventional analysis of Adam Smith, supplemented by Say's Law to prove the impossibility of permanent technological unemployment. The first and second editions of Ricardo's *Principles* touch only obliquely on the price-reducing effects of machinery and do not even mention technological displacement of labor; it is naturally assumed that machinery benefits all classes as producers and consumers.[4] A month after the publication of the *Principles* John Barton (1789–1852) published his *Observations on the Conditions of the Labouring Classes* in which he emphasized the fact that technical change always involves the conversion of one portion of capital "circulating" as a fund of consumption goods available for wage payments to another portion "fixed" in machinery and equipment; in the latter form, capital no longer serves as a source of demand for labor, except indirectly and to a lesser extent. Hence employment tends to lag continually behind the growth of cap-

2. *Commerce Defended* (2d. ed. London, 1808), pp. 81–2.

3. The term "Say's Identity" is suggested by G. S. Becker and W. J. Baumol to denote the strict version of Say's Law which logically implies a barter economy ("The Classical Monetary Theory. The Outcome of the Discussion," *Economica,* November 1952). See also D. Patinkin, *Money, Interest, and Prices* (Evanston, Ill., 1956), pp. 119–21, 249–52, 472–3.

4. Ricardo, *1,* 62. For other indications of Ricardo's earlier views see *1,* lvii–lviii.

ital investment with consequent adverse effects on wages. McCulloch assented to this view, at least so far as to agree that the introduction of machinery depresses wages initially.[5] But Ricardo soon persuaded him of his error and McCulloch now produced what must be regarded as the first satisfactory statement of the theory of "automatic compensation."

McCulloch seems to have realized that something more was needed than the naïve and fallacious argument that all technically displaced labor is necessarily reabsorbed in the construction of new machines. If the new machinery is labor-saving in character, as all the classical writers assumed, then the same volume of output will be produced with less labor but not necessarily with a sufficiently larger quantity of capital goods. The growth of output, therefore, is a necessary prerequisite to the absorption of all displaced labor. It was this conclusion which formed the basis of McCulloch's argument: cost reductions are usually reflected in price reductions which increase the quantity demanded of the product affected by the technical improvement, leading to an expansion of the industry concerned. But if consumers do not respond to lower prices, the saving on the price of that product gives rise to an increased demand for other articles. Wherever commodity prices are not lowered in accordance with the reduction in costs, the surplus profit accruing to the entrepreneur results in increased expenditures on consumption or additional investment in labor and machines.[6] Directly or indirectly, the introduction of machinery carries with it a proportionate increase in output, and the consequent reabsorption of displaced labor.[7]

McCulloch's approach was never taken up by any other classical author. Ricardo's startling admission in the third edition of his *Principles,* to the effect that the process of mechanization may prove injurious to the working class, produced a drastic reorientation to the whole machinery question. Thereafter the discussion was largely dominated by the wages fund approach which Ricardo adopted in the new chapter "On Machinery." "My mistake," Ricardo explained, "arose from the supposition, that whenever the net income [profits plus rents] of

5. *Edinburgh Review,* January 1820, p. 171.

6. Of course, the same output can be produced at lower cost *after* the machinery has been installed. Even so, McCulloch's argument ignores the consideration that profits need not rise to the full amount of the reduction in labor costs; the improved machinery (being capital-using) is likely to be more costly than the old machinery. Hence increased profits, even if fully invested, will not guarantee re-employment of all labor released by the improvement. See H. Neisser, " 'Permanent' Technological Unemployment," *American Economic Review,* March 1942.

7. *Edinburgh Review,* March 1821, pp. 111–16. McCulloch drew to some extent on the fourth of Say's *Letters to Malthus* (1820).

a society increased, its gross income would also increase"; now he saw grounds for believing that the introduction of a machine might lower output for a period of time so as to "render the population redundant, and deteriorate the condition of the labourer" (*1*, 388).

Ricardo illustrates this contention by a single numerical example, that of a producer conducting "the joint business of a farmer, and a manufacturer of necessaries" who diverts one-half of his annual labor force, hitherto employed in the production of consumers' goods, to the construction of a machine. Since the introduction of the machine under these circumstances implies the direct conversion of circulating capital into fixed capital, the means of employing labor (the wages fund) is reduced by the full value of the machine; in the next "year" half of annual "gross income" is irretrievably lost but "net income" is unaffected.[8] Now it is immediately conceded that "it could not fail to follow from the reduction in the price of commodities consequent on the introduction of machinery that with the same wants he [the capitalist] would have increased means of saving"; with an increased "power of saving from revenue to add to capital," output would be expanded so that "a portion of the people thrown out of work in the first instance would be subsequently employed." [9]

Whether wage cuts would accelerate the re-employment of displaced labor, Ricardo did not say. In fact, his entire analysis focused attention on the disruptive impact of technological change without depicting the nature of the adjustment process to a new state of equilibrium.[10] For once he was not interested in the permanent effects. If anything, the implication of the argument at this stage is that some labor may never again find employment: "The case which I have supposed is the most simple that I could select; but it would make no difference in the result, if we supposed that the machinery was applied to the trade of any manufacturer." In every case, the use of machinery reduces current output below previous levels while the rate of profit remains the same; as the quantity of wage goods utilized declines the demand for manufactured articles falls accordingly and some labor is permanently displaced. Thus, whatever the eventual repercus-

8. Ricardo, *1*, 388–89. Profit and rent here represent a physical residual, and all variables in the example are expressed in money and not in value terms. As Schumpeter has said, Ricardo's "exact reasoning is always in the terms of the labor-embodied approach; but this approach does not lead to any results about anyone's distress or welfare which were what interested him in this chapter. And so he mixed up the two" (*op. cit.*, p. 684).

9. Ricardo, *1*, 390. The reasoning is incorrect: prices cannot fall *before* output rises beyond previous levels.

10. This is the gist of Wicksell's criticism: *Lectures on Political Economy* (London, 1934), *1*, 137 ff.

sions, the possibility remains that the demand for labor may be lessened for "a considerable interval" in consequence of a smaller wages fund (*1*, 391–2).

Up to this point Ricardo's argument is confined to the case in which the new machinery is a genuine innovation that alters the production functions of entrepreneurs. Unless technological progress involves such discontinuities there is no reason to assume that the use of new machinery requires the diversion of labor previously employed in the production of wage goods. When technical change is gradual and continuous the cost of new machinery is financed out of retained earnings and not out of the wages fund.[11] This is the case taken up in the closing pages of the chapter on machinery where Ricardo shifts his grounds radically. "To elucidate the principle, I have been supposing, that improved machinery is *suddenly* discovered and extensively used; but the truth is, that these discoveries are gradual, and rather operate in determining the employment of the capital which is saved and accumulated, than in diverting capital from its actual employment" (*1*, 395).

In the process of economic expansion, rising food prices, reflected in rising money wages, encourage the introduction of labor-saving devices: "Machinery and labour are in constant competition, and the former can frequently not be employed until labour rises" (*1*, 395).[12] The "Ricardo effect" under British conditions, where "food is high, and costs much labour for its production," implies a constantly rising ratio of machinery to labor.[13] Hence "the demand for labour will continue to increase with an increase of capital, but not in proportion to its in-

11. In these cases, the introduction of a machine may be due to a change in factor prices, involving a substitution of factors within an unchanged production function. Yet the change in factor prices may stimulate the discovery of new methods which might have been used even before the change if only they had been known. It is really questionable whether one may fruitfully distinguish between an "induced" invention in a given state of knowledge and an invention which involves a change in knowledge. For Ricardo, at any rate, we must assume that a new machine represents a change in the technical horizon of entrepreneurs. See J. Robinson, *The Rate of Interest* (London, 1952), p. 53, and Schumpeter, *op. cit.*, pp. 679–80 n., where the reference to Barton might refer to Ricardo just as well.

12. A footnote to the same effect was added to the first chapter on value immediately before a passage (carried over from the first two editions) which pointed out that "the public benefited by machinery" (*1*, 41–2).

13. Ricardo assumes that wages rise relative to the price of machines; naturally this leads to the substitution of machines for labor. Strictly speaking, the Ricardo effect in modern business cycle theory refers to a situation in which machine prices rise proportionately when wages rise; additional conditions are then required to bring about factor substitution. See F. and V. Lutz, *The Theory of Investment of the Firm* (Princeton, 1931), p. 137.

crease; the ratio will necessarily be a diminishing ratio."[14] But without elaborating upon this fundamental generalization Ricardo faces about once more to observe that a rapid rate of technical advance will assure steady improvements in the laborer's standard of living:

> I have before observed, too, that the increase of net incomes, estimated in commodities, which is always the consequence of improved machinery, will lead to new savings and accumulations. These savings, it must be remembered are annual, and must soon create a fund, much greater than the gross revenue, originally lost by the discovery of the machine, when the demand for labour will be as great as before, and the situation of the people will be still further improved by the increased savings which the increased net revenue will still enable them to make [*1*, 396].

A warning against state action to discourage technological progress brings the chapter on machinery to a close.

Though his contemporaries were quick to scoff at the example in which a machine was used not to increase output but to derive the same profit from a smaller output, Ricardo insisted on the importance of his analysis of "sudden" technical change. When McCulloch objected that the short run effects on output had nothing whatever to do with the benefits of machinery, Ricardo seized on his admission that the use of machinery might conceivably diminish the gross produce under some circumstances. If so, Ricardo asserted triumphantly, it did not matter that prices would rise; the decline of total output could not fail to diminish the demand for labor.[15]

On another occasion, however, Ricardo posed the question squarely in terms of the rate of capital accumulation. Some members of Parliament had praised Cobbett's *Letters to the Luddites* as an able reply to the continued complaints against the introduction of labor-saving devices.[16] In the course of the debate, Ricardo remarked that he was not "altogether satisfied with the reasoning contained in that pamphlet; because it was evident, that the extensive use of machinery, by throwing a large portion of labour into the market, while, on the other hand, there might not be a corresponding increase of demand for it, must, in some degree, operate prejudicially to the working classes" (*5*, 303).

Ricardo never integrated his revised views on the machinery ques-

14. This proposition is ignored in Schumpeter's treatment of Ricardo's machinery analysis and destroys his claim that Ricardo was the "father of what Marx called the Theory of Compensation" (*op. cit.*, p. 683).

15. *8*, 383–4, 391–2, 399–400.

16. See G. D. H. and M. Cole, *The Opinions of William Cobbett* (London, 1944), pp. 149–71. Cobbett changed his mind subsequently (see *ibid.*, p. 181).

tion with the rest of his analysis and it is difficult to decide what significance he ultimately attached to them. The distinction which he drew between sudden and gradual technical change merely clouds the issue. Only the former entails an absolute decline of employment as a portion of the wages fund is converted into assets of a fixed nature. Yet this case, Ricardo confessed, was entirely conjectural. In the instance of gradual technical change accumulated savings provide the source of additional investment in machinery and no technological unemployment is necessarily involved. On the other hand, the Ricardo effect implies that technical progress takes the form of rising capital requirements per unit of output and per unit of labor—"capital deepening" in Hawtrey's terminology—resulting in a secular lag of employment behind the growth of capital investment. Reabsorption of displaced labor therefore depends exclusively upon "capital widening"—upon the increase of capital formation proportionate to the increase in total output.[17] But in the absence of the corn laws, Ricardo supplies no reason for believing that new investment opportunities tend to disappear so as to confine all technical improvements to the "induced" type, dependent upon changes in the relative price of labor to capital.

In fact, the machinery chapter opens up a whole series of unanswered questions about Ricardo's system. Firstly, the chapter abandons the assumption of fixed technical coefficients of production, the concept of a composite dose of capital and labor varying in constant proportions per unit of land cultivated; the elasticity of substitution between capital and labor is no longer assumed to be zero. Granting now that a rise in wages will induce a substitution of capital for labor, on the premise that costs in the machinery goods industries do not rise proportionately,[18] what is the ratio of the relative decline in the quantity of labor employed to the relative increase in wages? Ricardo's remarks on the declining volume of employment per unit of output imply an elasticity of substitution greater than unity: every increase in money wages is accompanied by a more than proportionate decline in the quantity of labor hired. If this is so, aggregate returns to labor and also labor's relative share of national income must fall in the course of technological progress. Hence the same factors which tend to raise labor's money share in the absence of technical change (namely, diminishing returns in agriculture) tend also to produce the kind of improvements which counteract this effect. Once again we are re-

17. Or upon a "thinning" of capital, a decline in capital per unit of output. Capital-saving inventions, however, do not occur in the Ricardian universe.

18. "The same cause that raises labour, does not raise the value of machines, and, therefore, with every augmentation of capital, a greater proportion of it is employed on machinery" (Ricardo, *1*, 395).

minded that the Ricardian system is not, in essence, concerned with the secular aspects of economic growth.

Ricardo had unwittingly discovered the offsetting effect of factor-saving inventions. It is not surprising that he failed to carry through with the analysis; for to have done so would have vitiated the simple model which he had constructed to convey the undesirable consequences of the corn laws.

2. The Machinery Question in Classical Economics

The history of the discussion after Ricardo is quickly told. His followers never advanced beyond Ricardo's own formulation of the problem; they did nothing to remedy the incompleteness of his analysis. On the whole, it is doubtful whether they understood it. Torrens dismissed Ricardo's numerical example summarily—"the case supposed never yet occurred"—and left it at that.[19] James Mill was silent on the question. McCulloch never departed from the position taken up in his correspondence with Ricardo: "I will take my stand with the Mr. Burke of the American war not with the Mr. Burke of the French revolution—with the Mr. Ricardo of the first not of the third edition." [20] The earlier essay on the "Effects of Machinery and Accumulation" was reproduced in his *Principles*, supplemented by a brief discussion of "the case supposed by Mr. Ricardo" which concludes with the observation: "It has never hitherto actually occurred, and . . . it is extremely unlikely it ever will. Capitalists never resort to machines, unless when they expect to produce, by their means, the same supply of commodities as before, at a cheaper rate." [21]

In an article on the machinery question, which John Stuart Mill later described as "the most scientific treatment of the subject which I have met with," William Ellis (1800–81) drew on Ricardo's own concessions to attack the "lump-of-labour" fallacy which the chapter on machinery had fostered:

> The grand source of all the false reasoning upon machinery is to be found in the supposition that every new application of capital to other purposes than that of paying wages is a deduction from the fund devoted to that purpose . . . [But] every improvement in the arts of production is uniformly attended with an increase of profit which acts as a stimulus to an increase of capital; or, more

19. *The Production of Wealth*, pp. xi–xii. See also R. Torrens, *Wages and Combinations* (London, 1834), pp. 33–4.

20. Ricardo, 8, 384.

21. McCulloch, *Principles*, p. 187. See also the attack on Barton's views in the second edition of McCulloch's *Principles* (1830), pp. 541 ff.

> correctly, it is attended with an increase of capital by which the rise in the rate of profit is anticipated. The capital, therefore, attracted to a new and more profitable employment, is not drawn from that fund to which the labourers look for support, but from fresh savings.[22]

One solitary voice was raised on behalf of Ricardo's position. In an *Essay on the Distribution of Wealth,* Sir George Ramsay accepted the thesis that the introduction of machinery may conflict with the interests of the working class. Likewise, he followed Ricardo in the belief that the capital-output ratio tends to rise through time; this led him to the strange deduction that "every augmentation . . . in the national stock destined for reproduction, comes, in the progress of society, to have less and less influence upon the condition of the labourer." Nevertheless, he refused to concede the possibility of a chronic pool of unemployment; among other factors, he singled out the likelihood of a progressive reduction in the length of the working day as an element making for the reabsorption of displaced labor.[23]

Senior reviewed the problem once again in 1836, linking his analysis firmly to the doctrine of the wages fund as the source of demand for labor.[24] His treatment of the subject merely added minor glosses to Ricardo's analysis. Like everyone else he too paid no attention to Ricardo's observation on the trend of investment into the capital-intensive industries, accompanied by a secular lag in the demand for labor.[25]

This brings us down to John Stuart Mill's *Principles* (1848), in which Ricardo's argument is not only faithfully reproduced but in the very same paradoxical manner of asserting one thing on one page and retracting it all on the next. Every conversion of circulating to fixed capital is temporarily injurious to workers: "All attempts to make out that the labouring classes as a collective body *cannot* suffer temporarily by the introduction of machinery, or by the sinking of capital in permanent improvements, are, I conceive, necessarily fallacious." But this holds only when the introduction of machinery diverts circulating capital from other uses: "I do not believe that, as things are actually transacted, improvements in production are often, if ever, injurious, even tempo-

22. *Westminster Review,* January 1826, p. 119.

23. *Essay on the Distribution of Wealth* (Edinburgh, 1836), pp. 74–5, 88–93, 95, 121.

24. See also J. Tozer, "Mathematical Investigation into the Effect of Machinery," *Transactions of the Cambridge Philosophical Society* (1838), 6, Pt. III, 507–22, for a thorough review of the arithmetical examples employed by Sismondi, Barton, Ricardo, and McCulloch in their analyses of the machinery question.

25. Senior, *Political Economy,* pp. 162–6.

rarily, to the labouring classes in the aggregate." In particular, "there is probably no country whose fixed capital increases in a ratio more than proportional to its circulating"; though why this is true Mill did not explain. And whereas Ricardo had frowned on state interference with the rate of technical advance, Mill did not hesitate to argue that if technological progress were so rapid as to diminish the wages fund, "it would be incumbent on legislators to take measures for moderating its rapidity." [26]

Most surprising of all, Malthus showed no sympathy for Ricardo's new position on the machinery question. Malthus simply pointed to the growth of manufacturing towns like Manchester and Glasgow to demonstrate that the accumulation of capital did not entail a decline in the demand for labor. "There is no occasion . . . to fear," he declared, "that the introduction of fixed capital, as it is likely to take place in practice, will diminish the effective demand for labour; indeed, it is to this source that we are to look for the main cause of its future increase." [27] If the rate of accumulation were too rapid, Malthus believed, then a lack of markets for the increased supply might result in distress and unemployment. But in general, the use of machinery tends to reduce costs, thereby opening up new markets and stimulating luxury spending. Consequently, when Ricardo in 1821 proposed the machinery question for discussion at the Political Economy Club, Malthus expressed the view that so long as technological progress "be accompanied by a proper proportion of *unproductive* expenditure it will certainly raise both profits and wages and greatly advance the wealth of the country." [28]

Ricardo's chapter on machinery might have suggested the possibility of a general rapprochement between the two thinkers. Indeed, in McCulloch's eyes Ricardo's recantation was tantamount to a surrender of Say's Law.[29] But Ricardo denied that his new position on the machinery question implied any concession to Malthus' doctrine of the possibility of gluts: "Mr. Malthus' objection to machinery is that it adds so much to the gross produce of the country that the commodities produced cannot be consumed—that there is no demand for them: mine, on the contrary, is that the use of machinery often diminishes the quantity of gross produce, and although the inclination to consume is unlimited, the demand will be diminished, by the want of

26. J. S. Mill, *Principles of Political Economy*, ed. W. J. Ashley (London, 1909), pp. 96–9; also pp. 714–15.

27. *Principles*, p. 238; also pp. 351–60. See also an extensive critique of Barton's views written in 1822: G. W. Zinke, "Letters of Malthus to His French Translator Pierre Prévost," *Journal of Economic History*, November 1942.

28. Ricardo, 9, 11.

29. *Ibid.*, 8, 382.

means of purchasing. Can any two doctrines be more different?" (*8*, 382). Ricardo, it would seem, exaggerated the difference between the two views; particularly since he related Malthus' argument exclusively to his own fictional example of "sudden" technical change. Had he stressed the implications of the Ricardo effect and the danger of insufficient capital-widening the sharp contrast between his conclusions and Malthus' might have disappeared altogether. As a matter of fact, having envisaged the possibility of diminished employment opportunities, Ricardo went so far as to agree with Malthus that "unproductive expenditures" play a significant role, not so much in determining the pace of capital investment as in governing the distribution of its benefits. Laborers have an interest in the manner in which revenue is expended, Ricardo pointed out in the chapter on machinery, because a given expenditure on "menial servants" gives employment "to much more labour" than an equivalent expenditure on luxury goods. This serves to demonstrate that Ricardo did not assume that labor was always fully employed since in that case a shift of consumption spending toward the more labor-intensive services would prove abortive. That this is not what Ricardo meant is clear from his comments in elaboration of the theme:

> A country engaged in war, and which is under the necessity of maintaining large fleets and armies, employs a great many more men than will be employed when the war terminates, and the annual expenses which it brings with it, cease . . . At the termination of the war, when part of my revenue reverts to me [through tax reductions], and is employed as before in the purchase of wine, furniture, or other luxuries, the population which it before supported, and which the war called into existence, will become redundant, and by its effect on the rest of the population, and its competition with it for employment, will sink the value of wages, and very materially deteriorate the condition of the labouring classes (*1*, 393–4).

This is in harmony with Ricardo's observations elsewhere that manufacturing is particularly prone to the type of unemployment that accompanies "temporary reverses and contingencies" (*1*, 263). But if Ricardo did not deny the possibility of something like "cyclical" underemployment of labor and at the same time emphasized the incidence of technological unemployment, what is the meaning of his espousal of Say's Law?

3. Marxian Unemployment and Keynesian Unemployment

In the early stages of an Industrial Revolution capital equipment is usually in scarce supply relative to an abundant and almost unlimited supply of labor; as a consequence, a certain amount of actual and disguised unemployment is inevitable, not due to a deficiency of effective demand but owing to a lack of complementarity in the available factors of production. This type of unemployment corresponds to Marx' "industrial reserve army," denoting the excess of current labor available over the amount of labor required to absorb the existing stock of capital at its normal capacity. It is in this sense that "industry is limited by capital" in overpopulated underdeveloped countries and that full utilization of equipment may well coexist with underemployment of labor.[30]

In an era when the number of individuals on public relief hovered steadily around one million (about 10 per cent of the population of England and Wales),[31] the existence of a hard core of surplus labor must have been taken for granted.[32] Ricardo himself may have come across Patrick Colquhoun's estimate for 1812 which found 9 per cent of the population of Great Britain on relief. And, of course, the Malthusian theory of population alone suggested the fact that in "old" countries the stock of capital would frequently prove inadequate to absorb the available supply of labor. For Ricardo full employment meant nothing more than full-capacity use of the existing stock of capital; too little thrift, not insufficient demand, impeded the expansion of output. For that reason, Ricardo could never seriously entertain the remedy of putting idle labor to work on public projects; this would

30. See J. Robinson, *Collected Economic Papers* (New York, 1951), pp. 141, 169; also M. Fukuoka, "Full Employment and Constant Coefficients of Production," *Quarterly Journal of Economics*, February 1955, pp. 23–9. For an extensive discussion of the argument see W. A. Lewis, "Economic Development with Unlimited Supplies of Labour," *Manchester School,* May 1954; D. Hamberg, *Economic Growth and Instability* (New York, 1956), pp. 162–5.

31. See S. and B. Webb, *English Local Government. English Poor Law History* (London, 1929), Pt. II, 2, 1040, where the number of relief recipients during this period is roughly estimated on the basis of local expenditure figures.

32. As Jean Baptiste Say remarked with respect to the Poor Law: "It is probable that in the time of the reign of Queen Elizabeth, when England had not half the population of the present day, they had then discovered that there were more laborers than work. I desire no other proof of this than that very law which was then passed in favor of the poor . . . Its principal object is to furnish work for the unfortunate who can find no employ. *There was* no employ in a country which since then has been able to furnish enough for a double and triple number of laborers." *Letters to Malthus* (London, 1821; reprinted 1936), pp. 4–5.

simply raise the demand for consumption goods and so create inflation by straining capacity output. Similarly, he could and did recommend wage cuts as an effective device for clearing the labor market.[33] So long as the wage cuts are confined to unskilled labor there is every likelihood that output and employment will rise when "Marxian unemployment" rather than "Keynesian unemployment" is the dominant consideration. The prevalence of labor-saving innovation in an environment marked by the relative abundance of labor would at the same time account for Ricardo's concern with the machinery question and the attendant problem of technological unemployment.[34]

This is not to say, of course, that Ricardo himself recognized the distinction between full employment of capital and full employment of labor.[35] But there is nothing in his writings which denies this interpretation and it permits us to place a somewhat more favorable construction on many of his ideas than is customarily accorded to them.

In the depression years of 1816 and 1817 relief work in the form of road building was provided in London and in the provinces, financed by private subscription. Writing to Malthus, Ricardo expressed his misgivings over "the measures lately adopted for the relief of the poor": "I am not one of those who think that the raising of funds for the purpose of employing the poor is a very efficacious mode of relief, as it diverts those funds from other employments which would be equally if not more productive to the community. That part of the capital which employs the poor on the roads for example cannot fail to employ men somewhere and I believe every interference is prejudicial."[36] And again in 1819, a year of mass unemployment and labor unrest, he addressed Parliament to discourage the use of state-financed public works schemes: "When he heard honourable members

33. See, for instance, Ricardo, 9, 25.

34. There is some evidence that the labor-saving effects of improvements in this period overshot requirements as determined by relative factor scarcities. But even if the evidence were acceptable this would not be incompatible with the attested rise in the real wages of *employed* labor in the generation following Waterloo. See W. Fellner, *Trends and Cycles in Economic Activity* (New York, 1956), pp. 238–9.

35. Certainly Ricardo never saw the issue as clearly as Bentham had done 20 years earlier: in an unpublished MS Bentham considered the effect of an increase in the quantity of money on prices when there is unemployment of labor as contrasted with the situation in which "all hands capable of employ were full of employment" (*Jeremy Bentham's Economic Writings*, ed. W. Stark [London, 1952], 2, 286; also pp. 303–8). Oddly enough, Bentham also arrived at similar conclusions to Ricardo's with respect to the machinery question, again in an unpublished MS (*ibid.*, 3, 333).

36. 7, 116. Malthus agreed with Ricardo, and on almost identical grounds. See the recently discovered letter of Malthus, published by P. Sraffa, *Economic Journal*, September 1955.

talk of employing capital in the formation of roads and canals, they appeared to overlook the fact, that capital thus employed must be withdrawn from some other quarter. The causes of the insufficiency of capital . . . were to be attributed to many circumstances, for some of which government were not to blame" (*5*, 32).

The scarcity-of-capital doctrine is also evident in everything which Ricardo wrote on the public debt. He regarded all state expenditures as unproductive of economic growth (*1*, 185). Whether government funds are raised by taxation or by borrowing, their effect is always to divert capital from productive employment. For Ricardo the primary "burden" of the debt is not the annual interest charge or the necessity of eventual redemption but rather the wasteful nature of public expenditures as such.[37] "The capital of the stockholder [of the public debt]," he wrote, "can never be made productive—it is, in fact, no capital. If he were to sell his stock, and employ the capital he obtained for it, productively, he could only do so by detaching the capital of the buyer of his stock from a productive employment" (*1*, 249 n.).

Just as there can be no general glut of commodities, "there cannot . . . be accumulated in a country any amount of capital which cannot be employed productively, until wages rise so high in consequence of the rise of necessaries, and so little consequently remains for the profits of stock, that the motive for accumulation ceases" (*1*, 290). Adequacy of demand is assured because human wants are insatiable: "Nothing is required but the means, and nothing can afford the means, but an increase of production" (*1*, 292). This is not to be read as a denial of the postwar crisis of whose existence, as we have seen, Ricardo was perfectly well aware. What separates Ricardo from Malthus in this respect is that Ricardo did not regard the depression as a harbinger of secular stagnation. "The distress which proceeds from a revulsion of trade," Ricardo observed, "is often mistaken for that which accompanies a diminution of the national capital, and a retrograde state of society" (*1*, 265). But the slump of 1816–17 was simply the result of "sudden changes in the channels of trade" following upon the conversion to a peacetime economy; basically the outlook for investment was favorable (*7*, 67).

Four years later Ricardo was still looking forward hopefully to an early revival of trade despite the persistence of restrictive legislation such as the corn laws. McCulloch, inclined to gloomier views, expressed his dissent in characteristically forceful language: "If Political Economy be worth one straw as a science . . . if it is not a mere holyday bauble—we are entitled boldly and confidently to affirm that so long as the present taxation and corn law system is kept up the

37. For a detailed analysis see R. O. Roberts, "Ricardo's Theory of Public Debts," *Economica*, August 1942.

country can never rise superior to the difficulties" (Ricardo, *8*, 354). He reminded Ricardo of the ever present danger of capital migration while the corn laws were in force: only the unsettled state of the Continent and the great distance of America prevented the flight of capital. But Ricardo's reply was to throw doubt on the supposition that the rate of profit was lower in Britain than elsewhere. Granted that profits would be higher if the corn laws were repealed, he told McCulloch, nevertheless, "I am by no means ready to admit that we may not have a more limited measure of prosperity notwithstanding the continued operation of our corn laws, and the continued existence of our debt." [38]

Not that Ricardo's arguments were always so reasonable; in defending Say's Law he took a position which hardly allowed for fluctuations in the rate of investment or the temporary occurrence of idle savings. At no time did he permit himself to conceive of a break in the income stream through the influence of hoarding (*1*, 291). Moreover, like most of his contemporaries he had no conception of the nature of derivative deposits and steadfastly denied that bank credit can "create capital." [39]

The blind spots in Ricardo's thinking are strikingly illustrated by his critical comments on a pamphlet by William Blake which appeared in 1823. Blake was one of a number of writers in the deflationary phase of the bullionist controversy who argued that government spending during the war period had actually stimulated production and augmented capital; the conversion of idle funds into public expenditures by means of taxing "unproductive consumption," while it operated to increase prices, accelerated the rate of economic growth.[40] Hence the postwar deflation was simply the result of the sudden decline in public spending. In holding this doctrine Blake was led to criticize the prevailing view that government borrowing always involved the transfer of capital from productive to unproductive employment: "The error lies in supposing, first, that the whole capital of the country is fully occupied; and, secondly, that there is immediate employment for successive accumulations of capital as it accrues from saving." [41] Blake

38. *8*, 357–8; also *9*, 158. But in Parliament Ricardo was unable to resist the convenient flight-of-capital argument against the Corn Laws (*5*, 38, 50, 187).

39. *5*, 436–7. For the same view expressed by Tooke and McCulloch, see *Political Economy Club*, pp. 240–1; also a typical essay on "Credit," Supplement to the *Encyclopaedia Britannica* (1824), *3*, 439–42. For Ricardo's denial of the "forced saving" effect, see Ricardo, *1*, 143; *3*, 121–3, 302, 319, 329; *5*, 445–6; *6*, 17, 233.

40. See Viner, *op. cit.*, pp. 192–7.

41. W. Blake, *Observations on the Effects Produced by the Expenditure of Government* (London, 1823), p. 54.

regarded a lack of profitable investment outlets as a normal consequence of capital accumulation. He admitted that the Law of the Market was unimpeachable, given the fact that "new tasks and wants spring up with the new capital." But he saw no reason to believe that this would necessarily follow. Unlike Malthus, however, Blake felt that public, rather than private, spending could be relied upon to provide a source of effective demand.[42]

Ricardo doubted whether Blake's views on currency were so very different from his own, but as to his ideas on "the effects of a war expenditure," "I cannot say one word in defence of this theory" (9, 287). Blake's evidence for the existence of gluts proved that "great mistakes are made in the application of capital . . . but . . . it does not impugn the general principle that if there were no mistakes there would be no gluts" (*4*, 345). Ricardo could see no reason to warrant the belief that government could find a market for unused funds when private producers had tried and failed. How can "the increased quantity of commodities, required by Govt . . . be produced," Ricardo queried, "without occasioning any diminished supply of commodities in any other quarter? If industry be encouraged in one department it is discouraged in another."[43] Ricardo failed utterly to meet Blake's point that full employment of capital was simply being posited as an assumption; in that Ricardo was in good company, Malthus not excepted. Blake was in fact the only writer in the first quarter of the century to draw explicit attention to this hypothesis underlying the controversy over Say's Law. It is to this controversy that we now turn.

42. *Ibid.*, pp. 54–5, 58–9, 69–70.

43. *4*, 356. John Stuart Mill employed similar arguments in a review of Blake's tract for the *Westminster Review*, July 1824: Blake's fallacy, as he saw it, lay in "conceiving that capital which being borrowed by government becomes a source of demand in its hand, would not have been equally a source of demand in the hands of those from whom it is taken" (pp. 38–9).

CHAPTER 5

Malthus' Heresy on Gluts

> Ricardo . . . and Mr. Tooke . . . appeared to me to regard the state of the country in much too favourable a point of view, the only circumstance upon which they laid any stress was the transfer of capital abroad. But as to loss of capital at home, deterioration of fixed capital, wages without adequate return, lessening of consumption, agricultural sufferings—they made light of these things. It was enough that they were provided for and classed under their proper heads with their natural remedies in books of Political Economy.
>
> JOHN LEWIS MALLET, *Diary*, JANUARY 1820

1. Malthus' Opposition to Ricardo

FROM THE MOMENT of their first meeting in 1811 Malthus and Ricardo disagreed on almost all the fundamental topics of political economy. In the beginning such differences concerned relatively incidental matters apropos of the bullion controversy, but by 1813 the dispute had spread to the problem of capital accumulation and its effect on the distributive shares. Their quarrel came into the open with the corn laws debate of 1815 which found them respectively on the side of protection and free trade. On the face of it, they adopted the same theory of rent. The conflict of interpretation, however, had to do with the nature and origin of rent and the relation of agriculture to the national welfare. The circumstances of the Napoleonic Wars had given rise to "a political inducement to represent the landlord as fattening on diminishing returns." [1] Stirred to protest, Malthus bent his efforts to demonstrate that rent constitutes a genuine addition to wealth, and not a mere transfer of purchasing power as Ricardo intimated.

While conceding that the cost of producing food often exerted a controlling influence on the rate of profit, Malthus refused to regard rising production costs in agriculture as the sole or dominant reason for reduced profits.[2] Firstly, he was not barred as Ricardo was from stressing the offsetting effect of improvements in agricultural methods. Secondly, he had his eyes on another source of weakening investment incentives, based upon the distinction between "necessaries of life"

1. E. Cannan, *A Review of Economic Theory* (London, 1929), p. 249.
2. See, for example, Ricardo, *6*, 117–18, 139–40, 154–5.

which "create their own demand" and "conveniences and luxuries" whose demand is dependent upon the consumption habits of the nonproductive elements of the population.[3]

What Malthus seems to have had in mind is this: The landlord's income, being a return to a nonproduced natural factor, is not destined to be respent like other income; consequently, unless the landlord can be induced to spend his receipts upon consumer goods and personal services, the "circular flow" ceases to be self-perpetuating. Hence what is wanted to ensure the expansion of output is a steady source of effective demand rather than the importation of cheap food. The prime mover of production is not the yield of land but the spending power of landlords. This is the whole content of Malthus' objection to Say's Law which, he argued, neglects to consider "the wants and tastes of mankind." For the rest, Malthus' writings represent nothing more than an attempt to give alternative formulations to this line of reasoning.

By the time he came to write his *Principles* (1820) Malthus saw the necessity of taking issue with Ricardo's theory of value so as to bring out the pivotal role of effective demand. At the outset Malthus repudiated the prevailing treatment of "demand" and "supply" as physical quantities actually bought and sold at given prices in the market. He chose deliberately to measure purchasing power by what he called the "intensity" of demand rather than the "extent" of demand. An increase in the intensity of demand indicates "the will and power to make a greater sacrifice in order to obtain the object wanted . . . It is in this latter sense alone that demand raises prices." An excess of supply, on the other hand, implies a situation which renders "a fall of price necessary in order to take off a temporary abundance."[4] A glut of a particular commodity may now be taken to mean an excess of supply relative to the intensity of demand so as to cause its price to fall below prime costs. By inference, a general glut or a deficiency of aggregate demand is an instance in which the sum of all income payments is not adequate to purchase the mass of commodities at remunerative prices to producers.

Malthus came close in these arguments to the distinction between price-determined and price-determining changes of demand and, in all, his discussion marked a considerable advance over Ricardo's rather flippant treatment of the short run aspects of price determination.[5]

3. See Ricardo, *6*, 168; *2*, 114–16. See also Ricardo's refutation of this distinction (which nevertheless is implicit in Ricardo's assumption of a demand curve for corn of zero elasticity): *1*, 406; *8*, 235–6, 245–8.

4. *Principles*, pp. 68–9.

5. See *ibid.*, p. 64, and Ricardo, *1*, 382–5; *8*, 207. Following standard practice, Ricardo confined demand-and-supply explanations to the determination of the *market* price. However, there is no reason to believe that he conceived of cost

Nevertheless, the micro-economic concept of intensity of demand is logically unrelated to the question of the sufficiency of aggregate demand; in fact, nothing more is heard of it in Book II of the *Principles* where Malthus deals specifically with the problem of general overproduction.[6]

The alleged foundation for the theory of gluts is Malthus' measure of value, defined as the quantity of "unskilled agricultural labour" rewarded at the current corn wage which a commodity will normally command in exchange.[7] This standard of value, Malthus argues, permits both international and intertemporal comparisons of real income; the value of total output at any time and place is simply estimated by the corresponding number of wage units which it can command.[8] Clearly, if bygones are forever bygones, it is possible that the number of wage units currently commanded by present output may fall short of the quantity of direct and indirect labor embodied in its production; it follows that the power to produce may not generate an equal power to consume.[9]

All this proves nothing but nevertheless is quite unobjectionable if we are willing to assume that changes in the level of output are uniquely associated with changes in the volume of employment. Unlike Ricardo's invariable measure of value, Malthus' measure really is a price deflator.[10] But Malthus never succeeded in explaining the implications of his measure or in relating it to Ricardo's standard.[11] The unsatisfactory character of Malthus' value theory, however, is of no great moment to his basic theme. Though designed to serve as a theoretical warrant for the contention that general gluts are possible, the entire analysis of Book I of Malthus' *Principles* is strictly speaking irrelevant to that proposition.

---

factors as influencing long-run *natural* price except insofar as they affected supply (see for instance *2*, 45–9). On this matter see Schumpeter, *op. cit.*, pp. 600–1, and Viner's review of Schumpeter's *History*, *op. cit.*, p. 905.

6. For a more detailed discussion of Malthus' demand analysis, see Bowley, *op. cit.*, pp. 87–9; Myint, *op. cit.*, pp. 35–8; V. E. Smith, "The Classicists' Use of Demand," *Journal of Political Economy*, June 1951, pp. 249–53.

7. T. R. Malthus, *The Measure of Value Illustrated* (London, 1823), pp. 18–19.

8. *Ibid.*, pp. 56, 65; also *Principles*, pp. 96 ff.

9. *Principles*, p. 317.

10. Ricardo overlooked this point in criticizing Malthus' measure (Ricardo, *4*, 361–2, 390–3, 406–10).

11. For a charitable interpretation, see Myint, *op. cit.*, pp. 38–40. It is difficult to see how Professor Myint can say that "the Glut controversy, in fact, cannot be fully appreciated except in terms of the different measures of value adopted by Malthus and Ricardo" (p. 85).

2. The Optimum Propensity to Save

Malthus' ideas are best expressed in terms of the doctrine of productive labor which he took over from Adam Smith. The distinction which Smith had in mind was between the accumulatable and the non-accumulatable. At first glance it seems obvious that goods can be stored but services cannot. Hence Adam Smith's famous definition of productive labor: labor is productive if it produces tangible commodities which are used in the further reproduction of wealth; unproductive labor, on the other hand, produces "luxuries" or perishable services for immediate consumption.[12] In this sense, productive labor alone creates an economic surplus, a net physical addition over and above wages. But productive laborers cannot buy back the commodities they have produced, Malthus argued, since they would not have been employed if the value of the product did not exceed the value of wages paid out: "No power of consumption on the part of the labouring classes can ever . . . alone furnish an encouragement to the employment of capital."[13] It follows that a certain volume of "unproductive consumption" or spending on luxury articles and labor services by households is necessary to sustain purchasing power and ensure continued reproduction. This conclusion, however, is based on the crudest underconsumptionist reasoning.

Malthus had grounds more relevant than this. He took his cue from Ricardo's admission that some supernumerary expenditure on luxury articles was necessary to absorb the output of an expanding productive capacity. In his *Principles* Ricardo speculated briefly on the possibility of a general glut in the event of a sharp rise in the propensity to save and invest:

> There is only one case, and that will be temporary, in which the accumulation of capital with a low price of food may be attended with a fall of profits; and that is, when the funds for the maintenance of labour increase much more rapidly than population; wages will then be high and profits low. If every man were to forego the use of luxuries, and be intent only on accumulation,

12. Two separate versions of the doctrine of productive labor may be found in *The Wealth of Nations.* Professor Myint has conveniently dubbed these the "storage" version and the "value" version (*ibid.*, p. 73). According to the former, productive labor, in Smith's words, "fixes or realises itself in some particular subject or vendible commodity"; according to the latter, productive labor produces goods which "can afterwards, if necessary, put into motion a quantity of labour equal to which had originally produced it." Malthus employs both verisions of the doctrine (*Principles,* pp. 34–49).

13. *Ibid.*, p. 404; also pp. 315, 322.

> a quantity of necessaries might be produced, for which there could not be any immediate consumption. Of commodities so limited in number, there might undoubtedly be an universal glut.

He felt confident, however, that in a country like England there could not be "any disposition to devote the whole capital and labour of the country to the production of necessaries only." [14] Even so, Ricardo's concession is rather curious; in the short run, heavy investments in fixed assets cannot greatly increase the flow of consumption goods; the assertion that the case is only "temporary" spoils the whole argument.[15]

Nevertheless, Malthus seized on Ricardo's remarks as supporting the thesis that "an inordinate passion for accumulation must inevitably lead to a supply of commodities beyond what the structure and habits of such a society will permit to be profitably consumed."

> Even if we suppose with Mr. Ricardo, what is not true, that an increase of population would certainly remedy the evil; yet as from the nature of population, an increase of labourers cannot be brought into the market, in consequence of a particular demand, till after a lapse of sixteen or eighteen years, and the conversion of revenue into capital by saving may take place much more rapidly; a country is always liable to an increase in the quantity of the funds for the maintenance of labour faster than the increase of population. But if, whenever this occurs, there may be an universal glut of commodities, how can it be maintained, as a general position, that capital is never redundant . . . ? [16]

Surely this is an extraordinary argument from the author of the *Essay on the Principle of Population.*[17] It did not, however, prevent Malthus from explaining the postwar depression by an increase of population "not only faster than the demand for labour, but faster than the actual produce." [18]

What Malthus failed to make explicit is that Ricardo's observation regarding the effect of a sudden contraction of "unproductive consumption" implies the possibility of a rate of saving in excess of the

14. *1*, 292–3; also *2*, 8–9; *9*, 131.

15. See G. J. Stigler, "Sraffa's Ricardo," *American Economic Review,* September 1953, p. 595.

16. *Principles,* pp. 319–20.

17. When Malthus resorted to this argument in correspondence with Ricardo, the latter cited the principle of population to refute the supposition (Ricardo, *7*, 70, 72).

18. *Principles,* p. 417. The contradiction between Malthus' population and employment theories is not adequately resolved, it seems to me, by Professor Spengler's restatement of "Malthus's Total Population Theory," *Canadian Journal of Economics and Political Science,* February 1945, particularly pp. 95–7.

optimum—optimum in the sense of maximizing the rate of capital formation. Now, the notion of an optimum propensity to save is one of Malthus' pet ideas:

> No considerable and continued increase of wealth could possibly take place without that degree of frugality which occasions, annually, the conversion of some revenue into capital, and creates a balance of produce above consumption; but it is quite obvious that they are not true to an indefinite extent, and that the principle of saving, pushed to excess, would destroy the motive to production . . . If consumption exceed production, the capital of a country must be diminished, and its wealth must be gradually destroyed from its want of power to produce; if production be in great excess above consumption, the motive to accumulate and produce must cease from the want of an effectual demand. . . . The two extremes are obvious; and it follows that there must be some intermediate point, though the resources of political economy may not be able to ascertain it, where, taking into consideration both the power to produce and the will to consume, the encouragement to the increase of wealth is the greatest.[19]

Malthus' belief that saving can be "pushed to excess" is capable of substantiation on a number of grounds.[20] He could have argued that the money flow normally fails to keep pace with the increasing volume of transactions; hence an expansion of output may be accompanied by prices falling more rapidly than costs; if wages are rigid downward (perhaps because wages are already at the subsistence level) any deflationary tendencies generate adverse changes in entrepreneurial receipts relative to outlays, leading to general losses throughout the economy. Or he might have pointed out that income received is sometimes used to liquidate debts or retained as idle cash balances; or that, for any other reason, individuals do not promptly disburse the proceeds of sales.

But Malthus did not resort to any of these explanations. Like Ricardo and Say, he rejected all purely monetary causes of general overproduction; apart from a parenthetical criticism of other economists for their neglect of the "importance" of money, and a few comments on the postwar deflation,[21] the *Principles* contains no analysis of the

19. *Principles*, pp. 6–7; also pp. 326, 432–4.

20. The only rigorous argument is that of Harrod and Domar: Given the capacity-creating character of investment, there is a propensity to save such as to maintain a rate of growth of income required for full employment equilibrium; any greater rate of saving produces excess capacity and unemployment. But of course there is nothing in Malthus to suggest this way of looking at the problem.

21. *Ibid.*, pp. 324 n., 386–8.

monetary aspects of economic activity. Nor did Malthus rely upon the notion that wages are inflexible; indeed, he fully allowed that wage cuts had stimulated the re-employment of servicemen released after Waterloo.[22] Furthermore, like all his contemporaries, Malthus regarded the process of saving and the making of investment as strictly interdependent activities; individuals save to invest and investment is financed out of profits rather than out of bank credit. Theoretically, there was nothing to bar Malthus from asserting that the decision to save is not always associated with a desire to purchase newly manufactured assets. In the classical tradition saving is viewed as the difference between past income and present consumption; the implicit reference to a time lag in the generation of income makes it possible to consider the consequences of saving to hoard. But Malthus simply could not entertain "hoarding" as a normal phenomenon; as he remarked: "No political economist of the present day can by saving mean mere hoarding." [23]

But if Malthus identified the act of saving with the act of investment, why did he speak of an optimum "principle of saving" and not of an optimum rate of investment? The explanation lies in the fact that he had continuous appeal to the intuitive notion that saving acts simultaneously to diminish the demand for consumers' goods and, insofar as it is promptly reinvested, to increase the supply of consumers' goods. Malthus' theory is "an underconsumption theory, of the oversaving type," [24] not in the usual sense that wage income is inadequate to buy back the whole product at cost-covered prices but in the sense that the reduced demand of nonwage earners cannot absorb the increased output which their savings have made possible. What is left out of the picture is that the double effect of saving does not take place simultaneously, owing to the time-consuming character of production. The decreased demand for consumers' goods is matched initially by an increase in the demand for capital goods which subsequently reduces costs, thereby freeing purchasing power for the reabsorption of additional output. That this process is fraught with the danger of a cumulative downturn is undeniable and, with appropriate additions, it may furnish the basis for a theory of business cycles. But as an ex-

22. *Ibid.*, p. 393. But in correspondence with Ricardo, Malthus did resort to wage rigidities to justify the possibility of gluts (Ricardo, 9, 20).

23. *Principles*, p. 38. Only once did Malthus refer explicitly to the existence of idle savings: in the last pages of the *Principles* he remarks on the fact that "In our own country very many persons have taken the opportunity of saving a part of their returned property-tax . . . This saving . . . contributes to explain the cause of the diminished demand for commodities, compared with their supply since the war" (p. 421).

24. Schumpeter, *op. cit.*, p. 740.

planation of the possibility of secular stagnation this argument falls flat. Nothing at all has been accomplished so long as the market forces which fail to preserve the optimum rate of saving are left unspecified. It is precisely on this score that Malthus' theory is vacuous.

It cannot be too strongly emphasized that Malthus' objection to Say's Law bears no resemblance to the modern doctrine of a "mature economy" in which private investment proves inadequate to ensure full employment of labor. This despite a certain superficial resemblance of language:

> Fully acknowledging that there is hardly a country in the four quarters of the globe where capital is not deficient, and in most of them very greatly deficient, compared with the territory and even the number of people; and fully allowing at the same time the extreme desirableness of an increase of capital, I should say that where . . . the capitalists were at a loss where and how to employ their capitals to advantage, the saving from revenue to add still more to these capitals would only tend prematurely to diminish the motive to accumulation, and still further to distress the capitalists.[25]

Since the capital stock was thought to be fully utilized it was current doctrine that, as Ricardo put it, "capital may . . . be increased by an increased production, or by a diminished unproductive consumption." [26] Therefore, for an expanding economy, saving is complementary to consumption. "The fortune of a country," wrote Malthus, "is made in the same way as the fortunes of individuals . . . —by *savings* certainly; but by savings which are furnished from increased gains, and by no means involve a diminished expenditure on objects of luxury and enjoyment" (*Principles*, p. 367). But in the circumstances of the postwar depression, Malthus argued, more thrift meant less consumption: "As soon as the capitalists can begin to save from steady and improving profits, instead of from diminished expenditure . . . we may then begin safely and effectively to recover our lost capital by the usual process of saving a portion of our increased revenue to add to it" (p. 430).

Hence, it is "vain and fruitless . . . to recommend saving"; "where are the under-stocked employments, which, according to this theory, ought to be numerous, and fully capable of absorbing all the redundant capital, which is confessedly glutting the markets of Europe in so many different branches of trade?" (pp. 418, 420). May we infer that everything saved is not automatically invested? If so, we are at loss what to

25. *Principles*, p. 328.
26. Ricardo, *1*, 150.

make of Malthus' assertion: "It is stated by Adam Smith, and it must be allowed to be stated justly, that the produce which is annually saved is as regularly consumed, as that which is annually spent, but that it is consumed by a different set of people. If this be the case, and if saving be allowed to be the immediate cause of the increase of capital . . . ," and so forth (p. 38). Ricardo was not wrong when he observed that this passage represents "an important admission from Mr. Malthus" which "will be found to be at variance with some of the doctrines which he afterwards maintains" (2, 15).

Malthus' general conclusion is that capital accumulation should precede slowly so that new tastes and wants for "conveniences and luxuries" may be cultivated to accommodate the increased supply. As for immediate palliatives he recommended the gradual removal of protective tariffs on manufactured goods and, of course, any and all measures to encourage "unproductive consumption." His advice to "landlords and men of property" is to alleviate unemployment by hiring "workmen and menial servants" to improve their estates. The state might contribute by promoting public works, "the results of which do not come for sale in the market." An increase of taxation would be required to finance such relief projects; this could have the effect, Malthus admitted, of reducing the stream of new investment and depressing the quantity of productive labor employed. But this is precisely Malthus' object:

> The objection to employing a large sum in this way, raised by taxes, would not be its tendency to diminish the capital employed in productive labour; because this, to a certain extent, is exactly what is wanted; but it might, perhaps, have the effect of concealing too much the failure of the national demand for labour, and prevent the population from gradually accommodating itself to a reduced demand. This however might be, in considerable degree, corrected by the wages given.[27]

The cure for depression, therefore, is not to stimulate investment by activating idle balances, but to scale down production to fit the existing level of demand. The nature of Malthus' approval of public works as a recovery measure should correct the impression that he was chiefly preoccupied with the barriers to economic growth in the form of gluts and unemployment. On the contrary, his stress on the negative aspects of economic development is a function of his concern with the agrarian sources of social welfare; since the landowner is the principal unproductive consumer, the prosperity of the community depends on the

27. *Principles*, pp. 429–30. See also T. R. Malthus, *Essay on the Principle of Population* (6th ed. London, 1826; reprinted 1890), p. 353.

wealth and spending power of landlords. Indeed, Malthus' defense of the corn laws and his theory of gluts are cut out of the same cloth.

3. The Defense of the Law of Markets

Almost the first public rebuttal to Malthus' strictures on the Law of Markets came from Say himself in a set of *Letters to Malthus on Political Economy and Commerce.* In the anxiety to score a watertight victory Say reformulated the law once again by excluding unsold commodities.[28] The only effective point which he made against Malthus dealt with the side issue of population pressures: "After having written three justly admired volumes to prove that the population always rises to the level of the means of existence, can you admit the case of *a great increase of productions, with a stationary number of consumers, and wants reduced by parsimony.* Either the Author of the *Essay on Population* or the Author of the *Principles of Political Economy* must be wrong." [29]

Say admitted the existence of a "general over-stock of all the markets of the universe" and a "universal difficulty . . . in obtaining lucrative employ"; this he attributed to miscalculations on the part of producers, lack of confidence in the stability of political institutions leading to the withholding of money, and barriers to the mobility of resources owing to government restrictions and poor means of transportation.[30] But these difficulties will be overcome by the decline in the bank rate which must eventually stimulate an offsetting rise in investment. Say's argument is projected by way of a criticism of Ricardo for ignoring the function of the interest mechanism in synchronizing saving and investment:

> Mr. Ricardo pretends that, in spite of taxes and other obstructions, there is always as much industry as capital employed, and that all capitals saved are still employed, because capitalists will not lose the interest. There are on the contrary, many savings unemployed on account of the difficulty in employing them, or being employed are lost in consequence of bad management. Besides, Mr. Ricardo is contradicted by what happened to us in 1813, . . .

28. *Letters to Malthus,* p. 28. For a detailed analysis of Say's numerous, and by no means identical, statements of the Law of Markets, see the brilliant treatment by Schumpeter, *op. cit.*, pp. 615–22, and the still useful discussion by E. v. Bergmann, *Geschichte der nationalökonomischen Krisentheorieen* (Stuttgart, 1895), pp. 67–78.

29. *Letters to Malthus,* p. 28. The italicized words in the quotation are Malthus' (see *Principles,* p. 317).

30. *Letters to Malthus,* pp. 2, 5, 8, 9, 35, 67.

> when interest of money fell so low, for want of good opportunities of employing it—and by what is happening to us at this moment in which the capitals sleep at the bottom of the coffers of capitalists.[31]

Nevertheless, Say affirmed the Law of Markets as an expression of the long-run tendency of the economy to full employment equilibrium which "shows mankind the source of real wealth and warns them of the danger of corrupting that source." The cure for overproduction is not to encourage wasteful luxury spending but to furnish such conditions as will stimulate the over-all expansion of industry.

Although in accord with Say's underlying argument, Ricardo objected (*8*, 227–8) to the manner in which Say tended to brush aside the problem of the correct composition of output with respect to consumers' demand; unfortunately, this thought was never developed in Ricardo's published writings. In addition, Ricardo refused to concede that the level of investment demands for loans was functionally dependent upon the rate of interest.[32] After reminding his readers that profits never fall but for a rise in the cost of producing wage goods, he asked: "Is the following quite consistent with M. Say's principle? 'The more disposable capitals are abundant in proportion to the extent of employment for them, the more will the rate of interest on loans of capital fall.'" But, Ricardo remonstrated, "if capital to any extent can be employed by a country, how can it be said to be abundant, compared with the extent of employment for it?" (*1*, 290 n.). Although the expansion of output up to the full utilization of the available capital stock is assumed to take place independently of the interest mechanism, Ricardo was perfectly aware of the function of price-interest variations in bringing about an equilibrium of industries *within* total output. But as usual, Ricardo dismissed this adjustment process as but of "temporary duration" (see *1*, 297–8).

That he failed to emphasize the corrective effects of automatic market forces was due not only to the primitive level of his analysis but to his conviction that Malthus' argument was geared to the bogey of capital saturation in the near future. And in this sense, Malthus' thesis did not call for a refined answer. In a letter to a friend Ricardo pointed out that Malthus believed that a chronic slump is "the specific

31. *Ibid.*, pp. 45–6 n. Malthus cited this passage in a letter to Ricardo and claimed that it "fully concedes all that I contend for. . . . The fall in the interest of money and the difficulty of finding employment for capital are universally acknowledged" (Ricardo, *8*, 260). Yet nowhere in the *Principles* did Malthus exploit Say's line of reasoning.

32. Niether Say nor Ricardo contemplated a connection between the rate of real saving and the rate of interest. On this point see R. L. Meek, "Thomas Joplin and the Rate of Interest," *Review of Economic Studies, 18,* third series, No. 47 (1950–51).

evil under which are *at present* suffering," and to Malthus himself he wrote:

> I have rather understood you to say that vast powers of production are put into action and the result is unfavourable to the interests of mankind, and you have suggested as a remedy either that less should be produced, or more should be unproductively consumed . . . You often appear to me to contend not only that production can go on so far without an adequate motive, but that *it actually has done so lately,* and that we are now suffering the consequences of it in stagnation of trade, in a want of employment for our labourers &c. &c., and the remedy you propose is an increase of consumption.
>
> . . . . .
>
> We appear then not to differ very widely in our general principles, but more so respecting the applications of them. Such and such evils may exist, but *the question is, do they exist now?* I think not, none of the symptoms indicate that they do, and in my opinion increased savings would alleviate rather than aggravate the sufferings of which we have lately had to complain.[33]

To avoid misunderstanding Ricardo drew a distinction between general overproduction in Malthus' sense and the so-called "stationary state" where "all motive for further savings will cease, but there will be no stagnation—all that is produced will be at its fair relative prices and will be freely exchanged" (9, 25). The economic system tended to "run down" in terms of real output but Say's Law precluded the possibility of "breakdown" from causes inherent in the process of capital accumulation.

Ricardo's incessant appeal to the insatiability of human wants is similarly understood as a reaction to Malthus' reliance on "the influence of so general and important a principle in human nature, as indolence or love of ease."[34] Malthus did not seek to justify his belief in the importance of this "principle of human nature"; by itself, however, it is incapable of *generating* a universal glut.[35]

Ricardo's followers did not contribute anything very important to the gluts controversy. In a preface to the *Essay on the Production of Wealth,* Torrens posited Say's Law as "the very key-stone of economical science" but expressed dissatisfaction with "the general unqualified sense" in which James Mill and Say had expounded it. In the course

33. 9, 15–16, 26–7 (my italics); also 8, 257.

34. *Principles,* p. 320.

35. It may be an element, of course, in explaining a very different matter: the lack of economic development in a backward area. Malthus employed it for that purpose as well (see *ibid.,* pp. 340–50).

of his analysis he came to grips with the empirical objections to the Law of Markets: "If the theory of effectual demand, which I have ventured to unfold, does not explain in a satisfactory manner that overstocking of the market, and want of profitable vend for commodities, *the existence of which is a matter of general experience,* I am ready to admit that such a theory must be essentially defective and incorrect." After a review of the measures that might be adopted to avert gluts, Torrens concludes with Ricardo that "the only limits to the increase of effectual demand will be the limits which are set to increased production, by the scarcity of fertile lands, or by a rate of wages so high as to deprive the capitalists of that *minimum* rate of profit which is necessary to induce him to continue his advances." [36]

James Mill took up Ricardo's concession to Malthus' theory involving the case of "every man consuming nothing but necessaries." On this question he was *plus royaliste que le roi* for he insisted that even here Say's Law holds without qualification. Malthus' doctrine is summed up in these words: "If saving were to go on at a certain rate, capital would increase faster than population; and that if capital did so increase, wages would become very high, and profits would sustain a corresponding depression"—an interesting example of how difficult it was for contemporary writers to grasp the meaning of Malthus' confusing and many-sided argument. High wages, "Mr. Malthus further says," would produce idleness among laborers. If so, Mill retorts, this amounts to higher wages for less work; "it is therefore the same thing as a rise of wages" which would "infallibly produce its own remedy" by discouraging investment. Furthermore, Malthus contends that "were the annual produce to go on increasing, its *value* would be diminished." But this is "merely a play upon the word." Likewise, Malthus states that "this rapid increase of capital would tend to diminish production," which is a contradiction in terms.[37]

McCulloch reduced Malthus' theory to an insistence on "the indisposition to consume" and pointed out that "there is no such indisposition in any country of the world." He spoke slightingly of Malthus' agricultural sympathies and concluded: "It is not to increased facilities of production, but to the restraints imposed on the freedom of trade, that those commercial revulsions, *we have so frequently experienced,* are really to be ascribed." [38]

It seems clear that no one in this period held Say's Law as a short-run proposition except in the heat of debate to ward off all final objections; even then there was no attempt to deny the obvious fact of

36. *Essay on the Production of Wealth,* pp. ix, 371, 399 (my italics).
37. J. Mill, *Elements,* pp. 242–4.
38. McCulloch, *Principles,* pp. 162, 170, 172 (my italics).

recurring distress and unemployment. The matter in dispute was the possibility of secular stagnation, not cyclical depression.[39] And in this context Say's Law is neither a truism nor a trivial proposition; it asserts that there are no inherent obstacles in a capitalist economy that would prevent the absorption of a constantly expanding output; therefore, "crises can never be *causally explained* solely by everybody's having produced too much." [40]

But this is not to say that any of the participants in the controversy ever did justice to the analytical issues involved. The proponents of Say's Law were generally so anxious to exploit its practical implications that they neglected to provide anything like a rigorous description of the dynamic adjustment process to full employment.[41] The cavalier treatment of monetary forces and, in particular, the failure to restrict the time period relevant to the assertion that any increase in output, being ultimately spent either on consumption goods or on investment goods, generates an equivalent increase in aggregate demand, reduced most of the gluts controversy to a battle over the strength of historical forces working to develop new tastes and wants.[42]

Malthus' attack upon Say's Law failed owing to his insistence that vanishing investment incentives can be explained solely by insufficient consumers' demand; had he stressed instead insufficient consumers'-plus-investors' demand he would have been forced to link the latter to diminishing returns to capital due to growing scarcities of cooperating resources. But time and time again Malthus denied the need to consider this connection. Ricardo, on the other hand, was placed in the comfortable position of showing the deficiency in Malthus' reasoning without being made to explain why consumption should necessarily rise to the level required for full employment if scarcities of cooperating factors do indeed lead to declining returns on capital. Thus Malthus' deficient analysis of Say's Law led both thinkers to circumvent the very essence of the problem of effective demand.

39. For the same interpretation see Patinkin, *op. cit.*, p. 474, and the sources cited there.

40. Schumpeter, *op. cit.*, p. 618.

41. Having in mind the real-balance effect of a falling level of prices and the influence of automatic price and interest variations, Professor Patinkin has justly remarked: "Even if we accept this secular interpretation of Say's Law—and the evidence in favor of it is convincing—we must again emphasize that classical economists failed to specify the market mechanism which would make this law valid" (*op. cit.*, p. 475; see also pp. 253–5).

42. On the role of money in classical theory vis-à-vis Say's Law, see A. W. Marget, *The Theory of Prices* (New York, 1942), 2, 25–51; Becker and Baumol, *op. cit.*, pp. 363–75. On the question of income disbursement and the appropriate clock period, see Marget, 606–21.

4. Physiocracy and the Theory of Gluts

Whatever the theoretical merits of Malthus' case, and they were few, his approach entailed a theory of society so out of keeping with the prevailing "climate of opinion" that it faced defeat at the very outset.[43] To the Ricardians the theory of gluts must have appeared identical to the ideas of the physiocrats which James Mill had attacked over a decade before in his *Commerce Defended.* "The Economists [the physiocrats] and their disciples," Mill had written, "express great apprehensions lest capital should increase too fast, lest the production of commodities should be too rapid. There is only, say they, a market for a given quantity of commodities, and if you increase the supply beyond that quantity you will be unable to dispose of the surplus."[44] Mill's essay was a reply to a tract by William Spence (1783–1860) who, like Malthus, believed that "the production of national wealth depends upon the expenditure of the class of land-proprietors . . . in countries constituted as this and those composing the rest of Europe are, the increase of *luxury* is absolutely essential to their necessities."[45] Similarly, Malthus' arguments seemed to hark back to Lauderdale's diatribes against parsimony and sumptuary legislation, which Mill had dismissed along with Spence's defense of prodigality.[46] Malthus' support of the corn laws also fitted the pattern; both Lauderdale and Spence favored a policy of agricultural protection.[47]

By 1820, the year that Malthus published his *Principles,* the theory of gluts was already firmly associated with an emphasis on consumption and the agrarian basis of wealth. And for a generation to come the status of agriculture in the economy was to be a subject of furious debate, reflecting the widening breach between urban and rural life produced by the Industrial Revolution. In the context of that controversy Malthus seemed to take the position of an apologist for the landed classes, voicing their apprehension at the rapid pace of indus-

43. See R. B. Simons, "Thomas Robert Malthus on British Society," *Journal of the History of Ideas,* January 1955.

44. J. Mill, *Commerce Defended,* p. 80.

45. Quoted by J. Mill, *ibid.,* p. 66. We are not concerned with the accuracy of Mill's interpretation of physiocracy; in point of fact, it was Spence who converted the theories of Quesnay into a doctrine of gluts and a vindication of luxury spending. See R. L. Meek, "Physiocracy and the Early Theories of Under-Consumption," *Economica,* May 1951; J. J. Spengler, "The Physiocrats and Say's Law of Markets. II," *Journal of Political Economy,* December 1954.

46. J. Mill, *op. cit.,* p. 96.

47. See Lauderdale's *Letter on the Corn Laws* (London, 1814), and Spence's *Objections against the Corn Bill Refuted* (London, 1815).

trialization. The doctrine of the physiocrats, transmuted and qualified, was widely felt to be the key to his general economic theory.[48]

No difficulty is encountered if we wish to find a basis for this impression in Malthus' writings. In several places he as much as declares his agricultural bias. In the *Essay on Population* three whole chapters are devoted to a discussion of the relative advantages of agriculture and manufacturing, leading to the conclusion that the "ideal state" is one in which "the commercial part of the population never essentially exceeds the agricultural part" (p. 382). Industry, however, had prospered under the circumstance of the war and threatened to surpass agriculture. That is why the corn laws were necessary to restore the balance: "The practical restrictions thrown in the way of importing foreign corn during the war . . . have been the means of giving a spur to our agriculture, that it has not only kept pace with a very rapid increase of commerce and manufactures, but has recovered the distance at which it had for many years been left behind, and now marched with them abreast" (p. 410). In theory he was a proponent of free trade (p. 415) but in practice he continued to advocate protection for corn on the grounds that it directed capital to agriculture.

Ricardo never saw fit to refute Malthus' theory of the "ideal" economic system. But in 1817, when Malthus announced a new edition of the *Essay on Population,* Ricardo wrote to James Mill: "He ought candidly to confess that he has committed great errors in his chapters on the Agricultural and Mercantile systems, as well as in that on bounties."[49] In his *Essay on Profits* Ricardo attacked Malthus directly for endorsing Adam Smith's lapses into physiocratic theory: "I cannot agree with Mr. Malthus in his approbation of the opinion of Adam Smith, 'that no equal quantity of productive labour employed in manufactures, can *ever* occasion so great a re-production as in agriculture.' I suppose that he must have overlooked the term ever in this passage, otherwise the opinion is more consistent with the doctrine of the Economists, than with those which he has maintained."[50] But Malthus had not misunderstood Smith's remark. Five years later, in the first edition of his *Principles* (1820), Malthus imagined a scale of productive labor graded according to the size of the net physical product created by each type of labor. In this hierarchy agricultural labor was to rank first, owing to "the natural pre-eminence of agriculture" (p. 39). Ricardo

48. See J. Bonar, *Malthus and His Work* (London, 1924), pp. 245–52.

49. *6,* 314; also *7,* 2.

50. Ricardo, *4,* 37. The same remark is cited in Ricardo's *Principles,* followed by the comment: "If Adam Smith speaks of value, he is correct; but if he speaks of riches, which is the important point, he is mistaken" (*1,* 429). Let it be remembered that for Ricardo "value" is a negative index of riches or productive efficiency.

objected to this scheme because it contradicted the concept of marginal rent [51] and no more is heard of it in the second edition of the *Principles.* But expressions of profound displeasure at the rapid spread of the factory system never entirely disappeared from Malthus' writings. In 1820 he had said: "Late events make us contemplate with no small alarm a great increase in the *proportion* of our manufacturing population, both with reference to the happiness and to the liberty of our country." [52] Sixteen years later he still refused to admit that England's comparative advantage in industry exceeded that of agriculture: "The fertility of the land, either natural or acquired, may be said to be the only source of a permanent high national returns for capital. If a country were exclusively manufacturing and commercial, and were to purchase all its corn at the market prices of Europe, it is absolutely impossible that the national returns for its capital should for any great length of time be high." [53]

In his hostility to industrialization, Malthus joined forces with the Lake poets and the followers of Robert Owen, and like them he drew on the support of popular belief which viewed manufacturing as a mere appendage to agriculture. An article in the *Quarterly Review* of 1827 provides an eloquent exposition of this viewpoint:

> Because a greater number of persons happen in this country to be employed in manufactures and commerce, than in the cultivation of the soil, a notion has been actively propagated, . . . that the manufacturing and commercial classes are more important and beneficial to the state than the classes engaged in agriculture. . . . Nothing can be more fallacious, more unphilosophical, more mischievous, than these opinions. The manufacturing and commercial interests, when estimated, not according to the number of hands, but according to the amount and productive character of the capital employed, are not entitled to that superiority over agriculture which is too frequently conceded them. It should be recollected that the manufacturer does not create wealth: he merely modifies that which has already been produced by the labours of the agriculturalist . . . It is, therefore, not a little surprising that

51. *2,* 18–19. Since profits in manufacturing are regulated by rentless returns in agriculture, the marginal productivity of labor is the same in both industries. The inframarginal productivity of labor on superior grades of soil is not, in Ricardo's system, due to the "bounty of nature." According to the "storage" version of the productive-labor doctrine, it is true, as Ricardo admitted, that "a given capital employed in agriculture, on any but the land last cultivated, puts in motion a greater quantity of labour than an equal capital employed in manufactures and trade"; but this simply implies that capital is more efficiently employed in manufacturing (*1,* 350).

52. *Principles* (1820), p. 223 n.

53. *Principles* (1836), p. 213.

> political economists, and even practical statesmen, should appear frequently to forget that the reward of manufacturing and commercial industry must depend upon the produce raised by the cultivation of the soil.[54]

To the followers of Ricardo there seemed little difference between such physiocratic ideas and Malthus' argument that production might outstrip consumption unless the traditional weight of agriculture in the economy were artificially preserved. The writings of Malthus' most famous disciple only confirmed that impression. In 1832 Thomas Chalmers (1780–1847), a leading Scottish divine, published a work *On Political Economy, in Connexion with the Moral Progress of Society,* which expounded the possibility of general overproduction along the lines laid down by Malthus. Earlier Chalmers had joined William Spence in deprecating commerce; now he attempted to dispel the illusion that "trade or manufacturing . . . bore any creative part in augmenting the public revenue." Since all taxes are ultimately borne by the landlord, argued Chalmers, the landed classes ought to give public notice of their importance by openly assuming the entire burden of national taxation. This, of course, is nothing but an erratic deduction from classic physiocratic doctrine.[55]

It should be apparent now why Malthus could never have become "the parent stem from which nineteenth-century economics proceeded."[56] The secular decline of British agriculture and the uninterrupted march of the Industrial Revolution made it impossible seriously to entertain the Malthusian doctrine of gluts. Though the controversy continued it was never again conducted on Malthus' intellectual terms.

5. The Outcome of the Debate

The debate between Malthus and Ricardo was carried on in the absence of any experience of cyclical booms and depressions. Evidence of depressed conditions were plentiful enough; the years 1818 and

54. *Quarterly Review,* October 1827, pp. 423–4. Throughout this period a small trickle of pamphlets kept the physiocratic tradition alive. For the years 1800–20, see R. L. Meek, "Physiocracy and Classicism in England," *Economic Journal,* March 1951. Mr. Meek cites William Reid, author of *Inquiry into the Causes of the Present Distress* (1833), as the only "out-and-out Physiocrat" in the Ricardian phase of classical economics. But see J. Pinsent, *Conversations on Political Economy* (London, 1821) and *Letter to David Ricardo* (London, 1822); A. Smythe, *Outlines of a New Theory of Political Economy* (London, 1822); P. Plough, *Letters on the Rudiments of the Science, called Catallactics* (London, 1842).

55. *Select Works of Dr. Chalmers,* ed. W. Hanna (Edinburgh, 1856), 9, 99 ff., 186–8, 338–9. For an analysis of Chalmers' theories, see Bergmann, *op. cit.,* pp. 157–63.

56. J. M. Keynes, *Essays in Biography* (New York, 1951), p. 120.

1819 in particular were notable for declining yields in the capital market and a reduction of traditional forms of investment in canals, turnpikes, and enclosures; the partial recovery of 1820–24 was accompanied in 1821 and 1822 by severe agricultural distress.[57] Nevertheless, such variations in business prospects had not yet acquired a clearly periodic and self-perpetuating character. The speculative frenzy of 1824–25, embracing both domestic and foreign securities on an unprecedented scale, marks "the first truly modern cyclical boom in British economic history."[58] Similarly, the crash which came in the winter of 1825 marks the first truly cyclical downturn of the capitalist economy. Though the familiar pattern of phases in industrial activity can be traced back to the closing decades of the eighteenth century, loan-financed government expenditures during the Napoleonic Wars cushioned such fluctuations and all but hid them from view.[59]

It is not surprising then that the periodic alternation of booms and slumps was not appreciated by economists until the third or fourth decade of the nineteenth century. Earlier it was possible to argue, as Ricardo did, that every crisis arose out of adventitious and nonrecurring circumstances. The depressions of 1811, 1816–17, and 1818–19 could be explained by pointing to obvious exogenous factors such as the Bank Restriction Act, the strains of waging war, the difficulties of postwar conversion, or the influence of the weather in producing poor or abundant harvests.

It took some time before old habits were shed. A treatise by George Poulett Scrope (1797–1876), published in 1833, contains an excellent but standard treatment of the reasons for "times of general embarrassment." These are "phenomena of which sad experience has of late too frequently attested the real existence, in spite of what theory may urge of their impossibility"; at the same time, Scrope emphasized, "such phenomena are anomalies . . . occasioned by the force of some artificial disturbing cause."[60]

A popular *History of the Middle and Working Classes*, published two years later, gave a clear definition of "the commercial cycle" as "ordinarily completed in five or seven years." There was no analysis of the factors that would necessarily impart cyclical fluctuations to the economic system, but the notion of periodicity is firmly grasped: "Spring is not a more sure harbinger of summer, than great commercial activity of depression, or stagnation of trade of its subsequent revival."[61]

57. See Gayer *et. al., op. cit., 1*, 149–51.

58. *Ibid.*, p. 171.

59. *Ibid., 2*, 568.

60. G. P. Scrope, *Principles of Political-Economy* (London, 1833), pp. 36, 214.

61. J. Wade, *History of the Middle and Working Classes* (3d ed. London, 1835), pp. 211, 254.

By the 1840's the concept of the business cycle was well established and frequently discussed in the pamphlet literature.[62] But the cyclical character of commercial depressions was still not clearly distinguished from Say's Law as a proposition about the adequacy of purchasing power in the long run. Some writers attributed the recurrence of crises to commercial restrictions, going so far as to suggest that free trade would render the economy crisis-proof.[63] Others really did insist on the fact of chronic overinvestment of capital which, they argued, aggravated the cyclical swings of the economy. In a powerful work on *England and America* (1834), Edward Gibbon Wakefield (1795–1862) depicted the contemporary English scene as a contrast between "gorgeous palaces and wretched hovels." "It does not follow," he declared, "that, because labour is employed by capital, capital always finds a field in which to employ labour. This is the non-sequitur always taken for granted by Bentham, Ricardo, Mill, McCulloch and others."[64] The glut is general, he contended, because no alteration in the distribution of capital between trades could by itself repair the situation. Hence colonization of Australia and New Zealand was recommended as an outlet for excess capital and surplus population.

Almost immediately, the colonization movement made one important convert among economists. In his provocative publication, *The Budget*, Robert Torrens made a case for public support of emigration schemes and repudiated his previous stand on the Law of Markets:

> There is a school of political economists, who assume, that capital possesses some occult quality, or influence, by which it creates for itself the field in which it is employed, and renders demand co-extensive with supply. Economists of this school contend, that though there may be a partial, there cannot be general overtrading . . . To those who regard political economy as an inductive science, the principles of which are nothing more than general facts established by experience, I confidently submit the following considerations, as showing . . . that, in any particular country exporting wrought goods in exchange for raw produce, there may exist a contemporaneous over-trading, throughout all the departments of manufacturing and commercial industry.[65]

62. For some representative samples, see Bergmann, *op. cit.*, pp. 189–98.

63. See, for instance, J. Wilson, *Fluctuations of Currency, Commerce, and Manufacturers* (London, 1842), p. 93; also a tract by W. R. Greg, *Not Over-Production, but Deficient Consumption, The Source of Our Suffering* (London, 1842).

64. Quoted by T. W. Hutchison, *A Review of Economic Doctrines, 1870–1929* (Oxford, 1953), p. 352 n. See H. O. Pappe, "Wakefield and Marx," *Economic History Review*, second series, *4*, No. 1 (1951), which goes some way toward rectifying the neglect of Wakefield as a serious economic thinker.

65. *The Budget* (London, 1844), p. 91.

Only a few authors drew a sharp distinction between business cycles and secular stagnation, but among these was John Stuart Mill. Yet another was Thomas Corbet, whose *Inquiry into the Wealth of Individuals* (1841) emphasized the fact that "periods of activity and relaxation, or prosperity and depression, must, although in a less degree, be at all times in operation or progress, so as to return periodically, independently of war or any other cause than the irregular exertion of human industry." After citing the crises of 1825 and 1836 as illustrations of his thesis, Corbet went on to expound the Law of Markets in the classic Say-Mill manner.[66]

John Stuart Mill's *Essay on Some Unsettled Questions in Political Economy*,[67] written in 1830 but published in 1844, provides perhaps the best exposition of Say's Law in the entire literature of English political economy. At the outset of his analysis Mill grants that the free operation of the market does not automatically assure full employment of capital; indeed, "perpetual non-employment of capital" is "the price we pay for the division of labour," and "except during short periods of transition, there is almost always a great briskness of business or great stagnation" (p. 68). This is followed by a discussion of Say's Identity and the reasons it fails to hold when money is used. In fact, the onset of a depression is characterized as a liquidity panic, leading to a fall in prices and the accumulation of unsalable inventories (pp. 69–72). However, and here Mill was not explicit, such a situation is supposed to prepare the way for a subsequent recovery. But the essential point is that these "well-known facts" have nothing in common with the contention that "a country may accumulate capital too fast; that produce in general may, by increasing faster than the demand for it, reduce all producers to distress" (p. 73). In general, the meaning of Say's Law is preserved when it is asserted that "there cannot be a permanent excess of production, or of accumulation; though it be at the same time admitted, that as there may be a temporary excess of any one article considered separately, so may there of commodities in general, not in consequence of overproduction, but of a want of commercial confidence" (p. 74).

Throughout this essay Mill confined himself to inventory cycles involving speculative trading in commodities. After the "railway mania"

66. T. Corbet, *An Inquiry into the Causes and Modes of the Wealth of Individuals* (London, 1841), pp. 105–11. By way of contrast see the discussion of business depressions combined with an attack on Say's Law in *Commercial Economy* (London, 1830), pp. 30–57, by E. S. Cailey (1802–62), later president of the Agricultural Protection Society; also *Outlines of Political Economy* (London, 1832), pp. 108–13. Neither Cailey nor the anonymous author of *Outlines* makes any reference to Malthus.

67. London, 1844; London Reprints No. 7, 1948.

of the 1840's, however, the role of investment cycles in the capital goods industries began to attract his attention. Consequently, the discussion of these issues in the *Principles* (1848) includes an analysis of fluctuations in fixed capital formation. Moreover, Mill gave the subject an entirely novel slant by linking the problem of the periodic cycle to the problem of economic growth. The prevailing rate of capital accumulation, he observes, has reduced the rate of profit within "a hand's breadth of the minimum," despite the influence of counteracting factors—foreign trade, capital exports, labor-saving devices, and new industries.[68] The waste of capital in a depression, however, tends to raise profits: "That such revulsions are almost periodical is a consequence of the very tendency of profits which we are considering." [69] Although Mill supplies no definite theory of the turning points [70] there is no doubt whatsoever that he regarded the cycle as endogenous in character. Nevertheless, he retained Say's Law and denounced Malthus, Chalmers, and Sismondi for advocating in effect a slower pace of capital formation. The "irrational" doctrine of gluts has drawn support from the recurrence of crises for "at such times there is really an excess of commodities above the money demand: in other words, there is an undersupply of money." But the fall of prices in such instances is cured eventually, not by a voluntary contraction of supply, but by a revival of investment incentives and a restoration of confidence. And as Mill observed correctly: "The permanent decline in the circumstances of producers, for want of markets, which those writers contemplate, is a conception to which the nature of a commercial crisis gives no support." [71]

The reader who at this stage has any interest left in the controversy on gluts should now turn to Marshall's *Principles*, where he will discover that nothing new was added between 1850 and 1890.[72]

68. J. S. Mill, *Principles*, p. 731.

69. *Ibid.*, p. 734.

70. The nearest approach to it is to be found in Mill's discussion of the "two states of the markets," *ibid.*, pp. 653–5. For Mill's theory of the trade cycle see A. H. Hansen, *Business Cycles and National Income* (New York, 1951), pp. 259–66; Rogin, *op. cit.*, pp. 301–9.

71. *Principles*, pp. 556–63. For a less sympathetic discussion of Mill's treatment of Say's Law, see Hutchison, *op. cit.*, pp. 348–54.

72. Pp. 710–11.

CHAPTER 6

Population and Wages

> How often have we read in Malthusian benefactors of the species: "The working peoples have their condition in their own hands: Let them diminish the supply of labourers, and of course, the demand and the remuneration will increase!" Yes, let *them* diminish the supply: but who are they? They are twenty-four millions of human individuals . . . each distinct within his own skin; *They* are not a kind of character that can take a resolution, and act on it, very readily . . . O wonderful Malthusian prophets! Millenniums are undoubtedly coming, must come one way or the other: but will it be, think you, by twenty millions of working people simultaneously striking work in that department; passing in universal trades-union, a resolution not to beget any more till the labour-market become satisfactory?
>
> THOMAS CARLYLE, *Chartism* (1839)

1. MALTHUS' PRINCIPLE OF POPULATION

THE RAPID GROWTH of population which marked the age of Malthus (roughly 1790–1835) was the result of a high birth rate combined with a declining death rate, a decline which must be credited, not to improvements in medical treatment (for these had little effect on the prevention and cure of disease until the twentieth century), but to improvements in economic and social conditions affecting housing, sanitation, and nutrition.[1]

The essential demographic facts are as follows: The birth rate had been rising throughout the eighteenth century; after 1790 it began to fall, first imperceptibly and then somewhat more markedly in the 1820's. On the other hand, the marriage rate showed no definite secular trend for the whole period; it declined slightly from 1800 to 1817, rose

1. The outstanding work on the question is G. T. Griffith's *Population Problems of the Age of Malthus*, Cambridge, 1926. Griffith's data and conclusions should be supplemented by T. H. Marshall's "The Population Problem During the Industrial Revolution," *Essays in Economic History*, ed. E. M. Carus-Wilson (London, 1954). For recent contributions to the debate, see H. J. Habakkuk, "English Population in the Eighteenth Century," *Economic History Review*, second series, 6, No. 2 (1953); T. McKeown and R. G. Brown, "Medical Evidence Related to English Population Changes in the Eighteenth Century," *Population Studies*, November 1955.

until 1824, and fell in the next two decades. Although the fall in the marriage rate after 1824 was counteracted by a rise in the fertility of marriage, due to a downward shift in the age distribution of the population and a lower average age of marriage, the birth rate continued to decline until 1850. The spectacular fall in the death rate, alluded to above, began around 1780 and reached a minimum point in 1811. Mortality rose again from 1811 to 1830, probably due to the deterioration of town conditions. The important factor in the fall of the death rate was the decline of infant mortality; there was in fact no increase in the average span of adult life. Although the over-all size of the population continued to expand throughout the period, the annual rate of increase reached a maximum in the years 1810–20. By 1831 the decennial census revealed a decline in the rate of population growth which was confirmed by the census of 1841 and 1851.[2]

These facts are of significance because they bear directly upon the population controversy of the 1830's and 1840's. Moreover, they serve to remind us that Malthus himself never clearly grasped the nature of the "population explosion" which he had set out to analyze. He seems to have been aware of the decline in the death rate but underestimated its significance; in addition, he virtually ignored any factors influencing the mortality rate other than shortage of food. His emphasis was always on the more questionable changes in the birth and marriage rates.[3]

The Malthusian theory of population contends that man's power to propagate exceeds his power to produce subsistence: this is a simple but complete statement of the doctrine. In general, population is said to be limited by preventive and positive checks, consisting of all the forces that reduce the birth rate and raise the death rate. An unchecked population would double in size every twenty five years (implying a rate of growth of 3 per cent per annum),[4] whereas the means of subsistence, it is held, cannot possibly increase at that rate over the same

2. The average annual percentage rates of growth of population by decades for the period under review are as follows: 1.3 for 1801–11; 1.7 for 1811–21; 1.5 for 1821–31; 1.2 for 1831–41; 1.2 for 1841–51. For the years 1793–1815 the figure is 1.4% but for 1815–47 the figure is only 1.1%, close to the 1% average for the whole period 1793–1912. See W. W. Rostow, *British Economy of the Nineteenth Century* (London, 1948), p. 8.

3. *Essay on Population*, pp. 222–30, 292–3, 466–70, 549–50.

4. Malthus' 3% per annum rate of increase was derived from spurious American data purporting to show a death rate of 20 per 1,000 and a birth date of 50 per 1,000. The actual birth and death rates in 18th-century Britain averaged something around 35 to 40 per 1,000, with the birth rate slightly larger than the death rate. In fact, no country in the 18th or 19th centuries ever attained a growth rate of 3% per annum in population. See W. A. Lewis, *The Theory of Economic Growth* (London, 1955), pp. 304–19.

period. Though Malthus could find no examples of an unchecked population, he concluded nonetheless that "the pressure arising from the difficulty of procuring subsistence, is . . . one which not only actually exists at present . . . but, with few exceptions, has been almost constantly acting upon all the countries of which we have any account." [5]

Much of the appeal of Malthus' theory lay in its striking simplicity when expressed in terms of the geometric and arithmetic ratios. Malthus cherished the ratios as essential to his doctrine but most of his followers dismissed them as irrelevant to the fact of a latent, if not actual, disparity between population and subsistence.[6] The arithmetic ratio, the weakest point in Malthus' armory, rested on the notion of a declining capacity to feed a growing population. But, strangely enough, Malthus never emphasized the law of diminishing returns in the *Essay on Populaton,* though he had been one of the first to develop the concept in his tracts on the corn laws.[7] The Ricardian economists, however, were quick to relate the arithmetic ratio explicitly to the assumption of diminishing returns in agriculture, thereby linking the Malthusian theory of population to Ricardo's theory of rent.

In the hands of James Mill, McCulloch, and others, the historical fact of decreasing returns to *extensive* cultivation, confirmed by the experiences of the Napoleonic Wars, is converted into a pseudodynamic law of diminishing returns: though technological progress postpones the effect, the specter of diminishing returns is held to be ever present and operative in the short run.[8] The statement that Britain is already overpopulated could be taken to mean that per capita output would be larger with a smaller population, or, rather, that further increases in population would reduce per capita output.[9] However, the Malthu-

5. T. R. Malthus, *Summary View of the Principle of Population* (London, 1830; reprinted in *Introduction to Malthus,* ed. D. V. Glass [London, 1953]), pp. 149–50.

6. The outstanding proponents of this interpretation in later years were John Stuart Mill and Alfred Marshall. But Ricardo too supported this view (see 8, 368). The statement of the Malthusian theory of population in Ricardo's *Principles* (*1,* 98–9) makes no mention of the ratios.

7. For statements involving the law of diminishing returns, see *Essay on Population,* pp. 5–6, 384–5. In one place Malthus states quite clearly why he is unwilling to resort to decreasing returns as the basis of the arithmetic ratio. If food were produced under conditions of increasing returns, he argued, population would only grow that much faster and the checks "necessary to keep the population on a level with the means of subsistence" would consequently operate with greater force, to the detriment of the working class (*Summary View of Population,* p. 151).

8. See Cannan, *Theories of Production and Distribution,* pp. 132–43.

9. This formulation suggests the concept of an optimum population. The optimum theory is suggested for the first time in Senior's *Political Economy* and is clearly stated by J. S. Mill in his *Principles.* See M. Gottlieb, "The Theory of Optimum Population for a Closed Economy," *Journal of Political Economy,* December 1945, p. 292 n.

sian thesis was often supported by a much simpler notion of overpopulation, namely, a population too large to be fed with domestic resources. Due to the rising cost of growing food on British soil, the subsistence fund or "capital" was supposed to lag behind the increase in numbers engendered by unrestrained childbearing. Proof of the principle of population now took the form of a syllogism: If capital had a tendency to increase faster than population, conditions would be prosperous; conditions are not prosperous; therefore population has a tendency to increase faster than capital.[10]

Malthus himself shied away from this type of argument. On the one hand, he insisted that the "pressure" of population on the means of subsistence was "constantly in operation"; on the other, he pointed out that his doctrine was not incompatible with gradual improvements in the standard of living.[11] Under certain circumstances and in some countries, he admitted, subsistence had actually increased faster than population.

As presented in the first edition of the *Essay on Population* (1798), the Malthusian theory was susceptible to empirical confirmation. But with the addition of a new preventive check—namely "moral restraint" —in the second edition of the *Essay* (1803), Malthus deprived his opponents of any means of empirical verification. By "moral restraint" he meant the practice of postponing marriage until the husband had adequate means to support a family, accompanied by strict premarital continence. This concession (and a concession it surely was)[12] provided the theory with a perfect escape clause making it almost impossible to grapple with it successfully. Whenever the growth of population was accompanied by a rise instead of a fall in the standard of living, the "contradiction" was resolved by crediting the result to the operation of the moral check.[13] In the same way, Malthus pointed to the principle of population as the perennial barrier to all efforts at social amelioration, while at the same time speaking of it as the motive force behind economic progress in the sense that it provided a stimulus to the poor.

Malthus' plea for moral restraint was as utopian in its own way as Godwin's claim that the progress of the human mind would bring about universal benevolence. Both required an entire change in human

10. J. Mill, *Elements*, pp. 43–4.

11. *Essay on Population*, pp. 3, 542–3; also *Summary View*, pp. 149–50; *Principles*, pp. 228–9.

12. See G. J. Stigler, "The Ricardian Theory of Value and Distribution," *Journal of Political Economy*, June 1952, p. 191.

13. On the tautological nature of Malthus' theory, see Rogin, *op. cit.*, pp. 165–70. A recent defender of the Malthusian doctrine seems fairly to revel in its truistic character: see G. F. McClearly, *The Malthusian Population Theory* (London, 1953), p. 157.

conduct but provided no means for bringing it about. When Malthus attacked the poor laws he cited the improvidence of the poor as evidence of the harmful effects of public relief, but when he counseled moral restraint he found support for his recommendation in the increasing frugality of the lower classes. Malthus' appeal to the working class to practice abstinence had, of course, nothing in common with the defense of birth control. He strongly disapproved of so-called neo-Malthusian checks "both on account of their immorality and their tendency to remove a necessary stimulus to industry. If it were possible for each married couple to limit by a wish the number of their children, there is certainly reason to fear that the indolence of the human race would be very greatly increased." [14] For the same reason he opposed public relief for the aged and infirm or the use of cash subsidies to encourage the deferment of marriage. In the end, he placed all his hopes, somewhat skeptically it is true, on the inculcation of prudent forethought as "the only effectual mode of improving the condition of the poor." [15]

2. Neo-Malthusianism

Despite Malthus' principled stand against birth control, his reliance on moral restraint, implying that the growth of population was within human control, paved the way for the advent of neo-Malthusian ideas. The argument that the birth rate could be limited by voluntary decision to postpone marriage was now subtly transformed by hinting at the existence of "physical checks" that might accomplish the same result without ascetic restraint. The first to commit himself in print was James Mill.[16] In an article on "Colony" for the 1818 edition of the *Encyclopaedia Britannica,* he spoke cautiously of "expedients" which could quickly dispose of the problem of overpopulation if only "the superstitions of the nursery were discarded." [17] In the *Elements of Political Economy* (p. 67) he referred again to some sort of preventive artifice to check the growth of population. But beyond such veiled remarks he did not venture.

Francis Place (1771–1854) had more courage: in his *Illustrations of*

14. *Essay on Population,* p. 572. For Malthus' attitude to birth control, see Griffith, *op. cit.,* ch. 4; N. E. Himes, App. A to his edition of Place's *Illustrations of the Principle of Population* (London, 1930).

15. *Essay on Population,* p. 455.

16. Privately, Bentham and Owen had already declared themselves in favor of birth control. See J. A. Field, *Essays on Population,* ed. H. F. Hohnmann (Chicago, 1931), ch. 1; N. E. Himes, "Jeremy Bentham and the Genesis of English Neo-Malthusianism," *Economic History,* August 1928.

17. Quoted by McCleary, *op. cit.,* p. 85.

the Principle of Population (1822) he explicitly recommended contraception as a means of limiting the number of births (p. 165). In the following year he was responsible for the circulation of broadsheets which contained direct instructions as to methods. In the meantime, he bombarded the working-class press, under a variety of signatures, with numerous communications advocating birth control.

The vehemence with which Place and James Mill expounded the Malthusian theory of population [18] was the direct result of their conviction that birth control provided an effective means for improving the conditions of the poor; for them Malthus' theory was an instrument of propaganda in the effort to overcome public prejudices. And in that effort they had the full support of John Stuart Mill, then seventeen years of age. In 1823 the young Mill contributed an anonymous article to *The Black Dwarf*, and unstamped London weekly; in it he spoke of "a remedy, which if adopted, would provide high wages," but which "the clergy will do all in their power to prevent." When the editor of the journal denied the validity of Malthus' principle of population, John Stuart replied with extracts from his father's article on "Colony." [19] At the same time, he took an active part in the campaign, distributing Place's handbills in the backyards of slum tenements. On one of these occasions he was arrested but, so far as is known, the indictment was quashed.[20] This act of youthful enthusiasm was not mentioned in his *Autobiography* (1873), but the description given there of the views held by the younger generation of utilitarians is suggestive of the buoyant mood of the neo-Malthusians.

> Malthus's population principle was quite as much a banner, and point of union among us, as any opinion specially belonging to Bentham. This great doctrine, originally brought forward as an argument against the indefinite improvability of human affairs, we took up with ardent zeal in the contrary sense, as indicating the sole means of realizing that improvability by securing full employment at high wages to the whole labouring population through a voluntary restriction of the increase of their numbers.[21]

18. "Wages are *already* at the lowest point, to which they can be reduced," Mill remarked; "That is, just sufficient to keep up the number of labourers and no more; the state of wages which seems to have been contemplated, by Mr. Ricardo, throughout his disquisitions on political economy, and which the tendency of population to increase faster than capital, undoubtedly leads us to regard as the natural state" (*Elements*, p. 258).

19. *The Black Dwarf*, Nov. 27, 1823, pp. 748–56; Feb. 25, 1824, pp. 238–44.

20. See N. E. Himes, "The Place of J. S. Mill and Robert Owen in the History of English Neo-Malthusianism," *Quarterly Journal of Economics*, August 1928; M. St. J. Packe, *The Life of John Stuart Mill* (London, 1954), pp. 56–9.

21. J. S. Mill, *Autobiography* (New York, 1924), p. 74.

Within the Ricardo circle McCulloch seems to have been the only one to share Malthus' sentiments on birth control. Place did his best to involve McCulloch in the movement by circulating a set of notes based on McCulloch's Ricardo Memorial Lectures which made great play of moral restraint as the alpha and omega of social reform. The *Trades' Newspaper and Mechanics Weekly Journal,* one of the first trade union papers in England, detected support of birth control in McCulloch's Lectures and made it the occasion for an attack on the neo-Malthusian movement. Birth control propaganda, it was argued, diverted the attention of workers from the pursuit of their real interests. The journal pledged itself to expose the campaign and called upon McCulloch to declare himself: "It is certain that other persons, who talk *very like* the Ricardo lectures on this subject, *do* mean a great deal more than merely to discourage improvident marriages." McCulloch disavowed such "revolting opinions" in a publicly printed letter, but the working-class press refused to accept his statement at face value; it was simply assumed that he lacked the courage to face the scandal that would follow upon approval of neo-Malthusianism.[22] To avoid future misunderstanding McCulloch inserted the following remarks in the second edition of his *Principles* (London, 1830):

> The schemes proposed for directly repressing population in the ancient and modern world, have not only been for the most part, atrocious and disgusting, but have really been opposed to the ultimate objects their projectors had in view. Could we subject the rate of increase to any easily applied physical control . . . the most effective stimulus to exertion [would be] destroyed . . . It is, therefore, to the principle of moral restraint, or to the exercise of the prudential virtues, that we should exclusively trust for the regulation of the principle of population [p. 228].

The movement in favor of birth control gained ground with the publication of Richard Carlile's outspoken *Every Woman's Book* (1826), but the subject continued to invoke moral indignation and religious censure.[23] Place was virtually ostracized by respectable society for his defense of contraception,[24] and the Mills, father and son,

22. See N. E. Himes, "McCulloch's Relation to the Neo-Malthusian Propaganda of His Time," *Journal of Political Economy,* February 1939.

23. Even Cobbett, the undisputed spokesman of the common people, attacked Carlile as a "disciple of Malthus" who sought "to recommend to wives and daughters of the labouring classes the means of putting Malthus' principles in practice . . . the horrible means of living and indulging without the *inconvenience,* as the monster calls it, of being mothers" (quoted by G. D. H. Cole, *The Life of William Cobbett* [London, 1924], p. 285).

24. See G. Wallas, *Life of Francis Place* (4th ed. New York, 1951), pp. 169–70.

suffered frequent abuse at the hands of journalists and pamphleteers. T. R. Thompson, himself an ardent Benthamite, appended a review of Mill's *Elements* to his *Catechism on the Corn Laws* (1826) in which he rebuked Mill for his hints at family limitation by means of "expedients." Thompson argued that neo-Malthusian propaganda would merely encourage earlier marriages; since contraceptive devices could never come into general use, the result would be an increased density of population.[25]

Another economist expressed the same sentiment in still more opprobrious language:

> It was darkly, but confidently and sedulously hinted at, . . . that means were in reserve, and ready to be circulated, of eluding the passions implanted by the Creator in the original constitution of the human race . . . Over the daring details with which this miserable philosophy was invested—its enduring robe of shame —and over the circumstances by which it was brought into actual contact with a part of the population, we must here draw a veil . . . their industrious dissemination by ready agents, worthy of the task, has begun the vile work of effecting self-degradation, and extinguishing all sentiment of moral dignity or worth, among a part of the lower orders.[26]

In view of such attacks the "ready agents" of the "miserable philosophy" never committed themselves explicitly. A special style of circumlocution, marked by laconic references, was invariably adopted to propagate birth control. The standard approach is nicely illustrated by John Wade's *History of the Middle and Working Classes* (1835). "The first condition of any preventive," Wade remarks, "is, that it should be practicable . . . For instance, to recommend infanticide, abortion, or any artifice to frustrate conception, might be positively mischievous, since, by the disgust it would excite, like an indecent attack on the established religion, it would prevent the temperate investigation of a subject of national importance" (p. 327). After this one would hardly imagine that the author entertained any neo-Malthusian ideas. But that would be to underestimate the subtlety of the question. Only ten pages later he asserts:

> The idea of making chastity the rule of a community has been abandoned by all men in despair . . . A virtuous celibacy, therefore, is hopeless, and *matrimony* or *vice* the only alternative. To meet this dilemma a class of philosophers has appeared, who have

25. *The Pamphleteer* 27 (1826), 359–61.
26. R. Jones, *Essay on the Distribution of Wealth* (London, 1831), pp. xiii–xiv.

> sought to divest marriage of its impoverishing consequences. I am venturing on delicate grounds I am aware, but I do not see how I can discharge my duty to our present subject without some notice of a matter that has excited considerable attention . . . The theory that has been put forth may, perhaps, be collected in the subjoined extracts from the writings of its most logical and philosophical expounder [pp. 336–7].

This is followed by a half-dozen quotations from the writings of James Mill. Without further comment the author takes leave of his subject.

Not until the famous Bradlaugh-Besant trial in 1877, and the subsequent formation of the Malthusian League, was contraception a topic that could be publicly discussed. As late as 1873 the dread of neo-Malthusian ideas was so strong that a public memorial for John Stuart Mill was rejected when the story of his youthful activities was recalled. Under the circumstances we will understand why John Stuart Mill never again mentioned birth control in print, althout it is known that he did not abandon his belief in the restraint of population by "the artificial check." [27]

As a close friend of James Mill and Francis Place, what was Ricardo's attitude toward neo-Malthusian checks? Ricardo had seen a manuscript copy of Place's book and liked it so well that he took it upon himself to take it to his own publisher. On some points he had reservations; consequently he sent Place a list of his criticisms (9, 49–57) which did not, apparently, include the advocacy of birth control. But to Malthus he wrote: "Place speaks of one of Owen's preventives to an excessive population—he does not dwell upon it, but I have a little doubt whether it is right even to mention it" (9, 62). Likewise, Ricardo's critical comments on Mill's *Elements* do not refer to the "expedients" which Mill had recommended.[28] We may infer that Ricardo believed in birth control or that, at any rate, he viewed the question with none of the moral reprobation so common in his time. The fact that in abandoning Judaism he adopted Unitarianism (*10*, 39–40), the most liberal of the nonconformist churches, gives credence to this interpretation. Of course, he may have had practical objections to Place's campaign. We shall never know. When Malthus remarked in his *Principles* that workers are "the arbiters of their own destiny; and what others can do for them is like the dust of the balance compared with what they can do for themselves," Ricardo added the comment: "This is excellent and cannot be too often and too clearly inculcated on the minds of the labouring classes" (2, 262). Obviously Ricardo's asser-

27. See N. E. Himes, "J. S. Mill's Attitude Towards Neo-Malthusianism," *Economic History*, January 1929.

28. Ricardo, 9, 126–33; also 9, 118.

tion is compatible with a belief in either the Malthusian or the neo-Malthusian remedy. Birth control was so explosive a topic that Ricardo may well have felt that open declaration of belief was premature.

3. The Eclipse of the Malthusian Doctrine in the 1830's

While the philosophical radicals put their faith in the spread of birth control techniques, others approached the problems of over-population by stressing the rise in living standards and the accompanying forces which made people desire to have smaller families. In either version the effect was to lighten the darker hints of the principle of population. By 1835 the Malthusian theory of population was, if not repudiated, so decisively shorn of its short-run implications that virtually nothing was left of it. With the decline of confidence in Malthus' population doctrine, the Ricardian system lost much of its logical rigor and became incapable of specifying the strength and direction of movement of the major economic variables with which it was concerned. It was, in fact, in the area of population controversy that the weaknesses of Ricardian economics first became decisively manifest.

The publication of a correspondence between Malthus and Nassau Senior, now professor of political economy at Oxford, marked the first break with Malthus' doctrine by a leading economist. Senior traced his disagreement with Malthus to a verbal ambiguity in the term "tendency." "The only difference between us," he asserted, "is one of nomenclature."

> You would still say, that, in the absence of disturbing causes, population has a *tendency* to increase faster than food, because the comparative increase of the former is a mere compliance with our natural wishes, the comparative increase of the latter is all effort and self-denial. I should still say, that, in the absence of disturbing causes, food has a tendency to increase faster than population, because, in fact, *it has generally done so,* and because I consider the desire of bettering our condition as natural a wish as the desire for marriage.[29]

Malthus, however, was not persuaded by Senior's conciliatory approach and insisted that "whether population were *actually* increasing faster than food, or food faster than population, it was true that, except in new colonies, favourably circumstanced, population was always pressing against food, and was always ready to start off at a faster rate than

29. N. W. Senior, *Two Lectures on Population.* The correspondence is reprinted in McCleary, *The Malthusian Population Theory,* pp. 114–15.

that at which the food was actually increasing." He cited the low standard of living in "old countries" as proof of his contention.[30]

In his second letter Senior turned to the issue that troubled him most, namely, "the effect which your mode, or my mode, of stating the law of population, is likely to produce on the reader's mind." Whatever Malthus may have intended, Senior pointed out, the principle of population was frequently represented as an insurmountable obstacle to the improvement of social conditions.

> Because additional numbers *may* bring poverty, it has been supposed that they necessarily *will* do so. Because increased means of subsistence *may* be followed and neutralised by a proportionate increase in the number of persons to be subsisted, it has been supposed that such *will* necessarily be the case. These were the doctrines which I found prevalent when I began my Lectures . . . You found the principle of population disregarded, or rather unknown . . . I found that principle made the stalking-horse of negligence and injustice, the favourite objection to every project for making the resources of the country more productive.[31]

Malthus neither affirmed nor disowned these inferences but replied that "we do not essentially differ as to facts when they are explained as you have explained them." But he persisted in recommending moral restraint rather than efforts to increase the food supply as the effective means of raising living standards.[32] There the discussion rested without a clear-cut decision on either side.[33]

Senior's critique, however, had turned the tide. A new skeptical attitude toward Malthus' theory made itself felt in the debates at the Political Economy Club. On April 15, 1831, the discussion turned once again to "the merits of Ricardo," and now some of the members were ready to question Ricardo's acceptance of Malthus' population theory. "One of the errors of Ricardo," Mallet reported, "seems to have been to have followed up Malthus' principles of population to unwarrantable conclusions."

30. *Ibid.*, pp. 115–16, 117; also p. 120.

31. *Ibid.*, pp. 126–7.

32. *Ibid.*, pp. 124–5.

33. See K. Smith, *The Malthusian Controversy* (London, 1951), pp. 180–9. Senior thought he had gained a victory. "If you will look at his correspondence with me," he wrote to Mallet, "you will find that he has nearly abandoned or rather disavowed the doctrine that population has a uniform tendency (in the sense of probability) to exceed subsistence" (*Political Economy Club*, p. 305). On the other hand, Malthus' friends felt that the correspondence had ended in mutual agreement (see Bishop Otter's "Memoirs of Robert Malthus" which was added as a preface to the second edition of Malthus' *Principles*, p. liii).

> For, in the first place it is clear that from the progress of social improvement . . . Capital, or the means of Employment—the fund for labour—increases in a greater ratio than population; that men generally reproduce more than they consume . . . he [Ricardo] looks forward from the gradual demand for food and the use of land, to the gradual lowering of wages [sic] and profits till nothing remains but rent to the Landlords. But long before that, modification would take place in the state of society which would make such conclusion all wrong.[34]

A few weeks prior to the publication of the Malthus-Senior correspondence Torrens had published a new edition of the *Essay on the External Corn Trade* in which he declared: "There is no tendency in population to increase faster than capital, and thus to degrade wages."[35] Afterwards he claimed credit for being the first to deny the Malthusian doctrine: The "correct and consolatory view of the question, was subsequently taken, I believe, in a correspondence which was published between Mr. Malthus and Mr. Senior . . . The doctrine, therefore, that population has a tendency to increase faster than capital may be considered as exploded."[36]

For a moment Malthus' *Essay* was overshadowed by Sadler's *Law of Population* (1830), which substituted a biological principle of declining fertility for the Malthusian check of moral restraint.[37] Macaulay gave the work notoriety by a derisive attack in the *Edinburgh Review;* the *Quarterly Review* featured an analysis of the controversy by Scrope which condemned Malthus and Sadler alike and criticized Senior for his concession to Malthus' arguments.[38] Richard Whately (1787–1863), Senior's successor to the Drummond Chair at Oxford, rose to Senior's defense with another semantic clarification.[39] Two years later Scrope published a *Principles of Political Economy* which had as one of its primary objects, he told his readers, the refutation of "that most per-

34. *Political Economy Club,* p. 225.

35. R. Torrens, *An Essay on the External Corn Trade* (5th ed. London, 1829), p. 473.

36. R. Torrens, *Letters on Commercial Policy* (London, 1833), pp. 43–4.

37. For an analysis of Sadler's *Law of Population,* see K. Smith, *op. cit.,* pp. 190–7.

38. *Quarterly Review,* April 1831, pp. 97–145. This and other anonymous articles by Scrope for the *Quarterly* are identified by R. Opie in "A Neglected British Economist: George Poulett Scrope," *Quarterly Journal of Economics,* November 1929. James Wilson, better known as "Christopher North," ridiculed Senior's manner of contradicting Malthus while, at the same time, minimizing the area of disagreement (*Blackwood's Edinburgh Magazine,* February 1831, pp. 395–400).

39. R. Whately, *Introductory Lectures on Political Economy* (2d ed. London and Dublin, 1832), pp. 249–50; quoted by Senior, *Political Economy,* p. 47.

nicious dogma which has so long been palmed upon the public as the fundamental axiom of political-economy: namely the 'tendency of population to exceed the procurable means of subsistence.'"[40]

Malthus' dedicated followers only brought the doctrine into further disrepute by carrying the argument to absurd lengths. Chalmers' *Political Economy* (1832), for example, expounded the Malthusian theory of population with a fervor that bordered on monomania. In Chalmers' hands political economy has no other *raison d'être* than to promote the view that progress is impossible without individual prudence and self-control. In the absence of "a virtuous and well educated commonalty," he declared, "starvation is the ultimate state of every industrious nation; a state from which it can only be saved, not by the multiplication of its products, but by a wholesome and moral restraint on the multiplication of its people." The gloom is barely relieved by what Chalmers called a "delightful conclusion," namely, that "the people collectively speaking, decide whether the remuneration for their work shall be a scanty or a sufficient one."[41] The book was reviewed by the major quarterlies with the respect appropriate for a professor of divinity at the University of Edinburgh, but neither Scrope in the *Quarterly Review* nor McCulloch in the *Edinburgh Review* managed to conceal their distaste for Chalmers' didactic admonitions.[42] McCulloch objected strenuously to Chalmers' principal conclusion that the growth of population and the necessary recourse to inferior soils had steadily reduced the English standard of living over the last fifty years.[43] Citing the annual increases in meat and grain consumption, the fall in the death rate, and the mounting funds of savings banks, whose depositors consisted largely of wage earners, McCulloch observed: "Though wages have declined since the peace, they have not declined to anything like the extent to which prices have declined; and . . . the condition of the labourers has been decidedly improved."[44] Ten years later Mc-

40. *Principles of Political Economy,* p. xvi. The theory of population is discussed in ch. 11, pp. 257–92.

41. *Selected Works of Dr. Chalmers,* 9, 103, 312–13.

42. *Quarterly Review,* October 1832, pp. 39–69; *Edinburgh Review,* October 1832, pp. 52–72. See also the sharply critical review in *Fraser's Magazine,* August 1832, pp. 113–18; September 1832, pp. 239–48.

43. Cannan claims that Chalmers was the first writer of eminence to question the historical validity of the law of diminishing returns (*Theories of Production and Distribution,* pp. 335–6). Chalmers did argue that the extension of cultivation to inferior soil was not itself proof of the decreasing productive power of agriculture; nevertheless, he spoke of "a limit to the augmentation of our physical resources" in virtue of which "there must, especially in old countries, be a felt pressure and discomfort throughout every community" (*Selected Works,* 9, 334–43).

44. *Edinburgh Review,* October 1832, p. 62. For the same view about the rise of real wages between 1815 and 1830, see *Political Economy Club,* pp. 234–5.

Culloch could declare without hesitation that "Mr. Malthus had overlooked and undervalued the influence of the principles which countervail the tendency to increase of population . . . The principle of increase is not the bugbear, the invincible obstacle to all improvements it appeared to be as described by him, and still more by Dr. Chalmers and his school. A vast improvement has everywhere taken place." [45]

After the passage of the Poor Law Reform Act in 1834 and the early efforts of Edwin Chadwick to improve sanitary conditions, the Malthusian bogey was all but vanquished and ceased to carry conviction. Senior's view of the doctrine now prevailed without opposition at the Political Economy Club. When "the value and truth of the Principles of the Essay on Population" came up for discussion in 1835, Mallet reports that "the whole artillery of the Club was, strange to say, directed against it." "Far from population having a tendency to increase faster than subsistence, Senior and Tooke held that there were facts enough to prove that the reverse was the case, and as to McCulloch, who is always bitter against Malthus, the workings of an envious and mean disposition, he held that there was in human nature a principle of improvement and exertion that was at all times sufficient to counteract and overcome the principle of population, and therefore that Malthus' theory was altogether erroneous." [46]

Clearly enough, the Malthusian check of moral restraint had dropped out of the discussion. Malthus himself had demonstrated that a reduction in the birth rate could not affect wages in less than sixteen to eighteen years. Obviously, it was pointed out, no wage earner will ever be actuated by such remote consequences.[47] Already in 1817 Barton had observed that "it is not by any nice comparison of the recompense of labour with the expense of living that the poor are discouraged from undertaking the charge of maintaining a family: uneducated man is guided very little by abstract reasoning, very much by custom." [48] Now McCulloch, at the Political Economy Club, derided "the notion of inculcating provident feelings among the poor—said that a poor man has no inducement to be provident." [49] Furthermore,

45. *The Literature of Political Economy*, p. 260. See also McCulloch's *Principles* (2d ed., 1830), p. 227; also (4th ed. 1849) p. 238.

46. *Political Economy Club,* pp. 265–6. The "new" view of population even crept into the seventh edition of Mrs. Marcel's *Conversations* (1839), p. 136.

47. Read, *Political Economy*, pp. 162–6. As for saving the cost of bearing children, it was probably thought to be too slight to afford an incentive for family limitation.

48. *Observations on the Condition of the Labouring Classes of Society*, p. 27.

49. *Political Economy Club,* p. 252. See also *Edinburgh Review,* May 1828, pp. 316–17. The doctrine of moral restraint had long been a favorite butt of the Owenites: see, for example, J. M. Morgan, *The Revolt of the Bees* (London, 1826), pp. 94–7.

it was argued, the level of wages might conceivably be raised by concerted efforts but not by individuals acting in isolation. "Universal distress fails to suggest . . . any motive for individual restraint," declared Whately's successor at Oxford.[50] Hortatory appeals to the working class, it came to be realized, had little effect on the supply of labor, and more could be accomplished by direct improvements in the standard of living; habit and custom would convert the new amenities into conventional necessities and a taste for these additional comforts would provide the wage earner with an effective motive for family limitation.[51]

In rejecting Malthus' solution to overpopulation economists also rejected Malthus' one-sided emphasis on the natality factor as the cause of the population spurt after 1780. Again it was John Barton who seems to have been the first to deny that the rising number of births was responsible for the increase in population.[52] McCulloch in 1825 laid great stress on the sharp decrease in the death rate which he credited to "the greater prevalence of cleanliness and sobriety of the poor, and the improvements that have been made in their diet, dress, and houses, partly to the drainage of bogs and marches, and partly, and since 1800 chiefly, perhaps, to the discoveries in medical science, and the extirpation of the small-pox." He even noted the fact that the death rate was lower in factory towns than in agricultural areas.[53]

Three years after the death of Malthus, McCulloch produced his *Statistical Account of the British Empire* (1837), which provided a wealth of data to support the thesis that the increase in population after 1800 was largely due to a marked reduction in the death rate; McCulloch also drew attention to the decennial census of 1831, revealing a decline in the rate of population growth.[54]

By the mid-1830's most economists realized that the growth of population was largely due to influences working on the side of the death rate. Moreover, the inverse relationship between living standards and births was singled out as the crucial element in Britain's new demographic balance. In his *On Wages and Combinations* (1834) Torrens

50. W. F. Lloyd, *Two Lectures on the Checks to Population* (Oxford, 1833), p. 22. Lloyd was familiar with neo-Malthusian ideas: Place had written to him expounding the need for birth control (see Himes' edition of Place's *Illustrations*, pp. 332–6).

51. See, for example, Senior, *Political Economy*, p. 42.

52. *An Inquiry into the Progressive Depreciation of Agricultural Labour* (London, 1820), pp. 40–3.

53. *Principles*, pp. 158–9. See also Place's *Illustrations*, pp. 251–8.

54. *A Statistical Account of the British Empire* (London, 1837), *1*, 417–20. See also G. R. Porter, *The Progress of the Nation* (London, 1836), *1*, 25. It is often assumed, incorrectly as we have seen, that all the classical economists were ignorant of the relevant demographic forces. See Packe, *op. cit.*, p. 56 n; H. A. Boner, *Hungry Generations* (New York, 1955), p. 122.

tried to give precision to the notion that the size of the family tended to decline with the increase in per capita wealth. His argument illustrates the prevailing departure from classic Malthusian doctrine. In countries where an abundance of fertile soil remains to be cultivated, he reasoned, a large family is an economic asset; but in densely populated areas, such as England, the unmarried worker finds himself at a financial advantage compared to the married worker. Therefore, he concluded: "As a country approaches the limits of her agricultural resources [and food prices mount], marriages become less frequent; and the *power* 'to increase and multiply' . . . is checked and controlled by the prevailing efficacy of these causes to such an extent, that the tendency in every civilized community is . . . for capital to increase faster than population."[55]

After 1835 no economist expounded the Malthusian theory without taking note of the empirical evidence that contradicted it. When Herman Merivale, newly appointed professor of political economy at Oxford, defended the Malthusian thesis in 1837, he was almost unconsciously driven into apologetic language:

> The doctrine of population is, in Political Economy, what that of original sin is in theology—offensive to philosophical pride, and irksome to sanguine temperaments; and hence the endless attempts which are made to contradict or to evade it. It is humiliating to feel that society must rely on the slow and painful process of moral restraint as the only corrective of a necessary evil . . . We prefer to be told . . . that machinery and science, and facilities of communication, are outstripping the rapid march of numbers, and rendering our sage apprehensions wholly imaginary. *The extraordinary advance of England in these respects, in the course of the last few years, has no doubt had an effect in lessening the practical belief in economical doctrines.*[56]

4. John Stuart Mill on Population

In John Stuart Mill's *Principles* (1848) the Malthusian theory of population becomes, once again, the analytical cornerstone of the Ricardian theory of distribution. In restoring Malthus' arguments Mill affected something of a counterrevolution. Why he did so is best left for later consideration.[57] What is to be stressed, however, is that on

55. R. Torrens, *On Wages and Combinations* (London, 1834), pp. 30–1. Torrens' argument would be unimpeachable if he had spoken of a decline in births rather than marriages.

56. *Edinburgh Review*, October 1837, pp. 94–5 (my italics).

57. See below, Ch. 9.

all the essential points he did not differ from the conclusions arrived at in the population controversy of the 1830's.

In the chapter on wages Mill attacked "several writers" who, in belaboring the different meanings of the term "tendency," asserted that in fact population had slackened its rate of increase relative to subsistence.[58] Mill had in mind not only Senior and Whately but also the new Drummond professor of political economy at Oxford and the Whately professor at Trinity College, Dublin, both of whom had recently given support to this interpretation of the Malthusian theory.[59] Waiving "the verbal question," Mill retorted, population still presses "too closely upon the means of subsistence" and any tendency for that pressure to diminish has been "extremely faint." It was his opinion that the optimum density of population had long been attained in almost all Western European countries, and certainly in Great Britain. "Is it true, or not," Mill queried in the *Principles*, "that if their number were fewer they would obtain higher wages? This is the question, and no other" (p. 358). Consequently he condemned any scheme to improve the material conditions of labor which failed, at the same time, to encourage further capital accumulation.

But nowhere did Mill invoke the plea of self-restraint in the manner of Malthus. Despite his obeisance to the orthodox position on population, Mill denied anything like a Malthusian obstacle to the relief of poverty.[60] As a cure for low wages he suggested a national system of compulsory education, accompanied by measures for immediate relief, such as foreign and home colonization by means of government grants-in-aid to distressed localities (pp. 352–3, 380–4). Moreover, he joined the demand for full equality of women with the hope of voluntary family limitation (pp. 378–9); his belief in the efficacy of birth control showed through in a diffident comment on the possibility of "continence" in marriage: "That it is possible to delay marriage, and to live in abstinence while unmarried, most people are willing to allow; but when persons are once married, the idea, in this country, never seems to enter anyone's mind that having or not having a family, or the number of which it shall consist, is amenable to their own control" (p. 375).

Having defended the Malthusian theory of population as analyti-

58. J. S. Mill, *Principles*, p. 359.

59. See T. Twiss, *Certain Tests of a Thriving Population* (London, 1845), pp. 27–8; *View of the Progress of Political Economy* (London, 1847), p. 222; J. A. Lawson, *Five Lectures on Political Economy* (London, 1844), pp. 53–77.

60. There is a hint of it in the earlier sections of the book where Mill remarks gloomily: "It is but rarely that improvements in the conditions of the labouring classes do anything more than give a temporary margin, speedily filled up by an increase of their numbers" (p. 161).

cally "correct," Mill was forced to admit that the census reports did not uphold the theory: "Subsistence and employment in England has never increased more rapidly than in the last forty years but every census since 1821 showed a smaller proportional increase of population than that of the period preceding." [61] In short, population had not "pressed" upon the means of subsistence throughout the period 1800 to 1850:

> So gigantic has been the progress of the cotton manufacture since the inventions of Watt and Arkwright, that the capital engaged in it has probably quadrupled in the time which population requires for doubling. While, therefore, it has attracted from other employments nearly all the hands which geographical circumstances and the habits or inclinations of the people rendered available; and while the demand it created for infant labour has enlisted the immediate pecuniary interest of the operatives in favour of promoting, instead of restraining, the increase of population; [62] nevertheless, wages in the great seats of the manufacture are generally so high, that the collective earnings of a family amount, on an average of years, to a very satisfactory sum; and there is as yet, no sign of permanent decrease, while the effect has also been felt in raising the general standard of agricultural wages in the counties adjoining [*Principles*, p. 350].

When Mill came to deal with "the probable futurity of the labouring classes" in the closing section of the *Principles* he went so far as to support the Senior-Whately viewpoint: "It appears to me impossible but that the increase of intelligence, of education, and of the love of independence among the working classes, must be attended with the corresponding growth of the good sense which manifests itself in provident habits of conduct, and the population, therefore, will bear a gradually diminishing ratio to capital and employment" (p. 759).

To convince ourselves that the Malthusian theory by this time meant anything one cared to make of it, we need only look briefly at a book which Mill commended to his readers: *Over-population and Its Remedy* by William Thornton (1813–80), Mill's colleague at the East India Company and the writer subsequently responsible for Mill's retraction of the wages fund theory. As we have seen, Malthus himself and some of his followers defined the condition of overpopulation as an

61. *Principles* (5th ed. 1862), p. 161. The same statement, but for the phrase "in the last forty years," appears in the first edition.

62. Oddly enough, neither Mill nor anyone else pointed out that the Factory Acts of 1833, 1844, and 1847, by prohibiting or restricting the employment of children, had provided an important incentive to the limitation of numbers.

inadequacy of domestic food supplies. John Stuart Mill regarded it as an analytical statement about declining per capita returns in the instance of an upward shift of population, everything else being held constant. But in this sense even Senior admitted in *Political Economy* that "there are few portions of Europe the inhabitants of which would not be richer if their numbers were fewer, and would not be richer hereafter if they were now to retard the rate at which their population is increasing" (p. 42). But Thornton advanced yet another definition of overpopulation, denoting the existence of Marxian unemployment and submarginal wages: "a deficiency of employment for those who live by labour, or a redundancy of the labouring class above the number of persons that the fund applied to the remuneration of labour can maintain in comfort." [63] Since the volume of unemployment had grown with the rapid spread of the factory system the cause resides in an excess multiplication of numbers. This is "the essence of Malthusianism" in all its "naked simplicity," Thorton declared.[64] But instead of recommending emigration as the solution,[65] Thornton's remedy boils down to a practical rule: "People ought not to marry until they are able to maintain the children they are likely to have"; a reduction in the marriage rate becomes the be-all and end-all of social reform, every other measure being but a step in that direction.[66] But in contradiction to all this, Thornton granted the utter futility of demanding prudential restraint from marriage on the part of the poor and even entertained the notion that an upward drift of per capita income tends of itself to reduce the birth rate.[67]

5. The Wages Fund Doctrine

It was one thing to reject the Malthusian theory of population but quite another to deny its corollary, a perfectly elastic supply of labor in the long run. If the rate of population growth was not a unique function of earnings, no level of wages could be said to represent an equilibrium level. For analytical purposes, this seemed to imply that the wage share of national income was indeterminate. An alternative approach was to assume the existence of a permanent reservoir of unemployed labor which, by providing incessant competition for employment, exerted a downward pressure on wages. Marx chose this explana-

63. *Over-population and Its Remedy* (London, 1846), p. 3.

64. *Ibid.*, p. 268.

65. Thornton's concept of overpopulation followed the view taken by the proponents of government-aided emigration. See R. T. Wilmot-Horton, *Causes and Remedies of Pauperism, Fourth Series* (London, 1830), pp. 18–19.

66. Thornton, *op. cit.*, pp. 270, 385.

67. *Ibid.*, pp. 121, 387 ff.

tion when he rejected Malthus' law of population. But with the classical economists, as Thornton's case bears out, the recognition of chronic underemployment only strengthened a belief in the Malthusian doctrine. Within the framework of the prevailing indentification of "population" with "labor force" it was impossible to postulate a horizontal long-run supply curve of labor without recourse, implicitly or explicitly, to Malthus' principle of population.

In retaining Malthus' theory, it was not necessary to follow James Mill in the extreme view that "wages are already at the lowest point, to which they can be reduced"; all that was required was the notion that the propensity of men to multiply had a constant tendency to maintain the standard of living at the customary level. Thus, in analyzing the secular tendencies of the distributive shares, one could treat wages as given by what laborers "have to have," while admitting that the actual level of wages at any moment in time is almost always above the biological and even the cultural minimum. This had been Ricardo's method and we find it again in John Stuart Mill's *Principles*.[68]

The opponents of Malthus' theory, however, were either left with no wage theory at all or else were forced to reintroduce the wages-population mechanism in the course of their analysis. Senior, for instance, never related his discussion of population to the question of wages.[69] Samuel Read, another adversary of Malthus, devoted a chapter of his treatise to "the causes which regulate the natural rate of wages," only to conclude that the natural rate is governed by "the number of individuals who compete for employment"—which is hardly a theory of wages.[70] Similarly, Scrope's chapter in his *Principles* says nothing about the determination of aggregate or per unit wages and is taken up with a discussion of personal talent and its effect on relative wage differentials.[71]

In view of the possibility of lags in the response of the birth rate, the population theory of wages, of course, could not be anything but a statement of secular tendencies. Consequently, it was often irrelevant to the kind of practical questions which arose with respect to factory legislation, trade unions, and the like. For these purposes wages were explained in terms of demand and supply, or, simply, the ratio of capital to population. Adam Smith had stressed the intimate connection between "the demand for those who live by wages" and "the funds

68. See J. S. Mill's perfectly circular definition of the subsistence level: "Wages are habitually at the lowest rate to which in that country the labourer will suffer them to be depressed rather than put a restraint upon multiplication" (*Principles*, p. 689).

69. See Bowley, *op. cit.*, pp. 173–6.

70. Read, *Political Economy*, p. 325.

71. Scrope, *Principles*, pp. 85–95.

which are destined for the payment of wages." Malthus had employed similar language in the *Essay on Population,* although he had at least pointed out that "the funds for the maintenance of labour do not *necessarily* increase with the increase of wealth and very rarely increase in *proportion* to it." [72]

By the 1820's it was elementary doctrine that the rate of wages depends on the relative magnitude of the laboring population and the capital fund. "Roundabout" production requires a stock of finished goods to meet the current needs of producers; specifically, a certain quantity of wage goods, crudely labeled "capital," must be advanced to workers for their maintenance during the cycle of production. Such goods are supposed to consist for the most part of agricultural produce which becomes available, not continuously, but at regular intervals determined by the annual harvest. Hence at the outset of every year, the amount of capital or wages fund, in the sense of an inventory of consumer goods, is predetermined by technical conditions which set an upper limit to the size of the wage bill. Though the fund is not necessarily a rigidly determinate amount at any moment of time, an increase of aggregate wages must, it was held, wait upon a prior expansion of production; in the absence of an increase in the rate of capital accumulation, no human agency can increase wages as a whole.

The wages fund doctrine is certainly present in Ricardo's *Principles.* At times Ricardo used the term "circulating capital" to stand for that part of capital which constitutes demand for labor,[73] but often he spoke carelessly of the "capital that is to support labour." Scattered remarks here and there and, particularly, the discussion in the chapter "Taxes on Raw Produce" do intimate a rigid predetermined wages fund, consisting of the harvest of past seasons. But on the whole Ricardo did not emphasize the idea.[74] Nevertheless, in measuring both wages and capital in terms of corn (the invariable measure of value) Ricardo adumbrated a proposition that was to become fully articulated in the hands of Mill and McCulloch.

No longer was the fund taken to mean a stock of material commodities; even the distinction between circulating capital and total capital was lost sight of. Already in the first edition of her *Conversations* Mrs. Marcet had said: "The rate of wages varies directly as the quantity of capital, and inversely as the number of labourers" (p. 130). "The

72. *Essay on Population,* p. 416. See also Malthus, *Principles,* pp. 234–6.

73. Ricardo drew a formal distinction between fixed and circulating capital in terms of technical durability but, in practice, his concept of circulating capital is identical to Marx' variable capital, consisting of wages only. See Ricardo, *1,* 30–8; *4,* 312. See also Cannan, *Theories of Production and Distribution,* pp. 73–4.

74. For a detailed discussion of Ricardo's wages fund theory, see F. W. Taussig, *Wages and Capital* (London, 1896; London Reprints No. 13, 1932), ch. 9.

rate of wages," James Mill now declared, "depends on the proportion between Population, and Employment, in other words, Capital."[75] Presumably wages are determined by dividing the number of laborers into the total sum of money set aside for wage payments. This indeed is the vulgar meaning of the wages fund theory: to raise wages, raise the dividend or lessen the divisor, produce more or procreate less.

Upon reading the *Elements* Ricardo pointed out to James Mill that "it is not strictly correct" to say that "the demand for labour and the power of employing it will be in proportion to the increase of capital . . . The power of employing labour depends on the increase of a particular part of capital, not on the increase of the whole capital (See my Chapter on Machinery)" (*9*, 127). The chapter on machinery had introduced the principle of factor substitution as governed by the relative prices of capital and labor. On this ground alone, the demand for labor might vary independently of changes in the amount of capital.[76] Furthermore, Ricardo's chapter on value should have reminded Mill and McCulloch that an increase in the rate of capital formation, even with fixed coefficients of production, may affect the demand for labor very differently depending on how the new investments are distributed among industries. This suggests, once again, that Ricardo's disciples failed to develop the logical implications of the system which they had inherited.

With the gradual abandonment of the Malthusian theory of population, the wages fund theory came to supplant the subsistence theory, or rather "in the matter of wages a huge 'short run' practically replaced the long run."[77] In general, the rate of wages was said to be dependent upon the volume of past production, the current rate of propagation of the working class, and the capitalist's propensity to save and invest out of present income. The better writers assumed no rigidity in the amount of wage goods available in the short run for payment as wages: depletion of the stock of finished goods and curtailment of consumption by nonwage earners might allow for temporary variations in aggregate labor income. The whole doctrine, however, was so loosely strung together that its practical import depended more often on the particular

75. *Elements*, p. 41; also McCulloch, *Principles*, pp. 327–8. For commentaries on Mill's and McCulloch's versions of the wages fund doctrine, see Taussig, *op. cit.*, ch. 10; Cannan, *op. cit.*, pp. 204–8; A. Salz, *Beiträge zur Geschichte und Kritik der Lohnfondstheorie* (Berlin, 1905), pp. 53–61.

76. In fact, as Wicksell showed, the weakness of the wages fund theory was that it made wages depend on the division of a given amount of capital into fixed and circulating portions, whereas Ricardo had demonstrated that this division in turn depends on the wage rate (see Stigler, *Production and Distribution Theories*, pp. 284–5).

77. Schumpeter, *op. cit.*, p. 665.

predispositions of a writer than on any systematic analytical implications. Most of the time it was never clear whether "capital" was supposed to include revenue expended on unproductive labor, or whether an increase in "wealth" always involved a larger wages fund. Was the whole of the fund necessarily exhausted in any period? Was the fund as inelastic for the individual employer as for the economy as a whole? The writings of the period do not yield an unequivocal answer to these questions.[78]

For example, the wages fund doctrine is often supposed to have been designed to sustain an attack on unionism. Yet McCulloch, one of its leading exponents, was instrumental in securing a repeal of the combination laws which prohibited the formation of unions.[79] And in this effort he had the full approval of Ricardo (*8*, 316). In part, McCulloch's desire to see the combination laws repealed was the result of a belief that unions were a passing phenomenon, likely to disappear once their activity was legalized.[80] But, more importantly, McCulloch thought that trade union action to raise wages above the "natural" level must automatically "cure itself"; moreover, in the absence of unions, the monopsomy power of the employer frequently results in wages below the competitive level. Therefore McCulloch welcomed labor unions as a countervailing force:

> Not only is a combination unaccompanied by violence, a fair exercise of the right of judging for themselves on the part of the workmen, but when it is entered into for the purpose of raising wages that have been unduly depressed, its object is proper and desirable. No master ever willingly consents to raise wages; and the claim either of one or of a few individuals for an advance of wages is likely to be disregarded, so long as their fellows continue to work at the old rates . . . hence it is obvious, that without the existence of either an *open and avowed,* or of a *tacit and real combination,* workmen would *never* be able to obtain a rise of wages *by their own exertions,* but would be left entirely dependent on the competition of their masters. . . . every attempt to prevent combination in such cases as this, is neither more nor less than an attempt to hinder workmen from making use of *the only*

78. For this reason there seems to be little point in arguing over the validity of the theory. Formally, there is nothing wrong with the idea of a predetermined wages fund; the only question is, what are the limits of its variations, at any moment of time? See Schumpeter, *op. cit.,* pp. 662–71, and a sharply contrasted assessment by K. Boulding and P. A. Samuelson: *The Impact of the Union,* ed. D. McCord Wright (New York, 1951), pp. 148, 316–17.

79. See Wallas, *op. cit.,* pp. 206–7; S. and B. Webb, *The History of Trade Unionism, 1666–1920* (London, 1920), pp. 93–112.

80. See Wallas, *op. cit.,* p. 217.

> *means* by which their wages can be speedily and effectually raised to their *just level.*[81]

The Essay on Wages containing these words was endorsed by Francis Place and recommended by him to working-class readers; it was also quoted with approval in at least two sets of trade union rules.[82]

Contrary to the prevailing impression, the wages fund doctrine was far more popular with those who minimized the economic importance of unions than with those who attacked labor organizations. Nassau Senior, whose attitude to trade unions was hostile in the extreme, never really based himself on economic considerations, much less on the wages fund theory.[83] Likewise, the spate of antilabor tracts which appeared in the year 1834, in response to the movement to form a General Union of Trades, rarely cite the laws of political economy against unions. Only occasionally do they invoke the immutable laws of demand and supply; generally the arguments rely on the conspiratorial character of unions.[84] By contrast, the wages fund doctrine is prominently displayed in Torrens' *Wages and Combinations* (1834); yet the worst that Torrens finds to say about unions is that they normally fail to achieve their object. He grants that unions can affect "a permanent increase in wages." But so long as the corn laws remain in force efforts to raise wages will be neutralized by the flight of capital.[85]

The concept of the wages fund was criticized almost as soon as James Mill and McCulloch had given definite expression to it. By and large, however, the critics addressed themselves to the form, rather than the substance, of the theory. Edward West was the first writer to assail the doctrine: "The opinion that the demand for labour is regulated solely by the amount of capital . . . has led perhaps to more false conclusions in the science than any other cause." After this bold assertion West's criticism seems a little tame: the demand for labor is not governed by the stock of wage goods inherited from the past

81. J. R. McCulloch, *An Essay on the Circumstances Which Determine the Rate of Wages* (Edinburgh, 1826), pp. 186–8. See also *Edinburgh Review,* January 1824, pp. 319–20.

82. See Wallas, *op. cit.,* pp. 161–2; W. H. Hutt, *The Theory of Collective Bargaining* (Glencoe, Ill., 1954), p. 28.

83. See Bowley, *op. cit.,* pp. 277–81; Levy, *op. cit.,* pp. 155–60.

84. See, in particular, E. C. Tufnell's *Character, Objects, and Effects of Trades' Unions* (London, 1834; reprinted, Manchester, 1933), which the Webbs described as "perhaps the best statement of the case against Trade Unionism." See also the favorable review of Tufnell's book by an unknown author in the *Edinburgh Review,* July 1834, pp. 341–59. Some of the pamphlets on trade unions published in the early 1830's are reviewed by R. K. Webb, *The British Working Class Reader* (London, 1955), ch. 8.

85. Torrens, *On Wages and Combinations,* pp. 57, 73, 81, 99.

but by the total level of investment and consumer expenditures in the economy; in addition, the supply of labor may vary independently of the size of population. It follows that "the demand for and money-wages of labour may be increased without any increase of the capital of the country." [86] In the same year, T. P. Thompson questioned James Mill's formulation of the theory: "It is never stated why the proportion between population and capital is different at one time and place from what it is at another, or what it is that induces such conditions of things as makes the shares different." [87]

Richard Jones (1790–1855), in a lecture delivered in 1833 at King's College, London, reiterated most of the points made by West: a change in the rate of growth of population is not identical with a change in the supply of labor, the demand for labor is affected by the prevailing pattern of consumption expenditures, hence wages are not regulated exclusively by any "fund for the maintenance of labour." [88] In one form or another, the same criticism is touched upon by Senior who, nevertheless, retained the wages fund theory in its orthodox form.[89]

One critic went a little further. In a work entitled *Great Britain for the Last Forty Years* (1834), Thomas Hopkins pointed out that in the wages fund doctrine "demand" (a quantity of capital available at any time to purchase labor) and "supply" (the present size of the labor force) are interdependent. In this sense, the theory fails to define a true equilibrium wage rate.[90] In embryonic form, this criticism foreshadows the decisive attack on the wages fund doctrine by Longe and Thornton in the 1860's.

It is hardly necessary to say that J. S. Mill's *Principles* gave expression once more to the concept of the wages fund as one of the undisputed verities of political economy. Mill's famous exposition avoided some of the looser expressions associated with earlier formulations of the doctrine. Like his predecessors, however, he presented the wages fund theory as an ordinary case of the workings of the law of demand and supply. And although he was fully cognizant of the distinction between intended and realized demand, his statements of the doctrine still come down to a comparison of a given quantity of money capital with a given quantity of labor in the market. Since the share of national income going to labor is fixed unalterably in any production period,

86. West, *Price of Corn and Wages of Labour,* pp. 80–6.

87. Thompson, *The True Theory of Rent,* p. 16. See also G. Higgins, "Observations on Mr. McCulloch's Doctrines Respecting the Corn Laws and the Rate of Wages," *The Pamphleteer,* 27 (1826), 250–3.

88. R. Jones, *An Introductory Lecture on Political Economy* (London, 1833), pp. 45, 50, 56.

89. Senior, *Political Economy,* pp. 153 ff.

90. *Great Britain for the Last Forty Years* (London, 1834), pp. 56–8.

trade union action is held to be essentially incapable of raising the level of wages. Nevertheless, "it is a great error to condemn, *per se* and absolutely, either trade unions or the collective action of strikes." Adopting McCulloch's argument, Mill concluded that trade unions, "far from a hindrance to a free market for labour, are the necessary instrumentality of that free market." [91]

6. An Alternative Theory of Wages

The critics of Malthus, we have seen, failed utterly to supply an alternative theory of wages. On the other hand, the wages fund doctrine, for what it is worth, was throughout this period every man's theory of wages, notwithstanding the objections of West and Jones. In fact, no aspect of classical economics was as little developed as wage theory. The only new contribution came from Trinity College, Dublin, in the shape of a series of *Lectures on Political Economy* (1834) by Mountifort Longfield (1802–84). Although Longfield was well known in Irish economic circles, this book attracted absolutely no attention in Great Britain, either from the press or from other writers on political economy.[92] Nevertheless, his treatment of wage theory affords a revealing contrast to the orthodox stream of discussion.

First of all, Longfield repudiated the "value of labour theory" of wages because "the expression . . . 'cost of production,' is merely metaphorical when applied to such a case"; in addition, the subsistence theory, referring as it does to a limiting state of equilibrium, is practically immune to factual attack.[93] Something like a wages-population mechanism no doubt tends to adjust wages in the long run, but "all I am contending for is, that the wages of the labourer depend upon the value of his labour, not upon his wants, whether natural or acquired, and that if his wants and necessities exercise, as they do, some influence upon the wages of his labour, it is indirect and secondary, produced by their effect upon the growth of population, and that this effect is not analogous to the effect which cost of production has upon the price of commodities." Present labor is not paid out of capital or out of past production but from the proceeds of current sales. Wages, therefore,

91. J. S. Mill, *Principles*, pp. 936–7. See Taussig, *op. cit.*, ch. 11.

92. Yet T. P. Thompson reviewed another of Longfield's books (*Three Lectures on Commerce, and One on Absenteeism*) for the *Westminster Review*, October 1835, pp. 411–15.

93. M. Longfield, *Lectures on Political Economy* (Dublin, 1834; London Reprint No. 8, 1931), pp. 202–6. Longfield did not criticize the Malthusian theory of population but merely asserted: "I do not apprehend that in the natural course of things, the increase of population, with all its attendants and consequences, will be prejudicial to the labourer" (pp. 238–9).

are governed by the supply of labor and the demand for labor "caused by the utility or the value of the work which they are capable of performing." [94] Ricardo treated profits as the leavings of wages; Longfield reversed the order of determination—with him wages become the residual variable. "The share of the article which each labourer will receive, is found by computing how much of the entire value consists of labour, and how much of profit, and by dividing the former share among the labourers, in proportion to the quantity and value of each man's labour." [95]

Longfield's argument is a cross between a productivity theory of wages and a produce-less-deductions theory. Longfield's infelicitous summary of his own theory reads: "The wages of labour depend upon the rate of profit and the productiveness of labour employed in the fabrication of those commodities in which the wages of labour are paid." This suggests the standard Ricardian theory. But actually Longfield's argument points in a different direction. By shifting the focus of attention from the determination of real wages, as governed by the cost of the laborer's upkeep and the quantity of wage goods accumulated in the past, to the present level of profits and the current productivity of labor, Longfield had succeeded in shedding all the trappings of the wages fund doctrine as well as the population theory of wages.

In the entire British literature of the day only one writer made any reference to Longfield's *Lectures*. In a *Treatise on the Industry of Nations* (1839), John Eisdell paid homage to Longfield's theory of distribution and made it his own.

> I have attempted to establish the positions that the employment of labour does not depend, as is generally supposed, upon capital . . . but that such employment and demand proceed from the skill of the workman to perform those kinds of work which the demands of the consumers call for . . . That though wages in each separate class are determined almost wholly by demand and supply, and the competition of labour in that class, the rewards of labour as a whole, and the condition of the working classes, are yet fixed chiefly by the productiveness of labour.[96]

94. *Ibid.*, p. 210.

95. *Ibid.*, pp. 211–12.

96. *Treatise on the Industry of Nations* (London, 1839), *1*, vi; also p. 136. Professor Viner has cited Eisdell's *Treatise* as being indebted to Longfield's arguments on international trade (Viner, *Studies in the Theory of International Trade*, p. 494 n.).

CHAPTER 7

Political Economy to Be Read as Literature

> The science, which from its object ought to be pre-eminently the people's science, has yet made but little way to popular power and favour. That this is so has arisen in part from a prevalent ignorance of its aim and promises. The consequence has been a vague scepticism concerning the extent of its actual attainments. . . . Discoverers are seldom the best teachers. The moment, however, comes at last, when the revealers of hidden mysteries meet with disciples who prove more successful missionaries than themselves . . . Miss Martineau's predecessors broke the ice only here and there. The letters of introduction which she has devised on behalf of her favourite science, have already won their way beyond what any body could have ventured to anticipate. We have heard more political economy during the last three months, than we believe was ever before heard out of the Political Economy Club. It has flowed smoothly, too, from off the tongues of people so very unlikely to trouble themselves with such investigations.
>
> W. EMPSON, *Edinburgh Review,* APRIL 1833

IN THE DECADES that followed the passage of the Reform Bill political economy became more popular than it had ever been before. A steady flood of didactic pamphlets and leaflets in the 1830's attests to the rising enthusiasm for economic science. Perhaps the best example of this kind of literature is the *Illustrations of Political Economy* by Harriet Martineau (1802–76). As an attractive medium for imbibing the lessons of economic science the *Illustrations* was without equal in its day—its success was astounding. The first of the thirty-four tales which comprise the work appeared in 1832 and within a few weeks sold thousands of copies; by 1834 the monthly sale of the series had reached ten thousand.[1] Almost the entire periodical press, daily, weekly, and monthly, received it with glowing praise. Readers as diverse as Victoria and Coleridge waited anxiously for each new num-

1. H. Martineau, *Autobiography,* ed. M. W. Chapman (Boston, 1877), *1,* 135, 201. The above figure may be compared to the sale of the most successful economic treatise in the first half of the century: J. S. Mill's *Principles,* which sold 3,000 copies in four years. Even at the height of its reputation, the *Edinburgh Review* had a circulation of 13,000. Many of Dickens' novels had a sale of 2,000 or 3,000 copies, and yet were judged remarkably successful.

ber. Sir Robert Peel sent a private letter of congratulation and Richard Cobden publicly endorsed the work. Members of Parliament and cabinet ministers showered the author with bluebooks and suggestions for new tales to pave the way for legislation. Nor was the tumult confined to Britain. Dutch, German, and Spanish translations appeared immediately; Louis Philippe ordered his ministers to introduce a French translation into the national schools, and the Emperor of Russia followed suit.[2]

Even the economists were won over, although at first they had been skeptical. For instance, shortly before the publication of the first number James Mill advised Miss Martineau's publisher that economic principles could never be successfully conveyed in fiction. Subsequently he admitted that his doubts had been unfounded.[3] McCulloch too had ridiculed "the idea of such illustrations" but was now assured by Macvey Napier that "they are of extraordinary merit."[4] Even John Stuart Mill gave the tales a favorite review, although he quarreled with the presentation of economic doctrine on some points.[5]

The economic ideas embodied in the stories were put forward as the settled and undisputed conclusions of an established science. Since Harriet Martineau disavowed any pretense at originality she saw no need to cite her authorities. "When the woodman finds it necessary to explain that the forest is not of his planting," she remarked in a preface to one of her stories, "I may begin to particularize my obligations to Smith and Malthus, and others of their high order."[6] In her *Autobiography* (*1*, 149–50) she gave an extensive list of her sources but without mentioning a single economic treatise. She did acknowledge her debt to Mrs. Marcet's *Conversations* as the first book she had read on economics.[7] Possibly the inspiration for the *Illustrations* came from "Mrs. B.'s" chance remark that such tales as Maria Edgeworth's "Cherry Orchard" might serve as a means of instructing children in political economy.

Be that as it may, her autobiography contains a description of her method of work which is in itself revealing of an uncritical approach to economic opinion. First she would furnish herself with "all the

2. *Ibid.*, pp. 177–9, 197–200.

3. *Ibid.*, pp. 129, 329.

4. Napier, *Selected Correspondence,* p. 136.

5. *The Examiner,* Oct. 27, 1833, pp. 676–8; *Monthly Repository,* May 1834, pp. 318–22.

6. *Illustrations of Political Economy* (London, 1834), *9*, vii.

7. *Autobiography*, *1*, 105. But when asked about the popularity of political economy prior to her *Illustrations* she claimed that "it was never heard of outside of the Political Economy Club, except among students of Adam Smith" (*ibid.*, *2*, 507).

standard works on the subject of what I then took to be a science."[8] Then would follow a skeleton plan of the course and a reading of that particular subject in each of the books available, while "restraining myself from glancing even in thought toward the scene and nature of my story till it should be suggested by my collective didactic materials." "It was about a morning's work to gather hints by this reading." A summary of the principles illustrated was then drawn up to be placed at the end of each number. "An hour or two sufficed for the outline of my story." Occasionally she would send to the library for travel books to supply local color; "the collecting, and noting down hints from these finished the second day's work." On the third day the material was reduced to chapters and a table of contents was constructed, noting the action of the characters, the features of the scene, and the economic principles to be exemplified. "This was not always completed at one sitting, and it made me sometimes sick with fatigue: but it was usually done in one day." After that "the story went off like a letter."[9]

An examination of the tales shows clearly that she relied very heavily on Malthus' *Essay on Population* and James Mill's *Elements;* Smith's *Wealth of Nations* and McCulloch's *Principles* were among her sources; there is no evidence that she ever read Ricardo. She seems to have been oblivious of any distinction between schools of economic thought and on the whole her opinions are an indiscriminate mixture of the best and the worst of classical doctrine. But she was a journalist, not an economist: that she oversimplified is only to be expected. What is of interest for our purpose is that on certain critical questions she took a distinctly Ricardian stand à la James Mill and, in that sense, she must be classed as a disseminator of Ricardian economics.

The flavor of Harriet Martineau's tales can hardly be captured by quotations, and what follows does not pretend to be an exhaustive discussion of the tales.[10] But her treatment of a half-dozen fundamental topics is sufficient to bring out her relationship to the school of Ricardo.

8. The phrase "what I then took to be a science" is not unintentional; by the time she came to write her autobiography, she had long since revolted against her earlier ideas. "After an interval of above twenty years," she remarked. "I have not courage to look at a single number—convinced that I should be disgusted by bad taste and metaphysics in almost every page" (*ibid., 1,* 194–5).

9. *Ibid.,* pp. 147–8.

10. But see N. E. Rivenberg, *Harriet Martineau. An Example of Victorian Conflict* (Philadelphia, 1932); E. Escher, *Harriet Martineau's sozialpolitische Novellen* (Zürich, 1935). Unfortunately, both studies are unsatisfactory: for one thing they assume that Harriet Martineau was a perfect representative of classical economics.

1. The Malthusian Theory of Population

At a time when most economists were beginning to doubt the relevance of "Malthus' devil," Harriet Martineau made the pressure of population upon the means of subsistence the fountainhead of economic reasoning; it is the ultimate and most pervasive theme of the *Illustrations.* In the story "For Each and All" she employed the Malthusian theory of population, as Malthus had, to attack the theories of Robert Owen.

> "When, then, comes all this misery? all this tremendous inequality?"
>
> "The misery arises from a deficiency of food. . . ."
>
> "Well: whence this deficiency of food?"
>
> "From the tendency of eaters to increase faster than the supply of food."
>
> "But if we can raise more food by co-operation than without it. . . ."
>
> "Even supposing we could,—unless co-operation also checked the increase of numbers, it could prove no more than a temporary alleviation of our grievances. In my opinion, it would, if it included equality of conditions, leave us in a worse state than it found us, in as far as it would relax the springs of enterprise and industry, and, in time, bring the community down into a deplorable state of sameness; it would, if persevered in, make us into a nation of half-naked potato eaters, and water-drinkers." [11]

The doctrine itself is expounded in a tale of life on a remote Hebridean island which concludes with the heroine's brother choosing friendship rather than marriage with the woman he loves lest their union result in more mouths to feed. The heroine explains his viewpoint to the puzzled object of his chaste affections:

> We have not the power of increasing food as fast as our numbers may increase; but we have the power of limiting our numbers to agree with the supply of food. This is the gentle check which is put into our hands; and if we will not use it, we must not repine if harsher checks follow. If the passionate man will not restrain his anger, he must expect punishment at the hands of him whom he has injured; and if he imprudently indulges his love, he must not complain when poverty, disease, and death lay waste his family.[12]

11. *Illustrations, 4,* 38.
12. *Ibid., 2,* 97.

This preposterous solution to the evils of overpopulation is more drastic than anything Malthus ever entertained. Ambiguous allusions elsewhere in the story to "the mild preventive check" and to "prudence in marriage" must have left the reader wondering just what was being proposed as a remedy.

Under the circumstances it is hardly surprising that she was misunderstood and accused of advocating birth control. The *Quarterly Review* lashed out at her bald defense of the theory of population in an article ostensibly written by the editors themselves.[13] "Has the young lady . . . been entering into high and lofty communion on such subjects with certain gentlemen of her sect, famous for dropping their gratuitous advice on these matters into areas, for the benefit of the London Kitchenmaids?" [14]

The emphasis in the tales on overpopulation as the root cause of all social ills seems to have outraged not a few readers, for in a later number the author added a prefatory note asking her audience to "give me time to show that I do not ascribe all our national distresses to over-population, but think as ill as they do of certain monopolies and modes of taxation." [15] But even in "The Morals of Many Fables," which brought the series to a close, she insisted on the basic principle that "owing to the inequality of soils (the ultimate capital of society), the natural tendency of capital is to yield a perpetually diminishing return;—and that the consumers of capital increase at a perpetually accelerated rate." [16]

2. Poor Laws

Like Malthus, Harriet Martineau attributed most of the rapid growth of population to the unstinted relief of indigence and destitution under the old poor law system.[17] Hence in "Cousin Marshall" she condemned

13. George Poulett Scrope acknowledged authorship of "the political economy of the article" but disavowed the "ribaldry" which had been inserted by Messrs. Lockhart and Croker (Martineau, *Autobiography, 1,* 156–7).

14. *Quarterly Review,* April 1833, p. 151. As it happens, Francis Place had sent her a copy of Robert Dale Owen's *Moral Physiology* which made a case for birth control. But this book reached her after the second number had appeared. See Himes' edition of Place's *Illustrations,* pp. 324–9.

15. *Illustrations, 5,* preface to "Berkeley the Banker."

16. *Ibid., 9,* 133. Years later, in 1855, she still thought the Malthusian doctrine indisputable, although "in my opinion, recent experience shows that it does attack a difficulty at the wrong end. The repeal of the corn-laws, with the consequent improvement in agriculture, and the prodigious increase of emigration have extinguished all present apprehension and talk of 'surplus population' " (*Autobiography, 1,* 159).

17. See below, Ch. 10, sec. 2.

all forms of private and public assistance to the poor as "bounties on improvidence." Only casualty hospitals and asylums for the blind were safe from her indictment: "With this exception, all arbitrary distribution of the necessaries of life, is injurious to society, whether in the form of private almsgiving, public charitable institutions, or a legal pauper-system." [18] Once set in motion, she argued, the practice of giving outdoor relief had a constant tendency to increase the burden thrown upon the poor rates. "We are rolling faster and faster towards the gulf, and two of our three estates, Lords and Commons, have declared that we shall soon be in it;—that in a few more years the profits of all kinds of property will be absorbed by the increasing rates, and capital will therefore cease to be invested; land will be let out of cultivation, manufactures will be discontinued, commerce will cease, and the nation become a vast congregation of paupers." [19]

Her solution is exactly that suggested by Malthus in the *Essay on Population,* namely, an enactment prohibiting parish relief to children born two years after the passage of the laws; within two generations this measure would abolish the poor laws entirely.[20] Unfortunately "Cousin Marshall" was published in 1833; the year before a Royal Commission had been appointed to devise a Poor Law Amendment Bill. It now appeared that complete abolition of the poor laws was inexpedient and that the principle of public relief, or rather indoor relief, was to be recognized as a permanent feature of national policy. As John Stuart Mill observed in one of his reviews, wholesale repudiation of the poor laws was no longer seriously contemplated: "Political economists having abandoned this among other exaggerated conclusions to which naturally enough they had pushed the principle of population when they first became acquainted with it." [21]

Members of the government were quick to recognize the propaganda value of Harriet Martineau's stories and secured her services for a new series of tales, based upon the recent findings of the poor law commissioners.[22] Miss Martineau's *Poor Laws and Paupers Illustrated,* containing a plan of reform identical to the *Report of the Poor Law Inquiry Commission,* was in the bookstores before Parliament met to debate the Poor Law Amendment Act of 1834.[23] Though less successful than the *Illustrations of Political Economy,* it played a part in mobilizing public opinion in favor of that controversial measure.

18. *Illustrations, 3,* 130; also pp. 36–43.
19. *Ibid.,* p. 49; also p. 112.
20. *Ibid.,* p. 119.
21. *The Monthly Repository,* May 1834, p. 321.
22. Martineau, *Autobiography, 1,* 165–8.
23. The second tale of *Poor Laws and Paupers Illustrated* contains the suggestions of the "workhouse test" and the "less-eligibility principle," both of which were embodied in the Poor Law Amendment Act (see below, Ch. 10, sec. 2).

3. Free Trade

On the question of population Harriet Martineau took her cue from Malthus but on rent and on gluts she followed the Ricardians.[24] In "Sowers not Reapers" she made a strong plea for free trade grounded upon Britain's comparative advantage in manufacturing.[25] Free trade was a sensitive political issue, as evidenced by the fact that she thought it necessary to preface the tale with a disavowal of any party allegiance: "I take my stand upon *Science*." But she was not afraid to be quite precise about the effects of the corn laws: "We pay as a nation 12,500,000 more for corn than we should pay if our ports were open to the world. Of this, not more than one-fifth goes into the pocket of the landowners, the rest being for the most part buried in poor soils." Also, she asserted confidently in the *Illustrations*, the price of wheat would fall at least six to nine shillings a bushel once the ports were thrown open to foreign corn (*7*, 88, 130–1). Many of her arguments foreshadow some of Cobden's later speeches. Like the leading spokesman of the Anti-Corn Law League she felt convinced that "very little can be done to improve the condition of the people till the Corn Laws are repealed. All practicable retrenchments, all ordinary reductions of taxation, all reforms in the organization of Church and State, improved as they are, are trifles compared with this. The only measure of equal consequence is the reduction of the Debt; and this ought to accompany or immediately precede the establishment of a free trade in corn" (*9*, 118).

4. The Ricardian Theory of Distribution

The essential ingredients of Ricardo's system are all present in the *Illustrations* but they are nowhere brought together in any systematic way. In "French Wines and Politics" an attempt is made to explain that labor "regulates" value, that since profits are a reward for labor as much as wages, value is governed by the sum of present and hoarded labor embodied in commodities (*4*, 38–9). But, of course, this concept is not carried over into any of the other stories. Perhaps the nearest approach to a statement of Ricardo's system comes in the tale called "For Each and All."

> "Of course, if land produces less and less, there must be a smaller produce to be divided between the capitalist and his labourer; and

24. *Illustrations, 2,* 76, 144; *8,* 40–1.

25. Of all her stories she thought that "Sowers not Reapers" was "the most successful for the incorporation of the doctrine with the narrative" (*Autobiography, 1,* 184).

> on the whole, they must share the decline pretty equally; since the farmer would not farm unless he could make some profit, and the labourers would not labour but for subsistence. But I am afraid this decline pulls down the profits of manufactures too; for farmers would turn manufacturers if they could earn higher profits thereby; and then there would be a new demand for corn; the price would rise; farmers would return to farming, and would take in new land, the diminished produce of which would lower profits again."
>
> "Yes, madam: this is the way that *agricultural profits determine all profits;* and that all are perpetually sinking. You see *labour become dearer when corn is;* that is, the labourer must have a certain quantity of corn in return for his labour, be its price what it may; and *these higher wages lessen profits again, without any advantage to the labourer* [*4,* 80–1; my italics].

Nevertheless, such thoughts were never permitted to override the principle of a natural identity of interests which was, in fact, her patent medicine for every difficulty. For that reason, although following Mill's *Elements* to the letter, she would not acquiesce to the proposal that the state should tax the unearned increment of land values (*9,* 46–7).

5. The Wages Fund and Trade Unions

The concept of a real wages fund, expressed in money merely for convenience, is invoked in most of the stories dealing with labor unions (*1,* 21, 51–2). It is at the back of what is perhaps the most interesting tale in the series, entitled "A Manchester Strike." The strike action which is described is aimed at equalizing wage rates among three local firms, a demand which can be justified by the wages fund doctrine. Both employers and employees agree that wages depend on the proportion of capital to labor (*3,* 58–60). But the employers plead innocence in the face of the irresistible forces of competition.[26] The union leaders defend their position by appealing to the inherent monopsony of the labor market (*3,* 46–51). And this view is presented with so much eloquence and passion that one would take it to be the author's own were it not for the fact that, elsewhere, she positively denies that the capitalist has any bargaining advantage.[27] Yet another viewpoint is put forward as coming from trade union leaders in London: Unions can succeed in "cases of special grievance from multiplication of apprentices, or from unfair methods of measuring work, or from gross in-

26. *Illustrations, 3,* 34; also pp. 126–33.

27. *Ibid., 9,* 51–2. See also H. Martineau, *The Tendency of Strikes and Sticks to Produce Low Wages and of Unions Between Masters and Men to Insure Good Wages* (Durham, 1834).

equality of wages, & c.; but for a general and permanent rise of wages, no strike could ultimately prevail, where there was a permanent proportion of unemployed labour in the market. A proportion of three per cent of unemployed labour must destroy their chance against the masters." [28]

After the strike is settled on a compromise basis one of the capitalists informs the men that only a part of the work force can be re-employed because the strike had wasted "the fund out of which your wages are paid." Pointing out that strikes are useless because they diminish the capital without reducing the numbers that seek work, he concludes with a word of "sound advice":

> All that you can do now, is to live as you best may upon such wages as the master can give, keeping up your sense of respectability and your ambition to improve your state when better times shall come. You must watch every opportunity of making some little provision against the fluctuations of our trade, contributing your money rather for your mutual relief in hard times, than for the support of strikes. You must place your children out to different occupations, choosing those which are least likely to be overstocked; and above all, you must discourage in them the imprudent, early marriages to which are mainly owing the distresses which afflict yourselves and those which will for some time, I fear, oppress your children. You ask me what you must do. These things are all that I can suggest.[29]

This humorless piece of advice is of a class with another which Harriet Martineau puts into the mouth of a foundry owner:

> Mr. Wallace told her that it was his constant endeavor to impress upon his people that it is the duty of well-paid labourers to become capitalists if they can as a security against a reverse of fortune. The difficulty he always found was to persuade them that the earnings which are only enough to maintain them for a few days, may, by being properly disposed of, be made sufficient for the maintenance of years. He wished his labourers to furnish themselves and their families in the first place with food, clothing, and habitation, and then put out at interest, or invest in some other profitable way, their surplus wages, that they might have something with which to begin a new employment, in case of their present work being taken from them.[30]

28. *Illustrations, 3,* 120–1.
29. *Ibid.,* pp. 102–3.
30. *Ibid.,* pp. 63–4. The idea was borrowed from Charles Knight's *The Results of Machinery* (London, 1831), p. 197.

6. Functions of Government

Whatever else Harriet Martineau may have preached in the *Illustrations,* the vulgar advocacy of *laissez faire,* pure and simple, is often supposed to be its hallmark. "Harriet Martineau reduces the *laissez-faire* system to absurdity," wrote John Stuart Mill to Thomas Carlyle, "by merely carrying it out in all its consequences." [31] Actually, there is no ground whatsoever for this opinion and it seems less than fair to condemn her for what is after all a perfectly standard treatment of the proper scope of government. Of course, we meet with such typical statements as the following from the *Illustrations:* "Government should protect the natural liberty of industry by removing all obstacles,—all bounties and prohibitions,—all devices by which one set of people tries to obtain unfair advantages over another set. If this were fairly done, industry would find its natural reward and idleness its natural punishment" (*1,* 92–3). But like all her contemporaries, she allowed important exceptions. In other words, she adopted the position of Adam Smith: the duties of government included protection against violence and invasion, the administration of education and justice, and the erection and maintenance of roads and canals which could never be undertaken by private persons (*7,* 134–5). Moreover, she saw no valid objections to the state provision of "useful and innocent amusements for the people," such as parks, museums, theaters, and libraries (*8,* 97, 100). And although she had rather extreme views, even for that time, about the undesirability of legislation to limit the hours of work of children, she kept such views out of the *Illustrations.*[32]

The *Illustrations* impart an overwhelming air of finality to economic doctrines. No doubt this impression is simply the result of the effort to popularize. Still, on some points Harriet Martineau went well beyond her scientific mentors. Moreover, at a time when political economy itself was in a state of flux, the *Illustrations* tended to support ideas which had already been partly discredited. Her emphasis on the Malthusian pressures and on harmony doctrine, for example, was no longer representative of the body of professional economic opinion. The *Illustrations* promulgated ideas which might have been considered authoritative fifteen or twenty years earlier but were no longer so; as such, the tales helped to create that vulgar and already outmoded image of "the dismal science" which passed for economic thought among

31. *Letters of John Stuart Mill,* ed. H. S. R. Elliot (London, 1910), *1,* 46.
32. For her views on factory acts in 1833 see *Autobiography, 2,* 87–8. For her later views see Rivenberg, *op. cit.,* p. 40.

the general public up to the 1870's. It is true that most contemporaries who read the tales were struck by their literary quality (it is extraordinary how much they were admired as fiction) rather than by their doctrinal content; but it is precisely for that reason that the economic ideas which they conveyed entered so deeply into the minds of the readers. New ideas are not likely to be welcome when everyone is already furnished with easy answers to difficult questions. Thus, by depriving Ricardo's critics of a receptive audience, the *Illustrations* played a significant role in holding back the reaction to Ricardian economics.

CHAPTER 8

Voices in the Wilderness

> The student who should take up the works of Mr. Jones, Mr. Malthus, and Mr. Senior, for the first time, would be led to apprehend that each of these distinguished economists had a separate system or school of his own; that each was opposed to the others, and all to Ricardo; and that the pseudo science of Political Economy was a chaos of unsettled and discordant elements. But . . . doctrines put forth in refutation of the principles of Ricardo are not unfrequently mere extensions of these principles.
>
> R. TORRENS, *The Budget. Introduction* (1844)

1. The Ricardian Socialists

THE NAMES OF Ravenstone, Gray, Hodgskin, Thompson, and Bray have gone down in social history under the label, perhaps the misnomer, of the "Ricardian socialists," denoting that small band of economic radicals who between 1820 and 1840 put forth the claim of labor to the whole product of industry. In their writings, this argument was justified as a simple logical deduction from the labor theory of value. And insofar as that theory of value was sanctioned by the authority of Ricardo, the growth of Ricardian socialism stimulated an attitude of iconoclasm among professional economists toward the teachings of Ricardo. In fact much of the theoretical development of the 1830's, particularly that related to the nature of profit as a source of income, was the result of a more or less conscious effort to counter the spread of socialist ideology.

The term "socialism," of course, had not yet acquired its modern connotation. No Ricardian socialist advocated nationalization of the means of production or central economic planning by the state. Prior to the revolutionary upsurge of 1848, British socialism was virtually synonymous with Owenism, suggesting a mixture of airy speculations about the virtues of a collective organization of society combined with a vigorous attack on the profit motive and the principle of free competition. The Owenites did not dwell on the concept of the class struggle; theirs was not a militant, still less a revolutionary, political program. Members of the working class were to subscribe to cooperative societies and these would gradually and peacefully supplant the surrounding structure of individualism by sheer demonstration of economic superiority. The road of transition to what Owen called the New Social System lay in inducing the upper classes to abandon the existing economic order and to sponsor cooperative projects in industry and agriculture. In this sense, the anticapitalist critics of the 1820's and 1830's were all, properly speaking, "utopian socialists."

If we exclude Owen himself, the first of the so-called Ricardian socialists was Piercy Ravenstone. His book, *A Few Doubts on the Subjects of Population and Political Economy* (1821), contains all the familiar ingredients of the Owenite case: labor is the source of all wealth; capital is essentially appropriated labor; capitalists make no real contribution to production; competition is wasteful and produces sharp inequality in the distribution of income. Characteristic too is Ravenstone's attack on the Malthusian theory of population.[1] Ricardo read Ravenstone's book but its full significance escaped him. "I . . . have looked with some interest at a work on Polit. Econ. by Mr. Piercy Ravenstone," he wrote to McCulloch, "which though full of the greatest error has some good things in it—he is a strenuous and an able advocate for Reform . . . The cause of the distress of the labouring class is well stated, but he appears not to be aware of the difficulty of providing a remedy" (9, 45, 63). Though Ricardo had no sympathy for Owen's social gospel, he did not realize that Ravenstone was a follower of Owen. Still less did it occur to him that Ravenstone was a socialist; at this stage the issues did not present themselves in these terms.[2]

Ravenstone's pamphlet was followed by a tract entitled *The Source and Remedy of the National Difficulties* (1821), which built its critique of the prevailing order on Smith's theory of productive labor. The anonymous author buttressed his argument with Colquhoun's wartime estimate of the distribution of the national income of Great Britain. This was to become standard procedure with the Ricardian socialists. Time and again they drew on Colquhoun's observation that "more than one fifth part of the whole community are unproductive labourers, and . . . these labourers receive from the aggregate labour of the productive classes about one third part of the new property created annually."[3] These unproductive laborers, Colquhoun hastened to add, do "eminently tend to promote, invigorate, and render even more pro-

1. See K. Smith, *op. cit.*, pp. 142–52, 164–9.

2. The Owenites were still hopeful at this time of winning Ricardo's favor. George Mudie, one of Owen's close associates, addressed an open letter to Ricardo entitled *Mr. Owen's Proposed Arrangements for the Distressed Working Classes Shown to be Consistent with Sound Principles of Political Economy* (London, 1819). See Robbins, *The Theory of Economic Policy*, pp. 126–34.

3. Colquhoun, *op. cit.*, p. 109.

ductive the labour of the creating classes," but this comment was easily overlooked. More grist for the mill was the unhappy assertion that "without a large proportion of poverty there could be no riches in any country; since riches are the offspring of labour; while labour can result only from a state of poverty." [4] This furnished the socialist writers with all the arguments they needed to support their prescriptions for a co-operative commonwealth.[5]

A work by John Gray, published in 1825, also made use of Colquhoun's data to arraign the existing mode of distribution, to which he added the contention that free competition acts as "an unnatural limit to production" by creating chronic insufficiency of demand.[6] William Thompson's *Inquiry into the Distrubution of Wealth* (1824) represents the philosophical wing of Owenism, joining Bentham's premise of maximum happiness to Owen's egalitarian ideals. It need not, however, concern us here. A new note is struck in Hodgskin's *Labour Defended against the Claims of Capital* (1825), which attacks the capitalist system with the aid of Locke's contrast between natural and artificial rights of property. In an age when "socialism" stood for the principle of mutual cooperation, Hodgskin was not a socialist but an anarchist.[7] Yet when the Ricardian socialists came under attack it was Hodgskin, and not Gray or Thompson, who was singled out as representative of the whole movement.

The usual Owenite denunciations of competition are not found in the writings of Hodgskin. Without stopping to indict the system of private enterprise, he went directly to the central theoretical issue: If labor is the source and measure of value it has a prior right to the entire fruits of industry. To define capital as "accumulated labor" does not justify the capitalist's expropriation of a portion of the product. Moreover, nothing can be achieved by calling for the establishment of cooperative units because the root of the problem is private ownership

4. *Ibid.*, p. 110.

5. Simon Gray, alias George Purves, had foreseen the dangerous implications of the theory of productive labor. "The unproductive theory," he wrote in a somewhat hysterical tone, "not only leads to everything false or incorrect in statistics, but to what is pernicious in morals and dangerous in politics . . . It is gloomy and malevolent, and calculated to set the various classes of society against one another, as well as to inspire general discontent, and a spirit hostile to subordination among the lower classes" (*All Classes Productive of National Wealth* [London, 1817], pp. 227–8).

6. J. Gray, *A Lecture on Human Happiness* (London, 1825; London Reprint No. 2, 1931), p. 60. For a detailed study of Gray's ideas, see J. Kimball, *The Economic Doctrines of John Gray, 1799–1833* (Washington, D.C., 1948).

7. Hodgskin was, in fact, attacked by some of Owen's disciples for his extreme individualism; see W. Thompson, *Labor Rewarded. The Claims of Labor and Capital Conciliated* (London, 1827).

of the means of production, maintained by the coercive apparatus of the state. "It is the overwhelming nature of the demands of capital," Hodgskin declares, "sanctioned by the laws of society, sanctioned by the customs of men, enforced by the legislature, and warmly defended by political economists, which keep, which ever have kept, and which ever will keep, as long as they are allowed and aquiesced in, the labourer in poverty and misery." [8]

Unlike Gray and Thompson, who show no signs of having read Ricardo, Hodgskin derived his exploitation theory of profit directly from Ricardo's version of the labor theory of value. In 1818, upon reading McCulloch's summary of Ricardo's *Principles* in the *Edinburgh Review,* he wrote to his friend Francis Place that it seemed clear to him that "profits are purely and simply a portion of the product of labour which the capitalist, without any right other than that conferred upon him by law, takes for himself." [9] In his book, Hodgskin fell back on Ricardo's theory of rent to dismiss the landlord as a passive agent in the productive process. Furthermore, he declared, the theories of political economy have amply demonstrated that wages and profits are inversely related, thereby revealing the fundamental character of the conflict between labor and capital. Ricardo, "that ingenious and profound writer," is invoked to support the notion that the recipients of profit and rent have no "natural" claim to any share of the total income: "His theory confirms the observations I have just made—viz. that the exactions of the capitalist cause the poverty of the labourer." [10] Favoring a stateless society of self-supporting producers, Hodgskin offered no remedies but urged workers to join trade unions as their only means of defense in the class war.

There is no doubt that the theories of the Ricardian socialists made deep inroads into working-class thought in the 1820's. And throughout this decade economists had no other answer to these arguments than the Malthusian theory of population. When John Stuart Mill attended a meeting of the London Co-operative Society in 1826, where he spoke

8. *Labour Defended against the Claims of Capital* (London, 1825; reprinted London, 1932), p. 80; also p. 55.

9. Quoted by E. Halévy, *Thomas Hodgskin (1786–1869)* (Paris, 1903), p. 120. In 1819 Hodgskin sent Place an outline of a critical study of Ricardo's theory (see *ibid.*, pp. 53–72), but the book was never written.

10. *Labour Defended,* pp. 80–1. See also Hodgskin's *Popular Political Economy* (London, 1827), consisting of four lectures to the London Mechanics' Institute. The institute, of which Hodgskin had been one of the founders, was established in 1823 to provide technical and popular education for workingmen. For a systematic exposition of Hodgskin's economic ideas, see G. H. Schütze, *Die Lehre von der Verteilung in der Volkswirtschaft bei Thomas Hodgskin* (Leipzig, 1930); also W. Stark, *The Ideal Foundations of Economic Thought* (London, 1943), pp. 51–103.

in opposition to Owen's schemes in the name of "the laws of political economy," his entire argument rested on the supposition that a collectivist economy would remove the individual's incentive to limit the size of his family.[11] That was also the gist of James Mill's analysis of Owen's case which bade the poor look to the principle of population as the remedy for their plight.[12] Curiously enough, Ricardo did not share the Malthusian objection to "the system of equality," but unfortunately he did not make his views public. Writing to Francis Place, he said:

> I believe, that under such a system [of equality], mankind would increase much faster than it now does, but so would food also. A large proportion of the whole capital of the country would be employed in the production of food-necessaries, and a less proportion in the production of luxuries, and thus we might go on, even with an increase of capital, without any increased difficulty, till that distant time, which because of its distance, Mr. Malthus says should not damp our ardour. Whether this would be a more happy state of society is another question which it is not now necessary to discuss [9, 50].

The first economist to meet the socialists on their own grounds was Samuel Read; being an opponent of Malthus' theory of population he was forced to resort to other arguments. "Labourers have been flattered and persuaded that they produce all," he remarked. "The Ricardo economists" maintain that "labour is the *only* source of wealth" while others (such as the author of *Labour Defended against the Claims of Capital*) have even denied the right of capitalists to any share of the product. But, on the contrary, workers must be made to understand that "they *do not* produce all wherever they take the assistance of capital." Of course, machinery unaided by labor can produce nothing; but it is the union of the factors of production, organized by the capitalist, which has produced the wealth of the country: "The capitalists are in reality the greatest of all benefactors to the community."[13] This was the type of reasoning which now gained wide currency. In a lead article *The Examiner* drew attention to the importance of teaching the poor that "want and labour spring from the niggardliness of nature, and not from the inequality which is consequent on the institution of prop-

11. Two of J. S. Mill's speeches on that occasion have been published by H. J. Laski (*Journal of Adult Education*, October 1929). "It was a *lutte corps-à-corps*," wrote John Stuart Mill years later, "between Owenites and political economists, whom the Owenites regarded as their most inveterate opponents: but it was a perfectly friendly dispute" (*Autobiography*, p. 87).

12. J. Mill, *Elements*, pp. 66–7.

13. S. Read, *Political Economy* (1829), pp. xxix–xxxiv, 56, 125–32.

erty. . . . In effect, though not in law, the labourers are co-proprietors with the capitalists who hire their labour." This "most exhilarating truth" is furnished by "the invaluable science of Political Economy" which ought to be diffused among the people without further delay.[14]

It must be remembered that while Smith and Malthus had endorsed popular education, including the principles of political economy, there was still much misgiving in the press of the day about the advisability of teaching economics to workingmen. Indeed, some were strongly opposed to the idea.[15] By the 1830's, however, it was beginning to be realized that the economic education of the working class could no longer be neglected.[16] For example, Richard Whately, lecturing at Oxford in 1831, warned his audience particularly against individuals who talked of the danger of too much education for the lower classes of society: "Can the labouring classes . . . safely be left to suppose, as many a demagogue is ready, when it suits his purpose, to tell them, that inequality of conditions is inexpedient, and ought to be abolished?" [17] In the same year the Society for the Diffusion of Useful Knowledge, founded for the express purpose of supplying cheap reading matter to the pupils of the Mechanics' Institutes, broke new grounds in popular education by publishing a work entitled *The Results of Machinery*. In a series of graphic parables, the author illustrated the attendant benefits of machinery and warned against combinations to raise wages by holding out the threat of capital migration and consequent national impoverishment.

This book was followed almost immediately by a companion volume, with the pointed title of *The Rights of Industry*, in which Hodgskin's

14. *The Examiner*, Dec. 26, 1830, pp. 817–18.

15. When Lord Brougham published his *Practical Observations upon the Education of the People* (1825), favoring adult education for workingmen, *Blackwood's Edinburgh Magazine* retorted: "We believe to a certain extent in political economy, for it comprehends a number of old stale truths which were familiar to all men before the name was ever heard of; but we may say that it combines with these truths many falsehoods . . . Its doctrines bring into question a very large portion of our political system; they strike at some of the main pillars of British Society; they seek the destruction of many sentiments and regulations which, in our judgement, are essential for binding man to man and class to class —for cementing together and governing the community . . . This is sufficient to convince us that a large part of political economy is yet anything but knowledge, and that it is therefore unfit to be taught to the working classes" (quoted by Smart, *op. cit.*, p. 288 n.). See M. J. L. O'Connor, *Origins of Academic Economics in the United States* (New York, 1944), pp. 90–5, for other references to this question.

16. The new approach to working-class education is discussed by R. K. Webb, *op. cit.*, ch. 3.

17. Whately, *op. cit.*, pp. 217–18. See also Longfield, *Lectures*, pp. 16–17.

writings were attacked by way of preaching the paramount importance of the profit motive in affording a livelihood to the working class.[18]

These appeals, however, fell on deaf ears as a wave of syndicalist thought enveloped the labor movement after the passage of the Political Reform Bill of 1832. The collapse of Owen's National Equitable Labour Exchange exacerbated the disillusionment of the working class with cooperative schemes and contributed to the emergence of militant Chartism. The Owenites, who had previously eschewed political activity, created the National Union of Working Classes to promote a program of manhood suffrage, secret ballot, equal electoral districts, and annual Parliaments. Place said of this group that they entertained "absurd notions . . . that everything which was produced belonged to those who, by their labour, produced it, and ought to be shared among them . . . They denounced everyone who dissented from these notions as a *political economist,* under which appellation was included the notion of a bitter foe to the working classes, enemies who deserved no mercy at their hands." [19]

These views caught the attention of Longfield. In his *Lectures* (1834) he led up to the analysis of profits with a reproof to those who taught the right of labor to the whole produce; their object, he said, was "to create disturbance, by stimulating the passions of the poor and ignorant, and persuading them their poverty is caused by oppression or misrule" (p. 158). Likewise, Scrope's *Principles* (1834) harks back to Hodgskin and others like him who "declaim against capital as the poison of society, and the taking of interest by its owners, as an abuse, an injustice, a robbery of the class of labourers." Perhaps it is not to be wondered at, Scrope admitted in his *Principles,* that those who observe "the prevalence of great misery among the inferior classes of workmen in this and other wealthy countries" and who surmise that "the share of the gross production which falls to the common labourers does not increase—perhaps even diminishes," should conclude that something is wrong with the present mode of distribution. "But that any sane person should attribute the evil to *the existence of capital* . . . is indeed wonderful." Savings will not be invested without the promise of a reward and to deprive capitalists of their profit is to deprive society of the production of wealth (pp. 150–1).

18. *The Rights of Industry* (London, 1831), pp. 56–7. Both *The Results of Machinery* and *The Rights of Industry* are sometimes erroneously attributed to Lord Brougham. But Charles Knight claimed authorship in the preface to a reprint of the two books under the title of *Capital and Labour* (London, 1845). *The Rights of Industry,* in particular, was widely circulated in digest form in what was at this time a veritable breviary for the working class: *Chambers' Information for the People* (London, 1835), No. 15, pp. 113–20.

19. Quoted by Wallas, *op. cit.,* p. 273.

The late 1830's found the more radical advocates of factory reform, the opponents of the new poor law, and the mass of urban laborers rallied around the People's Charter. The interest in socialist propaganda dwindled away as the immediate problems of political agitation took an upper hand. By now the prominent Ricardian socialists had all but disappeared from the scene. Thompson was dead and Hodgskin had become a journalist and lecturer for the free trade movement.[20] Gray joined the currency cranks in *Efficient Remedy for the National Distress* (1842), and in his *Lectures on the Nature of Money* (1848) denied that he had ever been a socialist. In 1839 there appeared the last and the most powerful "manifesto of Owenism": Bray's *Labour's Wrongs and Labour's Remedy.* But it was little read and passed unnoticed in the major journals; even the labor press damned it with faint praise.[21]

In itself, the neglect of Bray's book is not surprising. What Thompson had said in 1827 holds true for the whole period: "The leaders of the school of *Competitive* Political Economy" were reluctant to discuss "the system of *Co-operative* political economy."[22] Despite the attacks on Hodgskin by some writers, the sparseness of references to the views of the Ricardian socialists is truly striking. Both James Mill and McCulloch knew Hodgskin personally, yet never mentioned his books, nor gave any public hint of knowledge of the "labour theorists."[23] Even John Stuart Mill, the only contemporary economist to make a serious inquiry into the merits of the socialist case, based his analysis almost wholly on the writings of Saint-Simon, Fourier, and Cabet. He identified the British school of socialist thought with Robert Owen and regarded it as a distinctly inferior product compared to its French counterpart.[24] Yet he was personally acquainted with William Thompson and probably had read some of Thompson's books.[25] In an article

20. See Halévy, *Thomas Hodgskin,* pp. 156 ff.

21. See H. J. Carr, "John Francis Bray," *Economica,* November 1940.

22. Thompson, *Labor Rewarded,* p. 46.

23. Hodgskin resided in Edinburgh from 1818 to 1822 and visited McCulloch several times: McCulloch reviewed Hodgskin's *Travels in the North of Germany* in *The Scotsman* (see Halévy, *Thomas Hodgskin,* p. 36). When Hodgskin arrived in London in 1822, Place and James Mill secured him a position with the *Morning Chronicle.* In a letter to Lord Brougham, written in 1833, James Mill spoke of the "mad nonsense of our friend Hodgkin [*sic*] 'about' the rights of the labourer to the whole produce of the country, wages, profits, and rent, all included . . . These opinions, if they were to spread, would be the subversion of civilised society; worse than the overwhelming deluge of Huns and Tartars" (quoted by A. Bain, *James Mill, A Biography* [London, 1882], p. 364).

24. J. S. Mill, *Autobiography,* p. 117.

25. See R. K. P. Pankhurst, *William Thompson (1775–1833)* (London, 1954), pp. 212–15.

for the *Edinburgh Review* in 1845 he referred to Knight's *Rights of Industry* which, as we know, quotes Hodgskin at length.[26] But nowhere did Mill intimate that the writings of Thompson and Hodgskin had any bearing on the subject matter of political economy or on the question of socialism.[27]

It is no accident that the writers who did criticize the Ricardian socialists—Read, Scrope, and Longfield—were not only opponents of Ricardo's theories but were also among the first to develop the abstinence theory of profit. This is not to say that they directly associated the socialist argument with the doctrines of Ricardo; they were not prone to think of Hodgskin and Bray, much less of Gray and Thompson, as *Ricardian* socialists. In fact, it needs to be said that there is little warrant for the common belief that "it was Ricardo, not Owen, who gave the really effective inspiration to English socialism."[28] Only Hodgskin showed any familiarity with Ricardo's *Principles* and even he did not base his position on Ricardian tenets. The socialist writers were all adherents of the labor theory of value; this affords their only meeting ground with Ricardo.[29] The dominant aspects in Ricardo's system, the action of the law of diminishing returns and the growth of rent as a barrier to economic progress, found no echo in their works. On the other hand, the theory of productive labor, which figures so prominently in the writings of Ravenstone, Gray, and Bray, is mentioned only incidentally in Ricardo's *Principles.* The notion that rent and profit constitute a deduction from values created by labor comes from *The Wealth of Nations,* as does the very phrase "the whole of the produce of labour belongs to the labourer."[30] McCulloch's and Mill's theory that profits are only "wages of labour" may of course have encouraged the radical deductions of the critics of capitalism. But there is no evidence that the genesis of British socialism was in any important way connected with the spread of Ricardo's doctrines. Consider Charles Hall, the first socialist critic of the Industrial Revolution; he is in a

26. See J. S. Mill, *Dissertations and Discussions* (London, 1859–75), *2,* 214.

27. See G. D. H. Cole, *Socialist Thought. The Forerunners, 1789–1850* (London, 1953), pp. 312–13.

28. H. S. Foxwell in his introduction to A. Menger, *The Right to the Whole Produce of Labour* (London, 1899), p. lxxxiii. This is the basis of Foxwell's celebrated diatribe against Ricardo (see *ibid.,* pp. xli–xlii).

29. E. Lowenthal concludes her definitive study of *The Ricardian Socialists* (New York, 1911) with the observation: "There is nothing in either the tone of these authors or the form of their arguments which points especially to Ricardo . . . The term Ricardian socialism is probably due to the fact that Ricardo was the dominant figure of a school in which the labor theory of value was a common doctrine."

30. See P. H. Douglas, "Smith's Theory of Value and Distribution," *Adam Smith, 1776–1926* (Chicago, 1928), pp. 95–103.

sense a typical Ricardian socialist, attacking property rights and the parasitism of the upper classes on the basis of labor's claim to the whole product. But Hall's book, *The Effects of Civilisation,* which was widely read in Owenite circles, appeared twelve years before Ricardo's *Principles.*[31] So long as the labor theory of value maintained its hold on contemporary thought, the notion that profit constitutes an alienation of surplus value produced by labor leaped readily to mind. The growth of industry and the development of a class-conscious proletariat was all that was needed to produce the argument that workers were exploited.

What really impressed the economists of the day was that Ricardo's system furnished no satisfactory answer to the arguments of the socialists. If anything, it opened the door to the destructive language of class warfare. Ricardo's system suggested a "natural" divergence of interests between the classes of society: the prospects of capitalists and laborers depended upon the demise of the landed classes. (That this was an erroneous interpretation of Ricardo's doctrine is beside the point.) A theory so fraught with disharmonious implications, Ricardo's critics asserted, could no longer be sanctioned. "All systems are essentially false and delusive," said Richard Jones, "which suppose that the permanent gain and advantage of any one class of the community, can be founded on the loss of another class."[32] No one stated this thesis more pungently than Scrope; writing in the *Quarterly Review* of 1831, he convicted Ricardo and his disciples "not merely of errors, but of *crimes.*"

> Surely the publication of opinions taken up hastily upon weak, narrow and imperfect evidence—opinions which, overthrowing, as they did, the fundamental principles of sympathy and common interest that knit society together, could not but be deeply injurious even if true,—does amount to a crime . . . In their theory of rent, they have insisted that landlords can thrive only at the expense of the public at large, and especially of the capitalists: in their theory of profits, they have declared that capitalists can only improve their circumstances by depressing those of the labouring and numerous class: in their theory of wages, they have maintained that the condition of the labourers can only be bettered by depriving them of . . . the feelings of the husband and the father; in their theory of population, they have absolved governments from all responsibility for the misery of the people committed to their care . . . In one and all of their arguments they have studi-

31. See M. Beer, *A History of British Socialism* (London, 1940), pt. I, pp. 126–32.

32. *Essay on the Distribution of Wealth,* p. 328.

> ously exhibited the interests of every class in society as necessarily at perpetual variance with every other class! [33]

Such complaints become more frequent in the literature of political economy after 1830, reflecting among other things the growing influence of socialist thought in the labor movement. In this sense, the Ricardian socialists must be counted among the sources of the increasing reaction against Ricardian economics.[34] The weakness of Ricardo's theory of value, insofar as it had nothing explicit to say about the nature of profit, now stood more strongly exposed. A host of innovators sprang to the fore to supply the missing element and in so doing did not scruple to attack the conclusions and sometimes the very premises of Ricardian doctrine. The result was to make the decade 1830–40 the outstanding period of creative debate in the history of classical economics.

2. Jones and the Theory of Rent

The law of diminishing returns, encompassed in the Malthusian "pressure" of population upon "the means of subsistence," stood at the center of the Ricardian system. In 1829 Nassau Senior had submitted the theory of population to the historical test and found it wanting. But he had not dislodged the law of diminishing returns, although, by implication, he had undermined its significance. All that was needed now was a stronger emphasis on the forces making for continuous improvements in cultivation, and Malthus' doctrine as well as Ricardo's system would go by the board. For as soon as it is asserted that rising cost curves in agriculture are constantly shifting downward as a result of incessant improvements in method, the Ricardian theory loses most of its practical importance.

In effect this was the essential argument of Richard Jones' *Essay on the Distribution of Wealth* (1831). In the long run, increasing returns in agriculture are as probable as decreasing returns: "In the progress of those improvements in the art of cultivation, by which its most profitable amount of produce is approached, it may be very possible, that every successive portion of the capital and labor concentrated on the land, may be more economically and efficiently applied than the last" (pp. 199–200). Not only the increasing mechanization of English farm-

33. *Quarterly Review,* November 1831, p. 116. See also Wakefield, *England and America,* p. 84.

34. But R. L. Meek ("The Decline of Ricardian Economics in England," *Economica,* February 1950) seems to attribute far too much importance to this factor.

ing but also the development of the means of transportation and the growth of a national market would, as likely as not, discount the effect of diminishing productivity in agriculture (pp. 217–44). Even the increase of rents during and after the Napoleonic Wars went hand in hand with a decline in the number of people employed on the land and a decrease in the landlord's share of the product, being the result of "better farming and greater produce" (p. 285).

In general, Jones' work takes the form of an oblique attack on Ricardo's theory of rent from the standpoint of what we would now call the "historical school." [35] In keeping with his method, Jones separates the phenomenon of rent into two distinct historical types: peasant's rent and farmer's rent. A major portion of the *Essay* is taken up with what John Stuart Mill was to describe as "a copious repertory of valuable facts on the landed tenure of different countries"; much of that deals with the existence of peasant's rent and tributes exacted by the landowner in precapitalist societies, which is entirely irrelevant to the critique of Ricardo and the concept of farmer's rent. Jones was anxious to show that Ricardo's theory was not only false but insignificant: "We shall be making on the whole an extravagant allowance, if we suppose them [farmer's rents] to occupy one-hundredth part of the cultivated surface of the habitable globe" (p. 14). Ricardo's conception of the manner in which land is taken up for cultivation is condemned as a piece of "conjectural history"; the genesis of rent is in fact characterized by an initial tribute from the farmer which is "wholly independent of any difference in the quality of the ground" (p. 11).

In the closing section of the book, Jones revealed his underlying motive: to vindicate the landowning class by undermining the assumptions of the free traders. The theories of Ricardo were no sooner current, he asserts, than they aroused "mistaken views and excited feelings as to the sources of the prosperity of the landed proprietors, like those which have lately prevailed in England" (p. 304). It is true, he admitted, "that there are cases in which the landlords *may* derive a limited advantage from circumstances which are diminishing the means of the body of people; but their permanent prosperity, and that gradual elevation of their revenue which sustains them in their relative position in the community, must emanate from more wholesome and more abundant sources." The interests of capital and labor also clash upon occasions "for it is not disputed that . . . wages may be increased

35. Only the first part of the projected work was published; the rest of the book, which would have covered the theory of profit and wages, was never written.

by a decrease of profits, and profits swelled by the decrease of wages, as certainly rents may be elevated by encroachments on the revenues of the producing classes." Ultimately, however, all classes benefit from the increase of wealth and "in this respect, there is no difference in the social position of the landlords, and that of the other classes which compose the state" (pp. 287–8).

Jones' *Essay* made an immediate, and on the whole favorable, impression on his contemporaries. Scrope reviewed the book in the *Quarterly Review* and praised it as having "dealt the finishing stroke to the miserable 'theory of rent' of the Ricardo school." [36] William Whewell (1794–1866) endorsed Jones' critique in an address before the Cambridge Philosophical Society; he concluded his remarks by observing: "Ricardo . . . neglected altogether the effects of an increase in the powers of agriculture, which, in England, has been a change at least as important and as marked, as the increase in the population. This being the case, it is evident that the whole of his assumption of the nature of the economical progress of this country, and the views of the distribution of wealth arising from this assumption, must fall to the ground." [37] McCulloch in the *Edinburgh Review*, however, rose to Ricardo's defense. He granted that a historical investigation in the nature of rent was much needed. And he disavowed the notion that Ricardo's *Principles* had "fixed and ascertained every principle of the science" so that "economists have nothing left but to comment upon and explain it." But with all the aplomb he could muster, McCulloch assured the reader that Jones' accomplishments were few: "We are not indeed aware that he has stated anything that was not already well known to every one who has the slightest acquaintance with such subjects. His review is extensive, but superficial." Ricardo's theory of rent, McCulloch declared, no doubt applies only to "one-hundredth part of the cultivated surface of the habitable globe." But Jones is tilting at windmills: "For the demolition of the theory of rent espoused by Mr. Ricardo, two-thirds of Mr. Jones' lucubrations are entirely irrelevant." McCulloch went on to scoff at Jones' objections to the law of diminishing returns

36. *Quarterly Review,* November 1831, p. 81. Scrope based a chapter of his *Principles* on Jones' institutional survey of rental payments in different parts of the world.

37. W. Whewell, "Mathematical Exposition of Some of the Leading Doctrines in Mr. Ricardo's 'Principles,'" *Transactions of the Cambridge Philosophical Society* (Cambridge, 1833), *4,* pt. 1, 169. A laudatory review of Jones' book in *British Critic. Theological Review,* July 1831, pp. 40–60, is probably by Whewell. For a discussion of Whewell's "inductive" approach to economic questions, see S. G. Checkland, "The Advent of Academic Economics in England," *The Manchester School,* January 1951, pp. 59–66.

and, nicely confusing statics and dynamics, offered a proof of the law by *reductio ad absurdum:* if the law did not hold, the food supply of the entire universe could be grown in a "flower-pot." [38]

Malthus redefined rent in the second edition of his *Principles* so as to include "all the different kinds of rent referred to by Mr. Jones" (p. 153). Others joined him in paying homage to Jones' analysis.[39] John Stuart Mill, on the other hand, paid no attention to Jones' critique of Ricardo; yet the material for the chapters on land tenure in Mill's *Principles* is drawn from Jones' *Essay.*

Jones' influence on the course of economic thought ceased with the publication of his first book. After a brief tenure at Kings College, London, he succeeded Malthus at Haileybury College in 1835. For the next two decades he was absorbed in the execution of the Act for the Commutation of Tithes, having been appointed in 1836 as one of the three supervisory commissioners. Most of Jones' best work was published posthumously in the 1850's but scarcely made any impression on men like Fawcett and Cairnes, the leading economists of that day.[40]

3. The Abstinence Theory of Profit

The classical economists, as is well known, made no distinction between the income of ownership and the income of management; interest was treated as a component of profit and no less a net return on physical capital than the portion retained by the employer of labor.[41] The neglect of the distinction between entrepreneur and capitalist was more than an analytical oversight. Until the "railway mania" of the 1840's trading on the stock exchange was largely confined to government bonds and public utility stocks. The domestic capital market

38. *Edinburgh Review,* September 1831, pp. 85–6, 94–5.

39. Torrens, *The Budget,* p. xv; T. C. Banfield, *Four Lectures on the Organization of Industry* (London, 1845), pp. viii, 49–53.

40. An incomplete textbook of *Lectures on Political Economy of Nations* appeared in 1852 and the rest of Jones' *Literary Remains* were published in 1859 by W. Whewell. Some writers have had the mistaken impression that Jones' *Essay* received little attention in his own lifetime; see, for instance, H. Weber, *Richard Jones. Ein früher englischer Abtrünniger der klassichen Schule der Nationalökonomie* (Zurich, 1939). Jones' status as a critic of Ricardo has, contrariwise, been exaggerated. Weber calls him "the first English critic of the Ricardian school" (*ibid.,* p. 105). N. Chao's study refers to Jones as "the first important writer to attack the doctrines of the Ricardian school, and who also should be considered as the founder of modern institutonal economics" (*Richard Jones: An Early English Institutionalist* [New York, 1930], p. 18).

41. See F. H. Knight, *Risk, Uncertainty, and Profit* (London Reprints, No. 16, 1931), pp. 23–5; Schumpeter, *op. cit.,* pp. 646–7.

was poorly organized and virtually all new industrial investment was financed out of undistributed profits.[42] There was, consequently, little basis in practice for considering the investment function independently of the level of saving. Without distorting reality, it was possible to think of the active entrepreneur as identical with the inactive investor of capital.

The institutional setting helps to explain why Say's concept of the coordinating entrepreneur as a fourth factor of production made so little headway among English economists of the classical school. As late as 1836 George Ramsay, after pointing out that "the person who owns the capital, and he who directs the work may be, and indeed frequently are, different," was able to say: "All English writers on political economy with whom I am acquainted, treat of the two latter as forming but one class of men, to whom . . . the term ["capitalists"] is applied."[43] But the remark is not altogether accurate. A full decade before, William Ellis had drawn a clear line of separation between "the remuneration for the productive employment of . . . savings," which he called interest or "neat profit," and "the remuneration for . . . time and skill, which remuneration may be called agency for superintendence."[44] By the early 1830's the theory that profit constitutes a reward for enterprise as distinct from interest on money loans had found its way into a number of articles and books. The term "profit," however, continued to be used to denote the payment for ownership in lieu of what was later called "pure interest." For example, Samuel Read complained of the fact that the Ricardians had never provided a technical definition of profit. He offered to fill the gap: Profit is the sum that "can be got for the use of it [capital] without the labour of personally applying it, or superintending its application in business or production."[45] Two years later, Scrope's essay on "The Political Economists" in the *Quarterly Review* likewise defined profit (after Bailey) as "the compensation for abstinence from immediate gratification" and distinguished the latter from the payment for risk, the wages of management, and the gains of monopolized scarcity.[46]

Scrope pursued the theme further in his *Principles* (1833) and attacked the advocates of the labor theory of value for their failure to recognize that profit represents a compensation for "the time during which the owner of capital has allowed it to be employed productively with a view to its ultimate remuneration, instead of consuming it immediately on his personal gratification" (pp. 197–8). This did not, how-

42. See Gayer *et al.*, *op. cit.*, *1*, 410.
43. *Essay on the Distribution of Wealth*, p. 82.
44. *Westminster Review*, January 1826, p. 107.
45. *Political Economy*, pp. 244–5.
46. *Quarterly Review*, January 1831, p. 18.

ever, stop him from declaring that "the primary element of value in most things is *cost of procurement;* and the cost of procurement consists almost wholly of the trouble or labour necessary for producing the article" (p. 45).

This whole line of reasoning was brought to a head in Senior's *Outline of the Science of Political Economy* (1836). With Senior the traditional triad of land, labor, and capital gives way to a new division of the factors of production into labor, natural agents, and abstinence. Labor is no longer conceived as an expenditure of human energy measured in time units but simply as another subjective sacrifice incurred in production, governed by the strength of the disinclination to work. As for natural agents, it comprises all instruments of production which are cost-free to society as a whole; land is included therein as a species of the genus. Abstinence, on the other hand, is defined both as "the *conduct* of a person who either abstains from the unproductive use of what he can command, or designedly prefers the production of remote to that of immediate results," and as "that *agent,* distinct from labour and the agency of nature, the concurrence of which is necessary to the existence of Capital, and which stands in the same relation to Profit as Labour does to Wages." [47] Senior put so much stress on the psychic cost of deferring consumption that he found the case of inherited property a little difficult to handle. The returns on a legacy obviously represent quasi-rents, being in the nature of revenue which "fortune bestows either without any exertion on the part of the recipient, or in addition to the average remuneration for the exercise of industry or the employment of capital." [48] In a sense it might be said that even this revenue is "the reward for the owner's abstinence in not . . . spending its price in enjoyment." But, as Senior noted correctly, "the same remark applies to every species of transferable property. Every estate may be sold, and the purchase money wasted. If the last basis of classification was adopted, the greater part of what every Political Economist has termed rent must be called Profit." [49]

Abstinence, therefore, is a subjective real cost of new capital which accounts for the scarcity of capital and hence for the fact that ownership of capital commands an income. Senior linked this pain cost to the phychological underestimation of the future which, like Bailey before him and Böhm-Bawerk after him, he took for granted as an inherent feature of economic behavior. It never struck Senior that this view involved a sharp break with the older classical treatment of saving. For Adam Smith as for Ricardo, for all his talk of profit as only

47. Senior, *Political Economy,* pp. 58–9 (my italics).
48. *Ibid.,* pp. 91–2.
49. *Ibid.,* p. 129.

a "just compensation" for waiting, saving was a cultural and social phenomenon. The greater part of the community was thought to discount the present in favor of the future so that, in the aggregate, time preference was negative. Let us recall Adam Smith's comments in *The Wealth of Nations:*

> The principle which prompts to expense, is the passion for present enjoyment; which, though sometimes violent and very difficult to be restrained, is in general only momentary and occasional. But the principle which prompts to save, is the desire of bettering our condition, a desire which . . . comes with us from the womb and never leaves us till we go into the grave . . . An augmentation of fortune is the means by which the greater part of men propose and wish to better their condition . . . and the most likely way of augmenting their fortune, is to save and accumulate some part of what they acquire . . . Though the principle of expense, therefore, prevails in almost all men upon some occasions, and in some men upon almost all occasions, yet in the greater part of men . . . the principle of frugality seems not only to predominate, but to predominate very greatly [pp. 324–5].

The odd thing is that it was this very passage which Senior employed against Malthus; we may say that food has a tendency to outgrow population, Senior argued, because "in fact, it has generally done so, and because I consider the desire of bettering our conditions as natural a wish as the desire for marriage." One may say that Senior had simply not thought the matter through. But the point to be emphasized is that Senior in no way justified his belief in the relative preponderance of improvident over provident individuals.

Moreover, at times Senior actually seems to adopt the traditional view that investment is typically self-financed out of previous earnings: "Capitals are generally formed from small beginnings by acts of accumulation, which become in time habitual. The capitalist soon regards the increase of his capital as the great business of his life; and considers the greater part of his profit more a means to an end than as a subject of enjoyment." [50] In this case, abstinence as such is not involved at all in the saving-investment process, unless it is to be understood not as refraining from present consumption so as to augment future income but rather as refusing to increase present consumption

50. *Political Economy*, p. 192. In unpublished notes, written in the late 1840's, Senior characterized the middle classes as "the great accumulators of wealth" and launched into an amazing discussion of the "demonstration effect" and its impact on the rate of saving (*Industrial Efficiency and Social Economy*, ed. S. L. Levy [London, 1929], *1*, 65–9).

so as not to deplete future income. But in treating income derived from inherited property as a quasi-rent Senior had cut himself off from the former interpretation of "abstinence" in which profit is simply a reward for not encroaching upon capital.

Senior's abstinence theory suffers from an additional weakness which is not present in John Stuart Mill's subsequent formulation of the doctrine. Senior did not recognize a supply schedule of saving and ignored differences in the relative sacrifice involved in individual saving; in other words, he thought of saving as carried out under conditions of constant cost. In order to save the theory from the familiar objection that abstaining from present enjoyment is hardly a pain cost to the average saver in the upper income brackets, it would be necessary to point out, as Senior failed to do, that interest is governed by the *marginal* supply price of abstinence. And the latter may well exceed the rate necessary to induce saving on the part of many individuals.[51]

Although Senior did not acknowledge the writings of Bailey (nor of Jones, Read, or Scrope for that matter), his influence is writ large in Senior's book. It is evident in the generalization of the rent concept and in the attack on the assumption of "perfectly equal competition": whenever an appropriated natural agent concurs in the production of a commodity the value of such an article contains a "rent" payment which is not governed by any general rule. Since the assistance of natural agents may comprise all the advantages of soil or situation, personal talent and skill, patents and copyrights, most commodities are not really subject to the laws of competitive value.[52]

But while Senior's theory of value and capital derives from sources almost diametrically opposed to Ricardo, his theory of income distribution conforms to the pattern of the Ricardian school. There is a difference, however. Firstly, Senior defined the law of diminishing returns as holding only at a given level of skills.[53] And in actual fact "improvements in the art of agriculture generally accompany . . . an increase of the capital as well as of the population of a Country." There is every reason to think that "the total amount of the annual agricultural produce of Great Britain has much more than doubled during the last hundred years; but it is highly improbable that the amount of labour annually employed in agriculture has also doubled." [54] In addition, manufactured articles are produced under conditions of increasing returns; this notion is indeed elevated to the status of one of "the four elementary

51. On this point see G. Cassel, *The Nature and Necessity of Interest* (London, 1903), pp. 38–9; P. H. Douglas, *The Theory of Wages* (New York, 1934), pp. 423–5.

52. Senior, *Political Economy*, pp. 103–14.

53. *Ibid.*, p. 26.

54. *Ibid.*, p. 86; also p. 108.

propositions of the science of political economy." Nevertheless, Senior insists, in the long run the diminishing productivity of agriculture is an irrepressible barrier to economic growth. In this sense, even the Malthusian theory of population is part of his analytical scheme.[55]

On the vital question of free trade Senior not only agrees with Ricardo but even frames his argument in a typical Ricardian manner. Restrictions on the importations of corn constitute, as it were, restrictions on the exportation of manufactured articles; by limiting the scale of production, the tariff diminishes the efficiency of industry and makes it necessary to raise additional quantities of food on domestic soil at rising cost. Since workers consume chiefly "raw or slightly manufactured produce," the advantages of economies of scale in manufacturing are to no avail: the net effect is always "a constant tendency towards an increase of capital and population, and towards a fall in the rate of profit." [56]

That the book made so little stir at the time is largely the result of Senior's compromises with the Ricardian theory of distribution (poor organization of material and repetitiousness may have helped). At one point in his book Senior remarked: "Mr. Ricardo . . . is, perhaps, the most incorrect writer who ever attained philosophical eminence"; the general impression which Senior conveyed was that Ricardo had been right but infelicitous in expression. "It was principally because Senior failed in this way to connect his modifications of the Ricardian theory of value with any definite conclusions on the incomes of the factors of production, that his work attracted so little notice." [57] Herman Merivale, writing in the *Edinburgh Review,* welcomed the concept of abstinence but dismissed Senior's "encyclopaedic definition of rent" as an impractical refinement.[58] But even the abstinence theory of profit did not establish itself until John Stuart Mill adopted it in his *Principles.* Torrens dismissed it as a misleading innovation in the introduction to a reprint of *The Budget* (1844). His criticism, even if it had not been couched in the language of the mark-up theory, did not amount to much. It was impossible to resolve the cost of production into labor and abstinence, he argued, because the two are not correlative terms. Profit, being the excess of value over and above the sum of required outlays on production, is "not proportionate to abstinence." Abstinence is "that

55. As Marian Bowley has said, Senior's position is "somewhat peculiar. He considered Malthus' theory of great importance, and the connection between rent, population and distribution as elucidated by Ricardo to be formally correct, but while admitting all this he neither made it a fundamental part of the theory of value nor of wages" (*op. cit.,* pp. 173–4).

56. Senior, *Political Economy,* pp. 178, 193.

57. Bowley, *op. cit.,* p. 104.

58. *Edinburgh Review,* October 1837, pp. 98–102.

which causes the accumulation of capital." But "accumulation of capital is not cost of production; and much less can the cause of accumulation be a portion of the expenditure in which productive cost consists . . . To create profit we must both expend and reproduce. Abstinence does neither." [59] A similar thought had occurred to J. S. Mill; in a set of notes on Senior's book which he prepared in 1837, he commented: "I question if abstinence can be called an agent or an instrument of production. Could you not call it a *condition?* . . . Besides in order to employ productively what serves to feed me, I do not *abstain* from the enjoyment of it, I merely labour while I consume it." [60] But this line of reasoning was not followed up in Mill's *Principles.*

4. Longfield's Lectures

Of all the treatises on political economy which appeared in the 1830's the most original was Longfield's *Lectures.* We consider it here not because it had any influence on British economic thought [61] but because it affords yet another example of that tendency to compromise with Ricardian economics which we have seen at work in Senior's *Political Economy.* Longfield did not attack Ricardo; in some places he defended him against misinterpretation. Above all, he showed no disposition to help the reader reconcile the standard treatment with his own original contributions. The concluding chapter of the *Lectures,* which is devoted to the theory of distribution, contains a number of important insights but hardly a connected theory, much less a definite break with the Ricardian approach. If it be true that "new ideas, unless carefully elaborated, painstakingly defended, and 'pushed,' *simply will not tell,*" [62] we may say that Longfield's neglect is partly due to the fact that he chose the most inauspicious manner of presenting his ideas.

After an introductory lecture on the necessity of studying political economy, Longfield proceeds to expound the theory of value. He admits that labor is an adequate and, in fact, the best intratemporal measure of value (he followed Bailey in rejecting the concept of index

59. *The Budget,* pp. xxxvii–xxxviii.

60. J. S. Mill, "Notes on Senior's *Political Economy,*" *Economica,* August 1945.

61. Longfield's book did create a definite school of thought in Ireland (see R. D. Black, "Trinity College, Dublin, and the Theory of Value, 1823–1863," *Economica,* August 1945). Throughout this period there seems to have been little or no communication between Irish and British economists. Longfield, for instance, contributed an article to the *Dublin University Magazine* in 1840 on the views of the "banking school." One student of currency discussions in the period regards this contribution as clarifying "the most important controversial point in the theory of free banking. No attempt was made in subsequent literature to reply to it" (V. C. Smith, *The Rationale of Central Banking* [London, 1936], p. 76).

62. Schumpeter, *op. cit.,* p. 464.

numbers): "Subject to few exceptions, no permanent change can take place in the relative values of any two commodities without its being occasioned by some alteration in the quantity, or nature, or value of the labour required to produce one or both of those commodities." And like Ricardo, Longfield excludes nonreproducible goods from the purview of his analysis.[63]

The fourth lecture interrupts the sequence of topics to comment upon the nature of demand and its influence upon price. In the short span of five pages we get a remarkable discussion of the market-demand schedule made up of the separate action of individuals each endowed with diminishing grades of demand intensity for the product: value depends upon the marginal group of buyers who constitute potential demand at every decrease in price.[64] The analysis moves on to a typical Ricardian explanation of rent, with this exception, that rent is not made to depend upon differences in the fertility of soil.[65]

"Of capital," Longfield goes on to say, "there is not, properly speaking, any cost of production, except that sacrifice of the present to the future which is made by the possessor of wealth, who employs it as capital instead of consuming it for his immediate gratification. The amount of sacrifice varies very much in different ages and countries, and even in different persons of the same age and country." It is true that "many persons save without any prospect of profit, but merely from the love of accumulation, or, the preference of the future to the present." And the existence of a positive rate of interest is in itself a strong inducement to saving. However, for "my present purpose," Longfield declares, the supply side of capital may be passed over.[66] What interested him was rather the factors governing the demand for capital.

Additional units of capital, unaccompanied by an increase in population, must yield additional increments of product at a diminishing

63. *Lectures,* pp. 32, 35–6. I am at a loss to understand Schumpeter's observation that Longfield's "argument against the labor theory of value is one of the best ever penned" (*op. cit.,* p. 465).

64. Longfield, *Lectures,* pp. 111–15. In the same year, Lloyd at Oxford came to the verge of formulating a marginal utility theory of value (see Seligman, *op. cit.,* pp. 87–95). Lloyd's *Lecture on the Notion of Value* was as neglected as Longfield's book despite the fact that E. G. Wakefield quoted from it in his well-known edition of *The Wealth of Nations* (London, 1835), *1,* 64. Although Lloyd, like Senior, stated the principle of diminishing marginal utility, he did not apply it to any economic problem. Longfield, on the other hand, who did discuss exchange in terms of utility, did not develop the principle of diminishing marginal utility. See G. J. Stigler, "The Development of Utility Theory," *Journal of Political Economy,* August 1950, p. 313.

65. *Lectures,* pp. 116–57.

66. *Ibid.,* p. 196.

rate and, hence, result in lowering the rate of profit. The rate of profit is, in short, determined by "that portion of capital which is employed with the least efficiency, which I shall call the last portion of capital brought into operation." As a principal reason for the diminishing incremental product, Longfield cites the deterioration in the quality of the labor using the additional instruments which, though a sufficient, is not a necessary cause of the diminishing marginal productivity of capital. Then, confusing physical productivity with value productivity, he noted that the rate of profit must fall because the additional quantity produced must be sold at lower prices, while the new machinery employed must rise in price "in order to find employment for all the increased capital." [67] Having explained profit and rent by the principle of diminishing marginal productivity, he left wages to be accounted for as a residual.[68]

Surprisingly enough, in the *Lectures* Longfield defends Ricardo's dictum that wages vary inversely with profits (pp. 172–7), defends it in fact against Torrens' criticism and McCulloch's "misapprehension." Furthermore, he states it correctly as depending for its validity on Ricardo's invariable measure:

> The rate of profits depends upon the proportion which exists between the advance made by the capitalist, and the return which he receives, and the length of time for which that advance is made. For the sake of simplicity, let us suppose that all advances are made at the same interval, say, a year, from the time of sale . . . Let us also suppose that this advance is always made in the form of wages paid to the labourer, and it will follow, that the rate of profit depends upon the proportion in which the value of any commodity is divided between the labourer and the capitalist. . . . This proposition may be considered useless or untrue, as depending upon false suppositions. It is, however, true in those cases in which it does apply, and all other cases may, with a little care be reduced to them. And such reduction must be made, whenever we resort to labour as a common measure for comparing the values of commodities [pp. 170–1; also pp. 266–7].

But Longfield did not support the corollary of the Ricardian theorem, namely, that profit depend upon the productivity of labor in agriculture: "I have come to the very contrary conclusion that the decreas-

67. *Ibid.*, pp. 194, 197. Longfield assumes that capital is fully employed: in explaining why he confined his analysis to interest on fixed capital, he observed: "I conceived that its profits admitted more readily of a comparison with labour, being regulated by that portion which the necessity of employing all the capital within the country compels to be the least efficiently employed" (p. 198).

68. See above, Ch. 6, sec. 6. See also Douglas, *op. cit.*, pp. 32–4.

ing fertility has scarcely any direct effect upon the rate of profits, and that it exercises only a remote influence, if any, by its effect in retarding the increase of population" (p. 183). There follows a series of doctrinal revisions: The opposition between the tendency toward diminishing returns and the constant introduction of improvements in agriculture keep the price of corn "nearly stationary"; the laborer "will gain more by the diminished price of all other articles, than he will lose by the dearness of food and all raw materials"; rents tend to rise with the growth of population but the number of landholders increases proportionately, leaving "the relative situation of the classes . . . as before" (pp. 224–5, 238–9). In particular, there is no ground for pessimism in the tendency for the rate of profit to decline: the declining yield of investment, by rendering "the future and the present period of nearly equal importance in pecuniary speculation," will open up a whole series of long-term investments which previously were not profitable (pp. 230–1).

Longfield, Lloyd, and Senior may have kept "the torch of demand theory burning," as Jevons put it, but the subjective theory of value failed to advance after the publication of Senior's *Political Economy.* Thomas Banfield, lecturing at Cambridge in 1844 on the views of the continental economists, such as Rossi, Hermann, von Thünen, and Rau, boldly pronounced that "M. de Rossi's assertion, that value is essentially *subjective,* or conferred by the estimating party rather than an inherent quality in the object valued, causes a total revolution in economical science. It makes the wants, the tastes and the feelings of men the standard of value, whose exponent is then to be sought in the extent to which an object is consumed." [69] But Banfield's lectures failed to live up to their promise and, apart from a definition of the graduated scale of wants "according to which we have to economize," they lacked any systematic exposition of ideas. A protectionist by sentiment, Banfield spoke sharply against Ricardo's theories; [70] Jones and Senior were almost the only British writers whom he quoted with any approval. The lectures disappeared in the maelstrom of the corn laws debate, and the "total revolution in economic science" did not materialize until twenty-five years later.

69. *The Organization of Industry,* p. v.

70. Banfield's hostility to Ricardo is revealed by the title of one of his pamphlets: *Six Letters to Sir Robert Peel, Being an Attempt to Expose the Dangerous Tendency of the Theory of Rent Advocated by Mr. Ricardo and by the Followers of His School* (London, 1843).

5. Robert Torrens' Volte-Face

The year of Senior's treatise also saw the publication of an article on methodology by John Stuart Mill which remained for decades the classic statement of the nature and postulates of economic science. Political economy, it was Mill's opinion, is an abstract science employing the a priori method. It is concerned with man "solely as a being who desires to possess wealth, and who is capable of judging the comparative efficacy of means for obtaining that end." But the method a priori, presupposing "an arbitrary definition of man," is not a mode of reasoning entirely disassociated from experience. It is distinguished from the method a posteriori, Mill observed, by not requiring any concrete experience of economic behavior to sustain its conclusions.[71]

Mill's essay was incorporated in his *System of Logic* (1843). Robert Torrens had no sooner digested Mill's views but he put out a new edition of *The Budget,* subtitled *On Commercial and Colonial Policy. With an Introduction in Which the Deductive Method, as Presented in Mr. Mill's System of Logic is Applied to the Solution of Some Controverted Questions in Political Economy.* Deserting his faith in the inductive method, Torrens came to reconsider his critical stand on the theories of Ricardo:

> In the works of that profound and original thinker, more than in those of any other writer of our times, Political Economy is presented as an abstract science. All his reasonings are hypothetical. His conclusions are necessary truths, . . . under the premises assumed, and enabling us, if we will make the necessary corrections for the difference between the hypothetical circumstances and the circumstances which actually exist, to arrive at conclusions practically true under all the varying conditions of society . . . The impression that his conclusions are at variance with facts . . . involves a misconception. His conclusions are in strict conformity with the facts which he assumes; and, modified by the proper corrections, on account of the difference between the assumed and the existing facts will be found to be in tried conformity with existing facts [p. xiii].

"Succeeding economists have controverted his leading doctrines," and "have fallen into the . . . pernicious fallacy of seizing upon some modifying circumstances, and applying it to disprove the abstract proposition." Torrens confessed to the same mistake in his earlier writ-

71. *London and Westminster Review.* October 1836; reprinted, with minor alterations, in *Essays on Some Unsettled Questions,* pp. 137–46.

ings but felt assured by the fact that he had erred in distinguished company. He invited others to adopt his own self-critical attitude (p. xxii). "Mr. Ricardo explained, and explained correctly," Torrens declared, "the laws which regulate rent, wages, and profits, *under the circumstances which he assumed.* In doing this he rendered important service to the science of Political Economy."

> Mr. Ricardo investigated the laws which determine the *proportions* according to which the produce is divided between the three classes . . . and for the convenience of measuring *proportions,* and of reasoning upon them, he invented an artificial or ideal money, in which he estimated rents, profits, and wages. This ideal or hypothetical money is an invariable quantity of gold, always produced by an invariable quantity of labour, to which wages only are advanced. If rent, profits, and wages, be estimated in this ideal money, there can be no rise of rents without a fall in the sum of wages and profits; and if rent be deducted, there can be no rise of profits without a fall of wages, and no fall of profits without a rise of wages [pp. xxii–xxiii].

But what Ricardo had demonstrated under certain assumptions his followers held to be true under all circumstances, contending that a rise of wages always causes a fall in prices and that the rate of profit can never increase without deteriorating "the condition of the labourer." Granting Ricardo's assumption, in which the whole of the capital advanced consists of wages, profits rise and fall in exact proportion with the cost of producing wage goods; but when machinery is employed (and here Torrens harks back to his own theory), the rate of profit is determined by the wages of "proximate" or indirect labor, that is, by the quantity of fixed capital employed.

Given the necessary modifications, however, the Ricardian dictum that profits vary with wages is still "demonstrably true" as an abstract proposition (p. xxxv). "Doctrines put forth in refutation of the principles of Ricardo," Torrens concluded, after a glance at the objections of Malthus, Jones, and Senior, "are not unfrequently mere extensions of these principles" (p. xxxviii).

One of the first of Ricardo's critics had traveled the full circle and was now ready, once more, to pay homage to the master.

CHAPTER 9

The Half-Way House of John Stuart Mill

> The moment you admit that one class of things, without reference to what they respectively cost, is better worth having than another; that a smaller commercial value, with one mode of distribution, is better than a greater commercial value with another mode of distribution, the whole of that curious fabric of postulates and dogmas, which you call the science of political economy, and which I call *politicoe oeconomicae inscientia,* tumbles into pieces.
>
> T. L. PEACOCK, *Crochet Castle* (1831)

1. MILL'S INTELLECTUAL SOURCES

SHORTLY after the appearance of the second edition of Ricardo's *Principles* James Mill decided to take his thirteen-year-old son through a complete course in political economy. "It was one of my father's main objects," wrote John Stuart Mill in later life, "to make me apply to Smith's more superficial view of political economy, the superior lights of Ricardo." [1] From that day on the young Mill never deserted his faith in "the superior light of Ricardo." Nevertheless, other influences were in time to transform his Ricardianism into a unique blend of all the antithetical intellectual currents of the age.

It was after his "mental breakdown" in 1826, when he steeped himself in Wordsworth and Coleridge, that Mill began to break away from his doctrinaire belief in Benthamism. At the same time he was rapidly becoming convinced of the validity of Saint-Simon's views. By 1830 he regarded himself as a "convert." But he refused to become personally involved in the movement. In the first place he prided himself on being an "independent thinker"; furthermore, he was convinced that the followers of Saint-Simon "have yet much to learn in political economy from the English economists." [2]

A reading of Comte's *Cours de philosophie positive* added force to Mill's reaction against his earlier views. To Comte he owed the ex-

1. *Autobiography,* p. 20.
2. J. S. Mill, "Unpublished Letters to Gustave d'Eichtal," *Cosmopolis,* May 1897, pp. 353, 356, 362. See also the introduction by F. A. Hayek to a reprint of Mill's *Spirit of the Age* (Chicago, 1942).

plicit introduction into economics of the difference between static and dynamic analysis and, more important still, the distinction between the immutable laws of production constituting "physical truths" and the provisional laws of distribution referring to "human institutions" and "the laws and customs of society." [3] The latter distinction became one of the chief props of Mill's intellectual system; with its aid he was able to defend the substance of Ricardo's system as bearing upon questions of productive "efficiency" while denying most of its traditional implications for matters pertaining to distributive "equity."

The idea that propositions about the size of the "cake" were of a different order from those referring to its "slices" was not original with Comte or with Mill. Whately and Senior had employed it earlier as a general principle, separating the analysis of "universal economic truths" from the discussion of issues in which value judgments are involved. For them it implied a restriction of the scientific province of economics. The attention of the economist, Whately had argued, should be directed to the means by which wealth may be preserved or increased: "to inquire how far wealth is *desirable,* is to go out of his proper province." If such an inquiry is made at all, Whately added, it should be "so introduced as not to lose sight of the circumstance that it *is* a digression." [4] Mill did not disagree with this methodological position,[5] but in his view it was precisely the digressions of "welfare economics" which gave importance to the science of political economy. The types of problems involving competing social ends, which Senior wanted to excise as forming no part of "the business of a Political Economist," [6] were of the deepest concern to Mill. As he confessed in a letter to a friend: "I regard the purely abstract investigations of political economy . . . as of very minor importance compared with the great practical questions which the progress of democracy and the spread of socialist opinions are pressing on." [7]

With respect to the purely abstract questions of political economy, however, Mill was not simply Ricardo's echo, as is so often suggested.

3. For a discussion of Comte's influence on Mill, see I. W. Mueller, *John Stuart Mill and French Thought* (Urbana, Ill., 1956), ch. 4.

4. *Introductory Lecture on Political Economy,* pp. 20, 22. This is why Whately rejected the name "political economy" as conveying "no clear idea of the science denoted by it" and suggested instead "catallactics" or the "science of exchange."

5. See, for example, Mill's reply to an attack on Whately's position: *The Examiner,* Jan. 30, 1831, p. 68.

6. Such as: "To what extent and under what circumstances the possession of Wealth is, on the whole, beneficial or injurious to its possessor, or to the society of which he is a member? What distribution of Wealth is most desirable in each different state of society? and What are the means by which any given Country can facilitate such a distribution?" (*Political Economy,* p. 2).

7. *The Letters of J. S. Mill, 1,* 169–70.

On a number of points he was certainly original; moreover, he was the only disciple of Ricardo to make any significant improvements in the doctrine.[8] Nor did he ignore the theoretical innovations of Ricardo's critics. Indeed, few economists in the period were as well acquainted with the literature of English political economy. From Bailey and from Senior Mill derived the abstinence theory of profit, the generalization of the rent concept, and the classification of types of "imperfect competition." Jones' *Essay* was responsible for the chapters in Mill's *Principles* on the effects of different systems of land tenure. The treatment of value theory owes a debt to de Quincey's *Logic of Political Economy* (1844), while the analysis of the factors governing the propensity to save stems largely from John Rae's *New Principles of Political Economy* (1834).[9] To be sure, Mill had read none of the better continental economists. But it is difficult to understand how it could be asserted that "since . . . 1829, he had read virtually no economics at all. His utter failure to take any account of the advances that had been made in the intervening twenty years, had the effect of retarding the development of the science for an entire generation." [10]

As Mill conceived it his task was to incorporate the new ideas in the traditional body of Ricardian doctrine, or, at any rate, to reformulate the Ricardian system so as to anticipate the major objections of Ricardo's critics. In attempting this, he only succeeded in upholding an emasculated version of Ricardo's system while yielding to the anti-Ricardians on a number of crucial analytical questions. If we ask why, under these circumstances, Mill defended Ricardo at all, we do not need to resort to intellectual inertia as the sole explanation. Ricardo's system was eminently suited to Mill's central purpose, that of providing a rationale for a program of land reform and income redistribution. And in the final analysis, Mill was less interested in "the principles of political economy" than in "their applications to social philosophy." This goes a long way toward accounting for that eclecticism which is the outstanding feature of Mill's *Principles.*

8. Mill's contribution to the theory of international values is well known. Professor Stigler has drawn attention to several other original contributions by Mill: (1) the idea of noncompeting groups; (2) the analysis of the problem of joint products; (3) the concept of opportunity costs; (4) the treatment of economies of scale of the firm; (5) the correct statement of the "law of supply and demand"; and (6) the clarification of the meaning of Say's Law (Stigler, "The Nature and Role of Originality in Scientific Progress," *Economica,* November 1955).

9. There are other references in Mill's *Principles* to Rae's treatment of taxation and the division of labor. But there is no basis for the extravagant claim of Rae's modern editor that "it was Rae, more than any other, who modified the Ricardian basis of Mill's thought" (John Rae, *The Sociological Theory of Capital,* ed. C. W. Mixter [New York, 1905], p. xxxii).

10. Packe, *op. cit.,* p. 310.

2. Harmony or Disharmony of Interests?

John Stuart Mill's intellectual position may be brought into sharper focus by contrasting it with the social outlook of Ricardo's other disciples. From the beginning the "new" school of political economy had contained, as it were, a left wing and a right wing, represented respectively by James Mill and McCulloch. McCulloch did not subscribe to radicalism in politics,[11] nor did he share the enthusiasm of the utilitarians for land reform. In his *Elements* James Mill had coined the argument that any future increments of rental values could be taxed away to defray the expenses of government without affecting "the industry of the country" (pp. 248–55). McCulloch attacked this thesis in an article on "Taxation" for the 1824 Supplement of the *Encyclopaedia Britannica* [12] and, moreover, took strong exceptions to Mill's general hostile attitude toward the landed aristocracy. McCulloch favored primogeniture and the entailing of estates on the grounds that large holdings promoted efficiency of cultivation and served to maintain a scale of expenditures among the landed gentry which acted as an economic stimulus to other classes.[13] Some of McCulloch's strongest language was reserved for the liberal French law of succession and the system of peasant proprietorship that flourished on the Continent. "A powerful and widely ramified aristocracy, like that of England, not resting for support on any oppressive laws, and enjoying no privileges but which are for the public advantage," he insisted, "is necessary to give stability and security to the government and freedom to the people." [14]

Ricardo and James Mill were quite prepared to face the fact of a conflict of interests among the classes of society; McCulloch, however, was always disposed to emphasize the harmonious character of the economic universe.[15] Ricardo himself had taken McCulloch to task in 1824 for declaring that "where industry is free, the interest of the individual can never be opposed to the interests of the public." "In the case of machinery," Ricardo pointed out, "the interests of master and workmen are frequently opposed. Are the interests of the landlords

11. See McCulloch's opinion of James Mill's political views: Napier, *Selected Correspondence*, p. 39.

12. Ricardo likewise disapproved of Mill's plan. See above, Ch. 3, sec. 2.

13. *Edinburgh Review*, July 1824, p. 374. See also McCulloch's *Principles* (2d ed., 1830), pp. 257–61. McCulloch's argument here is almost identical to that in Malthus' *Principles* (pp. 380–1).

14. J. R. McCulloch, *A Treatise on the Succession to Property Vacant by Death* (London, 1848), p. 172.

15. See Halévy, *The Growth of Philosophical Radicalism*, p. 356.

and those of the public always the same? I am sure you will not say so" (9, 194). But McCulloch was not convinced. In the second edition of his *Principles* (pp. 452 ff.) he criticized Ricardo's treatment of technological progress in agriculture from the standpoint of harmony doctrine. And in the *Edinburgh Review* he wrote: "In treating of rent, Mr. Ricardo doubtless made discoveries . . . still, however, it is not to be denied that this part of his work is infected with grave errors. He supposed that the effect of improvements, which are so beneficial to every other class, was to reduce rent, and that, consequently, the interest of the landlord was opposed to that of the rest of the community." [16] After the repeal of the corn laws McCulloch was pleased to observe: "It can no longer be said that the price of food is enhanced by our legislation; and the interests of all classes of producers are now admitted, on all hands, to be as they always have been, identical . . . The more, indeed, that these matters are inquired into, the more clearly it will appear that there is not at bottom any real opposition between the interests of the owners of land and those of the other classes." [17]

The same apologetic strain makes itself felt in a work by another "faithful" disciple of Ricardo, *The Logic of Political-Economy* by Thomas de Quincey. Like Jones and Scrope, de Quincey expressed alarm at the growth of a class of "systematic enemies of property" who found comfort in the disharmonious implications of Ricardo's system:

> It happens that in no instance has the policy of gloomy disorganising Jacobinism . . . received any essential aid from science, excepting in this one painful corollary from Ricardo's triad of chapters on Rent, Profit and Wages . . . Separate, the doctrine of rent offers little encouragement to the anarchist; it is in connexion with other views that it ripens into an instrument of mischief the most incendiary . . . The class of landlords, they urge, . . . prosper, not pending the ruin, not in spite of the ruin, but *by* the ruin of the fraternal classes associated with themselves on the land [pp. 250–1].

These considerations did not weigh heavily with John Stuart Mill. On the contrary, throughout the *Principles* he lost no opportunity to accentuate those aspects of Ricardo's system which seemed to affirm the divergence of interests between the landed and industrial classes of the community.

> The ordinary progress of a society which increases in wealth is at all times tending to augment the incomes of landlords; to give them both a greater amount and a greater proportion of the

16. *Edinburgh Review,* September 1831, p. 97.
17. *Notes on The Wealth of Nations* (3d ed., 1849), p. 524.

> wealth of the community, independently of any trouble or outlay incurred by themselves. They grow richer, as it were in their sleep, without working, risking, or economizing. What claims have they, on the general principle of social justice, to this accession of riches? In what would they have been wronged if society had, from the beginning, reserved the right of taxing the spontaneous increase of rent, to the highest amount required by financial exigencies [p. 818].

Ever since the late 1830's Mill had been an ardent supporter of peasant proprietorship as the solution to Ireland's economic ills.[18] The validity of the scheme depended on the alleged efficiency of small-scale peasant farming. Hence Mill was anxious to defend the Ricardian proposition that "the interest of the landlord is decidedly hostile to the sudden and general introduction of agricultural improvements."[19] This despite his admission elsewhere that a strong impulse toward improvements in methods had become manifest in British agriculture "during the last fifteen or twenty years."[20]

The assertion that landlords "grow richer, as it were in their sleep" was the basis of the proposal to tax the "unearned increment" and of the scheme for breaking up the larger estates by means of the abolition of primogeniture.[21] In addition, Mill's *Principles* called for severe restrictions on the power of bequest: inheritance was to be limited to living heirs only and was not to exceed a sum adequate to finance their education (pp. 223–4, 897). Characteristically, Mill opposed a progressive income tax because "it is not the fortunes which are earned, but those which are unearned, that it is for the public good to place under limitation" (p. 808). But he strongly recommended progressive death duties in order to reduce inequalities in the distribution of income (p. 809).

With respect to measures for economic reform, Mill had traveled far beyond Ricardo and, indeed, all economists of his generation. There was no doubt about Mill's intentions. He fully expected to be severely censured for his legislative proposals on inheritable wealth. As Alexander Bain recollected: "What I remember most vividly of his talk pending the publication of the work, was his anticipating a tremendous outcry about his doctrines on Property. He frequently spoke of his pro-

18. See R. D. Collison Black, "The Classical Economists and the Irish Problem," *Oxford Economic Papers,* March 1953.

19. *Principles,* p. 718; also pp. 231–2.

20. *Ibid.,* p. 704.

21. *Ibid.,* pp. 817–19. In advocating these measures Mill made a point of refuting McCulloch's views on the inheritance of landed property (*ibid.,* pp. 891–3).

posals as to Inheritance and Bequest, which, if carried out, would pull down all large fortunes in two generations. To his surprise, however, this part of the book made no sensation."[22]

3. The Theory of Value

The order of presentation of subject matter in Mill's *Principles* is modeled on his father's *Elements* rather than on Ricardo's *Principles:* first Mill deals with the factors governing the volume of total output, considered as strictly technological in character,[23] then with the distribution of income, and only thereafter with the theory of exchange. We will ignore Mill's arrangement, however, and take up the theory of value before proceeding to the laws of production and distribution.

Like Ricardo, Mill in his *Principles* simplifies the treatment of value by "getting rid of rent." But he refines Ricardo's theory by taking into account the competing uses of agricultural land for purposes of mining, fisheries, and residence, cases in which rent *is* an expense of production which affects price (pp. 473–6). The principle of marginal costs is generalized to apply to manufacturing as well as to agriculture; hence both ground rent and "extra profit analogous to rent" are simply "the price paid for a differential advantage in producing a commodity" which "cannot enter into the general cost of production of the commodity" (pp. 476–7).

In his *Essays on Some Unsettled Questions* Mill had defended the Ricardian theorem of the inverse relationship of wages and profits as a proposition about per unit wages. Whereas gross profits vary with the magnitude of total output and the size of the wages bill, the rate of profit depends upon "the proportional wages of one labourer: that is, the ratio between the wages of one labourer and (not the whole produce of the country, but) the amount of what one labourer can produce" (p. 97).[24] In this sense, a "high-wage economy" does not contradict Ricardo's doctrine because "an increase of the labourer's real comfort was not considered by him as a rise of wages. In his language wages were only said to rise when they rose not in mere quantity but in value." Mill concluded the analysis by saying that the Ricardian theorem, restated to read, "the rate of profits varies inversely as the cost of production of wages," remains "strictly true . . . for all cases" (p. 103).

22. A. Bain, *John Stuart Mill* (London, 1882), p. 89.

23. Although Bk. I is supposed to be concerned solely with the "physical laws" of production the discussion is frequently tied to the institutional setting in which economic activity takes place (see, for example, Bk. I, chs. 7, 11).

24. This is a misleading interpretation of Ricardo's proposition (see above, Ch. 1, sec. 4).

This argument is carried over to the *Principles* without substantial change. None of McCulloch's or James Mill's hesitations [25] are permitted to cast doubt upon Ricardo's dictum: "Instead of saying that profits depend on wages, let us say (what Ricardo really meant) that they depend on the *cost of labour*" (p. 419). The "cost of labour" is alleged to be a function of the efficiency of labor, the rate of money wages, and the price of wage goods. "These . . . are also the circumstances which determine the rate of profit; and it cannot be in any way affected except through one or other of them." [26] This has nothing to do with the so-called opposition between capital and labor or their inability to prosper except at each other's expense:

> Diminished wages, when representing a really diminished Cost of Labour, are equivalent to a rise of profits. But the opposition of pecuniary interests thus indicated . . . is to a great extent only apparent. Real wages are a very different thing from the Cost of Labour, and are generally highest at the times and places where, from the easy terms on which the land yields all the produce as yet required from it, the value and price of food being low, the cost of labour to the employer, notwithstanding its ample remuneration, is comparatively cheap, and the rate of profit consequently high, as at present in the United States.[27]

What has this to do with the theory of value? Simply this: Mill does not derive the theorem about profits and wages, as Ricardo had done, from the concept of an invariable measure of value. Even the standard Ricardian thesis that "general wages, whether high or low, do not affect values" is entirely divorced from the notion that value is to be measured by an invariant yardstick.[28] Furthermore, the chapter in Mill's *Principles* which offers a "Summary of the Theory of Value"

25. See above, Ch. 3, sec. 4.

26. J. S. Mill, *Principles*, p. 420; also pp. 681–2.

27. *Ibid.*, p. 693. As late as 1864 Mill was still worried about the wages-profits theorem. Writing to Cairnes he inquired: "Have you formed any opinion or can you refer me to a good authority, respecting the ordinary rate of mercantile and manufacturing profit in the United States? I have hitherto been under the impression that it is much higher than in England because the rate of interest is so. But I have lately been led to doubt the truth of this impression, because it seems inconsistent with known facts respecting wages in America. High profits are compatible with a high reward to the labourers through low prices of necessaries, but they are not compatible with a high cost of labour; and it seems to me that the very high *money* wages of labour in America, the precious metals not being of lower value there than in Europe, indicates a high cost as well as a high remuneration of labour" (quoted by G. O'Brien, "J. S. Mill and J. E. Cairnes," *Economica*, November 1943).

28. *Principles*, pp. 460–6.

does not even mention the question of a measuring rod. But after having disposed of the theory of money, Mill does devote a brief chapter to the "Measure of Value": "It is necessary . . . to touch upon the subject, if only to show how little there is to be said on it" (pp. 564–8). True to the tradition established by Bailey, Mill rejects the possibility of a measure of the purchasing power "of the same thing at different times and places"; the idea of solving the difficulty by an index number of prices is not even contemplated. Mill goes on to argue that "a measure of exchange value, therefore, being impossible, writers have formed a notion of something, under the name of a measure of value, which would be more properly termed a measure of cost of production." Without mentioning Ricardo by name, he proceeds to delineate the meaning of Ricardo's yardstick concluding that "a measure of cost, though perfectly conceivable, can no more exist in fact, than a measure of exchange value." There is no mention in Mill's discussion, however, of the important role assigned to the invariable measure of value in Ricardo's system. The little that Mill has to say on this score is interesting, however. Noting the difference between a labor-commanded and a labor-embodied theory of value, he declares that "to confound these two ideas, would be much the same thing as to overlook the distinction between the thermometer and the fire." The concept of "a measure of cost of production" for purposes of social accounting is distinguished from a labor cost theory of value dealing with relative prices: "The idea of a Measure of Value must not be confounded with the idea of the regulator, or determining principle of value. When it is said by Ricardo and others, that the value of a thing is regulated by quantity of labour, they . . . mean . . . the quantity required for producing it. This, they mean to affirm determines its value; causes it to be of the value it is, and no other."

The trouble with Mill's analysis is that cost value is nowhere clearly separated from exchange value. The scant attention paid to the invariable measure of value is the result of Mill's insistence on the essential relativity of the term "value": "The value of a commodity is not a name for an inherent and substantive quality of the thing itself, but means the quantity of other things which can be obtained in exchange for it," and "there is no such thing as a general rise or a general fall of values." [29] Careful reading of the text shows conclusively that Mill repudiates the concept of cost value, enshrined in Ricardo's contrast between value and riches: "Absolute wages paid have no effect upon values . . . neither has the absolute quantity of labour . . . If, for instance, the general efficiency of all labour were increased, so that all things without exception could be produced in the same quantity

29. *Ibid.*, p. 459–68; also pp. 437–8.

as before with a smaller amount of labour, no trace of this general diminution of cost of production would show itself in the value of commodities" (p. 461). No effort is made to show how all this differs from Ricardo's treatment. Mill does not doubt that labor is the principal cost factor, "so much the principal as to be nearly the sole";[30] but the emphasis which he places on differences in costs due to natural scarcities and special immobilities in the supply of productive factors (see pp. 442–5) indicate adherence to the "anemic" version of the labor theory of value, which is satisfied with stressing the long-run importance of relative labor costs. All this may be good economic theory but it is poor discipleship. The result of Mill's treatment was to perpetuate the confusion endemic in the traditional statements of the Ricardian theory of value; one might read straight through the commentaries of McCulloch and both Mills and yet never be quite sure as to the exact meaning and significance of the labor theory of value.[31]

Mill's theory of profit follows in Senior's footsteps. Although unable wholly to divest himself of the suggestion of an exploitation theory,[32] Mill reduced gross profits to a reward for abstinence (measured by the market rate of interest on "the best security"), an indemnity for risk, and the wages of superintendence (p. 406). Interest, as a reward for abstinence, is governed by "the comparative value placed, in the given society, upon the present and the future" (p. 407). Mill defined abstinence as "forbearing to consume capital" without noticing that Senior had something else in mind, namely, to augment savings by refraining from present consumption (see pp. 70, 201–2). For Mill interest is a payment that prevents the depletion of capital; for Senior it is a reward for a sacrifice incurred in creating new capital. Mill recognized that "the savings by which an addition is made to the national capital usually emanate from the desire of persons to improve what is termed their conditions of life, or to make a provision for children or others, independent of their exertions," that is, by persons who undervalue the present rather than the future.[33] Nevertheless, he thought, there is a rate of interest "below which persons in general

30. *Ibid.*, p. 457; also pp. 479–80.

31. See above, Ch. 1, sec. 5.

32. "The cause of profit is, that labour produces more than is required for its support . . . the reason why capital yields a profit, is because food, clothing, materials, and tools, last longer than the time which was required to produce them; so that if a capitalist supplies a party of labourers with these things, on condition of receiving all they produce, they will, in addition to reproducing their own necessaries and instruments, have a portion of their time remaining, to work for the capitalist" (*Principles*, pp. 416–17; also pp. 163–4).

33. *Ibid.*, p. 729. And, like Marshall, Mill thought that there was a historical tendency for men to "become more willing to sacrifice present indulgence for future objects" (p. 730).

will not find sufficient motive to save," and this rate is conceived of as an average, not a marginal, reward for the sacrifice of saving based upon a relative equality of provident and improvident individuals (p. 729). In the sense that Mill's argument allows for a savers' surplus it marks a slight advance over Senior's formulation of the doctrine.

The upshot of the matter is that value is governed by money costs of production which, in the ultimate analysis, represent payments for the sum of disutilities incurred in the form of labor and abstinence. In other words, Mill's theory of value is really no different from Senior's and both are closely linked to Marshall's "real-cost" theory. It is only Mill's orthodox manner of expression which obscures his virtual rejection of the Ricardian theory of value.

4. Productive and Unproductive Consumption

The leitmotif of the first section of Mill's *Principles,* dealing with the laws of production, is the distinction between "productive labour" paid out of business capital and "unproductive labour" bought and consumed by households. Even in the *Essays on some Unsettled Questions* Mill had shown a strong desire to renovate Smith's doctrine which had all but disappeared from the literature of economics after a half-century of criticism. In a sense, Mill acted on sound instinct; the distinction between productive and unproductive labor had in fact remained an implicit feature of classical economics.[34] Although the terms "productive labour" and "unproductive labour" were discarded, the concept of wealth-creating employments reappeared in the guise of a distinction between productive and unproductive consumption. Its purpose was the same: to divide those investments which make a direct contribution to the growth of the total physical product from that class of expenditures which go to finance the incidental functions of marketing, defense, and other social services; incidental, that is, to the maximum growth of total output.[35] "In whatever manner political economists may have settled the definition of productive and unproductive labor or consumption," John Stuart Mill remarked, "the consequences which they have drawn from the definition are nearly all the same." [36]

34. See Schumpeter, *op. cit.*, pp. 628–31, and above, Ch. 5, sec. 2.

35. The word "incidental" is of course question-begging: there seems to be no short way of conveying the sense of the distinction. Despite the unhappy history of the classical doctrine of productive labor, a case can be made for it as a crude approach to the question of investment criteria in underdeveloped economies. But Adam Smith's terminology was ill suited to the purpose and the theory soon degenerated into a squabble about where to draw the line.

36. Mill, *Essay on Some Unsettled Questions,* p. 82.

Ricardo, for example, had agreed that wealth may be increased either by making present labor more productive or "by employing a greater portion of revenue in the maintenance of productive labour" (*1*, 278).[37] McCulloch, on the other hand, joined Lauderdale and Say in repudiating the distinction between productive and unproductive labor. Yet he defined consumption as productive "if it occasions, whether directly or indirectly, the production of the same or of a greater quantity of equally valuable products, and unproductive if it does not have that effect." [38] James Mill treated the accumulation of capital as a function of the volume of productive consumption and remarked that "whatever is unproductively consumed . . . is a diminution of the property, both of the individual and the community." [39] Even Senior, who dismissed "Adam Smith's well known division of labour into productive and unproductive" as a mere matter of nomenclature, made use of the concept of productive consumption, traditionally defined.[40] In short, productive consumption was always regarded as a means to an end, unproductive consumption as an end in itself, equivalent to a squandering of resources. The rate of economic growth was viewed as dependent solely upon the volume and efficiency of productive labor engaged in industry and agriculture. Unproductive labor or unproductive consumption, much as it added to "the sum of enjoyments," was thought to make no contribution whatever to the expansion of output.[41]

John Stuart Mill, therefore, was merely verbalizing a theory which in its broad outlines commanded general assent. This is not to say that he managed to overcome all the classic objections which had been advanced against Adam Smith's presentation of the doctrine. He did, however, stress the fact that the issue turns upon "the permanence rather than the materiality of the product"; by permanence he meant storability. But, he argued, insofar as the tacit reference to material goods in the concept of "wealth" is sanctioned by traditional usage,

37. Cannan is clearly mistaken when he asserts that Ricardo was "quite silent" on the doctrine of productive labor (*Theories of Production and Distribution*, p. 21).

38. McCulloch, *Principles*, pp. 391, 403–16. See also E. Whittaker, *A History of Economic Ideas* (New York, 1940), pp. 364–6.

39. *Elements*, p. 222. Malthus felt that "both Mr. Ricardo and Mr. Mill . . . fully allow the distinction between productive and unproductive labour" (*Definitions in Political Economy*, p. 92 n.).

40. *Political Economy*, pp. 51–7.

41. Malthus' attitude here was a rather special one. He agreed that unproductive consumption as such was "wasteful." Nevertheless, expenditures on luxury goods served to sustain demand for the output of manufacturing industry. Much as we today might regard spending on armaments as "unproductive" and yet stimulating to economic activity as a whole.

productive labor can be defined as labor employed in the production of "utilities embodied in material objects" (p. 48). The only productive consumers are productive laborers, "the labour of direction being of course included, as well as that of execution"; productive laborers may, however, purchase "luxuries" and so consume unproductively (pp. 51–2). Mill refused to admit that the term "unproductive labour" implied any sense of ethical disapproval, as Say and McCulloch had charged: It is "a great error to regret the large proportion of the annual produce, which in opulent countries goes to supply unproductive consumption." But he could not refrain from adding: "The things to be regretted, and which are not incapable of being remedied, are the prodigious inequality with which this surplus is distributed, the little worth of the objects to which the greater part of it is devoted, and the large share which falls to the lot of persons who render no equivalent service in return" (p. 53).

The object of Mill's discussion was to provide him with a handle to attack the Malthusian heresy that the spending of unproductive consumers could be conducive, and even indispensable, to the growth of national wealth. During the Napoleonic Wars, Mill observed, the income withdrawn by government loans for unproductive war expenditures should have reduced the annual product by restricting the volume of private investment. Surprisingly enough, the war period was actually one of unbounded prosperity which witnessed the rapid expansion of total output. The artificial boom gave rise to a multitude of "unfounded theories in political economy . . . almost all tending to exalt unproductive expenditure, at the expense of productive" (p. 76). We recall that Ricardo had attacked Blake for insisting upon the stimulating effects of war expenditures, an attack in which John Stuart Mill himself had joined.[42] But now Mill was at last prepared to admit the income-generating effects of public spending. In rich countries with low rates of interest, he argued, the income siphoned off by the government in wartime rarely takes the form of levies on productive investment, drawing instead on funds which otherwise would have been exported to the colonies or expended by the wealthy classes on luxury goods.[43] In this sense, the government can "create capital," and fiscal policy is capable of exerting a positive influence on the level of economic activity.[44]

42. See above, Ch. 4, sec. 3.

43. *Principles,* p. 78; also pp. 740–2.

44. McCulloch seems to have arrived at similar views but along a different path. "McCulloch gave us an episode in his own peculiar and paradoxical manner," wrote Mallet in 1835, "maintaining that wars had always been a source of increased wealth to this country. He held the debt to be a mere transference of income from one pocket to another and made very light of it—as did most of the speakers . . .

Nevertheless, Mill was unable to shed the notion that involuntary unemployment is somehow impossible. "If there are human beings capable of work," he observed, in his *Principles,* "they may always be employed producing something" (p. 66). In complete contradiction to his previous analysis of war expenditures he remarked, in a footnote, upon the fact that government revenues during the Napoleonic Wars were derived from taxes on circulating capital, at the expense of the wages of the civilian labor force: "England employed comparatively few additional soldiers and sailors of her own, while she diverted hundreds of millions of capital from productive employment, to supply munitions of war and support armies for her Continental allies. Consequently, . . . her labourers suffered, her capitalist prospered, and her permanent productive resources did not fall off" (p. 77 n.). And while admitting, as we have seen, that some domestic capital is unable to find investment outlets at home, he was yet able to assert with reference to the passage of the Corn Law of 1815: "Had legislators been aware that industry is limited by capital, they would have seen that, the aggregate capital of the country not having been increased, any portion of it which they by their laws had caused to be embarked in the newly-acquired branch of industry must have been withdrawn or withheld from some other; in which it gave, or would have given, employment to probably about the same quantity of labour which it employs in its new occupation" (p. 64).

The same kind of confusion is at the back of Mill's celebrated proposition: "Demand for commodities is not demand for labour" (p. 79). This dictum is supposed to emphasize the fallacy of the doctrine that "the unproductive expenditure of the rich is necessary to the employment of the poor." Since the decision as to whether the proceeds of sales will be used to reconstitute the wages fund rests with the capitalist, demand for commodities is not *necessarily* demand for labor. The effect upon employment from a rise in demand depends upon the technical structure of production and the inducement to invest. It is a perfectly familiar classical argument [45] even though, as Mill said, "I can hardly point to any except Mr. Ricardo and M. de Say who kept it constantly and steadily in view." Nevertheless, Mill's comments on the proposition are fraught with misunderstanding because (among other things) it is never made clear whether it is supposed to hold regardless

he held that the pressure of taxation was the greatest of all incentives to industry, and during a war, when taxes come pelting in, it stimulates the industrious man to greater and greater exertions; so that 20 years of war were more likely, according to his view, to benefit the country and add to its wealth, than 20 years of peace" (*Political Economy Club,* pp. 270–1; also p. 226).

45. See the discussion between A. C. Pigou and H. G. Johnson, *Economic Journal,* June 1949 and December 1949.

of the existence of unemployed resources. If all resources are fully employed, demand for commodities is not demand for labor: an increased demand for consumers' goods means a decrease in investment, hence a decline in the amount of employment demanded at any given wage rate.[46] Moreover, Mill's proposition recalls Ricardo's argument that the individual consumer can influence the demand for labor by substituting the purchase of direct labor services for commodities of personal consumption. Such a redistribution of expenditures would clearly have no effect on the volume of employment if labor were already fully employed. Ricardo was perfectly aware of this,[47] but Mill seems hardly to have realized its importance: If some labor is unemployed, he should have said, "demand for commodities *is* demand for labour."

It is interesting to note that Senior commits the same error in his discussion of "Mr. Ricardo's theory," namely, that "it is more beneficial to the labouring classes to be employed in the production of services than in the production of commodities." [48] Now this statement already distorts the meaning of Ricardo's doctrine, which is concerned solely with an alternative between direct and indirect employment of *un*productive labor; but this is another matter. The important factor in Senior's as in Mill's analysis is the absence of any recognition that Ricardo assumed the existence of Marxian unemployment; the demand for soldiers and sailors during wartime, Senior declared, is not, as Ricardo has it, "an additional, it is merely a substituted demand." [49]

5. Secular Changes in Wages, Profits, and Rents

The law of diminishing returns, regarded as a law of dynamics uniquely operative in agriculture, was in Mill's opinion "the most important proposition in political economy. Were the law different, nearly all the phenomena of the production and distribution of wealth would be other than they are." [50] Taking a leaf from Senior's treatise Mill defined it as a self-evident axiom "in any given state of agricultural skill and knowledge," then qualified it by listing a number of checks or counteracting factors.

Like every other economist of his day, Mill time and again contrasted the tendency of agricultural prices to rise in the long run with "the natural effect of improvements to diminish gradually the real

46. See the commentary of F. A. Hayek, *The Pure Theory of Capital* (Chicago, 1941), App. III.

47. See above, Ch. 4, sec. 2.

48. *Political Economy*, p. 171.

49. *Ibid.*, p. 173.

50. *Principles*, p. 177.

prices of almost all manufactures." On the formal level, this amounts to what has been called "a bad mixture of a dubious 'law' of economic history on the one hand, and a truncated part of the static principle of combining proportions on the other." [51] More loosely interpreted, however, this was simply a way of pointing to the fact that the secular prospects of the economy depended upon the conflict between technological progress in industry and the diminishing productive powers of agriculture. Ricardo hesitated to ascribe a significant influence to cost-reducing innovations in manufacturing (sometimes he denied that it had any influence whatever) and never really made up his mind whether changes in the composition of wage goods might mitigate the effect of diminishing returns in agriculture. But Mill took a definite stand on these questions. Although he did not wish to follow Senior in asserting an inherent "law" of increasing returns in industry, he agreed that

> In manufactures . . . the causes tending to increase the productiveness of industry, preponderate greatly over the one cause which tends to diminish it [the increased costs of raw materials drawn from the land]: and the increase of production, called forth by the progress of society, take place, not at an increasing, but at a continually diminishing proportional cost.
>
> . . . .
>
> Manufactured articles, tend as society advances to fall in money price. The industrial history of modern nations, especially during the last hundred years, fully bears out this assertion.[52]

And it must not be imagined that this "tendency . . . to a perpetual increase of the productive power of labour in manufactures" does not seriously affect "the necessaries or indulgences which enter into the habitual consumption of the labouring class." "Seldom is a new branch of trade opened without, either directly or in some indirect way, causing some of the articles which the mass of the people consume to be either produced or imported at a smaller cost. It may be safely affirmed, therefore, that improvements in production generally tend to cheapen the commodities on which the wages of the labouring class are expended." [53] The tendency of improvements to cheapen wage goods is not, in actual fact, opposed by rising prices for agricultural products. Although the law of diminishing returns was said to be "the most important proposition in political economy," it had not been operative in agriculture since 1825 or thereabouts:

51. H. S. Ellis and W. Fellner, "External Economies and Diseconomies," *Readings in Price Theory* (London, 1953), p. 243.

52. *Principles*, pp. 185–6, 703; also pp. 444–5.

53. *Ibid.*, p. 715.

> During the twenty or thirty years last elapsed [1857], so rapid has been the extension of improved processes of agriculture, that even the land yields a greater produce in proportion to the labour employed; the average price of corn has become decidedly lower, even before the repeal of the corn laws had so materially lightened, for the time being, the pressure of population upon production.
>
> . . . . .
>
> There are times when a strong impulse sets in towards agricultural improvement. Such an impulse has shown itself in Great Britain during the last fifteen or twenty years [1848]. In England and Scotland agricultural skill has of late increased considerably faster than population, insomuch that food and other agricultural produce, notwithstanding the increase of people, can be grown at less cost than they were thirty years ago.[54]

Of course, Mill voiced the familiar contention that the operation of the law of diminishing returns would eventually result in a weakening of investment incentives and a rising share of income going to the landlord class, with laborers receiving higher money, but the same real, wages.[55] In other words, he subscribed to the Ricardian theory of distribution. Nevertheless, whenever he faced up to the evidence he found the Ricardian theory falsified in every respect.

Mill was aware that almost none of the predictions of the Ricardian system had been borne out by the train of events. In particular, he knew perfectly well that the corn laws had not succeeded in maintaining the price of corn or the rent of land. In the attempt to square these facts with the deductions of Ricardian theory, he sought to close the door against any possibility of disproof on empirical grounds.

> The difference between a country without corn laws, and a country which has long had corn laws, is not so much that the last has a high price or a larger rental, but that it has the same price and the same rental with a smaller aggregate capital and a smaller population. The imposition of corn laws raises rents, but retards that progress of accumulation which would in no long period have raised them fully as much. The repeal of corn laws tends to lower rents, but it unchains a force which in a progressive state of capital and population restores and even increases the former amount.[56]

54. *Ibid.*, pp. 193, 704. The first quotation was added in the fourth edition; the second quotation appeared in the first edition and was retained thereafter with appropriate changes in the words "during the last fifteen or twenty years."
55. See, for instance, *ibid.*, pp. 723–4.
56. *Ibid.*, pp. 849–50.

In other words, the corn laws did not really affect the *distribution* of income between "the three main classes of society"; neither could the repeal of the corn laws have any influence in the long run on the factor shares. Is it possible to conceive of anything more contrary to the tenor of Ricardian economics?

Yet this is but one comment among many, easily overlooked in a treatise of such bulk. Nassau Senior, at any rate, was more impressed by Mill's formal obeisance to the traditional Ricardian viewpoint. "We must dismiss Mr. Mill's exposition of the theory of Profit and of Rent," he wrote in the *Edinburgh Review,* "with the single remark that it does not differ materially from that of Ricardo." [57]

6. The Empirical Relevance of Ricardian Economics

To appreciate Mill's equivocal position, in which Ricardo's analytical system is defended while its predictive value is denied, we must retrace our steps to consider the factual material which had been accumulated in the years preceding the publication of Mill's *Principles.*

Much as Ricardo was addicted to "the abstract method," he had never objected, in principle, to the procedure of submitting "speculations" to "the test of fact." As he wrote in his *Reply to Mr. Bosanquet:* "I have long wished that those who refused their assent to principles which experience has appeared to sanction, would either state their own theory . . . or . . . would point out those facts which they considered at variance with that which, from the firmest conviction, I have espoused" (*3,* 160–1). Some of Ricardo's early critics did just that: they cited whatever data was available to show that diminishing returns had not yet set in even on the worst soil, that the average price of wheat had declined in the eighteenth century despite the rapid growth of population, and that rents and profits rose and fell together in contradiction to the conclusions of Ricardo's system.[58] But his method of approach commanded little attention. It was not until the late 1830's that economists began to be generally aware of adequate statistical information bearing upon economic questions.

57. *Edinburgh Review,* October 1848, p. 328. Most of the review is devoted to a discussion of Mill's methodological views; there is also a brief criticism of Mill's treatment of the law of diminishing returns, the doctrine of productive labor and the concept of the wages fund (*ibid.,* pp. 303, 308–14, 320–2).

58. See T. W. Buller, *A Reply to a Pamphlet by David Ricardo on Protection to Agriculture* (1822), pp. 17–19; J. Lowe, *The Present State of England* (1823), pp. 148–50; "The Opinions of the Late Mr. Ricardo and of Adam Smith on Some of the Leading Doctrines of Political Economy," *The Pamphleteer* (1824), *24,* 57–8.

Descriptive statistics had received official recognition as a separate branch of inquiry as early as 1832 with the addition of a statistical department to the Board of Trade. Within a year the British Association for the Advancement of Science formed a statistical section, and in the same year a statistical society was founded in Manchester and in London (later the Royal Statistical Society). Richard Jones and Charles Babbage were instrumental in launching the London society's *Quarterly Journal*, and by 1835 the "Index of Fellows" included Chadwick, Malthus, McCulloch, Merivale, Scrope, Senior, Tooke, and Torrens.[59]

The function of the new society, as announced in its prospectus, was to "procure, arrange and publish facts to illustrate the conditions and prospects of society"; members were cautioned, however, to observe the distinction between statistics and economics: "The Science of Statistics differs from Political Economy, because, although it has the same end in view, it does not discuss causes, nor reason upon probable effects; it seeks only to collect, arrange, and compare, that class of facts which alone can form the basis of correct conclusions with respect to social and political government." [60] But before long some members gave expression to the hope that "the study of Statistics will, ere long, rescue Political Economy from all the uncertainty in which it is now enveloped." [61] And, indeed, the tabulation and interpretation of the body of data gathered over years by government departments and royal commissions soon provided a means for testing a number of widely held economic propositions. George Porter's *Progress of the Nation* (1836), the first serious attempt at a statistical manual of the British economy, succeeded in framing a simple factual argument to invalidate the rule of historical diminishing returns in agriculture. From 1801 to 1831 the population of the United Kingdom had increased by nine million; yet "where the people are deprived of any considerable proportion of their accustomed supply of food, it is highly improbable that their number should increase." Since grain imports had never risen above the average annual figure of 500,000 quarters of wheat (only exceeding one million quarters in five separate years of deficient harvest), it followed that "a most important extension of agriculture must have taken place within the Kingdom." Moreover, while the number of families in Great Britain rose by 34 per cent between 1811 and 1831, the number of families employed in agriculture increased by only 7 per cent. "It is impossible . . . to arrive at any other conclusion," Porter wrote, "than that a larger amount of

59. *Annals of the Royal Statistical Society* (London, 1943), pp. 14–15.
60. *Quarterly Journal of the Statistical Society of London,* May 1838, pp. 1–3.
61. *Ibid.,* September 1838, p. 317.

produce has of late been continually drawn from a given portion of ground than was obtained in general at the beginning of the century"; although cultivation has been extended, "the produce of equal surfaces of ploughed land has increased in a still greater ratio." [62]

Much of this, of course, was still inspired guesswork; the available data on the yield of different classes of arable soil were too scanty to allow for any definite conclusions about the productivity of agriculture.[63] Porter himself despaired eventually at the lack of adequate statistical material; in an address before the Statistical Section of the British Association in 1839 he voiced the complaint that "to this day the public is without any authoritative document from which to know even the quantity of land under cultivation in any county of England." He went on to say that almost no information existed regarding "the productiveness of the soil" and "the proportion required for reproduction," and blamed the landed interests for obstructing statistical inquiries on the ground that the publication of the facts might damage their claim to protection.[64]

McCulloch's *Statistical Account of the British Empire* (1837) followed Porter's argument in every detail. By comparing the growth of population with the quantity of wheat imported McCulloch showed that home production had, to a remarkable extent, kept pace with increasing domestic needs.[65] By 1846 McCulloch was prepared to commit himself further. Firstly, he noted again that "between 1813 and the present period . . . the supply of produce has been increased, partly by the extension of cultivation; but far more by its improvements. A much greater quantity of produce is now obtained from the same *breadth of land* than in 1812." [66] Now Porter had been convinced that "the revenue drawn in the form of rent, from the ownership of the soil, has been at least doubled in every part of Great Britain since

62. *The Progress of the Nation* (London, 1836), *1*, 145, 148, 162.

63. Official agricultural statistics in England begin only in 1866. But there are isolated official and unofficial estimates of the yield and acreage of the three main British cereals for the first half of the century, all of which strongly suggest a sharply rising output of wheat and barley per acre for the years 1800–60. See M. K. Bennett, "British Wheat Yield Per Acre for Seven Centuries," *Economic History*, February 1935; G. E. Fussell and M. Compton, "Agricultural Adjustments after the Napoleonic Wars," *Economic History*, February 1939; L. Drescher, "The Development of Agricultural Production in Great Britain and Ireland from the Early Nineteenth Century," *Manchester School*, May 1955.

64. *Quarterly Journal of the Statistical Society of London*, October 1839, pp. 291–6.

65. *A Statistical Account of the British Empire, 1*, 551–2; also *Edinburgh Review*, January 1836, pp. 319–45.

66. *Statistical Account of the British Empire* (3d ed. 1847), *1*, 549.

1790."[67] But McCulloch pointed out that this increase of "gross rents" was only partly due to the extension of cultivation to less fertile and less accessible soils. Difficult as it was to distinguish "pure" intramarginal rent from gross rent, McCulloch nevertheless ventured to assert that "estimating the whole rental of Great Britain at *forty-five* millions, if we set apart *twenty* millions as real rent, and regard the remaining *twenty-five* millions as interest on account of buildings, fences, drains, roads, and other improvements of the soil, we shall certainly be within the mark." While gross rents had indeed risen by 30 per cent from 1815 to 1845, McCulloch remarked, rents on the whole were "moderate in England," because of "a disinclination on the part of many landlords to raise rents, and a wish not to remove tenants, and to keep their estates always underrented."[68]

Three years later the analysis of rent in the third edition of McCulloch's *Principles* gave no hint that the law of diminishing returns, the exclusive dependence of rent on differences in the quality of soils, and the tendency of pure rents to rise with the progress of wealth and population—all fundamental tenets of the Ricardian system—had been contradicted by data which the author himself had gathered. But the knowledge of these facts is probably responsible for McCulloch's qualified approval of Ricardo's theories in later years. In 1828 he had been most insistent in denying the allegation that Ricardo's doctrines were "merely speculative."[69] Twenty years later, however, he regretted to say that they were mostly "theoretical rather than practical conclusions"; "Mr. Ricardo did not sufficiently attend to the circumstances which practically countervail several of the principles on which he laid great stress."[70] But such admissions did not lead McCulloch to abandon the Ricardian system; he made no effort to re-examine his theoretical views in the light of the failure of Ricardo's theory to yield useful predictions.

The leading economists of the period all maintained this curious separation between abstract theory and empirical work. All the major debatable issues in Ricardian economics hinged upon the relative weight of forces making for diminishing and increasing returns in the production of wage goods. This question was essentially capable of

67. *Progress of the Nation, 1,* 164.

68. *A Statistical Account of the British Empire, 1,* 561, 557–8. Recent research has shown that the sharp rise in rental values which characterized the period 1800–20 was not sustained in the years that followed; contrary to the prevailing contemporary impression, there was no clear trend in the rental series from 1820 to 1840 and only a slight increase in the 1840's (Gayer *et al., op. cit., 2,* 927).

69. *Notes on the Wealth of Nations,* p. xcvi.

70. *Ibid.* (3d ed. 1849), p. lv. See also Ricardo, *10,* 370.

being resolved along empirical lines, given the fact that some information on money wages and the composition of working-class budgets had been made available by this time [71] and that the concept of a price index (pioneered by Joseph Lowe and George Scrope) was now fairly common knowledge.[72] As a matter of fact, John Stuart Mill as much as intimated that the outcome of the race between "population" and "agricultural improvements," upon which depended so many of Ricardo's generalizations, could be determined by a time series of wheat prices, deflated by an appropriate index and adjusted for seasonable variations.

> Which of the two conflicting agencies [population or agricultural improvements] is gaining upon the other at any particular time, might be conjectured with tolerable accuracy from the money price of agricultural products (supposing bullion is not to vary materially in value), provided a sufficient number of years could be taken, to form an average independent of the fluctuations of seasons. This, however, is hardly practicable, since Mr. Tooke has shown that even so long a period as half a century may include a much greater proportion of abundant and a smaller proportion of deficient seasons than is properly due to it. A mere average, therefore, might lead to conclusions only the more misleading, for their deceptive semblance of accuracy. There would be less danger of error in taking the average of only a small number of years, and correcting it by a conjectural allowance for the character of the seasons, than in trusting to a larger average without any such correction. It is hardly necessary to add, that in founding conclusions on quoted prices, allowance must also be made as far as possible for any changes in the general exchange value of the precious metals.[73]

Needless to say, he did not carry out the investigation; it would merely have revealed what he already knew.

The body of doctrine which Ricardo bequeathed to his followers

71. See, for example, budget studies of 31 working-class families for the years 1836–41 in *Quarterly Journal of the Statistical Society of London,* January 1842, pp. 320–34.

72. Other statistical techniques, such as the Gaussian law of error and the method of least squares, had also been developed by the 1830's but were not employed with respect to social phenomena until the 1860's. See H. M. Walker, *Studies in the History of Statistical Methods* (Baltimore, 1929), ch. 2; Schumpeter, *op. cit.,* pp. 524–6.

73. J. S. Mill, *Principles,* p. 704. In the third edition (1852) he added: "A still better criterion, perhaps, . . . would be the increase or diminution of the amount of the labourer's wages estimated in agricultural produce."

rested on a series of definite predictions about the course of economic events which were subject to empirical verification, in the strictest sense of the term. And the statistical data and methods of the times, crude as they may have been, were adequate to test the validity of Ricardian theory, in terms of its predictive accuracy for the class of phenomena which it was intended to explain. Moreover, as we have seen, such evidence was within the purview of all the economists of the day. Yet almost none of the classical thinkers was willing to surrender economic propositions on the grounds that they were contradicted by the available evidence. Just as the Malthusian theory of population was often upheld despite the knowledge that population was not "pressing" upon the food supply, so the undeniable rise of productivity in agriculture was not permitted to contradict the notion that in England, as John Stuart Mill put it, "the rate of profit is habitually within, as it were, a hand's breadth of the minimum." Only one of Ricardo's disciples was willing to go so far as to deny this fundamental inference. Agreeing with Ricardo that "it is the land which gives the original impulse to profits," and forced to admit that the tendency for rents to rise had been more than offset by improvements in method, Thomas de Quincey concluded:

> Amongst all men . . . there is a misgiving that profits, and by consequence interest, must be under a fatal necessity of gradually sinking, until at length they touch the point of extinction. Even Ricardo had too much authorised this false idea. There is no *essential* tendency downwards in profits, more than upwards . . . During these two centuries [the 17th and 18th centuries] it has not uniformly declined: on the contrary, it has *oscillated* in all directions; and by that one fact, so abundantly established, we are released from all apprehension of a downward *destiny*.[74]

Apparently John Stuart Mill did not deem this argument worthy of consideration: no mention is made of it in Mill's laudatory review of de Quincey's book.[75]

The divorce between theory and facts was probably never more complete than in the heyday of Ricardian economics. And it is clear that the explanation is not, as is sometimes supposed, that a paucity of statistical material in the period made it impossible to entertain any but an abstract and deductive approach to economic reasoning.[76] Whatever may have been the cause it was certainly not a state of factual

74. *Logic of Political-Economy*, pp. 293–4.

75. *Westminster Review*, June 1845, pp. 318–31.

76. This "justification" is implicit in virtually every history of economic doctrines. For an explicit statement of this view see W. C. Mitchell's *Lecture Notes on Types of Economic Theory* (New York, 1949), *1*, 160–1.

ignorance. Rather, despite the wealth of evidence, methodological predilections barred the way to a serious consideration of the empirical relevance of theory. Both the disciples and the critics of Ricardo agreed that economics was a deductive science based on simple premises derived from experience and conscious introspection.[77] Methodological disputes took the form of disagreement over the relative significance and sufficiency of the underlying assumptions on which the whole deductive structure was built.[78] Whether the structure itself was empirically meaningful was a question which was never squarely considered. Witness the grounds of Torrens' reappraisal of Ricardo: Ricardo's conclusions are "in strict conformity with the facts which he assumes; and modified by the proper corrections, on account of the difference between the assumed and the existing facts, will be found to be in tried conformity with existing facts." [79]

To be sure, all the classical writers paid lip service to the Baconian method of "direct induction." As John Stuart Mill observed in his essay on methodology, "We cannot too carefully endeavour to verify our theory, by comparing . . . the results which it would have led us to predict, with the most trustworthy accounts we can obtain of those which have been actually realized. The discrepancy between our anticipations and the actual fact is often the only circumstance which would have drawn our attention to some important disturbing cause which we have overlooked." [80] The reference to a "disturbing cause" contains the whole of classical teachings on the problem of testing the predictive success of economic hypotheses.

7. The Stationary State and Socialism

In the years 1815–48 the rate of increase in industrial production in England reached a maximum for the whole of the nineteenth century. It was the classic period of the Industrial Revolution and it left its mark in significant improvements in the material conditions of life. But for other reasons these years "have a bad name in economic history." [81] The total picture is mixed: on the one hand, better consumption goods and rising real wages resulting from the secular downward trend of prices; on the other, the hardships attendant upon a burgeoning factory system, the unprecedented crowding of towns, and the

77. Richard Jones was, perhaps, the only thinker in the period to take a different view.

78. See Bowley, *op. cit.*, pp. 33–9.

79. See above, Ch. 8, sec. 5.

80. *Essays on Some Unsettled Questions*, p. 154.

81. W. W. Rostow, *British Economy in the Nineteenth Century*, p. 19.

persistence of dire poverty in rural districts.[82] Is it any wonder that the early Victorians often regarded the spectacular economic developments of the times with some misgivings?

John Stuart Mill is a striking but by no means an unrepresentative example.[83] "Ever since the great mechanical inventions of Watt, Arkwright, and their contemporaries, the return to labour has probably increased as fast as the population," he observed in the *Principles;* "wages in the great seats of manufacture are . . . so high, that the collective earnings of a family amount on an average of years, to a very satisfactory sum" (pp. 192–3, 350). But yet he questioned whether "all the mechanical inventions yet made have lightened the day's toil of any human being. They have enabled a greater population to live the same life of drudgery and imprisonment, and an increased number of manufacturers and others to make fortunes" (p. 751). While "mechanical inventions . . . have not yet begun to effect those great changes in human destiny, which it is in their nature and in their futurity to accomplish," it is nevertheless "only in the backward countries of the world that increased production is still an important object: in those most advanced, what is economically needed is better distribution" (p. 749). And again: "While I agree and sympathize with socialists in this practical portion of their aims, I utterly dissent from the most conspicuous and vehement part of their teachings, their declamations against competition . . . one of their great errors, as I conceive, is to charge upon competition all the economical evils which at present exist" (p. 792). But at the same time he confessed: "I am not charmed with the ideal of life held out by those who think that the normal state of human beings is that of struggling to get on; that the trampling, crushing, elbowing, and treading on each other's heels, which form the existing type of social life, are the most desirable lot of human kind, or anything but the disagreeable symptoms of one of the phases of industrial progress" (p. 748). What of America which has "the six points of chartism, and . . . no poverty"? "All that these

82. With respect to money wages and real wages in the period, much quantitative evidence is available in the studies of Bowley, Wood, Silberling, Tucker, Gilboy, and Ashton, but actually no clear-cut conclusion has been reached. (For a review of the debate see W. Woodruff, "Capitalism and the Historians: A Contribution to the Discussion on the Industrial Revolution in England," *Journal of Economic History*, March 1956.) All the classical economists, however, were convinced that the material welfare of the working class had improved over the whole period and particularly after 1830 (see above, Ch. 6, sec. 3).

83. One other example must suffice: Samuel Laing (the younger), author of *National Distress; Its Causes and Remedies* (London, 1844), an eloquent indictment of the social conditions of the day. Yet Laing did not deny that total output had grown rapidly and laid great stress on the increase of "the national wealth in faster *ratio* than population" (pp. 73–4).

advantages seem to have yet done for them . . . is that the life of the whole of one sex is devoted to dollar-hunting, and of the other to breeding dollar-hunters" (p. 748 n.). The "saint of rationalism" was also something of a romantic.

For Ricardo the stationary state was hardly more than a conceptual device which defined the abstract limits of capital accumulation. For Mill, however, "this irresistible necessity that the stream of human industry should finally spread itself out into an apparently stagnant sea" was a concrete historical prospect. And it was not, as Ricardo had thought, as yet "far distant"; old countries were ever on the verge of stationariness: "The mere continuance of the present annual increase of capital, if no circumstances occurred to counteract its effect, would suffice in a small number of years to reduce the rate of net profit to one per cent," at which all induced saving would disappear (p. 731).

But Mill's stationary state is of a rather special kind. It is the result of "the joint effect of the prudence and frugality of individuals and a system of legislation favouring equality of fortune"; it would not preclude some technical advance, at least of the labor-saving variety, and would afford "as much scope as ever . . . for improving the Art of Living, and much more likelihood of its being improved, when minds ceased to be engrossed by the art of getting on." In short, the description of this "apparently stagnant sea" is more a disavowal of the preoccupation with market values and the physical yardstick of output than a serious analysis of the nature of economic activity in the absence of continuous economic growth. Before divesting the stationary state of all the unpleasant connotations associated with it in the writings of "the political economists of the old school," Mill remarked upon McCulloch's treatment of the question as particularly unsatisfactory. "With Mr. McCulloch," Mill declared, all that is "economically desirable" is identified with "the progressive state" and with that alone, namely, with the rapid increase of wealth irrespective of its distribution. There is an unintentional irony in this criticism because McCulloch was even then approaching Mill's own pessimistic attitude toward the process of industrialization.[84]

Little needs to be said here (for it is a well-canvassed question) about what is perhaps the most unorthodox feature of Mill's *Principles*, the generous appraisal of the views of Saint-Simon and Fourier and the defense of consumers' cooperatives and profit-sharing schemes in industry. Two things stand out in Mill's discussion. Firstly, he made short shrift of two popular objections to socialism which he had himself professed in his youth: [85] the lack of population restraints under a system of collective ownership and the alleged necessity of private

84. See below, App. C.
85. See above, Ch. 8, sec. 1.

pecuniary incentives (pp. 204–7). Secondly, he repudiated any notion of central planning: the supposition that "a few human beings" could allocate the resources of the community is "almost too chimerical to be reasoned against" (p. 213). Granting that labor under capitalism is remunerated "almost in an inverse ratio" to the irksomeness of work and that "the restraints of communism would be freedom in comparison with the present condition of the human race," yet capitalism had not yet had "a fair trial in any country." In the balance, Mill thought it premature to dispense with the profit motive while there were still prospects of improvements under the present economic order (pp. 208, 210).

In the first edition of the *Principles,* as Mill himself said, "the difficulties of Socialism were stated so strongly that the tone was on the whole that of opposition to it"; but in the third edition (1852) the treatment was altered so as to leave only one important objection standing, namely, "the unprepared state of mankind in general and the labouring classes in particular." [86] These changes were largely due to the events of February 1848 in France and the growth of "Christian socialism" in England. By 1850 the state of public opinion fairly invited a more sympathetic consideration of socialist doctrine.[87] "Socialism seems making progress in England as well as abroad," observed *The Economist.* "It is patronised by some of the clergy, and by some of the literati . . . It is said to be the fulfilment of science, to reconcile the past with the future, political economy with progress; and so it makes its way in the land." [88] And the *British Quarterly Review* asserted that "socialism . . . has become 'a great fact' . . . In Germany, and other parts of the Continent, socialism is epidemic; and in England, let our readers take our words for it, there are far more socialists than people are aware of." [89]

In fact, it needs to be said that the general radical tone of Mill's *Principles* was not unrelated to its date of publication. There are few ideas in it which had not been his property in 1835 or thereabouts but they were never made public prior to 1848 except in unsigned articles. The 1840's saw a resurgence of socially conscious literature [90] and a

86. *Autobiography,* p. 164. For a discussion of Mill's position on socialism in the successive editions of the *Principles,* see N. Grude-Oettli, *John Stuart Mill zwischen Liberalismus and Sozialismus* (Zürich, 1936), pp. 119–37; Robbins, *The Theory of Economic Policy,* pp. 142–68; Schumpeter, *op. cit.,* pp. 531–2.

87. Possibly the alterations in favor of socialism in the third edition were due to Harriet Taylor's influence (see Packe, *op. cit.,* pp. 306–14).

88. *The Economist,* May 4, 1850, p. 479.

89. *British Quarterly Review,* May 1850, p. 467.

90. I have in mind such novels as Disraeli's *Coningsby* (1844), *Sybil* (1845), and *Tancred* (1847), Mrs. Gaskell's *Mary Barton* (1848), Mrs. Trollope's *Michael Armstrong* (1848), Kingsley's *Yeast* (1848) and *Alton Locke* (1850), and Charlotte Brönte's *Shirley* (1849).

sudden but decided turn of public opinion toward state intervention to effect social reform. The *Principles* appeared in a period which had all the earmarks of a renaissance of statism.[91] Mill himself, in a letter to Comte written in 1847, observed that the country had "embarked on a system of charitable government." "Today the cry is to provide the poor not only with money, but, it is only fair to say, whatever is thought beneficial, shorter hours of work, for example, better sanitation, even education . . . That is to say, they are governed paternally, a course to which the Court, the nobility and the wealthy are quite agreeable." [92] It is not really so surprising, therefore, that Mill's proposals to "pull down all large fortunes in two generations" attracted little attention and that not a single contemporary reviewer felt it necessary to comment upon Mill's suggestion for fundamental changes in the economic basis of society.[93]

91. Some historians point to the Factory Act of 1847, rather than to the repeal of the corn laws in '46, as the turning point of the age; see G. M. Young, *Victorian England* (2d ed. New York, 1954), ch. 8.

92. Quoted by E. Halévy, *The Victorian Years, 1841–95* (2d ed. London, 1949), p. 167.

93. See *Edinburgh Review*, October 1848; *The Economist*, May 27, 1848, pp. 603–4 (a review by Thomas Hodgskin); *Blackwood's Edinburgh Magazine*, October 1848, pp. 407–28; *Westminster and Foreign Quarterly Review*, July 1848, pp. 291–314.

CHAPTER 10

Matters of Economic Policy

> In the numerous and great debates which have lately taken place on subjects that Mr. Ricardo discussed, his authority has been rarely appealed to. We turn to his two works . . . "The influence of a low price of corn on the profits of stock," and on "Protection to agriculture"; and we find in them very little that resembles the arguments, or refers to the facts, by which the corn laws have been overturned . . . we cannot say that his writings . . . have done much to bring about that abolition which a real deficiency of food has been the great means of forcing on. All honour, certainly, to the gentleman who, as early as 1815, though from reasoning which has not turned out to be very influential, foresaw some of the economical evils of laws which, *ab initio*, were thoroughly immoral and unjust.
>
> THOMAS HODGSKIN, in *The Economist*, NOVEMBER 28, 1846

1. THE FRAMEWORK OF THE DEBATE

DISCUSSIONS about economic policy in the years between Waterloo and the Great Exhibition revolved in the main around some half-dozen concrete issues: first of all the corn laws, then banking and currency reform, taxation and debt financing, combination laws, factory acts and the related question of compulsory free education, health and sanitary legislation, and public relief for the poor, the sick, and the aged.

The banner of laissez faire did not furnish unambiguous answers to any of these policy issues. Even the most zealous proponent of "leaving things to their course" might accept state intervention in a specific case without derogation from the purity of his creed if the problem in question seemed incurable by means of the economic process "working itself out." Without abandoning belief in the normative character of the market mechanism, the classical economists could and did propose remedial legislation on pragmatic grounds. It made no difference if they were Ricardian economists or not, since Ricardo had never paid much attention to the scope and functions of government. Of course, he believed that "the aim of the legislature should be . . . to interfere as little as possible with the natural equilibrium which would have prevailed if no disturbance whatever had been given."[1] Yet

1. Ricardo, *8*, 101; also *5*, 68; *7*, 106; *8*, 173.

he also sanctioned the view that "there are a few, and a very few exceptions to it, where the interference of government may be beneficially exerted" (*4*, 71–2). By way of example, he cited such things as government minting of coins, the inspection of drugs, the examination of doctors and the like, which are meant to prevent fraud or to certify a fact, and the whole area of banking. It was open to anyone else to extend the list as new problems for regulation arose.

Thus McCulloch approved of public control of utilities, railroads, and town dwellings, state supervision of charitable foundations, medical education, and accident insurance in mines and factories.[2] "Non-interference should be the leading principle," he declared, but the government should intervene whenever "it can be clearly made out that it will be productive of *public* advantage."[3] John Stuart Mill proposed legislation as a cure for nearly every social evil not deemed positively incurable; the province of government, he asserted, cannot be circumscribed by any general rule except "the simple and vague one" that state interference "should never be admitted but when the case of expediency is strong."[4] Senior advocated state regulation of housing and sanitation as well as compulsory education[5] while Torrens, in a pamphlet attacking the Ten Hours Bill, repudiated the principle of laissez faire as "an absolute truth, applicable under all circumstances."[6] When the question of public control of railroads came up for discussion at the Political Economy Club in 1842, it is not surprising to learn that the members unanimously approved of placing railroads under the jurisdiction of the state.[7]

There was no such thing as a Ricardian theory of economic policy. More than that, however: on many of the concrete policy issues under discussion in the period Ricardo offered no guidance whatever; on others, his proposals were either universally rejected or else outmoded by the course of events. In short, the Ricardian economist had no special position of his own on *any* question of economic policy.

The corn laws would seem to be an exception to this statement, but even here, we will see, the issue was not settled in Ricardo's terms; since all the leading writers were free traders, repeal of the corn laws was not a question dividing Ricardo's followers from his critics. In

2. *Principles* (2d ed. 1830), pp. 249–88.

3. *Ibid.* (4th ed. 1839), pp. 308–9. For a useful summary of McCulloch's views on the role of government, see C. J. Ratzlaff, *The Theory of Free Competition* (Philadelphia, 1936), pp. 83–91.

4. *Principles*, p. 800.

5. See Bowley, *op. cit.*, pp. 237–72.

6. R. Torrens, *A Letter to Lord Ashley* (London, 1844), pp. 64–5.

7. *Political Economy Club*, pp. 282–3; also p. 286.

a sense, of course, this is a perfect measure of Ricardo's influence. Nevertheless, by the 1840's, when the controversy over free trade reached its height, the case against the corn laws bore little resemblance to the arguments which Ricardo had employed.

The major plank in Ricardo's program for currency reform was a return to the gold standard. The resumption of specie payments in 1819, however, is only partly attributable to the influence of Ricardo's monetary pamphlets; in addition, Ricardo did not approve of the manner in which cash payments were resumed.[8] After 1820 monetary discussions took the form of a controversy between the currency and the banking school, culminating in the Bank Charter Act of 1844 which embodied the views of the currency school. The "currency principle" was derived from bullionist doctrine, which Ricardo espoused, and the basic features of the Bank Act came close to adopting the suggestions of Ricardo's *Plan for the Establishment of a National Bank* (1824). In this sense, "Ricardo was the father of the system adopted by the Bank of England after its internal revolution at the beginning of the forties."[9] Nevertheless, disciples and critics of Ricardo were to be found on both sides of the dispute, Torrens being a prominent member of the currency school, McCulloch on some points holding with the banking school, and John Stuart Mill occupying an intermediate position.[10] The discussion involved so many complex considerations that it is difficult to distinguish one camp from the other, much less delineate a Ricardian as against an anti-Ricardian point of view.[11]

On tax matters Ricardo offered a detailed analysis of the incidence of various taxes but little practical advice to the chancellor of the exchequer other than "the golden maxim . . . that the very best of all plans of finance is to spend little, and the best of all taxes is that which is the least in amount" (*1*, 242). He was, however, an adamant opponent of the income tax (*1*, 160–1), which, having been abolished in 1816, was re-enacted by Peel in 1842. And he called for the immediate redemption of the public debt by means of a capital levy,[12] a "chimerical project" he admitted, which met with derision. Though he wrote extensively against the Sinking Fund (finally eliminated in 1839),

8. See Viner, *Studies in the Theory of International Trade,* pp. 174–8; F. W. Fetter, "The Bullion Report Re-Examined," and R. S. Sayers, "Ricardo's Views on Monetary Questions," both in *Papers in English Monetary History,* ed. T. S. Ashton and R. S. Sayers (Oxford, 1953).

9. Sayers, *op. cit.,* pp. 92–3.

10. See Viner, *op. cit.,* ch. 5.

11. See M. R. Daugherty, "The Currency-Banking Controversy," *Southern Economic Journal,* October 1942.

12. Ricardo, *1,* 247–9; also *4,* 196–7; *5,* 21–2, 34–5, 38–9, 249–50.

it was already a discredited instrument of fiscal policy before Ricardo's time. In general, the tax reforms under Huskisson and later under Peel owe nothing to Ricardo's works.

Ricardo approved of McCulloch's efforts to secure the repeal of the combination laws because "like all other contracts, wages should be left to the fair and free competition of the market, and should never be controlled by the interference of the legislature," [13] but otherwise he did not think twice about trade unions or the activities of workingmen to secure higher wages.

When Peel's Cotton Factories Regulation Act was passed in 1819 Ricardo was already a member of Parliament. The act did not attract much attention outside the House of Lords, still it is surprising that Ricardo never mentioned it either in his published writings or in correspondence with friends. Malthus, for one, came out in favor of legislation to restrict child labor in the fifth edition (1817) of his *Essay on Population* (p. 282). In the 1830's, when the factory acts became a topic of heated debate, economists generally took a position which had no particular relationship to their views on economic theory.[14] A few writers had resort to the argument that shorter hours would reduce output and depress wages but, in the main, the issue was posed in terms of the competence of factory operatives to recognize their own interests. Insofar as child labor was concerned, it was agreed that legislation was necessary; the only question in dispute was the proper age of consent at which to draw the line. With the possible exception of John Stuart Mill, all the economists of the day condemned the Ten Hours Bill and similar efforts to regulate the hours of adult males. It is clear that they would have adopted the same attitude if Ricardo had never written. The same thing, of course, is true of health and sanitary legislation.

Public relief is an issue that deserves more careful discussion. We will consider it at some length. Without further ado, however, we may say that Ricardo's proposals on the poor laws, being identical to Malthus', were quietly dropped in the process of public discussion.

2. The Poor Laws

In the eyes of the classical economists the demoralizing effects of the English poor law system dated from the passage of Gilbert's Act of 1782 which introduced the principle of outdoor relief for able-bodied paupers. Prior to this act relief was only afforded by residence in a

13. *Ibid., 1,* 105. See also above, Ch. 6, sec. 5.

14. I have dealt with this question in some detail elsewhere: "The Classical Economists and the Factory Acts—A Re-Examination," *Quarterly Journal of Economics,* May 1958.

workhouse, the necessary costs being met by an annual levy on the landed property of the parish. A decade after Gilbert's Act the seventeenth-century law of settlement, which made every pauper chargeable upon and removable to his parish of legal settlement, was amended to exclude the sick and the aged. A still more drastic modification of the system came with the decision of a group of county magistrates, meeting at Speenhamland, Berkshire, in 1795, to alter the method of administering relief. The so-called Speenhamland system, which was rapidly adopted throughout southern England, directed the poor law authorities to supplement wages so as to provide a subsistence standard of living; the scale of allowances was to vary with the size of the household and the price of a quartern loaf. The effect was to give farmers an incentive to reduce wages, while relying on the rates to keep their laborers from starvation. Furthermore, under the provisions of the new bread scale, family income increased automatically with the number of children, each child constituting an additional claim for relief. The poor laws, which had once checked the growth of population by discouraging improvidence, now came to be regarded as a major stimulus to the increase of population.

The second edition of Malthus' *Essay on Population,* which appeared in 1803, concentrated its fire upon the practice of subsidizing wages out of public funds. But Malthus went further and called for the repeal of the entire poor law system, without distinction between relief for the able-bodied and assistance to the aged and infirm. The poor laws did not alleviate poverty, Malthus argued, but in fact contributed to its increase by weakening individual responsibility and destroying the motive for prudence and self-restraint. The poor had no right to claim relief because "dependent poverty ought to be held disgraceful. Such a stimulus seems to be absolutely necessary to promote the happiness of the great mass of mankind." This incentive argument was accompanied by broader economic objections: the poor laws raised the price of provisions by creating an inelastic demand for corn, thus depressing real wages and discouraging capital investment. Once set in motion, the allowance system had a constant tendency to increase the burden of relief. Consequently, Malthus advocated "the *gradual* and *very gradual* abolition of the poor laws . . . so gradual as not to affect any individuals at present alive, or who will be born within the next two years." [15]

In the period of widespread unemployment after Waterloo, the rising cost of public relief drew renewed attention to Malthus' analysis. In the peak year of 1818, the number of paupers relieved, in part or in whole, amounted to one and a half million. When Ricardo's *Principles*

15. *Essay on Population,* pp. 334–5, 343, 357.

appeared the poor laws were in general disfavor, and Ricardo followed Malthus in demanding their abolition by "the most gradual steps" in order "to eradicate them with safety from our political system" (*1*, 106). In correspondence with Trower, however, Ricardo said something rather different; while agreeing that "great evils . . . result from the idea which the Poor Laws inculcate that the poor have a *right* to relief," still, he remarked, "I would gladly compound for such a change in the Poor Laws as should restore them to what appears to have been the original intention in framing them; namely, the relieving only the aged and infirm and under some circumstances, children." [16] And at one place in the *Principles* Ricardo spoke of the Speenhamland system as a "misapplication of the poor laws" (*1*, 162).

Despite the general outcry against the poor laws the propertied classes continued to regard the system as a necessary instrument to assuage social discontent. Even the parliamentary *Report on the Poor Laws* (1817), which did much to publicize the evils of the prevailing method of giving relief, came to the conclusion that "the general system of Poor Laws interwoven with the habits of the people, ought in any measure for their improvement, be essentially maintained." [17] The Peterloo Massacre in 1819, the Cato Conspiracy in 1821, the recurrence of machine wrecking and rick burning in the twenties, and "the last labourers' revolt" in 1830 impressed the upper classes with the danger of abolishing or reducing relief. This probably accounts for the fact that most of the changes which were made in the poor laws after the Napoleonic Wars were in the direction of greater leniency.[18]

The number of paupers on relief declined all through the twenties. In 1831, however, they rose again above one million. In the following year the government appointed a royal commission to devise appropriate changes in the poor laws. Nassau Senior and Edwin Chadwick were among the more prominent members of the commission and Senior wrote the greater part of the *Report of Inquiry*.[19] Complete abolition of the poor laws being inexpedient, the commissioners proposed to do away with the allowance system and to furnish relief in the workhouse on the basis of "the less-eligibility principle"—by making the workhouse "an uninviting place of wholesome restraint" paupers would be encouraged to avoid being thrown on the rates. Furthermore, they recommended that the tradition of parish administration be replaced by centralized control in the form of a triumvirate of poor law commissioners.

The new poor law was introduced amidst a carefully planned cam-

16. Ricardo, *7*, 248; also 124–5; *5*, 1, 6.
17. Quoted by S. and B. Webb, *English Local Government*, Pt. II, *1*, 33.
18. *Ibid.*, Pt. I, *1*, 346–9, 391–5.
19. See Levy, *op. cit.*, ch. 9; Bowley, *op. cit.*, pp. 282–334.

paign which sought to mobilize public opinion in favor of the measure; [20] in the closing months of 1834 the bill passed through Parliament without serious opposition.

Although the Poor Law Amendment Act represented a retreat from the proposals of the *Essay on Population*, the measure was defended along classic Malthusian lines: by making relief less attractive than the rewards of independent work, the new system would destroy the inducement to raise large families and promote individual prudence. "The Essay on Population and the Poor Laws Amendment Bill will stand or fall together," wrote Bishop Otter in 1836; "they have the same friends and the same enemies." [21] Actually, we can only speculate whether Malthus himself approved of the new legislation for he never expressed an opinion on the matter (he died in 1834). But, like Ricardo Malthus had never been sympathetic to centralization of the rates. Moreover, the Poor Law Bill of 1834 violated the Malthusian canon that every amendment of the poor laws must constitute a step toward their ultimate elimination. As Edwin Chadwick observed, prior to the commissioners' report of 1834 "eminent economists and statesmen, and indeed most people of intellectual rank in society, adopted this [the Malthusian theory] as a settled conclusion. [They] prescribed, as the necessary remedy, the absolute repeal and disallowance of any legal provision of relief . . . and were of the opinion that all measures for dealing with the Poor Law in England ought to tend to its discontinuance." [22]

Although the new poor law was anything but a popular measure most economists were soon won over to the new system of public relief, drastically transformed and centrally administered. Even James Mill changed his mind and now supported the measure.[23] There were exceptions, however: Longfield and Lloyd, for example, as well as Read and Scrope.[24] They all affirmed the pauper's right to adequate relief, and Scrope, for one, suggested an alternative national insurance scheme, financed by contributions from employers. But the most prominent and outspoken opponent of the Poor Law Amendment Act was none other than McCulloch.

20. R. K. Webb, *op. cit.*, ch. 6. See also above, Ch. 7.

21. W. Otter, "Memoir of Robert Malthus," prefixed to the second edition of Malthus' *Principles*, p. xix.

22. Quoted by S. and B. Webb, *English Local Government*, Pt. II, *1*, 87 n.

23. See A. Bain, *James Mill. A Biography*, p. 372; also *Letters of John Stuart Mill*, *2*, 14.

24. M. Longfield, *Four Lectures on Poor Laws* (Dublin, 1834); W. F. Lloyd, *Four Lectures on Poor-Laws* (London, 1835) and *Two Lectures on the Justice of Poor-Laws* (London, 1837); Read, *Political Economy*, p. 364; Scrope, *Principles*, pp. 303–4, 316–24.

McCulloch had never adopted the Malthusian attitude to public relief. As early as 1820 he denied the contention that the poor laws were instrumental in promoting the rapid growth of population.[25] In 1821 McCulloch indicated his position in a letter to Napier: "I am by no means clear that in a highly manufacturing country like England, where periods of privation must necessarily be of frequent recurrence, and where they must necessarily affect a large proportion of the population, a provision calculated to meet these contingencies . . . may not balance the evils which every such provision brings along with it."[26] In 1828 McCulloch devoted an entire essay in the *Edinburgh Review* to the subject of public relief, in which he argued that the poor law had in fact checked the growth of population prior to the adoption of the Speenhamland system; all that was needed, therefore, was to return to the original provisions of the Elizabethan statute.[27] In 1830, testifying before a parliamentary committee, he warned against any change from the method of parish control of relief. Abolition of the poor laws was out of the question, he asserted, because common law gave the poor, whether able-bodied or infirm, a right to employment and subsistence. The chairman of the committee reminded him that in Ricardo's opinion "no scheme for the amendment of the poor laws merits the least attention, which has not their abolition for its ultimate object." McCulloch was not in the least put out: "I believe, however, that had Mr. Ricardo been as well acquainted with the history of the English Poor Laws as he would have been had he been alive at the present, he would have changed it. Mr. Ricardo was a person of utmost candour, and never attempted to support an opinion merely because he had once advanced it."[28]

In the second edition of his *Principles* (1830) McCulloch came out strongly in support of the poor law system, including outdoor relief to the able-bodied in periods of commercial depression.

> I have endeavored to set the objections to a compulsory provision in the strongest point of view; and it is not to be denied that they are very formidable. I acknowledge that at one time they appeared to me to be quite unanswerable . . . But a closer examination of the subject, and especially of the history of the poor laws, had led me to doubt the correctness of this opinion; and I

25. *Edinburgh Review,* January 1820, pp. 159, 169. McCulloch took his cue from John Barton's *Observations;* see G. Sotiroff, "John Barton (1789–1852)," *Economic Journal,* March 1953, pp. 90–2.

26. Napier, *Selected Correspondence,* p. 30.

27. *Edinburgh Review,* May 1828, p. 326.

28. *Third Report from the Select Committee on the State of the Poor in Ireland* (July 1830), pp. 580–1, 590.

> am now satisfied that the evils incident to a poor's rate may be, and in fact have been, so far repressed by regulations as to its management, as to render them innocuous.[29]

A few years after the passage of the Poor Law Amendment Act McCulloch attacked it as "a measure of very questionable policy." By vesting control in the hands of a central body, it made government an official protector of the poor: "Government has made itself their dry nurse and foster-mother; it is responsible for every real or fancied abuse that may anywhere exist in their treatment; and it must stoop to interfere in every workhouse squabble." The solution was to decentralize the system and to place the administration of relief once more in the hands of landlords: "give property its proper influence,—take from justices all power to interfere in the concerns of the poor, and leave the rest to the self-interest of the parties." The workhouse rule ought to be confined to the idle and disorderly, McCulloch insisted, and able-bodied workers should receive outdoor relief in periods of distress.[30]

McCulloch's opposition to the new poor law may have been the cause of his break with the *Edinburgh Review* in 1837. The *Review* had become the semi-official organ of the Whigs, publishing lead articles by Chadwick and Senior in defense of the Poor Law Amendment Act, and McCulloch must have found it difficult to go along with the new editorial policy. Whatever the explanation for the break [31] it set the seal on McCulloch's declining influence. New editions of his works continued to appear but his reign of authority was over. By the 1840's he was no longer regarded as a leading economic writer.

It should be noted that the Poor Law Act of 1834 never succeeded in abolishing outdoor relief to the able-bodied, particularly in the industrial centers of the North. The system was relaxed once again after 1852, but even before this the new poor law showed a continuous increase in the proportion of outdoor over indoor relief.[32] By 1850 it should have been clear that the framework of the 1834 Amendment

29. Pp. 408–9. See also Walter Coulson's review of the book, *Edinburgh Review,* January 1831, pp. 346–55.

30. J. R. McCulloch, *Notes on The Wealth of Nations* (2d ed. 1838), pp. 595–8.

31. McCulloch resented the fact that Napier was allowing others to write economic articles for the *Review.* (See F. W. Fetter, "The Authorship of Economic Articles in the *Edinburgh Review," Journal of Political Economy,* June 1953, p. 240.) McCulloch was appointed in 1838 to the post of Comptroller of Her Majesty's Stationery Office; knowledge of the appointment, which would render him financially independent, may have influenced him in severing his connections with the *Edinburgh Review.*

32. See E. Halévy, *The Age of Peel and Cobden* (2d ed. London, 1947), pp. 146–7.

Bill was hopelessly inadequate to deal with the problem of destitution and unemployment.[33] Nevertheless, John Stuart Mill defended it warmly, holding that the Malthusian objections to the poor law system were irrefutable until the Inquiry Report of 1834 showed how the guarantee of relief could be freed from its injurious effects by means of the principle of less-eligibility.[34]

3. Free Trade and the Manchester School

A theory which attributed the fall of profits and the rise of rents to the high price of corn, artificially maintained by the legislature in opposition to the interests of "the producing classes," lent itself with little difficulty to a vituperative attack on the landowning aristocracy. Zealots adulterated Ricardo's arguments to suit the tastes of popular opinion.[35] Tract after tract depicted the landlord as a social parasite, living off the "bread tax" which he and his kind had foisted on the poor. The incendiary tone of the campaign is best illustrated by T. P. Thompson's *Catechism on the Corn Laws; With a List of Fallacies and Answers* (1826), a work that went through fifteen editions in the short space of five years.

> What is the answer to the proposition, That the agriculture of the country is the great basis of its wealth . . . A. It is not agriculture that is the basis, but *having corn.* If by agriculture is meant having two bushels of corn where there might have been four, it is not the basis of the wealth of the country, but its impoverishment . . . It may be information to the home agriculturalists to state, that there would be no physical impossibility in living without them altogether. Not that it would be either politic or just. . . . But it would be *no more;* the consequence would not be that there would be no corn. The corn produced by the exportation of manufactures, even though the whole of the raw materials should be of foreign production, is just as substantial, unvisionary corn, as what is grown at home. The home growers would seem to have some doubts of this, by the way in which they speak of themselves

33. See S. E. Finer, *The Life and Times of Sir Edwin Chadwick* (London, 1952), pp. 82 ff., for an excellent critique of the assumptions underlying the *Report of Inquiry.*

34. *Principles,* pp. 365–8, 968–9.

35. Ricardo's writings certainly furnished all the essential ingredients for such an attack despite his own protestations that "I meant no invidious reflection on landlords—their rent is the effect of circumstances over which they have no control, excepting indeed as they are lawmakers, and lay restrictions on the importation of corn" (*8,* 182; also pp. 207–8).

as if they were the *only* machines nature has created for affecting the apparition of corn.

. . . . .

Q. That land and trade must work together—A. True, as long as they go on honestly in company. Not true if one is endeavoring to wax by the robbery of the other. Q. That the landed and commercial interests are not opposed to each other—A. They *are* opposed to each other when one is in the act of plundering the other. And there is no use in attempting to conceal it.[36]

Another popular pamphlet, *The Iniquity of Landholders* (1826), charged the landlords with being "the great oppressors of the country"; "it will be clearly proved, by their own admissions, as well as by the records of undoubted authority, that their power has been uniformly employed in enriching themselves at the expense of the other classes of the community." [37]

The corn laws became an obsession as much with the apostles as with the critics of free trade. Protectionists denounced the free trade movement as a menace to the security of property, "subversive of the true foundations of society," while the free traders hailed cheap bread as the panacea to remedy every ill.[38] The theories of Ricardo were analyzed, not so much for their logical coherence and practical validity as for their tactical consequences in the settlement of controversies provoked by the issue of free trade. When the exigencies of the moment made it necessary to excite odium against the landlords, the disharmonious implications of the Ricardian system were thrown into relief; at such times the landlord was depicted as having no pecuniary interests in the improvement of methods. When it was thought politic to conciliate the conflict of interests the theory was suitably amended to allow for the counteracting influence of technological progress, or else discarded altogether with no more explanation but that "it sowed dissension." [39] On the one hand it was said that the corn laws forced the extension of cultivation to inferior soils and kept the price of wheat at famine levels, on the other hand it was comfortably predicted that repeal would not bring a serious drop in prices nor throw much cul-

36. *Catechism on the Corn Laws* (Sutro Branch California State Library: Reprint Series No. 16, 1940), pp. 6–7, 86.

37. *The Iniquity of the Landholders* (London, 1826), p. 6.

38. As Torrens remarked in one of his pamphlets: "So long as the existing Corn Laws remain, so long will it be found impracticable, either to diminish the hours of labour, or to increase wages" (*Three Letters to the Marquis of Chandos* [London, 1843], p. 5).

39. See the opinions of Jones and Scrope (above, Ch. 8, sec. 1), and McCulloch and de Quincey (above, Ch. 9, sec. 2).

tivated land into pasture.[40] Each writer had his own hobbyhorse and adapted Ricardo as he saw fit. For the purpose of stifling creative thought it would have been difficult to invent anything so effective as the campaign in favor of free trade.

With the formation of the Anti-Corn Law League, under Cobden and Bright, the debate moved into a new phase. For the first time, the proponents of free trade began to make a serious effort to convince the public that repeal would benefit the agricultural classes as much as the rest of the community, an argument which already occurs in the Merchant's Petition of 1820 and in Ricardo's *On Protection of Agriculture* (1823).[41] With the publication of James Wilson's *Influences of the Corn Laws* (1839) and George Porter's *Effects of the Restrictions on the Importation of Corn* (1839), the essential harmony of class interests under free trade became a byword of the movement for repeal.[42] Abolition of the corn laws, Cobden was soon saying, would lower costs of production and stimulate foreign demand for British manufactured goods; wages would rise as markets were expanded, and so far from injuring agriculture, free trade would benefit it by stimulating the demand for wheat.[43]

In his anxiety to secure the widest support for his cause, Cobden fell between two stools. He declared without hesitation that rents had doubled since 1793 and had risen steadily since 1828.[44] "If Corn-laws keep up the price of food, they maintain the amount of rents also. The Corn-law is a rent law, and it is nothing else." [45] Without this consequence, it is clear, it would have been impossible to impugn the motives of landlords in maintaining the corn laws. But on the eve of

40. McCulloch combined both arguments: see, for example, *Edinburgh Review*, September 1826, p. 323.

41. *On Protection of Agriculture* is much milder in tone than any of Ricardo's earlier writings. Although a system of protective duties is most advantageous to landowners, Ricardo asserted, it is incompatible with a stable price of corn and a calculable steady income. Therefore, the gradual abolition of the corn laws, and a more moderate price of corn, might yet be beneficial to landlords as well as to the other classes of society (*4*, 237–8).

42. The two pamphlets are analyzed by S. Gordon, "The London *Economist* and the High Tide of Laissez-Faire," *Journal of Political Economy*, December 1955, pp. 464–5.

43. In 1843 Cobden frankly admitted that "most of us entered upon this struggle with the belief that we had some distinct class interest in the question . . . in the progress of the last five years, we have found, gradually but steadily, that every interest and every object, which every part of the community can justly seek, harmonises perfectly with the views of the Anti-Corn-Law League" (*Speeches on Questions of Public Policy, 1*, 97–8).

44. *Ibid.*, pp. 53–4; also p. 402.

45. *Ibid.*, p. 192.

repeal, Cobden declared that free trade would not diminish rents;[46] three years later he denied that he had ever dwelt upon a reduction of rents or a shifting of resources from land to manufacturing as a consequence of repeal. Greater profits for farmers and augmented rents for landowners would naturally follow upon the rising demand for foodstuffs due to the increased purchasing power of wages.[47]

The relationship between the price of corn and the rate of wages was always a moot point in the discussion over free trade. If the corn laws did maintain the price of home-grown produce above the international price, repeal might exert a downward pressure on money wages. Was this not the basis of the argument that free trade would permit Britain to compete on the world market? But, if so, there was no guarantee that the abolition of the corn laws would be in the interest of the working class. As Thompson put it in his *Catechism*, in the form of an assertion from the interlocutor, "if corn falls, wages must fall; and consequently cheap corn can be of no advantage to the labourer." The answer was this: "This must depend on whether wages fall *as much* as corn. No foreign corn will be brought into the country, unless more can be had for a given quantity of industry than can be got from the growers at home. If therefore, foreign corn comes in at all, there must be a greater share for the labourers; or in other words, wages will *not* fall so much as corn" (p. 18).

Obviously, this was not wholly comforting and the protectionists made the most of it. John Almack's *Character, Motives, and Proceedings, of the Anti-Corn-Law League* compiled a long list of quotations from Ricardo, Thompson, and Cobden, to name only a few, purporting to show that they supported repeal because it would lower the price of bread, reduce wages, and raise profits.[48] The League's true purpose, he charged, was "the decoying of the labouring poor into the cheap-labour trap" for the aggrandizement of the manufactures.[49]

Another protectionist writer culled a long list of contradictory statements from the *Anti-Corn Law Circular*, the League's paper, and

46. *Ibid.*, p. 382.

47. *Ibid.*, p. 402; also pp. 122–3.

48. *Character of the Anti-Corn-Law League* (London, 1843), pp. 32–48. Almack's knowledge of the literature, however, was anything but thorough. He cited Ricardo as "the very highest authority with all repealers and free-traders" and then declared: "The next authority in point of eminence, in the estimation of free traders, was Mr. Malthus" (pp. 46–7).

49. *Ibid.*, p. 95. It is noteworthy that Almack still adhered to physiocratic ideas: "Manufacturers are in reality only subsidiary appendages to agriculture, and entirely sustained thereby"; "foreign commerce never was to England, nor ever will be, a source of national wealth" (p. 71, pp. 74–5).

from Cobden's public addresses. Though Cobden denied that free trade would necessarily lower the price of food, the *Circular* stated unequivocally that "the Corn Law compels us to pay three times the value for a loaf of bread"; "if the Corn Laws were abolished, the workingman would save 3½d. up every loaf of bread"; "as a consequence of the repeal of the Corn Laws we promise cheaper bread . . . its price will be reduced 33 per cent." [50]

Almost all writers on free trade up to the 1840's undoubtedly had insisted that cheap food meant cheap labor; certainly Ricardo, James Mill, and McCulloch all assumed that wages were regulated by the price of corn and, therefore, that a reduction in the price of bread entailed lower money wages. As McCulloch said: "A rise of wages is seldom indeed exactly coincident with a rise in the price of necessaries, but they can never be very far separated"; it is understood that the chief necessary is corn.[51] By the 1840's, however, the *Paralleltheorie,* as German critics call it,[52] gave way to the *Konträrtheorie:* the doctrine that a low price of food would be accompanied by an increase in money wages, as well as real wages, through the stimulus given to domestic industry. The League's cry was now: "Cheap bread, dear labour; dear bread, cheap labour." In fact, by this time the shift of consumption patterns away from land using products had gone far enough so as to make it possible to deny any relation whatever between corn prices and wages. It used to be said, James Wilson pointed out, that "the high price of labour in this country, as compared with the continent, is only the result of a higher price of provisions; and that the lower price of labour on the continent, consequent on a lower price of provisions, is the chief cause of whatever progress these countries have made in the arts and manufacturers." But this argument is "wrong, both as regards the facts, and the principles deduced." [53]

Cobden's very first speech in Parliament took up the "fallacy of wages" which is "at the bottom of all opposition to the repeal of the Corn-laws." "I see no relation between the price of food, or of any other article of consumption, and the price of labour . . . the rate of wages has no more connection with the price of food than with the moon's change. There [in manufacturing industry] it depends entirely on the demand for labour; there the price of food never becomes an ingredient in testing the value of labour. There the labour market is,

50. Quoted by D. G. Barnes, *A History of the English Corn Laws from 1660–1848* (Boston, 1930), pp. 255–7.

51. *Principles,* pp. 379–80; also p. 341. For some representative opinions on the relation between corn prices and wages in the 1820's and 1830's, see Diehl, *Erläuterungen zu David Ricardos Grundgesetzen, 2,* 105–23.

52. See above, Ch. 1, sec. 2.

53. *Influences of the Corn Laws* (2d ed. London, 1840), p. 101.

happily, elastic, and will become more so, if you leave it unfettered." [54] But in the same speech Cobden estimated that 50 per cent of wages were on the average spent on food, that the corn laws raised the price of bread by 40 per cent and, hence, taxed wages by 20 per cent. He left it to his audience to resolve the contradiction.[55]

It is not surprising that the League rarely invoked Ricardo's writings to sanction the demand for repeal. Ricardo held out, we must remember, for a duty of twenty shillings a quarter on all wheat imported, with annual reductions of one shilling till the duty reached ten shillings, at which it should stand permanently to allow for the special tax disabilities of landowners.[56] But the League's program called for total and immediate abolition of the corn laws. A nominal fixed duty on corn was advocated as a compromise measure by the Whigs (without reference, however, to Ricardo's arguments), and the League was naturally reluctant to give any support to this proposal.[57] The hero of the League was Adam Smith, not Ricardo. Cobden's speeches contain frequent references to *The Wealth of Nations* and its proofs of the advantages of "commercial liberty," [58] but only a single incidental reference to the writings of Ricardo.[59] Although the League made it a practice to publish and distribute authoritative pamphlets on free trade,[60] no effort was made to reprint the *Essay on the Profits of Stock* or the tract *On Protection to Agriculture*. Both were out of print until McCulloch issued an edition of *The Works of Ricardo* in 1846.

The leading economists of the day held themselves aloof from the popular debate on free trade. For the most part they agreed with Cob-

54. *Speeches on Questions of Public Policy*, 1, 6–7; also pp. 120–1, 196–7, 200–2, 252, 279.

55. In all his writings I have been able to discover only one statement that indicates an understanding of the "high-wage economy" theory (*ibid.*, p. 19).

56. See above, Ch. 1, sec. 4.

57. The Whig attitude is indicated by the statement of Lord Melbourne, the Whig prime minister, in 1839: "To leave the whole agricultural interest without protection, I declare before God that I think it the wildest and maddest scheme that has ever entered into the imagination of man to conceive" (quoted by Barnes, *op. cit.*, p. 242). It was only in 1845, when Peel announced his intention of opening the ports by immediate Order of Council, that Lord John Russell put the Whigs on record with a hasty manifesto to his constituents abandoning the principle of a fixed duty and declaring for total repeal.

58. *Speeches on Questions of Public Policy*, 1, 89, 180, 202–3.

59. *Ibid.*, p. 384.

60. Writing to Edward Baines, Cobden explained the League's methods: "Recollect that our primary object is to work the printing press, not upon productions of our own, but producing the *essence* of authoritative writers such as Deacon Hume, Lord Fitzwilliam, etc., and scatter them broadcast over the land" (quoted by Barnes, *op. cit.*, p. 254). In a single year, such as 1843, the League published 9 million tracts.

den that the rate of wages did not vary with the price of food; this Ricardian notion, Thornton declared, is "an oft-refuted but still common opinion." [61] But John Stuart Mill refused to concede the validity of the Kontrārtheorie. Temporary fluctuations in the price of food, he thought, probably affect wages in the opposite direction; but in the long run, "wages do adapt themselves to the price of food, though after the interval of almost a generation." "I cannot, therefore, agree," Mill declared, "in the importance so often attached to the repeal of the corn laws, considered merely as a labourer's question, or to any of the schemes, of which some one or other is at all times in vogue, for making the labourers *a very little better off*." [62] This certainly suggests a disavowal of the vulgar propaganda of the Anti-Corn Law League. As we saw earlier, Mill doubted that the corn laws as such had raised corn prices or rents to any significant degree.[63] In the *Principles* his prediction for the future, ambiguous as it was, was not calculated to support Cobden's brighter visions of the free trade era:

> There is every reason to expect that under the virtually free importation of agricultural produce, at last extorted from the ruling powers of this country, the price of food, if population goes on increasing, will gradually but steadily rise; though this effect may for a time be postponed by the strong current which in this country has set in (and the impulse is extending itself to other countries) towards the improvement of agricultural science, and its increased application to practice [p. 850].

McCulloch alone persisted in advocating the Ricardian proposal of a fixed duty on corn, while ignoring the activities of the League.[64] Thomas de Quincey, never a keen enthusiast for free trade, commented on "the monstrous delusions of the Corn-Law agitators" in his *Logic of Political Economy:* "Well I knew that the working poor man would find the ultimate *bonus* upon his bread to be next to nothing under whatsoever the changes of the Corn-Law; assuming even the stationariness of wages and assuming also that no such reaction of evil should arise from the injury to our domestic agriculture as unavoidably would arise." [65]

61. *Over-population and Its Remedy* (1846), p. 305. See also Longfield, *Lectures on Political Economy* (1834), pp. 262–6; Lawson, *Five Lectures on Political Economy*, p. 8 n.; Senior, *Industrial Efficiency and Social Economy*, ed. Levy, 2, 256–7.

62. *Principles*, pp. 347–8.

63. See above, Ch. 9, sec. 5.

64. See his *Statements Illustrative of the Probable Consequences of the Proposed Repeal of the Corn Laws* (London, 1841). See also *Political Economy Club*, pp. 262–3, 278, 294.

65. *Collected Writings of Thomas de Quincey*, 9, 125 n.

But Torrens delivered a frontal attack on the viewpoint of the Manchester school. Cobden had based his position on the conviction that free trade would break down the barriers of nationalism and inaugurate an era of universal friendliness among the nations of the world: "I believe that if you abolish the Corn-Law honestly, and adopt the Free Trade in its simplicity, there will not be a tariff in Europe that will not be changed in less than five years to follow your example." [66] It was Torrens' contention, however, that unilateral repeal of protective duties, without guaranteed reciprocal action on the part of other countries, would prove a disastrous policy. Its consequence would involve "throwing land out of cultivation, destroying the capital invested in the cultivation of inferior soils, and lowering the wages of agricultural labour by diminishing the demand for it." [67] This was a desertion from the camp of free trade. Disraeli echoed Torrens' arguments a few years later when he asked if Peel meant to fight "hostile tariffs with free imports"; the notion goes back to Malthus who, some thirty years before, had defended the corn laws on the ground that open ports would place England "at the mercy of restrictions imposed by other countries." [68]

Taking a broad view of the scene it seems evident that though Ricardo's writings gave the initial impetus to the free trade movement their practical influence was largely dissipated in the controversies of the twenties and thirties. The campaign which finally secured the repeal of the corn laws in 1846 based itself, more often than not, on arguments directly contrary to the spirit and letter of Ricardo's works. The free traders of the 1840's were the progeny of a parent they disavowed. It is an ironic commentary on the history of Ricardian economics that the fundamental theorem of profits depending upon wages and wages upon the price of wheat proved to be the Achilles heel of the anti-corn law agitation, and that John Stuart Mill should have been unable to put much stock in the benefits of repeal, the most basic of all the conclusions of Ricardo's system.

4. Post-Mortem on the Corn Laws

In the years that followed repeal of the corn laws the price of bread failed to decline; wheat prices averaged only a little less in the free trade forties than in the five years preceding abolition. After a sharp

66. *Speeches on Questions of Public Policy, 1*, 360.

67. *The Budget*, pp. 418–19. The attack was somewhat misconceived: Torrens asserted that Cobden's advocacy of one-sided free trade was contrary to the import of Ricardo's and Senior's writings on free trade, a statement which Senior immediately denied (see Bowley, *op. cit.*, pp. 225–8).

68. *The Grounds of an Opinion on the Policy of Restricting the Importation of Corn* (London, 1815).

fall in 1850 the price of corn rose again in the 1850's due to bad domestic harvest, accompanied by droughts in Europe, and to the Crimean War which interrupted imports from the Baltic and raised freight charges on the remaining sources of supply. In and of itself, of course, there is no reason why the repeal of the corn laws should have guaranteed cheap bread. When the home supply was inadequate, free imports could at most be expected to keep down domestic prices by assuring Britain of access to the widest available market. But the effect of free trade on corn prices had been the principal bone of contention in the corn law debates with both sides pressing exaggerated claims.

As it happened, the question was never clearly settled because the discovery of gold in California and Australia in 1849–50 soon exerted an independent influence on the level of prices and radically altered Britain's terms of trade. In other respects, however, the course of events in the thirty years following repeal was such as to support the viewpoint of the Manchester school. A larger quantity of grain was imported in the decade after 1846 than in all the thirty-one years between Waterloo and repeal, yet there was no ruinous drop in wheat prices or in acreage under cultivation. In fact the period between repeal and the 1870's was the golden age of British farming.[69] Moreover, the rise in corn imports did serve to stimulate the export of British manufactures; a considerable part of the increased foreign supply after 1846 was derived from the Levant, and by 1855 this area constituted the major foreign outlet for Manchester cotton goods. Judged by the results, the hopes of Cobden and Bright had been broadly vindicated.

There remains the question: Did the corn laws have a material influence on prices, and, if so, what was the magnitude of the effect? Firstly, there is the notion that the corn laws accentuated the amplitude of fluctuations in wheat prices brought about by the vicissitudes of harvests. Ricardo had used this argument against fixed import duties as laid down in the Act of 1822. Under this system a bumper crop must cause the domestic price to fall to the level of the world price before the farmer can be relieved by exportation (*4*, 240–2). With the adoption of the sliding scale of duties in 1828 this aspect of the question took on new significance.

Ostensibly the sliding scale was designed to stabilize prices: the duty was to be lowered when the price rose and to be raised when it fell. But the practical effect, it is said, was precisely the opposite. Traders were able to drive up the price by withholding supplies; the consequent reduction in the duty, being regarded as temporary in nature, led to heavy importation which caused the price to fall and the duty

69. See J. H. Clapham, *Economic History of Modern Britain. Free Trade and Steel, 1850–66* (New York, 1932), pp. 2–9.

to rise once again; before foreign supplies were dried up, further speculative hoarding would produce a repetition of the entire cycle. The result was to aggravate the repercussions of variable harvests upon the general level of economic activity, via the effect of grain imports on the money market.[70]

Thus free trade was expected to reduce the fluctuations, as well as the level, of corn prices. Yet repeal did not bring greater stability, at least not until the 1880's. Edgeworth once compared the period 1821–44 with that of 1850–73 with respect to fluctuations in the price of corn as tested by the mean deviation of the annual price from the average of each period respectively; he found significantly greater instability in the years after abolition than in the years before. This was true even when he tested monthly and weekly, instead of annual deviations. Again, taking a smaller period of thirteen years (1829–41 and 1851–63) and then of six years (1836–41 and 1851–56) he obtained the same results.[71]

Still, the matter of price variability was a secondary element in the Ricardian attack on the corn laws. On the key question—whether or not the level of wheat prices would have been lower over the whole period in the absence of import restrictions—it is much more difficult to arrive at a definite answer.

The problem of estimating the repercussions of the Corn Law of 1815, for example, is essentially that of measuring "the indirect effects of a non-existent tax."[72] Under the provisions of that act, foreign grain entered freely or was shut out entirely. Between 1816 and 1824 bread went literally untaxed. Even under the sliding scale of 1828 corn was not imported until the price rose above a certain level; therefore it was not uncommon for months and sometimes years to pass when no revenue was derived from corn import duties. Moreover, the failure of continental harvests often prevented the shipment of grain to England even when the British price warranted importation. As a matter of fact, years of scarcity in European grain areas almost always coincided with poor harvests in England and Ireland; the available foreign supply was normally limited to meeting a one-tenth deficiency of

70. The mechanism was clearly recognized by contemporary observers: see Wilson, *Fluctuations of Currency, Commerce, and Manufactures,* p. 45; J. R. McCulloch, *Statements Illustrative of the Consequences of Repeal,* p. 20; Torrens, *The Budget,* p. 398. On the relation between the corn laws and cyclical change, see Rostow, *British Economy of the Nineteenth Century,* pp. 50–1; R. C. O. Matthews, *A Study in Trade-Cycle History* (Cambridge, Eng., 1954), ch. 4.

71. F. Y. Edgeworth, review of *The History of the English Corn Laws* (1904) by J. S. Nicholson, reprinted in *Papers Relating to Political Economy* (London, 1925), *3,* 134–5.

72. C. R. Fay, *The Corn Laws and Social England* (London, 1932), p. 119.

the British harvest.[73] If this is so, as it seems to be for the period up to the 1840's, living costs would have been much the same without the corn laws.

Moreover, improvements in agriculture in Great Britain and Ireland made it possible in the twenties and thirties to keep pace with the rising demand for corn, resulting from the increase in population and in per capita income, without an increase in price. It was only in the 1840's that Britain was no longer able to feed herself, even in years of abundant harvests.[74]

The price of wheat in the postwar period actually showed a discernible declining trend and never again approached the famine levels of 1816–20; this would put an end to the matter were it not for the appreciation in the value of money throughout the years 1815–50. Jevons showed subsequently that the price of corn never fell as low from 1815 to 1850 as the average price of forty basic commodities and that the price of wheat considered separately did so only once, namely in 1835. On the other hand, both fell below the base-year price (1782) in 1822 and 1850, but neither fell as much as the average of the entire forty commodities combined.[75] Hence Jevons' calculations suggest that the secular decline in the price of agricultural produce during the period was not so great as that of prices in general. This is to say that agricultural prices were preserved at relatively higher levels.[76] But it would be difficult to say whether this "price scissor" was due to the superior productivity of industry or to the existing scheme of protection for agriculture. In view of the available data this is an issue which probably will never be settled.

73. See Matthews, *op. cit.*, pp. 35–6.

74. See *ibid.*, p. 32; Fay, *op. cit.*, pp. 116–18.

75. W. S. Jevons, "The Variations in Prices and the Value of Currency since 1782," *Investigations in Currency and Finance* (London, 1909), pp. 112–42. For a summary of Jevons' findings see Barnes, *op. cit.*, pp. 205–8.

76. This was Marshall's reading of the evidence: *Industry and Trade* (4th ed. London, 1923), pp. 754–7.

CHAPTER 11

The Closing Decades: Fawcett and Cairnes

> Our free-trade friends have two axioms for us, axioms laid down by their justly esteemed doctors, which they think ought to satisfy us entirely. One is, that, other things being equal, the more population increases, the more does production increase to keep pace with it . . . The other is, that, although population always tends to equal the means of subsistence, yet people's notions of what subsistence is enlarge as civilisation advances, and take in a number of things beyond the bare necessaries of life; and thus, therefore, is supplied whatever check on population is needed. But the error of our friends is precisely, perhaps, that they apply axioms of this sort as if they were self-acting laws which will put themselves into operation without trouble or planning on our part, if we will only pursue free-trade, business, and population zealously and staunchly.
>
> MATTHEW ARNOLD, *Culture and Anarchy* (1869)

IN THE YEARS between the Great Exhibition and the Franco-Prussian War economic science failed to make any substantial advance. As a result of Mill's catholic presentation of doctrine, which stifled theoretical progress by yielding to every viewpoint, political economy showed definite signs of becoming moribund. A shallow optimism engendered by free trade and a prolonged industrial boom diverted attention from central analytical questions.[1] Government policy, methodological issues, trade unions, and the effects of the gold discoveries were topics that attracted the bulk of the literature.[2] From the standpoint of later developments the works of Lardner, Jennings, and MacLeod were not without significance; [3] but these did not come within the ken of fundamental Ricardian doctrine. The central ideas of Ricardian economics, handed down in the writings of Fawcett and Cairnes, stood where Mill had left them in 1848.

1. This and other explanations of the state of theoretical quiescence are canvassed by S. G. Checkland, "Economic Opinion in England as Jevons Found It," *Manchester School*, May 1951.

2. See Hutchison, *A Review of Economic Doctrines*, ch. 1. On the discussions about the role of trade unions apropos of the wages fund doctrine, see Taussig, *op. cit.*, ch. 12. On the debate about the influence of gold on prices, see R. S. Sayers, "The Question of the Standard in the 1850's," *Economic History*, January 1933.

3. See R. M. Robertson, "Jevons and His Precursors," *Econometrica*, July 1951.

Henry Fawcett (1833–84) was "a man of one book"; his *Manual of Political Economy*, published in 1863, the year of his election to the professorship at Cambridge, was simply an abridgment of Mill's *Principles* with some additional material on cooperatives and poor laws. The only points of interest in it are a series of obiter dicta; these are revealing of that blatant discrepancy between theory and observation which had long sapped the vitality of the Ricardo-Mill line. The rise in per capita income, despite the Malthusian theory of population, and the failure of wheat prices to reflect the alleged tendency toward diminishing returns were conveniently credited by Fawcett to the "disturbing influence" of free trade. That the same facts had been in evidence when the population of England was largely restricted to its own soil for food supplies was of course ignored.

"In no epoch, probably, has the land of England been so greatly improved as during the last few years"; "it can . . . be conclusively proved that capital has increased more than population and wages have consequently advanced"; nor have profits fallen "during the last quarter of the century"; there is no reason to entertain a "prospective augmentation of food in an advancing country" which at one time had "thrown a gloom over the speculations of those Political Economists, who apparently failed to foresee the great results of Free Trade." Everyone had prospered, even the landlord. Though the price of wheat had fallen since repeal, Fawcett observed (incorrectly), "a more than corresponding rise has taken place in the price of other kinds of agricultural produce"; hence "the rent of land has, no doubt, in this country, rather increased than diminished since the passing of free trade." Fawcett reminded his readers that when Mill said "the interest of the landlord is opposed to that of the labourer and capitalist" he meant to say that an increase in the share of one claimant diminished the share of the others; obviously, "all the three classes may participate in any general improvement."[4]

The works of John Elliot Cairnes (1823–75) are of far greater importance. Cairnes had made his reputation with a study of *The Character and Logical Method of Political Economy* (1857), a series of lectures delivered at Trinity College, Dublin. *Essays on Gold Questions* (1859–60) and *The Slave Power* (1862) enhanced his fame. With his appointment in 1865 to the professorship at University College, London, Cairnes became at once the most prominent economist of the day. His *Leading Principles of Political Economy Newly Expounded* (1874) was the last treatise in the classical tradition. Al-

4. H. Fawcett, *Manual of Political Economy* (2d ed. London, 1865), pp. 147, 150, 478, 572; *idem*, *Economic Position of the British Labourer* (London, 1865), pp. 137, 147.

though it took the form of a critical commentary on Mill's *Principles,* the net result of Cairnes' book was to undermine Mill's authority and open the way to the historism of Rogers, Leslie, and Ingram.

The Character and Logical Method of Political Economy opens with a complaint at the anarchic character of economic discussions since the repeal of the corn laws. All the fundamental propositions of economic science—"such questions as those respecting the laws of population, of rents, of foreign trade, the effects of different kinds of expenditure upon distribution, the theory of prices"—are once again regarded as open and unsettled questions. Why? Because of "the effect which the practical successes achieved by Political Economy (as exemplified in the rapid and progressive extension of the commerce of the country since the adoption of free trade) have had on the method of treating economic questions." [5] These remarks set the tone for Cairnes' writings on methodology; his concern was to warn against those who would bend economics to political purposes, who would condemn it because it stood for laissez faire and who would refute its abstract principles by factual evidence. "The discussions of Political Economy have been constantly assuming more of a statistical character," he declared; "results are now appealed to instead of principles; the rules of arithmetic are superseding the canons of inductive reasoning; till the true course of investigation has been well-nigh forgotten." [6] Economic laws, Cairnes insisted in his *Logical Method,* are rules deduced from "human nature and external facts," not "from the statistics of society, or from the crude generalization of history."

> An economic law expresses . . . a tendency; therefore, when applied to external events it is true only in the absence of disturbing causes, and consequently represents a hypothetical, not a positive truth; that, being deduced by necessary consequences from certain mental and physical principles, it can be established only by establishing the existence of the principles assumed, and showing that by logical necessity they involve the tendency asserted; and refuted only by proving that the principles do not exist, or that the reasoning is unsound [p. 118].

In this sense all of Ricardo's theories represent "hypothetical truths" holding "only in the absence of disturbing causes." And it is in connection with the discovery of disturbing causes—"those minor or dis-

5. Yet Cairnes held that "the doctrine of Free Trade is a product of systematic reasoning"; the prediction that free trade would enrich the country has been "verified by the event"; therefore, "to this extent Political Economy lays claim, and not without valid grounds, to the power of prediction" (*Essays in Political Economy, Theoretical and Applied* [London, 1873], p. 303).

6. *Logical Method of Political Economy* (2d ed. New York, 1875), p. 23.

turbing agencies which modify, sometimes so extensively, the actual course of events"—that "we find the proper place of statistics in economic reasoning" (p. 97).

This is not to be construed as asserting that economic laws can be upset by statistical evidence; on the contrary, Cairnes' aim was to discredit the empirical objections of Ricardo's critics. These objections were grounded on what Matthew Arnold labeled "the two axioms" of "our free trade friends": greater density of population enhances the scope of the division of labor, resulting in rising per capita output, and higher living standards automatically supply an effective prudential check.[7] The author under attack throughout Cairnes' book was G. K. Rickard, occupant of the Drummond Chair at Oxford, who expounded both of "the two axioms" and, in addition, was a vigorous opponent of Ricardo and Mill.[8] One of the propositions of Ricardian economics, which Rickard denied with factual data, was "the diminishing productiveness of soil," "the unpenetrable barrier," Cairnes called it, "against which all anti-Malthusian plans and arguments are ultimately shivered." "The attempt to meet the doctrine in question by statistical data implies . . . a total misconception, both of the fact which is asserted, and of the *kind* of proof which an economic doctrine requires. The doctrine contains, not an historical generalization to be tested by documentary evidence, but a statement as to an existing physical fact, which, if seriously questioned, can only be conclusively determined by actual experiment upon the existing soil." [9] No one, however, denied the law of diminishing returns as a "physical fact," that is, as a static principle governing the proportions in which the factors of production may be advantageously combined; what was in question were the historical predictions drawn from it. As Cairnes himself said:

> The influence of the physical qualities of the soil, as expressed by the law of its diminishing productiveness . . . is a principle most important with reference to the objects of Political Economy, and quite essential in enabling us to understand . . . that general tendency to a fall of profits and rise of rent, which, though frequently and sometimes for long periods interrupted, is nevertheless one of the most striking circumstances connected with the material interests of advancing communities [p. 216].

7. The confused status of population theory in the period between Mill and Marshall, particularly with respect to the dynamics of secular population changes, is discussed by J. J. Spengler in "Marshall on the Population Question. I," *Population Studies,* March 1955, pp. 265–77.

8. G. K. Rickard, *Population and Capital* (London, 1854).

9. Cairnes, *Logical Method,* p. 51 n.

Again and again the alleged hypothetical character of economic propositions is employed as a defense against those who would attack Ricardian economics for its failure to yield accurate predictions. Cairnes' method was to charge his opponents with "crude empiricism" while appealing to the time-honored ambiguities of the term "tendency." To be sure, Cairnes conceded, "as nations advance in civilization, the proportion between population and subsistence generally alters in favour of subsistence"; but this is "a proposition which, I think, can scarcely pretend to the dignity of a 'law' even in the loosest sense of the word" (pp. 18–81). And to assert, as Rickard did, that the tendency to diminishing returns *is* counteracted by "the progress of civilization" amounts to abandoning "all pretensions to solving the problems of wealth" and "to give up at once the cause of Political Economy as a branch of scientific research" (pp. 215–16).

This kind of argument, however, was not very persuasive, as Cairnes must have realized. In his *Leading Principles* he adopted an entirely new line of reasoning. Now he flatly declared that "it has never been found in the history of any country, that . . . inventions have kept pace with the declining rate of return yielded by natural agents." [10] Yet the real price of corn, he contended, shows no permanent tendency to rise in the course of economic progress; this is admitted to be in conflict with "Mr. Mill's teachings" but in conformity with Adam Smith's view of the long-run stability of corn prices.[11] The explanation is that the "normal" price of corn "after it attains a certain elevation" checks the growth of population, arrests the extension of cultivation, and so eliminates the pressures making for further increases in the price. "I venture to assert that, at all events since the beginnings of the seventeenth century, the normal price of wheat has not risen in England more than the depreciation of the precious metals since that time will fully account for . . . I have little doubt that if the question were gone into statistically, and due allowance made for changes in the value of money, the results would bear out the conclusion at which, on purely economic grounds, I have arrived." [12]

That the price of meat and dairy produce tends to rise through time while the price of manufactured articles tends to fall is of no special theoretical significance since corn is "the staple food" and "the principal article of the laborer's consumption." [13] It should have followed that Ricardo's prognosis of the secular changes in the functional distributive shares was unfounded. If the price of wheat is unaffected

10. *Some Leading Principles of Political Economy* (London, 1874), p. 119.
11. *The Wealth of Nations,* pp. 240–2.
12. *Leading Principles,* p. 126; also p. 143.
13. *Ibid.,* pp. 124–35.

by the corn laws, or by the diminishing productivity of agriculture, neither rents nor profits need to fall as a result of the increased cost of producing wage goods. Cairnes only escaped this conclusion by relying on the short memory of his readers. Barely a hundred pages after declaring, in his *Leading Principles,* that the real price of corn had not risen since the seventeenth century, he contradicted himself in the course of explaining Ricardo's maxim that profits depend upon wages. "Ricardo . . . has laid it down that profits are inversely as wages [*sic*], but any tolerably careful student of Ricardo would see that by wages he meant 'proportional wages'—that is to say, the laborer's share of the product, or, if wages in the ordinary sense, then that the statement was to be received subject to the condition that the efficiency of labor remained the same." [14] As everyone knows, "by simply observing the events now passing before our eyes" wages have been steadily advancing "for some years," "advancing not merely in its money amount, but in the real reward it procures for the laborer" (p. 53). But labor has nevertheless not received its full share of the growth of output: "Within the last century an enormous increase has taken place in the productiveness of industry in Great Britain . . . yet the rate of wages . . . measured by the real well-being of the laborer —though some improvement no doubt has taken place in his condition during this time—has certainly not advanced in anything like a corresponding degree; while it may be doubted if the rate of profit has advanced at all" (p. 275). It must be remembered, Cairnes noted, that "the productiveness of industry only affects the rate of wages and profits in so far as it results in a cheapening of the commodities which enter into the consumption of the laborer" (p. 277). Wage goods consist for the most part of "commodities of raw produce, or in which the raw material constitutes the chief element of value (clothing is, in truth, the only important exception)"; and "of all such commodities it is the well-known law that an augmentation of quantity can only be obtained, other things being the same, at an increasing proportional cost." In consequence, "the large addition to the wealth of the country has gone neither to profits nor to wages, nor yet to the public at large, but to swell a fund ever growing even while its proprietors sleep—the rent-roll of the owners of the soil" (pp. 278–89).

With respect to the theory of value Cairnes' attitude is clearly set out in an essay on Comte, written in 1870.

> On the governing principle of "natural" value in domestic transactions, Ricardo left little for his successors to supply. Mr. Senior improved the exposition by giving a name—Abstinence—

14. *Ibid.,* p. 236. Cairnes had a firm grasp of the high-wage economy theory (see *ibid.,* pp. 384–5).

> to an element of cost, not unrecognized by Ricardo, and implied in his exposition but not brought into sufficient prominence by him; and Mr. Mill, in his chapter on the "ultimate analysis of cost of production," has affected some modifications in detail, and given greater precision to some of the conceptions involved; but in essentials the doctrine remains as it came from the master's hand.[15]

Actually, the treatment of value in Cairnes' *Leading Principles* is wholly in the "real cost" tradition; there are no concessions to a physical labor cost theory such as are occasionally found in Mill's *Principles* and the invariable measure of value is never heard of.[16] The common Ricardian assumption of imperfect mobility of resources in trade between countries is carried over by Cairnes to domestic trade; hence domestic values are said to be governed by the reciprocal demand of "noncompeting groups" (pp. 66–73, 89–96). This simple but ingenious generalization of Mill's theory of international values remained a suggestion, nothing more, for Cairnes dismissed the solution of short-period pricing problems as of "slight help" in resolving questions of "large or permanent interest" (p. 111).

What Cairnes called "the Malthusian difficulty" looms large in all his writings. In the *Leading Principles* he did not trouble himself to expound the doctrine anew; it was enough to point to "the influence of Mr. Darwin's great work, in which . . . the tendency of human beings to increase faster than subsistence . . . was shown to be merely a particular instance of a law pervading all organic existence." Besides, Cairnes declared, "those attacks upon the economic doctrines of wages which were based upon objections to the Malthusian doctrines—attacks upon what we may call the *supply* side of the wages problem—have for some time come to an end" (p. 157). Yet a few pages earlier Cairnes had coined an argument with respect to "the supply side of the wages problem" which, after being taken up by Marshall, finally led to the excision of the Malthusian doctrine of population from the body of economic theory.

Whenever we attempt to advance a general formula governing the supply of productive factors, Cairnes observed, we are brought "face to face with the fact that the motives which influence human beings in the production and supply of commodities are not those which influence them in the production and supply of labor; in other words, that the conditions operative in the two cases are essentially distinct." The

15. *Essays in Political Economy*, p. 292.

16. On the other hand, Cairnes dismissed the utility theory of value which, he said, has "quite lately been revived by Professor Jevons," but failed even to expound it correctly (*Leading Principles*, pp. 17–21).

"production" of children is determined by cultural forces and not by any pecuniary calculus; "human beings, at least out of slave countries, are not produced to meet the requirements of the market." When children arrive at the age of maturity they will take decisions "distinctly governed by industrial considerations, or at least considerations bearing upon material success in life; but at this point the supply of labor *has already been determined.*" Therefore, though "in a certain irregular way, and taking considerable periods of time, the supply of labor as a whole follows the demand for labor," nevertheless "strictly commercial motives" operate "not upon the aggregate supply of labor, but merely upon the mode of its distribution" (pp. 152–4). In other words, the size of the labor force is largely an indeterminate variable and, insofar as economic reasoning is concerned, rigorous propositions about its behavior cannot be introduced as necessary links in the chain of arguments.[17] And with that (Cairnes should have realized) all the comparisons of the increase of population with the increase of food, which had for over half a century provided material for endless debate among economists, went by the board.

It is difficult to find any explanation for Cairnes' adherence to Ricardian economics other than personal deference to John Stuart Mill and desire to be aligned with "the great names." Cairnes was often original in his thinking and vigorous in his criticism, even of Mill himself. It is obvious that he had no sympathy for the labor theory of value. Nor was he influenced, as Mill and Fawcett were, by an overriding concern with social reform.[18] Moreover, all the practical questions which had once motivated the Ricardian economists were now settled issues. We do not expect that he could have joined Jevons in a wholly novel approach to economic questions. Yet it is surprising that in repudiating so much that was central to Ricardo's system, he did not treat Ricardo as he treated Adam Smith: a source from whom one might adopt ideas without regard to doctrinal filiation. In the last analysis, Cairnes' defense of Ricardo seems to emanate from a desire to stem the tide of shallow empiricism which was sweeping over contemporary economic thinking. Bad theory was better than no theory at all. And as he surveyed the scene he saw no satisfactory substitute for the general approach of Ricardo and his followers.

17. I do not mean to suggest that economic calculations are never operative in determining the rate of growth of population. But as yet the question has defied generalization.

18. Cairnes supported the proposal to tax the unearned increment and favored workers' cooperatives, but these ideas are barely mentioned in *Leading Principles.*

CHAPTER 12

Conclusion. The Evolution of Ricardian Economics

THE TASK of propagating Ricardian economics with a view to supplanting the "old" political economy of Adam Smith was largely over by 1830. While the rack renting days of the Napoleonic Wars and the Corn Law of 1815 were still fresh in the public mind Ricardian economics thrived on the current enthusiasm for free trade. These were the years when Ricardo's writings were directly associated, as Bailey put it, with "the political measures of the age" and when loyalty to the new dispensation overrode all critical objections.

Those who lacked any sympathy for the Ricardian approach failed to rally round a definite viewpoint. Malthus' criticism of Say's Law, which might have provided a point of departure, suffered from confused formulation and was, moreover, hitched to the defense of an unpopular cause: no theory which pleaded the case of the landed aristocracy and warned of the dangers of rapid industrialization could hope to succeed in an era dominated by the vision of unbounded economic expansion. The apparent contradiction between the Law of Markets and the recurrence of gluts was resolved as soon as it was recognized that business cycles are a regular feature of an industrial economy. Thereafter the chief function of Say's Law in the classical schema was not to deny the occurrence of periodic depressions but to emphasize the fallacy of the idea that "the unproductive expenditure of the rich" is necessary to prevent stagnation and breakdown.

Rapid as had been the ascent of Ricardian economics in the 1820's, significant deviations from Ricardo were in evidence almost from the start. James Mill and McCulloch attempted unsuccessfully to reformulate the labor theory of value so as to remove the difficulties created by differences in the turnover periods of different industries. Their exposition altered the character of the Ricardian theory of value. Instead of concentrating, as Ricardo did, on the conceptual problem of a measuring value so as to trace the effect of historical diminishing returns upon the rate of capital accumulation, Mill and McCulloch sought to give a strict labor cost explanation of relative prices. In so doing they were led to call profits "the wages of accumulated labour," which virtually suggested the exploitation theory of profit. It was not long before the followers of Owen recognized the connection, thus drawing support for their views from a theory identified with Ricardo. Bailey's devastating, if somewhat misconceived, attack on intertemporal comparisons of value served further to discredit Ricardo's invariable yardstick which thereupon practically disappeared from the literature of economics. Even John Stuart Mill shunted it into an isolated chapter of his *Principles* and treated it as an esoteric issue not deserving of the attention which it had received.

Ricardo's strong preference for paradoxical maxims led to much misunderstanding. The proposition that "profits depend upon wages," while valid as he expressed it, was difficult to expound and difficult to grasp. Even McCulloch and James Mill were anxious to convert it into a self-evident argument lest it provide a stumbling block to the spread of Ricardian economics. Their compromise was to say that it applies only when profits and wages are defined as relative shares of output. This ignores the fact that Ricardo's analysis clearly refers to the rate of profit on capital and, moreover, fails to show how a declining relative share of capital can affect the incentive to invest. Still another weak version of Ricardo's theory, favored by West, Senior, and J. S. Mill, is that ceteris paribus, the profits of a firm depend upon wage costs. This proposition, while true, is trivial and fails to convey Ricardo's meaning.

But most economists in the period, including most of Ricardo's critics, did believe that the amount of profit and, given the stock of capital, the rate of profit are governed by the efficiency of labor in agriculture. And this is the substance of Ricardo's theory of profit. However, in rejecting Ricardo's rigorous proof of the fundamental theorem they forgot the assumptions upon which it was based. Instead of investigating the changing composition of wage goods, thus raising the question of the usefulness of Ricardo's theory,[1] they clung to a vaguely defined connection between the rate of profit and diminishing returns in agriculture which somehow always overcame the forces making for increasing returns in industry.

Ricardo's seminal views on the machinery question were never taken up in earnest by any of his disciples. Bogged down in Ricardo's somewhat confusing presentation and unwilling to relax the simple verities of the wages fund doctrine, they took refuge in an expression of faith: whatever the analytical complexities, rapid capital accumulation would suffice to absorb all technically displaced labor. No one bothered to clear up the difference between innovations resulting from a change of technical knowledge and innovations induced by a change in factor

1. Even Longfield and Torrens, who did grasp the logical structure of Ricardo's argument, did not go on to question its empirical significance.

prices—a distinction which Ricardo had broached and then passed over. The whole topic of technological unemployment sank into oblivion. When John Stuart Mill came to discuss the machinery question in his *Principles* he reproduced Ricardo's arguments in full, adding the standard disclaimer with respect to Ricardo's major conclusion that employment would necessarily lag behind the growth of output.

After 1830 a series of new revisions served to undermine the supremacy of Ricardian economics. The census returns of 1831 took the sting out of the Malthusian theory of population, one of the chief props of Ricardo's system. Senior and Torrens went on record as denying the danger of an excessive increase of population. Jones and Whewell were quick to argue that Ricardo's underestimation of technical advances in agriculture had led to an entirely false view of the process of economic growth; McCulloch, and later de Quincey, were driven to admit that agricultural improvements had neutralized the tendency toward historical diminishing returns. Ricardo's *Principles*, McCulloch conceded, was not "a practical work"; and this was only one of the many flashes of impiety which now made their appearance in McCulloch's writings as the tone of professional economics became ever more hostile to Ricardo's teachings.

Writers such as Bailey, Read, Scrope, Lloyd, Longfield, and Senior had already laid the basis for an alternative body of doctrine. In their works the labor theory of value was replaced, more or less explicitly, by a utility theory. The popular approach was to redefine labor in terms of the disutility of effort; labor costs were thus made commensurate with the real cost of capital in the form of a premium for those willing to forego present consumption. The concept of rent was then generalized with reference to all forms of income; immobilities of resources and productive services were bundled together under the label of "monopoly" as exceptions to the Ricardian theory of value. Ricardo's clear-cut distinctions between wages, profits, and rents were in this manner shown to be nothing more than matters of terminology.

Insofar as there were any motivating political causes for the opposition to Ricardo they issued from the disharmonious implications of his theory of rent. Scrope convicted the Ricardian school not only of errors but of "crimes" for expounding the notion that the pecuniary interests of the landlord ran counter to the general welfare. Jones practically asserted that any theory which denied the spontaneous harmony of interests was necessarily wrong. The Ricardians themselves were divided on this question. McCulloch did his best to minimize any suggestion of a natural or even an artificial conflict of interests; de Quincey expressed profound alarm at the fact that "gloomy disorganizing Jacobinism" found support in certain corollaries of Ricardo's theory;

James Mill and John Stuart Mill, however, made the most of the image of the parasitical landlord as a justification for land reform proposals; Fawcett, on the other hand, was a firm advocate of harmony doctrine. In each case Ricardo's system was appropriately revised to suit the social orientation of the writer in question without regard to the analytical issues involved.

Something like this is what Marx had in mind when he spoke of Ricardo's successors as "vulgar economic apologists." The disintegration of Ricardian economics, he argued, was simply the result of the fact that "Political Economy can remain a science only so long as the class-struggle is latent or manifests itself only in isolated and sporadic phenomena."

> Let us take England. Its political economy belongs to the period in which the class-struggle was as yet undeveloped . . . With the year 1830 came the decisive crisis . . . Thenceforth, the class-struggle, practically as well as theoretically, took on more and more outspoken and threatening forms. It sounded the knell of scientific bourgeois economy. It was thenceforth no longer a question, whether this theorem or that was true, but whether it was useful to capital or harmful, expedient or inexpedient, politically dangerous or not. In place of disinterested enquirers, there were hired prize-fighters; in place of genuine scientific research, the bad conscience and evil intent of apologetics.[2]

Leaving aside the alleged material basis of scientific economics, here at least is a fairly concrete explanation of the decline of Ricardian economics. Whether or not the Six Acts and the Peterloo Massacre were "isolated and sporadic phenomena" at a time when the class struggle was only "latent," there is no doubt of the increase in social tension after 1830. It shows itself in the struggles around the Reform Bill, the attempts of the labor movement at General Union, the rise of Chartism, the emergence of the Ten Hours movement, and the agitation against the Poor Law Amendment Act. In the light of the incendiary language of the free trade pamphleteers and the use of the labor theory of value by the Ricardian socialists it is not surprising that many economics began to see the need for a new approach to fundamental questions of theory. In this connection it is significant that the writers who attacked the views of the "labour theorists"—Scrope, Read, and Longfield—were also among the first to advance the abstinence theory of profit. In this sense, the theoretical innovations of the "neglected British economists" were not unrelated to the nature of the

2. Preface to the second edition of *Capital, 1*.

class struggle after 1830. Whether this is what Marx himself meant to imply is not clear [3] but it is certainly an interpretation which others have placed upon his remarks.[4] And if we choose to regard the labor cost theory of value as the kernel of Ricardian economics we are driven to assert that the vital influence of Ricardo came to an end in the 1830's. The major treatises published in that decade give ample evidence of what Mr. Dobb describes as "the shift towards subjective notions and towards the study of exchange-relations in abstraction from their social roots" which became the outstanding characteristic of economic thought after 1870.

The difficulties with this argument are twofold. Firstly, it fails to account for the unmistakable Ricardian stamp of Scrope's and Senior's theory of production and distribution—not to speak of many of Ricardo's other critics—when, as this reasoning goes, the Ricardian influence had already disappeared. Secondly, it leaves us wondering why Mill and Cairnes, for example, took such pains to defend Ricardo's basic propositions even when the evidence pointed the other way. The fact is that Ricardo's influence never really made itself felt in the realm of value theory. From this point of view there is little justification in talking at all about a Ricardian school. The formal problems of value may loom all-important when relative prices are placed in the foreground of economic enquiry. But the classical era was largely preoccupied with the issue of economic growth. This is why the subjective theory of value did not succeed in gaining general approval. The kind of value theory that is to be found in Senior's *Political Economy* (1836) had all the characteristics of viable and successful economic theory. It made use of fewer special assumptions than the labor theory of value and, by including nonreproducible goods, encompassed a wider range of phenomena. Yet it failed to supplant the labor cost approach.

It was simply that these were not the issues that interested contemporaries by and large. No doubt Senior's book provided a more elegant, and certainly a more symmetrical, theory of prices than Ricardo's *Principles*. But what matter such logical refinements or the greater tractability of Senior's schema if it bore the same conclusions as Ri-

3. Marx was not aware of the writings of Lloyd and Longfield; he denounced Senior's abstinence theory but ignored Senior's criticism of the labor theory of value. McCulloch was put among the "vulgar economists" but John Stuart Mill was exempted from the charge: while Marx had no high opinion of Mill's "shallow syncretism" he thought it wrong to class him with "the herd of vulgar economic apologists."

4. M. Dobb, *Political Economy and Capitalism* (New York, 1945), pp. 133–4; Roll, *op. cit.*, pp. 404–11; R. L. Meek, "The Decline of Ricardian Economics in England," *Economica*, February 1950.

cardo's system on the specific economic problems of the day?[5] After all, Senior did subscribe to the basic Ricardian link between the productivity of agriculture and the rate of capital accumulation, and he concluded from this, again on Ricardian lines, that free trade would constitute a bulwark against the stationary state. Torrens reflected the prevailing attitude when he denied that either Malthus, Jones, or Senior had succeeded in establishing "a separate system or school of his own." "Doctrines put forward in refutation of the principles of Ricardo," Torrens concluded, "are not infrequently mere extensions of these principles."

The Ricardian emphasis on economic growth and the changes in the distributive shares so permeated economic thinking in the period that even those who revolted against Ricardo's authority in fact accepted its essential outlook.[6] To be sure, "it was a *minority* which swept the public off its feet . . . the advocates of the complete Ricardian case were almost ludicrously few."[7] But it is just as true that the advocates of the complete Keynesian case in the years, say, 1936 to 1946, were "ludicrously few"—yet who would deny the pervasive influence of Keynesian economics in that decade? What is at issue here is an influence that cannot be measured by the number of avowed disciples. As Jevons said: "There were economists, such as Malthus and Senior, who had a far better comprehension of the true doctrines (though not free from the Ricardian errors), but they were driven out of the field by the unity and influence of the Ricardo-Mill school."[8] The weight of "the Ricardian errors" was so strong that even the critics and outspoken opponents of Ricardo came under their spell. Consequently the original

5. "I should be inclined to argue," writes Professor Stigler, "that most of our modern economics of price was deemed by the classical economists to be pedestrian stuff, inappropriate to a treatise. The problems of the firm and the industry are important, they would say—no doubt of it. But they are tolerably well handled by the journalist and the businessman. For us, they would say, there are greater problems: the true basis of value, the laws of distribution of national income, the foundations of national prosperity, the growth and decline of nations. Why should we fuss over the minutiae of a firm's costs, or over its timid elements of monopoly? These are the proper subjects for later, and lesser, men. As for us, we seek the great eternal truths and the laws of history" (*Five Lectures on Economic Problems* [London, 1949], p. 36).

6. As Professor Robbins put it: "What is relevant here in this connection is not whether analysis of value and distribution of Senior and J. S. Mill—not to mention money and international trade—followed Ricardo in all respects but whether it conformed to the type of analysis of which his works are the arch type" (*Quarterly Journal of Economics,* February 1955, pp. 10–11).

7. S. G. Checkland, "The Propagation of Ricardian Economics in England," *Economica,* February 1949.

8. Preface to the second edition of *The Theory of Political Economy* (London, 1889).

contributions of men like Malthus, Bailey, Scrope, Jones, Longfield, and Senior took the form of isolated theoretical innovations, carrying no practical import, which were either brushed aside or assimilated without disturbing the mainstream of Ricardian economics. The shortcomings of anti-Ricardian economics—its eclectic character, its failure to carry through—far more than the dogmatism of Ricardo's disciples was the factor responsible for its lack of success.[9]

While Ricardian economics remained the ruling doctrine of the age it paid a price in the gradual but steady dissolution of the original theoretical structure. At first a purely spontaneous process of self-criticism led to a number of amendments in the whole body of doctrines inherited from Ricardo. Thereafter, the attempt to assimilate the ideas of the dissenters gave rise to further modifications in the Ricardian system. By the 1840's, however, it was the growing quantity of statistical data, revealing the failure of Ricardo's theory to yield accurate predictions about the phenomena to which it referred, which provided the fundamental impetus to doctrinal revision.

As it appears in Mill's *Principles* (1848) or in Cairnes' *Leading Principles Newly Expounded* (1874), the Ricardian system stands hedged about with serious qualifications and even the admission of directly contradictory arguments. Neither Mill nor Cairnes was willing to assert that greater density of population had actually raised wheat prices relative to manufactures or that rents had risen and profits fallen as a result of the corn laws. Nor did they claim that the tendency toward diminishing returns could be retarded if, and only if, manufactured articles were freely traded against cheap foreign corn. Free trade was no longer regarded as the panacea it had once been for Ricardo and the early votaries of the new political economy.[10]

Yet, as we know, Mill and Cairnes clung to Ricardo's theories despite quantitative evidence to the contrary; their explanation of the dis-

9. Nothing is explained merely by pointing to the intellectual tenacity of Ricardo's disciples. Not even McCulloch exhibited an obsequious regard for every one of Ricardo's dicta. James Mill was not dissuaded by Ricardo's disapproval from prescribing a far-reaching program of land reform. Robert Torrens first accepted, then rejected Ricardo's system, only to retract his objections in the end. And John Stuart Mill carried the Ricardian theory into realms never envisaged by Ricardo himself.

10. The insidious weakness of the Ricardian model was its assumption of the preponderance of wheaten bread in the workers' budget. When the Paralleltheorie, stressing the casual dependence of money wages on corn prices, ceased to be factually tenable, the Ricardian case for free trade lost most of its force. Add to this the fact that Ricardo had never advocated the total repeal of all tariffs on agricultural produce and we see why Hodgskin could say that there is little in Ricardo's writings which "resembles the argument, or refers to the facts, by which the corn laws have been overturned."

crepancy was that the deductions of Ricardo had been upset by "disturbing causes." Now, in principle, it is true that economic relationships hold only in the absence of changes in all the unenumerated, and often unmeasurable, variables. If this is all that Mill and Cairnes were saying one could hardly quarrel with it. But unless the omitted "disturbing causes" can be said to exert their influence with some accountable regularity the asserted relationship lacks any empirical content. When McCulloch found evidence of rising wheat yields per acre as early as 1837 and no tendency for the growth of population to reduce per capita income, he ascribed the result arbitrarily to the landlord's sudden enthusiasm for improvements; this was not allowed to affect the Ricardian indictment against the corn laws. When Fawcett insisted that the introduction of free trade "disturbed" the conclusions of Ricardo, he ignored the empirical evidence which had been collected prior to repeal. Cairnes went so far as to cast general doubt on the use of statistics as a means of testing economic propositions, asserting irrelevantly that "the diminishing productiveness of the soil" was an indisputable "physical fact."

The Malthusian principle of population is a perfect example of a doctrine which was defended on logical grounds as pertaining to a "tendency" operating in the absence of counteracting checks. And when every increase in output was not followed by additional mouths to feed, the term "tendency" became "a smoke-screen to cover a withdrawal of indefinite extent." [11] The strength of the Malthusian theory, of course, lay in the fact that it supplied at once a hypothesis about the action of the population variable in economic growth, a statement of the land using tendencies of capital accumulation, and an explanation of the equilibrium adjustment of wages in the long run. The principle of population was the cement which held these strands together. When it was rejected in one sense it was often retained in another.[12] Thus Senior attacked the Malthusian thesis on the one hand and on the other made it one of the four elementary propositions of economic science. Not until Cairnes did anyone realize that the so-called pressure

11. Hutchison, *op. cit.*, p. 73.

12. A letter from Chadwick, written in 1836, affords a striking example of this (all the more striking because Chadwick was not an economic theorist): "Everywhere the apparent surplus of labourers has been absorbed, and what may be said of the results is not that they prove the principle of population as to the tendency to be untrue but that they show it to be inapplicable to England in its present condition: as if we were to say that the proof that no stones actually fall to the centre of the earth was to disprove the principle of gravitation or a tendency of all stones to fall to the centre, &c . . . But I do not think that the statement of the fact will militate against the sounder theories on the subject" (quoted by H. L. Beales, "The Historical Context of the *Essay on Population,*" in *Introduction to Malthus,* pp. 15–16).

of population upon the means of subsistence was a question separate and distinct from the wages-population mechanism.[13] But even Cairnes did not realize the implications of his discusson. If it be true that strictly pecuniary motives operate "not upon the aggregate supply of labor but merely upon the mode of its distribution," the connection between demographic changes and economic growth becomes an empirical question outside the domain of abstract theory.

The amazing thing is not that Ricardian economics survived but that it lasted down to the 1870's long after it had become palpably incongruent with reality and top-heavy with the infusion of antithetical ideas. In the final analysis the explanation lies in the fact that nothing better was found to take its place. In an era of rapid industrial expansion, dominated by the conflict between the landed gentry and the manufacturing interests, a theory which dealt with the major issues of capital accumulation and functional distribution in terms of a few aggregate variables had all the advantages of popular appeal and practical significance. On this level of analysis Ricardo had no competitors. The discrepancy between Ricardo's predictions and the actual course of events made it necessary to admit that the Ricardian system was not quite correct. But so long as the corn laws remained on the statute books Ricardian economics appeared to be relevant to the contemporary scene: it addressed itself to the vital policy question and provided a rationale for a definite course of action. There was always the fear that in rejecting Ricardo entirely the case for free trade might be jeopardized. In the absence of an alternative structure of equal scope and practical import, yielding superior predictions for as wide a range of phenomena, there was every incentive to retain the Ricardian system in its broad outlines.

Ricardo's model was geared to an "insulated economy" which refrains from reaping the benefits of comparative advantage by placing restrictions on the importation of raw produce. Hence with the achievement of free trade the Ricardian system ceased to be applicable. If it had not been for the subtle shift of emphasis which John Stuart Mill imparted to received doctrine the matter would have ended in 1846. But by then the weight of tradition had achieved a momentum of its own which stemmed the tide against Ricardo for yet another two decades. When Jevons came to publish his *Theory of Political Economy* (1871) he did not attempt to provide a substitute for Ricardian economics; rather, he altered the nature of the central problem: "Given, a certain population, with various needs and powers of production, in possession of certain lands and other sources of material: required, the mode of employing their labour which will maximize the utility of the produce."

13. Although Longfield had said as much in 1834.

APPENDIX A

Ricardo and Marx

THE FIRST TASK of value theory is to explain the ratios at which commodities exchange. By assuming that commodities are produced under conditions of constant cost, this explanation may be confined to the supply side. By its very nature, the labor theory of value must abstract from differences in the capital structure of different industries. When capital per worker varies in different lines of production, while the rate of profit on capital is everywhere the same, it can never be true that relative prices are strictly proportionate to the amount of direct and indirect labor employed. Commodities requiring more capital per worker will have a lower ratio of wage costs to prices. Moreover, the scope of the labor theory is restricted to long-run prices of reproducible goods under perfect competition. For most problems in micro-economics it is hopelessly inadequate. But so far as it goes it is a valid first approximation. The labor theory of value in this sense is simply a special case of the Marshallian theory of value.

However, the labor theory of value is more than a theory of relative prices, and this is where the controversies begin. Both Smith and Ricardo employed the theory as a method of social accounting and Marx used it to deduce, from additional corollaries, that profit is appropriated labor. The first of these is tied up with Ricardo's misleading criticism of Adam Smith's labor-commanded theory of value. Adam Smith made the power of purchasing labor itself, rather than the power of purchasing the products of labor, the measure of the value of a commodity. Ricardo accused Smith of identifying the two measures (*1*, 14) although there is ample evidence in the *Wealth of Nations* that Smith recognized the distinction between a labor-commanded and a labor-embodied theory. Ricardo dismissed Smith's measure because it is subject to "as many fluctuations as the commodities compared with it," which is irrelevant in the context of relative price determination. If two commodities embody equal quantities of labor they command an equal amount of labor (or, for that matter, any other commodity). In a profit economy the labor which a commodity can purchase always exceeds the labor required to produce it. Hence Ricardo (and Marx after him) implies that different relative prices will be obtained from the use of the two measures. This is a fallacy. Given any two commodities, in the one case we have ratios of purchasing power over a common wage unit, in the other we have ratios of man-hours; either method yields the same equilibrium ratios of exchange.

But the labor-commanded theory hardly constitutes an adequate explanation of relative prices. The value of the wage unit itself is not accounted for.

The labor-embodied theory has at least the virtue of employing the same rule to explain the value of output and the value of input. In Adam Smith's language we would have to say that the value of wage goods is determined by the labor it can purchase, which explains nothing. However, this only shows that Smith's measure was not intended to deal with the problem of relative prices but rather with secular changes in wealth. Starting with the notion that the disutility of labor is invariant "at all times and places," Smith was led to the view that a man's real wealth is best measured by the amount of other men's "toil and trouble" which he can purchase in the market. A nation's wealth, he concluded, ought to be similarly estimated. The value of total output is the number of wage units it commands.

As a unit of social accounting, a labor-commanded measure is useful only insofar as both money wages and real wages remain constant through time.[1] It is obvious why Ricardo rejected Smith's measure. In the Ricardian system, diminishing returns in agriculture raise money wages but leave real wages unchanged. Ricardo, in turn, postulated a measure invariant in cost value and money price (given constancy in the purchasing power of money). There is no logical choice between these two approaches; everything depends on the purpose of the analysis and each has its own drawbacks.

The attempt to account for relative prices by relative wage costs can be called the "labor cost theory of value"; it has had no enthusiastic adherents since Marx. The device of expressing certain aggregate variables in terms of physical man-hours or the money value of man-hours can be described as the "labor standard theory"; on this definition, Smith and Malthus are adherents of the wage unit version of the labor standard theory, while Ricardo, Marx, and Mrs. Robinson[2] advocate the man-hour version.[3]

We come now to Marx's unique contribution to the labor theory of value, the exploitation theory of profit. Marx divides output into constant capital (c), variable capital (v), and surplus value (s). Surplus value, and therefore profit, is derived solely from employing labor directly; it is nothing else but output net of depreciation (c) minus the wages bill (v).[4] In the first volume of *Capital* Marx assumes that relative prices are strictly proportional to relative labor costs and that profit per worker or "the rate of exploitation" $\left(\frac{s}{v}\right)$ is the same in all industries. This implies that capital-labor ratios (the organic compositions of capital) are everywhere equal. The moment it is

1. Smith's measure is at the same time an index number employed to measure changes in real income: if money wages are held constant the real value of the quantity of money is held constant.

2. See Joan Robinson, *The Accumulation of Capital* (London, 1956), pp. 118–22.

3. The utility theory of value can be treated in the same way: Subjective value theory deals with ratios of utilities while subjective welfare economics deals with additive utilities or conditions under which someone may be said to be "better off." The history of utility theory is reminder enough of the importance of keeping these two strands of thought separate and distinct.

4. Depreciation allowances are assumed to be equal to replacement needs.

granted that capital per worker varies widely from industry to industry, the assumption of uniform profits per worker produces the paradoxical result that the rate of profit on capital varies inversely with the degree of mechanization. But the rate of profit on total capital invested tends to equality regardless of the composition of capital. It follows that profit per worker is not independent of capital per worker and, hence, that relative prices do not correspond to labor values.

This is the so-called "great contradiction" which Marx solved in the third volume of *Capital* by transforming all values $(c + v + s)$ into "prices of production," the latter denoting money costs of production $(c + v)$ including profits at the going rate $\left(\frac{s}{c + v}\right)$. With the aid of elementary algebra it can be shown [5] that when the value of both inputs and outputs is transformed into supply prices,[6] either total profits equal total surplus value or "total value equals totalprice." Both equalities cannot be preserved unless prices are measured in terms of a commodity produced with a composition of capital equal to the social average.

In the end, Marx' laborious transformation of values into prices brings us circuitously to a result which Ricardo achieved directly by measuring prices with an invariable yardstick. In terms of Ricardo's measuring rod it is strictly true that relative prices correspond to relative labor values and that profits are independent of the amount of constant capital employed. In the Ricardian universe a commodity sells at its value if it sells at its supply price because differences in capital structure are explicitly assumed away.

It is not surprising, therefore, that Marx secures the same answers as Ricardo when he considers a Ricardian problem: the effect of a change in wages upon prices.[7] Marx considers a three-industry economy, holds "total value equal to total price," and finds that a rise in money wages leaves the price of goods produced with average technique unaffected while changing other prices inversely to the degree of mechanization.[8]

This result is helpful in understanding Marx' strange formula in which a sum of relative prices is said to be equal to a sum of relative values. What it implies is that the labor theory of value holds only when differences in capital structure are ignored. Granted, Marx would say, the organic composition of capital is not everywhere the same; nevertheless, if the calculus of value is "correctly" translated into the calculus of price certain aggregate

5. See R. L. Meek, "Some Notes on the Transformation Problem," *Economic Journal*, March 1956, and the literature cited there.

6. Marx himself made the mistake of transforming output values only.

7. *Capital*, 3, ch. 12.

8. McCulloch had remarked that when prices are estimated in the invariable measure, changes in wages, while causing "some variation in the exchangeable value of particular commodities," "neither add nor take away from the *total value* of the entire mass of commodities" (*Principles*, p. 312). As A. C. Whitaker points out, this observation may have suggested the transformation problem to Marx (*History and Criticism of the Labor Theory of Value* [New York, 1904], p. 62.

relations persist: labor costs determine surplus value, which determines average profits, which govern the rate of profit. In other words, the labor cost theory can be employed to show that the rate of profit depends upon the ratio of man-hours required to produce wage goods to the man-hours required to produce total output. This, Marx seems to feel, is all that is needed to vindicate the theory of surplus value.

But this proposition, established by Ricardo, does not itself yield the theory that profit is in the nature of an unearned income. This Marxian conclusion follows only from the additional argument that the rate of exploitation is equal in all industries. The transformation problem would not arise were it not for the fact that Marx wanted to show that despite the fact that profit per worker seems to vary with capital per worker, nevertheless each worker generates the same surplus per man-hour.[9] Yet all that he succeeded in demonstrating was that in the aggregate the amount of profit and, given the stock of capital, the rate of profit depend upon the ratio of real wages to net output. Unfortunately, this has nothing to do with the question of whether profit is an unearned income and is perfectly compatible with the notion that it is an indispensable and moral reward for "waiting."

For Marx the central difficulty is always that of "harmonising the mutual exchange of capital and labour with the Ricardian law of determining value by labour." [10] To explain profit by "living labor" alone is to suggest that the rate of profit on capital depends upon the composition of capital; this is the celebrated contradiction. But Ricardo never noticed this contradiction. It did not occur to him to think of capitalists as claimants without function. He argued that value is determined by the amount of living and stored-up labor embodied in commodities.[11] It does not follow from this that the more mechanized processes should earn relatively less profit per worker. Ricardo's philosophical reflections about labor being "the foundation of value" are still a far cry from the theory of surplus value.

And yet there is a "contradiction" in Ricardo's version of the labor cost theory. A change of wages alters the price structure, and, so, while commodities are still produced in the same way, relative prices have altered. A special measuring rod is introduced to abstract from this difficulty. This automatically prevents any divergence between labor values and actual sup-

9. Marx's transformation actually assumes what it is designed to prove. As Mrs. Robinson puts it, Marx's solution is "purely formalistic and consists in juggling to and fro with averages and totals": "the *values* of commodities are imputed by crediting each group of workers with an average rate of exploitation of labor as a whole and the 'transformation of values into prices' consists of breaking the average up again into the separate items from which it was derived . . . if the imputation and the transformation are both done according to the rules, the answer is bound to come out right" (*Collected Economic Papers,* pp. 150–1).

10. *Capital,* 2, 205.

11. Strictly speaking, the notion of adding present man-hours to something called "stored-up labor" has no obvious meaning since the latter is a flow of future values discounted at a ruling rate of interest. The main task of the labor standard theory is to specify how capital values might be measured, a task which Ricardo avoided by his device of an invariable measure of value.

ply prices and thus seems to preserve the Marxian theory of surplus value free of "the great contradiction." But it is a strange exploitation theory of profit which requires for its validity the assumption that there is no variety in the capital structure of an economy.[12]

It is sometimes said that Marx's greatest contribution is the explicit recognition that the key to the nature of profit is to be sought in the historical process by which workers have been rendered legally free but effectively destitute. However, a well-known theory of profit, which appears in the *Wealth of Nations* and was shared implicitly by Ricardo, accounts for the reward of mere ownership of capital by the fact that laborers cannot wait for the proceeds of time-consuming production; those that can, exact a price for the service of waiting. Whatever may be wrong with this theory it fits the facts of a dispossessed working class.[13]

Actually neither Smith nor Ricardo exhibited any particular interest in the nature of profit. What Ricardo did say about the problem lays stress upon the element of waiting (*4*, 365–6) and therefore points away from, not toward Marx. This would hardly need saying were it not that the labor theory of value is frequently regarded as evolving, almost purposively, toward the theories of Karl Marx. The concept of surplus value, one Marxist asserts, was not derived from the labor theory of value; no, the labor theory of value was developed "precisely in order to explain the manifest existence of surplus value in the real world." [14] Smith and Ricardo are simply muddled forerunners of Marx.

Marx himself set the fashion for this style of criticism. In his *Theories of Surplus Value,* intended as a final volume of *Capital,* we are presented with a "*critical* history of the *main* point of political economy, the theory of surplus value." A third of the book is given over to a criticism of Ricardo: Ricardo should have realized that the fact of a uniform rate of profit contradicts the determination of value by labor time; Ricardo merely identifies value with price and therefore profit with surplus value; Ricardo ignores the nature of labor as "the substance of value" and deals only with "the magnitude of value"; and, most crushing of all, Ricardo failed to investigate "the origin of surplus value." [15] But Ricardo's discussion of the invariable measure of value brings out quite clearly that prices will diverge from values owing

12. Bortkiewicz takes the view that since both Ricardo and Marx regard profit as originating in "a withholding of some of the produce of labour" they should be classed together as advocates of the "withholding theory of profit"—his name for the exploitation theory ("Value and Price in the Marxian System," *International Economic Papers,* No. 2 [London, 1952], pp. 32, 51). But the notion that profit is governed by the ratio of wages to output, both expressed in man-hours, is not a theory of the origin of profit, nor does it imply that some of labor's product is withheld.

13. Marx tried to refute this doctrine; his refutation proceeds entirely by way of a repeated assertion that "the fund out of which the capitalist pays the wage earner is nothing but the latter's own product" (*Theories of Surplus Value,* trans. G. A. Bonner and E. Burns [London, 1951], pp. 96–9).

14. R. L. Meek, *Studies in the Labour Theory of Value* (London, 1956), p. 126.

15. *Theories of Surplus Value,* pp. 203, 210, 212, 213, 260, 283, 310, 342.

to the existence of an average rate of profit coupled with differences in capital-labor ratios. Ricardo discovered the "contradiction," which makes it a little strange that Marx should accuse him of ignoring it.[16]

What is so puzzling is that Marx pays practically no attention to Ricardo's invariable measure of value. When Marx does touch on it he interprets it incorrectly as designed solely to show that a change in wages will not affect "the price of production of gold." Ricardo's choice of gold as the invariable yardstick is deemed "absurd"; here Marx shows clearly that he could not grasp the concept of a numéraire which is at the same time the circulating medium. Section 6 of chapter 1 of Ricardo's *Principles,* "On An Invariable Measure of Value," is dismissed as saying nothing of importance: "The connection between value—its immanent measure in labor-time—and the necessity for an eternal measure of the values of commodities is not understood; it is not even raised as a problem." [17] For Marx the attempt to find "a commodity of unchanging value which would serve as a constant measure for others" is an attempt "to square the circle": the measure of value must be "an immanent measure which at the same time forms the substance of value." [18] The sense of this is that the measure of value must be independent of what is to be measured; this is of course Ricardo's own requirement for an invariable measure of value. That the measure of value must also constitute "the substance of value" is Marx's requirement for the theory of surplus value and has nothing to do either with relative prices, social accounting, or Ricardo's system.

Marx's critique of Ricardo is a comedy of errors. Just as Böhm-Bawerk in *Karl Marx and the Close of his System* took it for granted that Marx was trying to analyze relative prices, and criticized him from that standpoint, Marx assumes that Ricardo should have been interested in "harmonising the mutual exchange of capital and labour with the . . . law of determining value by labour" and condemned him for not arriving at the theory of surplus value.

Addendum

F. Seton, in an article which appeared as this book went to press ("The Transformation Problem," *Review of Economic Studies,* 24, third series, No. 65), provides a rigorous proof of the argument sketched above. Discarding the three-industry model for an n-fold division of the economy, he shows that the principle of equal profitability is sufficient to transform labor values into a unique set of relative prices. In order then to determine absolute prices

16. See Bortkiewicz, *op. cit.,* pp. 27–36, for an incisive analysis of Marx's tendentious critique of Ricardo.

17. *Ibid.,* pp. 241–4.

18. *Ibid.,* p. 116. For Marx, the "immanent measure" is labor as distinct from labor power. The value of labor power is determined by the "amount of labor" required to produce wage goods; "value of labor" has no meaning; labor is simply a certain number of man-hours. Marx was very proud of this distinction but it is merely a verbal clarification of an obvious point.

any one of the following invariance postulates or numéraires will do: (1) a value of unity for all "luxury goods" consumed only by capitalists; (2) a value of unity for the weighted average of all prices, i.e., "total value equals total price"; and (3) a value of unity for the total surplus, i.e., "total profits equals total surplus value" (this comes to the same thing as (1) if net investment is zero). On the other hand, the Ricardian postulate that the organic composition of capital in the wage goods industry is equal to the national average necessarily guarantees invariance of the wages-output ratio. But since this invariance is expressed in terms of price ratios it fails to determine absolute prices. Marxists surmount this difficulty by assuming equal rates of exploitation in all industries. But this assumption is precisely what the transformation-solution is meant to prove.

APPENDIX B

Malthus and Keynes

IN CLAIMING Malthus as a predecessor Keynes has set a fashion in the history of economic thought which has thrown the whole debate on gluts out of focus. Historical perspective, contemporary relevance, and even analytical incisiveness have been thrown to the winds in the effort to prove that "the almost total obliteration of Malthus's line of approach and the complete domination of Ricardo's for a period of a hundred years has been a disaster to the progress of economics." [1] And yet, as Professor Robbins has said, "the more thoroughly Malthus is studied, the more slender appear his claims to be regarded as a precursor of the *General Theory*." [2]

Let us briefly examine two examples of the Keynesian interpretation. In his book, *The Keynesian Revolution*, Professor Klein likens the Ricardo-Malthus dispute on gluts to the struggle between Keynes and his contemporaries: "The issues in each case were essentially the same." He declares that Malthus alone understood that "both savings and consumption could increase in a period of unemployment"; as evidence he supplies a statement by Malthus which has no reference to unemployment but merely to the fact that saving and consumption may be complementary "in consequence of a previous increase in the value of national revenue." There follows a series of assertions about Malthus' insights which run true for all the classical economists; namely, "that savings depend upon income such that an increase in income leads to an increase of savings," "that investment is entirely a function of national income," "that income and wealth distribution have some effect upon the level of savings." Professor Klein concedes, however, that Malthus had no adequate theory of the determinants of effective demand, that he never went adequately behind the motives for investment, that he took a strict classical position on wage cuts as a stimulus to employment, and that, at best, he offered a basis for a theory of the savings function. He sums up by stating that Malthus' main contribution to the problem of unemployment was the concept of unproductive consumption, and finds similarities between Malthus' ideas and the crude underconsumption theory of Foster and Catchings.[3] Surely this is not only a misrepresentation of

1. Keynes, *Essays in Biography*, p. 117.
2. *The Theory of Economic Policy*, p. 30 n.
3. *The Keynesian Revolution* (New York, 1949), pp. 125–9. For a contrasting treatment by another warm admirer of Keynes, see the judicious analysis by Hansen, *op. cit.*, pp. 241–54.

Malthus but actually undermines belief in *any* relation between Malthus and Keynes.

Another protagonist of Malthus has declared that "once the veil of agricultural illustrations has been lifted, Malthus' underlying theory . . . unfolds itself with a remarkable Keynesian flavor." [4] But his conclusions speak for themselves.

> Malthus explained the fall of profits in terms of an inadequate consumer demand which grows out of the saving process. Somewhere in the circular income flow, funds become stagnant. He was never very implicit, but he seemed to imply that because of slowly changing consumption habits laborers tend to retain increasingly large amounts of idle money as their incomes expand. It is very difficult to ascertain whether he did or did not think everything saved is invested . . .
>
> It seems fair to conclude then that Malthus's theory assumed that excessive savings lead to a damming up of idle purchasing power, although he was hazy as to where the damming-up process occurs.[5]

Despite the Keynesian phraseology of "effective demand," Malthus' theory contains not a hint of the concept of underemployment equilibrium; even the idea of a business cycle never entered Malthus' imagination. Instead of an alternative between individual decisions to save and to consume, with income variations equating *ex ante* saving and investment, we get an alternative between saving to invest and spending on luxury goods, with employment governed by the market for services and tertiary products. Instead of an influence of income distribution on the volume of savings, there is the notion that oversaving is connected with the preponderance of certain social classes in the community imbued with an irrational propensity to save.

The attempt to treat Malthus as an early exponent of the use of fiscal policy to promote aggregate demand misses the mark entirely. Whereas with Keynes public works have the object of stimulating production by making net additions to purchasing power, for Malthus they serve the aim of contracting productive investment by taxing available capital. Malthus' whole argument is rooted in the belief that further industrialization of the British economy is undesirable. Modern adherents of the Keynes-Hansen stagnation thesis have often been accused of generalizing particularly severe cyclical fluctuations into a secular lack of opportunities to invest; by contrast, Malthus must be charged with a myopic exaggeration of the difficulties experienced after the Napoleonic Wars, difficulties for which he offered exactly the wrong remedy. In view of these and other differences

4. J. J. O'Leary, "Malthus and Keynes," *Journal of Political Economy,* December 1942. See also P. Lambert, "The Law of Markets Prior to J.-B. Say and the Say-Malthus Debate," *International Economic Papers,* No. 6 (1956), in which the author goes so far as to describe Keynes' *General Theory* as "essentially a rigorous exposition of Malthus."

5. J. J. O'Leary, "Malthus' General Theory of Employment and the Post-Napoleonic Depressions," *Journal of Economic History,* November 1943, pp. 195–6.

between Malthus and Keynes, it would seem that the claim of doctrinal precedence rests on nothing more than their common rejection of Say's Law.[6]

6. For a review of some genuine forerunners of the Keynesian view in this period, see S. G. Checkland, "The Birmingham Economists, 1815–1850," *Economic History Review,* second series, *1,* No. 1 (1948).

APPENDIX C

McCulloch's Critique of the Factory System

In the years that McCulloch wrote for the *Edinburgh Review* (1818–37) he acquired the reputation of an apologist for the factory system. "McCulloch was ready to turn the whole country into one vast manufacturing district, filled with smoke and steam engines and radical weavers," remarked Mallet bitterly, "and to set adrift all the gentlemen and farmers now constituting our agricultural population." [1] The successive editions of McCulloch's *Principles,* however, reveal a sense of growing alarm at the social and political consequences of the Industrial Revolution. Indeed, McCulloch's nervous fear of public unrest, which colored his stand on all policy questions, led him eventually to doubt the benefits of industrialization as such.

In the first edition of the *Principles* McCulloch attacked Adam Smith's statement that the division of labor in industry necessarily renders the workman "as stupid and ignorant as it is possible for a human creature to become." [2] On the contrary, McCulloch declared, specialization has promoted literacy and education: "The intelligence of the workmen employed in manufactures has increased as their number has increased, and as their employments have been more and more subdivided." [3] In the second edition of the *Principles* (1830) McCulloch takes note of the objection that the extension of manufacturing subjects an ever growing portion of the population to unstable employment: With every trade depression "public tranquility and the security of property are apt to be endangered." But such instances of distress are really the result of artificial restrictions on commerce; at worse, McCulloch asserts, they represent the "growing pains" of an industrial civilization. And at the same time the turbulence and political excitement which is thereby generated is creative of popular agitation for better legislation. This is why "the introduction and establishment of extensive manufactures and commerce have everywhere been the era of public freedom, and of an improved system of government." [4]

In the next edition of the *Principles* (1843) the tone is radically different. The shadow of Chartism has put its spell on the land of promise. The factory system is now described as productive of a state of "perpetual helotism." The year before, at the Political Economy Club, McCulloch had taken the side of those who held the view that the specialized skill of the

1. *Political Economy Club,* p. 234.
2. *The Wealth of Nations,* p. 734.
3. *Principles,* p. 162.
4. *Ibid.* (2d ed. 1830), pp. 175–7.

factory worker was acquired "at the expense of his intellectual, social and martial virtues." "The education given to workers encouraged them to revolt," he added, "and they have no chance whatever to better themselves." [5] In his *Principles* he elaborated upon the theme: A worker must be conscious of the advantages he derives from established institutions "before any species of training will make him anxious for their preservation." But workingmen who contrast their lot with the rich will be apt to conclude that "there is something radically wrong in a system productive of such results" and will lend a willing ear to "workshop agitators" who "represent the privations of the work-people . . . as the necessary consequence of a defective system of domestic economy, having regard alone to the interests of the higher classes." While judicious legislation may bring greater stability to the factory system in the future, the beneficial effects of industry, McCulloch concedes, depend largely on its subordination to agriculture "and other more stable businesses." This is not to be taken as an expression of "any doubts or misgiving as to the continued advantages resulting from the progressive improvements of the arts," he adds ingenuously, for it has reference only to "the excessive growth of manufactures in particular countries." The question arises whether "artificial means" ought to be used to check the disproportionate growth of manufacturing. For some time, however, McCulloch assures his readers, all questions of this sort will be "decided in the negative." And then, on an unusual note of humility, he concludes: "Notwithstanding its vast importance, the solution of this class of questions must be left to the economists of some future age." [6]

The relentless spread of those "dark satanic mills" had shattered even McCulloch's habitual self-confidence. The most orthodox of Ricardo's disciples had come at last to share Malthus' fear of the rapid pace of technological progress.

As late as 1859 we find McCulloch asserting sentiments identical to those voiced by John Stuart Mill: "There seems, on the whole, little room for doubting that the factory system operates unfavourably on the bulk of those engaged in it . . . It is certain, too, that the demand for the services of children and other young persons, and the ease with which factory labour may in general be learned, has had a powerful influence in depressing wages, and, consequently, in preventing the wonderful inventions and discoveries of the last half century from redounding so much to the advantage of the labouring classes as might otherwise have been anticipated." [7]

5. *Political Economy Club,* p. 380.
6. *Principles* (3d ed. 1843), pp. 182–7; also (4th ed. 1849) pp. 189–94.
7. J. R. McCulloch, *Treatises and Essays* (Edinburgh, 1859), p. 455.

BIBLIOGRAPHY

PRIMARY SOURCES *

Almack, John, *Character, Motives and Proceedings of the Anti-Corn-Law Leaguers, with a Few General Remarks on the Consequences That Would Result from a Free Trade in Corn*. London, 1843.

[Bailey, Samuel], *A Critical Dissertation on the Nature, Measure, and Causes of Value; Chiefly in Reference to the Writings of Mr. Ricardo and his Followers*. London, 1825. London School of Economics Reprints, No. 7, 1931.

[———], *A Letter to a Political Economist; Occasioned by an Article in the Westminster Review on the Subject of Value*. London, 1826.

[Bailey], "On the Nature, Measure and Causes of Value," *Westminster Review*, January 1826, pp. 157–72.

Banfield, Thomas C., *Six Letters to the Right Hon. Sir Robert Peel, Bart., Being an Attempt to Expose the Dangerous Tendency of the Theory of Rent Advocated by Mr. Ricardo and by the Writers of His School*. London, 1843.

———, *Four Lectures on the Organisation of Industry; Being Part of a Course Delivered in the University of Cambridge in Easter Term, 1844*. London, 1845. 2d ed. 1848.

Barton, John, *Observations on the Circumstances which Influence the Condition of the Labouring Classes of Society*. London, 1817. Reprinted: Ed. J. H. Hollander. Baltimore, Johns Hopkins Press, 1934.

———, *An Inquiry into the Causes of the Progressive Depreciation of Agricultural Labour in Modern Times*. London, 1820.

———, *A Statement of the Consequences Likely to Ensue from our Growing Excess of Population, if not Remedied by Colonization*. London, 1830.

Bentham, Jeremy, *Economic Writings*, ed. W. Stark. 3 vols. London, Allen & Unwin, 1952.

Blake, William, *Observations on the Effects Produced by the Expenditure of Government during the Restriction of Cash Payments*. London, 1823.

Bray, John Francis, *Labour's Wrongs and Labour's Remedy; or, the Age of Might and the Age of Right*. Leeds, 1839. London School of Economics Reprints, No. 6, 1931.

* For the authorship of unsigned articles by McCulloch, Malthus, Scrope, Senior, and J. S. Mill, see F. W. Fetter, "The Authorship of Economic Articles in the *Edinburgh Review*, 1802–47," *Journal of Political Economy*, June 1953; J. Bonar, *Malthus and His Works* (London, 1924); R. Opie, "A Neglected British Economist, George Poulett Scrope," *Quarterly Journal of Economics*, November 1929; N. W. Senior, *Industrial Efficiency and Social Economy. Original Manuscripts*, ed. S. L. Levy (London, 1929); *Bibliography of the Published Writings of J. S. Mill*, ed. N. MacMinn *et al.* (Evanston, Ill., 1945).

Broadhurst, John, *Political Economy*. London, 1842.

Buchanan, David, *Inquiry into the Taxation and Commercial Policy of Great Britain, with Observations on the Principles of Currency and of Exchangeable Value*. Edinburgh, 1844.

Buller, Thomas Wentworth, *A Reply to a Pamphlet, by David Ricardo, Esq., M. P., on Protection to Agriculture*. London, 1822.

Cairnes, John Elliot, *The Character and Logical Method of Political Economy*. London, 1857. 2d ed. New York, 1875.

———, *Essays in Political Economy, Theoretical and Applied*. London, 1873.

———, *Leading Principles of Political Economy Newly Expounded*. London, 1874.

Cayley, Edward Stillingfleet, *On Commercial Economy, in Six Essays*. London, 1830.

[Cazenove, John], *Considerations on the Accumulation of Capital and its Effects on Profits and on Exchange Value*. London, 1822.

———, *An Elementary Treatise on Political Economy; or, A Short Exposition of its First and Fundamental Principles*. London, 1840.

Chalmers, Thomas, *On Political Economy, in Connection with the Moral State and Progress of Society*. Glasgow and Edinburgh, 1832. 2d ed. 1840. Reprinted in *Selected Works of Dr. Chalmers*, ed. W. Hanna, Edinburgh, 1856. Vol. 9.

"Chalmers on National Economy," *Fraser's Magazine*, August 1832, pp. 113–18; September 1832, pp. 239–48.

Chambers, William and Robert, eds., *Chambers' Information for the People* (London, 1835), No. 15: "Political Economy," pp. 113–20; 2d ed. Edinburgh, 1842, *1*, No. 45: "Political Economy," pp. 705–20; No. 46: "Population—Poor Laws," pp. 721–36; *3*, No. 70: "Social Economics of the Industrious Orders," pp. 305–20.

Cobbett, William, *The Opinions of William Cobbett*, ed. G. D. H. Cole and M. Cole. London, Cobbett, 1944.

Cobden, Richard, *Speeches on Questions of Public Policy*, ed. J. Bright and J. E. T. Rogers. 2 vols. London, 1878.

Colquhoun, Patrick, *A Treatise on the Wealth, Power and Resources of the British Empire*. London, 1814. 2d ed., 1815.

Corbet, Thomas, *An Inquiry into the Causes and Modes of the Wealth of Individuals; or the Principles of Trade and Speculation Explained*. London, 1841.

Cotteril, Charles Forster, *An Examination of the Doctrines of Value, as Set Forth by Adam Smith, Ricardo, M'Culloch, Mill, the Author of 'A Critical Dissertation', Torrens, Malthus, Say, &c. &c. Being a Reply to those Distinguished Authors*. London, 1831.

Craig, John, *Remarks on Some Fundamental Doctrines in Political Economy; Illustrated by a Brief Enquiry into the Commercial State of Britain, since the Year 1815*. Edinburgh, 1821.

Eisdell, John S., *A Treatise on the Industry of Nations; or, the Principle of National Economy and Taxation*. 2 vols. London, 1839.

[Ellis, William], "Effect of the Employment of Machinery &c. upon the Happiness of the Working Class," *Westminster Review*, January 1826, pp. 101–30.

Fawcett, Henry, *Manual of Political Economy*. London, 1863. 2d ed. 1865.

———, *Economic Position of the British Labourer*. London, 1865.

Fitzwilliam, Earl (Viscount Milton), *Address to the Landowners of England, on the Corn Laws*. London, 1832. 2d ed. 1832.

Gray, John, *A Lecture on Human Happiness*. London, 1825. London School of Economics Reprints, No. 2, 1931.

Greg, William Rathbone, *Not Over-Production, but Deficient Consumption, the Source of Our Suffering*. London, 1842.

Higgins, George, "Observations on Mr. McCulloch's Doctrines Respecting the Corn Laws and the Rate of Wages," *The Pamphleteer*, 27 (1826), 240–56.

[Hodgskin, Thomas], *Labour Defended Against the Claims of Capital, or the Unproductiveness of Capital Proved with Reference to the Present Combinations amongst Journeymen*. By A Labourer. London, 1825. 2d ed. 1831. Reprinted: Ed. G. D. H. Cole. London, Labour Publishing Co., 1922.

———, *Popular Political Economy. Four Lectures Delivered at the London Mechanics' Institution*. London, 1827.

[———], "On *Works of David Ricardo*," *The Economist*, Nov. 28, 1846, pp. 1556–8.

[———], "On J. S. Mill's *Principles*," *ibid.*, May 27, 1848, pp. 603–4.

Hopkins, Thomas, *Economical Inquiries Relative to the Laws which Regulate Rent, Profit, Wages and the Value of Money*. London, 1822.

———, *On the Rent of Land, and its Influences on Subsistence and Population*. London, 1828.

———, *Great Britain for the Last Forty Years; Being a Historical and Analytical Account of its Finances, Economy, and General Condition, During that Period*. London, 1834.

Horton, Sir Robert John Wilmot, *Causes and Remedies of Pauperism in the United Kingdom Considered. Fourth Series. Explanation of Mr. Wilmot Horton's Bill, in a Letter and Queries Addressed to N. W. Senior Esq. with his Answer*. London, 1830.

The Iniquity of the Landholders . . . in Regard to the Corn Laws. London, 1826.

Jemmett, Henry, "Observations on Mr. Ricardo's Principles of Political Economy and Taxation," *The Pamphleteer*, 27 (1826), 142–51.

Jones, Richard, *An Essay on the Distribution of Wealth, and on Sources of Taxation*. London, 1831.

———, *An Introductory Lecture on Political Economy, Delivered at King's College, London, 27th. February, 1833. To which is Added a Syllabus of a Course of Lectures on the Wages of Labour*. London, 1833.

[Knight, Charles], *The Working Man's Companion. The Results of Machinery, Namely Cheap Production and Increased Employment, Exhibited*. London, 1831.

[———], *The Working Man's Companion. The Rights of Industry*. London, 1831. 2d ed. as *Capital and Labour; Including the Results of Machinery*. London, 1845.

Laing, Samuel (the younger), *National Distress; its Causes and Remedies. Atlas Prize Essay*. London, 1844.

Lauderdale, Earl of (James K. Maitland), *An Inquiry into the Nature and Origin of Public Wealth, and into the Means and Causes of its Increase*. Edinburgh, 1804. 2d ed. 1819.

———, *A Letter on the Corn Laws*. London, 1814.

Lawson, James Anthony, *Five Lectures on Political Economy; Delivered Before the University of Dublin in Michaelmas Term, 1843*. London, 1844.

[Lewis, George C.], "Legislation for the Working Classes," *Edinburgh Review*, January 1846, pp. 64–99.

Lloyd, William Forster, *A Lecture on the Notion of Value, as Distinguished not only from Utility, but also from Value in Exchange. Delivered Before the University of Oxford in Michaelmas Term, 1833*. London, 1834. Reprinted in *Economic History*, Supplement to the *Economic Journal*, May 1927.

———, *Two Lectures on the Checks to Population, Delivered Before the University of Oxford, in Michaelmas Term, 1832*. Oxford, 1833.

———, *Four Lectures on Poor-Laws, Delivered Before the University of Oxford, in Michaelmas Term, 1834*. London, 1835.

———, *Two Lectures on the Justice of the Poor-Laws, and one Lecture on Rent, Delivered in the University of Oxford in Michaelmas Term, 1836*. London, 1837.

Longfield, Mountifort, *Lectures on Political Economy, Delivered in Trinity and Michaelmas Terms, 1833*. Dublin, 1834. London School of Economics Reprints, No. 8, 1931.

———, *Four Lectures on Poor Laws, Delivered in Trinity Term, 1834*. Dublin, 1834.

Lowe, Joseph, *The Present State of England in Regard to Agriculture, Trade, and Finance; with a Comparison of the Prospects of England and France*. London, 1822. 2d ed. London and Edinburgh, 1823.

[McCulloch, John Ramsay], "On Ricardo's 'Principles of Political Economy and Taxation,'" *Edinburgh Review*, June 1818, pp. 59–87.

[———], "Taxation and the Corn Laws," *ibid.*, January 1820, pp. 155–87.

[———], "The Opinions of Messrs. Say, Sismondi, and Malthus, on Effects of Machinery and Accumulation," *ibid.*, March 1821, pp. 102–23.

[———], "On Combination Laws, Restraints on Emigration, &c.," *ibid.*, January 1824, pp. 315–45.

[———], "French Law of Succession," *ibid.*, July 1824, pp. 350–75.

[———], "Political Economy," Supplement to the fourth, fifth, and sixth editions of the *Encyclopaedia Britannica* (1824), *6*, pt. I, 216–78. Ed. with Notes J. M. Vickar. New York, 1825.

———, *The Principles of Political Economy: with a Sketch of the Rise and Progress of the Science*. Edinburgh and London, 1825. 2d ed. London, 1830. 3d ed. Edinburgh, 1843. 4th ed. Edinburgh, 1849.

———, *An Essay on the Circumstances which Determine the Rate of Wages and the Condition of the Working Classes.* Edinburgh, 1826. 2d ed. London, 1851.

[———], "On Commercial Revulsions," *Edinburgh Review,* June 1826, pp. 70–93.

[———], "Abolition of the Corn Laws," *ibid.*, September 1826, pp. 319–59.

[———], "Rise, Progress, Present State, and Prospects of the British Cotton Manufacture," *ibid.*, June 1827, pp. 1–39.

———, *The Wealth of Nations, by Adam Smith, With a Life of the Author, an Introductory Discourse, and Supplementary Dissertations.* 3 vols. Edinburgh and London, 1828. 2d ed. 1838. 3d ed. 1849. 4th ed. 1855. 5th ed. 1859. 6th ed. 1863.

[———], "On Poor Laws," *Edinburgh Review,* May 1828, pp. 303–29.

[———], "Jones on the Theory of Rent," *ibid.*, September 1831, pp. 84–99.

[———], "Chalmers on Political Economy," *ibid.*, October 1832, pp. 52–72.

———, *A Descriptive and Statistical Account of the British Empire, Exhibiting its Extent, Physical Capacities, Population, Industry, and Civil and Religious Institutions.* 2 vols. London, 1837. 2d ed. 1839. 3d ed. 1847. 4th ed. 1854.

———, *The Literature of Political-Economy.* London, 1845. London School of Economics Reprints, No. 5, 1938.

———, *The Works of David Ricardo, Esq., M.P., With a Notice of the Life and Writings of the Author.* London, 1846. 2d ed. 1853.

———, *Statements Illustrative of the Policy and Probable Consequences of the Proposed Repeal of the Existing Corn Law.* Edinburgh and London, 1841. 2d–16th eds. 1841.

———, *A Treatise on the Succession to Property Vacant by Death.* London, 1848.

———, *Treatises and Essays.* Edinburgh, 1859.

Malthus, Thomas Robert, *An Essay on the Principle of Population.* London, 1798. 2d ed. 1803. 3d ed. 1806 (2 vols.). 4th ed. 1807. (2 vols.) 5th ed. 1817 (3 vols.). 6th ed. 1826 (2 vols.). Reprinted: Ed. G. T. Bettany. London, 1890.

———, *The Grounds of an Opinion on the Policy of Restricting the Importation of Foreign Corn.* London, 1815.

———, *An Inquiry into the Nature and Progress of Rent, and the Principles by which it is Regulated.* London, 1815. Reprinted: ed. J. H. Hollander. Baltimore, Johns Hopkins Press, 1903.

———, *The Principles of Political Economy, Considered with a View to their Practical Application.* London, 1820. 2d ed. 1836. Reprinted: New York, Kelley, 1949.

———, *The Measure of Value Stated and Illustrated, With an Application of it to the Alterations in the Value of English Currency since 1790.* London, 1823.

[———], "Tooke—On High and Low Prices," *Quarterly Review,* April 1823, pp. 214–39.

[———], "Political Economy," *ibid.*, January 1824, pp. 297–334.

———, *A Summary View of the Principle of Population.* London, 1830. Reprinted in *Introduction to Malthus,* ed. D. V. Glass (London, Watts, 1953), pp. 117–81.

———, *Definitions in Political Economy.* London, 1827. 2d ed. with Preface, Notes, and Supplementary Remarks by J. Cazenove. London, 1853. Reprinted: New York, Kelley & Millman, 1955.

———, "Letters of Malthus to his French Translator Pierre Prévost," ed. G. W. Zinke, *Journal of Economic History,* November 1942.

———, "Letter to Ricardo," ed. P. Sraffa, *Economic Journal,* September 1955.

Marcet, Jane, *Conversations on Political-Economy; in which the Elements of that Science are Familiarly Explained.* London, 1816. 2d ed. 1817. 3d ed. 1819. 4th ed. 1821. 5th ed. 1824. 6th ed. 1827. 7th ed. 1839.

Martineau, Harriet, *Illustrations of Political Economy.* 9 vols. London, 1832–34.

———, *Poor Laws and Paupers Illustrated.* 4 vols. London, 1833–34.

———, *The Tendency of Strikes and Sticks to Produce Low Wages and of Unions between Masters and Men to Ensure Good Wages.* Durham, 1834.

———, *Autobiography,* ed. M. W. Chapman. 2 vols. Boston, 1877.

[Merivale, Herman], "Senior on Political Economy," *Edinburgh Review,* October 1837, pp. 37–102.

Mill, James, *Commerce Defended; an Answer to the Arguments by which Mr. Spence, Mr. Cobbett and Others, have Attempted to Prove that Commerce is not a Source of National Wealth.* London, 1808.

———, *Elements of Political Economy.* London, 1821. 2d ed. 1824. 3d ed. 1826.

[Mill, John Stuart], "Two Letters on the Measure of Value," *The Traveller,* Dec. 6, 13, 1822. Reprinted as *John Stuart Mill on the Measure of Value,* ed. J. H. Hollander. Baltimore, Johns Hopkins Press, 1936.

[———], "Questions of Population," *The Black Dwarf,* Nov. 27, 1823, pp. 748–56; Feb. 25, 1824, pp. 238–44.

[———], "War Expenditure," *Westminster Review,* July 1824, pp. 27–48.

[———], "Quarterly Review–Political Economy," *Westminster Review,* January 1825, pp. 213–32.

[———], "Review of Miss Martineau's Tales," *Examiner,* January 1830, p. 68; Oct. 27, 1833, pp. 676–8; *Monthly Repository,* May 1834, pp. 318–22.

———, *Essays on Some Unsettled Questions of Political Economy.* London, 1844. London School of Economics Reprints, No. 7, 1948.

[———], "Claims of Labour," *Edinburgh Review,* April 1845, pp. 498–525. Reprinted in: *Dissertations and Discussions, Political, Philosophical and Historical.* London, 1859–75. 2, 181–217.

———, *Principles of Political Economy with Some of Their Applications to Social Philosophy,* ed. W. J. Ashley. London, Longmans, Green, 1909.

———, *Letters of John Stuart Mill,* ed. H. S. R. Elliott. 2 vols. London, Longmans, Green, 1910.

———, *Autobiography.* New York, Columbia University Press, 1924.

———, "Unpublished Letters to Gustave d'Eichtal," *Cosmopolis,* May 1897.

———, "Two Speeches on Education," ed. H. J. Laski, *Journal of Adult Education,* October 1929.

———, *Spirit of the Age,* ed. F. A. Hayek. Chicago, University of Chicago Press, 1942.

———, "Notes on Senior's *Political Economy,*" *Economica,* August 1945.

"J. S. Mill on Political Economy," *Blackwood's Edinburgh Magazine,* October 1848, pp. 407–28.

"J. S. Mill's *Principles,*" *Westminster and Foreign Quarterly Review,* July 1848, pp. 291–314.

Morgan, John Mintner, *The Revolt of the Bees.* London, 1826. 2d ed. 1830. 3d ed. 1839.

[Mudie, George], *Mr. Owen's Proposed Arrangements for the Distressed Working Classes, Shown to be Consistent with Sound Principles of Political-Economy; in Three Letters Addressed to David Ricardo, Esq., M. P.* London, 1819.

Napier, Macvey, *Selections from the Correspondence of the Late Macvey Napier.* London, 1879.

"On Agriculture and Rent," *Quarterly Review,* October 1827, pp. 391–437.

"The Opinions of the Late Mr. Ricardo and of Adam Smith on Some of the Leading Doctrines of Political Economy, Stated and Compared," *The Pamphleteer, 23* (1824), 518–26; *24* (1824), 50–8.

Outlines of Political Economy, Being a Plain and Short View of the Laws Relating to the Production, Distribution, and Consumption of Wealth. London, 1832.

Parliamentary Papers, *Third Report from the Select Committee on the State of the Poor in Ireland.* July, 1830.

Pinsent, John, *Conversations on Political Economy; or, a Series of Dialogues, with Remarks on our present Distress, their Causes and the Remedies Applicable to Them.* London, 1821.

———, *Letter to the Chairman of the Honourable House of Commons on the Agricultural Distress, and to David Ricardo, Esq., M.P. in Answer to his Speech of the 7th. March 1821, Designed to Demonstrate the Errors of the Theory which that Gentleman Advocates.* London, 1821.

Place, Francis, *Illustrations and Proofs of the Principles of Population.* London, 1822. Reprinted: With Introduction, Notes, and Appendices by N. E. Himes. London, Houghton, Mifflin, 1930.

Plough, Patrick [pseudonym], *Letters on the Elements of the Science, Called Formerly, Improperly, Political Economy, Recently, More Pertinently, Catallactics.* London, 1842.

Political Economy Club, *Centenary Volume. Minutes of Proceedings.* London, 1921. Vol. *6.*

Porter, George Richardson, *The Progress of the Nation in its Various Social and Commercial Relations, from the Beginning of the Nineteenth Century to the Present Day.* 3 vols. London, 1836–43. 2d ed. 1846. 3d ed. 1851.

———, "On the Collection of Statistics in Agriculture," *Quarterly Journal of the Statistical Society,* October 1839, pp. 291–6.

Purves, George (Simon Gray), *All Classes Productive of National Wealth; or, the Theories of M. Quesnai, Dr. Adam Smith, and Mr. Gray, Concerning the Various Classes of Men, as to the Production of Wealth to the Community, Analysed and Examined.* London, 1817. 2d ed. 1840.

[de Quincey, Thomas], "Dialogues of the Three Templars on Political-Economy, Chiefly in Relation to the Principles of Mr. Ricardo," *London Magazine,* March–October 1824. Reprinted in *Collected Writings of Thomas de Quincey,* ed. D. Mason. Edinburgh, 1890. 9, 37–112.

———, *The Logic of Political-Economy.* Edinburgh, 1844. Reprinted in *Collected Writings,* Vol. 9.

Rae, John, *The Sociological Theory of Capital,* ed. C. W. Mixter. New York, Macmillan, 1905.

Ramsay, George, *An Essay on the Distribution of Wealth.* Edinburgh, 1836.

Ravenstone, Piercy, *A Few Doubts as to the Correctness of Some Opinions Generally Entertained on the Subjects of Population and Political-Economy.* London, 1821.

Read, Samuel, *Political Economy. An Inquiry into the Natural Grounds of Right to Vendible Property, or Wealth.* Edinburgh, 1829.

Ricardo, David, *Works of David Ricardo,* ed. P. Sraffa. 10 vols. Cambridge, The University Press, 1951.

"Ricardo's *Principles,*" *Edinburgh Monthly Magazine,* May 1817, pp. 175–8.

"Ricardo on *Political Economy,*" *The Monthly Review,* December 1820, pp. 416–30.

"Ricardo's *Principles,*" *Farmer's Magazine,* May 1820, pp. 129–46, 152–5.

[Rogers, Edward], *An Essay on Some General Principles of Political Economy, on Taxes upon Raw Produce, and on Commutation of Tithes.* London, 1822.

Rooke, John, *An Inquiry into the Principles of National Wealth, Illustrated by the Political Economy of the British Empire.* Edinburgh, 1824.

Say, Jean Baptiste, "Letter to Malthus on Political Economy and Stagnation of Commerce," *The Pamphleteer, 14* (1820), 289–345. Reprinted: Wheeler Economic and Historical Reprints, No. 2. London, 1936.

———, *A Treatise on Political-Economy; or the Production, Distribution, and Consumption of Wealth,* trans. C. R. Princep from the fourth French edition. 2 vols. London, 1821.

———, *Oeuvres diverses.* Paris, 1848.

[Scrope, George Poulett], "The Political Economists," *Quarterly Review,* January 1831, pp. 1–52.

[———], "Malthus and Sadler, on Population and Emigration," *ibid.,* April 1831, pp. 97–145.

[———], "The Archbishops of Dublin on Political Economy," *ibid.,* November 1831, pp. 46–54.

[———], "Jones on the Doctrine of Rent," *ibid.,* November 1831, pp. 81–117.

———, *Principles of Political-Economy. Deducted from the Natural Laws of Social Welfare, and Applied to the Present State of Britain.* London,

1833. 2d ed. published as *Political Economy for Plain People Applied to the Past and Present State of Britain.* London, 1873.

[Senior, Nassau William], "Report On the State of Agriculture," *Quarterly Review,* July 1821, pp. 466–504.

[———], "Some Ambiguous Terms Used in Political Economy," Appendix to R. Whateley's *Elements of Logic, Encyclopaedia Metropolitana* (1826). Reprinted as an Appendix to *An Outline of the Science of Political Economy.*

———, *Three Lectures on the Transmission of the Precious Metals from Country to Country and the Mercantile Theory of Wealth, Delivered before the University of Oxford in June, 1827.* London, 1828. London School of Economics Reprints, No. 3, 1931.

———, *Two Lectures on Population, Delivered before the University of Oxford in Easter Term, 1828. To Which Is Added, a Correspondence between the Author and the Rev. T. R. Malthus.* London, 1829. 2d ed. 1831. The correspondence is reprinted in G. F. McCleary, *The Malthusian Population Theory* (London, 1953), pp. 114–27.

———, *On the Cost of Obtaining Money, and on Some Effects of Private and Government Paper Money.* London, 1830. London School of Economics Reprints, No. 5, 1931.

———, *An Outline of the Science of Political Economy. Encyclopaedia Metropolitana* (1836), Vol. 6, pt. 43. Reprinted: New York, Kelley, 1951.

[———], "J. S. Mill on Political Economy," *Edinburgh Review,* October 1848, pp. 293–339.

Smith, Adam, *An Inquiry into the Nature and Causes of the Wealth of Nations,* ed. E. Cannan. New York, Modern Library, 1937.

Smythe, Anthony, *Outlines of a New Theory of Political Economy.* London, 1828.

"Socialism in England," *The Economist,* May 4, 1850, pp. 479–80.

Spence, William, *Tracts on Political-Economy. Viz. 1. Britain Independent of Commerce. 1808; 2, Agriculture the Source of the Wealth of Britain. 1808; 3. The Objections against the Corn Bill Refuted. 1815; 4. Speech on the East India Trade. 1812. With Prefatory Remarks on the Causes and Cure of Our Present Distress.* London, 1822.

[Thompson, Thomas Perronet], "The True Theory of Rent, in Opposition to Mr. Ricardo and Others. Being an Exposition of Fallacies of Rent, Tithes, &c. in the Form of a Review of Mr. Mill's Elements of Political Economy." *The Pamphleteer* 27 (1826), 305–62. 2d ed. 1827.

[———], "Catechism on the Corn Laws, with a List of Fallacies and the Answers." *The Pamphleteer,* 27 (1826), 363–413. 21st ed. 1841. Reprinted: San Francisco, Sutro Branch California State Library, 1940.

[———], "Professor Longfield on Absenteeism," *Westminster Review,* October 1835, pp. 411–15.

[Thompson, William], *Labor Rewarded. The Claims of Labor and Capital Conciliated; or, How to Secure to Labor the Whole Produce of Its Exertions. By One of the Idle Classes.* London, 1827.

Thornton, William Thomas, *Over-population and Its Remedy*. London, 1846.

Tooke, Thomas, *Thoughts and Details on the High and Low Prices of the Last Thirty Years, from 1793–1822*. London, 1823. 2d ed. 1824.

Torrens, Robert, *An Essay on the External Corn Trade*. London, 1815. 2d ed. 1820. 3d ed. 1826. 4th ed. 1827. 5th ed. 1829.

[———], "Strictures on Mr. Ricardo's Doctrine Respecting Exchange-Value," *The Edinburgh Magazine and Literary Miscellany. A New Series of the Scots Magazine*, October 1818, pp. 335–8. Reply by [McCulloch, John Ramsay], *ibid.*, November 1818, pp. 429–31.

[———], "Mr. Owen's Plan for Relieving the National Distress," *Edinburgh Review*, October 1819, pp. 453–77.

———, *An Essay on the Production of Wealth; with an Appendix in which the Principles of Political Economy are Applied to the Actual Circumstances of this Country*. London, 1821.

———, *Letters on Commercial Policy*. London, 1833.

———, *On Wages and Combinations*. London, 1834.

———, *Three Letters to the Marquis of Chandos*. London, 1843.

———, *A Letter to Lord Ashley, on the Principles which Regulate Wages and on the Manner and Degree in which Wages would be Reduced by the Passing of a Ten Hour Bill*. London, 1844.

———, *The Budget. A Series of Letters on Financial, Commercial, and Colonial Policy: With an Introduction in which the Deductive Method, as Presented in Mr. Mill's System of Logic, is Applied to the Solution of Some Controversial Questions in Political Economy*. London, 1844.

Tozer, James, "Mathematical Investigations into the Effect of Machinery on the Wealth of the Community in which it is Employed, and on the Fund for the Payment of Wages," read May 14, 1838. *Transactions of the Cambridge Philosophical Society* (Cambridge, 1838), *6*, pt. III, 507–22.

[Tufnell, Edward Carlton], *Character, Objects and Effects of Trades' Unions; with Some Remarks on the Laws Concerning Them. By "An Anti."* London, 1834. Reprinted: Manchester, Express Co-operative Pt. Co., 1933.

"Trades' Unions and Strikes," *Edinburgh Review*, July 1834, pp. 341–59.

Twiss, Thomas, *On Certain Tests of a Thriving Population. Four Lectures Delivered Before the University of Oxford, in Lent Term, 1845*. London, 1845.

———, *View of the Progress of Political Economy in Europe Since the Sixteenth Century. A Course of Lectures Delivered before the University of Oxford in Michaelmas Term, 1846, and Lent Term, 1847*. London, 1847.

Wade, John, *History of The Middle and Working Classes*. London, 1833. 2d ed. 1834. 3d ed. 1835.

[Wakefield, Edward Gibbon], *England and America. A Comparison of the Social and Political State of both Nations*. London and New York, 1834.

———, *An Inquiry into the Nature and Causes of the Wealth of Nations, by Adam Smith, with a Commentary*. 4 vols. London, 1835–39.

West, Sir Edward, *Essay on the Application of Capital to Land, with Ob-*

servations Shewing the Impolicy of any Great Restriction of the Importation of Corn. London, 1815. Reprinted: Ed. J. H. Hollander. Baltimore, Johns Hopkins Press, 1934.

———, *Price of Corn and Wages of Labour, with Observations upon Dr. Smith's, Mr. Ricardo's and Mr. Malthus's Doctrines upon these Subjects.* London, 1826.

Whately, Richard, *Introductory Lectures on Political Economy. Being Part of a Course Delivered in Easter Term, 1831.* London and Dublin, 1831. 2d ed. 1832. 3d ed. 1847. 4th ed. 1855.

Whewell, William, "Mathematical Exposition of Some Doctrines of Political Economy," read March 2 and 14, 1829. *Transactions of the Cambridge Philosophical Society* (Cambridge, 1830), *3*, pt. I, 191–230.

———, "Mathematical Exposition of Some of the Leading Doctrines of Mr. Ricardo's 'Principles of Political Economy and Taxation,'" read April 18 and May 2, 1831. *Ibid.* (1833), *4*, pt. I, 155–98.

Wilson, James, *Influences of the Corn Laws, as Affecting all Classes of the Community, and Particularly the Landed Interests.* 2d ed. London, 1840.

———, *Fluctuations of Currency, Commerce, and Manufactures, Referable to Corn Laws.* London, 1840.

"Working Classes in Manchester and Dukinfield," *Quarterly Journal of the Statistical Society,* January 1842, pp. 320–34.

Secondary Sources

Adams, T. S., "Index Numbers and the Standard of Value," *Journal of Political Economy,* December 1901.

Annals of the Royal Statistical Society, 1834–1934. London, Royal Statistical Society, 1934.

Ashley, W. J., "The Rehabilitation of Ricardo," *Economic Journal,* September 1891.

Bain, Alexander, *James Mill. A Biography.* London, Longmans, Green, 1882.

———, *John Stuart Mill.* London, Longmans, Green, 1882.

Barnes, D. G., *A History of the English Corn Laws from 1660–1848.* London, Routledge, 1930.

Baumol, William, *Economic Dynamics.* New York, Macmillan, 1951.

Beales, H. L., "The Historical Context of the *Essay on Population,*" *Introduction to Malthus,* ed. D. V. Glass. London, Watts, 1953.

Becker, G. S., and Baumol, W. J., "The Classical Monetary Theory. The Outcome of the Discussion," *Economica,* November 1952.

Beer, M., *History of British Socialism.* London, Allen & Unwin, 1948.

Bennett, M. K., "British Wheat Yield Per Acre for Seven Centuries," *Economic History,* February 1935.

Bergmann, Eugen von, *Geschichte der nationalökonomischen Krisentheorieen,* Stuttgart, Kohlhammer, 1895.

Biaujeaud, H., *Essai sur la théorie ricardienne de la valeur.* Paris, Librairie du Recueil Sirey, 1934.

Black, R. D., "Trinity College, Dublin, and the Theory of Value, 1823–63," *Economica,* August 1945.

———, "The Classical Economists and the Irish Problem," *Oxford Economic Papers,* March 1953.

Böhm-Bawerk, Eugene von, *Capital and Interest.* London, Macmillan, 1932.

Bonar, James, *Malthus and His Work.* London, Allen & Unwin, 1924.

Boner, H. A., *Hungry Generations.* New York, King's Crown, 1955.

Bortkiewicz, Claudius von, "Value and Price in the Marxian System" (1907), *International Economic Papers,* No. 2. New York, Macmillan, 1952.

Bowley, Marian, *Nassau Senior and Classical Economics.* New York, Kelley, 1949.

Brown, E. H. P., *The Framework of the Pricing Process.* London, Chapman and Hall, 1936.

Bruce, T. W., "The Economic Theories of John Craig, A Forgotten English Economist," *Quarterly Journal of Economics,* August 1938.

Cannan, Edwin, *A History of the Theories of Production and Distribution in English Political Economy from 1776 to 1848.* London, Staples Press, 1953.

———, *A Review of Economic Theory*. London, P. S. King and Son, 1929.
Carr, H. J., "John Francis Bray," *Economica*, November 1940.
Cassel, Gustav, *The Nature and Necessity of Interest*. New York, Macmillan, 1903.
Cassels, J. M., "A Reinterpretation of Ricardo on Value," *Quarterly Journal of Economics*, May 1935.
Chao, N., *Richard Jones. An Early English Institutionalist*. New York, Columbia University Press, 1930.
Checkland, S. G., "The Birmingham Economists, 1815–50," *Economic History Review*, second series, *1*, No. 1 (1948).
———, "The Propagation of Ricardian Economics in England," *Economica*, February 1949.
———, "The Advent of Academic Economics in England," *Manchester School*, January 1951.
———, "Economic Opinion in England as Jevons Found It," *ibid.*, May 1951.
Clapham, J. H., *Economic History of Modern Britain. Free Trade and Steel, 1850–86*. New York, Macmillan, 1932.
Cole, G. D. H., *The Life of William Cobbett*. London, Home & Van Thal, 1947.
———, *Socialist Thought. The Forerunners, 1789–1850*. London, Macmillan, 1953.
Cole, G. D. H., and Postgate, Raymond, *The Common People, 1746–1946*. London, Methuen, 1949.
Cournot, Augustin, *Researches into the Mathematical Principles of the Theory of Wealth*. New York, Macmillan, 1929.
Daugherty, M. R., "The Currency-Banking Controversy," *Southern Economic Journal*, October 1942.
Deane, Phyllis, "Contemporary Estimates of National Income in the First Half of the Nineteenth Century," *Economic History Review*, April 1956.
Diehl, Karl, *Sozialwissenschaftliche Erläuterungen zu David Ricardos Grundgesetzen*. 2 vols. Jena, Fischer, 1922.
Dobb, Maurice, *Political Economy and Capitalism*. New York, International Publishers, 1945.
Douglas, Paul H., "Smith's Theory of Value and Distribution," *Adam Smith, 1776–1926*, ed. J. M. Clark. Chicago, University of Chicago Press, 1928.
———, *The Theory of Wages*. New York, Macmillan, 1934.
Drescher, L., "The Development of Agricultural Production in Great Britain and Ireland from the Early Nineteenth Century," *Manchester School*, May 1955.
Drummond, J. C., and Wilbraham, A., *The Englishman's Food*. London, Cape, 1940.
Edelberg, V., "The Ricardian Theory of Profits," *Economica*, February 1933.
Edgeworth, F. Y., *Papers Relating to Political Economy*. London, Macmillan, 1925. Vol. 3.
Ellis, H. S., and Fellner, W., "External Economies and Diseconomies," *Readings in Price Theory*. London, Allen & Unwin, 1953.

Escher, E., *Harriet Martineau's sozialpolitischen Novellen.* Zürich, Thomas & Hubert, 1925.

Fay, C. R., *The Corn Laws and Social England.* Cambridge, The University Press, 1932.

Fellner, William, *Trends and Cycles in Economic Activity.* New York, Henry Holt, 1956.

Fetter, F. W., "Lauderdale's Oversaving Theory," *American Economic Review,* June 1945. Reply by M. Paglin, *ibid.,* June 1946.

———, "The Authorship of Economic Articles in the *Edinburgh Review,* 1802–47," *Journal of Political Economy,* June 1953.

———, "The Bullion Report Re-Examined," *Papers in English Monetary History,* ed. T. S. Ashton and R. S. Sayers. Oxford, The Clarendon Press, 1953.

Field, James Anthony, *Essays on Population,* ed. H. F. Hohnmann. Chicago, University of Chicago Press, 1931.

Finer, S. E., *The Life and Times of Sir Edwin Chadwick.* London, Methuen, 1952.

Fraser, L. M., *Economic Thought and Language.* London, A & C. Black, 1937.

Fukuoka, M., "Full Employment and Constant Coefficients of Production," *Quarterly Journal of Economics,* February 1955.

Fussel, G. E., and Compton, M., "Agricultural Adjustments After the Napoleonic Wars," *Economic History,* February 1939.

Gayer, Arthur D., *et al., The Growth and Fluctuations of the British Economy.* 2 vols. Oxford, Clarendon Press, 1953.

Gide, Charles, and Rist, Charles, *A History of Economic Doctrines.* London, Harrap, 1948.

Gourvitch, Alexander, *Survey of Economic Theory on Technological Change and Employment.* Philadelphia, Works Projects Administration, 1940.

Gordon, S., "The London *Economist* and the High Tide of Laissez-Faire," *Journal of Political Economy,* December 1955.

Gottlieb, Manuel, "The Theory of Optimum Population For a Closed Economy," *Journal of Political Economy,* December 1945.

Grampp, W. D., "Malthus on Money Wages and Welfare," *American Economic Review,* December 1956.

Griffith, G. T., *Population Problems of the Age of Malthus.* Cambridge, The University Press, 1926.

Grude-Oettli, N., *John Stuart Mill zwischen Liberalismus und Sozialismus.* Zürich, Bleicherode, Nieft, 1936.

Habakkuk, H., "English Population in the Eighteenth Century," *Economic History Review,* second series, *6* (1953).

Halévy, Élie, *Thomas Hodgskin (1786–1869).* Paris, Societé Nouvelle de Librarie et d'Édition, 1903.

———, *England in 1815.* London, T. F. Unwin, 1937.

———, *The Age of Peel and Cobden.* London, T. F. Unwin, 1947.

———, *The Growth of Philosophic Radicalism.* New York, Kelley, 1949.

Hamberg, D., *Economic Growth and Instability.* New York, Norton, 1956.

Hansen, Alvin H., *Business Cycles and National Income.* New York, Norton, 1951.

Hayek, Friedrich A., *The Pure Theory of Capital.* Chicago, University of Chicago Press, 1941.

N. E. Himes, "Jeremy Bentham and the Genesis of English Neo-Malthusianism," *Economic History,* August 1928.

———, "The Place of J. S. Mill and Robert Owen in the History of English Neo-Malthusianism," *Quarterly Journal of Economics,* August 1928.

———, "J. S. Mill's Attitude Toward Neo-Malthusianism," *Economic History,* January 1929.

———, "McCulloch's Relation to the Neo-Malthusian Propaganda of His Time," *Journal of Political Economy,* February 1939.

Hollander, Jacob H., "The Concept of Marginal Rent," *Quarterly Journal of Economics,* January 1895.

———, *David Ricardo. A Centenary Estimate.* Baltimore, Johns Hopkins Press, 1910.

———, *Introduction to 'Notes on Malthus' by David Ricardo.* Baltimore, Johns Hopkins Press, 1928.

Hutchison, T. W., *Review of Economic Doctrines.* Oxford, The Clarendon Press, 1953.

Hutt, W. H., *The Theory of Collective Bargaining.* Glencoe, Ill., The Free Press, 1954.

Jevons, W. S., *The Theory of Political Economy.* London, Macmillan, 1898.

———, *Investigations in Currency and Finance.* London, Macmillan, 1909.

Johnson, H. G., "An Error in Ricardo's Exposition of His Theory of Rent," *Quarterly Journal of Economics,* November 1948.

———, "Demand for Commodities is *Not* Demand for Labour," *Economic Journal,* December 1949.

Kaldor, N., "Alternative Theories of Distribution," *Review of Economic Studies, 23, second series,* No. 61 (1955–56).

Keynes, J. M., *The General Theory of Employment Interest and Money.* New York, Harcourt, Brace, 1936.

———, *Essays in Biography.* New York, Horizon Press, 1951.

Kimball, Janet, *The Economic Doctrines of John Gray, 1799–1833.* Washington, Catholic University of America Press, 1948.

Klein, Lawrence R., *The Keynesian Revolution.* New York, Macmillan, 1949.

Knight, Frank H., *Risk, Uncertainty and Profit.* London School of Economics Reprints, No. 16, 1933.

———, "The Ricardian Theory of Production and Distribution," *Canadian Journal of Economics and Political Science,* June 1935.

Levy, S. L., *Nassau W. Senior, The Prophet of Modern Capitalism.* Boston, B. Humphries, 1949.

Lewis, W. Arthur, "Economic Development with Unlimited Supplies of Labour," *Manchester School,* May 1954.

———, *The Theory of Economic Growth.* London, Allen & Unwin, 1955.

Lowenthal, Esther, *The Ricardian Socialists.* New York, Columbia University Press, 1911.

Lutz, Friedrich and Vera, *The Theory of Investment of the Firm.* Princeton, Princeton University Press, 1951.

McCleary, G. F., *The Malthusian Population Theory.* London, Faber and Faber, 1953.

McKeown, T., and Brown, R. G., "Medical Evidence Related to English Population Changes in the Eighteenth Century," *Population Studies,* November 1955.

Marget, Arthur W., *The Theory of Prices.* 2 vols. New York, Prentice-Hall, 1942.

Marshall, Alfred, *Principles of Economics.* London, Macmillan, 1936.

———, *Industry and Trade.* London, Macmillan, 1923.

Marshall, T. E., "The Population Problem During the Industrial Revolution," *Essays in Economic History,* ed. E. G. Carus-Wilson. London, E. Arnold, 1954.

Marx, Karl, *Theories of Surplus Value.* London, Lawrence & Wishart, 1951.

———, *Capital.* New York, International Publishers, 1939.

Matthews, R. C. O., *A Study in Trade-Cycle History.* Cambridge, The University Press, 1954.

May, K., "The Structure of Classical Value Theory," *Review of Economic Studies, 17,* first series, No. 42 (1949–50).

Meek, R. L., "The Decline of Ricardian Economics in England," *Economica,* February 1950.

———, "Thomas Joplin and the Rate of Interest," *Review of Economic Studies, 17,* third series, No. 47 (1950–51).

———, "Physiocracy and the Early Theories of Underconsumption," *Economica,* May 1951.

———, "Physiocracy and Classicism in England," *Economic Journal,* March 1951.

———, *Studies in the Labour Theory of Value.* London, Lawrence & Wishart, 1956.

Menger, Anton, *The Right to the Whole Produce of Labour.* London, Macmillan, 1889.

Mitchell, Wesley C., *Lecture Notes on Types of Economic Theory.* New York, Kelley, 1949.

Mueller, I. W., *John Stuart Mill and French Thought.* Urbana, Ill., University of Illinois Press, 1956.

Myint, Hla, *Theories of Welfare Economics.* Cambridge, Harvard University Press, 1948.

Neisser, Hans, " 'Permanent' Technological Unemployment," *American Economic Review,* March 1942.

O'Brien, G., "J. S. Mill and J. E. Cairnes," *Economica,* November 1943.

O'Connor, M. J. L., *Origins of Academic Economics in the United States.* New York, Columbia University Press, 1944.

O'Leary, J. J., "Malthus and Keynes," *Journal of Political Economy,* December 1942.

———, "Malthus' General Theory of Employment and the Post-Napoleonic Depressions," *Journal of Economic History,* November 1943.

Opie, Redvers, "A Neglected British Economist. George Poulett Scrope," *Quarterly Journal of Economics,* November 1929.

Oppenheimer, Franz, *David Ricardos Grundrententheorie.* Jena, G. Fischer, 1927.

Packe, Michael St. John, *The Life of John Stuart Mill.* London, Secker and Warburg, 1954.

Palgrave, R. H. I., ed., *Dictionary of Political Economy.* 3 vols. London, Macmillan, 1893–99.

Pankhurst, R. K. P., *William Thompson (1775–1833).* London, Watts, 1954.

Pappe, H. O., "Wakefield and Marx," *Economic History Review,* second series, *4,* No. 1 (1951).

Paquet, André, *Le Conflit historique entre la loi des débouchés et le principe de la demande effective.* Paris, Librairie Armand Colin, 1953.

Patinkin, Don, *Money, Interest, and Prices.* New York, Row, Peterson, 1956.

Peacock, Allan T., "Theory of Population and Modern Economic Analysis," *Population Studies,* November 1952.

Pigou, A. C., "Mill and the Wages Fund," *Economic Journal,* June 1949. Reply, H. G. Johnson, *ibid.,* December 1949.

Plummer, A., "Sir Edward West (1782–1828)," *Journal of Political Economy,* October 1929.

Ratzlaff, C. J., *The Theory of Free Competition.* Philadelphia, University of Pennsylvania Press, 1936.

Rivenberg, N. E., *Harriet Martineau, An Example of Victorian Conflict.* Philadelphia, 1932.

Robbins, Lionel, *An Essay on the Nature and Significance of Economic Science.* London, Macmillan, 1946.

———, *The Theory of Economic Policy in English Classical Political Economy.* London, Macmillan, 1952.

———, "Schumpeter's *History of Economic Analysis,*" *Quarterly Journal of Economics,* February 1955.

Roberts, R. O., "Ricardo's Theory of Public Debts," *Economica,* August 1942.

Robertson, R. M., "Jevons and His Precursors," *Econometrica,* July 1951.

Robinson, Joan, *The Rate of Interest and Other Essays.* London, Macmillan, 1952.

———, *Collected Economic Papers.* New York, Kelley, 1951.

———, "The Labor Theory of Value," *Science & Society,* spring 1954.

Rogin, Leo, *The Meaning and Validity of Economic Theory.* New York, Harper, 1956.

Roll, Erich, *A History of Economic Thought.* New York, Prentice-Hall, 1956.

Rostow, W. W., *British Economy in the Nineteenth Century.* Oxford, The Clarendon Press, 1948.

———, "Adjustments and Maladjustments after the Napoleonic Wars," *American Economic Review,* March 1942.

Salaman, R. W., *The History and Social Influence of the Potato.* Cambridge, The University Press, 1949.

Salz, Arthur, *Beiträge zur Geschichte und Kritik der Lohnfondstheorie.* Berlin, J. G. Cota'sche buchhandlung nachfolger, 1905.

Sayers, R. S., "The Question of the Standard in the 1850's," *Economic History,* January 1933.

———, "Ricardo's Views on Monetary Questions," *Papers in English Monetary History,* ed. T. S. Ashton and R. S. Sayers. Oxford, The Clarendon Press, 1953.

Schumpeter, Joseph A., *History of Economic Analysis.* New York, Oxford University Press, 1954.

Schütze, G. H., *Die Lehre von der Verteilung in der Volkwirtschaft bei Thomas Hodgskin.* Leipzig, Ernst'sche Vertlh., 1930.

Seligman, E. R. A., *Essays in Economics.* New York, Macmillan, 1925.

Sidgwick, Henry, *The Principles of Political Economy.* London, Macmillan, 1901.

Simons, R. B., "Thomas Robert Malthus on British Society," *Journal of the History of Ideas,* January 1955.

Smart, William, *Economic Annals of the Nineteenth Century, 1821–30.* London, Macmillan, 1917.

Smith, Kenneth, *The Malthusian Controversy.* London, Routledge & Kegan Paul, 1951.

Smith, Vera C., *The Rationale of Central Banking.* London, P. S. King & Son, 1936.

Smith, V. E., "The Classicists' Use of Demand," *Journal of Political Economy,* June 1951.

Sotiroff, G., "John Barton (1789–1852)," *Economic Journal,* March 1953.

Spengler, J. J., "Malthus' Total Population Theory," *Canadian Journal of Economics and Political Science,* February 1945.

———, "The Physiocratics and Say's Law of Markets. II," *Journal of Political Economy,* December 1954.

———, "Marshall on the Population Question. I," *Population Studies,* March 1955.

Spring, D., "Earl Fitzwilliam and the Corn Laws," *American Historical Review,* June 1954.

Sraffa, P., "The Laws of Returns Under Competitive Conditions," *Readings in Price Theory.* London, Allen & Unwin, 1953.

Stark, W., *The Ideal Foundations of Economic Thought.* London, Routledge & Kegan Paul, 1948.

Stigler, George, *Production and Distribution Theories.* New York, Macmillan, 1941.

———, *Five Lectures on Economic Problems.* New York, Longmans, Green, 1949.

———, "The Ricardian Theory of Value and Distribution," *Journal of Political Economy,* June 1952.

———, "Sraffa's Ricardo," *American Economic Review,* September 1953.

———, "The Development of Utility Theory. I," *Journal of Political Economy,* August 1950.

———, "The Nature and Role of Originality in Scientific Progress," *Economica,* November 1955.

Swann, E., *Christopher North.* Edinburgh, Oliver and Boyd, 1934.

Taussig, F. W., *Wages and Capital.* London School of Economics Reprints, No. 13, 1935.

Turgeon, Charles I., and Turgeon, C.-H., *La Valeur d'après les économistes anglais et français.* Paris, Librairie du Recueil Sirey, 1925.

Viner, Jacob, *Studies in the Theory of International Trade.* New York, Harper, 1937.

———, "Schumpeter's *History of Economic Analysis,*" *American Economic Review,* December 1954.

Walker, Helen M., *Studies in the History of Statistical Methods.* Baltimore, Williams & Wilkins, 1929.

Wallas, Graham, *The Life of Francis Place.* New York, Burt Franklin, 1951.

Walsh, Correa M., *The Fundamental Problem in Monetary Science.* New York, Macmillan, 1903.

Webb, R. K., *The British Working-Class Reader, 1790–1848.* London, Allen & Unwin, 1955.

Webb, Sidney and Beatrice, *The History of Trade Unionism, 1666–1920.* New York, Longmans, Green, 1920.

———, *English Local Government. English Poor Law History.* London, Longmans, Green, 1929.

Weber, Hans, *Richard Jones. Ein früher englisher Abtrunniger der klassischen Schule der Nationalökonomie.* Zürich, H. Girsberger, 1939.

Wermel, M. T., *The Evolution of the Classical Wage Theory.* New York, Columbia University Press, 1939.

Whitaker, A. C., *History and Criticism of the Labor Theory of Value in English Political Economy.* New York, Columbia University Press, 1904.

Whittaker, Edmund, *A History of Economic Ideas.* New York, Longmans, Green, 1946.

Wicksell, Knut, *Value, Capital and Rent.* London, Allen & Unwin, 1954.

———, *Lectures on Political Economy.* 2 vols. New York, Macmillan, 1934.

Wieser, Fredrich von, *Natural Value.* London, Macmillan, 1893.

Woodruff, W., "Capitalism and the Historians. A Contribution to the Discussion on the Industrial Revolution in England," *Journal of Economic History,* March 1956.

Wright, D. McCord, ed. *The Impact of the Union.* New York, Harcourt, Brace, 1951.

Young, G. M., *Victorian England.* New York, Doubleday, 1954.

[illegible] "The Nature and Role of Originality in Scientific Progress," *Eco*[illegible]

[illegible] Edinburgh, Oliver and Boyd, 1951.
[illegible] London School of Economics Reprints, [illegible]

[illegible] Librairie du Recueil Sirey, 1925.
[illegible] *International Trade*, New York, Har[illegible]

[illegible] *History of Economic Analysis*," *American Economic Review*, [illegible]
[illegible] *the History of Statistical Method*, Baltimore, [illegible] 1929.
[illegible] *Francis Place*, New York, Burt Franklin, 1951.
[illegible] *The Fundamental Problem in Monetary Science*, New York, Macmillan, 1903.
[illegible] *The British Working Class Reader, 1790–1848*, London, Allen [illegible]

[illegible] *The History of Trade Unionism, 1666–1920*, [illegible] 1920.
[illegible] *English Local Government: English Poor Law History*, London, [illegible] 1929.
[illegible] Zurich, H. Girsberger, 1951.
[illegible] New York, [illegible] 1936.
[illegible] *of the Labor Theory of Value in* [illegible] New York, Columbia University Press, 1904.
[illegible] *of Economic Ideas*, New York, [illegible]

[illegible] London, Allen & Unwin, 1934.
[illegible] 2 vols., New York, Macmillan, 1934.
[illegible] London, Macmillan, 1955.
[illegible] A Contribution to the [illegible] Industrial Revolution in England," *Journal of Economic His*-[illegible]

[illegible] New York, [illegible]

[illegible] New York, Doubleday, 1954.

INDEX OF NAMES

INDEX OF SUBJECTS

YALE STUDIES IN ECONOMICS

1. Richard B. Tennant, The American Cigarette Industry. A Study in Economic Analysis and Public Policy
2. Kenneth D. Roose, The Economics of Recession and Revival. An Interpretation of 1937–38
3. Allan M. Cartter, The Redistribution of Income in Postwar Britain. A Study of the Effects of the Central Government Fiscal Program in 1948–49
4. Morton S. Baratz, The Union and the Coal Industry
5. Henry C. Wallich, Mainsprings of the German Revival
6. Lloyd G. Reynolds and Cynthia H. Taft, The Evolution of Wage Structure
7. Robert Triffin, Europe and the Money Muddle
8. Mark Blaug, Ricardian Economics. A Historical Study